Text Book of Computers for Hotel Management

Sonia Rahul Sharma

AMAN PUBLICATIONS
NEW DELHI

Published by
Rajiv Jain for Aman Publications
LG-4A, Ganpati Bhawan,
4675-B/21, Ansari Road,
Darya Ganj, Delhi - 110002
PH: 23255012, 23282127
E-mail: sshjbs@yahoo.com

First Published - 2013

ISBN No.: 81-8204-0396
ISBN No.: 978-81-8240-039-7

SOLE DISTRIBUTOR
JINDAL BOOK SERVICES
LG-4A, Ganpati Bhawan,
4675-B/21, Ansari Road,
Darya Ganj, Delhi - 110002

Jacket Designed by :
S.M. Graphics

Printed by:
Indus Printwell, Delhi, India

Dedicated to 'Shirdi Sai', my respected Parents
&
my loving husband

Preface

As we begin to foray into the technological era, computerization has become an inseparable part of all organizations. Computers have made their presence felt in all spheres of activities. Computers today are affecting our lives in more ways than we are probably aware of it. As it can be said that information is lifeblood of society. **Toni Carbo Bearman** as has very well described the impact of information as-

> ". . . how we make financial transactions, control the supply and movement of goods and services, educate people, communicate information, entertain....work or shop from home; communicate from virtually anywhere to virtually anywhere.... Consult medical experts, sharing patient information, from remote areas....the list goes on..."

All these applications require processing of information by computer, which in turn has given rise to a field i.e. Information Technology (IT).

SONIA SHARMA

Acknowledgement

The successful completion of this project is due to GOD, the one, the only and the indivisible creator and sustainer of the worlds. To Him, we belong and to Him, we will return. I wish to thank Him for all that he has gifted me with, although, He can never be praised or thanked enough.

I would also like to express my gratitude to my loving husband who supported me entirely during the project and my respectable parents for teaching me values that are precious irrespective of time and place.

I also feel obliged for the professional support and motivation given by our Director, Mr. A.P Rastogi.

SONIA SHARMA

Salient Features Of The Book

- Simple & Easily understandable language is used through out the book
- It encompasses sixteen units.
- Every new topic in a unit is highlighted by a picture 

- Precise explanation of each topic is provided in the book
- Visuals like pictures, charts, diagrams etc are used to maintain the enthusiasm of reader.
- This book contains a special section *"Update Your Net Knowledge"* to keep the reader in pace with the advancing internet technology (both theoretically & practically)
- It also includes Appendices that contains the following-
  - o Glossary
  - o Memory Units
  - o ASCII Chart
  - o Shortcut Keys
  - o Abbreviations
  - o List of URLs & e-mail ids of hotels of metropolitan cities
  - o List of Best Top Ten Websites of India

Note:

Extra points of a respective topic is highlighted by a picture 

CONTENTS

1

Computer Fundamentals

Introduction:

Anyone who has lived in a modern society within the last few years is aware of what a computer is. We all have seen them, and we have all used them. Even though we know what a computer looks like, and we might know something about what it does, there are some puzzling things about the nature of this machine that make understanding it a little more elusive than other machines. In this section, we will examine what actually happens deep inside the computer and see how it really works. Computers are almost completely universal, capable of doing all kinds of complex processes. The simple tasks are combined in complex ways to make the computer capable of performing complicated jobs. Computers deal with every kind of information from words to numbers to pictures and music.

A computer is composed of hardware and software, and can exist in a variety of sizes and configurations.

Therefore, a computer can be defined in this way: "A computer is a universal information manipulator".

Definition of Computer

Computer is a fast and accurate electronic data manipulating device that's designed to automatically accept and store data (input), process them and produce results (output) under the direction of a stored set of instructions/programs.

Or

"A Computer is a tool or an instrument that can perform the computations fast and accurately using the precise instructions given to it by a human user."

Or

"An electronic device for the storage and processing of information"

Or

"A computer is a device or machine for making calculations or controlling operations that are expressible in numerical or logical terms"

Or

"An electronic device that performs pre-defined or programmed computations at a high speed and with great accuracy; a machine that is used to store, transfer, and transform information"

INFORMATION

1. Computers are designed to work with information.
2. Information is more conceptual. Numbers, words, and instructions are good examples of information.
3. The input given by means of some input device (Examples: keyboard, mouse, modem, scanner) to the computer is called data.
4. This data is processed by the computer i.e. several manipulations of data is done.
5. Output is the way the computer communicates the results to us. It is displayed through output devices. e.g. Monitor, Printer, Plotter etc.

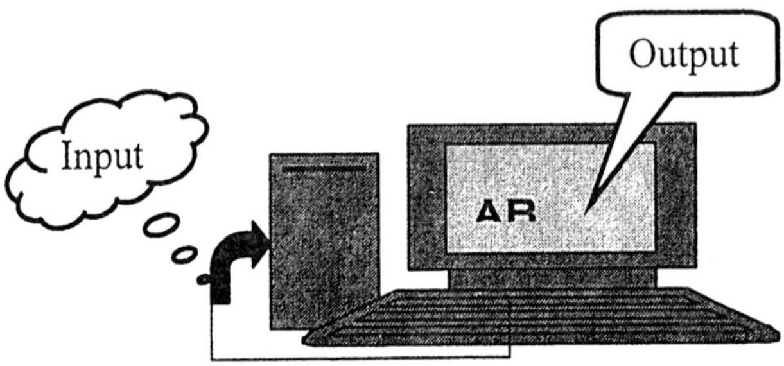

6. The processed data (or output) so obtained or we can say the meaningful data obtained after it's processing is called Information.

FULL FORM OF TERM "COMPUTER": -

Commonly **O**perating **M**achine **P**urposely **U**sed **F**or **T**raining **E**ducation & **R**esearch

Characteristics & limitations

1.SPEED :- As computer is an electronic device. It's internal speed is virtually instantaneous. They can process millions of instructions per second. The unit of measuring computation time is-

- Microsec (millionths of a second)
- Nannosec (thousand-millionths of a sec)
- Picosec (Million-Millionths of a sec)

Therefore, The computer can work much faster than human beings. In a computer, a specialized oscillator, called the clock, serves as a sort of pacemaker for the microprocessor. Today's personal computers run at a clock speed in the hundreds of megahertz (MHz) and some exceed one gigahertz (GHz). The clock speed is determined by a quartz-crystal and is an important factor in determining the rate at which a computer can perform instructions.The speed of computer is closely related to the amount of data it processes. The terms used to describe the amount of data handled by a computer system are volume and frequency. Volume represents the overall quantity of data and frequency describes how often a specific data item is used in processing.

2.AUTOMATION :- For doing every work, computer requires or needs a human user. Once a program is in the computer's memory, the individual instructions are then transferred, one after the other to the control unit for execution. It simply means that computers are not intelligent as human beings. They always need to be programmed by a human being.

3. VERSATILITY OR MULTIPURPOSE :-Computers are capable of performing almost any task, provided that the task can be reduced to a series of logical steps. This is because, the computer has only limited ability and it can perform only four basic functions-

1. Input/output operations.
2. Text manipulation & calculation
3. Logic/comparison operations
4. Storage and retrieval operations

Computers can do a variety of jobs depending upon the instructions fed to them and their hardware characteristics. Modern computers can be used in railways, air reservations systems, process controls, nuclear reactors, manufacturing plants, scientific laboratories, hospitals and hotels etc.

4. ACCURACY : The accuracy of computers is consistently high. The circuits in a computer have no mechanical parts to wear and malfunction. Almost without exception, the errors in computer are due to human rather than to technological weaknesses. This is due to the fact that human being gives the basic instructions to the computer for carrying out various operations. But, modern computers have a special error detecting and error correcting features, due to which they have become highly accurate.

5. DILIGENCE : Being a machine, a computer does not suffer from the human traits of tiredness and lack of concentration Diligence is the property by virtue of which a computer can work continuously without getting tired & without loosing concentration. **e.g.** If five million calculations have to be performed, it will perform the 5 millionth calculation with the same accuracy & speed as the first.

6. MEMORY AND STORAGE : Memory is that area in computer where the storage of data takes place. A computer can store unlimited data. The stored data can be retrieved back easily in fraction of seconds.The information is stored in the form of files, but on disks and tapes. This helps in easy and speedy retrieval of information. This storage is known as electronic storage system. For example, in a company or an organization the details of employees are given such as name, address, basic salary, unique code number etc., that may be required by accounts department as well as personnel department. In case, an employee resigns or is promoted, then the updation of the information is required only once and at one place. Now a days standard storage capacity of a computer is in the range of 20 GB-100 GB.

7. PROGRAMMABILITY : Computers can do nearly anything with information, but they have to be taught (by humans, for now) how to store and manipulate that information. They can only do what we teach them to do. Programmers obviously do a lot of this teaching, but users do, too. If we can imagine how to translate an operation into the core operations, we can get a computer to do it. This process is the art of programming and using a computer. Likewise, if we can imagine how any value can be represented digitally, we can teach a computer how to store and manipulate that value. Using computer languages like C, C++, Java etc, a program can be developed for accomplishing a certain task. Do you know? What is Program? Program is basically a group of instructions given to the computer.

LIMITATIONS OF COMPUTER

As the speed and size of computing technology continues to improve, we are seeing fewer and fewer technical limitations. We can already make computers do many kinds of operations by combining the ones we have. The hardware is not the limiting factor in computing. The limiting factor is absence of following human traits-

- Cannot think.
- Cannot learn by experience.
- Cannot take independent decisions i.e. requires human intervention to do each and every step.

Computer Applications

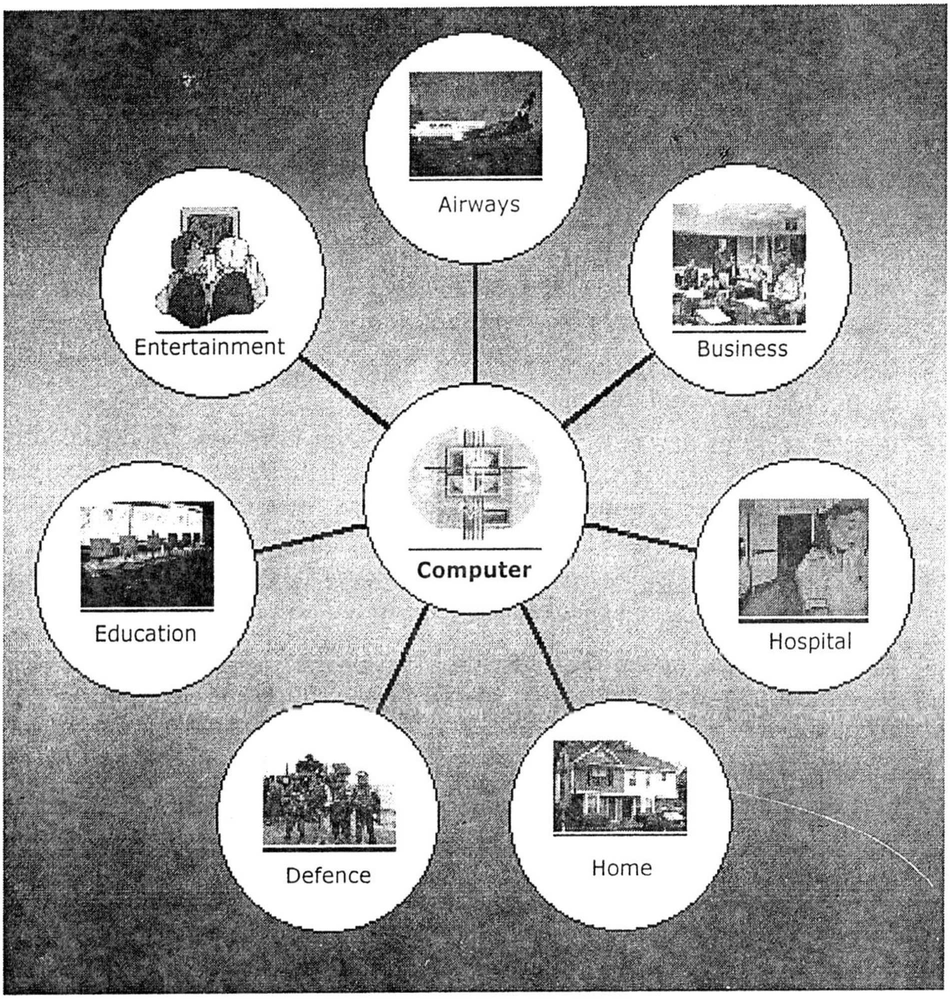

➢ BUSINESS :-

- Computers began their business careers in the banking and insurance industries, where massive amounts of data have to be processed daily. Computers are used in banks for magnetic coding of checks, and for the **ATM** facility.

- Credit cards are used for automatic and instantaneous banking transactions through computers.
- The concept of "bank anywhere, anytime" depends on the computer based expansion of **EFT** (Electronic Fund Transfer) technology.
- A person can perform all the banking transactions sitting at home via Internet.
- Computers are used for almost all aspects of business administration bookkeeping, accounting, inventory control, forecasting and record keeping.
- In the field of Office Automation, computers interconnected by telecommunication are applied to such tasks as the text and document processing and keeping in touch with the outside world through electronic mail and information browsing.

➢ EDUCATION :-

- In Education, Computers are becoming increasingly useful tools of education. Thus, computers are used for computation, design and research.
- For some applications, such as routine instructions, they can be superb adjuncts to the teacher.
- They are ideally suited for self-placed instructions where the course objectives and contents are well defined.
- Computers are not good at teaching "fuzzy" situations, where tasks cannot be defined in simple terms.
- Virtual libraries are nowadays replacing paper libraries. In virtual libraries, the books are stored using small silicon chips. Using computers, student can enter the book name and thus able to retrieve data from corresponding e-books.
- Used in development of CBT (Computer Based Teaching) and CAT (Computer Aided Teaching) programs for education.
- Computers are thus widely used by the students for developing projects, presentations and even the notes using the audio visual features of computers.
- Various educational publishing houses are successfully implementing the concept of Educational CDs.
- Teachers can use computers to develop & maintain question banks, test papers and scores of students.

➢ HOME :-

- Computers have entered the homes in large numbers.
- Many home computers are used mainly for entertainment but have great potential for education, household management and household control.
- There are some other examples of some automated systems like microwave ovens, fully automatic washing machines, programmable recorders and radios, home security systems and intelligent telephones. These all are consist of built-in computing devices.

- Home budget and expenditure analysis can be done using computers.
- Addresses of friends and relatives can be maintained using electronic address book.
- Meetings can be scheduled using computers.
- PCs are coming in which you can view all your television channels and even you can pause your program in between and resume it later.
- Many games can be played using computers like Cricket, Chess, Snooker, Solitaire etc.
- Computers can be used for listening to music and viewing movies at home.
- Computers can be used to upgrade you with the latest inventions and news happening round the world using internet at home.

➢ ELECTRONIC MAIL: -

- An electronic system, which can store and deliver message that, would otherwise be sent through postal services or over telephone lines.
- Using a computer and having Internet connection you can send mails to different people, just sitting at home.

➢ FASCIMILE MACHINES :-

- These are used to electronically send copies of documents to distant places.
- Facsimile machines can be connected to computers in order to send fax using computers.

➢ TELECONFERENCING FACILITY :-

- This is an Electronic method of bringing together geographically apart conferring groups, face to face at the same time.
- It is a facility where audiovisual equipment like cameras, microphones etc together with communication facilities are used to hold meeting of various people sitting geographically apart.
- All the members of the meeting will be able to see and hear each other, with the help of cameras and microphones, sitting at their own offices.

➢ WEATHER :-

- To forecast the weather.

➢ HOSPITALS :-

- Computers are widely used in retrieving information of patients, diseases and drugs etc.
- Used in hospitals and nursing home for maintaining medical records, prescription writing, and diagnostic applications and computerized scanning (CAT Scanning).
- Doctors can discuss a disease or problem with his colleagues by using teleconferencing facility.

- Some expert systems have been developed. Although, such systems cannot substitute doctors, however they can provide help to doctors. The databases used in these expert systems need to be checked and updated time to time **e.g MYCIN** (expert system for diagnosing Meningitis)
- There are various devices that scans images and diagnose diseases e.g. Positron Emission Tomography (**PET**), Magnetic Resonance Imaging (**MRI**), Computerized Axial Tomography (**CAT**)
- Computers are also used in pathological tests such as Haemoglobin test, glucose test, white and red blood cell count etc.

➢ PUBLISHING :-

- Nowadays, publishing houses are using several application programs like PageMaker, Word Processing, Corel Draw, Photoshop etc for designing books, thesis, brochures etc.
- Laser printers are connected to the computers in order to take out the hard copy or print of the designed material (textual or pictorial).
- Thus, the final copy produced is sent to the author for proof reading.
- The errors pointed out by the author are again corrected and then a negative of the actual copy is produced.
- Finally, the negative is used for offset printing. In this way, the mass printing of books is carried out.
- The software package that is specially designed for publishing is DTP. DTP stands for Desktop Publishing. It consists of PageMaker, Corel Draw and Photoshop.

➢ ENGINEERING :-

- Design of any piece of engineering whether an aeroplane, ship, car, building need the help of computers to eliminate technical faults and human error.
- Some of the examples are: CAD (Computer Aided Designing), CAM (Computer Aided Manufacturing), CAE (Computer Aided Engineering), CAM (Computer Aided Manufacturing) and CIM (Computer Integrated Manufacturing)
- Computers are used for guiding spacecrafts on moon.
- Various satellites and spacecraft are launched that need no intervention of human beings (unmanned satellites or spacecrafts). Thus, such satellites and spacecrafts are automatically guided and monitored by computers alone.
- Using computers, various equipments are developed that proves to be beneficial in determining or predicting natural calamities like volcanoes, earthquakes, hurricanes etc. Besides this, such equipments can also determine the impact of these calamities on human beings. **E.g.** Richter Scale is used to measure the intensity of an earthquake.

➢ DEFENCE :-

- Used to operate war planes, ships, radars and many advanced weapons.
- ENIAC was the first computer developed for the Army of US.

- The defence personnel of US Army had developed a network useful for connecting remote offices of US defence to communicate with each other. The network was called ARPANET. This network was upgraded from time to time to develop a global network of computers i.e. Internet.
- Computers are used to communicate by radio in air, under water and on surface with land based network.
- Computers can also be used to compute internal shell trajectories for various distances and weather conditions.
- Computers can also be used as Smart Bombs ie. Missiles (but that is a destructive use of computers)
- To computerize geographically separated defence organizations through networking.
- To update the necessary information about the conspiracy of enemy countries using radars, satellites, transmitters etc.
- In America, MDT (Mobile Data Terminals) are used by the crime branch that have data regarding the car numbers, car owners, license numbers etc. Thus, using MDT's help, the crime organizations perform their duties efficiently.
- Smart weapons use microprocessor based control systems.
- Computers allow pilot to interact with the entire air-traffic control system.
- ENIAC was the first computer developed for the Army of US.
- The defence personnel of US Army had developed a network useful for connecting remote offices of US defence to communicate with each other. The network was called ARPANET. This network was upgraded from time to time to develop a global network of computers i.e. Internet.

newtopic Historical Development of Computers

Human beings are different from animals because of the ability to invent tools, improve upon and make the best use of tools for improving the way of working and communication etc. The evergreen curiosity of man to invent new things has led the whole world today to a situation where we have high speed and multipurpose machines called computers. Machines were invented to help man in his calculations, to increase his skills of work and speed of work. Calculator was invented for computing purpose at a speed more than that of a human being. The first truly general purpose computer was designed to meet the defence need of World War II. Gradually, the journey from calculator to high-speed computers started and today we have reached a stage where we will see the fifth generation computers to think like human beings. That day is not far when computers will perform almost all the tasks that a human brain can do. Depending upon the needs the man has developed computers generation after generation. But this is not the end. We have to go miles and miles ahead to improve the technology and bring computers in our life in such a way that they become our good friends and help us in day-to-day life. The efforts of man are on.

The history of evolution of computers will prove the fact that man is capable of doing much more and bring a revolutionary change as early as possible. From huge size of computer to very small size computer man has taken around 30 years. This is due to the microprocessor revolution in last ten years and this revolution has changed the entire world of computers.

1. ABACUS OR SOROBAN :-

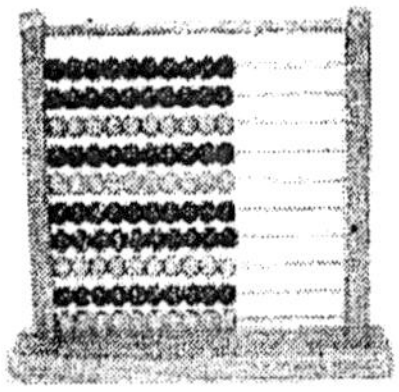
Abacus

1. The word "abacus" comes to us from a Greek word "abax." meaning "sand"
2. It was developed by Egyptians in 450 B.C
3. It was the first actual calculating aid or mechanism. It is basically a mechanized pebble counter.
4. According to the original concept, abacus is a flat stone covered with sand (or dust) into which numeric symbols were drawn. The first abacus was almost certainly based on such a stone, with pebbles being placed on lines drawn in the sand. Over time a wooden frame supporting thin sticks, braided hair, or leather thongs, onto which clay beads or pebbles with holes were threaded, replaced the stone.

2. NAPIER S BONES :-

John Napier

1. It is a set of rods used for multiplication.
2. A Scottish mathematician, **John Napier** devised it in 1614 A.D.
3. This device was designed by using bones or wood. He actually inscribed multiplication tables on strips of wood or bone.

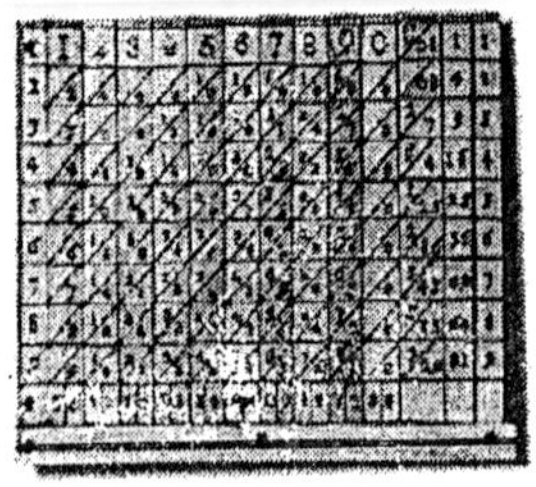
Napier's Bones

3. PASCAL S ARITHMETIC MACHINE:

1. A French mathematician **BLAISE PASCAL** devised it in 1642.
2. However, Pascal's device could only add and subtract, while multiplication and division operations were implemented by performing a series of additions or subtractions. In fact the Arithmetic Machine could really only add, because subtractions were performed using complement techniques, in which the number to be subtracted is first converted into its complement, which is then added to the first number. Interestingly, modern computers also employ similar complement techniques.
3. It could only perform multiplication by repeated addition and division by repeated subtraction.

4. LEIBNIZ DEVICE

1. Gottfried von Leibniz developed Pascal's ideas and devised a machine in 1671.
2. It was a device, which, as well as performing additions and subtractions, could multiply, divide, and evaluate square roots by series of stepped additions.
3. However, it was not reliable because of insufficient accuracy.

5. PUNCHED CARDS OR HOLLERITH CARDS

1. **Herman Hollerith** introduced it in early 1800 A.D.
2. The basic principle is the presence of one or the other two states i.e. absence or presence of a hole in the punched card.
3. Earlier, Hollerith's cards were punched with round holes. But, the data storage capacity of such punched card was limited. For example, a Hollerith's card supported 45 columns, where each column could be used to represent a single character value or data value.
4. For further improving pucnched cards, IBM responded by using rectangular holes, which allowed them to pack 80 columns of data onto each card.
5. Each card contains 12 rows of 80 columns, and each column is typically used to represent a single piece of data such as a character. The top row is called the "12" or "Y" row; the second row from the top is called the "11" or "X" row; and the remaining rows are called the "0" to "9" rows.

6. DIFFERENTIAL ENGINE & ANALYTIC ENGINE :

In 1822, Babbage proposed a machine called the Difference Engine to automatically calculate mathematical tables.

IBM 80-column punched card format

Punched Cards

Charles Babzbage

After it's partial completion, In 1834, Charle's Babbage started to work on Analytic Engine (an enhanced form of Differential engine), which could make decisions based on the results of previous computations. It was also known as automatic calculator.

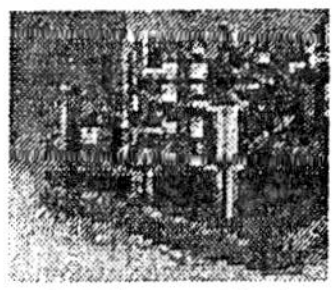

Differential Engine

Basic reason due to which "Charles Babbage" is called the "Father of Computer"

Analytic Engine consists of all the basic components, which are present in modern computers i.e. input unit, output unit, memory unit and a computation unit. This machine was also intended to employ several features subsequently used in modern computers, including sequential control, branching, and looping.

Analytical Engine

Augusta Ada Lovelace, the daughter of the English poet Lord Byron, developed the program for Analytic engine. Ada. She was a splendid mathematician. Therefore, she was credited as being the first computer programmer. In 1979, a modern programming language was named "**ADA**" in her honor.

7. MARK- 1 :-

1. It is the first electromechanical computer built by Howard Aiken with the support of IBM in 1937-44.
2. The machine contained more than 750,000 components, was 50 feet long, 8 feet tall, and weighed approximately 5 tons.
3. It sounds like a "roomful of ladies knitting."
4. Switches and relays (One of the earliest forms of switches, which were formed from a metal bar surrounded by a coil of wire) were used in developing this machine.
5. This machine was based on numbers that were 23 digits wide — it could add or subtract two of these numbers in three-tenths of a second, multiply them in four seconds, and divide them in ten seconds.
6. Although the Mark I is considered to be the first digital computer, its architecture was significantly different from modern machines.

IBM automatic sequence controlled calculator (ASCC) (Courtesy of IBM)

8. ENIAC :-

1. It refers to Electronic Numerical Integrator and Calculator.
2. It is the first general-purpose true electronic computer, developed using vacuum tubes.
3. J. Presper Eckert and John Mauchly devised it at Pennysylvania University in 1946.
4. It was 10 feet tall, occupied 1,000 square feet of floor-space, weighed in at approximately 30 tons, and used more than 70,000 resistors, 10,000 capacitors, 6,000 switches, and 18,000 vacuum tubes.
5. ENIAC required 150 kilowatts of power, which was enough to light a small town.
6. The major drawback of ENIAC was that it was hard-wired; i.e. it did not have any internal memory as such. Therefore, it was needed to be physically programmed by means of switches etc.
7. It also required frequent replacement of burnt out vacuum tubes (say approximately 19,000 tubes every year)

ENIAC

newtopic Classification of Data Processing Devices

❖ **Manual or Mechanical Devices:** The devices, which are based on simple mechanisms and are powered by hand, are called manual devices.
e.g. Abacus, Slide Rule etc.

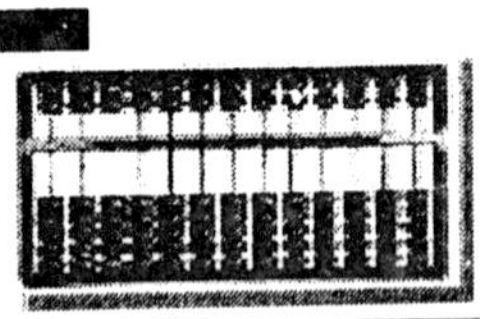

Abacus

Punched Card Reader

❖ **Electromechanical Devices:** The devices, which are powered by an electric motor and involve the usage of switches and relays, are called electromechanical devices.

e.g. Household appliances, Punched card processing equipments.

Electronic device

❖ **Electronic Devices:** The devices that make use of electronic components such as transistors, microprocessors etc.

e.g. Personal Computers.

newtopic Ages & Generations of Computer

AGES OF COMPUTERS :-

- Dark Age (5000 B.C –1890 A.D) (Manual devices)
- Middle Age (1890-1944) (Electronmechanical Devices)
- Modern Age (1944 onwards) (Electronic Devices)

GENERATION OF COMPUTERS :-

YEAR	GENERATION	TECHNOLOGY USED	GRAPHICAL REPRESENTATION
1946-55	I	Valves (Vacuum Tubes or Diodes)	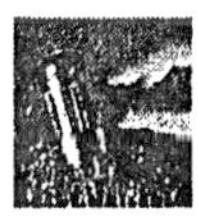
1955-64	II	Transistors	
1964-75	III	IC (Integrated Circuits) with LSI (Large Scale Integration)	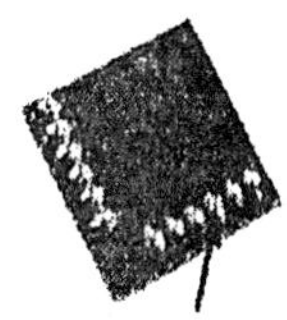
1976-1990	IV	VLSI (Very large scale integration)	
Late 1990'S	V	Optic fibre technology to handle AI (Artificial Intelligence)	

→ ZEROTH GENERATION OF COMPUTERS :-

It consists of all the calculating devices discussed here from ABACUS to MARK-II.

→ FIRST GENERATION COMPUTERS:

The main trends that were started during the time of first generation computers-

1. The first generation computer control was centralized in a single CPU, and all operations required direct intervention of the CPU.
2. Concepts such as use of virtual memory and index register.
3. Punched cards were used as input device.
4. Magnetic tapes and magnetic drums were used as secondary memory.
5. Binary code or machine language was used for programming.
6. Use of ferrite-core main memory was started during this time.
7. Towards the end due to difficulties encountered in use of machine language as programming language, the use of symbolic language, which is now called assembly language started.
8. Assembler, a program, which translates assembly language programs to machine language, was made.
9. Computer was accessible to only one programmer at a time (Single user environment.)
10. Advent of von-Neumann architecture.

Disadvantages of I Generation :-

- Large number of vacuum tubes are used
- Too bulky in size
- Generated heat
- Air conditioning was required
- Unreliable
- Frequent Hardware Failure
- Constant maintenance required.
- Very expensive
- Consume more power
- Not portable.

ADVANTAGE OF I GENERATION :-

1. Vacuum tubes were used for internal logic and capacitors were used for storage. Only these electronic components were available during that period.
2. First generation computers could accomplish mathematical operations like addition, subtraction, multiplication, division, table reference etc., at a good speed and these computers were the fastest calculating machines of their time.

EXAMPLES OF I GENERATION COMPUTERS: -

- **ENIAC** (*Electronic Numerical Integrator and Calculator*) (1946)

  Limitation: *ENIAC needed to be programmed manually by setting switches and plugging or unplugging. Thus, passing instructions to the computer was cumbersome and time-consuming.*

- **EDVAC** (Electronic Discrete Variable Automatic Calculator) (1951)

  EDVAC (Electronic Discrete Variable Automatic Computer) was designed on stored program concept. The concept of 'stored program' was developed by **Dr. John Van Neumann**. This new concept solved the problem of ENIAC. The instructions and the data were stored in the binary form instead of decimal numbers.

- **EDSAC** (*Electronic Delay Storage Automatic Calculator*) (1949)

  EDSAC

  EDSAC (Electronic Delay Storage Automatic Calculator) was developed by Britishers during 1947-1949. Addition was completed in 1500 microseconds and multiplication was completed in 4000 microseconds. This machine utilized stored program concept.

- **UNIVAC** *(Universal Automatic Computer) (1951)*

  UNIVAC

- **ACE** *(Automatic Computer Engine) (National Physics Lab in 1951)*

- **LEO** *(Lyons Electronic Office) First Commercial Computer by M.V Vikies in 1951)*

- **IAS Machine** *(New version of EDVAC, built by Von Neumann) (1952)*

  IAS Machine

Note: **IAS MACHINE HAS FIVE BASIC PARTS-**

- Memory
- ALU
- C.U
- Input Unit
- Output Unit

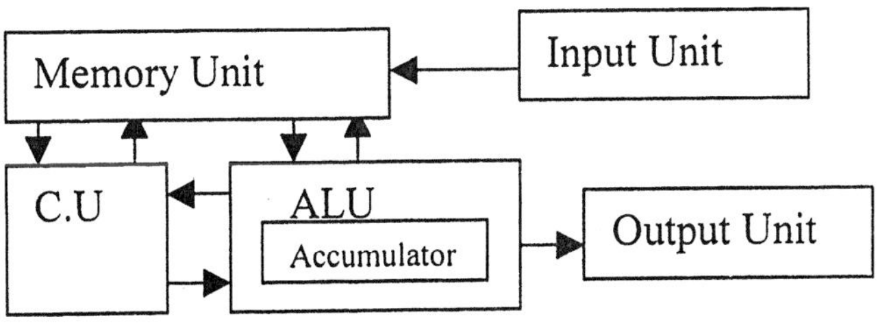

➔SECOND GENERATION COMPUTERS:

Transistor: The transistor is an electronic device, which was invented by Bardeen, Bratain and Shockley in 1951. It consists of three parts, which are called emitter, base and collector. Semi-conducting materials like silicon are used in manufacturing transistors. Pure silicon is heavily doped with materials like aluminum, phosphorus, arsenic, indium etc but these materials must be either trivalent(valency should be three) or pentavalent (valency should be five).

Disadvantages of II Generation Computers:-

- Manual Assembling of components required
- Air conditioning is required
- Constant maintenance required.
- Expensive

Advantages Of II Generation :-

- Smaller size.
- Less heat generation
- Less power consumption
- More reliable
- Less prompt to hardware failure
- Faster
- Portable
- Low maintenance
- More advanced in terms of arithmetic logic unit (ALU) and control unit (CU).
- Computational time reduced from milliseconds to microseconds.

Examples of II Generation:-

- PDP-1, developed by DEC, It was the first minicomputer.
- NCR 304 (National Cash Register)

➔ THIRD GENERATION COMPUTERS:

Chips & ICs : The advent of micro-electronics technology started the method of integrating large number of circuit elements into very small (less than 5mm square) surface of silicon known as 'chips'. This new invention of **integrated circuits (ICs)** defines the third generation of computers. Thousands of transistors, capacitors & resistors could be fabricated on a single wafer of

SSI & MSI : Different circuits are constructed on different wafers. The packaged circuit chips are interconnected on **PCB** (Printed circuit board) to produce several complex electronic circuits such as computers, digital diaries etc. Initially, the integrated circuit contained only 10 to 20 components. This technology was named **small-scale integration (SSI)**. Later on, with the advancing technology in microelectronics, hundreds of components were fabricated on a chip. This technology was named **medium scale integration (MSI)**. Third generation computers mainly used SSI chips.

THE MAJOR DEVELOPMENTS OF THE THIRD GENERATION COMPUTERS ARE AS FOLLOWS-

1. IC circuits were used
2. Semiconductor (Integrated circuit) memories were used as main memory
3. The CPU design was made simple and a technique called microprogramming (a scheme where programs controls the generation of signals) was introduced.
4. Multiprocessing & Pipelining techniques were used to reduce execution time of programs.
5. The operating systems were facilitated with the efficient methods of sharing the facilities or resources such as processor and memory space, automatically.

Disadvantages

- Highly sophisticated technology required for the manufacture of ICs.
- Temperature control is required but this requirement is less than that in second generation computers.

Advantages of III Generation:

- Even smaller size as compared to second generation computers
- Lower heat generation
- Less power required
- Computing time reduced from microseconds to nanoseconds.
- More reliable
- Faster
- Portable
- Low maintenance cost
- Production is rather easier and cheaper.

Examples of III Generation Computer-

- IBM 360, developed by IBM in 1964.
- PDP-8, developed by DEC in 1965, first mass-market minicomputer.
- PDP-11, developed by DEC in 1970, was the first highly successful minicomputer.
- CRAY-1, developed by Cray in 1974, first supercomputer.
- VAX, developed by DEC in 1978.

→ FOURTH GENERATION COMPUTERS:

With the rapid advancement of IC technology, it became possible to integrate 30,000 components on a single chip. This technology was known as Large Scale Integration (LSI). Efforts are still on for integrating more than 1 million components on a single chip. This technology is known as Very Large Scale Integration (VLSI).

Disadvantage of IV Generation:

None

Advantages of IV Generation:

- Even smaller size
- Negligible heat generation
- No AC (Air conditioner) required
- Less power required
- More reliable
- Faster
- Portable
- Low maintenance cost
- Production is rather easier and cheaper.
- Chances of hardware failure are very low and hence, minimal maintenance is required.

Examples of IV Generation:-

- IBM PC developed in 1981, having Intel 8088 memory chip.
- IBM PC/AT developed in 1982, having Intel 80286 chip.
- 386, developed in 1985 having Intel 80386 chip.
- CRAY-2, developed in 1985, was the fourth generation supercomputer.
- 486, developed in 1989, had Intel 80486 memory chip.
- Pentium, developed in 1995, has Pentium (80586) memory chip.

→FIFTH GENERATION COMPUTERS :-

These are some of the limitations of fourth generation computers. Unlike the human brain a computer cannot think on its own, cannot learn by experience and cannot handle real-time situations. It has to be given step-by-step instructions to make it perform a task. Scientists are working on the fifth generation computers.

The main aim of the development of fifth generation computers will be to bring about machines with genuine I.Q i.e. the ability to reason logically, and the real knowledge of the world.

In such computers, technology of AI (Artificial Intelligence) is used for making "expert systems" which can perform tasks with as much intelligence as the human beings i.e. they have special abilities to think and make decisions.

Japanese have named fifth generation computers as KIPS (Knowledge Information Processing System).

- ***Common characteristics of expert systems-***
    - o Performance is almost equivalent to an human expert.
    - o Explain their reasoning
    - o Can provide alternative solutions to a problem

Note:

- **Artificial Intelligence**: AI is concerned with designing and programming machines to accomplish tasks that represent intelligent behavior. Recently, AI technology is used to determine how to program computers for learning and discovery. The development of intelligent programs employs databases and complex set of rules.
- **Virtual Reality**: It is a concept that is helpful in analyzing the practical aspect of a thought or an imagination. Thus, it is a way for humans to visualize, manipulate and interact with computers and extremely complex data. e.g. Air traffic control systems, engine simulators etc. It is the other name given to Artificial Reality. Virtual Reality is also called Cyberspace or Simulator technology.

- ***Example:***

Yet to develop, but ROBOTS have a few feature of fifth generation computers.

- ☐ e.g.1 a robot has been developed in Tokyo, which is named as Piplio. The special feature of this robot is that it can recognize the voice and faces of human beings)
- ☐ e.g. 2.a ballroom dance partner (lady) robot

Courtesy: Eddidraws

Note:

COMPARITIVE FEATURES OF VARIOUS GENERATION OF COMPUTERS

CRITERIA	I GEN.	II GEN.	III GEN.	IV GEN.	V GEN.
Basic Electronic component	Vacuum Tubes or Valves	Transistors circuits	Integrated Circuits (IC) with LSI	IC with VLSI	IC with ULSI

Speed	Slowest	Slow	Medium	Faster	Fastest
Size	Largest	Large	Medium	Smallest	
Medium					
Reliability	Unreliable	Less Reliable	More Reliable	Most judge	Yet to
Availability	Out-dated	Out-dated	Out-dated	Current	Yet to build

newtopic Human Brain Vs Computer

Similarity :-

- Both use electrical signals.
- Both transmit information.
- Both have a memory that can grow.
- Both have evolved over time.
- Both can adapt and learn.
- Both need energy.
- Both can be damaged.
- Both can do math and other logical task.
- Both brains and computers are studied by scientist.

Differences :-

SNO.	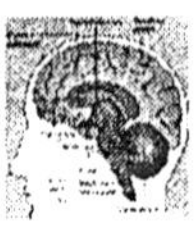 **HUMANBRAIN**	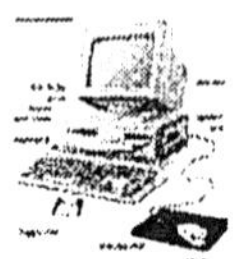 **COMPUTER**
1	The brain uses chemicals to transmit information.	The computer uses electricity.
2	The electrical signals travel at high speeds in the nervous system.	Comparitively much faster rate of traveling of signals.
3	A neuron in the brain is either on or off by either firing an action potential or not firing an action potential.	A computer uses switches that are either on or off.
4	A human memory in the brain grows by stronger synaptic connections.	Computer memory grows by adding computer chips.

5	It is much easier and faster for the brain to learn new things	The computer can do multiple complex tasks at the same time, which are difficult for the brain.
6	The brain needs nutrients like oxygen and sugar for power.	The computer needs electricity to keep working.
7	The brain is always changing and being modified. There is no "off" for the brain - even when an animal is sleeping, it's brain is still active and working.	The computer only changes when new hardware or software is added or something is saved in the memory. There is an "off" for a computer. When the power is turned off, signals are not transmitted.
8	The brain is better at interpreting the outside world and coming up with new ideas. The brain is capable of imagination.	The computer is faster at doing logical computations

newtopic Calculator Vs Computer

SNO.	 CALCULATOR	 COMPUTER
1.	Performs mathematical calculations	Performs mathematical and logical calculations
2.	Operate at high speed	Operates at incredibly faster speed
3.	Small temporary memory	Large or permanent memory
4.	No facility for secondary storage	Various secondary storage devices are available
5.	Needs an operator continuously	Once initiated, is capable of functioning automatically.
6.	Handles small data in the form of calculation	Handles large volume of data from highly complex operations

Note:

CYBERPHOBIA: - Some people are scared of using the computers. It is known as cyber phobia.

Components/Elements of Computer

The entire computer system is classified into two-

- Central Processing Unit
- Peripheral devices connected to and controlled by the CPU

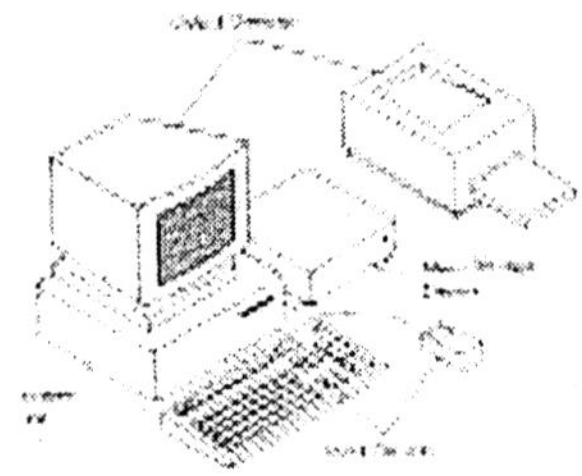

Hierarchical Representation of Elements of Computer

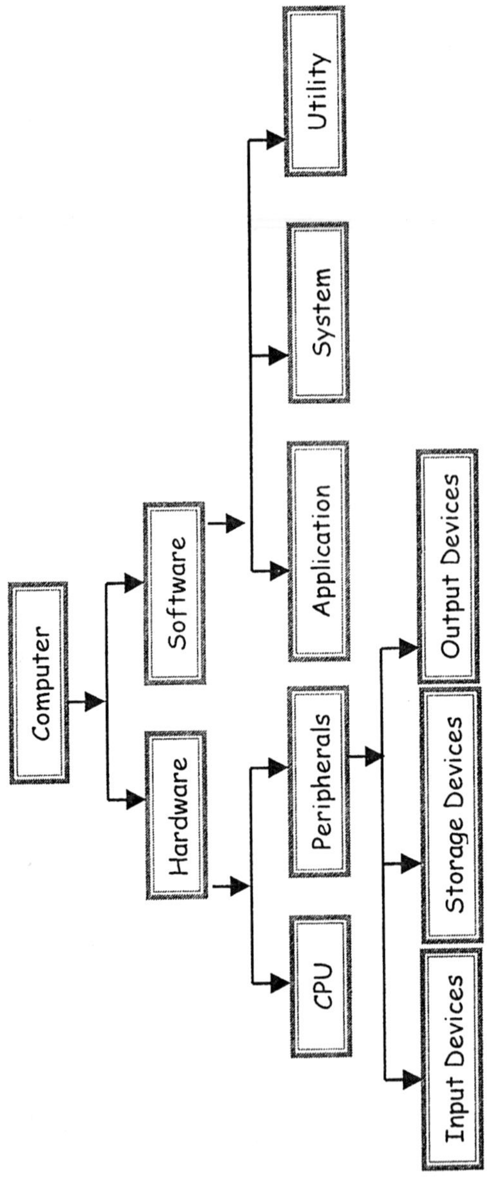

Hardware Concepts

The term hardware refers to the physical components of computer i.e. it includes the touchable and visible parts of the computer. It consists of all the electrical and mechanical components of the computer.

The basic functions performed by hardware are as follows-

- Accepts and store data
- Process the data accepted
- Output the processed result

Peripherals or Peripherals Devices: All those devices which can be connected to the computer (or CPU) externally are called peripherals or peripheral devices.

Peripheral devices includes-

- Input Devices
- Output Devices
- Storage Devices

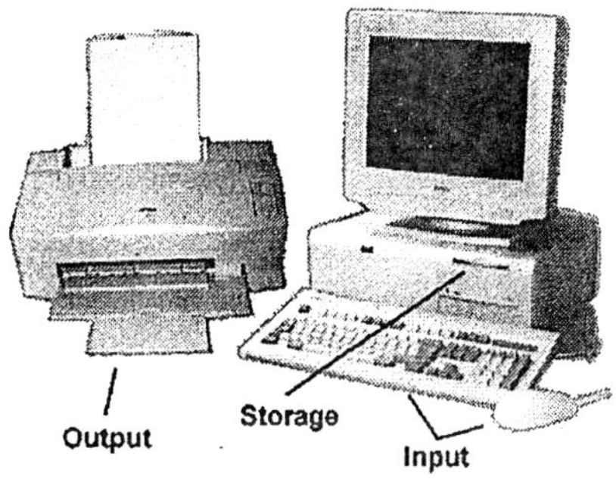

Input Devices:

Input devices are those devices through which data can be fed into the computer. In other words, Input devices accepts data from outside world and converts the data in binary form (acceptable by computer) and finally sends it to the computer for further processing.

Examples of Input Devices:

1. Keyboard
2. Mouse
3. Joystick
4. Light Pen
5. OMR
6. OCR
7. OBCR
8. MICR
9. Speech Synthesizer
10. Scanner
11. Digitizers
12. Floppy Disk Reader
13. Microphones
14. WebCam

KEYBOARD

1. Keyboard is called "**QWERTY**" Keyboard because the alphabetical keys are arranged so that the upper left row of letter begins with the following six letters- Q W E R T Y

2. ASCII codes (i.e. 8 bit code) are supported by QWERTY keyboards. Thus, it supports 256 characters (2^8)
3. The keys of computer can be divided among the following categories-
   a. Alphabetical keys (A – Z)
   b. Numeric Keys (0-9)
   c. Control Keys (Shift, Ctrl, Del, Enter, Esc & Insert)
   d. Functional keys (F1- F12 : these keys have different functionality in different software)
   e. Multimedia keys
   f. Utility keys (PrintScreen, Pause/Break, PageUp, PageDown)

MOUSE

1. The mouse is basically a pointing device.
2. It is an input device, but instead of sending character to the CPU, it sends the coordinates of the point on the screen, at which the mouse pointer is placed or clicked.

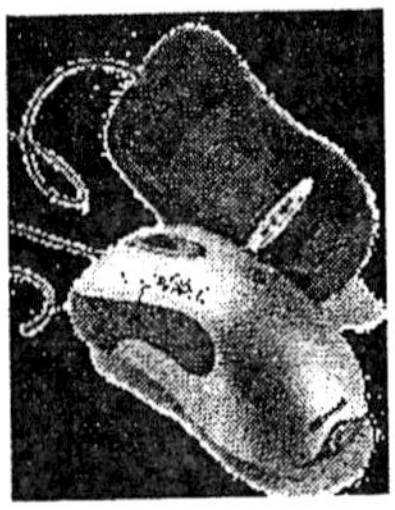

3. The mouse has a roller underneath, which enables it to move across a flat surface and thus leading to change in the cursor position on the screen correspondingly.
4. The mouse may be mechanical or optical and comes in many shapes and sizes.
5. There may be two or three buttons on the mouse.
6. With a mouse, you can draw, select options from a menu and modify or move text.
7. Commands are issued by pointing with the pointer and clicking a mouse button.
8. Left mouse button is generally used for clicking and double clicking. Right mouse button (i.e. right click) is used to open and selecting pop-up or context menus

JOYSTICK

1. The joystick is also a pointing device like mouse, but it is normally used in games.
2. In joystick, a stick can be moved right, left, backward or forward.
3. The electronics in joystick measures the movement of the stick from its central position and sends the information for processing.

LIGHT PEN

1. It is a pointing device that can be used to point to areas on the screen and to choose a menu option.
2. The pen consists of a photocell placed in a tube.
3. With this device, the user can directly communicate with PC without using keyboard or mouse.
4. A pen can be used to draw pictures on the screen and saves time when trying to produce accurate screen designs.

OMR

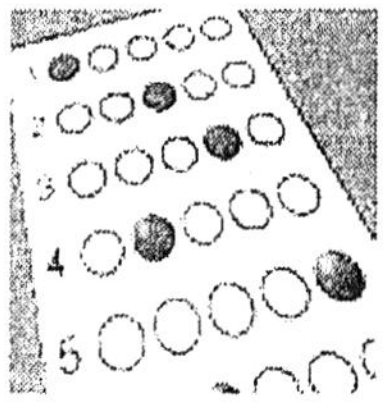

1. OMR stands for **O**ptical **M**ark **R**eader.
2. It is an optical scanner that employs light source and sensors for reading information recorded on paper.
3. This device can recognize pen/pencil marks.
4. It is basically used for objective answer sheets evaluation or processing of forms on a large scale basis.

OCR

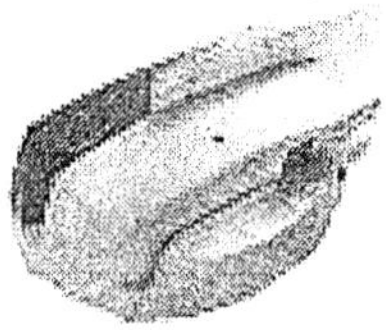

1. OCR stands for **O**ptical **C**haracter **R**eader.
2. It can read typewritten document i.e. used for evaluating telephone bills or objective papers
3. OCR optically reads and scans the written data, converts it into electrical codes and finally transmits to the computer very speedily.

OBCR

1. It stands for **O**ptical **B**ar **C**ode **R**eader.
2. It is used for reading the Universal Product Code and prices, directly from the bar code imprinted on the packets of the consumer products like grocery, books, toys etc.

MICR

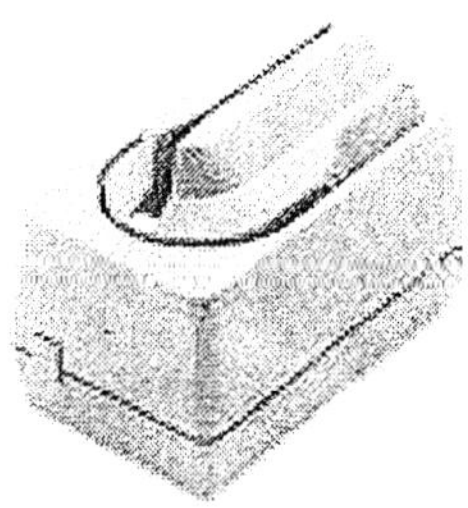

1. It stands for **M**agnetic **I**nk **C**haracter **R**ecognition.
2. It is used in banks to process huge number of cheques in banks.
3. When the cheque is paid in at a bank it undergoes a chain of processing events and only then is money transferred from one bank account to another. The method of processing the cheque is called **cheque clearing**. This normally takes several days.

4. The numbers at the bottom of the cheque are written in special magnetic ink. These are :
   a. the account number
   b. the branch number
   c. cheque number
5. The cheques with the characters marked in ink are passed through a magnetic field where the ink coded characters (like amount of the cheque, signature of the account holder etc) get magnetized due to iron deposits in the ink. These are then sensed by the MICR. This process is of reading characters written in magnetic ink is called MICR or Magnetic Ink Character Recognition.

SPEECH SYNTHESIZER

1. Voice-input system is one of the recent ways of inputting data.
2. The device has a microphone through which spoken words are input to the computer.
3. Within the computer, there is a pre-stored vocabulary of about 100 to 200 words in the form of a typical "***sound patterns***"
4. The voice input word is then recognized and compared with the vocabulary stored inside.
5. These devices are used in those areas of applications where one may not be free to use keyboards ***e.g.*** laboratories, quality control or even the disabled.

SCANNER

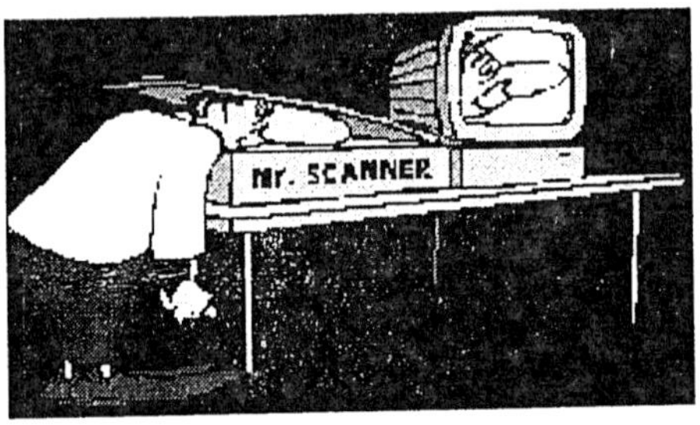

1. Scanner is a device that is capable of reproducing a drawing or a picture from a page on to the computer.
2. When the picture or any text is scanned with the light, it is broken into light and dark dots.
3. These are then converted into digital form for storage into computer.
4. Recently developed scanners use laser beam to create high-resolution color and black & white photograph.
5. The electronic components used by the scanner are-
   a. CCDs (Charged –coupled devices)
   b. PMTs (Photo-multiplier tube)
   c. CISs (Contact image sensors)

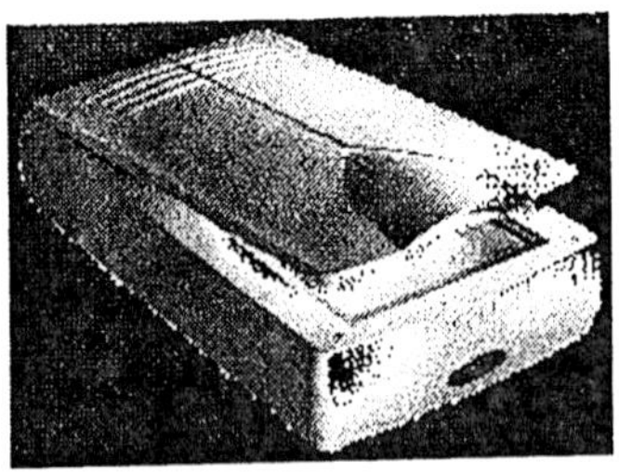

6. Scanners can be differentiated by their resolution.
7. ***Types of Scanners-***
   a. Drum Scanners

b. Sheet-fed Scanners

c. Flatbed Scanners

d. Handheld Scanners

DIGITIZERS OR DIGITIZER TABLET :-

1. Digitizers are also used for graphical work.
2. It is actually a work surface which has a grid of electric wires set in. The grid is connected to PC.
3. With a special pen, the user draws lines on a paper placed on the tablet. As the pen moves, the grid senses the exact position of the pen and signals to the PC.
4. Even the users, who do not have a very steady hand, will be able to draw straight lines because PC will straighten the irregular lines also.

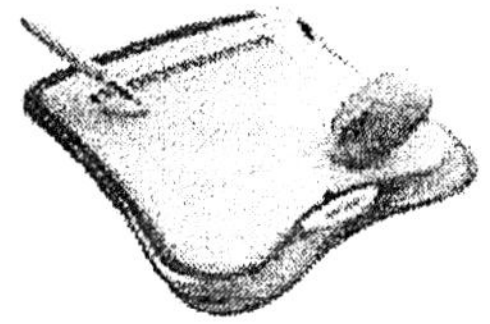

FLOPPY DISK READER:-

1. Data recorded on a floppy disk is read and stored in a computer's memory by a device called floppy disk reader.
2. A floppy disk is inserted in the slot of the floppy drive.
3. The disk is rotated at around 360 r.p.m.
4. A reading head is positioned touching a track.
5. A voltage is induced in a coil wound on the head when a magnetized spot moves below the head.
6. The polarity of voltage when a 1 is read is opposite to the voltage when a 0 is read.
7. The voltage sensed by the head coil is amplified, converted to appropriate signals and stored in the computer's memory.

MICROPHONES

1. It is also called ***"mic"*** *(pronounced as "mike")*
2. It is a device which converts sound into electrical representation of the sound wave, which can be amplified and recorded. It lets the user record speech and sound into the computer.

WEBCAM

1. A webcam is a real-time camera that is connected to a computer, either directly or wirelessly and gathers a series of images for remote display elsewhere.
2. It is called webcam because the images generated by it can be accessed and displayed on the World Wide Web through a web server.
3. Web cams are often used personally at home or used for videoconferencing.

Output Devices

Output devices are those devices through which output or processed information can be obtained. In other words, output devices accepts data in binary form from the computer and converts the coded data to human acceptable form and finally outputs the converted result to the outside world.

Examples of Output Devices

1. Monitor or V.D.U (Visual Display Unit)
2. Printer
3. Plotter
4. Microfiche

MONITOR

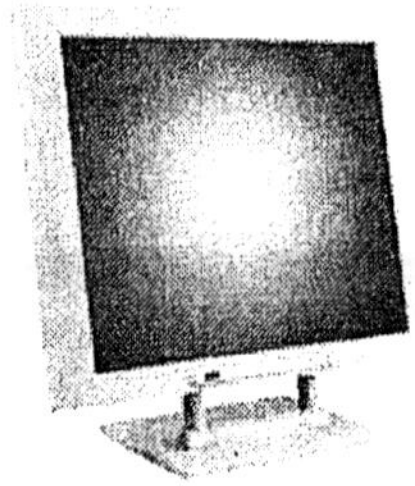

1. A monitor is also called V.D.U or Visual Display Unit.
2. Monitors can be MONOCHROME (black & white) or color models (V.G.A : visual graphics adapter)
3. An RGB monitor has three color guns, which shoot the colors simultaneously, producing a broader color range.
4. On the screen, PIXELS or PICTURE ELEMENTS (tiny dots or points) are present which can be illuminated by highly focused electron beam. These tiny dots are illuminated in such a pattern that we recognize the characters or the objects.
5. To avoid the fading of a picture displayed on the screen, the screen is coated with PHOSPHOR to retain the light.
6. Technologies used in Monitors may be – CRT (cathode ray tube) or LCD (Liquid Crystal Display).

EFT Monitors: EFT stands for **E**ye **F**resh **T**echnology. This technology is first launched by ***Samsung***. EFT Monitors are available in 15 and 17 inches. It is based on unique ***Magic Green*** technology. The monitor have a vital coating on the rear that emits anions and far infra red rays that serve to make the environment fresh, relax the human body & ease the strain on human eyes. The ***Silver Nano*** coating serves to remove odor from the environment making air fresh and clean. The technology offers specialized setting from highly used applications- Movie mode, Game mode, Internet mode & Text mode. This technique is used for both the categories of monitors – CRT & LCD.

DIFFERENCE BETWEEN 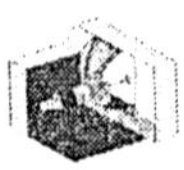 CRT MONITORS &  LCD MONITORS

Sno. CRT MONITORS	LCD MONITORS
1. CRT stands for Cathode Ray Tube	LCD stands for Liquid Crystal Display
2. It is too bulky (approx.13-23 kg)	It is comparatively less bulky (i.e. 4.5 kg)

SNO. CRT MONITORS	LCD MONITORS
3. It has comparatively higher depth	It is only 1-3 inch thick.
4. It is based on Passive-Matrix technology.	It is based on Active-Matrix technology.
5. It produces comparatively less sharper images.	It produces sharp images.
6. It is comparatively less brighter	It is more brighter (brightness is measured in Nits)
7. It consumes more electricity.	It consumes only one-third to one-half the electricity of their CRT counter parts.
8. The standard size varies from 15–21 inch or large; though the actual viewing screen will be about one inch smaller than the rated size.	It's standard size also varies from 15 -21 inch or large; though the viewing screen is the same size as the rated display.

PRINTER

Printers are the primary and the most popular output devices used to prepare permanent documents or Hard copy for human use. The speed of printing is measured in either ***cps*** (characters per second) or ***ppm*** (pages per minute). The output produced by printers is said to be either letter quality (as good as a typewriter), ***near letter quality***, or ***draft quality***. Only daisy-wheel, ink-jet, and laser printers produce letter-quality type. Some printers (daisy-wheel and line printers) can print only text. Other printers can print both text and graphics. Some printers, notably dot-matrix printers, are limited to one or a few fonts. In contrast, laser and ink-jet printers are capable of printing an almost unlimited variety of fonts. Daisy-wheel printers can also print different fonts, but you need to change the daisy wheel, making it difficult to mix fonts in the same document.

Classification of Printers-

- On the Basis of What they Print
- On the Basis of the Mechanism of Printing

On the Basis of What they Print

1. **Character Printer:** It prints one character at a time. It can print 30 to 400 characters per sec. ***e.g*** Dot Matrix Printers, Daisy Wheel Printer, Inkjet Printer
2. **Line Printer:** It prints one line of text at a time. It can print 300 to 3000 lines per min ***e.g.*** Drum Printers or Chain Printers
3. **Page Printer:** It prints one page at a time. It can print 8 to 600 pages per minute. It mostly uses cut sheets instead of continuous stationery. ***e.g.*** Laser Printer

On the Basis of Mechanism of Printing or How they Print

- Impact Printers
- Non-impact Printers

Impact Printer	Non-Impact Printer
It uses electromechanical mechanism to cause hammers or pin stud to strike against a ribbon and paper arrangement (like typewriter).	It does not have any striking mechanism. It uses chemical, thermal, electrostatic beam or inkjet technology for printers.
It is comparatively slower than non-impact printer.	It is comparatively faster than impact printers.
It is too noisy because printing heads strike the paper.	It does not make so much noise
It can produce more than one copy simultaneously (using stationery with interleaved carbon)	It cannot produce more than one copy simultaneously.
It is very economical.	It is comparatively expensive.
Print quality is comparatively low.	It has comparatively high print quality.
Examples: Dot Matrix Printers (DMP), Line Printers, Daisy wheel printer	***Examples:*** Thermal Printer, Laser Printer & Inkjet Printer

DOT MATRIX PRINTERS

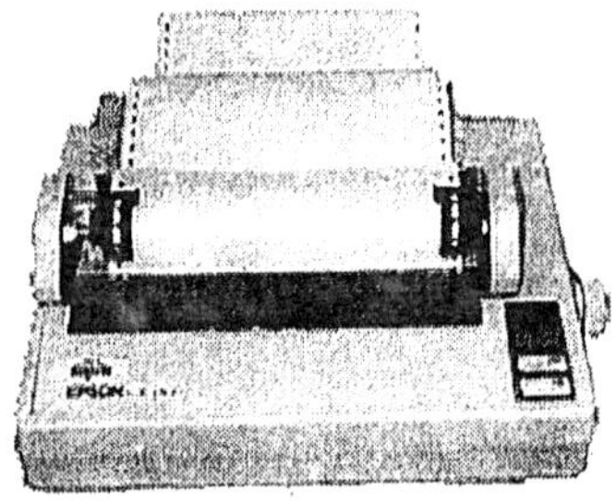

1. Characters are formed from a matrix of dots.
2. Each character is formed as the combination of x dots horizontally and y dots vertically, so that a matrix of x and y is formed therefore, it is called DMP.
3. The speed is usually 30 - 550 characters per second (cps).
4. This is the cheapest and noisiest of the printer family. The standard of print obtained is poor.
5. They are useful for low quality carbon copy printing.

DAISY WHEEL PRINTER

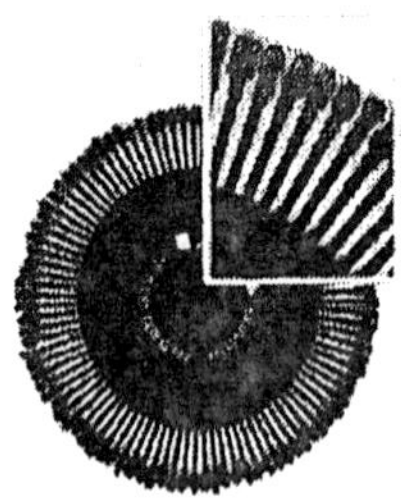

1. Molded metal characters like those in a typewriter are mounted on extensions attached to a rotating wheel and are printed onto the paper by means of a hammer and print ribbon.

2. The wheel is such that it rotates on its axis and then moves from left to right. However, the wheels are removable. One can use wheels of different fonts (because wheels are inexpensive)
3. This results in a great deal of movement and noise during the printing of documents, so printing is slow (less than 90 cps).
4. The standard of print is similar to that produced by an electric typewriter.

DRUM PRINTER

1. An old line printer technology that used formed character images around a cylindrical drum as its printing mechanism. When the desired character for the selected position rotated around to the hammer line, the hammer hit the paper from behind and pushed it into the ribbon and onto the character. ***Eg.*** *Cash Register*
2. It has a small drum having a set of characters embossed on the drum, such that each row belongs to a same character. So, it has a separate row for all characters to be printed.
3. Printing is little bit wavy because the drum rotates continuously; due to which the timing between character appearance at the desired position and hammer striking may vary.
4. Drum is expensive therefore; one user cannot own more than one drum.

INKJET PRINTERS

1. Characters are formed as a result of electrically charged or heated ink being sprayed in fine jets onto the paper. Individual nozzles in the printing head produce high resolution (up to 400 dots per inch or 400 dpi) dot matrix characters.

2. Inkjet printers use color cartridges which combine magenta, yellow and cyan inks to create color tones. A black cartridge is also used for crisp monochrome output.
3. This method of printing can generate up to 200 cps and allows for good quality, cheap color printing.
4. Being non-impact printers, they cannot print multi copies simultaneously.
5. Cartridges are easily replaceable.
6. It does not produce noise generally.
7. It is quite inexpensive.

THERMAL PRINTERS

1. Characters are formed by heated elements being placed in contact with special heat sensitive paper forming darkened dots when the elements reach a critical temperature. A fax machine uses a thermal printer
2. Thermal printer paper tends to darken over time due to exposure to sunlight and heat. The standard of print produced is poor.

3. Thermal printers are widely used in battery powered equipment such as portable calculators.

LASER PRINTERS

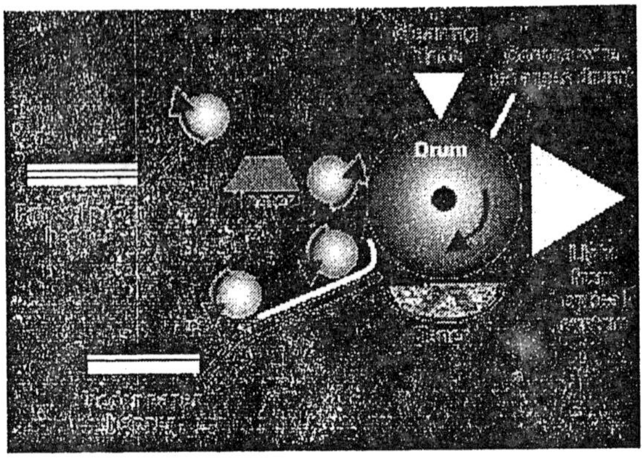

1. It is similar to a Xerox copier. Laser Printers use a laser beam and dry powdered ink to produce a fine dot matrix pattern. This method of printing can generate about 4 pages of A4 paper per minute.
2. The standard of print is very good and laser printers can also produce very good quality printed graphic images too.
3. A photoconductive drum is initially charged and then a high intensity laser beam is used to discharge selected areas on the drum. These discharged areas correspond to the white areas of the printed document.
4. Toner is then applied to the laser exposed areas of drum. So, this whole process creates an image of paper to the surface of drum. This image is then transferred and permanently fused on paper, when paper comes in contact with the drum. After this, the drum is automatically erased before the image of next page

5. It is suitable for screen printing or Book publishing.
6. It cost ranges 7,000 to 9 lakhs.
7. Both black & white and colored laser printers are available.

PLOTTER

1. Plotter is a graphics printer that draws images with ink pens.
2. These are output devices and are used to produce high resolution graphics and drawings.

3. It uses one or more pens that can be raised, lowered and moved over the printing media to draw graphics or text. The heart of the plotter is the printer head assembly, consisting of a horizontal bar and, attached to it, the head assembly holding the pen in use. The pen can be positioned horizontally by moving the pen assembly along the bar. Vertical positioning is achieved by either moving the bar (stationary page plotter) or the paper (rolling page plotter). Pen plotters are still the most affordable printing device for CAD use and offer resolution unlike any other printer. The lines are not made up of dots. They are actually drawn, providing infinite resolution.

4. There are two types of Plotter-

   a. ***Pen Plotter :*** In Pen Plotters, a special pen filled with one or more colors is used for making drawing, diagram etc. In this type of plotter, paper is fixed and pen moves across the page.

   b. ***Inkjet Plotter :*** In inkjet plotters, the paper is placed on a drum and a jet of ink of different colors is mounted on a carriage. In this type of plotter, Pen is fixed, and paper moves forward and backward on drum.

newtopic Memory

A memory is the storage place where data and instructions can be stored into and retrieved from whenever required by other functional blocks of a computer.

Types of Memory

→ Primary Memory

→ Secondary Memory

PRIMARY MEMORY: - It refers to computer's memory. All the information is processed and stored in chips.

Two Basic Kinds of Memory Chips:-

- RAM CHIPS
- ROM CHIPS

RAM CHIPS

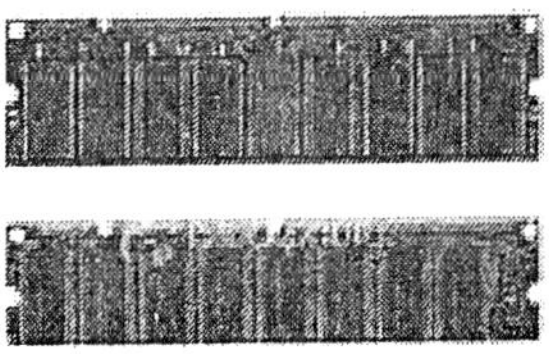

- Stands for **R**andom **A**ccess **M**emory.
- Both reading and writing can take place; therefore it is also called as "***Read-write***" memory.
- It holds information or data temporarily.
- It is volatile i.e. the data stored in RAM will get lost, if the power is turned off.
- The word ***"random"*** refers to the fact that any piece of data can be returned quickly, and in a constant time, regardless of its physical location and whether or not it is related to the previous piece of data. This contrasts with storage mechanisms such as tapes, magnetic disks and optical disks, which rely on the physical movement of the recording medium or a reading head.

ROM CHIPS

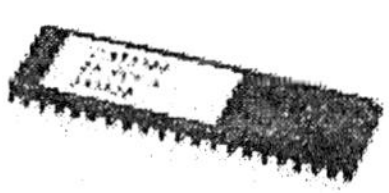

- It stands for **R**ead **O**nly **M**emory, because only reading can be done; writing is not allowed.
- Instructions are permanently imprinted on physical components by the manufacturer and are not accessible or changeable by the user.

- It is non-volatile i.e. the data will not get lost, if the power is turned off.
- It contains the instructions for booting the computer & loading Operating system from the hard into RAM.

SECONDARY STORAGE DEVICE OR MEDIA:

Computer's main memory is the primary storage. Additional storage facilities are needed to store information and retrieve it as and when it is required. Such storage facilities are referred as secondary storage media. It is used to store data permanently.

Secondary storage devices are -:

- Optical disk
- Magnetic disk (Hard disk & Floppy Disk)
- Magnetic tapes

OPTICAL DISK

1. An optical is an electronic data storage medium that can be written to and read using a low-powered laser beam.
2. An optical disk is impressed with a series of spiral pits in a flat surface.
3. It is placed in CD-Drive; it is read by means of laser beam and light detector which interprets the information etched on the surface of the disk.
4. Optical disks can store more data at lower costs therefore; they are still used as a complement to magnetic storage media.
5. **Examples:** CD (Compact disk), DVD (Digital Video Disk)

Advantages:

- It is physically harder to break or melt or warp.
- It is not sensitive to being touched, though it can get too dirty or scratched to be read. It can be cleaned.
- It is entirely unaffected by magnetic fields.
- Much powerful & preferred media for distributing software.
- It can store 600 – 700 MB of data.

STRUCTURE OF COMPACT DISK (CD)

1. The base of CD is a clear hard plastic known as polycarbonate.
2. The top of the plastic disk is coated with a reflective material such as aluminium that reflects the light of the reading laser. The entire disc is coated with a protective lacquer & a label is printed on the top of the disc.
3. Disc diameter equals to 120 mm & center hole diameter of the disc is 15 mm.

4. The area closed to the center hole is called clamping area and no data is written in this area. It is generally 26 mm to 33 mm wide.
5. The data area is approx. 38 mm wide & is divided into three sectors- table of contents, program area & read-out area (end of disc)
6. Inside a CD is a flat light reflecting layer called "***land***". On the land are many "***pits***" written in a spiral-shaped track. Lands (or reflective surface) and Pits (or holes) are used to store information.
7. When the laser strikes a land, most of its light is reflected back to the sensor. When the laser passes a pit, the light is diffused and less is reflected back to the sensor. The intensity of the light reflected back is converted to the digital signals your computer reads as 0s and 1s.
8. When you save photos, files, or MP3s to CDs using a CD burner on your PC, you are also creating lands and pits to store the information.

DVD

1. DVD stands for Digital Video Disk
2. It is a type of optical disk technology similar to the CD-ROM. A DVD holds a minimum of 4.7 GB of data, enough for a full-length movie.
3. DVDs are commonly used as a medium for digital representation of movies and other multimedia presentations that combine sound with graphics.

MAGNETIC DISK

It is a thin circular metal plate coated on both sides with a magnetic material. It is similar to a gramophone record. It is of two types:-

FLOPPY DISK

1. It is made of flexible plastic which is coated with magnetic oxide. Flexible disk is enclosed within a square plastic referred as cartridge, which gives handling protection to the disk surface.

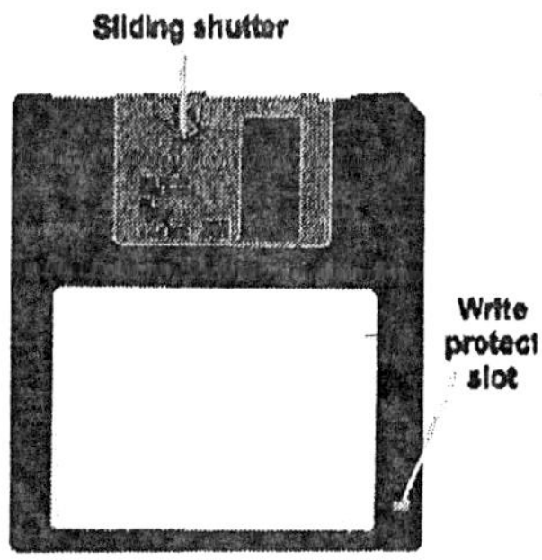

2. It is random access storage medium.
3. Data is stored in tracks (concentric) and sectors. Each sector holds 512 Bytes worth of data.
4. If you open the "***write protect slot or notch***" then disk becomes ***write-protected***. It means no data can be stored further on the disk until the notch is closed again.
5. It may be single sided or double sided. But, Single-sided disks are not in use any more. Floppy drives have two read/write heads - one for each surface. The position of the heads relative to each other is fixed.
6. **Density** is the number of bytes that can be stored on each track. ***Double density*** diskettes are no longer common. They are generally labelled ***DD or 2D. High density*** disks are usually labelled ***HD***
7. All disk drives have indicator lights that show when the disk is actually being used. A diskette should never be removed while this light is on. You should always glance at this light before removing a diskette.

Size	Density	Tracks per Side	Sectors	Storage Capacity
5.25"	Double	40	9	360 K
5.25"	High	80	15	1.2 MB
3.5"	Double	80	9	720 K
3.5"	High	80	18	1.44 MB

Size : The first floppy developed was of 8 inches. Generally, it comes in two size :-

- 5.25 inches
- 3.5 inches (standard size used nowdays;)

The total capacity of a disk is a multiplication of surfaces by tracks by sectors. So, a 3.5" high density disk can hold 2 x 80 x 18 x 512 = 1,474,560 bytes (1,024 = 1,440K).

HARD DISK :

1. Hard disks are the most popular medium for secondary storage. It is made up of a metal plate coated on both sides with a magnetic material.
2. It is known as "***hard disk***" because the plates are made up of metal.
3. A disk pack consists of a no. of these disks (3 or more) mounted about half an inch apart from each other on a central shaft.
4. Each disk consists of a no. of invisible concentric circles called tracks. The data is stored as magnetized spots arranged in concentric circles (tracks) on the disk. Each track is divided into sectors.

5. The number of tracks and sectors on a disk is known as its "***format***".
6. ***Cylinder:***. The two or more vertically adjacent tracks form an imaginary cylinder.
7. All the disk of a disk pack moves simultaneously, in the same direction and at equal speed.
8. Although the length of each track is different but the number of characters stored in each track is same.

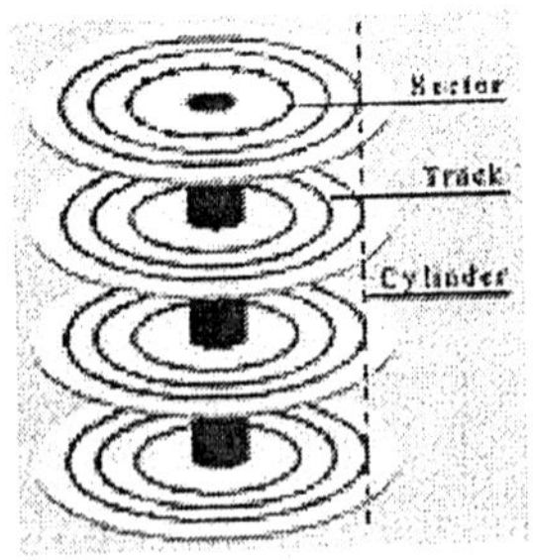

9. The hard disk is direct-access storage medium.
10. As the disk rotates read/write heads move to the correct track. The disk is sealed and lubricated and the head hovers on a cushion of air just above the disk to avoid damage. These are therefore called floating heads.

11. *Storage Capacity:* It generally ranges from 10 to 200 GB.

Some Related Terminology:-

1. **Memory access time:** It refers to the time taken by a character in memory to be transferred to or from the CPU.
2. **Disk access time:** is an average of the time between initiating a request and obtaining the first data character.
   - **Seek Time:** The time it takes for a read/write head to move to a specific data track
   - **Latency :** The time between initiating a request for data and the beginning of the actual data transfer. On a disk, latency is the time it takes for the selected sector to come around and be positioned under the read/write head.
   - **Transfer Time:** The time it takes to transmit or move data from one place to another. It is the time interval between starting the transfer and the completion of the transfer.

MAGNETIC TAPES

1. Magnetic tapes are similar to cassette tapes in being accessed only serially. (Serial Access Medium)
2. It is very popular medium for storage of voluminous amount of processing data.
3. Data is stored in frames across the width of the tape. The frames are grouped into blocks or records. These tapes have 556 to 6250 characters per inch.
4. Each record on a tape is separated by blank spaces called ***inter record gaps.***
5. Can be used either as a backup for disks or for easy transfer of information between two unconnected computers.

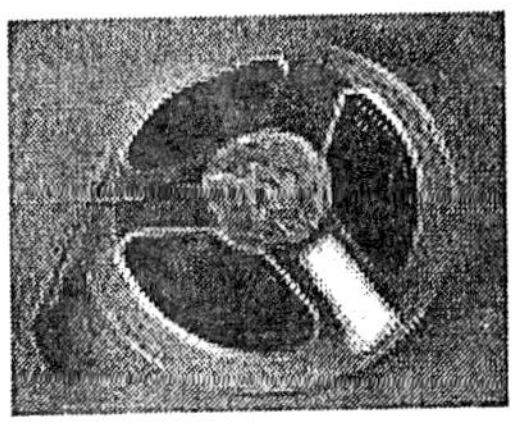

ADVANTAGES :-

- Voluminous storage.
- Low cost.
- Reusable and erasable.

DISADVANTAGES :-

- Not applicable for jobs which require rapid access of specific records because it is a sequential medium.
- An external label is required because each reel of tape is indistinguishable from the others.
- Tape is continuous in design so inserting of records is not possible.
- Some data is always lost when the tape is worn out.
- The environment of the tape must be tightly controlled from change of temp., humidity and dust.

newtopic Software Concepts

Instruction: The command executed by the computer for doing a particular task is called instruction. ***e.g.*** *DOS Commands*

Program: The collection or group of related instructions for performing a particular task is called a program ***e.g.*** Word, Excel etc.

Software or Software Package: The collection or group of various programs is called a software or software package. ***e.g.*** *Ms-Office (collection of application programs like Word, Excel, PowerPoint etc)*

TYPES OF SOFTWARE:

- ➔ System Software
- ➔ Application Software
- ➔ Utilities

System Software:

System software encompasses those programs that are used to manage the resources of computer at low level. System software is generally required for loading, supervising, controlling and execution of computer programs.

Examples: Operating System, Language Processors, Library Programs etc

1. ***Operating System:*** An operating system can be defined as integrated set of programs that control and supervise a system. These set of programs gets automatically loaded in the machine memory as soon as the computer power is put on. Operating system acts as an interface between the hardware and the software or we can say between computer and the user. The Operating system is loaded from the disk into the RAM during the booting procedure. It remains in memory until the power is switched off (or shutdown). Common examples of Operating system are- Ms-DOS, WINDOWS, UNIX and LINUX etc.
2. ***Language Processors:*** These programs are used to convert each instruction in the source program to machine understandable code (or binary code). These programs are unalterable and machine dependent. ***Examples:*** Compilers, Assemblers, Debuggers.
3. ***Library Programs:*** Library programs are set of programs specifically designed to be used by different users. These programs are stored on a secondary storage medium like magnetic tapes or disks. Thus, a programmer can directly access it rather than writing on it's own. ***Examples*:** Library files used in C or C++

➔ *Application Software*

Application software consists of programs that are designed for an end user. Thus, such programs serve as ready made solutions to give problems. These problems may be scientific or related to business. These application software are usually available on magnetic tapes or disks and can be loaded into the computer memory when desired.

Examples: Databases, Word Processors, Spreadsheets, Graphic Packages (like Flash, Corel Draw etc)

1. ***Databases:*** A database is an organized collection of interrelated data items or records ***e.g.*** *telephone directory, dictionary, student's database etc.* Some popular databases are- **dBase, FoxPro, Oracle, Sybase** etc. The system or software that manages the operations related to a database (like adding, deleting, modifying, sorting etc) is known as Database Management System (DBMS). In RDBMS (Relational Database Management System), the data is represented in terms of tables. The table consists of '***columns***' which represent the data elements and the '***rows***' represent the data. It provides user friendly and quick access to the data stored in the tables. Most of the business applications make use of the database concepts because RDBMS with 4GL tools together provide a very powerful tool for developing business applications.

2. ***Word Processor:*** It is a program that is used for typing, editing and formatting of text. It is somewhat similar to typewriter but with some advance features like saving, formatting and printing, word wrap etc. The most common word processor used nowadays is Ms-WORD.

3. ***Spreadsheets:*** A spreadsheet allows the user to organize text and numbers in rows and columns. In addition, "calculator-like" functions can be added to a spreadsheet to automatically calculate totals, averages, percentages, and much more. A spreadsheet is the computer equivalent of a paper ledger sheet. It consists of a grid made from columns and rows. It is an environment that can make number manipulation easy and somewhat painless. In a spreadsheet the ***COLUMN*** is defined as the vertical space that is going up and down the window. Columns are labelled as A, B, C, D...IV etc. In a spreadsheet the ***ROW*** is defined as the horizontal space that is going across the window. Rows are numbered as 1, 2, 3....65,536 etc. In a spreadsheet the ***CELL*** is defined as the space where a specified row and column intersect. Each CELL is assigned a name (or address) according to its COLUMN letter and ROW number.

   In a spreadsheet there are three basic types of data that can be entered.

   a. ***labels*** - (text with no numerical value)

   b. ***constants*** - (just a number — constant value)

   c. ***formulas*** - (a mathematical equation used to calculate)

4. ***Graphic Packages:*** Graphic packages refers to a collection of programs used for graphic design, multimedia development, specialized image development, general image editing or to access graphic file. Graphics packages can be classified as- Raster graphics & Vector Graphics. Several graphics program support animation or digital video. ***E.g.***PaintBrush, Corel Draw, Photoshop, Flash etc.

→ *Utility Programs*

Utilities are called "Service Programs" because these programs supports everyday use of the computers including memory management, virus protection, file compression, file management, searching of files, diagnostic routing to check the performance and current health of hardware. **E.g.** Editors, File Manager, Debugging tool, DOS prompt in Windows, Find or Search programs, Antivirus etc.

OTHER TYPES OF SOFTWARE-

Retail software: This type of software is used for managing various operations of the retail stores.

OEM software: OEM stands for "***Original Equipment Manufacturer***" and refers to software sold in bulk to resellers, designed to be bundled with hardware. For example, Microsoft has contracts with various companies including Dell Computers, Toshiba, Gateway and others. Microsoft sells its operating systems as OEM software at a reduced price, minus retail packaging, manuals and installation instructions. Resellers install the operating system before systems are sold and the OEM CD is supplied to the buyer. The "manual" consists of the Help menu built into the software itself. OEM software is not legal to buy unbundled from its original hardware system.

Shareware: This software is downloadable from the Internet. Licenses differ, but commonly the user is allowed to try the program for free, for a period stipulated in the license, usually thirty days. At the end of the trial period, the software must be purchased or uninstalled.

Crippleware: This software is similar to shareware except that key features will cease to work after the trial period has ended. For example, the "save" function, the print function, or some other vital feature necessary to use the program effectively may become unusable. This "cripples" the program. A purchase is necessary to unlock the crippled features.

Demo software: Demo software is not intended to be a functioning program, though it may allow partial functioning. It is mainly designed to *demonstrate* what a purchased version is capable of doing, and often works more like an automated tutorial. If a person wants to use the program, they must buy a fully functioning version.

Adware: This is free software that is supported by advertisements built into the program itself. Some adware requires a live Internet feed and uses constant bandwidth to upload new advertisements. The user must view these ads in the interface of the program. Disabling the ads is against the license agreement. Adware is not particularly popular.

Spyware: Spyware software is normally free, but can be shareware. For example, a multimedia player might profile what music and video files the software is called upon to play. This information can be stored with a unique identification tag associated with the specific program on a user's machine, mapping a one-to-one relationship.

Freeware: Freeware is also downloadable off the Internet and free of charge. Often freeware is only free for personal use, while commercial use requires a paid license. Freeware does not contain spyware or adware.

Public domain software: This is free software, but unlike freeware, public domain software does not have a specific copyright owner or license restrictions. It is the only software that can be legally modified by the user for his or her own purposes.

newtopic

Block Diagram of Computer (or Computer Architecture)

A chart that contains squares and rectangles connected with arrows to depict hardware and software interconnections.

Computer Block diagrams consists of following five units-

1. Input Unit
2. Output Unit
3. Memory Unit (RAM)
4. Control Unit (C.U)
5. Arithmetic & Logical Unit (A.L.U)

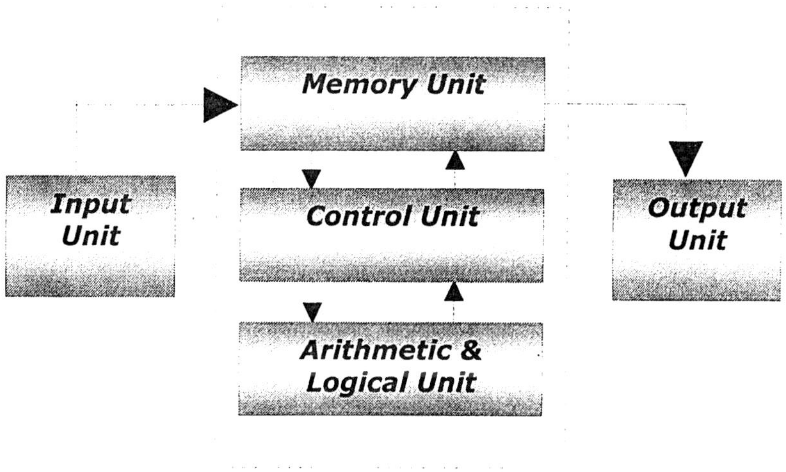

CPU

Input Unit: Input Unit refers to the input devices attached with the computer to feed input. ***E.g.*** Keyboard, Mouse etc.

Output Unit: Output unit refers to the output devices connected with the computer to display results or output. ***E.g.*** Printer, Monitor etc.

Memory Unit: It refers to RAM (Random Access Memory). It is also called Primary memory of computer. It is used to temporarily store the input fed through input devices or to store output to be displayed through the output device.

Control Unit: It acts as a bridge between RAM and ALU. It has no role in processing of data. Thus, it is just used for transferring data from memory unit to A.L.U and vice-versa.

Arithmetic & Logical Unit: A.L.U is responsible for performing all arithmetic and logical computations. A.L.U performs various operations like addition, subtraction, multiplication & division on numerical data. It also performs logical computations such as equal to, less than & greater than. A.L.U uses registers for the purpose of storing operators, operands and processed result. There are three basic types of registers used in ALU-

1. ***Storage Register:*** It temporarily holds data from or being sent to the primary storage section
2. ***Accumulator Register:*** It holds the result of the calculations until needed later on.
3. ***Adder:*** It receives the data from two or more sources perform the arithmetic and logical calculations and transfer the result to the accumulator.

Memory Unit, Control Unit and ALU all together forms the major unit i.e. CPU (Central Processing Unit). CPU is called the heart and nerve center of the computer. Its speed is regulated by an extremely accurate clock that is part of computer's circuitry. So, the speed of computer is called "clock speed". This clock is like a "pacemaker of heart", as a pacemaker regulates the heart beat, the clock ensures that computer operations are done in a proper time sequence.

Functioning of Computer Units

The input is fed through the input unit and is temporarily stored in memory unit. The control unit then fetches the required data from the RAM and transfers it to ALU for further processing. The processed data from ALU is again fetched by Control unit and is transferred to Memory unit, from where it is finally displayed to the end user through the output unit.

new topic Classification of Computers

- On the Basis of Type of Computations performed
- On the Basis of Size & Speed
- On the Basis of Manner of Processing

On the Basis of Type of Computations performed

1. ***Digital:*** Digital computer is a computer that stores data as discrete numbers or digits (i.e. 0 and 1) and processes them in distinct steps ***e.g.*** Digital clock, Thus, a digital computer uses symbolic representations of its variables. A digital computer can easily store and manipulate numbers, letters, images, sounds, or graphical information represented by a symbolic code.
2. ***Analog:*** An analog computer is a computer that processes, in parallel, a continuous source of fluctuating variables. Thus, in analog computers, variables are represented as continuous, varying physical quantities ***e.g.*** Speedometer, Analog clock (with needles) etc.
3. ***Hybrid:*** A hybrid computer is one that combines both digital and analog technology.

On the Basis of Size and Speed

1. ***Supercomputer:*** Supercomputers operate very fast and have multiple processors. These are characterized by very large size and very high processing speeds. There are very few of these machines in existence due to their cost. This type of computer has been developed for scientific applications usually involving complex arithmetic and mathematical operations. One such use is in weather forecasting. ***E.g.*** PARAM 10000 (developed by India & Japan in 1998)

2. ***Mainframe:*** Mainframe computers are large general purpose computers. Mainframe computers generally require special attention and are kept in a controlled atmosphere. These are characterized by extensive processing, storing and input/output capabilities. They are multi-tasking and generally used in areas where large databases are maintained ***e.g.*** government departments and the airline industry. Mainframe typically can run more than one Operating system at a time as well.

3. ***Mini computer:*** These perform multi-tasking and allow many terminals to be connected to their services. The ability to connect minicomputers to each other and mainframes has popularized them among larger businesses. This use is being challenged by the developments in the microcomputer range and the practice of sharing resources of microcomputers under a network. Minicomputers are still recognized as being able to process large amounts of data.

4. ***Micro computer:*** These are the smallest category of computers. Microcomputers use single chip processors and are known as PCs (personal computers). The rapid increase in the speed and memory of the PC has extended its use from single applications to multi-tasking applications. The general trend has been to have several PCs linked together in a network in order to share peripherals such as printers. This practice is reducing the popularity of mini-computers and mainframes.

❒ On the Basis of Manner of Processing

1. Timesharing System or Multiuser System:

i. A system which supports multiple users to access a single processing system through different remote terminals i.e. each terminal provides direct access to the processor.

ii. In this case, the attention of CPU is switched from one user to another and a job is done in an allocated time-slice. It all happens in such a manner that it appears that nobody else is using the computer.

iii. ***e.g.*** Consider a situation, in which a programmer working on terminal 1 is loading data onto a storage device. At the same time, another programmer, working on terminal 2 is loading his program in main memory and the CPU is busy in executing the program that is being run from terminal 3.

iv. In this case, each user gets the impression that only he is getting the full attention of CPU, but it is not true. Each user gets the equal attention for a small time slot.

v. ***Examples of O.S that supports this feature are -*** UNIX, LINUX & WINDOWS-NT.

2. Batch Processing system:

i. The main function of a batch processing system is to automatically keep executing one job to the next job in the batch.

ii. The main idea behind a batch processing system is to reduce the interference of the operator during the processing or execution of jobs by the computer.

iii. ***Turn Around Time:*** In a batch processing system, we generally make use of the "turn around time". It is defined as the time from which a user job is given to the time when it's output is given back to the user. This time includes the batch formation time, time taken to execute a batch, time taken to print results and the time required to physically sort the printed outputs that belong to different jobs. You can reduce the turn around time by recording the jobs or faster input output media like magnetic tape like magnetic tapes or disk.

iv. ***Job Scheduling:*** This term is also used in case of batch processing. It is the process of sequencing jobs so that they can be executed on the processor. It recognizes different jobs on the basis of first-come-first-serve basis.

v. It is because of the sequential nature of the batch, the batch monitor always starts the next job in the batch.

vi. Several batches could be performed on the same criteria of priorities. So, the batch having the highest priority could be made to run earlier than other batches. This would give a better turn around service to the selected jobs.

3. Multiprocessing System:

i. It refers to a system, where multiple processors are used to execute a certain tasks.

ii. Multiprocessing is possible due to multi-threading, which means that when an application has to e executed, it is divided into various small tasks called threads and each thread is simultaneously executed by each processor at the same time.

iii. Multithreading cannot be applicable in case of multiprogramming.

4. Multiprogramming System:

i. It refers to the existence of two or more programs in different parts of the memory hierarchy at the same time.

ii. In this way, it is possible to keep all parts of the computer busy by working with several programs in sequence ***e.g.*** a program is being executed in the CPU and an I/O transfer is required. The CPU initiates I/O processor to start executing the transfer. This leaves the CPU free to execute other programs.

5. *Multitasking System:* It refers to a situation in which different tasks are performed by the same processor; but each task is occupying a different portion of memory, so that if one task gets corrupted, the other task can independently remains continued ***e.g. O.S supporting multitasking feature:*** WINDOWS- 9x, 2000, Millenium, NT, XP, Vista etc.

6. *Real-Time System:*

i. It is that system which responds back fast so that it is able to have an impact on the environment in which it is working.

ii. The real time system is mostly applied in those systems where the response or the feedback is immediately required. ***E.g.*** Process Control Systems in factories or missile tracking system for defense.

iii. Another important example of real time system application is in the airline seat reservation system in whose case the availability of a seat is checked, reserved and booked while the operator is interacting with the customer.

iv. Thus, the interaction between the computer and the application environment has to be very quick in case of a real time system. Therefore, the O.S is designed in such a manner so that it is able to meet the need of quick response.

v. Since the response time of a real time system are critical, a general time sharing system may not be able to satisfy them.

vi. When a real time application is to be supported by a computer system along with the general time-sharing series, then the real time application is given the higher processing priority.

newtopic Type of Languages used in Computers

A language is basically used for communication or giving instructions. As human beings use different languages in order to communicate among them. Similarly, human being requires computer languages for aiding communication with computer.

1. ***Low level language or Machine language or binary Language (L.L.L):*** The language that a microprocessor can read and interpret is called low level language or machine language. It is also called binary language because low level language code consists of binary bits i.e. 0 and 1. These '0' and '1' represents the state of the pulse in the circuit. If there is pulse (or current) in the circuit then it is represented as "1" and the absence of pulse is indicated by "0"
2. ***High Level Language (H.L.L):*** It is a problem oriented language that is portable across several platforms. It is easily understandable by human beings because high level language code consists of English language like statements ***e.g.*** COBOL, PASCAL, BASIC, FORTRAN, Java, C, C++ etc.
3. ***Assembly Language:*** It is a programming language that uses symbolic codes called MNEMONICS for developing the program. But, before execution, the program written in assembly language is required to be translated into machine language. The task of translating assembly code into machine code is done by assembler.

DIFFERENT GENERATIONS OF COMPUTER LANGUAGES

- **1 GL or First Generation Languages:** It refers to the machine language. The machine language code run fast and efficiently as it is directly executed by the CPU. First generation languages require no translators or assemblers for their translation.
- **2 GL or Second Generation Languages:** It refers to Assembly language, which is platform specific (depends on the microprocessor). Assembly language code be easily read and written by human beings. However, it needs to be translated from assembly language to machine language using assembler, before it's final execution.

- **3 GL or Third Generation Languages:** It refers to a high level structured programming language. The term "structured" refers to procedural languages, which means such languages requires the specification of processing steps to accomplish a desired task ***e.g.*** C, COBOL, PASCAL, BASIC etc.
- **4 GL or Forth Generation Languages:** Forth generation languages refer to non-procedural languages. These languages are used by non-programming professionals because prior knowledge of language is not required. It includes certain commands that can be directly used to interact with the computer ***e.g.*** SQL, NATURAL, Informix-4GL etc
- **5 GL or Fifth Generation Languages:** It is a programming language that uses constraints (conditions) rather than algorithm. These languages are designed to make the computer solve the problem for you. These languages are mainly used in artificial intelligence research ***e.g.*** Prolog, MERCURY etc.

LANGUAGE PROCESSORS

1. ***Compiler:*** It is a translator program which reads the whole code written in H.L.L at once, and then converts it into machine language. It plays no role in execution. It requires large memory space because it is copied to main memory whenever compilation is required. Compilation process requires less time. Compiled program runs much faster. Thus, it is better than interpreter if we talk in terms of execution time. After making changes to a program, compilation is to be done again.
2. ***Interpreter:*** It is also a translator program which reads the code written in high level language line-by-line, converts it into machine language and also executes it. It requires comparatively less memory space for its storage. Interpretation method is much more time consuming. Interpreted program run at a slower rate. It gives fast response to changes in a source program. Thus, it is better than compiler if we talk in terms of debugging because it is the best debugger.
3. ***Assemblers:*** Assembler is also a translator program used to convert the code written in assembly language to machine language.

new topic Standards Adopted by Manufacturers to Represent Characters in Computer

1. ASCII:

a. It stands for American Standard Code for Information Interchange.

b. It is pronounced as "***ask- ee***"

c. Earlier ASCII used 7 bits to represent each character in the ASCII character set.

d. But presently, each character is represented by eight bit code.

e. Therefore, total number of character = 2^8 = 256 (i.e. from 0 to 255)

f. The chart containing the ASCII characters is called "***ASCII Chart***". The ASCII chart contains the ***"ASCII Codes"*** (0 to 255) and their corresponding characters. These characters may include- English alphabets (lowercase and uppercase), numeric digits (0-9), graphical symbols as well as mathematical symbols. ***For example:*** ASCII code of capital "A" is 65, Likewise, ASCII Code of small "a" is 97 and so on.

g. Text files stored in ASCII format are sometimes called ASCII files. Text editors and word processors are generally capable of storing files in ASCII format. However, executable files and most data files containing numeric data are never stored in ASCII format.

h. All PCs & Macintoshes support ASCII standard.

2. EBCDIC:

a. It stands for Extended Binary Coded Decimal Interchange Code

b. It is pronounced as "eb-see-dic"

c. These codes are designed by IBM (International Business Machine, an Indian Computer Company) in 1963 as an extension to older Binary Coded Decimal (BCD) standard (that uses 4 bits to represent a character)

d. According to EBCDIC representation, each character is represented using eight bits.

e. Therefore, total number of characters = 2^8 = 256 (i.e. from 0 to 255)

f. However, in recent years, EBCDIC has been expanded to 16-bit or 32-bit variants to allow representation of large non-latin character sets.

g. All IBM mainframe computers, even the most recent models continue to support EBCDIC standard.

3. UNICODE:

a. It stands for Universal Code, which is an internationalized code

b. It represents each character using 16 bits.

c. Therefore, total number of characters = 2^{16} = 65536

Number System and Related Conversion

1. ***Decimal Number System:*** It consists of ten digits from 0 to 9.

- **Convert from Decimal Number System to Any Base**
  - *Let's take an example of a number i.e. 1234. For converting it to* ***Base 10****, do the following: -*

```
          Quotient Remainder
       ----------------
1234/10 =   123      4 -----+
 123/10 =    12     3 ----+ |
  12/10 =     1    2 --+  | |
   1/10 =     0   1 -+ |  | | (Stop when the quotient is 0)
                     | |  | |
                     1 2 3 4(Base 10)
```

- **Conversion of a decimal number 1341 in binary notation.** *Note that the desired base is 2, so we repeatedly divide the given decimal number by 2.*

```
         Quotient Remainder
   ------------------
1341/2  =  670   1 -------------+
 670/2  =  335   0 ------------+ |
 335/2  =  167   1 -----------+ | |
 167/2  =   83   1 ---------+ | | |
  83/2  =   41   1 --------+| | | |
  41/2  =   20   1 -------+|| | | |
  20/2  =   10   0 ------+||| | | |
  10/2  =    5   0 -----+|||| | | |
   5/2  =    2   1 ---+|||||| | | |
   2/2  =    1   0 --+|||||| | | |
   1/2  =    0   1 -+ ||||||| | | |       (Stop when quotient is 0)
                    | ||||||| | | |
                    1 0 1 0 0 1 1 1 1 01  (BINARY; Base 2)
```

❐ **Conversion of the same decimal number 1341 in octal notation -**

```
       Quotient  Remainder
   ------------------
1341/8  =  167   5 -----+
 167/8  =   20   7 ---+|
  20/8  =    2   4 --+||
   2/8  =    0   2 -+ |||   (Stop when the quotient is 0)
                    | |||
                    2 4 7 5 (OCT; Base 8)
```

❐ **Conversion of the same decimal number 1341 in hexadecimal notation-**

```
         Quotient  Remainder
   ------------------
1341/16  =  83   13 ---+
  83/16  =   5    3 --+|
   5/16  =   0    5 -+ | |   (Stop when the quotient is 0)
                     | | |
                     5 3 D   (HEX; Base 16)
```

2. ***Octal Number System:*** It consists of eight digits from 0 to 7. To convert a value from octal to binary, you merely translate each octal digit into its 3-bit binary equivalent.

DECIMAL	HEXADECIMAL	BINARY	OCTAL
0	0	0000	000
1	1	0001	001
2	2	0010	002
3	3	0011	003
4	4	0100	004
5	5	0101	005
6	6	0110	006
7	7	0111	007
8	8	1000	010

(contd.)

DECIMAL	HEXADECIMAL	BINARY	OCTAL
9	9	1001	011
10	A	1010	012
11	B	1011	013
12	C	1100	014
13	D	1101	015
14	E	1110	016
15	F	1111	017

- **Conversion from Octal to Binary:** *to convert from Octal to Binary just replace the octal digit with the corresponding binary pattern*

  Octal: 17 Binary: 001 111

- **Conversion from Binary to Octal:** *to convert from Binary to Octal just replace the binary pattern with the corresponding octal digit (Start with making pair of three bits from right hand side)*

  Binary: 111 010 Octal: 72

2. **Hexadecimal Number System**: The other major numbering system used by a computer is hexadecimal, or Base 16. In this system, the numbers are counted from 0 to 9, then letters A to F before adding another digit. The letter A through F represents decimal numbers 10 through 15, respectively. The below chart indicates the values of the hexadecimal position compared to 16 raised to a power and decimal values. It is much easier to work with large numbers using hexadecimal values than decimal.

- **Conversion from Hexadecimal to Binary:** *To convert a value from hexadecimal to binary, you merely translate each hexadecimal digit into its 4-bit binary equivalent. Hexadecimal numbers have either and "0x" prefix or an "h" suffix. For example, the hexadecimal number:-*

  0x3F7A

  Is translated into Binary, Using the Binary chart above-

  3 F 7 A

  0011 1111 0111 1010

- **Conversion from Binary to Hexadecimal:** *To convert from Binary to Hexadecimal just replace the binary pattern with the corresponding hexadecimal digit (Start with making pair of four bits from right hand side)*

  Binary: 0111 1010 Hexadecimal: 0x7A

3. **Binary Number System:** It consists of only two digits i.e. 0 and 1. Computer memory is based on the electrical representation of data. Each memory position is represented by a bit which can be either 'on' or 'off'.

This makes it easier to represent computer memory using a base 2 number system rather than the base 10 decimai system. The binary system represents numbers by a series of 1's and 0's which correspond to 'on' and 'off' values. A "1" represents an 'on' position, a 0, an 'off' position. A byte is represented by 8 bits numbered 0 to 7 from left to right. The leftmost bit is called the high-order bit, the right most bit, the low-order bit in the decimal system, each position corresponds to a power of 10, in the binary system, each position corresponds to a power of 2

Conversion of Binary to Decimal: In this case, we index the binary numbers starting from right hand side and then follow the given steps for the conversion of binary to decimal-

e.g. $\mathbf{0^5\ 1^4\ 0^3\ 1^2\ 1^1\ 1^0}$

$= 0 * 2^5 + 1 * 2^4 + 0 * 2^3 + 1 * 2^2 + 1 * 2^1 + 1 * 2^0$

$= 0 + 16 + 0 + 4 + 2 + 1$

$= 23$

2

Operating System- DOS & WIN

Introduction:

An Operating System, or OS, is a software program that enables the computer hardware to communicate and operate with the computer software. Without a computer Operating System, a computer would be useless.

Thus an operating system is a large collection of specialized programs, which manages resources such as memory, processor, file system and input/output devices. It gets loaded in the computer's main memory as soon as the power is put on. It keeps track of the status of each resource and decides who will have a control over computer resources, for how long and when. In other words, it acts as an interface between the software and hardware; or between the user and computer.

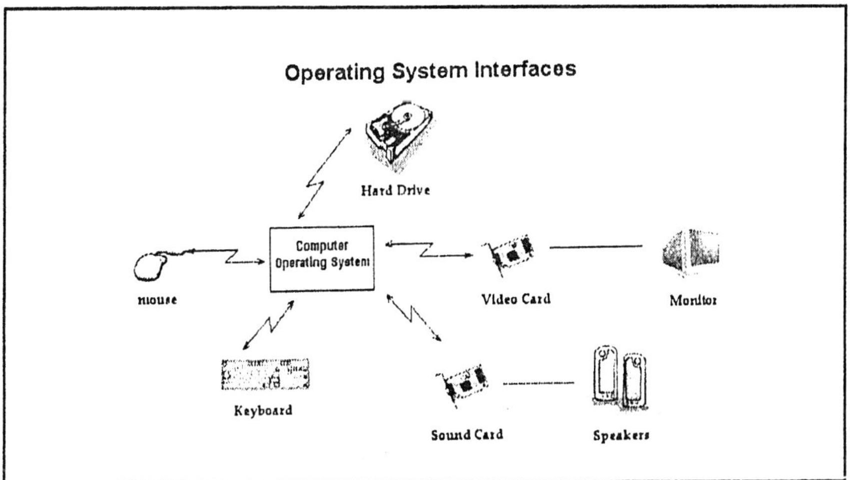

Examples: UNIX (first OS), DOS, LINUX, WINDOWS 3.1, 95, 98, NT, 2000, ME, XP, Vista etc.

new topic Functions or Services of Operating System

1. ***Memory Management:*** Current computer architectures arrange the computer's memory in a hierarchical manner, starting from the fastest registers, CPU cache, random access memory and disk storage. An operating system's memory manager coordinates the use of these various types of memory by tracking which one is available, which is to be allocated or deallocated and how to move data between them. This activity, usually referred to as virtual memory management, increases the amount of memory available for each process by making the disk storage seem like main memory.
2. ***Process Management:*** Every program running on a computer, be it background services or applications, is a process. Process management is an operating system's way of dealing with running multiple processes. Process management involves computing and distributing CPU time as well as other resources. Most operating systems allow a process to be assigned a priority which affects its allocation of CPU time.
3. ***Disk Management:*** These programs used to perform some "housekeeping" (i.e. inbuilt) functions such as-
    a. Formatting disk
    b. Displaying the contents of a disk
    c. Checking a disk for reading and writing
    d. Determining the space remaining on a disk
    e. Making a backup copy of the contents of a hard disk and restoring the contents from a backup copy.
4. ***File Management:*** All operating systems include support for a variety of file systems. A file system (often also written as file system) is a method for storing and organizing computer files and the data they contain to make it easy to find and access them. Microsoft Windows includes support for FAT12, FAT16, FAT32, and NTFS. The NTFS file system is the most efficient and reliable of the four Windows file systems.
5. ***Networking:*** Most current operating systems are capable of using the TCP/IP networking protocols. This means that one system can appear on a network of the other and share resources such as files, printers, and scanners using either wired or wireless connections.

new topic Types of Operating System

1. **Real time processing**: When the computer has to react within a guaranteed time to an input, a real time operating system is used. For example, the engine management system within a car uses a real time operating system in order to react to all the things going on within the engine. A real time operating system does not necessarily have to be fast. It simply has to be quick enough to respond to inputs in a predictable way. Computers operating in real time are often dedicated to the control

of systems such as industrial processes, planes and space flights. Another example of real time processing is computer games. ***For example,*** when an action is selected in a game, the data is fed back to the computer and the systems updated.

2. **Multi-programming:** Multi-programming is a method of operating such that several programs appear to be running at once. In this case, a single CPU divides it's time between more than one job. The jobs are usually given priorities. The operating system switches jobs in and out of processor time according to priority. For example, while one job is being allocated printer time, another will be being processed in memory. The processor is so fast that it seems that many jobs are being processed at the same time.

3. **Multi-tasking:** An Operating system that is capable of allowing multiple software processes to run at the same time. This isn't just about running more than one application at the same time. Multi-tasking allows multiple tasks to run concurrently, taking turns using the resources of the computer. In other words, it is capable of allowing multiple software processes to run at the same time. For example- running a couple of applications, sending a document to the printer and downloading a web page.

   However, operating systems are not truly multi-tasking - in order to do this, you would need parallel processors, which are now appearing on personal computers.

4. **Multi-access or multi-user:** A multi-access (or multi-user) system is one where a number of users are able to use the same system together. Modern personal computers can allow multi user access i.e. more than one person can make use of the computer resources at the same time via a LAN. The central processor deals with users in turn; clearly the more users, the slower the response time. Generally, however, the processor is so fast that the response time at the most is a fraction of a second and the user feels they are being dealt with immediately. **e.g. LINUX, UNIX, WINDOWS 2000**

5. **Batch processing:** A batch processing system is where programs or data are collected together in a batch and processed in one go. Typically the processing of payrolls, electricity bills, invoices and daily transactions are dealt with this way. This method of operation lends itself to jobs with similar inputs, processing and outputs where no human intervention is needed. Jobs are stored in a queue until the computer is ready to deal with them. Often batch processed jobs are done overnight.

new topic Booting

"Booting refers to the starting process of computer"

The term apparently derives from bootstrap which is a small strap or loop at the back of a leather boot that enables you to pull the entire boot on. There is also an expression, "pulling yourself up by your own bootstraps," meaning to leverage yourself to success from a small beginning. The booting of an operating system works by loading a very small program into the computer and then giving that program control so that it in turn loads the entire operating system.

To boot (as a verb; also "to boot up") a computer is to load an operating system into the computer's main memory or random access memory (RAM). Once the operating system is loaded (and, for example, on a PC, you see the initial Windows or Mac desktop screen), it's ready for users to run applications. The term "***reboot***" simply means to reload the operating system (this is done by pressing the Ctrl, Alt, and Delete keys at the same time).

1. Types of Booting

- ***Cold Booting or Hard Booting:*** Cold booting refers to switch on computer from a powered-down or off-state. It is done by pressing ***Power*** button of the CPU. It is also called hard booting.
- ***Warm Booting or Soft Booting:*** Warm booting refers to restarting the computer that is already turned on via an Operating system. Restarting is required whenever your system encounters certain errors or hangs problem. It is done either pressing ***Restart*** button of the CPU or by pressing Ctrl + Alt + Del keys simultaneously. It is also called soft booting.

2. Sequence of Booting or Bootstrap Process

1. As soon as the computer is turned on, the basic input-output system (BIOS) on your system's read-only memory (ROM) chip is "woken up" and takes charge. BIOS is already loaded because it's built-in to the ROM chip and, unlike random access memory (RAM), ROM contents don't get erased when the computer is turned off.
2. BIOS first does a power-on self test (POST) to make sure all the computer's components are operational. Then the BIOS's boot program looks for the special boot programs that will actually load the operating system onto the hard disk.
3. First, it looks on drive A (unless you've set it up some other way or there is no diskette drive) at a specific place where operating system boot files are located. If there is a diskette in drive A but it's not a system disk, BIOS will send you a message that drive A doesn't contain a system disk. If there is no diskette in drive A (which is the most common case), BIOS looks for the system files at a specific place on your hard drive.
4. Having identified the drive where boot files are located, BIOS next looks at the first sector (a 512-byte area) and copies information from it into specific locations in RAM. This information is known as the boot record or Master Boot Record.
5. It then loads the boot record into a specific place (hexadecimal address 7C00) in RAM.
6. The boot record loads the initial system file (for example, for DOS systems, IO.SYS) into RAM from the diskette or hard disk.
7. The initial file (for example, IO.SYS, which includes a program called SYSINIT) then loads the rest of the operating system into RAM. (At this point, the boot record is no longer needed and can be overlaid by other data.)
8. The initial file (for example, SYSINIT) loads a system file (for example, MSDOS.SYS) that knows how to work with the BIOS.

9. One of the first operating system files that is loaded is a system configuration file (for DOS, it's called CONFIG.SYS). Information in the configuration file tells the loading program which specific operating system files need to be loaded (for example, specific device driver).
10. The last step in the bootstrap process is to load COMMAND.COM; which in turn automatically searches for another special file (AUTOEXEC.BAT)
11. The above mentioned special file is loaded to tell which specific applications or commands the user wants to have included or performed as part of the boot process. In DOS, this file is named AUTOEXEC.BAT. In Windows, it's called WIN.INI.
12. After all operating system files have been loaded, the operating system is given control of the computer and performs requested initial commands and then waits for the first interactive user input.

newtopic Disk Operating System (DOS)

1. About DOS

It is an acronym that stands for Disk Operating System. It is written by BILL GATES & PAUL ALLEN in 1980s. It is a single user and unitasking system. The earliest version of DOS is known as QDOS (Quick & Dirty DOS) written by TIM PATERSON. DOS prepared by Microsoft Company is known as MS-DOS. It's current version is MS-DOS 8.0. Similarly, DOS developed by IBM (International Business Machine) is called PC-DOS. It's current version is PC-DOS 2000.

Important Files or Programs contained in DOS

Essential Files

1. **IO.SYS:** This program interacts with the computer's ROM-BIOS & calls from the MS-DOS.SYS program. IO.SYS shares with BIOS responsibility for:
   a. Console display and keyboard (CON)
   b. Line printer (PRN)
   c. Auxiliary device (AUX)
   d. Date and time (CLOCK)
2. **MS-DOS.SYS:** This is the Kernel of DOS. This program interacts directly with the application programs and IO.SYS program. It is like a bridge between application programs and IO.SYS as it intercepts program calls for printing, data storage and route these calls to the IO.SYS program, which responds to the request with the appropriate reaction. Thus, the DOS Kernel performs the following functions:
   a. File and record management
   b. Memory management
   c. Character device input/output
   d. Spawning other programs
   e. Access to real-time clock

3. **COMMAND.COM:** This program is also called as command processor or shell or command interpreter. It intercepts commands from the keyboard and executable command files. These files have the file extensions as .com & .exe The command processor is the user interface to DOS.

   The command processor is responsible for parsing and carrying out user commands, including the loading and execution of other programs from disk (external commands). The command processor also includes the code for many of the most commonly-used DOS commands, known as the internal commands.

Optional Files

1. **CONFIG.SYS:** It contains commands to handle-
   a. Commands to load memory managers
   b. Information on how memory should be configured
   c. Information about installed hardware
   d. Commands to load hardware drivers
   e. Settings including number of file handles and buffers
2. **AUTOEXEC.BAT:** BAT is a text file containing a set of commands to be carried out each time the computer is booted. This file is automatically executed whenever you boot the computer. This saves you from having to type the same commands (PATH, DATE, TIME, PROMPT, MODE, etc.) every time you start the computer.

2. Some Basic Terminology Related to DOS

- ***System Disk:*** The disk (hard disk or floppy disk) on which the three essential DOS programs (or files) reside is called system disk.
- ***POST:*** It refers to Power On Self Test. The POST is a built-in diagnostic program that checks your hardware to ensure that everything is present and functioning properly, before the BIOS begins the actual boot. It later continues with additional tests (such as the memory test that you see printed on the screen) as the boot process is proceeding.
- ***BIOS:*** It is the acronym used for Basic Input Output System. It is a in-built software contained in ROM chip. It contains all the code required to control the keyboard, display screen, disk drives, serial communications, and a number of miscellaneous functions. It contains the default resident drivers (like CON for Console display and keyboard) as well as installable drivers (like MOUSE.SYS, CLOCK.SYS etc)
- ***Shadowing:*** The process of copying the BIOS from ROM to RAM is called shadowing.
- ***DOS Prompt or Command Prompt:*** The message displayed on the screen, on loading DOS is called DOS prompt or command prompt. DOS prompt indicates that DOS is ready to accept the commands from the user. It displays the current working drive and directory name. **e.g. C:\WINDOWS\>** (where, C: indicates the default drive name, WINDOWS refer to the current directory name, "\" indicates root directory, "**>**" indicates output indirectional sign.

- ***Default Drive:*** The drive name that is displayed in the command prompt, when we just switch on the computer is called default drive.
- ***File:*** A file is a collection of interrelated data or information stored by DOS. The files are identified by a specific name. A filename is made up of a primary name and an optional extension. The primary name of a file is 1 to 8 characters long and the optional extension is 1 to 3 characters long. A period (.) is used to separate the primary name & extension. The primary name may consist of the following characters-
  a. ***Alphabetical characters: (***A to Z) or (a to z)
  b. ***Numerical characters:*** 0 to 9
  c. ***Special or wild card characters:***%, &, ^,# etc
- ***Directory:*** A directory is a named storage area of the disk that is used for storing one or multiple files and one or multiple subdirectories. The conventions (rules) of naming a directory are same as that of a file. However, a directory does not have any extension unlike file. It should be noted that a directory may contain subdirectory or file whereas a file can never contain any directory or subdirectory or file.
  a. ***Root Directory:*** The top directory in a file system is referred to as root directory. It is the basic inbuilt directory of the disk provided by the Operating system. The directory records the files that are stored on the disk. In directory entry (displayed using DIR command) it is indicated as (.) ***For example-***. If the command prompt is ***C:\WINDOWS\SERVER>*** then in this case **C:** would be the root directory.
  b. ***Parent Directory:*** The directory that contains the current directory is called its parent directory. In directory entry (displayed using DIR command) it is indicated as **(..)** ***For example-***. If the command prompt is ***C:\WINDOWS\SERVER>*** then in this case WINDOWS would be the parent directory.
  c. ***Current Directory:*** The directory in which the user works currently is called current directory. ***For example-***. If the command prompt is ***C:\WINDOWS\SERVER>*** then in this case SERVER would be the current directory.
- ***Directory Entry:*** For each file, there is a directory entry-
  a. Eight character file name
  b. Three characters extension
  c. The size of the file
  d. Date stamp
  e. Time stamp
  f. Starting cluster address
  g. File attributes (Hidden, Read only, System or Archive)
- ***File Attributes:*** Attributes means information about the file. A file can have more than one attribute attached to it, although only certain combinations really make any sense. Most of the attributes for files can

be modified using the DOS ***ATTRIB*** command. A file may have following attributes-

a. ***Hidden:*** It is used for hiding a file

b. ***Read-Only:*** It is used for protecting a file from being changed, overwritten or deleted

c. ***System:*** It indicates that file belongs to DOS

d. ***Archive:*** It is used to keep track of whether a file already has copies or backup copies or need backup copies.

- ***FAT:*** It stands for File Allocation Table. File storage does not occur sequentially. File is randomly stored on the disk in the form of clusters (chunks of data). The process by which files are assigned to clusters is called File Allocation. Thus, FAT is a table which keeps track of cluster number (i.e. address of the file) where the file is stored. The starting cluster address is stored in the root directory of the disk provided by the OS. An EOF makes the end of file i.e. final cluster of the file.

3. DOS Commands- Internal & External

Internal Commands

The internal commands are part of DOS' COMMAND.COM file. If you delete COMMAND.COM, you can no longer command DOS to do anything at the command line. These are simple and easy to use.

Internal Commands	**Purpose**	**Syntax**
CD	Used for changing directory i.e. for moving from one directory to another	CD <dir. Name>
CLS	Used for clearing screen	CLS
COPY	Used to copy file from one location (source) to another (target)	COPY <source> <target>
COPY CON	Used to create a file (on console). You can exit from file using Ctrl + Z or pressing F6 key	COPY CON <Filename>
DATE	Used to display or change the current date	DATE
DEL or ERASE	Used for deleting files	DEL <Filename>
DIR	• Lists the name of the directory and files present in the given directory • Displays the Page-wise list of directory and files i.e. pauses the output of the DIR command if there are more files than can be listed on your screen at once • Displays the Width-wise list of directory and files i.e. gives the directory listing wide across your screen without times, dates, and sizes listed	• DIR • DIR /P • DIR /W

Internal Commands	Purpose	Syntax
DEL or ERASE	Used for deleting files	DEL <Filename>
EXIT	If you are working in DOS prompt provided by WINDOWS then this command will let you exit from DOS window to WINDOWS session	EXIT
MD or MKDIR	It is used for making a directory or sub-directory	MD <Dir. Name>
PROMPT	It is used to set your system prompt. In the syntax, string refers to the text that you want to appear as prompt e.g. prompt $t would display current time as your command prompt	PROMPT <string>
RD or RMDIR	It is used for deleting or removing directory. The directory must be empty before deletion. "/s" switch must be used with RD command in order to delete all subdirectories and files contained in a given directory	RD <Dir name>
REN	It is used to rename a file	REN <old file name> <new file name>
TIME	It is used to display or change the current time	TIME
TYPE	It is used to display the contents of an existing file	TYPE <File name>
VER	It is used to display the version of the currently used Operating system in your system.	VER
VOL	It is used to display the current volume label of the hard drive or floppy disk	VOL

External Commands

The external commands are known as disk bound commands. They reside in individual files on disk and must be loaded into primary memory (RAM) before they can be executed. If any of those files are deleted accidentally or purposefully, you can still execute all of DOS' internal commands and any external commands that are still left on disk.

External Commands	Purpose	Syntax
ATTRIB	• It is used to change the characteristic or property of a file. (using certain options like +R for applying read only attribute; -R to remove Read only attribute from a file) • It is also used the display the preset attributes of a file	• ATTRIB +R <Filename> • ATTRIB

External Commands	Purpose	Syntax
CHKDSK	It examines the status of the selected disk. It displays the following information- • Total disk space • Total disk space occupied and the number of files. • The total disk space either lost or considered unusable by the system • The amount of disk space available for the system. • The memory occupied by the O.S and memory-resident programs.	CHKDSK
COMP	It is used to compare one file or set of files with a second file or a set of files. COMP only checks whether the given files are same or not and displays the message accordingly.	COMP <File1> <File2>
DEFRAG	It speeds up disk performance by reorganizing files i.e. it arranges defragmented files in continuous sectors so that no empty space falls between them. This makes file reading faster.	DEFRAG
DELTREE	It is used to delete a directory with all its subdirectories and files.	DELTREE
DISKCOPY	It is used to copy data of one floppy disk onto another floppy disk. It copies hidden files also (as it copies sector by sector) *This command only works with floppy disk.*	DISKCOPY <Drive 1:> <Drive 2:>
FDISK	It is used for partioning of hard disk. Each partition is assigned a logical drive letter like C, D or E etc. Each partition may have its own Operating system. This command can erase or overwrite your files, therefore used with caution.	FDISK**FDISK /Status** – this command displays the disk partition information
FORMAT	It is used to prepare a blank disk for storing data again. Thus, it should be kept in mind that when you format a disk (hard disk or floppy) all the contents of the disk get automatically deleted.	FORMAT <Drive name>
LABEL	It is used to display and set the volume label of the disk	LABEL <String>
MOVE	It is used to move a file from its current location to a new location on your hard disk	MOVE <source> <target>
MSBACKUP	It is used to backup data from hard disk to floppy disk. If the data, you intend to backup will not fit onto a single floppy disk, MSBACKUP will prompt you to insert another floppy	BACKUP C: A:
PATH	It displays or change the current path	PATH
RESTORE	This command restores files from disks made using the BACKUP command i.e. from floppy to hard disk.	RESTORE A: C:

External Commands	Purpose	Syntax
SCANDISK	It scans the disk for errors. It analyses the FAT and directory structure, report problems and repairs most of the problems it finds. It also tests the surface of the disk for physical flaws and rescues data from flawed areas.	SCANDISK
TREE	It displays the subdirectories contained in a given directory in hierarchical order (i.e. tree form)	TREE
XCOPY	It is used to selectively copy files from one disk to another. It copies file by file. It saves diskspace because it does not copy bad sector.	XCOPY <Drive 1:> <Drive 2:>

Illustration of Sequence of Commands used for making the given structure (Assuming C:\ as the root directory)

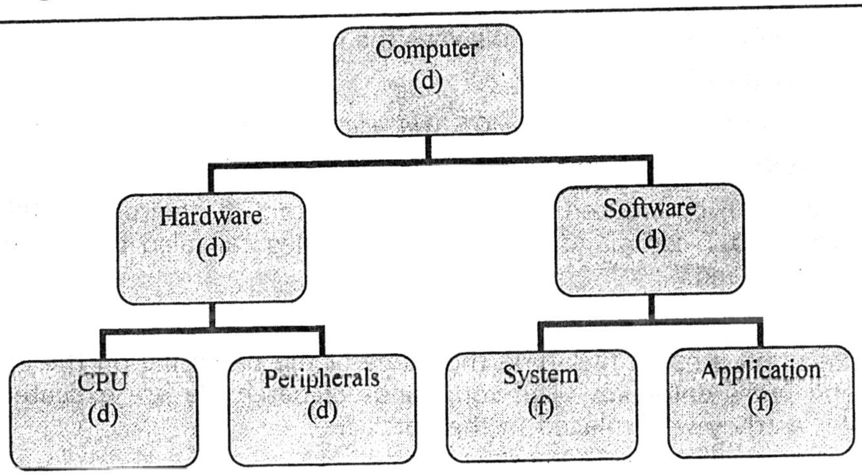

C:\> MD Computer

C:\> CD Computer

C:\Computer\> MD Hardware

C:\Computer\> MD Software

C:\Computer\> CD Hardware

C:\Computer\Hardware>MD CPU

C:\Computer\Hardware>MD Peripherals

C:\Computer\Hardware>CD..

C:\Computer\>CD Software

C:\Computer\Software>Copy con System

This is System file *(type the desired text that you want to store in file)*

^ Z

1 File Copied

C:\Computer\Software>Copy con Application

This is Application file *(type the desired text that you want to store in file)*

^ Z

1 File Copied

4. Batch Files & Configuring

Batch Files

Batch files are disk files containing one or more DOS commands. When we call the batch file by typing its name at the DOS prompt and pressing Enter, the commands in the batch file are executed one after another just as if they were typed individually. These files (which always have the extension .BAT), are useful in automating frequently used sequences of commands. To terminate a batch file at any time, **Ctrl + C** or **Ctrl + Break** shortcut key or BREAK command is used. On issuing BREAK command, DOS displays the message-

Terminate batch job (Y/N)?

Based on your answer Y or N DOS will accordingly execute the command.

Creating Batch Files

Batch files can be created using any text editor. The editor of DOS can be invoked using EDIT command. However, batch files can also be created using COPY CON command.

Executing Batch Files

For executing a batch file, type the name of the batch file on the command prompt and press enter key. The commands of batch file are executed in the same order as they were placed in the batch file.

Automatic Execution of Batch Files

If you want some commands to be executed automatically, whenever you start your computer, then for that AUTOEXEC.BAT file is used. AUTOEXEC.BAT file may include internal as well as external commands. Every time you boot the system, DOS automatically checks for the presence of the AUTOEXEC.BAT file on the drive containing your Operating system. If DOS finds such a file, it executes the statements in this file just after booting the system.

Batch File Commands

Batch File Commands	**Purpose**	**Syntax**
@	This command is used to suppress the command line. If you use @ with a command then that command is not displayed on the screen; instead of it only the output of the command is displayed	@ Command e.g. @ ECHO hello would only display "hello" as the output
ECHO	• The command **"@ ECHO OFF"** is almost always placed at the top of a batch file to switch off subsequent command echo.	

Batch File Commands	Purpose	Syntax
	• MS DOS batch files use two echo 'modes'. The default echo mode is ECHO ON. When ECHO is set to ON, every command in the batch file is displayed to the screen before it is run. • The command ECHO OFF sets the batch echo mode to OFF. In this mode, the commands are not printed to the screen prior to their execution. • As well as the echo modes, the ECHO command is used to print a message to the user. Messages are displayed to the user by preceding a line of text with ECHO.	ECHO ON ECHO OFF ECHO <Message>
REM	REM is used for making comments in a batch file. Comments are lines of code which are **not** executed by the batch file, but rather are used to convey information about the workings of the batch file itself. Good batch file programming practice demands a comment at the head of every batch file explaining its use and syntax.	REM <line containing comment>
PAUSE	The PAUSE command prints the message **"Press any key to continue..."** to the screen and waits for the user to respond.	PAUSE
GOTO	The GOTO command allows a batch file to branch to a different location to continue executing commands from. To tell the batch file *where* to go to, a label is placed after the GOTO command. (Label must be appropriately defined using colon (:) before actually using it.	GOTO <Label>
IF	The IF command is used in batch files to test whether a condition is met or not. This allows the batch file to perform a particular action only if a particular condition is met. There are several different variations of the IF command: IF EXIST, IF x == y	IF EXIST <File or Dir> <DOS COMMAND> IF NOT EXIST <File or Dir> <DOS COMMAND> **e.g.** IF NOT EXIST %1 MKDIR %1
SHIFT	The SHIFT command is often used in situations where an operation needs to be performed on several files or directories. SHIFT command increases the number of command-line parameters accessible by a batch file. Each time SHIFT is called, the value in the 1st parameter is discarded and replaced by the value of the 2nd parameter. The value in the 2nd parameter is replaced by the value in the 3rd parameter and so on.	SHIFT
CALL	The CALL command is used to run another batch file from within a batch file. Execution of the current batch file is paused and the called batch file is run. After the called batch file has finished running, the original batch file is resumed at the line after the CALL statement.	CALL batchfilename
FOR	FOR repeats a command for a number of files, directories, or text-strings i.e. The FOR command performs the same command for each element of a list. **e.g.** FOR %%f IN (*.*) DO TYPE %%f | MORE	FOR variable IN list DO command [parameters] [switches] Where :- **variable** is substituted for each element in the *list* & passed to *command*.

Batch File Commands	Purpose	Syntax
		list is a list of filenames or directory names, • **command** is a DOS internal or external command to be performed for each element of the *list*.
CHOICE	CHOICE makes it possible to accept various user-responses. *(This is used for designing menu in which the user may respond by selecting the desired menu item)*	CHOICE [/C:choices] [/N] [/S] [/T:choice, timeout][TEXT] Where: - **/C: choices**: specifies the choices that the user can choose from. The choices can only be single characters. **/N** : Do **not** display choices and the '?' at the end of the *TEXT* prompt. **/S** : Treat the choices as case sensitive, meaning that 'a' is a different choice from 'A'. By default, case is **not** sensitive - 'a' is equivalent to 'A'. **/T: choice, timeout**: Default to *choice* after *timeout* seconds. **TEXT**: The text to display as the prompt of the choice.

CONFIG.SYS

It is the configuration file. It contains the commands which are used to configure the system. If DOS does not find this file in the root directory, it supplies its own default values for all of the configuration command it requires. The configuration is done with the help of configuration directives supported in DOS. The parameters that can be configured or modified in the CONFIG.SYS file includes the following-

1. The Break status
2. The number of disk buffers
3. The Country specification
4. Additional device drivers
5. Maximum number of drives that you can access
6. Maximum number of files that can be opened concurrently by the file handlers (FILES)

Creating Config Files

You can create the Config.sys file in the same way as a batch file is created using either the COPY CON command or EDIT command. It should be noted that the file is saved with the extension .SYS and make sure that you are in the root directory before you create the file.

Configuration Directives (or Commands used in Config.Sys file)

Directives	Purpose
BREAK	It enables & disables the extended Ctrl +C and Ctrl + Break checking.
BUFFERS	It controls the number of internal disk buffers DOS sets for caching disk data
DEVICE	It loads an installable device driver into memory
FILES	It sets the maximum number of files that can be open in the system at any time
LASTDRIVE	It sets the highest drive letter that DOS will recognize
COUNTRY	It sets the time, date, currency and other display formats for countries other than United States.

newtopic Windows (98 & 2000)

1. Interfaces- CUI & GUI

A computer has many peripheral devices attached with it like mouse, keyboard, printer, scanner, modem etc. These are either input devices or output devices. OS does the allocation and release of these devices to and from jobs on user requisition. Thus, Operating system acts as an interface between these peripherals and the user. Interface can be of two types-

- CUI
- GUI

CUI	GUI
It refers to Character User Interface	It refers to Graphical User Interface
It provides a text-mode environment or interface	It provides a graphical mode environment or interface that contains icons & images to represent commands & options.

CUI	GUI
Commands are typed in order to interact with the OS.the OS	Mouse click is used to interact with
It is not user friendly	It is user friendly
Prior training or knowledge of commands is required	Prior training or knowledge of Windows commands is not required
It is unitasking	It is multitasking
It refers to a single user O.S	It refers to a multi user O.S
Example: DOS & UNIX	***Example:*** Windows & LINUX

2. About Windows

Windows is the most popular GUI based operating system that was developed by Microsoft Company of America. Bill Gates is the owner of Microsoft. Windows is very user friendly and easy to use. It has folders rather directories in DOS.

Versions of Windows: Windows 3.1, 9x (95, 98), NT, 2000, ME (Millenium), XP (Experience)

Latest Version of Windows: Windows Vista (launched in 2007)

Difference between Window & Windows: A Window refers to a rectangular area in which a program/ file or a message is displayed. On the other hand, Windows refers to Operating System.

3. Features of WIN-98 & WIN-2000

Features of Windows 98:

Windows 98 is an upgrade to Microsoft's Windows 95 operating system. It incorporates most of the features of its predecessor and includes some new features and additional device drivers, as well as fixing many of the bugs in Windows 95.

Windows 98 integrates the many new interface changes introduced by Internet Explorer 4.0, such as Active Desktop (which allows you to use a web page as a desktop) and single-click access to all your files and folders.

Following are some of the Windows 98 features:

- **Universal Serial Bus (USB) support:** USB ports allow for true Plug and Play on your computer. You can plug a device into the USB port (even while the computer is on), install the drivers for the device, and use the device, without a lengthy installation process or restarting. Common USB devices include removable media (e.g., Zip drives), digital cameras, and game controllers.
- **Power management features:** These configure your computer to turn your monitor and/or hard drive off after a period of inactivity, and allow you to create different schemes for use in different situations.

- **FAT32:** Windows 98 also introduces the FAT32 file system. FAT32 allows for more efficient use of your hard drive, so that less disk space is wasted. It also allows you to format and use a hard disk drive as big as 2TB (terabytes) without creating separate partitions on the hard drive. Previous versions of Windows allowed for only 2GB (gigabyte) partitions.

Features of Windows 2000:

Windows 2000 is an upgrade to Microsoft's Windows NT operating system, intended for business use. The Windows 2000 platform offers many different products, including Windows 2000 Professional, Server, Advanced Server, and Datacenter server. It has following important features-

1. **NTBackup and Advanced System Recovery:** This functionality is included in Windows 2000. NTBackup has been significantly enhanced for Windows 2000. It provides support for the Active Directory, Advanced System recovery, Remote Storage Manager, disk-to-disk operations and other new Windows 2000 storage functions.
2. **File System Support:** Windows 2000 Server supports multiple file systems. Windows 2000 continues to support all previous file systems as well as introduces new supported file systems. Other File systems supported in Windows 2000 include FAT, a Windows 95/98 compatible FAT32, the Compact Disk File (CDF) system and the Universal Disk Format (UDF) that is used with DVD read-only devices.
3. **The Volume Management:** This function is enhanced in Windows 2000 with the introduction of a new Volume Manager in addition to the fault tolerant disk manager. The new volume manager introduces a new disk partition layout that provides better manageability and recoverability.
4. **I20 Support:** New I2O (also called Intelligent Input/Output) architecture allows for higher input/output performance on your servers by offloading certain I/O operations to a secondary processor. I2O improves I/O performance in high-bandwidth applications such as networked video, groupware and client/server processing.
5. **Scalability:** The Windows 2000 Server family scales from small workgroups to enterprise data center developments. The Windows 2000 Server family includes products that support up to 32 processors and advanced I/O. It also integrates network load balancing and new multiprocessor optimizations for your business applications.
6. **Print Support:** With Windows 2000 Advanced Server, you can choose from among more than 2500 different printers.
7. **Reliability:** Windows File Protection protects core system files from being overwritten by application installs. Full 32-bit operating system minimizes the chance of application failures and unplanned reboots.
8. **Mobility:** ***Universal Serial Bus (USB)*** lets you connect and disconnect a wide array of peripherals such as joysticks, scanners, and camcorders without configuring or rebooting your computer. ***IrDA*** support provides secure, wireless communications between two Windows 2000 computers using the popular infrared protocol. ***Hibernate*** turns off your computer and monitor after a pre-determined time, while retaining your desktop on disk. ***Offline Viewing*** makes entire web pages with graphics available for viewing offline.

9. **Maintainability:** Multilingual support allows users to easily create, read, and edit documents in hundreds of languages. Windows 2000 offers 25% faster performance than Windows 95 or Windows 98 on systems with 64MB or more of memory. 32-bit architecture allows you to run more programs and perform more tasks at the same time than Windows 95 or 98. Windows 2000 can support up to 4GB of RAM and two symmetric multiprocessors.

4. Some Basic Terminology related to WINDOWS

1. ***Desktop:*** The Desktop is the working area (background) of the Windows displayed on your computer. When you start your computer, you will see several screens go by before you arrive at the main Windows screen, which is the Desktop. It is analogous to the surface of the desk, on which you keep your notebook to work on it because you work with electronic files on the desktop.
2. ***Taskbar:*** The taskbar is the horizontal bar along the bottom of the Desktop. It has the ***Start*** button on the left. Taskbar also displays the (rectangular) icons of currently running programs. Near the right side, you will see the programs or tasks that start automatically when you start Windows. On the far right, you will see the time displayed. The taskbar allows you to start your navigation process through all of the computer files.
3. ***Icon:*** An icon is a little picture that represents a program, command, or a file in Windows.
4. ***Pointer:*** A pointer is the arrow you use to choose things on screen.
5. ***File:*** A file is a collection of information, with a unique name, stored in your computer or on a removable disk.
6. ***Extension:*** The last three letters (suffix) of a file name designate an extension. An extension identifies the format of the file. It is preceded by a period. Extension tells computer about the format of file, each time you want to work with that file.
7. ***Folder:*** Folders are special files that can hold multiple documents. They allow you to organize information. Folders can hold both files and other folders (subfolders).
8. ***Titlebar:*** Title bar is the horizontal bar displayed at the top of every program window. It includes the title of the opened program, title of the file currently opened in the program window and control buttons like minimize, restore and close button.
9. ***Scrollbar:*** A scrollbar is a gray rectangle with small black arrows on both ends. It lets you select the portion of the window you want to see. It is on the right side of a window for vertical scrolling and on the bottom for horizontal scrolling. When a document is so big it cannot completely be displayed on the monitor, a scroll bar appears so you can see all of its contents by moving the document up and down the screen, or right and left.
10. ***Menu Bar:*** A menu bar is an onscreen display that lists available categories of commands. It is usually located at the top of the program window. To choose a category or command, just click on it.

11. ***Menu:*** A menu is a list of commands displayed on your screen, which allows you to perform tasks. When you click on any of the words in the menu, a list of choices drops down. Just as you would select your choices from a restaurant menu, you select the choices of what to do on your computer
12. ***Pop-Up or Context Menu:*** A shortcut menu is a hidden menu that can be opened at any time. Almost every object on your Desktop has one. If you right-click on the item, the shortcut menu will appear.
13. ***Grayed or Dimmed command Name:*** Grayed or Dimmed command refers to a choice that is currently not available ***e.g.*** If you right click on the title bar; assuming that the Window is already maximized, then the maximize command will be grayed in control box menu.
14. ***Ellipses:*** The command followed by ellipses (...) indicates that some dialog box will be displayed on clicking that command. ***E.g.*** Save...
15. ***Triangle:*** The command followed by triangle indicates that the command has additional sub-choices ***e.g.*** Toolbar, Zoom etc.
16. ***Radio Button:*** Radio button is also called option button. It lets you to choose one option out of given multiple options.
17. ***Check box:*** Check box lets you to choose more than one option out of given multiple options.
18. ***List box:*** List box is a collection of several items. You can choose the desirable item by simply clicking on that.
19. ***Text box:*** A text box refers to a rectangular box in which either text is displayed or you can type text in text box.
20. ***Combo box:*** It is a collection of a text box and a list box. The item that you select from the list box will be displayed in the text box. ***e.g.*** Font combo box in Font dialog box in Ms-Word.
21. ***Application Window:*** The window containing the most recently executed program is called the application window. Every application or program has got a separate application window. ***E.g.*** *Word window, Excel window etc.*
22. ***Document Window:*** The window containing the most recently opened file in an application window is called document window. ***E.g.*** Document window in Word, Workbook window in Excel etc.
23. ***Wallpaper:*** Wallpaper is the background that displays on your desktop.
24. ***Screensaver:*** Screensaver is a constantly changing image displayed on the screen whenever you leave your turned-on system untouched (or free). Some screensaver lets you to enter password to resume your work. Such screensavers protect your work from unauthorized persons.
25. ***Drives:*** Drives are used to store data. Almost all computers come with at least two drives: a hard drive (which is used to store large volumes of data) and a floppy drive. The hard drive is typically designated the C:\ drive and the floppy drive is typically designated the A:\ drive. If you have an additional floppy drive, it is typically designated the B:\ drive. If your hard drive is partitioned or if you have additional drives, the letters D:\, E:\, F:\, and so on are assigned.

26. ***Slider:*** You use a slider to increase or decrease a value. You increase a value by moving the slider from left to right; you decrease a value by moving the slider from right to left.

27. ***Spinner:*** A spinner is a set of arrows located on the side of a text box. You use the up arrow to increment a value and the down arrow to decrement a value. You can also type the value you want directly into the text box.

28. ***Dialog box:*** It refers to a rectangular window that is used to display certain messages or used to accept certain input from the user.

29. ***Tabs:*** Dialog boxes contain several pages of options. The headers of such pages are called tabs. You can switch among these tabs by pressing Ctrl + Tab.

5. Basic Windows Operations

• Opening a Window :-

1. ***Double click*** on the icon of the program or file displayed on the desktop. Similarly, a window can be opened by clicking on ***Start > Programs*** and choosing desirable program. In this case the selected program's window would be displayed on the screen.

• Closing a Window :-

1. For closing a window, click on ***Close*** button displayed at the top right corner of the window. A window can also be closed by choosing ***File > Exit*** option on the menu bar.

• Resizing a Window:-

You may want to change the size of the window to make it easier to read. There are several ways to resize a window-

1. Put the pointer on any of the window's borders, but not on the title bar. The mouse pointer turns into a two-headed arrow. Drag the border to change the size of the window.
2. If you click on the ***Minimize*** button, the window "***closes***". You will notice how the program button is still on the taskbar. This is different from actually exiting the program that you can do by clicking on the close button. Instead of quitting the program entirely, minimizing closes only the window of the program. The title of the program you minimized now appears as a button on the taskbar. To maximize or open the window again, click on the button (on the taskbar)
3. If you click on ***Restore*** button, then the window is displayed on the desktop in reduced sized. However, the original size of the window can be restored by clicking on the same button again.

• Moving a Window :-

1. Point to the window's title bar.
2. Drag the title bar to the location you want and release the mouse button.

- **Managing Multiple Windows on the Screen:-**

For this right-click on the mouse anywhere on the taskbar. A menu appears. Choose one of the following option to arrange the windows-

1. ***Cascade Windows:*** The Cascade command displays the windows so that the title bars of each window appear. Click on the title bar to bring its window to the front of each stack.
2. ***Tile Windows Horizontally:*** Tile horizontally stacks each window in horizontal panes
3. ***Tile Windows Vertically:*** Tile vertically stacks each window in vertical panes

- **To create a New Folder :-**

1. Double click **My Computer**, and then double click the disk drive or folder in which you want to create the new folder. (*To make a folder on the desktop simply right click on the desktop and then choose* ***New > Folder*** *option)*
2. Go to ***File*** menu, point to ***New,*** and then click on the ***Folder***, then a New Folder will appear on the screen.
3. Type the name of the new folder, and then press Enter.

- **To copy or move a file/ folder :-**

1. Double click on My Computer
2. Seek the file/folder you want to move or copy. Go to **Edit** Menu.
3. Select the option ***"Cut"*** to move the file/folder or ***"Copy"*** to copy the file/folder.
4. Open the drive or folder to which you want to move or copy the file/ folder.
5. Again Go to **Edit** Menu in the menu bar and choose **Paste** to paste the file/folder there.
6. The file will be either moved or copied to the new location, depending on whether you had chosen the ***Cut*** or the ***Copy*** Option at the source.

- **To delete a file or folder :-**

1. Double Click ***My Computer*** and then double click on the drive in which the file/folder exist.
2. Select the file or folder you want to delete, and then right click on it
3. Select the option ***Delete*** from the short cut menu
4. The file will be transferred to the ***Recycle Bin,*** from where you can restore or remove the file later.

- **To restore a deleted file or folder :-**

1. Double click on the ***Recycle Bin***. The Recycle Bin window will be displayed.
2. Select the file to be restored or undeleted by clicking it.

3. Go to ***File*** Menu and choose option ***Restore.***
4. The file or folder will be moved in the folder (or drive) from where it was deleted.

- **To permanently delete file/folder:-**

1. Double Click ***My Computer,*** then double click on the drive in which the file/folder is present. Select the file by clicking it.
2. Then Press ***Shift + Del*** from the keyboard. In this case, the file/folder will not get moved to the recycle bin.

- **To copy a file/ folder to a floppy disk :-**

1. Double click ***My Computer.***
2. Locate the file or folder you want to copy, and then right click on it.
3. From the short cut menu displayed, select the option ***Send To*** and choose the icon representing the floppy disk. (*In this case, your floppy should be already inserted in your active floppy drive)*

- **To copy a file/ folder from a floppy disk to a particular drive on your hard disk:-**

1. Double click ***My Computer.***
2. Double click on **A:** (floppy drive icon), then the file contained in floppy will be displayed.
3. Select the desired file and right click on it. Then choose either ***Cut*** or ***Copy*** option in order to move or copy the selected file.
4. Then move to **My Computer** window by clicking on ***Back*** button on the toolbar.
5. Double click on the desired hard drive (C: or D: or E: etc) and right click in the blank area and finally click ***Paste*** option.

- **To copy a file/ folder from a CD to a particular drive on your hard disk:-**

1. Double click ***My Computer.***
2. Double click on **E: or G:** (CD drive icon), then the file contained in CD will be displayed.
3. Select the desired file and right click on it. Then choose either ***Cut*** or ***Copy*** option in order to move or copy the selected file.
4. Then move to **My Computer** window by clicking on ***Back*** button on the toolbar.
5. Double click on the desired hard drive (C: or D: or E: etc) and right click in the blank area and finally click ***Paste*** option.

- **To copy a file/ folder from a HARD DRIVE to CD :-**

The process of transferring a file/folder from a hard drive to CD is called Burning (CD Writing). For this you cannot use simple Cut, Copy & Paste option. Instead of it, you need the following –

1. Hardware (CD Writer)
2. Software (CD Writer s/w like **Nero Start Smart)**

Starting Burning Process- *For starting burning process, a blank CD must be inserted in the CD writer (It should be noted that CD-ROM will not work in burning process)-*

1. Double click on the ***Nero Start Smart*** icon on the desktop or select ***Start > Programs > Nero Start Smart.*** Then following window is displayed-

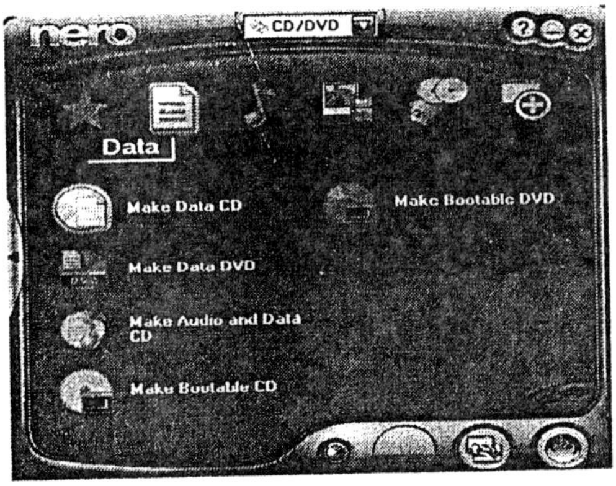

2. Click ***Make Data CD*** option to create a data CD. *(A data CD may contain programs or files/folders or graphics or audio files).* Then following window is displayed-

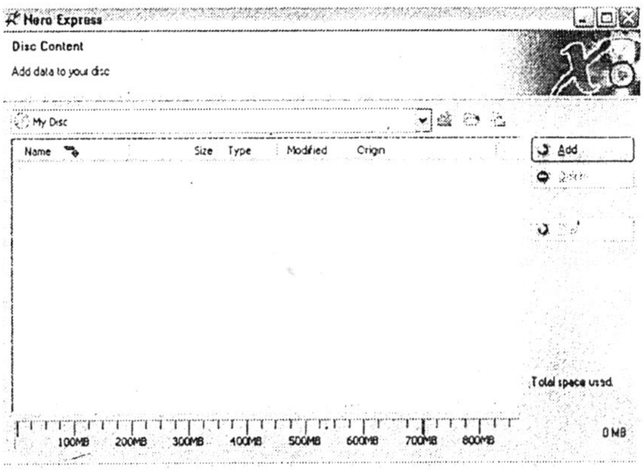

3. Then click on ***Add*** button to locate the files for transferring to CD (i.e. for burning). It is followed by the given window-

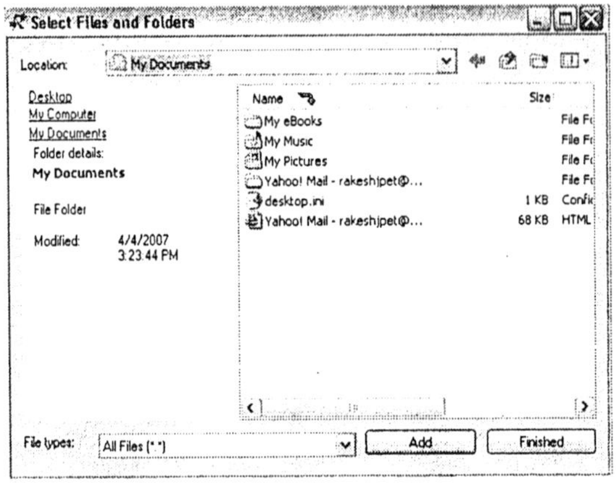

4. Select or Specify the location of file on your hard drive and then select the file and click ***Add*** button. The same process is repeated for adding "***n***" number of files (that can be stored on your CD) in the burning list. Finally click ***Finish*** button. This step is followed by clicking ***Next*** button.

5. Finally, click  button displayed in the Nero Express window and wait for the burning process to get successfully completed. After this, a message will be displayed to you that burn process is successfully completed and your CD will come out of your drive.

6. My Computer

My Computer is an icon that represents all of the drives on your system. To open folders and display files, you often start by opening My Computer. Once you open this window, you can then open any of your drives to see the folders and files contained on that drive.

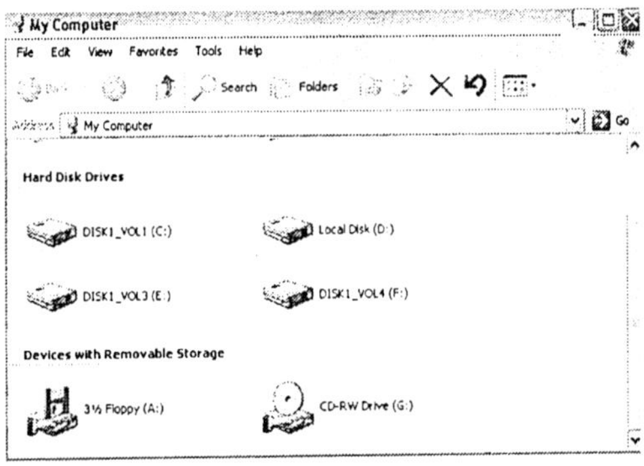

To open a particular drive, either *double click* on it or *right click* it & then choose ***Open*** or ***Explore*** option.

You can right click on any drive and then click ***Properties*** option to view the ***Used Space*** & ***Free Space*** on that drive.

7. Control Panel

It is used to view and manipulate basic system settings such as display settings, adding or removing hardware and changing accessibility options etc. It can be opened by choosing ***Start > Settings > Control Panel.***

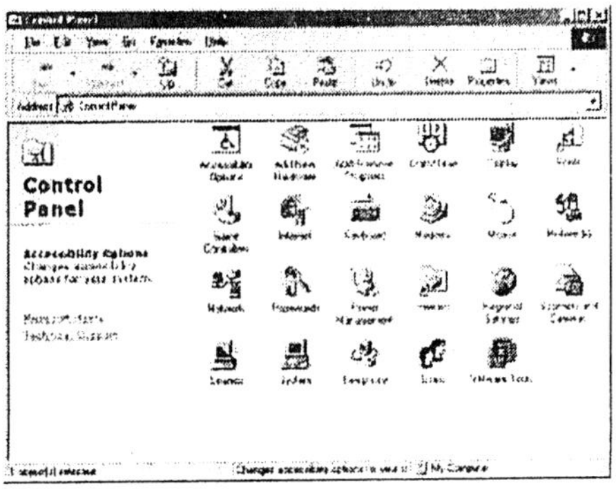

Control Panel consists of following applets that are used to modify different settings of the system-

Accessibility Options: Adjusts your computer settings for vision, hearing and mobility.

Add Hardware

Add Hardware: Installs and troubleshoot hardware

Add or Remov...

Add or Remove: Install or remove programs and Windows components.

Date and Time

Date and Time: It is used to set the date, time & time zone for your computer.

Display

Display: This option is used to change the appearance of your desktop such as background, screen saver, colors, font size and screen resolution.

Folder Options

Folder Options: It is used to customize the display of file and folders.

Fonts

Fonts: This option is used for adding, changing and managing fonts on your computer.

Internet Options

Internet Options: It is used to configure your Internet display and connection settings.

Mouse

Mouse: This option is used to customize your mouse settings, such as the button configuration, mouse pointers, and motion speed and double-click speed.

Keyboard

Keyboard: It is used to customize keyboard settings such as the cursor blink rate and the character repeater rate.

Sounds and Audio Devices

Sounds and Devices: This option is used to change the sound scheme for your computer or configure the settings for your speaker and recording devices.

Taskbar and Start Menu

Taskbar and Start Menu: It is used to customize the Start menu & taskbar, such as types of item to be displayed and how they should appear.

8. Recycle Bin

Recycle bin is an icon on the Windows desktop. It represents a directory where deleted files are temporarily stored. When you delete a file in Windows Explorer or My Computer, the file appears in the Recycle Bin. The file remains in the Recycle Bin until you empty the Recycle Bin or restore the file.

Double-clicking the Recycle Bin icon displays the folder listing of deleted files available for restoration. You can right click on the desired file *(in recycle bin)* and select ***Restore*** option. Restoring file refers to moving file from recycle bin to it's original location *(from where it was deleted)*

In case if you want to delete all files or folders from the recycle bin, then right click recycle bin and click ***Empty Recycle Bin*** option.

9. Windows Explorer

Windows Explorer is the software program that best lets you manage your computer's files. It represents your computer as one big filing cabinet.

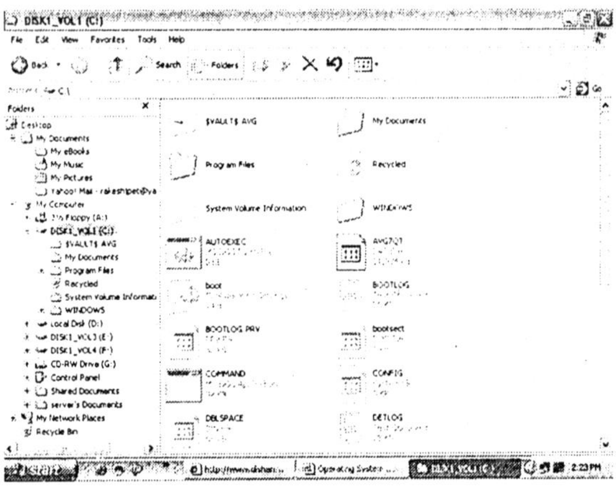

At the bottom left of your screen, there is the ***"Start"*** button. Use the Right button of your mouse to click on that button, and then left-click on ***"Explore".*** Then ***Windows Explorer*** window would appear on the screen.

As you view Windows Explorer, you see the screen broken into two halves. One side contains the folders, or directory tree. The Explorer view begins with Desktop, followed by My Computer, and lists all your drives, followed by other folders or programs contained within the Desktop and My Computer. The other side shows the files and folders inside the folder selected.

The ***plus (+)*** signs by certain folders indicate the folder has other sub-folders contained within. Click on the plus sign, and the tree will expand further. A ***minus(-)*** sign on a folder means that it is fully expanded.

When you want to see details of your files (i.e. size, date created/modified), click on ***View > Details.*** When you just want to see a list of files, click on ***View >List***.

10. Network Neighborhood or Network Places

Network Neighborhood icon will be displayed automatically on the desktop, if your computer is a part of a network. When this icon is double clicked, the Network neighborhood window will be displayed. It lists all the computers currently connected in the network. If you double click on a particular computer's icon then the sharable drives of that computer will be displayed. You can access these drives by simply double clicking on them. In order to know the name (i.e. network identity) of your system then right click on ***Network Places*** icon on the desktop. Then, click ***Properties*** option, which is followed by^a Properties dialog box. In this, click ***Identification*** tab to know the ***Computer Name.***

3

Networking & Data Communication

Introduction:

Many of you have probably heard of the term "***network***," but do you really know what it means? If you have no idea what a network is, this is the place to start. In this chapter, an overview of what a network is, how networks are classified and the parts of a network are given. This chapter will introduce you to the world of networks. You are probably more familiar with networks than you think.

Networks did not just spring up overnight. Rather, it took years for scientists and engineers to advance this technology. The first networks were relatively simple, but now, we have networks that span the whole world, like the Internet.

new topic DATA

1. The term data is derived from the Greek word "datum".
2. It refers to raw facts about an entity (entity means place, person or thing), which are gathered from the surroundings.
3. In other words, it simply means unprocessed data.
4. Data may be expressed or communicated using numbers, alphabets, symbols or pictures.
5. Data can be generated through various sources including human activity, measurements by man & machine etc.
6. It may or may not be useful to produce meaningful information.

   e.g. Ram has five balloons

   Two students are absent today etc.

1. Data Processing & Information

1. The process of converting data into meaningful information is called data processing.
2. Data processing involves-
   a. Collection or gathering of data
   b. Sorting of Data
   c. Storage & Retrieval of data
   d. Processing of data according to a specific set of criteria or norms to produce desirable information.

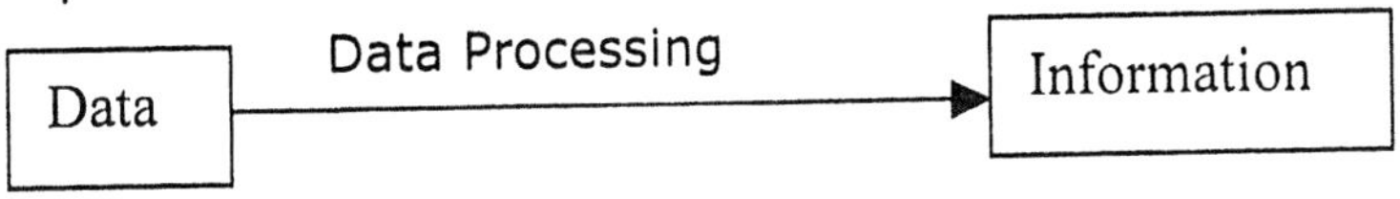

2. Digital Data Vs Analog Data

Sno.	Digital Data	Analog Data
1	Digital data refers to discrete values i.e. discontinuous voltage pulses **e.g.** text, integer etc.	Analog data refers to continuous values having continuously varying patterns of intensity **e.g.** Temp., Pressure, Sound etc
2	Signals are propagated through Repeaters.	Signals are propagated through Amplifiers.
3	Encoded using Modem to produce analog signal	Encoded using 'Codec' (Coder decoder) to produce a digital bit of stream.
4	Digital signals represent a stream of bits i.e. 1s and 0s	No such bits are present to represent analog signals.
5	Less suspectible to noise	More suspectible to noise

newtopic COMMUNICATION SYSTEM

1. Communication system is used for the exchange of data between two parties.
2. Components essential in a Communication System-
   a. **Source:** This is a device which generates the data to be transmitted e.g. telephone & PC
   b. **Transmitter:** A Transmitter is required to transform & encode the information in such a way as to produce electromagnetic signals that can be transmitted across some sort of transmission system. **E.g.** a

modem is used to convert digital signals to analog signals, which are handled by the telephone system.

c. **Transmission System:** It can be a single transmission line or a complex network connecting source & destination.

d. **Receiver:** It accepts the signal from the transmission systems and converts it into a form that can be handled by the destination device. **E.g.** a modem accepts an analog signal & converts it into digital bits acceptable by the computer.

e. **Destination:** It takes the incoming data from the receiver.

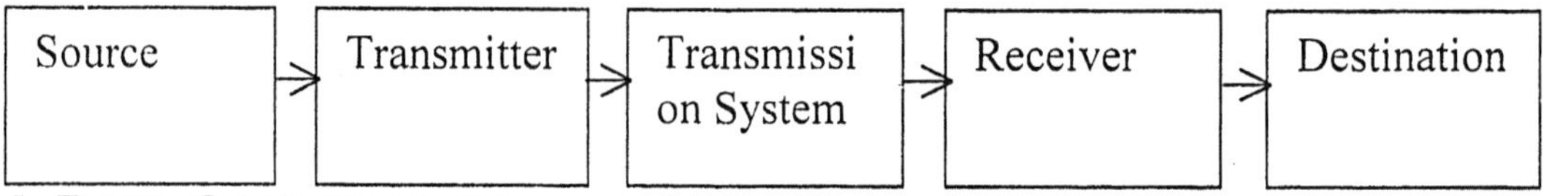

1. Data Communication or Data Transmission

In simple words, it refers to the transfer of data from one place to another by means of a suitable path. Technically speaking, it is the process of transferring data in the form of signals from source to destination by means of a reliable transmission medium. The term source and destination may be an electronic device, a sensor or human being.

1. Data is transmitted across the network in the form of bits and bytes translated into electrical signals (each bit being on or off, or positive or negative).
2. Before being transmitted, bytes are arranged into segments for transmission over a network. Each segment of data is attached to a header and a trailer.
3. The header precedes the data and identifies the data's destination and the protocols used by the packet.
4. The trailer follows the data and is used by some protocols for error checking.
5. The header and trailer are referred to as a frame and the entire package, frame and data, is called a packet.
6. Packets are transmitted (as bits and bytes) separately over the network.
7. At the receiving end, the headers and trailers are removed and the data from all the packets is reassembled into contiguous data.
8. On a PC, the process of breaking data down into packets and then reassembling them is carried out by the ***firmware*** on the network interface card.

2. Data Communication Vs Voice Communication

Sno.	*Data Communication*	*Voice /Video Communication*
1	Data is very sensitive or prone to errors	Voice and Video are error tolerable
2	Difficult to get back lost data	Lost or missed data can be made out of communication

Sno.	Data Communication	Voice /Video Communication
3	The perception of mood & tone of the sender could not be understood by the receiver	It is easy to understand the mood & tone of the sender
4	Data can be encoded for ensuring security.	Voice/Video cannot be encoded

3. Types of Data Transmission

1. **Digital Transmission:** In this case, the data is transmitted as a sequence of voltage pulses, over a wire medium **e.g.** a constant +ve (positive) voltage represents binary 1 and a constant –ve (negative) voltage represents binary 0.

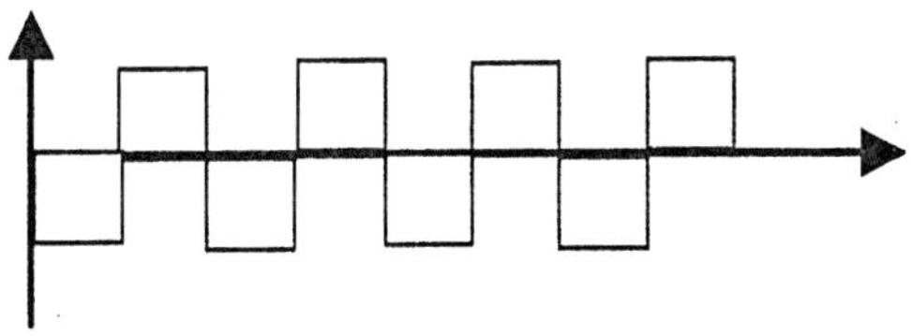

2. **Analog Transmission:** In this type of transmission, data is transmitted in the form of varying pattern of electromagnetic waves, over a transmission medium e.g. Human voice. One wave constitutes one cycle. The unit for measuring wavelength is Hertz i.e. one cycle per second.

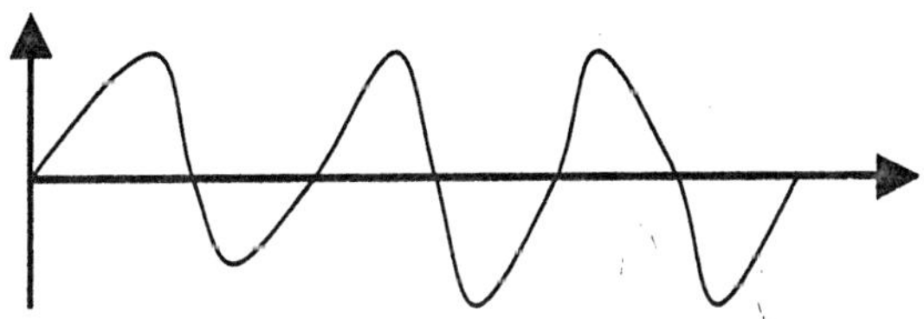

4. Modes of Transmission

Mode of Transmission refers to the direction of flow of information or signals between two stations or devices.

- **Simplex: -** In simplex mode of transmission, signals are transmitted only in one direction i.e. one station is the receiver and other is the transmitter. **e.g.** Printer can only be used as output device. To understand it in simpler terms, it can be compared to a lane allowing one-way traffic. Such mode is rarely used.
- **Half Duplex: -** In half duplex mode of transmission, both the stations may transmit, but only one station can transmit at a time. **e.g.** Radio. To understand it in simpler terms, it can be compared to a one-way lane, allowing bi-directional traffic. In this case, while vehicles are traveling in

one direction, the vehicles going the other way must wait. Such type of mode is common in use.

- **Full Duplex: -** In full duplex mode of transmission, both stations may transmit simultaneously i.e. the transmission is possible in both directions at the same time. **e.g.** Telephone Network (If two people are communicating by telephone, then both can speak & listen at the same time). For better understanding, it can be compared to a two-way lane allowing traffic to flow in both the directions at the same time. This mode is fast and common.

newtopic TRANSMISSION MEDIA

The physical media that is used for actual transmission of data is called transmission media. In this context, the term 'data' refers to stream of bits.

1. Categories of Transmission Media

- **Guided Transmission Media: -** In such transmission media, the waves or signals are guided or transmitted along a physical path. **e.g:** Twisted pair cable, coaxial cable & optical fiber. It may be point-to-point (only two devices sharing the same medium) or multi-point (more than two devices sharing the same medium)
- **Unguided Transmission Media: -** In such transmission media, signals or electromagnetic waves are not guided along a physical path. e.g. Propagation through vacuum, air & water.

2. Various Examples of Transmission Media

- Twin wire or Twisted Pair
- Coaxial Cable
- Fiber Optics or Optical Fiber

Twin Wire Or Twisted Pair

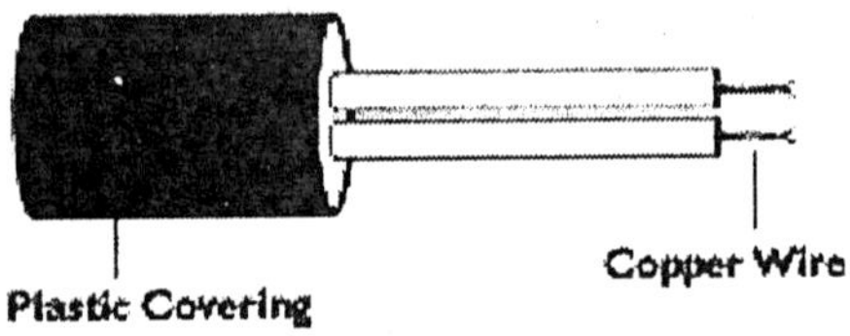

1. A twin wire consists of one or two pairs of insulated copper wires typically about 1mm thick.
2. The wires are twisted together in a helical form. It's structure can be compared to a DNA molecule.
3. **Purpose of Twisting:** The purpose of twisting the wires is to reduce electrical interference by canceling out cross-talk.
4. **Common Application:** It is the most common transmission medium. One of it's common application is the ***Telephone system***.
5. **Use of Repeaters:** Twisted pair can run several kilometers without amplification. However, repeaters are required for longer distances.
6. **Twisted Pairs running in Parallel:** When many twisted pair run in parallel for a considerable distance, they are bundled together & enclosed in a protective sheath.

7. **Bandwidth :** It refers to the difference between the limiting frequencies of a continuous frequency spectrum. Generally, bandwidth of twisted wire is 250 KHz. The bandwidth depends on-
   a. Thickness of the wire &
   b. Distance traveled
8. **Maximum Speed :** This cable can carry signals at a maximum speed of 100 Mbps (Mega bits per sec)
9. **Varieties of Twisted Pair:-** Both of these are referred to as Unshielded Twisted Pair (UTP). The two varieties only differ in twists per cm & type of insulation.
   a. Category 3 (Suitable for Telephone System)
   b. Category 5 (Suitable for Computer Communication due to more twists per cm & Teflon insulation, which results in less interference i.e. crosstalk)
10. **Advantage:**
    a. Good for short distance communications.
    b. Twisted pairs can be used for both analog & digital transmission.
    c. Twists greatly reduce crosstalk on the lines
    d. Inexpensive
    e. Adequate performance
    f. Quicker Installation
    g. Easy to cut strip; can fit easily into office furniture
    h. Used in LAN (UTP or 10baseT).
11. **Disadvantage:** Higher cable capacitance can reduce the data transfer speed.

Coaxial Cable

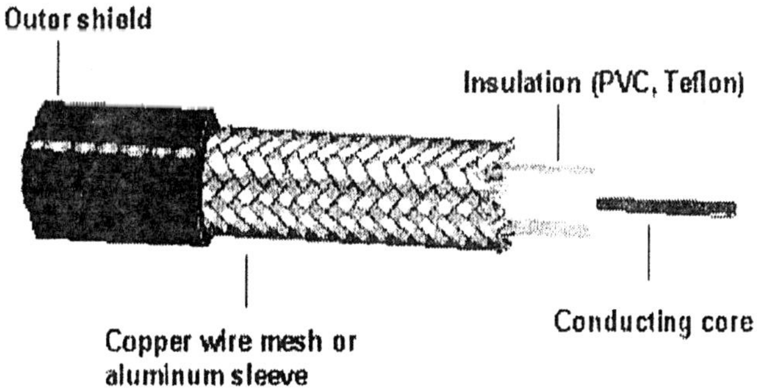

1. It consists of an insulated copper conductor, surrounded by a circular insulation layer and a conductive shield. The insulated copper conductor is termed as "***coax***".
2. A cylindrical conductor encases the insulator, as a woven braided mesh.
3. The outer conductor is covered in a protective plastic sheath.
4. The outer copper tube and the inner conductor have the same axis of curvature (i.e. concentric conductors share the same axis) that's why it is called "coaxial".

5. **Kinds of Coaxial Cable :-**

   a. **Baseband Coaxial Cable:**

      i. used for longer distances at higher speed because it has better shielding than twisted pair.

      ii. Have high bandwidth & excellent noise immunity

      iii. Extensively used in telephone system, cable television & some LANs.

      iv. **Types:-**

         1. **50 ohm** (used for digital transmission)
         2. **75 ohm** (used for analog transmission e.g. T.V cables)

   b. **Broadband Coaxial Cable:-**

      i. It is specially used for analog transmission.

      ii. However, may also be used for digital transmission, but in such a case, extra electronics are required for converting digital signals to analog signals.

      iii. Using it, television and data can be mixed on one cable.

      iv. It requires analog amplifiers periodically.

      v. **Types of Broadband Coaxial Cable:-**

         1. Dual Cable System
         2. Single Cable System

      vi. Technically, Broadband cables (having multiple channels) are inferior to baseband (having single channel) cables, because broadband cable is not so much suitable for sending digital data.

      vii. Practically, Broadband cables are widely used, due to the fact that they large area coverage.

6. **Advantages:-**

   a. High immunity to electrical interference.
   b. High quality of data transmission.
   c. Higher bandwidth upto 400 Mhz.
   d. Higher data transmission speeds i.e. approximately 350 Mbps
   e. Used extensively in LANs
   f. Supports baseband as well as broadband transmissions.

7. **Disadvantages:-**

   a. High cost of installation
   b. Expensive than twisted pair
   c. May not be able to fit into existing cable runaways, due to it's higher diameter.
   d. Signal loss at higher frequencies.

Fiber Optics Or Optical Fiber

1. Fiber cables are similar to coaxial cable, except these are without the braid.
2. **Components of Fiber Cables-**
   a. Glass core in the center
   b. Glass cladding
   c. Thin plastic jacket
3. The two glasses have different indexes of refraction.
4. Data is transmitted as Light pulses (photons)
5. **Components of Fiber Optics:-**
   a. **Light Source:** A pulse of light indicates 1 bit and the absence of light indicates a zero bit. Light sources used may be **LED** (Light emitting diode) or **ILD** (injection laser diode). **ILD** is more powerful and achieves higher data rates and over longer distance.
   b. **Transmission Medium:** It is an ultra thin fiber of glass.
   c. **Detector:** Detector generates an electrical pulse when light falls on it.
6. Light source is attached to one end of an optical fiber, with a detector at it's other end.
7. This system allows unidirectional transmission of data.
8. Light source accepts an electrical signal and converts it into light for transmitting it to other end. At the detector (or receiver) end, the output is reconverted to an electrical signal.
9. **Types of Fiber Cables on the basis of where the fiber cables are used-**
   a. **Terrestrial fiber sheaths** (laid in the ground)
   b. **Transoceanic fiber sheaths** (laid in the sea water)
10. **Types of Fibers on the basis of propagation of light:-**
    a) **Multimode Fiber:-** Multi-mode fiber uses multiple light waves to carry more than one signal at a time. But single-mode fiber can transfer data at higher rates in comparison because in multi-mode fiber light pulses will be reflected internally at different angles (i.e. modes). This results in overlapping of light pulses and non-axial travel (bouncing off the walls) which in turns increases the distance traveled. Thus, these are suitable for considerably shorter distances. It is less expensive
    b) **Singlemode Fiber:-** A fiber in which light propagates in straight line without bouncing is called a single mode fiber. It is used for longer distances. It is quite expensive.

    Both are usually used as a high-speed interconnection between LAN's or distant buildings.

11. Ways of Connecting Fibers-

a. Using Connectors

b. Mechanical Splicing

c. Fusion splicing

12. Total Internal Reflection: - Fiber optics system follows the principle of Physics- i.e. total internal reflection. According to this, when light ray travels from one medium to other medium at or above the critical angle, it is totally reflected back in the fiber i.e. it propagates for many kms with virtually no loss.

13. Advantages:

a. Very High frequency ranges (20, 000 Mhz)

b. High Speed of data transmission (400 Mbits and more)

c. Single fiber can support over 30, 000 telephone lines.

d. Becoming very popular for LAN & MAN, also used for intercontinental links.

e. High security i.e. data cannot be tapped from the cable (i.e. High signal to noise ration). Any attempt to tap the photons is detectable because it stops them.

f. Totally immune to electrical interference, capacitance or cross-talk.

g. High quality data transmission i.e. very low attenuation over long distances

14. Disadvantage: High cost of cable and it's installation is the biggest drawback currently.

3. Copper Cable Vs Fiber Optics

Sno.	*Copper Cable*	*Fiber Optics*
1.	Comparatively allows smaller bandwidth	Comparatively allows larger bandwidth
2.	Repeaters are needed at every 5 km distance.	Repeaters are needed at about every 30 km distance.
3.	Comparatively expensive	Comparatively cost saving
4.	Comparatively thick & heavy	Thin & light weight
5.	Provides less security	Do not leak light, therefore quite difficult to tap.
6.	Electrons move in a wire during electrical transmission. Movement of one electron affect another electrons & is itself affected by	Photons move in a fiber optic cable during optical transmission. Movement of one photon does not affect other photons and is itself

Sno.	*Copper Cable*	*Fiber Optics*
	the electrons outside the wire (because they have electric charges)	not affected by photons outside the fiber.
7.	Higher Installation cost	Comparatively less installation cost.
8.	Easily affected by electromagnetic interference, power failures or corrosive chemicals in the air.	Not affected by electromagnetic interference, power failures, lightning or corrosive chemicals in the air.

4. Wireless Technology

The excitement of wireless, obviously, is that you can dispense with all the wires. You don't need them to communicate. If you have a laptop and some kind of wireless modem, you can open up your laptop and spontaneously, at any given time, form a network with maybe 1,000 people on your campus or 100 people in your office building. This is what's called an ad hoc wireless network.

There's no prior infrastructure. For instance, in the morning there may only be 50 people in this building; in the afternoon, 100. So the number of nodes may change. The position of the nodes changes. But the network itself has to keep functioning.

Basically wireless networks can only provide the equivalent of nearest-neighbor communication, but not long-distance communication unless you're willing to sacrifice throughput. Throughput is the rate at which you can pump data into or out of network—the rate of communication. There are some limits to communication that can be supported by wireless networks.

Thus, according to **Dr. P. R Kumar** (*Professor of University of Illinois, USA*), ***"A wireless medium is more like a cocktail party than a telephone call."***

For WANs, satellites provide global communication over the world, receiving signals from transmitters and relaying them back to the receivers. With geostationary satellites senders and receivers always points the same direction. For MANs microwave radio technology is widely used (2 to 24 Mbit/s). For LANs Spread Spectrum radio technology is becoming very popular (up to 2 Mbit/s)..

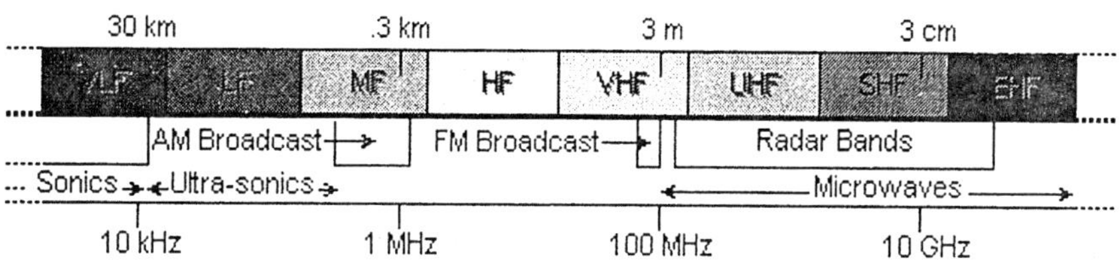

Two types of wireless:

- Infrared (two types: point-to-point and broadcast)
- Radio frequency

Advantages of wireless:

- No cables
- RF can penetrate physical obstructions

Disadvantages of wireless:

- Infrared requires ling-of-sight
- RF (Radio frequency) requires free portion of spectrum
- RF is vulnerable to eaves-dropping
- Currently, there are multiple RF standards

newtopic COMPUTER NETWORK

1. WHAT IS COMPUTER NETWORK?

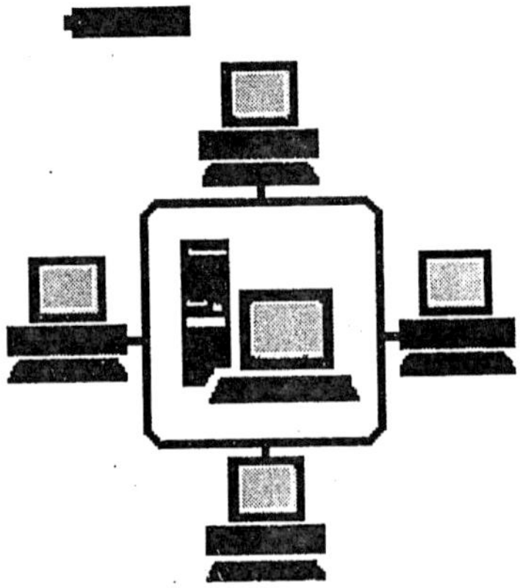

1. Computer Network is a collection of interconnected computers, which are able to exchange information between each other.
2. In other words, it is a collection of computers and peripheral devices connected by communication links that allows the network components to work together autonomously.

2. NETWORKING

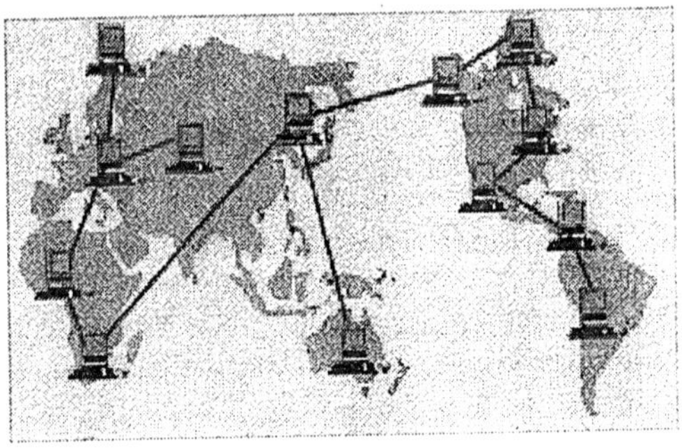

Networking refers to an art of arranging computers in a network.

According to Andrews and McFredries,

"Networking is a means of connecting computers together so that they can share resources, such as files and peripherals (printers, modems, CD-ROM drives, etc.) and services. It involves both hardware and software. "

3. GOALS OF NETWORKING

1. **Data Communication:** Computer network serves as a medium of data communication (i.e. exchange of information) among the nodes (or computers), participating in a computer network. Computer network is used to enhance human-to-human communication in long run.
2. **Resource Sharing:** The term '**resource**' refers to data, peripherals (**e.g.** printer, scanner etc), programs (like Word processors or databases etc) or administrative services (like installation, backup, security). A computer network ensures the sharing of all programs, peripherals and data among all the nodes of a computer network. The physical location of participating node plays no role in this regard. Resource sharing is useful in case if you have limited number of resources

3. **Cost Reduction:** Using a **client-server model** of computer network, the overall cost of installing a computer network can be reduced to a great extent. In this case, essential equipments are attached to server (**i.e.** high performance computer) and important programs & data is also stored on server. All the clients (**i.e.** computer or node) attached to the server can share the data, programs & equipments connected to the server. This will led in the reduction of overall cost of the system **e.g.** A common printer attached to server (assume that server is placed in IT Department) can be used by employees of various other departments like Housekeeping, Front Office and F&B Service etc.
4. **Reliability:** Computer Network is useful in ensuring reliability of data. This is achieved by storing copies of same data on various nodes or computers in a network. This is done to ensure consistent retrieval of data from other node, in case, if data is corrupted on one node of computer network. **For example**, the copy of **Room availability report** is maintained on more than one computer nodes in computer network, so that if one node in network goes down, then the same report can be retrieved from some other node.
5. **Scalability:** It means to expand the computer network desirably by adding more computers or nodes in the network. **e.g.** Assume a case of a hotel, where separate computers are provided to Managers of different departments. If more managers are employed further in an organization, then the respective number of computers is required to be added in the computer network of that hotel.
6. **Centralized Management & Allocation of Resources:** It means controlling the entire system (or various nodes) directly by server. Managing various nodes may include activities like allocation & deallocation of resources to various nodes or maintaining the entire information present on different nodes in a centralized manner (i.e. maintaining entire data of different nodes on a common server). For example, for every guest who check-in a hotel, a unique guest account is created and all the debits and credits of guests are posted to their respective accounts. Thus, the centralized information of guest accounts on server can be used for generating desirable reports such as telephone revenue analysis, Coffee sales analysis etc.

4. Types of Networks On the Basis of Geographical Area & Transmission Media

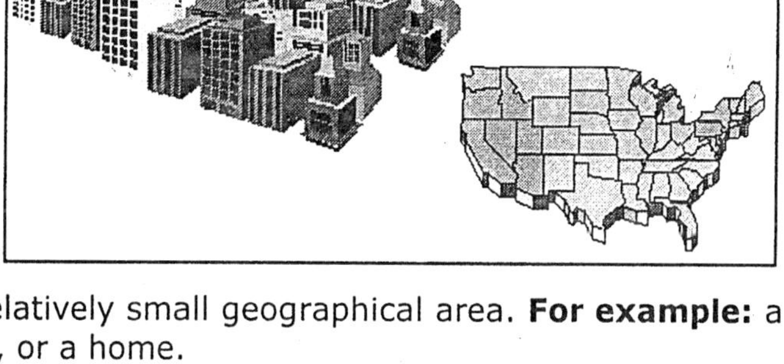

- LAN
- MAN
- WAN

LAN

Local Area Network: A network in which all nodes are connected with network cables and which occupies a relatively small geographical area. **For example:** a building, office, or department, or a home.

1. LAN is the acronym that stands for Local Area Network.
2. Such networks are used to interconnect computers in a single room or rooms; within a building or buildings on one site i.e. area of LAN is restricted to few meters to kilometers.
3. Traditional LAN runs at speeds of 10-100 Mbps (Megabits per sec; 1megabit= 1,000,000 bits)
4. LAN provides means for users to interconnect a wide range of devices together.
5. **For smaller LANs:** the number of computers may vary from 2 to 25
6. **For Large LANs:** the number of computers may be as many as 10,000 computers.
7. **Transmission Media used :** Coaxial cable, Twisted Pair, Optical fiber or Wireless
8. **Designs for building LAN:** Wangnet (Wang), Ethernet (Xerox) & Decnet (Digital Equipment), Token Ring *(less popular than Ethernet)*
9. **Characteristics of LAN-**
   a. **Topology:** Various topologies such as Bus, Ring, Star, Tree & Hybrid topologies are possible for LAN. Typically Buses or Rings.
   b. **Size:** The size of LAN is restricted **i.e.** In this case; the transmission time is bounded & known in advance.
   c. **Transmission Technology:** In case of LAN, a single cable is used for connecting all the participating nodes to server. Two technologies used for transmission are- Baseband & Broadband.

Advantages of LAN:-

1. Facilitate communication
2. Sharing of resources
3. Low cost per connection
4. Inexpensive transmission media
5. Enables unlike computer equipments to communicate.
6. Low Latency (except in case of high traffic periods)
7. Speed adequate for distributed systems

Disadvantages of LAN:-

1. Expensive than conventional system
2. Requirement of user training
3. Need of Routine Maintenance
4. Dependency on different LAN vendors
5. Need of extra security to protect the system from unauthorized systems.

COMPONENTS REQUIRED FOR LAN

- **Transmission Media or Cables:**
  - Establish physical connection between computers
  - Carry signals or messages across the network
  - Establish a communication link between various devices
- **NIC (Network Interface Card):**
  - It is a circuit board, plugged into one of the expansion slots of the workstation and server.
  - The server and the workstation should have the same type of NIC.
  - NIC's come in 8-bit, 16-bit, and 32-bit flavors. More expensive 32-bit NICs are usually reserved for servers.
  - NIC's include a component called the transceiver, which is responsible for converting data to a signal which is in a form appropriate to the network. For example, a FDDI card contains a laser diode that converts data signals to light pulses.

Network Interface Cards have two major functions:

- They create the physical connection between a node and the rest of the network (via a cable)
- Their firmware (programs encoded on NIC) is responsible for breaking data down into packets when transmitting data and reassembling the packets when receiving data. Typical packet size is 512 bytes.

Types of NICs are-

- o ARCNET (Attached Resource Computer Network) It offers a speed of 2.5 Mbps
- o ETHERNET CARDS : Data transmission speed is 10 Mbps
- o TOKEN RING CARDS: Available in two versions, one transmitting at 8 Mbps and the other at 16 Mbps.

- **Workstations:** The nodes or computers constituting the network are called workstations. In other words, the workstations, or clients, are the user's personal computers, which perform stand-alone processing and access the network servers as required. More precisely, the nodes having processing as well as data storage capabilities are referred to as ***"workstations".*** On the other hand, the nodes having no data processing as well as data storage capabilities are referred to as "***terminals***".
- **Server:** The computer that has the administrative abilities to handle the entire nodes or clients and providing services in a computer network is termed as a server. The hardware configuration of server is highly optimized according to it's various roles. In other words, servers are high-speed machines that hold programs and data shared by all network users.
- **Hubs or Concentrators:** Hubs are the devices used as central connecting points on star topology networks.

Hubs can have as few as 6 ports or as many as several dozen. Hubs are basically signal splitters - they take all the signals received through one port and redistribute them among the other ports Hubs are powered devices. They may include LED's which can monitor power, active connections, traffic, and collisions.

Types of Hubs

- ***Passive Hubs:*** Passive hubs are the simplest. They take all the packets received on any port and send them out all the other ports and that's about it.
- ***Active Hubs:*** Hubs which compensate for attenuation by amplifying or repeating the data signal are called active hubs. Active hubs may also include additional diagnostic capabilities.
- ***Intelligent Hubs:*** have all the features of active hubs and in addition can monitor the network and report problems to a central location from where they can be remotely controlled using network software.

⌖ Repeaters

Repeaters are devices that strengthen the data signal on a network. Signal attenuation is proportional to the distance the signal travels.

There are two types and they take different approaches to boosting signal strength:

- ***Amplifying repeaters:*** They simply amplify the entire signal. They have the disadvantage that as well as amplifying the data signal, they also amplify any existing noise or interference as well.

  Example: Used on broadband networks such as ATM. Broadband networks can transmit multiple data signals simultaneously because each (analogue) signal occupies its own band of frequencies. Data is represented by a shift in frequency within the frequency band assigned to that signal
- ***Signal Generating repeaters:*** This type of repeater "reads" the signal and then creates a (stronger) duplicate of the data signal before sending it on.

  Example: Used on baseband networks such as Ethernet. (Baseband networks can only transmit one (digital) signal at a time. Data is represented by the on or off state of the signal)

TRANSMISSION TECHNIQUES USED IN LAN

There are two techniques used for transmitting signals over the cable-

i. **Baseband:** According to this technique, a digital signal is directly applied on to the cable, and the entire cable is used to propagate the digital signal **e.g. Ethernet, Telephone** (used only for data communication)

Features of Baseband-

1. Transmission of analog or digital signals without any modulation.
2. Uses digital signals to transfer data. (restricted use)
3. Not suitable for video and voice.
4. Simple, inexpensive, reliable.

5. Limited to 1km distance.
6. Common in LANs (e.g. Ethernet, Token ring).

Advantage: Simple & inexpensive interface units

Disadvantage: Entire cable is allocated to a single channel.

ii. Broadband: According to this technique, total bandwidth is divided into a number of channels and information is transmitted in the form of radio-frequency signals. It can carry data communication, telephone & television on the same cable

Features of Broadband-

1. Modulate data before transmission.
2. Commonly referred to channel with bandwidth greater than 4Khz (voice)
3. Need modulation/demodulation devices
4. Greater bandwidth and coverage.
5. More useful for backbones to support more channels.

Advantage: Each channel is capable of carrying different types of information (data, video signals etc). **e.g. IBM'S PCNET**

Disadvantage: expensive modems are required & installation & maintenance of broadband cables is quite difficult.

MAN

1. MAN is the acronym that stands for Metropolitan Area Network.
2. Generally covers towns and cities (50 kms)
3. It is basically a bigger form of LAN. It was developed in 1980s.
4. It might be public or private
5. Plural of MAN is MANs.
6. Transmission Medium used is Cables or Optical Fibers.
7. It implements a standard called DQDB (Distributed Queue Dual Bus).
8. DQDB consists of two unidirectional buses or cables to which all the workstations are connected.
9. Each bus has a head-end and a device initiating transmission activity.
10. A distinguished feature of MAN is that it contains broadcast medium.
11. A MAN can support both voice & data.
12. Typical latencies is generally less than 1msec.
13. Message Routing is fast.
14. **Example-** A network of different branches of the same organization, located remotely in different areas of a bigger city or Cable Television network.

WAN

1. It is an acronym that stands for Wide Area Network. It was developed in 1960s.
2. WAN refers to a computer network spanning a regional (like different states of a country), national (like countries) or global area (like continents).
3. In WAN, several machines are used as hosts for serving the other machines in the network.
4. The hosts are connected by a communication subnet.
5. The subnet or intermediate host consists of –
   a. **Transmission lines** (channels, circuits or trunks): These are responsible for the actual transfer of bits between machines.
   b. **Switching elements:** These are specialized computers used to connect two or more transmission lines. ***e.g.*** Routers, Bridges, Gateways etc. Some of the switching techniques used are- Circuit switching, Message switching & Packet switching. Routers forwards packets from one to another following a route from the sender to the receiver. Hosts are typically connected (or close to) the routers.
6. Most common example of WAN is Internet.
7. **Typical speed:** 20 - 2000 Kbits/s.
8. **Typical Latencies:** 100ms - 500ms.
9. **Advantages of WAN:-**
   a. Facilitates remote data & job entry
   b. Facilitates centralized information
   c. Timesharing
   d. Resource sharing
   e. Large geographical coverage
10. **Disadvantages:-**
   a. High installation cost
   b. Security requirement for data
   c. User training requirement
   d. Complex design
   e. Problems with delays if using satellites.
   f. Not (yet) suitable for distributed computing.

5. LAN Vs WAN

Sno.	*LAN*	*WAN*
1	The area used for LAN is localized i.e. geographically confined.	The area used for WAN are geographically dispersed i.e. linked by microwave or telephone system
2	Comparatively reduced cost	Comparatively high cost

Sno.	LAN	WAN
3	**Hardware Requirements-** 1. Transmission channel 2. NIU 3. Servers 4. Workstation	**Hardware Requirements-** 1. Bridges 2. Routers 3. Gateways 4. X.25 standard interface
4	**Transmission Channel-** 1. Twisted pair cable 2. Coaxial cable 3. Fiber-optic cable 4. Radio waves	**Transmission Channel-** 1. Radio waves 2. Micro waves 3. Communication Satellites
5	It is under the complete control of the owner.	It needs the involvement of another authority like Telecom.
6	Lower error rate	Comparatively higher error rate
7	Usually have symmetric topology like Bus, Star etc	Typically have irregular topologies like Intersecting Rings, Complete etc.

6. Types of Network on the Basis of Architecture

1. Peer-to-Peer Network
2. Centralized Computing Model
3. Client-Server Model

- ***Peer-to-peer Networks***

"A peer-to-peer (P2P) network is created when two or more PCs are connected and share resources without going through a separate server computer".

In a peer-to-peer network model there is not necessarily a single designated server: each node has the potential to be a server and share its resources. Thus, peer-to-peer servers function simultaneously as servers and workstations.

Nearly all Operating Systems come with the ability to act as some kind of a server to share resources. You can setup different computers to allow others to use its peripherals such as printers or CDROM drives, and other computers to allow others to read or write to its hard disk allowing sharing of files, while other computers may allow access to its Internet connection. When you allow workstation computers to become servers and share things in this manner, it is called a Peer-to-peer network.

An Example of a Peer-to-peer Network

Peer to peer networking is usually found in small offices, shops, and nowadays even in homes. This method allows PC's to access information which is kept on any of the machines that are connected to the network, and to print to any of the printers on the network.

The Benefits of a Peer-to-peer Network

Peer-to-peer networks are very cheap to implement because it only requires the ability of O.S to share items with other computers on the network. Nearly all of the most popular desktop Operating Systems like Ms-Windows, Apple's Mac OS, Unix, Linux & BSD have this feature.

So the only cost will be the networking hardware (cards, wiring, hubs or switches), and the labor to configure the workstations for this type of network sharing.

Other Advantages of Peer to Peer Network are as follows-

- Easier to set up than client/server model(mostly because reduced security features)
- Performance is acceptable when only several computers are being used.
- Fairly inexpensive because they have light hardware requirements (no high-performance server, just NIC's and cabling) ......***As explained above***
- Operating system software costs are lower or non-existent (built-in to Win 9x OS).

Limitations of a Peer-to-peer Network

1. Without a central server, it is very difficult, or nearly impossible to secure this type of network in any way.
2. You can implement passwords on each different network share, but in order for the network to usable, the exact same username and password must be entered into each computer acting as a server. Thus, to change a password for a user could literally take hours of work, especially if the network consists of computers located in different buildings or different floors.
3. On a peer-to-peer network, it is also very difficult to implement a good backup system because important documents tend to be stored on different hard disks on different computers.
4. In Peer-to-peer networks, instead of maintaining a small handful of servers, you must maintain all of the workstations as servers, and as such any downtime with any computer on the network could cause considerable loss of labor or information
5. The users must be highly experienced so that he/she could solve small problems like that of password and network mapping etc.

When a peer-to-peer network would be appropriate for you organization:-

1. There are fewer than 10 people.
2. People should be well computer-educated.
3. Security is not an issue or the users can be trusted to maintain good security.
4. There is no one central administrator who set network policies.
5. Users are physically close together and there are no plans for further expansion of the network.

• CENTRALIZED COMPUTING MODEL:

This model uses one powerful, centralized computer to which are attached many "***dumb terminals***"

Dumb terminals are simply a keyboard and a monitor and have no local processor and no local storage, these being provided by the central computer.

This model was developed when processing and storage were extremely expensive and required a lot of physical space. In the past, corporate data communications involved accessing a "central" computer. Everybody went to this **one** computer to take care of a particular task or business process. This computer did all processing associated with that task. Wherever possible, this computer did other tasks also. After all, computers were very expensive.

Initially, input to the computer was performed using interactive "dumb terminals". Later, "smart terminals" provided for batched input to the mainframe. Batch terminals help to reduce network costs by taking advantage of switching networks. These are often found in retail chains where stores download sales information to the mainframe at the end of the day.

Features of Centralized Computing Model-

- Relies heavily on WAN technologies
- Ideally suited for mission-critical information
- High computer cost
- Low end-user equipment costs
- Lower network management costs
- Higher transmission facility costs
- Lacks flexibility and customization

• Client-Server Networks

In the client/server model, "intelligent" PC's are attached to a central computer. The central computer is the server and the attached pc's are called clients, nodes, or workstations. The server is usually a dedicated server, meaning that it is dedicated to its network functions and is not used locally to perform standard day-to-day applications.

Processing is done locally on the workstations while security and resources are managed centrally on a server.

Clients use their own processing power but rely on the server for resources and services such as:

- Printer, modem
- Files, including large databases
- Security (password verification)
- Server based applications (centralized installation, configuration)
- Network applications (email, groupware)
- Regular backups

The client/server model uses two types of software:

- **NOS - Network Operating System:** The NOS runs on the server and provides the network services to the clients. ***Examples*** of client/server NOS's include: NetWare, Windows NT Server, UNIX (LINUX) and IBM LAN Server.
- **Client software:** A set of programs which runs on top of the workstation's regular operating system and facilitates access to services provided by the server.

Client/server networks are often distributed: It means more than one dedicated server is used in order to maximize network performance. Server tasks can be distributed in a variety of ways:

- Among groups of users to reduce the volume of requests handled by any single server.
- Along the lines of function - a database server, a print server, a file server, etc.
- Any combination of the above.

Thus, the Client-Server network model usually consists of one or more server computers that provide services and information to a number of workstation computers. These services can consist of many different roles, including: file services, web services, email services, domain name lookup services, document version system services, Internet sharing services, etc.

Features of Client- Server Model

- Relies on both LAN and WAN technologies
- Flexible deployment - easily customized
- Low computer cost
- Increased end-user equipment costs
- Lower transmission facility costs
- Increased network management costs

Difference between Peer-To-Peer Network and Client-Server Network

This model differs from the Peer-to-peer network model in that the servers usually do not dually act as a workstation, and the workstations usually do not act as servers, and if they do act as a server, they should be configured to allow the central servers to provide access restrictions on the shares they provide the network.

An Example of a Client-Server Network

A great example of the Client-Server network model is actually the World Wide Internet. On the Internet clients, or computer with web browsers, access web sites that are hosted on servers.

The Benefits of a Client-Server Network

§ Security is relatively easy to implement with this type of network model.

§ Information control (like company's email & contact list) is also fundamentally easier.

§ Maintenance cost for the network drops because all the important information of the network actually resides on the servers, the workstation maintenance also drops since the users can access any information they need through any workstation, and a faulty workstation will have very little effect on the performance of network.

The Downsides of a Client-Server Network

§ The cost of this type of network is relatively high up front, not only must you purchase the server hardware, but most server software is very expensive, especially for larger networks since some software companies charge more for each client computer that will connect to the main server (although there are cheaper alternatives). Once the network is in place however, it is relatively easy to justify the cost since the overall cost to maintain the network becomes less expensive.

§ If you need 24x7 operability, you should allow in your budget a second "redundant" server, so if the main server goes down, the redundant server will step in and provide services until the primary server is back up again. An experienced administrator should be able to setup redundant servers that will assume control of failing servers without user intervention.

When a server-based network would be appropriate for you organization:-

1. There are more 10 people in the organization.
2. Many of the people are not sophisticated users.
3. Organization maintains such information that has to be centrally controlled.
4. A central administrator will set network policies and oversee network maintenance.

new topic TOPLOGIES OF LAN

1. Topology refers to the architectural drawing of the components used in a network. It is analogous to the architectural drawing of a home or building.
2. In other words, it can be defined as the manner by which the computers are physically connected together in a network.
3. Topology determines following -
   a. The complexity of network
   b. Strategy for physically expanding the network
   c. The cost of network installation.

1. KINDS OF TOPOLOGIES

- Linear Bus Topology
- Tree Topology
- Star Topology
- Ring Topology
- Mesh Topology

LINEAR BUS TOPOLOGY

In Bus network, a set of clients or nodes are connected through a bus. "***Bus***" simply refers to a communication line. It is the simplest network architecture.

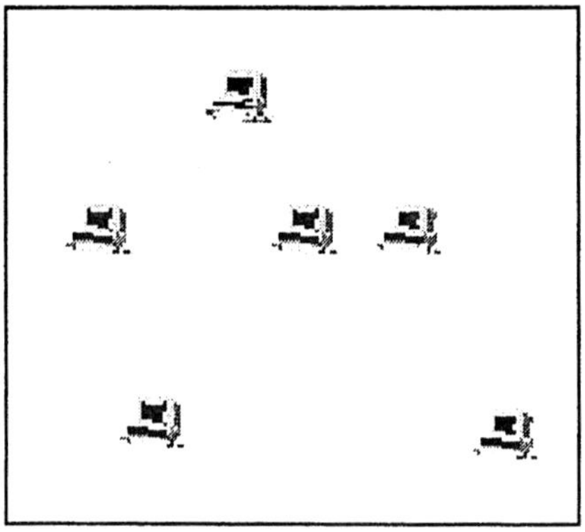

Features:

- A single cable connects all the nodes or terminals.
- Each node is connected to two other nodes except the nodes or terminals at either end of the cable.
- The network O.S keeps a unique electronic address for each node and manages the flow of data based on the addressing scheme.
  - Bus networks have problems when two nodes want to transmit at the same time on the same bus. Thus systems which use bus network architectures normally have some scheme of ***collision avoidance*** or ***collision handling***. (using CSMA or bus master, which controls access to the shared bus resource)
  - A true bus network is passive. It means the computers on the bus simply listen for a signal; they are not responsible for moving the signal along.
  - **Example:** Ethernet

Advantages:

- Easier to implement & further extend the network.
- Least amount of cable is required, therefore less expensive
- Simple wiring.
- For longer distance LANs, repeaters can be used to amplify the signals.
- Cost per station is generally lower than star networks but higher than ring networks.

Disadvantages:

- Efficient for small networks only.
- Performance can be slow at times because all the information traffic is dedicated a single cable.
- Each node can transmit, but the determination of transmitting node is done by a polling sequence. Polling sequence is a process, in which a token is passed from one node to another, but the node having the token can only transmit.
- Difficult to administer/troubleshoot.
- Limited cable length and number of stations
- If there is a problem with the cable, the entire network goes down
- Performance degrades as additional computers are added in the network

- High maintenance cost (in long run)
- Low security (All computers on the bus can see all data transmission)
- One virus in the entire network will affect all of them

TREE TOPOLOGY

A Tree network consists of star-configured nodes connected to switches/concentrators, each connected to a linear bus backbone. Each hub/concentrator rebroadcasts all transmissions received from any peripheral node to all peripheral nodes on the network. All peripheral nodes may thus communicate with all others by transmitting to, and receiving from, the central node only. The failure of a transmission line linking any peripheral node to the central will in the isolation of that peripheral node from all others, but the rest of the systems will be unaffected.

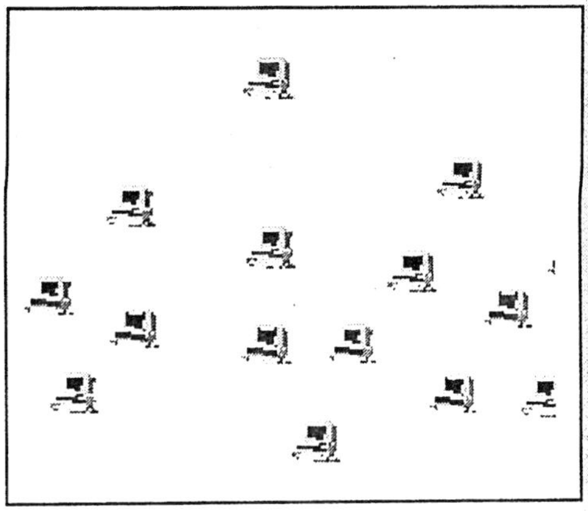

Features:

- It is a special case of star topology.
- All nodes and links are connected in a hierarchical order using a coaxial cable.
- The topmost node is called the root. The root may have zero or more child nodes, connected by links.
- Two or more than two nodes sharing the same parents are called **siblings**.
- All nodes in the tree are descendants of the root node.
- The main difference between the bus topology and tree topology is that the former uses baseband transmission whereas the latter use broadband techniques.

Advantages:

- Throughput (amount of work processed by a network) of broadband tree systems is high and limited only by the bandwidth of the cable.
- Cost is generally similar to linear bus systems.
- It uses some "traffic control" mechanism that determines when to allow traffic to travel up and down the branches of a tree.
- Allow easier troubleshooting.
- Message delay is low, when independent channels are provided by the technique of frequency division multiplexing.

Disadvantages:

- If there is disruption or error in any one branch of a tree, then the whole network goes down.
- This ensures that there is only one path from one node to any other node in the tree.

STAR TOPOLOGY

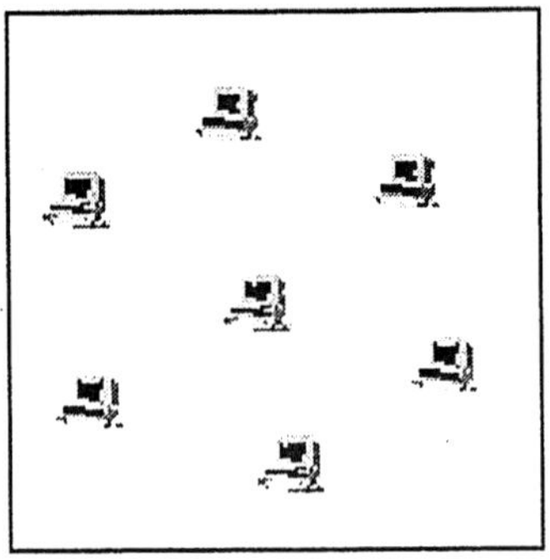

Star network is one of the most common network topologies. A star network consists of one central switch, hub or computer which acts as a router to transmit messages. The star topology reduces the chance of network failure by connecting all of the systems to a central node. When applied to a bus-based network, the central hub rebroadcasts all transmissions received from any peripheral node to all peripheral nodes on the network. All peripheral nodes may thus communicate with all others by transmitting to, and receiving from, the central node only. The failure of a transmission line linking any peripheral node to the central node will result in the isolation of that peripheral node from all others, but the rest of the systems will be unaffected.

Features:

- This topology consists of a central node to which all other nodes are connected.
- Star networks are most commonly employed to connect remote and local terminals to mainframe computers and in private branch exchanges (PABXs)
- Individual nodes are connected using a central concentrators or "hub". Hub can be passive or active.
- Active hub regenerates the electrical signal and sends it to all the computers connected to it. It is also called as **"multi-port repeater".** It requires electrical power to run.
- Passive hub merely acts as a connection point and does not amplify or regenerate the signal. It does not require electrical power to run.
- The throughput of computers in a star topology based network is constrained by the rate at which the central hub can accept and retransmit them.

Advantages:

- Easy to add and remove computers to a star network.
- Good performance
- Failure of a single computer does not necessarily bring down the whole star network.
- Network Administrator can easily determine the faultier node.
- Different cable types can be used in the same network with a hub that can accommodate multiple cable types.

Disadvantages:

- Large amount of cable is required, therefore expensive.
- The number of stations may be expanded only up to the limit of expansion permitted by the central hub.
- Many star networks require a device at the central point to rebroadcast or switch network traffic.

- If the central hub fails, the whole network fails to operate.
- The initial cost of a star network is high because the central hub must be installed with a margin of expansion. However, the incremental cost for additional stations is low.

RING TOPOLOGY

A ring network is a topology of computer networks where each node is connected to two other nodes, so as to create a ring. Ring networks tend to be inefficient as compared to star networks because in ring network, data must travel through more number of points before reaching its destination. ***Example:*** The Token ring network is a ring topology only at the logical level; it runs on a physical Star network, using central devices called MAUs or MSAUs.

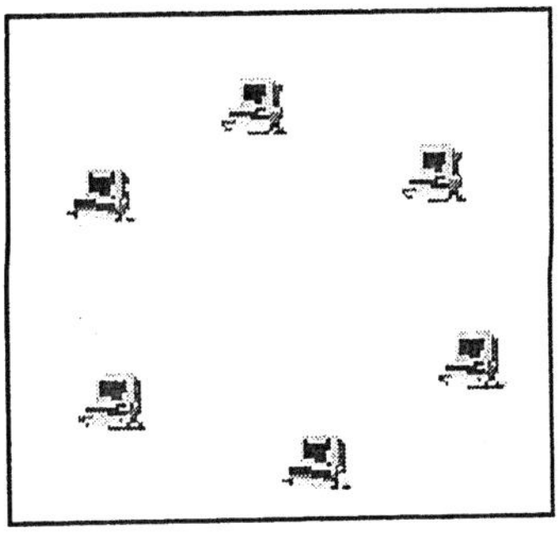

Features:

- In a ring topology, each computer is connected to the next or neighboring computer, in such a way a closed loop is formed.
- All nodes have transmitters & receivers.
- Data are transmitted only in one direction around the ring i.e. a node can expect transmission from a node before it and the node itself can send transmission to the following node.
- Thus, the opportunity to transmit data around the ring is passed on from node to node in a fixed order.
- The media and the capability of the repeater determine the thoroughput.

Advantages:

- Data are quickly transferred without a "bottle neck" (because, all data traffic is in the same direction)
- The cost per node is generally lower than other topologies offering similar performance.
- Every computer is given equal access to token therefore; a single computer cannot monopolize the network.
- Adding additional nodes has very little impact on bandwidth.
- It prevents network collisions.

Disadvantages:

- Data packets must pass through every computer between the sender and recipient, therefore this makes it slower.
- Difficult to troubleshoot.
- The amount of cable required is generally less than for a star topology.
- Message delay increases i.e. network degrades as more nodes are added to the ring.
- Failure of one computer in the ring can affect the entire network.
- Difficult to add or remove node in a ring i.e. each additional node involves system disruption and reduces performance.

- In order for all computers to communicate with each other, all computers must be turned on.
- Total dependence upon the one cable.

GRAPH OR MESH TOPOLOGY

A Mesh network is a networking technique which allows inexpensive peer network nodes to supply back haul services to other nodes in the same network. Mesh networks differ from other networks in that the component parts can all connect to each other via multiple hops, and they generally are not mobile.

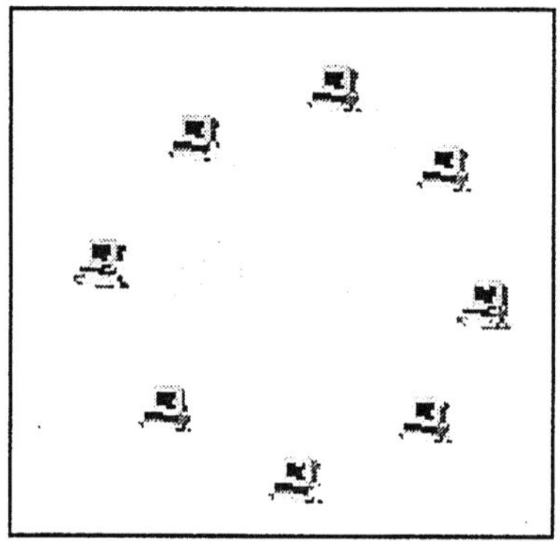

Features:

- In mesh topology, all the nodes are linked together in an arbitrary fashion.
- Nodes may have one or redundant links between them.
- A fully connected mesh linking **'n'** nodes requires n(n-1) links but it is usually not possible to provide all connections ***e.g.*** a network of six systems typically have 15 links (5+4+3+2+1)
- It is called as graph topology, because if we trace the path, then the graph is connected one.
- Eliminating redundant links can reduce the cost of mesh network.

Advantages:

- Mesh networks are self-healing i.e. the network can still operate even when a node breaks down or a connection goes bad. As a result, a very reliable network is formed.

Disadvantages:

- Guaranteed communication channel capacity.
- Message delay may be high because long distance transmission media have relatively low data rates.
- Easy to troubleshoot.

new topic PROTOCOLS

A protocol is a formal set of rules, conventions and data structure that governs how computer exchange information over a network.

Or

A protocol is a standard procedure & format that two data communication devices must understand, accept & use to be able to talk to each other.

Example of Protocol used by LAN :

ETHERNET

(*Popular LAN architecture based on CSMA/CD method, invented at Xerox Corporation's Palo Alto Research Center (PARC) during 1973*)

1. It generally employs Linear Bus topology (i.e. 10base2, coax, max. distance 200 mt.). However, it may use a star topology (10baseT, UTP, Max. distance 100 mt.)
2. Thus, it uses a single coaxial cable (or UTP cable) i.e. **"Ether".**
3. It also uses optical fibres (10baseF, Max. distance 2000 mt.)
4. All the computers or nodes in Ethernet share access to single communication medium or cable.
5. It is a baseband network as a single message (data in digital form) is carried over the wire at a time.
6. **Data Transmission Rate :** 10 Mbits/s (Fast Ethernet reaches 100 Mbit/s)
7. **Advantage :** Cabling is minimized
8. **Disadvantage:** A break in the cable can bring down the entire network
9. Most recent version operates at 1 Gbps (Gigabits per second)
10. Ethernet transmit data in the form of small units called ***frames***. All stations are continually listening to the bus looking for frame addressed to them. This is so, because, broadcasting of the frames is done to all stations on the network. A ***frame length*** may vary from 64 to 1518 bytes. The ***transmission time*** varies from 50 to 1200 msec.
11. **<u>Frame Format :</u>**
    a. Destination address (6 bytes)
    b. Source address (6 bytes)
    c. Type (2 bytes)
    d. Data (46 ... 1500 bytes)
    e. Check sequence/checksum (4 bytes).
    f. Type field is sometimes used to store the length of the frame.

6 Bytes	6 Bytes	2 Bytes	46 ... 1500 Bytes	4 Bytes
Destination Address	Source Address	Type	...... DATA	Frame Check Sequence

Layout of Ethernet Packet

12. A standard Ethernet segment is limited to 500m in length & the standard requires a minimum separation of 3m.
13. The requirements of an Ethernet cable can be determined by 5-4-3 rule i.e. according to this rule, the following can appear between any two nodes in the network-
    a. Upto 5 segments in a series
    b. Upto 4 concentrators or repeaters
    c. 3 segments of cable that contains nodes

14. Various topologies or varieties of Ethernet based on the transmission media and transmission speed- (*Below given standards are established by IEEE*)

	Media Type	***Max. Segment Length***	***Max. # Nodes/ Segment***
10Base5	Thick coaxial	500 meters	100
10Base2	RG58 (thin) coaxial	185 meters	30
10BaseT	UTP	100 meters	1024
10BaseF (FOIRL)	Fiber-optic	2,000 meters	1024k

In the above standards, the **"10"** refers to the *Ethernet transmission speed* - 10Mbit/s. The **"Base"** refers to *baseband* (single communications channel on each cable). Originally, the last character referred to the maximum cable distance in hundreds of meters. This naming convention changed, however, with the introduction of 10BaseT and 10BaseF. In these instances, the T and F refer to the cable types (twisted-pair and fiber-optic).

15. Ethernet is also referred to as a ***passive network***, which means that the networked computers and not some dedicated network device originate the signals used to manage network traffic.
16. Network traffic must be managed because if two or more nodes attempt to send data simultaneously a collision occurs and the potential exists for corrupted packets.
17. The method used by Ethernet networks to prevent concurrent transmission by more than one node is referred to as being ***contention-based*** because each node must contend for the opportunity to transmit on the network.
18. Mechanisms used by Ethernet for coordinating transmission-
    - CSMA
    - CSMA/CD

CSMA

1. CSMA stands for ***Carrier Sense Multiple Access***.
2. A network control scheme in which a node verifies the absence of other traffic before transmitting on a shared physical medium. Transmission of digital bits is done in the form of electrical signals.
3. "***Carrier Sense***" describes the fact that a transmitter listens for carrier wave before trying to send. If the ***carrier*** is present, then the computer must wait for previous transmission to be finished. On the contrary, if no ***carrier*** is present, then the computer can transmit the frame.

4. "***Multiple Access***" describes the fact that multiple nodes send and receive on the common medium i.e. same "***Ether***" (or cable). Transmissions by one node are generally received by all other nodes using the medium.
5. ***Procedure of CSMA:*** A node listens to medium and waits until it is free (when no one else is talking). Thus, it waits for a random back off time than start talking.
6. ***Advantage:*** Simple to implement and it is a functional scheme that works.
7. ***Disadvantage:*** cannot recover from a collision.
8. Concurrent transmission by multiple nodes results in frame ***collisions***. Collisions are of three types- Local, Remote & Late collision. There are three ways to address collisions in CSMA networks-
   a. In ***Pure CSMA***, only the carrier sense is used to avoid collision.
   b. In ***CSMA/CA*** (CSMA with Collision Avoidance), each node must inform other nodes of an intent to transmit.
   c. In ***CSMA/CD*** (CSMA with Collision Detection), sending nodes are able to detect when a collision occurs and stop transmitting immediately.
   d. In ***CSMA/BA*** (CSMA with Bitwise Arbitration), all of the nodes on the bus are assigned an identification number (or priority code). When a collision occurs, one of the nodes that are attempting to send at the same time will be given priority to transmit according to its priority code.

newtopic CSMA/CD

1. CSMA/CD stands for Carrier Sense Multiple access with Collision detect.
2. The term **'Collision detect'** refers to monitoring the cable for collisions during transmission.
3. If two or more computers transmit their respective frames at the same time, they may interfere with each other resulting in collision.
4. Thus, collision means the interference between two or more signals.
5. Collision can be detected by determining the difference between the transmitted frame and received frame. If a difference is found, then it may be due to the collision. However, collision does not affect hardware.
6. If a collision is detected, then each computer randomly delays the transmission, thus waiting for a longer time until the cable becomes idle again. In technical terms, doubling the random delays is called **binary exponential backoff.**
7. **To understand,** The CSMA/CD protocol functions somewhat like a dinner party in a dark room. Everyone around the table must listen for a period of quiet before speaking (Carrier Sense). Once a space occurs everyone has an equal chance to say something (Multiple Access). If two people start talking at the same instant they detect that fact, and quit speaking (Collision Detection.)

new topic WIRELESS NETWORKS

WiFi refers to "**W**ireless **F**idelity". WiFi is also known as 802.11 networking and wireless networking. The term **wireless** is normally used to refer to any type of electrical or electronic operation which is accomplished without the use of a "***hard wired***" connection.

Wireless networks are telephone or computer networks that use radio waves as their carrier or physical layer. Wireless networking allows the user to have the same access to the network as people with a traditional wired network, but with the freedom to move any where within approximately 100 feet of the wireless signal. Thus, wireless medium is a broadcast medium. A wireless network is comprised of devices with adapters communicating with each other using radio waves. These wireless devices are called ***nodes.*** A ***Base station*** is a special node in the network that is not mobile and is located in a central location. The "***Blue box"*** is a wireless router that is connected by a cable to a modem. The wireless router turns the network signal into a radio wave, which can be received by any wireless device within 100 feet.

There are many different standards of wireless access, but the most commonly used and most dependable is WiFi. ***For example,*** you can connect computers anywhere in your home or office without the need for wires.

Wireless network differs in the duplexing mechanism and the network architecture. There are two basic types of wireless networks (on the basis of architecture)-

- ✓ ***Distributed:*** Distributed wireless networks, also called ad hoc networks, are wireless terminals communicating with one another with no pre-existing infrastructure in place; therefore, they are also called ***infrastructure-less*** networks.
- ✓ ***Centralized:*** In centralized networks the downlink transmissions (from base station to wireless nodes) are broadcast and can be heard by all the devices on the network. The up link (from wireless terminals to the BS) is shared by all the nodes and is therefore a multiple access channel. A centralized network can operate both in TDD mode or FDD mode.

Disadvantages

With all of the positives of wireless networks, there are several downsides that have kept it from becoming industry standard. For example, wireless networks generally transmit at speeds that are slower than traditional wired networks. In addition, the equipment needed to establish a wireless network for a school size zone would be very costly.

4

HyperText MarkUp Language

Introduction:

1. HTML stands for **H**yper **T**ext **M**arkup **L**anguage.
2. It is a language of tags i.e. markup tags and attributes.
3. It is an Internet language.
4. An HTML file is a text file containing small markup tags (or html elements). The markup tags tell the web browser how to display the page.
5. Browser usually deals with html language i.e. Browser is used to execute a html code.
6. HTML files are used to design static web pages i.e. non-interactive or only readable pages, in which no dynamic changes can be done.
7. An HTML file must have an **htm** or **html** file extension.
8. An HTML file can be created using a simple text editor like ***Notepad*** or ***EditPlus.***
9. You can easily edit HTML files using a WYSIWYG (what you see is what you get) editor like ***FrontPage*** or ***Dreamweaver***, instead of writing your markup tags in a plain text file.
10. For making dynamic web pages HTML is used with any of the scripting language like ASP, VBScript, Jscript etc.
11. Internet files are called web pages. The collection of related web pages is called website.

newtopic Various Versions of HTML

- **HTML 2.0**: Developed in July, 1994.
- **HTML 3.2**: Developed in Jan, 1997.
- **HTML 4.0**: Latest version based on Unicode.

HTML Tags

- HTML tags are used to mark-up HTML **elements**
- HTML tags are surrounded by the ***angle brackets*** < > The angle brackets simply tell browsers that the text between them is a HTML command.
- HTML Tags can be-
  - **Paired :-**
    - A tag having it's opening (start tag) and closing tag (end tag). The text between the start and end tags is the **element content.**
    - Both opening and closing tag looks alike, except the closing tag, which includes a forward slash(/)
    - To apply tags to information in your document, place the opening tag before the information, and place the closing tag after the information.
  - **Single:-**
    - A tag having it's opening tag only.
    - HTML tags are **not case sensitive,** <b> means the same as <B>. However, the World Wide Web Consortium (W3C) recommends lowercase tags

Tag Attributes

1. Tags can have attributes.
2. Attributes can provide additional information about the HTML elements on your page.
3. Attributes always come in name/value pairs like this: **name="value".**
4. Attribute values should always be enclosed in quotes. Double style quotes are the most common, but single style quotes are also allowed. For example: In some cases, when the attribute value itself contains quotes, then the entire attribute value must be enclosed in single quotes— **name = 'Kalpna "Astronaut" Chawla'**
5. Attributes are always added to the start tag of an HTML element.

EXAMPLES OF TAGS & ATTRIBUTES:

1. ***<body>*** tag defines the body element of your HTML page. With an added ***bgcolor*** attribute, you can tell the browser that the background color of your page should be blue like this: ***<body bgcolor="blue">.***
2. ***<table>*** tag defines an HTML table. With an added ***border*** attribute, you can tell the browser that the table should have no borders: ***<table border="0">***

Structure of HTML Documents

§ HTML documents are plain text files.

§ They contain no images, no video, no animations, however, they can include "pointers" or "links" to other file types.

§ It consists of Tags and attributes.

§ HTML Documents consists of the following three parts-

- o **Head:** it is used to establish it's title.
- o **Body:** constitute contents of web page.
- o **Footer:** used for labeling of pages or for specifying it's author, date of creation and version number etc.

§ **Two Categories of Body Elements**

- Block-level Elements
- Text-level Elements

How To Write Simple Code Of HTML

If you are running Windows, start Notepad.

1. Type in the following text:

```
<html>
<head>
<title>Title of page</title>
</head>
<body>
This is my first webpage. <i>This text is italic </i>
</body>
</html>
```

2. Save the file as "***mywebpage.htm***".
3. Start your Internet browser. Select "***Open***" (or "Open Page") in the File menu of your browser. A dialog box will appear. Select "***Browse***" (or "Choose File") and locate the HTML file you just created - "***mywebpage.htm***" - select it and click "***Open***". Now you should see an address in the dialog box, for example - "***C:\MyDocuments\mywebpage.htm***". Click OK, and the browser will display the page.

   Or Simply type the address of the webpage in the address bar, displayed in the Internet Explorer window.

Explanation of Above HTML Code

The first tag in your HTML document is <html>. This tag tells your browser that this is the start of an HTML document. The last tag in your document is </html>. This tag tells your browser that this is the end of the HTML document.

The text between the <head> tag and the </head> tag is header information. Header information is not displayed in the browser window.

The text between the <title> tags is the title of your document. The title is displayed in your browser's caption.

The text between the <body> tags is the text that will be displayed in your browser.

The text between the <i> and </i> tags will be displayed in italicized font.

Note: When you write HTML text, you can never be sure how the text is displayed in another browser. Some people have large computer displays, some have small. The text will be reformatted every time the user resizes his window. Never try to format the text in your editor by adding empty lines and spaces to the text.

Syntax of HTML Tags

Sl. no.	*Tags*	*Purpose*
	Block Level Elements	
1	**<Html>.......</Html>**	First tag for starting html code. i.e. contains html document.
2	**<Head>** **<Title>.......</Title>** **</head>**	Used to display any information as the title of the page.(Title bar)Used inside head tag.
3	**</Body>.........</Body>**	Used to display any information on the web page.
4	**<P>.......</P>**	Paragraphs are defined with the <p> tag. HTML automati-cally adds an extra blank line before and after a paragraph. It is a bad habit to use empty paragraph tags in order to leave a blank line.
5	**<H1>.......</H1>**	Used to display level one headings.

Sl. no.	*Tags*	*Purpose*
6	**<H2>........</H2> ....<H6>....</H6>**	Used to display level two headings. **Note :** H1 is largest & H2 is smallest.
7	**<HR>**	For displaying horizontal ruler.
8	**<CENTER>**	Used to display the text in center.
	Text-Level Elements	
9	**<B>......</B>**	For converting text into bold. Used inside body tag.
10	**<I>........</I>**	For converting text into italics.
11	**<U>......</U>**	For underlying a given text.
12	** **	Single tag. The tag is used when you want to end a line, but don't want to start a new paragraph. The tag forces a line break wherever you place it. It should be noted that HTML automatically adds an extra blank line before and after some elements, like before and after a paragraph, and before and after a heading.Used for line break and it places the cursor to next line.
13	**<A HREF="URL">....</A>** **<a href=mail to:email address>.....</a>**	Anchor tagUsed to create hyperlinks.You can also use it to link to e-mail address, when someone clicks on this type of anchored link.
14	**<IMG SRC="URL">**	Single tag.Used to insert a picture within web page.
	Text Tags	
15	**<ABBR>.....</ABBR>** **OR** **<ACRONYM>........</ACRONYM>**	**E.g** <ABBR TITLE="Punjab National Bank">PNB </ABR> Title attribute is used with this tag

Sl. no.	Tags	Purpose
		to indicate that the given text is an abbreviation.It's expanded version can be seen in a pop-up appearing, when the mouse is over the acronym.
16	**<BLOCKQUOTE>....... </BLOCKQUOTE>**	Used to quote one or more para-graphs from an-other source.
17	**<CITE>......</CITE>**	Used to indicate that enclosed text is a citation from another source.The text within CITE is usually rendered in italics.
18	**<CODE>......</CODE>**	Used to enclosed programs or samples of code to offset them from normal text.Usually displayed in a mono-spaced font.
19	**<DEL>......</DEL>**	It marks text that has been deleted from a previous version of the web document.
20	**<INS>......</INS>**	Identifies sections of a web page that have been inserted in revision.
21	**<DFN>.......</DFN>**	It is used to mark terms that appear for the first time in the web document.Such definitions are often in italics.
22	**<EM>........</EM>**	It adds emphasis to enclosed text.
23	**<KBD>........</KBD>**	It marks the text to be entered by the user at the keyboard.
24	**<PRE>........</PRE>**	This element forces the browser to display the exact formatting, identation and white space that the original text contains.
25	**<Q>.........</Q>**	Used to highlight short quota-tion from outside resources.

Sl. no.	*Tags*	*Purpose*
26	**<STRONG>......</STRONG>**	It provides strong emphasis for keywords or phrases within normal body text, lists.Such text is displayed in bold and given a strident pronouncia-tion.
27	**_{......}**	Used to specify that the enclosed text is subscript.
28	**^{.......}**	Used to specify that the enclosed text is superscript.
29	**<VAR>........</VAR>**	It is used to mark up the variables of the programs.
30	**<STRIKE>.......</STRIKE>**	Used to strikethrough the enclosed text.
31	**<BIG>........</BIG>**	It makes text font one size larger than the <BASEFONT> size.So, single or multiple <BIG> tags can be used as per the requirement.
32	**<SMALL>.......</SMALL>**	It makes text font one size smaller than the <BASEFONT> size.So, single or multiple <SMALL> tags can be used as per the requirement.
33	**<TT>......</TT>**	It is used to make the enclosed text in Teletype i.e. monospac-ed (that look like a typewriter font)
	Lists—— Ordered, Unordered, Definition	
34	**<LI>**	Singleton tag.It is used to create a list item
35	**<UL>.......</UL>**	It is used to define Unordered list.**e.g.** <UL><LI TYPE = "DISC|SQUARE|CIRCLE> Body </UL>where, DISC|SQUARE refers to the type of bullets.

Sl. no.	Tags	Purpose
36	**<OL>.........</OL>**	It is used to define ordered list.**e.g** <OL> <LI TYPE = "1" |"A"| "a"|"i" |"I" |>Body</OL> where, a = Lowercase alpha-numericA = Upper case alpha-numeric
37	**<DT>**	To indicate the definition term.
38	**<DD>**	To indicate the actual definition of term.
39	**<DL>.......</DL>**	To define definition list.Both <DT> & <DD> tags are used within <DL> tag.
40	**<DIR>.......</DIR>**	It is used to define directory list i.e. list of short elements, such as filenames.
41	**<MENU>......</MENU>**	It is used to define menu list, in which each element is typically a word or short phrase that fits on a single line.
	Background Images & Colors	
42	**<Body Background="image.gif">**	Used to set the background of web page.
43	**<Body Bgcolor="BLUE">**	Used to fill the background of web page with a specific color.
	Frames	
44	**<frame >........</frame>**	For displaying multiple html files simultaneously, the page is divided into various no. of frames. So, for the creation of frame, frame tag is used.
45	**<frameset>.........</frameset>**	It is used to specify the percentage of area occupied by each frame.Note: body tag, head tag & title tag cannot be used, while using this tag. e.g<html><frameset cols = "50%, 50%"><frame src = "G:\a.html"> <frameset rows

Sl. no.	*Tags*	*Purpose*
		= "30%, 70%"><frame src = "b. html" ><frame src = "c.html"> </frameset></frameset> </html>

SOME ADDITIONAL TAGS

46	<! This is a comment >	The comment tag is used to insert a comment in the HTML source code. A comment will be ignored by the browser. You can use comments to explain your code, which can help you when you edit the source code at a later date. Note that you need an exclamation point after the opening bracket, but not before the closing bracket.
47	<Marquee>.........</Marquee>	To make a given text movable. By, default, it moves the text from right to left.
48	<blink>.........</blink>	To make a given text blink. Works only in Netscape Navigator.
49	<font>...........</font>	To set the font of text.
50	<meta>.........</meta>	For making comment in html code.
51	<form>.........</form>	For designing forms used inside <body> tag.
52	<object>........</object>	For including or embedding objects of other software.
53	<table> <tr> <td> field_name=value </td> </tr> </table>	Used for creating table.

Examples of HTML Code & Corresponding Output in Browser

EXAMPLE 1

```
<body>
<b>This text is bold</b>
<br>
<strong>
This text is strong
</strong><br>
<big>
This text is big
</big>
<br>
<em>
This text is emphasized
</em>
<br>
<i>
This text is italic
</i>
<br>

<small>
This text is small
</small>

<br>

This text contains
<sub>
subscript
</sub>
<br>
This text contains<sup>superscript
</sup>
</body>
</html>
```

OUTPUT

This text is bold

This text is strong

This text is big

This text is emphasized

This text is italic

This text is small

This text contains $_{\text{subscript}}$

This text contains ^{superscript}

EXAMPLE 2:

```
<html>
<body>
<abbr title = "United Nations">UN</abbr>
<br>
<acronym title = "World Wide Web">WWW</
acronym>

<p>The title attribute is used to show the
spelled-out version when holding the mouse
pointer over the acronym or abbreviation.</p>

</body>
</html>
```

OUTPUT

UN

WWW

The title attribute is used to show the spelled-out version when holding the mouse pointer over the acronym or abbreviation.

EXAMPLE 3:

Headings Headings are defined with the <h1> to <h6> tags. <h1> defines the largest heading. <h6> defines the smallest heading. HTML automatically adds an extra blank line before and after a heading.

```
<html>
<body>

<h1>This is heading 1</h1>
<h2>This is heading 2</h2>
<h3>This is heading 3</h3>
<h4>This is heading 4</h4>
<h5>This is heading 5</h5>
<h6>This is heading 6</h6>

<p>Use heading tags only for headings.
Don't use them just to make something bold.
Use other tags for that.</p>

</body>
</html>
```

OUTPUT

This is heading 1

This is heading 2

This is heading 3

This is heading 4

This is heading 5

This is heading 6

Use heading tags only for headings. Don't use them just to make something bold. Use other tags for that.

EXAMPLE 4:

Code	Output
<html> <body> <h4>An Unordered List:</h4> <ul> <li>Coffee</li> <li>Tea</li> <li>Milk</li> </ul> </body> </html>	**An Unordered List:** • Coffee • Tea • Milk

EXAMPLE 5:

Code	Output
<html> <body><h4>An Ordered List:</h4> <ol> <li>Coffee</li> <li>Tea</li> <li>Milk</li> </ol> </body> </html>	**An Unordered List:** 1. Cofee 2. Tea 3. Milk

newtopic Summary of HTML Tags

BASIC HTML TAGS

Tag	**Description**
<html>	Defines an HTML document
<body>	Defines the document's body
<h1> to <h6>	Defines header 1 to header 6
<p>	Defines a paragraph
 	Inserts a single line break
<hr>	Defines a horizontal rule
<!-->	Defines a comment
Text Formatting tags	
TEXT FORMATTING Tag	***Description***
<b>	Defines bold text
<big>	Defines big text
<em>	Defines emphasized text
<i>	Defines italic text
<small>	Defines small text
<strong>	Defines strong text
<sub>	Defines subscripted text
<sup>	Defines superscripted text
<ins>	Defines inserted text
<del>	Defines deleted text
List tags	
List Tag	***Description***
<ol>	Defines an ordered list
<ul>	Defines an unordered list
<li>	Defines a list item
<dl>	Defines a definition list
<dt>	Defines a definition term
<dd>	Defines a definition description
Form tags	
FORM Tag	***Description***
<form>	Defines a form for user input
<input>	Defines an input field

<textarea>	Defines a text-area (a multi-line text input control)
<label>	Defines a label to a control
<fieldset>	Defines a fieldset
<legend>	Defines a caption for a fieldset
<select>	Defines a selectable list (a drop-down box)
<option>	Defines an option in the drop-down box
<button>	Defines a push button
Image Tags	
Image Tag	***Description***
<img>	Defines an image
<map>	Defines an image map
Table Tags	
TABLE Tag	***Description***
<table>	Defines a table
<th>	Defines a table header
<tr>	Defines a table row
<td>	Defines a table cell
<caption>	Defines a table caption
<colgroup>	Defines groups of table columns
<col>	Defines the attribute values for one or more columns in a table
<thead>	Defines a table head
<tbody>	Defines a table body
<tfoot>	Defines a table footer
Frame Tags	
FRAME Tag	***Description***
<frameset>	Defines a set of frames
<frame>	Defines a sub window (a frame)
<noframes>	Defines a noframe section for browsers that do not handle frames
<iframe>	Defines an inline sub window (frame)
Link Tags	
LINK Tag	Description
<a>	Defines an anchor

"Computer Output" Tags	
Tag	**Description**
<code>	Defines computer code text
<kbd>	Defines keyboard text
<samp>	Defines sample computer code
<tt>	Defines teletype text
<var>	Defines a variable
<pre>	Defines preformatted text
Citations, Quotations, and Definition Tags	
Tag	**Description**
<abbr>	Defines an abbreviation
<acronym>	Defines an acronym
<bdo>	Defines the text direction
<blockquote>	Defines a long quotation
<q>	Defines a short quotation
<cite>	Defines a citation
<dfn>	Defines a definition term

newtopic Creating a Web Page or Web Site

- Create an HTML page with an ***editor*** such as Simple Text, BBEDIT, SimpleText (Mac) or Webford, Notepad (PC)
- Create an HTML page from a ***word processing*** document
- Create a WEB page with an ***Authoring tool*** such as Netscape Composer (free), Front Page Express (free), Front Page (available for small cost at library), Page Mill, etc

After creating web page (or website), you can view them in any of the available web browser like Internet Explorer or Netscape Navigator.

1. Steps of Creating a Web Page

1. Planning
2. Organizing
3. Creating
4. Testing

PLANNING :-

- It is an act of formulating a program for a definite course of action.
- In other words, it an act or process of drawing up plans or layouts for some project or enterprise.

ORGANISING:-

- The four basic steps in organizing are-
  - Divide the web page into logical units
  - Establish a hierarchy of importance and generality.
  - Use the hierarchy to structure relationships among chunks.
  - Analyze the functionality of your system.

CREATING:- Following steps are used for creating a web page-

- Gather information
- Determine the intended audience
- Create a Storyboard
- Plan your navigation tools
- Create an appealing web page.

TESTING :-

- By testing, we can evaluate the effectiveness of online library instructions and can understand how to create a more useable interface.

2. Components of a Web Page

1. Text
2. Pictures
3. Animated Graphics
4. Audio Files
5. Video clippings etc.

3. Points to remember while designing a Web Page

The World Wide Web is one of the three most popular applications of the Internet, along with Instant Messaging and Email. As easy as it has become to create a website, though, most novice designers still make a lot of mistakes which are simple enough to avoid if you know how.

⊙ *Keep it Simple*

The number one mistake that most web designers make is trying to be too fancy. For instance, lots of people have taken to adding embedded music or Flash animation to their sites. While this is all well and good if you're a musician or a Flash animator; Not only can this prove to be expensive for you, it can be annoying for surfers without a high speed connection. Additionally, it can be annoying, especially if your taste in music doesn't suit theirs.

The key is an acronym called ***KISS***, or *Keep It Simple, Stupid*. While not implying stupidity on anyone's part, it means that you should always keep in mind that simple is better. The less complex a system, the less often it will break, the less often you will need to maintain it, and the less annoyance you will cause the people browsing your site.

Identify Your Audience

Is the page that you are designing for customerss? Are you presenting scholarly materials to help move you towards your PhD? Are you creating an online birthday greeting card?

Once you have your target audience identified, you can focus your efforts on figuring out how to draw them. For a website on art, you would want thumbnails and full sized images to keep them interested. The is a world of possibility available for web designers, but it has to be focused on what you're targeting, otherwise you'll never gain interest.

Keywords

This is an especially important step for commercial websites and other sites trying to draw in an audience.

Keywords are like a candle and surfers are like moths. You want as bright a light as possible to draw as many moths as you can. But when the moths arrive, you don't want them flapping around wondering why they bothered showing up.

There are two mistakes that are commonly associated with keywords: not using them at all and using them too often. Not using them at all is fairly self-explanatory. Using them too much occurs when, in an attempt to create greater keyword density, you detract from the value of the content in your site. Repeating the term 'mother's day cards' fifty times on a single page would certainly cause it to register high on many search engines.

Content

Content is what separates the real web pages from the fake ones. Content can be anything at all. It can be articles. It can be pictures of your home. It can be any sound. It doesn't matter what it is as long as it is relevant to the people browsing your site. It shouldn't be hard to figure out what they want once you know who your audience is. And if you've used the proper key words and phrases with the right density, you know that people will come visit your site. Content is what keeps them there and keeps them coming back.

Eye Catching Design

It can be difficult to draw the line between ***'eye catching'*** and ***'over the top,'*** but the distinction is vitally important. When you are designing a page, you want it to stand out and be noticed. But if you don't keep it simple, you run the risk of annoying the people that you are trying to entice.

The key to a good, eye catching design is subtlety. Start out by writing the page as plain as possible. Review everything and decide which parts you feel need to stand out. When going through and editing the page, do something which helps draw the eyes of someone browsing the page to those parts. Something as simple as a slight increase in font size, italics, or making a few words bold can do the job better than a lot of over the top graphics, Flash animation, etc.

By limiting the number of eye-drawing areas on your page, you will cause the parts that you have emphasized to be that much more noticeable.

⊙ *Searchability*

Depending on what sort of site you are designing, you might need to have some tool in place to allow people to search it for information. There are many free search tools available, which allow administrators to integrate search engines into their pages. However, unless your site is very in depth, you might not need that much functionality.

At the very least, you should have a site map available to browsers. A site map is a simple tool that lists everything on your site in a simple manner. There are many formats used, but in general an essay-style outline, with specifics mentioned underneath general subheadings, is one of the easiest to use and write.

4. Organizing Web Page

Most Web sites have lots of information to convey to the visitor, which typically takes plenty of space. It is best to design a home page (e.g., index.html) that is essentially an introduction to what is available at your site, then provide links to additional information about each topic on separate pages. If you clutter the home page with excessive detail it will overwhelm the reader.

Resist the impulse and the pressure to put detailed information on the home page, no matter how important it may be. If there is something that viewers must see, provide a clearly visible link to this information that will draw attention to it.

One way to plan your Web site is to draw mock-up pages on separate sheets of paper. You can be sketchy while planning the general layout, indicating graphics, figures, and tables with blank areas. Having an outline of the planned text is also a good idea; the details can be filled in later once the overall organization plan unfolds.

You should have a pretty good idea of how your page(s) will be organized and what information they will contain before you even begin to create them online. Web pages may be organized using one of the following organization methods-

- Hierarchical
- Linear
- Webbed

The best way to organize your pages is usually hierarchically, and by topic. For example, if you are on the faculty, you might wish to divide your pages into personal and professional, with professional pages further divided into classroom and student information and information about your research or community activities. These pages might also be subdivided if information is extensive into more manageable "chunks" of information.

HIERARCHICAL ORGANISATION:-

- It is much like the technique used when creating an organizational chart for a company.
- The hierarchy starts with top officials, then shows the managers who work for them, the employees who work for those managers, and so on.

- Organizing information in a hierarchical structure, you present a first group of equally important topics, followed by another group of equally important topics and so on.
- e.g. UPTEC Web site uses hierarchical organization to structure the main page.

LINEAR ORGANIZATION:-

- In a linear organization, the information is organized in a particular order.
- At a web site that uses linear organization, a visitor can move forward and backward within a sequence of pages, but cannot jump to other pages.
- It may frustrate user, therefore it is only used, wherever necessary. ***e.g.*** Microsoft wizard.
- When using linear organization try to follow these two guidelines:
  - o Remember that the visitor cannot roam to other pages; therefore, be sure the linear process is essential to the task at hand.
  - o Keep the linear sequence as short as possible so that visitors focus on the process and complete it successfully.

WEBBED ORGANIZATION:-

- In this case, a visitor can link from one web page to many other pages at the same web site or at another.
- This organization results in disorientation of web surfers- **i.e.** they do not know where they are or where they have been.
- Following guidelines have to be used, while using this organization-
  - o Provide information on each page that allows visitors to orient themselves. ***e.g.*** including a footer or header on each page.
  - o Provide a link to your home page on all pages. If you do so, visitors can easily return to a familiar page.

new topic Features of an Effective WebSite

1. Content must be
   - o easy to find.
   - o easy to access.
   - o easy to understand.
2. The site must be informative, engaging, and entertaining.
3. The design must be compelling and comfortable.
4. Information must be offered to the visitors in the manner and form they expect.
5. Navigation tools should be well-marked and easy to understand.
6. The design and "feel" of the site should target the intended audience.

Publishing Your Web Site

- As you create your web site, you will build and test it on your hard drive. To put your site on the web so others can access it, you have to "***publish***" the site by putting all of the files (both HTML files and graphic files) on the web server that will host your site. To publish your work, you have to copy your files to a web server. Your own PC can act as a web server if it is connected to a network.
- If you are running Windows 98, you can use the PWS (Personal Web Server). PWS turns any Windows computer into a Web server. PWS is easy to install and ideal for developing and testing Web applications.
- Windows 2000's built-in Web server IIS, makes it easy to build large applications for the Web. Both PWS and IIS include ASP, a server-side scripting standard that can be used to create dynamic and interactive Web applications. IIS is also available for Windows NT.
- Some editor programs (or web publishing tools) have the ability to publish your pages. Some popular editors are- Netscape Composer, Front Page and Front Page Express, PageMill, HotDog Professional.

Publicizing Your Site

Once you've built your organization's Web site, the next task is to make sure you've publicized your site as widely as possible. There are two key audiences to which you need to publicize your site- people you already communicate with, and people you don't. Each audience is important, but the methods you'll use to reach them are different. Thus, after publishing, your site needs to be publicized. For this, you should register your site with some search engines, so that people doing on-line searches can find the site. The following methods can be used for publicizing-

- Get the URL of your site printed on your business cards, stationery, and in yellow pages.
- Add your URL to your signature block in e-mail and newsgroup messages.
- Include the URL in your return address whenever you send greeting cards or holiday cards.
- Have some bumper stickers printed showing your organization's URL.
- Post the URL on all school bulletin boards.

5

DBMS & RDBMS

What is Data?

It is a term derived from a Greek word "***datum***". It represents the raw facts gathered from the surroundings for the purpose of extracting information.

What is Database?

1. A database is a collection of relevant data, which is organized for easy storage and access.
2. Data is a single piece of information, and can include, but is not limited to, text, images, numbers, and media clips.
3. Databases help to organize data in a coherent way to help us in our everyday lives. Every single day, we can accumulate tons of data. Without a way to organize all of this, the world would be a complete mess of little pieces of scattered information.

1. TYPES OF COMMON OPERATIONS PERFORMED IN A DATABASE-

(Assuming Student's database)

1. **Adding** a new record. (**e.g.** admission of a new student)
2. **Deleting** existing record (**e.g.** a student withdrawing his/her admission from a particular course)
3. **Modifying/Editing** existing records (**e.g.** change of address of a student)
4. **Sorting** or arranging records (**e.g.** alphabetically)
5. **Searching** a particular record in the database (**e.g.** searching for those students who belongs to "***Delhi***")

2. Types of Databases-

On the Basis of Media used for storing data:

1. **Paper-based:** In such databases, paper media is used for the storage of data or records. They are cumbersome and hard to transport from one place to another. It is also quite easy to misplace a page or a portion of the database. Inefficient for performing simple database operations (above mentioned). **Examples of Paper-based Databases-**
   a. **Dictionary :** dictionaries are large databases of words. They organize words and their definitions in such a way to make it easy for us to use.
   b. **Library:** Library is also an example of a database. They store numerous books in a logical order.
2. **Electronic or Computerized:** These databases rely on computers to organize and store data. They are fast, compact, durable, and extremely reliable. Computerized database plays an integral part in record keeping and in the storage of data. These databases are often used by the government, by universities and colleges, and by businesses to keep track of data. Anybody could access these databases, providing that they had the proper hardware and software. Electronic databases are vital components of many websites like Amazon, dishant etc. Besides, it is used in many search engines to keep track of all the websites so that you can access them efficiently.

On the Basis of Function Performed by Database:

- **Analytic Databases:**
  1. Analytic databases are generally used for storing statistical data for long term use.
  2. Such databases are read-only; it means that you can only retrieve data, but you can't modify the data
  3. These databases are used for OLAP (Online Analytical Processing).
  4. **Example:**
     a. Inventory catalogs
     b. Target Sales Review
- **Operational Databases:**
  1. Unlike Analytic databases, these are used to store and manage dynamic data.
  2. You can easily modify such databases i.e. these databases lets you add, edit or delete the data.
  3. These are used for OLTP (Online Transaction Processing).
  4. **Example:**
     a. Railway Reservations
     b. Airway Reservations

ARCHICTECTURE OF A DBMS

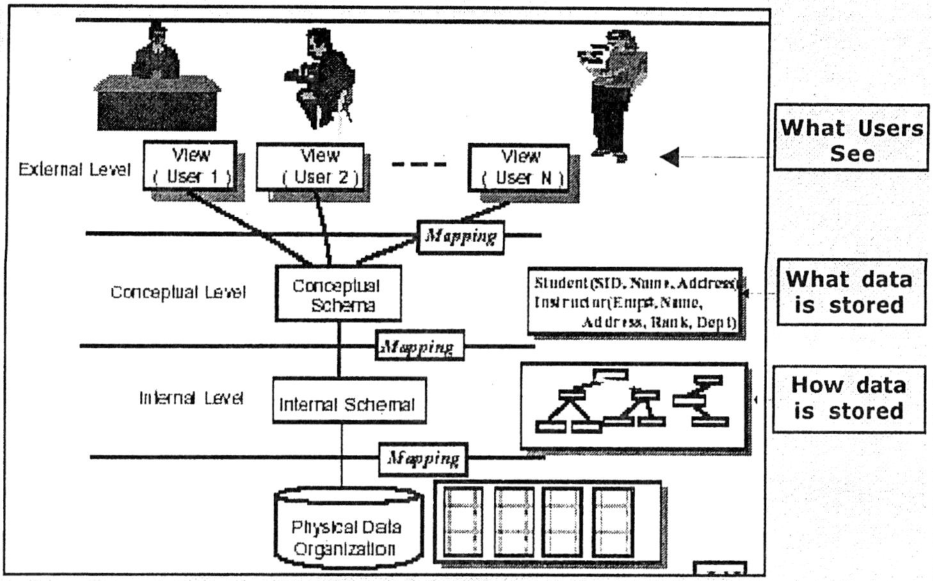

On the Basis of Architecture:

- **Client Server Database Systems**

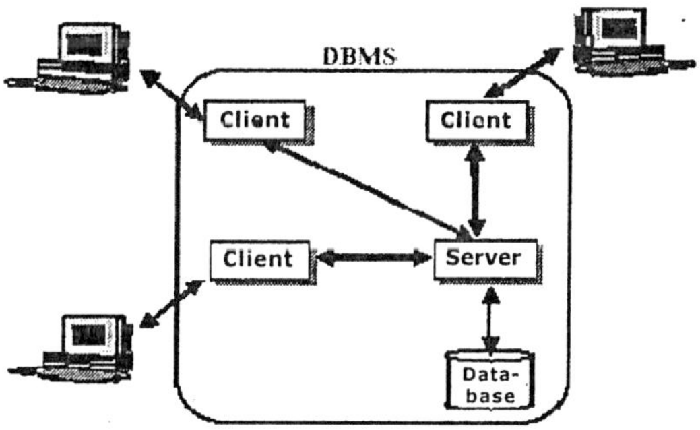

- **Centralized Database System**

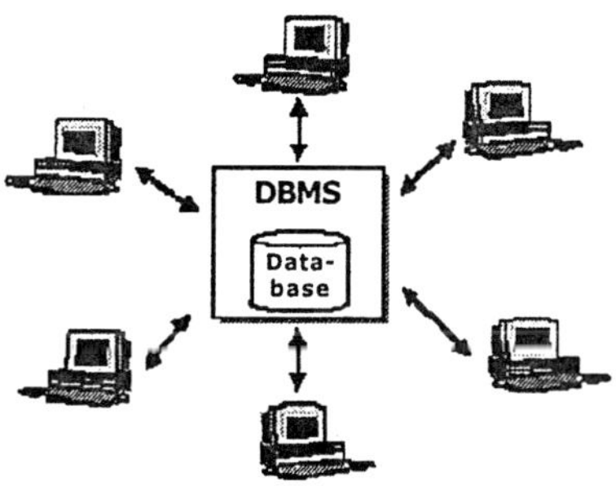

❖ Distributed Database System

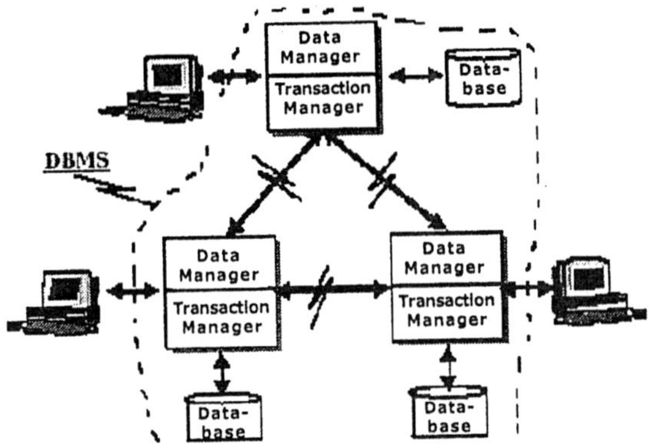

3. COMPONENTS OF A DATABASE-

1. Data:

1. Data is one of the key parts of a database because a database is maintained to organize data efficiently.
2. Data is a small bit of information, gathered from the surroundings.
3. Data may be in the form of pictures, text, numeric values, or audio samples.
4. For example-
   a. Suppose you are noting down the team scores of a quiz then your team scores will represent type of data.
   b. Contact details (names, addresses, phone numbers, and e-mail addresses) of your friends and relatives are the good examples of data.

Name	Address	Phone No.	E-mail
Anita	43, Chanakya puri, Delhi	4445126	anu@yahoomail.com
Sunita	543, Laxmi Nagar, Delhi	3276871	sunita@rediffmail.com
Sunaina	54, Shastri Nagar, Meerut	8627235	naina@yahoomail.com
Rashmi	12/6, Sadar, Meerut	3578892	rashmi@rediffmail.com

2. Field:

1. Fields are used to hold the data in a database.
2. **Example:** Name, Address, Phone number, E-mail – these columns (used in above database table) would be called **Fields**. The column headers/ headings are called **Field Names.**

3. All fields can contain different types of information. For example, the **"Name"** field above contains the names of the people, while the **"Address"** field contains the people's addresses. Some fields can contain text, some numeric values, some images, some a short movie clip, some an audio file- the list goes on and on.
4. Sometimes, you can control the type of data that can be placed in a certain field. For example, say you want to limit the **"Phone"** field in the above address book to only seven letters.

3. Records

1. The columns in a database table represent **"fields".**
2. The rows in a database table represent **"records"** except the first row because it generally contains the field names.
3. Thus, records begin with the second row.

4. Database Files

1. A computer file is a collection of data.
2. Different types of computer files are used for storing different data. **For example-** a WORD file is used to store textual information; a graphic file is used to store picture/image and so on.
3. Thus, database file is a special computer file used to store data.
4. Database files are composed of fields, records, and data.

4. Hierarchical Representation of Database Components

Database

↓

Files (in DBMS) / Tables (in RDBMS)

↓

Records

↓

Fields

5. Why a Database Is Used :-

- Redundancy can be reduced.
- Data are available at one place.
- Inconsistency can be avoided.
- Data can be shared.
- Data are independent.
- Complex queries can be easily answered.
- Provides fast response to user's request.

6. General Aspects of a Database Model

1. ***Structure:*** It specifies the data structures and schema used to represent data.

2. ***Integrity:*** It provides a language for the definition of data.
3. ***Manipulation:*** provides a language in which updates of the data can be expressed.
4. ***Querying:*** provides a language in which the data can be queried.

new topic What is DBMS?

1. It is the acronym used for "***Database Management System***".
2. In simple words, it is software that enables you to create and maintain databases.
3. In other words, a database management system (DBMS) is a set of computer-based application programs that support the processes of storing, manipulating, retrieving and presenting the data within the database. The data within the database are organized into database files, records, and fields.
4. ***Database File:*** A database file is a collection of records.
5. ***Record:*** Each record in a database file or table is composed of fields.
6. ***Fields***:
   i. The fields contain the actual data that describe and distinguish the items maintained in the table **e.g** The fields of "***Product***" table are "***name***", "**quantity**", "**price**," and so on.
   ii. Each field has certain characteristics, such as the type of data maintained (such as text, numbers, or dates), the length of the field (such as 15 characters), and the format of the data within the field (currency with three decimal places).
7. In other words, the DBMS is the major software component of an electronic/computerized database system.

   1. ***Advantages of DBMS:-***
      a. To create and organize data in centralized manner.
      b. Enhanced data quality
      c. To setup and maintain access path to the database so that any part of the database can be quickly accessed, without actually worrying about the implementation details. (Data Independence)
      d. To manipulate the data in response to the user's access.
      e. To maintain data integrity and security.
   2. ***Disadvantages of DBMS-***
      1. Problems associated with centralization
      2. Cost of H/W & S/W
      3. Complexity of backup and recovery

3. Example of a DBMS

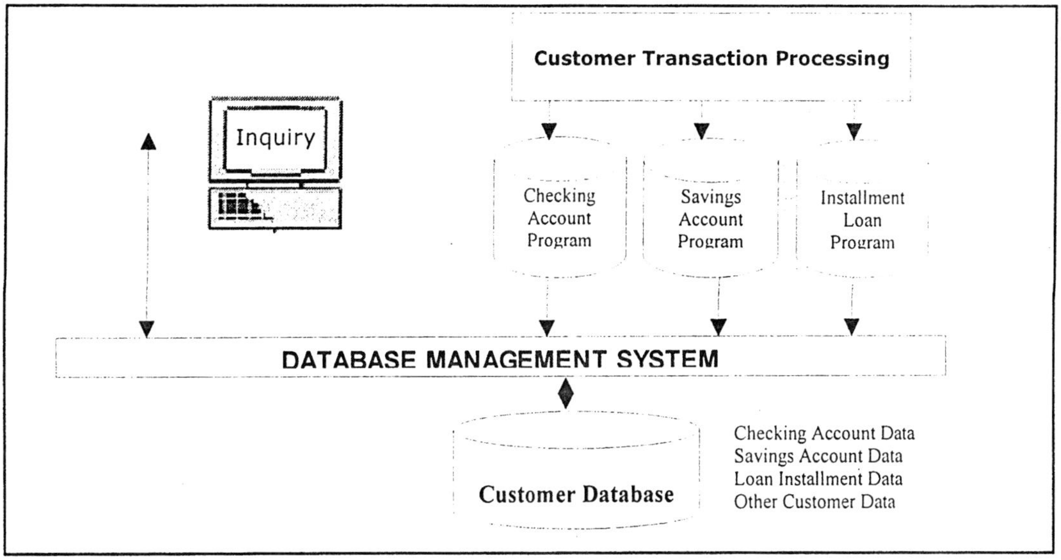

4. STRUCTURE OF DBMS :-

✓ *Data Definition Language Compiler :-*

1. The DDL compiler converts the data definition statements into a set of tables.
2. These tables contain the metadata (data about data) concerning the database.

✓ *Data Manager*

1. Central software component of the DBMS.
2. It converts operations in the user's queries coming directly via query processor or indirectly via an application program from the user's logical view to a physical file system.
3. It is responsible for interaction with the file system and also concerned with the backup and recovery operations.

✓ *File Manager*

1. It is responsible for the structure of the files and managing the file spaces.

✓ *Disk Manager*

1. It is a part of Operating system of the host computer and all physical input and output operations are performed by it.

✓ *Query Processor*

1. It is used to interpret the online user's query and convert it into a form that can be sent to the data manager.
2. It uses the data dictionary in order to prepare an optimal plan to access the database.

✓ *Data Files*

1. It contains the data portion of the end user.

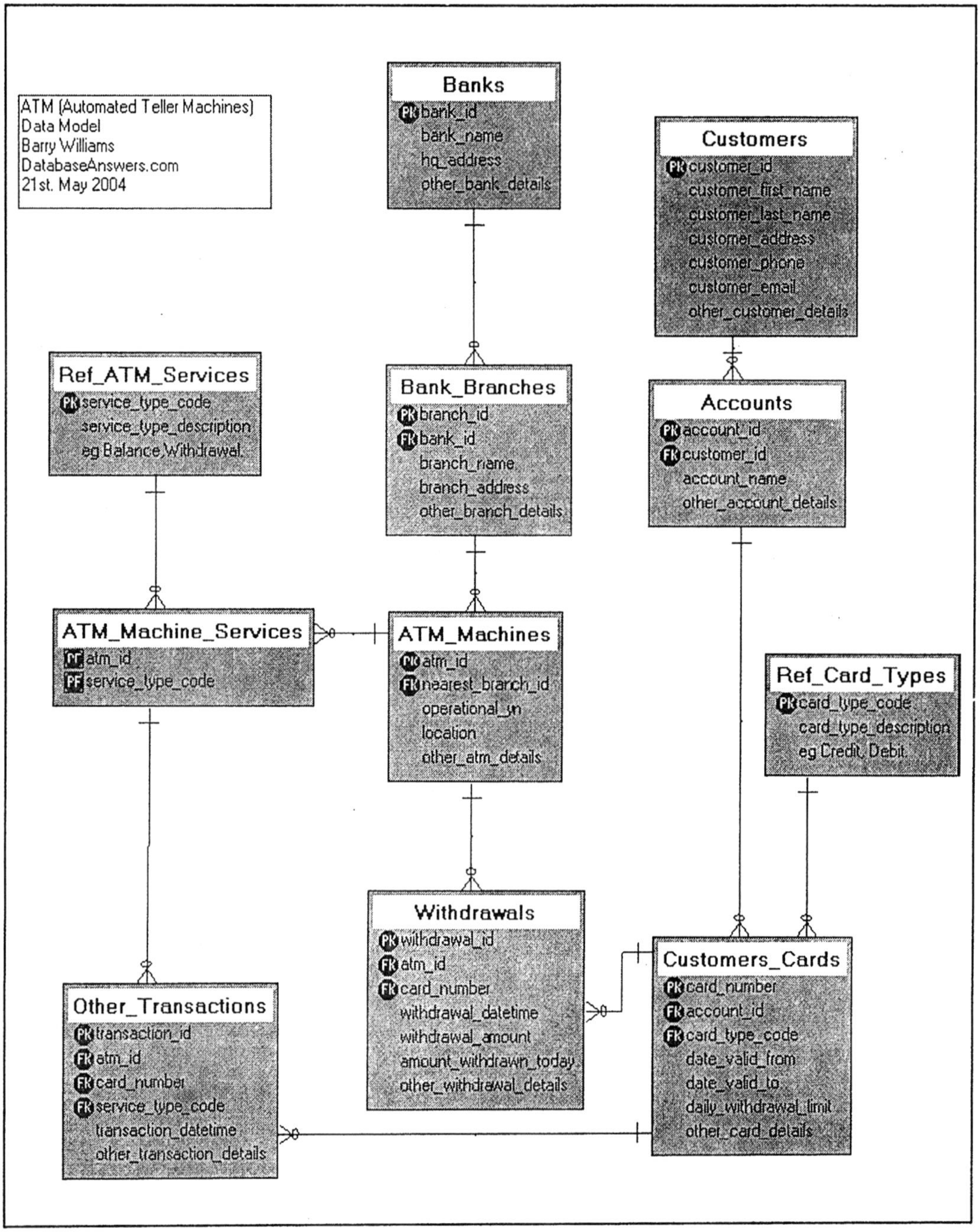

✓ *Data Dictionary*

1. The data dictionary does not store data but information about data i.e. metadata (data about data)
2. In other words, it stores the description of the structure of the data within the database, the description of data relationships and the integrity constraints on data

5. Different Forms of DBMS

DBMS (e.g. Dbase, FoxPro)

↓

RDBMS (e.g. Ms-Access)

↓

ORDBMS (e.g. Oracle —most advanced)

newtopic Terminologies used in context of Database Management Concepts

1. **Database:** A collection of related information stored in a structured format. The term "***Database***" can be used interchangeably with the term "***Table***" Technically, both the terms are different- a ***table*** is a single store of related information, whereas a ***database*** can consist of one or more tables of information that are related in some way.
2. **Data entry:** The process of entering information into a database. It is usually done by people through data-entry forms.
3. **Column: -** A column in a database table that represents an entity's attributes. It is often called a ***field** or **attribute.*** Thus, an attribute is a piece of information describing a particular entity.
4. **Field Size:** The maximum possible data or information stored in a particular field is referred to as Field size **e.g.** In ***guest*** database, a field "***guest_name***" can store maximum 20 characters, therefore, the size of the field is 20.
5. **Data Type:** The type of data stored in a field is called data type. **For example:** in guest database, a field "***guest_name***" accepts <u>*Character*</u> type data whereas the field "***bill_amt***" would accept <u>*Numeric*</u> type data and so on.
6. **Entity :-** A person, place, thing or an event about which information has to be kept is called an entity.
7. **Row: -** A row is a single set of entity attributes or column values in a database table.
8. **Record: -** It is the same as a row. In students table, each student's details (name, date of birth, contact details, and so on) will be contained in its own record.
9. **Relation: -** A collection of related information. A table is also called a relation. Every value in the relation i.e. each attribute/column in each tuple/row must be "***ATOMIC***", it means they cannot be decomposed further. (i.e. each column in a row contains only one value) **e.g.** In a student's database, the "name" column must be further subdivided into "***first name***" and "***last name***", in order to follow the rule of atomicity.
10. **Relationship:-**A relationship is defined as the association between two entities. In a relationship, one entity is defined as the parent and other entity is identified as the child.

11. **Cardinality:** - The number of tuples or rows in a table is called cardinality.
12. **Data Integrity: -** It refers to the maintenance of the same data throughout the database for maintaining data consistency.
13. **Flat file:** A database that consists of a single table is referred to as Flat file. E.g. Microsoft Works (also called ***Flat file Managers***). On the contrary, the database that consists of multiple tables is called relational databases (RDBMS).

    Example: Access, Oracle etc (also called ***Relational Database Managers***).
14. **Data Independence: -** It is a property of changing the physical structure of data without changing it's logical structure. **e.g.** column definitions in a table are independent of one another. We can modify a column's definition in a table without affecting any of the other columns (i.e. increasing width of a column). It is of two types-
    a. **Physical Independence:** It refers to immunity of conceptual schema to changes in the internal schema i.e. if an internal schema changes (**e.g.** using different storage structures or file organizations), then conceptual or external schema remains unaffected.
    b. **Logical Independence:** It refers to immunity of external schema to changes in the conceptual schema i.e. if conceptual schema changes (**e.g.** addition or removal of entities), then external schema remains unaffected.
15. **Domain :-** It means the range specified for an attribute. Every attribute/ column has one domain.
16. **Degree of Relation :-** The number of attributes in a table is known as degree of relation.
17. **Key: -** A key is an attribute having unique values, using which the tuples of a relation can be identified. **e.g. "Guest_id"** must be field of "**Guest"** table.
18. **Client-Server Databases:** It is a special type of database that provides an interface, that lets the clients submit certain data requests to the server's database. Then, the server's database will handle and process the requests and respond to each client explicitly.
19. **Object-oriented Databases:** Object-oriented database models let databases store and manipulate not only text, but also sounds, images, and all sorts of media clips etc. They are quite expensive due to their large size. Thus, they are only found in large commercial or government organizations.
20. **Data Modeling:** It is the process of structuring and organizing data using a database management system. It is a common term used for ***Data Analysis***.
21. **Abstraction :-**
    a. It literally refers to data hiding.
    b. It means that the user does not need to know the details of how data is physically stored and maintained in the system.

c. The major purpose of a good RDBMS will be to provide users an abstract view of the data.

22. Levels of Abstraction:-

a. ***View or External Level*** (i.e the actual output) : Highest level

b. ***Conceptual Level*** (Based on user's requirement) : deals with what type of data is stored in the database

c. Physical Level (Storage Level) : It deals with how the data is stored physically i.e. deals with how data structure is organized or managed.

23. Database State: The actual data values stored in the database is referred to as database state.

24. Database Language: The language that is used to interact with the database for performing various operations like inserting data, delete, update etc, is known as database language **e.g.** SQL, my-SQL etc.

25. Data Center: A Data Center is a physical place that is used to store computer network's most critical systems (like Mainframes, servers etc), including backup power supplies, air conditioning, and security applications. E.g. Bank's data center, University data center. Data centers are generally used to store & protect the data or information of an organization.

26. Database Logging: It simply refers to Data acquisition or procurement of data for later use. For Data Logging, you can use stand-alone Data Logger or PC-based Data Logger. Stand-alone data loggers are more efficient than PC-based logger because, they have more sensors; they are able to process the data at a much faster rate and so on. However, data from stand-alone data loggers can also be transferred to Personal computer (PC).

Example:

(1) a weather system logger used by meteorologists to detect temperature and pressure in order to determine upcoming weather conditions.

(2) a data logging device in a Supermarket store can assess which items you have bought using credit card , how many times a month you buy them and even, how many times you visit the store etc.

27. Database Mining: It refers to manipulation of large amount of data to filter or extract or find valuable information out of the database. It is also known as ***Knowledge-Discovery in Database***. The persons involved in database mining are known as ***Data miners***. It is generally used for predicting the trends and future.

28. Data Warehousing: Data warehousing is combining data from multiple and sources into one comprehensive and easily manipulated database. Common accessing systems of data warehousing include queries, analysis and reporting. It is commonly used by organizations, to analyze trends over time. This is so because data stored in data warehouses is updated frequently & regularly. Data warehouses are generally used for decision making and not for transaction processing.

29. **Data Scrubbing / Data Cleansing:** It refers to the process of detecting and correcting errors in data. A database may contain errors (or ***dirty data***) due to improper data entry, duplicate entry, merging of two databases or incorrect formatting of data. For this purpose, special software is used by the organizations. However, Data Scrubbing is sometimes missed as a part of Data warehousing.

30. **Data Migration:** Data migration is actually the translation of data from one format to another format or from one storage device to another storage device. **E.g.** For taking backups, the users transfer their data to CDs or DVDs and so on. Data migration typically has four phases: analysis of source data, extraction and transformation of data, validation and repair of data, and use of data in the new program. For achieving this, particular Data migration software is required **e.g** ***Nero Express*** or ***Nero Start Smart*** etc.

31. **Database Dictionary:** It is a set of metadata (data about data) i.e. it stores definitions & representations (how data is represented like integer, date, string etc) of various data elements. It also contains integrity constraints, space allocation information etc. It is basically read-only.

32. **Database Schema:** A schema is a collection of components and database objects under the control of a given database user. **e.g.** In FoxPro, schema refers to Database files & Fields ; In Oracle, schema refers to Tablespaces, Database, Table & Column etc.

33. **Schema Levels**

    a. Internal Level (Schema)

    - It describes the physical storage structure and paths to access data
    - It utilizes a physical data model

    b. Conceptual Level (Schema)

    - It describes the logical structure and access paths of the whole database
    - It utilizes Conceptual data model

    c. External Level (schema)

    - An external view or interface is used to interact with users
    - It utilizes a logical data model

newtopic What's a data model?

1. Data models are only a theoretical idea i.e. these are abstract concepts that you cannot touch.
2. Data model basically represents a methodology for storing and retrieving data from the database.
3. Data models are used to describe data, relationship between data and constraints on data.

4. Practically speaking, a data model may represent group of entities about which a company wishes to hold information, the attributes/properties of that information, and relationships among those entities.
5. **For example,** a data model might include an entity called "People", representing all the people (*In case of Hospitality, the entity People may represent Guest, Employee, Vendors etc*) who interact with an organization

1. Data Models Can Be Build For-

1. People, organizations and Relationships
2. Shipments and Deliveries
3. Work Order and Work Effort Management
4. Time Billing
5. Invoicing
6. Accounting
7. Budgeting
8. Contact and Geographical Information
9. Human Resources Management

2. Tools for Creating a Data Model for an Application

1. Entity Relationship Diagrams
2. Data Flow Diagrams
3. Classification of Data Models -

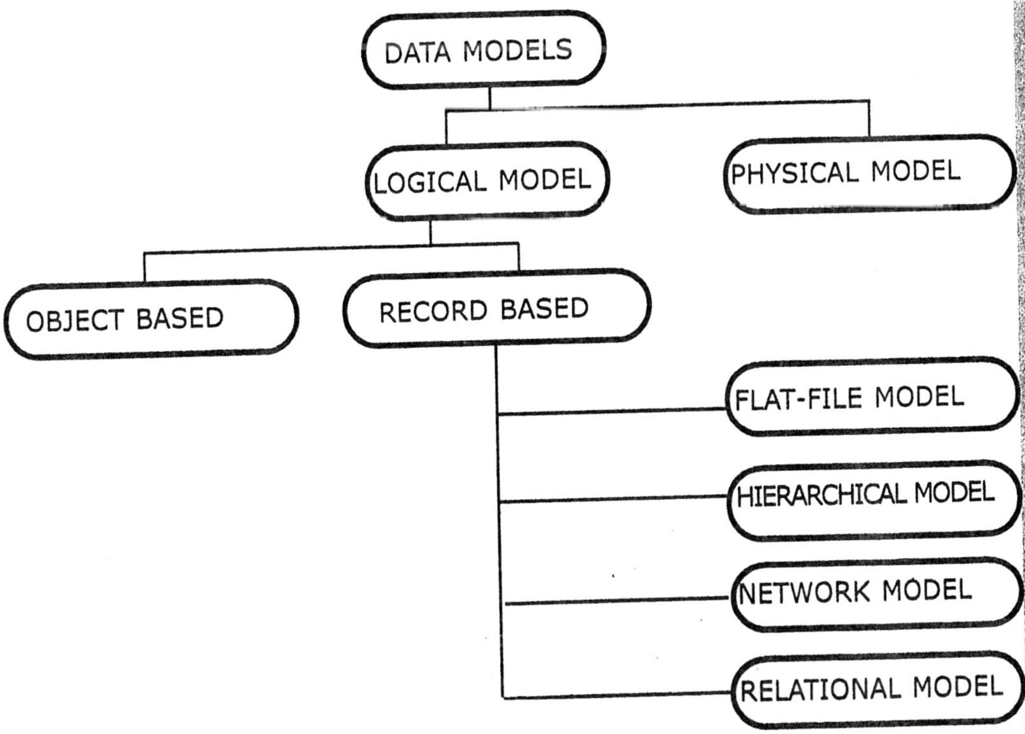

Logical Model

1. A logical model is a representation of both the data elements used and the relationships between them.
2. A logical model is an idealization of a real system.
3. A logical data model is dynamic rather than static.
4. It is necessary to develop a logical data model rather than directly making database design; because to develop a logical data model, we are forced to focus on data and its internal relationships without initially worrying about implementation details such as column's datatype, range and constraints etc.

• *Object Based Logical Model*

1. They are used in describing data at the conceptual and view levels.
2. Some of the examples are :-
   a. **ER Model :-** It consists of collection of entities and relationships among these objects.
      i. Entities are people, places, objects or concepts. Each entity is described by a set of attributes.
      ii. Relationship refers to the association among the entities.
      iii. e.g. Table is an object, whereas the columns are the entities; Database is an object, whereas the tables are the entities.
3. **Drawback:** The limitation of this model is that it cannot express the relationships among relationships.

• *Record Based Logical Model:-*

1. <u>Flat-file Database Model:</u>

a. The flat-file data model is generally used by the old paper-based databases.
b. In this model, data was stored in numerous files.
c. However, the files were not linked; therefore, data might be repeated in more than one file.
d. Drawback : Database redundancy (repetition of data)

2. <u>Hierarchical Database Model:</u>

1. The hierarchical data model organizes data in a tree structure.
2. The hierarchical database is used to overcome problem of repetitiveness of the flat-file database model. Although, it is not completely successful.

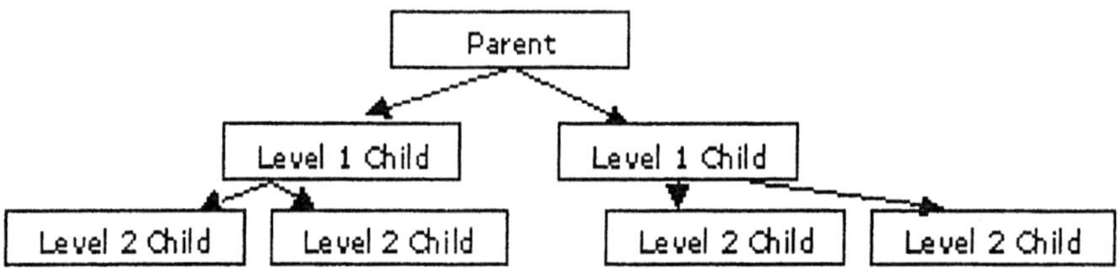

3. A hierarchical database consists of a series of databases that are grouped together to resemble a family tree.
4. There is a hierarchy of parent and child data segments.
5. In the above figure, each of the boxes represents one database. The top database in the hierarchical model is called the "parent" database. The databases under it are called "child" databases. One "parent" can have many "children," but a "child" can only have one "parent." The child databases are all connected to the parent database via links called "pointers."
6. The hierarchical model uses Parent Child Relationships, to create links between record types. (or component databases)
7. It has 1:1 (one-to-one) or 1: N (one-to-many) relationship between record types. For example, an organization might store information about an employee, such as name, employee number, department, salary. The organization might also store information about an employee's children, such as name and date of birth. In this example, the employee and children data forms a hierarchy; where the employee data represents the parent segment and the children data represents the child segment.
8. **Example:** "My Computer" in Windows. First you open the file "My Computer". Then you select one of the drives then subsequently you can select the folders or file displayed under each drive and so on.
9. ***Drawbacks of Hierarchical Model -***
   i. In the above figure, you might have seen that the child databases on the same level are not connected. This actually represents a problem in the hierarchical database model that makes searching for data extremely difficult.
   ii. Another problem is that data cannot be entered into the child databases until that field has been added to the parent database. This method was quite inefficient.
   iii. Operation like Insert, delete and update become cumbersome due to absence of many-to many correspondence between records.

Thus, although the hierarchical database model reduced some repetitiveness of data, it also presented many new problems.

3. Network Database Model:

1. The network database model was designed to help resolve some of the hierarchical database model's problems.
2. This model uses ***pointers or links*** to relate records, therefore, also called physical model.
3. Advantages of Network Model -
   a. This model is similar to hierarchical model except that it has many-to-many correspondence or relation between records.
   b. It reduces redundancy of data
   c. It facilitates easier searching of data.

   d. Another improvement of the network database model over the hierarchical model is that while in the hierarchical model a child database can only have one parent, in the network model, a child database can have more than one parent.
4. **Drawbacks:** Network database model had its share of problems. For one thing, it was difficult to execute and maintain. Only database experts could successfully use these databases. It was difficult for the general public to use network databases for real-life applications.
5. **Example:** The **CODASYL** network model.

4. Relational Model:-

1. The relational database model is different from the hierarchical and network database models in that there are no **"parent"** and **"child"** databases. Rather, all of the databases in the relational database model are equal.
2. It solved many of the problems displayed in the hierarchical and network database models.
3. It follows the ***relational database theory*** *(discussed later)* i.e. it uses the concept of **table** (a combination of rows and columns) to store data. A **database** is a collection of such tables.
4. Data can be stored in any number of separate tables. Then, these tables are connected by a **"key"** field.
5. Each table is used to store different types of data. **Example:** In a hotel, employee's details are stored in a separate database and guest details are stored in different database and so on.
6. All the tables and all the columns containing in each table must have a unique name.
7. This model uses ***values*** in the records for relating the records, therefore also called logical model.
8. **Advantages :**
   a. Reduced Redundancy
   b. Searching is faster
   c. Data can be retrieved from multiple tables by issuing a single query.
   d. Consistency of data is maintained.

Physical Model

The actual implementation of logical data model is called physical model. e.g. Network Model and Hierarchical Model.

newtopic Types of Relationships between Tables-

1. ***One-To-One Relationship:*** *In this example,* every employee is assigned one workstation, not all workstations are assigned to one employee.

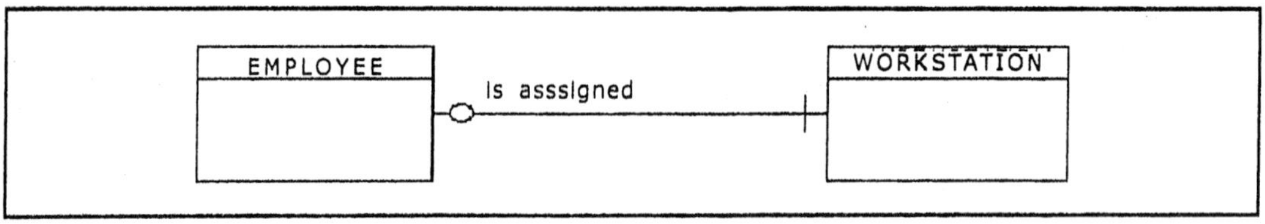

2. ***One-To-Many Relationship:*** In this example, a department may be responsible for many projects but each project is the responsibility of one department.

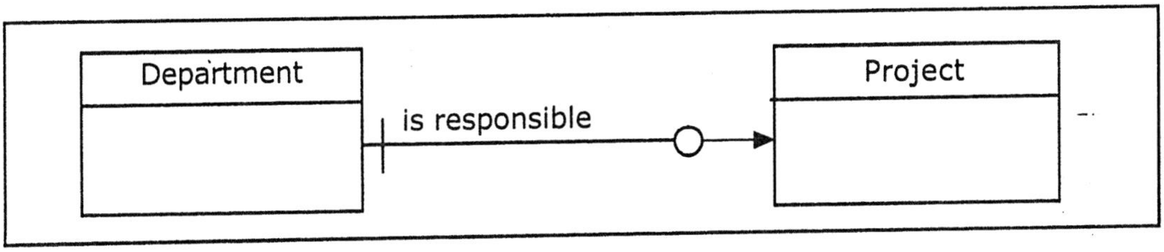

3. ***Many-To-Many Relationship:*** In this example, employees may be assigned many projects and every project has assigned to atleast one employee.

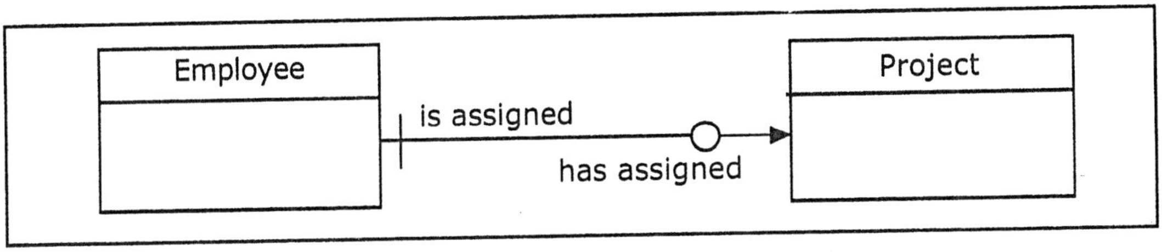

newtopic Relational Database Theory

1. A ***database*** consists of one or more tables.
2. Each ***table*** consists of rows and columns.
3. Rows are also called ***Tuples*** and columns are also called ***Attributes or Fields***. It should be noted that the ***record*** is the same thing as ***row***.
4. All the fields or attributes of a table must be unique.
5. Each row of a table is uniquely identified by a ***Primary Key***, which is composed of one or more columns. This implies that a table may not contain duplicate rows.
6. A column or group of columns that uniquely identifies a row in a table is called a ***Candidate key***. There may be more than one candidate key for a particular table. One of these will be chosen as the primary key.
7. The ***Entity Integrity Rule*** of the model states that no component of the primary key may contain a **NULL** value.
8. A column or combination of columns that matches the primary key of another table is called a ***Foreign Key***.
9. According to the ***Referential Integrity Rule***, for every foreign key value in a table there must be a corresponding primary key value in another table in the database.

RDBMS

1. It stands for Relational Database Management System.
2. It was proposed by **E.F Codd** in 1970. He is a member of the IBM Research Laboratory in San Jose, California.
3. This is based on the concept of ***Relational Model*** (described above). In RDBMS, a database may consist of multiple tables, which can be related to each other through a common field i.e. ***Key*** field.
4. The relational model consists of three components:
   - a. ***A Structural component*** — a set of ***Tables*** (also called *Relations*).
   - b. ***Manipulative component*** — consisting of a set of high-level operations or statements (or commands) which act upon tables.
   - c. ***A Set of Rules*** — for maintaining the integrity of the database.
5. The terminology associated with relational database theory originates from the branch of mathematics called ***set theory***.
6. The relational DBMS method retrieves information from the database by matching data values in common fields across several tables.
7. The tables within a relational DBMS contain information about a single type of business entity. **For example,** information about employees will be placed in a "***employee***" table, information about guests in a "***guest***" table, information about sales orders in a "***sales_order***" table, etc.

1. Advantages of the Relational Model:

1. It offers an abstract view of data **i.e.** it manages software complexity (hide the details of different processes from the users). It basically abstracts the physical structure of data storage, from the logical structure of data.
2. Ad-hoc queries can be made to retrieve desired data from the database.

2. Drawbacks:

- It's never been fully& faithfully implemented.

3. Examples of RDBMS

1. MS Access
2. MySQL
3. Oracle, Sybase, MS SQL Server

4. E.F CODD'S RULES

1. There are **12 (twelve)** rules devised by ***Dr. E.F Codd*** in 1985, that need to be satisfied for a DBMS to be called truly relational.
2. So far, there is no RDBMS in the industry, which satisfies all these twelve rules.
3. An RDBMS only gives full benefits, if it satisfies all these twelve rules

4. Oracle satisfies 10.5 (it is 10.5 because one rule (View Updating Rule) is partially followed) rules
5. FoxPro satisfies 6 rules.
6. The rules are as follows-

RULE 1: INFORMATION RULE :- *According to this rule-*

- All the tables have different information.
- All the tables and their attributes should have unique names.

RULE 2 : RULE OF GUARANTEED ACCESS- *According to this rule-*

- Data should be retrievable using certain logical addresses such as table name, primary key value and column name i.e. there should be one value or null at the intersection of a row and column.

RULE 3 : SYSTEMATIC TREATMENT OF NULL VALUES :- *According to this rule-*

- Null is treated in the same way through out the DBMS and is independent of the datatype of the field i.e. A null value in a character field must mean the same as null in an integer field.

RULE 4 : DATABASE DESCRIPTION RULE :- *According to this rule-*

- There must be a data dictionary within the RDBMS, in which the entire description of the objects can be stored so that it can be retrieved back even after dropping the objects.

RULE 5 :COMPREHENSIVE SUB-LANGUAGE RULE :- *According to this rule-*

- There must be a certain language having some predefined syntax for performing the following tasks-
  - Data definition
  - view definition
  - data manipulation
  - Integrity constraints
  - Authorization
  - Transaction boundaries

RULE 6: THE VIEW UPDATING RULE (not fully followed by Oracle) *According to this rule-*

- For any updation in the table, there must be a corresponding updation in a view related to the table in which the updations have been performed.
- But, in practice, there exists some cases in which views do not get updated with the updation of the corresponding table.

RULE 7: THE INSERT AND UPDATE RULE :- *According to this rule-*

- The major DML commands like SELECT, INSERT, UPDATE and DELETE must be available and operational on sets of rows in a table.

RULE 8: THE PHYSICAL INDEPENDENCE RULE :- *According to this rule-*

- An RDBMS consists of two layers which are independent of each other-
  - **Logical layer**
    - o It refers to the data which a user wants to retrieve.
    - o End users and application tools interact at logical layer

- **Physical layer**
  - o It refers to the implementation of logical layer.
  - o Data administrator interacts with both the physical and logical layer.
  - o Programmers interact only with physical layer.

RULE 9 : THE LOGICAL DATA INDEPENDENCE RULE :- *According to this rule-*

- ◆ The retrieval of data is independent of how the data is logically stored in the database i.e. data is consistently retrieved, if it is stored in two different tables (splitted from the base table) or even when it is stored in a table that is formed by the combination of two splitted tables.

RULE 10 : INTEGRITY INDEPENDENCE RULE :-

- ◆ According to this rule, a relational database should follow the given rules-
  - ***Entity Integrity :-*** No component of a primary key can have missing or null values.
  - ***Referential Integrity :-*** For each distinct foreign key value, there must exist a matching primary key value in the same domain.

RULE 11 : DISTRIBUTION RULE :-

- ◆ A RDBMS must have distribution independence i.e. it must have the capability to recombine the tables using SQL-JOIN, MINUS, INTERSECT, RESTRICT etc, even when the tables are decomposed in fragments.

RULE 12 : NO SUBVERSION RULE :-

- ◆ It literally means that there should be no divertion in the output i.e. it should be same.
- ◆ More precisely, If a RDBMS has a low level language, this language cannot be used to subvert or bypass the integrity rules and constraints expressed in the higher level relational language.

RULE ZERO :

- ◆ According to this rule, a RDBMS should be truly relational, i.e. it should be in the relational form (i.e. in the form of tables)

newtopic Database Design

1. An effective data model (or database design) completely and accurately represents the data requirements of the end users.
2. For designing a database, a basic model representing entities (tables) and relationships, is developed first. Then detail is added to the model by including information about attributes (or columns).
3. Thus, it is a bottom-up process.
4. Database design process or Data modeling must be preceded by planning and analysis. Planning defines the goals or objectives of the database. Analysis determines the requirements of the database.

5. The database design can be used by the database designer to actually build the database. This design is flexible (adaptive to change easily) as it is independent of any hardware and software.
6. The entire database design process can be viewed as a series of steps-
   a. Identification of data objects and relationships
   b. Constructing ER diagram with entities and relationships
   c. Refining the ER diagram
   d. Add key attributes to the diagram
   e. Adding non-key attributes
   f. Diagramming Generalization Hierarchies
   g. Validating the model through normalization
   h. Adding business and integrity rules to the Model
7. After constructing database by actually implementing the database design; test it with sample data, so that you can identify the problems caused by the design.
8. You can then, modify the design to rectify the errors or problems and so on.... This step of re-modifying database continues until the consistent and problem-free database design is developed.

newtopic Normalization

1. It is the study of relations(tables), attributes(columns) and the dependency of attributes upon one another.
2. Normalisation includes the achievement of following goals-
   a. Minimising redundant data.
   b. Avoiding update anomalies.
   c. Reducing inconsistent data.
   d. Designing data structures for easier maintenance.
3. Normalisation theory describes the desired arrangements of table and columns as Normal forms.

There are following kind of normal forms-

1. First Normal Form
2. Second Normal Form
3. Third Normal Form
4. Boyce Codd Normal Form (BCNF)
5. Fourth Normal Form
6. Fifth Normal Form (PJ/NF)

FIRST NORMAL FORM :-

- An entity is said to be in first normal form, if all of it's attributes are atomic i.e. each attribute consists of a single fact about the entity.

Name	Roll No.

Non-Atomic

First Name	Last Name	Roll No.

Atomic

SECOND NORMAL FORM-

- An entity is said to be in second normal form, if all of it's columns must depend on the primary key only. (i.e. full functional dependence)
- This rule implies that a table must not contain extraneous information.

Class ID	Course	Instructor_ID

✓

Class_ID	Course	Instructor_ID	Ins_Position

✗

THIRD NORMAL FORM-

- An entity is said to be in third normal form, if a table's columns must be entirely dependent on the primary key i.e. each column in the table must be dependent on the entire primary key, not just a portion of it.
- In other words, an entity is said to be in third normal form, if it is in 2NF and no attribute of the table should be transitively (i.e. indirectly) functionally dependent on the primary key.
- If B is dependent on A and C is dependant on B, then C is said to be transitively dependent on A. Transitive dependency causes problems in updation.

A	B	C

Primary key

newtopic Data Entry Forms or Screens

Data entry forms (front-end) act as an interface between the database and the user. Whatever data is entered and saved in each form would be added as an individual record in the database (at the back-end)

If you're designing a database, it would be of worth designing well-thought-out data entry screens. After all, why should you make life harder for yourself when a little effort in the design phase will make using your database easier for all time?

newtopic A sample design process

Let's try to build a design for "***Guest***" database-

Step 1: Create a Guest table containing all the fields: guest's name, age, Gender, Company, Contact number, Contact address date, reservation date, arrival date, departure date etc..

Step 2: Test the Guest table with some sample data. When you create sample data, you should see which type of data must be stored in which field. However, you can enter same name for two different guests. Ask some questions regarding to retrieving of data like "*you want to extract those guest whose arrival date is same"*. Try to find the solution to this problem.

Step 3: Analyse the data: In this step, you need to analyze the data whether it has been entered correctly i.e. a field having character datatype should contain characters or text and so on. Besides this, try to find a way to identify each guest uniquely.

Step 4: Modify the design: You can identify each guest uniquely by giving each one a unique ID, a new field that we add, called **ID**. Thus, ID field is a *key field* for "***Guest***" table. Therefore, it contains a unique value in each record. We can use that field to retrieve any specific record. This will also help you in preventing duplicacy.

Step 5: Elliminate Recurring Fields: Suppose, you have one field named as "*payment_ amount"* and other field named as "*total_amount*" in the "**Guest**" table. Here, in this example both fields are used to hold same information, therefore, delete one of the unwanted field from the "***Guest"*** table.

Step 6 : Elliminate Data entry anomalies: Sometimes, there are potential problems when we add or delete records in a database-

- ***Example of Deletion anomalies***: If a guest cancels his/her reservation then, all the information about him disappears from our system. So, if a guest again wishes to withdraw the cancellation of his/her reservation, then the entire entries have to be made again. Therefore, a new field "***res_status***" must be introduced or added to the ***"reservation"*** table (re-modifying database design)

Step 7: Normalise table data: According to first normal form, all the fields should be "***atomic***" **i.e.** the fields cannot be decomposed further. But, if take the above mentioned example of ***"guest"*** table- it contains a field named "***guest_name***" that can be further decomposed into "***first_name***" and "***last_name***". Therefore, for making the database design simpler, remove the field "***guest_name***" and introduce two new fields named as "***first_name***" and "***last_name***" respectively. Likewise, analyze your database to see that at least it should follow first three normal forms. (1NF, 2NF, 3NF)

Step 8: Analyse the results. Finally, again analyze your data, if you find the following results, then it means you have build a successful database design-

- **No redundant information:** You need to enter each guest record only once.
- **No inconsistent data:** There's only one place (i.e. one table) where you can enter guest information to prevent inconsistent data. Also, if there's any change in guest information like departure date etc then, you need to do is update the departure date in one place.
- **No addition or insert anomalies:** If a guest makes a reservation in a hotel and then cancels it on the same date. Then, on next day, he wishes to withdraw his cancellation, then in this case the same record is entered two times in the database that would violate the *rule of no duplicacy*. Therefore, this design is faultier. To correct it, you have to add a new field ***"res_status"*** and you just need to update this field on cancellation/ withdrawal of cancellation of reservation.
- **No deletion anomalies:** If a guest check out from the hotel or cancels his/her reservation, you still retain the details about that guest.

Example 1: Tables used in Reservation Database Design

Fields of "Reservation" Table	***Fields of "Guest" table***
Res_id (PK)	Guest_id (PK)
Arrival_Date	Res_id (FK)
Departure_Date	First_name
Depart_time	Last_name
Arr_Flightno	Designation
Dep_Filghtno	Company_Name
Nightno	Compnay_Add
Roomno	Ctel_no
Roomtype	Mob_no
Rate	Resi_Add
Paymode	Rtel_no
Res_Status	Guest_type

Example 2: ATM Database Design (Courtesy: Databaseanswers.com)

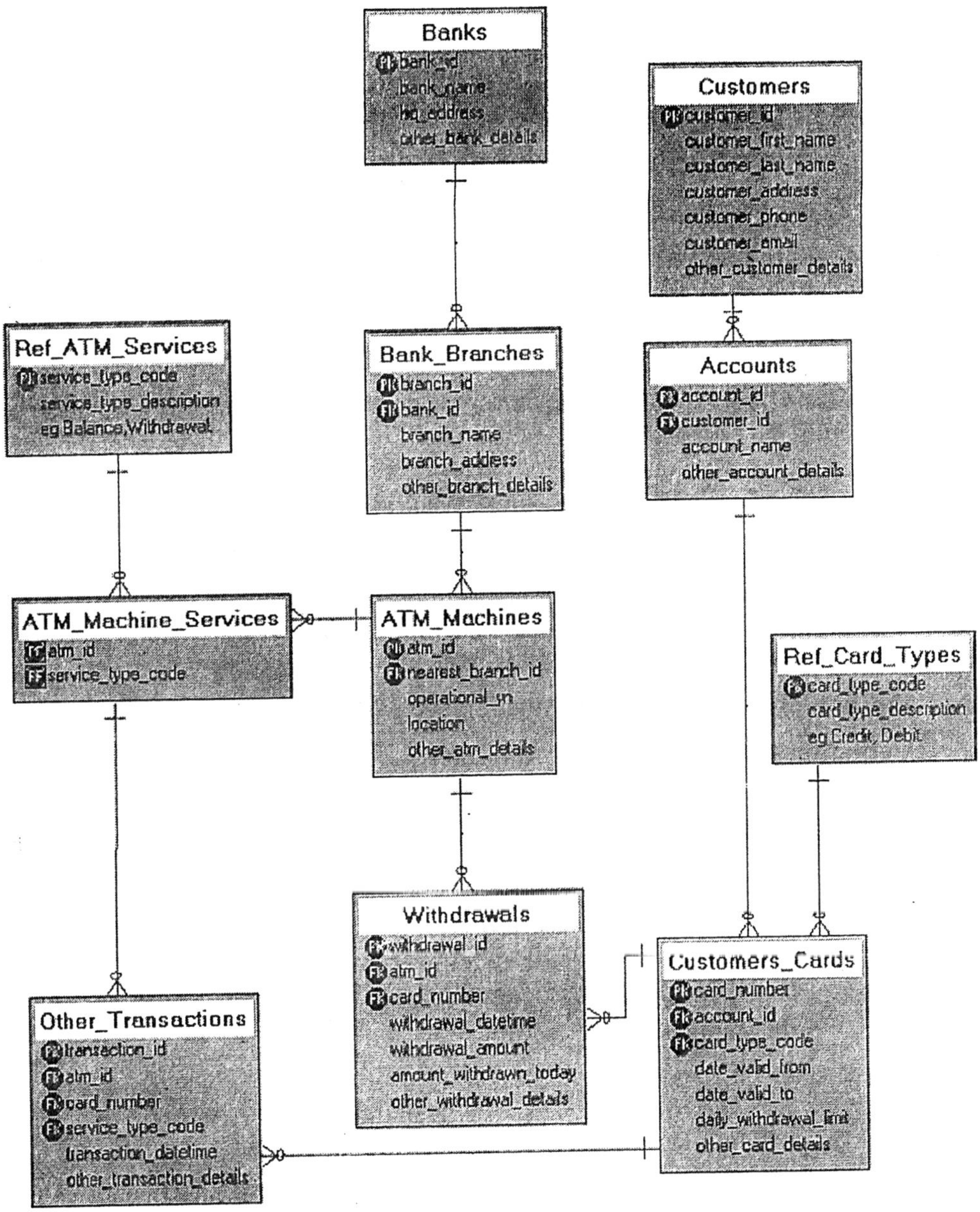

Simple guidelines to effective data entry screen design

The design of your data entry screens will depend on the following factors-

- Database program
- Amount of data in the database
- Requirements of the data entry personnel, or
- Application-specific requirements

If you're designing a database, it would be of worth designing well-thought-out data entry screens. By putting your efforts in the design phase, you can make your database easier for all time. You should consider the following guidelines for making a data-entry screen design-

1. Always build your screen from scratch don't use already existing screens (developed by some different personnel).
2. Logical organization of fields
3. Don't overload a screen with unnecessary fields to maintain visual clarity
4. Don't use scrollbars unnecessarily i.e. all the components (e.g. text box, list box, field name) of the screen should be simultaneously visible.
5. Make use of simple and readable fonts
6. Make use of good color contrast for the components of the screen.
7. Maintain uniformity upto a certain extent
8. After designing the screen, check the tab order (it should be from left to right & top to bottom)
9. Try to include help (wherever required) associated with the data entry in a particular component (text box or list box etc)
10. Validate your data as soon as it is entered on the screen. **For example:** the "***name***" field should not accept any numeric data; "***bill_amt***" field should not accept character data.

6

FoxPro

Introduction:

FoxPro 2.6 is a DBMS (Data Base Management System). It helps to enter and manage the data in database files. Once the database is ready, we can access selected data out of it. Multiple databases can be linked up together. The first DBMS was developed by Ashton Tate i.e. dBase II. Some of the advanced versions of dBase II were dBase III and dBase III PLUS. Latest version of FoxPro is Visual FoxPro. FoxPro is compatible with the following Operating System- DOS, Windows, UNIX & MAC.

FEATURES OF FOXPRO 2.6

1. Queries can be made on a single or multiple databases that are grouped together by some field.
2. Reports can be generated by grouping some fields with suitable headings from a single or multiple databases.
3. You can design customized screens with FoxPro Screen designer.
4. You can generate your own Application and Projects with FoxPro Application Generator.
5. You can import data from other databases, and can export FoxPro databases to others.
6. You can make use of View windows to see selected fields from a single or multiple database.

STARTING FOXPRO

1. Click on ***Start*** button.
2. Choose ***Programs > FoxPro*** for Windows.

Then FoxPro will start and command window will be displayed at the right hand corner with blinking cursor for the Command to Input. You can type the commands in command window. All the commands (that you enter) are stored sequentially for later use. You can select any command from command window to execute it. You can close the Command window and reopen it by choosing Window > Command or by pressing Ctrl + F2 shortcut key.

Terminologies used in FoxPro

- ***Database:*** A database is a collection of related data organized in a tabular form.
- ***File / Table:*** It is a two-dimensional structure. A Database file is a collection of fields and records in a tabular form. The extension of a database file is ***.dbf***
- ***Record:*** It refers to a row in a table. In other words a record is a set of column values or field values of a single entity.
- ***Fields:*** It refers to a column in a table. In other words a field is the smallest part of the record that can be accessed.
- ***Record Pointer:*** It is a pointer that is used to point a particular record. The record currently pointed by the record pointer is termed as current record.
- *BOF:* It is the position before the first record.
- *EOF:* It is the position after the last record.

DataTypes Used in FoxPro

A datatype refers to type of information/data a field can store. It can be of the following types-

DataTypes	***Purpose***	***Max. Width***
Character *Numeric*	Character or string For digits, decimal point, positive and neg. sign	256 20 digits wide upto 18 decimal places
Float (not commonly used because it is used in business applications)	Used for scientific calculations	20 digits wide
Date	Used for dates	8 (fixed)
Logical	When there are two possibilities of an information i.e. T or F, Y or N	1
Memo	Long textual matter	Max. 10000 characters
General	For Scanned bitmaps	10 bytes

Conventions Used for Naming Fields

The following conventions are used while naming fields in a database file-

- Must begin with an alphabet
- Alphabets, Numbers and Hyphens are allowed
- No blank space or special characters are used
- Maximum 10 characters long

FoxPro Commands for Working with Data

Sno.	Commands & Syntax	Purpose
1	CREATE	To create a database file (.dbf file)
2	CLOSE ALL	To close all opened files
3	CLOSE <Filename>	To close specified file
4	USE	To close recently opened files
5	USE ?	To open a particular file (it will display the Open box on the screen, so that you can select the file name and click Open)
6	CLEAR	It is used to clear the screen of FoxPro window (where the output of executed commands are displayed)
7	MODI STRU	To make modification in the structure (i.e. field name, datatypes etc) of the recently opened database file
8	LIST	To display records of the current database file irrespective of the record pointer position.
	LIST NEXT 2	It will display two records from the current record pointer position i.e. if record pointer is on second record, then it will display second and third record.
	LIST OFF	It will display all the records excluding their record number.
	LIST FOR <field name> = <value>e.g. LIST FOR cust_name = "Rajesh"	It displays all the records with the name "Rajesh"

Sno.	Commands & Syntax	Purpose
	LIST FOR cust_code = 6	It will display all records having cust_code equivalent to 6.
	LIST <fields> or LIST FIELDS <fields>e.g. LIST cust_name, cust_city	It will display all the records including fields cust_name and cust_city only
	LIST TO PRINT	It will sent the list of records to the printer
15	DISPLAY	It displays the current record (where the record pointer is currently placed) of the recently opened database file.
	DISPLAY NEXT 2	It will display 2 records from where the record pointer is currently placed
	DISPLAY OFF	It will display all the fields of the current record excluding record number.
	DISPLAY FOR cust_city = "Delhi"	It will display all the records where cust_city is equivalent to "Delhi"
	DISPLAY TO PRINT	It will sent the current record to the printer.
	DISPLAY <Fields>	It displays only specified fields.
	Display All	It will display all the records irrespective of the current record pointer.
16	GOTO or GO <Record_no>	It is used to place the record pointer at specified record.
	GOTO TOP	It is used to place the record pointer at the top most record (i.e. first record) in the database file
	GOTO BOTTOM	It is used to place the record pointer at the last record in the database file
17.	SKIP <record_no> **e.g.** SKIP -2	It is used to jump or move record pointer from the current position by the specified record number. The command SKIP -2 will move the record pointer back by 2 records from the current record pointer position.

Sno.	Commands & Syntax	Purpose
	SKIP 2	Likewise, the command SKIP 2 will move the record pointer forward by 2 records from the current position
18	EDIT	It is used to modify records of a database file
	EDIT RECORD <Record_no>	It will display the specified record for editing
	EDIT FOR cust_code = 7	It will display the records having cust_code equivalent to 7 for editing.
	EDIT FIELDS <fields>	It will display the current record with specified fields for editing.
19	BROWSE	It is used to modify records of currently opened database file. It displays multiple records together.
	BROWSE FIELDS <fields>	It will allow the editing of fields listed with **FIELDS** clause.
	BROWSE FOR cust_name = "abc"	It allows editing in the record having cust_name as "abc"
	BROWSE FIELDS cust_code, cust_name, cust_city FREEZE cust_name	It displays all the fields listed with **FIELDS** clause but allows editing only in the freeze field
20	APPEND	To add records in the currently opened .dbf file. Using this command, the record will be added at the end of the file i.e. after the last record.
21	QUIT	To exit out of the FoxPro window.
22	DELETE	It marks the current record for deletion.
23	DELET ALL	It marks all records of the database for deletion.
	DELETE NEXT 2	It marks two records for deletion from the current record pointer position.

Sno.	Commands & Syntax	Purpose
	DELETE FOR <condition> e.g. Delete for cust_city = "Delhi"	It will mark all those records for deletion where City is Delhi.
	RECALL	It unmarks the current record if it is marked for deletion.
24	RECALL ALL	Umarks all records of the database that are marked for deletion
	RECALL NEXT 2	Unmarks two records that are marked for deletion from the current record pointer position.
	RECALL RECORD FOR cust_city = "Delhi"	It will unmark all those records that are marked for deletion where CITY is DELHI.
	PACK	It physically removes or deletes those records from the database which are already marked for deletion. Packed records cannot be recalled.
25	ZAP	It will remove all records from the database irrespective of the fact whether they have been marked for deletion or not. So, you have to be very sure before you zap the database, else you might end up losting information, which cannot be retrieved.
26	REPLACE <field> WITH <New expression> FOR <condition>e.g. REPLACE cust_name WITH "Aastha" FOR cust_code = 24	It is used to replace the contents of a specified field with some new expression.

Difference between-

DISPLAY ALL	LIST
It displays all the records. However, it pauses after each screen of records is displayed.	It also displays all the records. But, the screen scrolls away the output so that only the last screen of records is displayed.
EDIT	**BROWSE**
In this all the fields of one record is displayed sequentially. Due to this, you can edit only one record at a time.	In Browse window, all the fields of entire records are displayed in a tabular form so that you can modify multiple records at a time.

GOTO	SKIP
GOTO command is used to move the record pointer to a desired record number.	It is used to move the record pointer forward or backward by the specified record number.

Sorting and Indexing

SORTING

- Sorting is the physical rearrangement of records in a database.
- Sorting can be done in both ascending order s well as in descending order.
- By default, sorting is done in ascending order.
- After performing sorting, a new sort file is created having extension .dbf.
- Sorting consumes more time to rearrange records.
- Sorting takes same space as the space occupied by the file being sorted but this space is four times more than the index file.
- Sorting has to be performed each time whenever any record is appended in the database because a record is always appended at the end of the file.
- Sorting can be done on one or more than one field but sorting on more than one field will be performed only if the database is large.
- Sorting can be done on any field i.e. character, numeric, float etc except general and memo.
- It should be noted that the database on which sorting has to be performed must be in use.
- Sorting can either be done-
  - o By using Sort command or
  - o By using Sort Dialog box.

Syntax : SORT ON <Field1> TO <Filename> /A /D /C, <Field2> /A /D /C <Scope> [FOR <exp>]

Where, /A : Ascending order.
/ D : Descending order.
/ C : Ignore the case of character field

Scope : NEXT <exp>
RECORDS <exp>
REST
ALL

FOR : FOR <Any criteria>

VIEWING THE SORTED FILE :-

USE <sorted file name>

List

DISADVANTAGES OF SORTING :-

- Requires diskspace as occupied by the original database.
- Slow process.
- Data in sorted file is not automatically updated on appending any record in the database, i.e. sorting has to be done again and again.

INDEXING

- Indexing means to arrange the records in ascending order.
- Records are not physically arranged in the database.
- A new file i.e. an index file is created which contains the memory address of the records.
- The extension of index file is .idx or .cdx
- The index file occupies one fourth space as compared to the index file.
- It consumes less time.
- When database file is updated, the index file will automatically get updated if it is in use otherwise it can be updated using REINDEX command.
- Different index files are created separately for performing indexing on different fields. But we can use only one index file at a time.
- In case of indexing no duplicate copy of database is created as in case of sorting.
- In case of Reindex (i.e. Recreate index) used for updating index file, no new file is created.

Syntax :-

INDEX ON <field> TO <index file name>

SYNTAX FOR USING INDEX FILES OR ACTIVATION OF INDEX FILE

USE <name of dbf file> INDEX <index file name1> <index file name2> **OR**

USE <name of dbf file>

SET INDEX TO <index file name>, <index file name2>

The first index file is called master or controlling index.

If we want to see the records according to the second index file then, we can use following command :-

SET ORDER TO <name of 2nd index file>

SET ORDER TO <2> (i.e no. of index file in the index file list)

POINTS TO REMEMBER:-

- For sorting more than one field, only a single sort file is created.
- For indexing more than one field, different index file is created.
- Using REINDEX command, no new file is created.

DIFFERENCE BETWEEN .IDX AND .CDX

.IDX	.CDX
It is a unique index file	It is a compact index file.
It takes four times more disk space as compared to .cdx file.	It takes only one fourth of the size of .idx file.
We have to open corresponding .idx file when a database is opened.	When we open the database, .cdx file will automatically get opened.
It performs indexing only in ascending order.	It performs indexing both in ascending as well as descending order.
We have to close index file also after closing the database.	It will get automatically closed after closing database.

newtopic Rushmore Technology

- Rushmore is a data access technique that permits sets of records to be accessed very efficiently.
- Rushmore is an exclusive technology for rapidly selecting sets of records from tables. It can reduce query response times from hours or minutes to seconds.
- FOR clause searches for the desired text sequentially, whereas WHILE works with indexed database file. Therefore, FOR clause works slower than WHILE loop in case of a large database, containing thousands of records. Therefore, in order to increase the performance of FOR clause, Rushmore technology is introduced.
- The Rushmore technology uses all types of index files automatically, if they are available and open, thus in order to enable the Rushmore technology, all the index files related to a file are kept open. (Exception : Structural compound index file automatically gets opened, with the opening of corresponding database file)
- The following commands can make use of Rushmore technology :-
    - o EDIT, BROWSE, CHANGE, LIST, SORT, INDEX, LOCATE, REPORT, DELETE, RECALL and COPY.
- Thus, using the Rushmore technology, it becomes much simple to search the desired information by using the FOR clause in the search criteria.

newtopic Relational Query By Example

- **RQBE** provides an easy way of selecting database files (or selecting particular fields from database files) and helps us to set relations.

- RQBE generates a SQL (Structured query language, used for making queries in case of relational database) SELECT command that FoxPro executes to give the results.
- For entering query, we must open the RQBE window. This window lets us open files, select all or desired fields, sort order, the output file etc.
- It should be noted that all the open databases must be closed using CLOSE DATABASES command before opening the RQBE window.
- Select File, New from the FoxPro menu system, then select the Query file type. Finally, select OK push button.
- By default name of the query is called "Untitled". We give a desired name to the query, during saving and closing it. The extension of the query is .QPR. This query file proves to be useful when you want to re-execute the same query.
- We can also start the RQBE window with a specific query file with CREATE QUERY <Filename> command.
- Thus, from the RQBE window, we can select the name of different database files, even particular fields from them, sort order etc to generate a particular query.
- When a table in a query (.QPR) file cannot be found, the Relational Query By Example (RQBE) tool loads the remaining (found) tables in the query, but doesn't generate the FROM clause unless the table set is modified
- You can also use the NOT check box to invert the relation.

newtopic Working with Multiple Database Files

- To open a database file, we have used USE command.
- In case, we have to open more than one database at a time, we have to open them in different work areas.
- Work areas are just the portion of RAM that FoxPro uses to open a database file.
- We can open at maximum 225 databases because FoxPro allows only 225 workareas.
- However, it should be noted that in one work area, only one file can be opened i.e. not more than one.
- SELECT command is used to select work area. With SELECT command you have to specify the work area reference (or name). ***e.g.*** any letter from A to Z can be used as a work area reference.
- In order to retrieve data from more than one file, a relation has to be set among the selected files using the following sequence of command :-

```
SELECT A
    USE CUST_M
    INDEX ON cust_code TO cust
```

```
SELECT B
    USE BILL_M
    INDEX ON cust_code TO bcust
SELECT A
    USE CUST_M INDEX cust
    SET RELATION TO cust_code INTO B
```

- This command sets the relation between both the databases. Before setting the relationship, we have to index both the tables on the common field and we can set the relationship on that common field.
- Once the relation is set, we can access the information from both the database files.

  e.g. ? cust_name, B->bill_date, B->bill_tot

Generating Reports and Labels

<u>*REPORTS*</u>

*Reports are used to display data in a presentable form. Before creating the report, the database must be opened. By default extension of a FoxPro report file is **.frx***

<u>Creating a report</u>:- One of the following methods can be used for creating report-

- **<u>By giving command</u>**- *CREATE REPORT* (report screen gets opened)
- **<u>By Menu options</u> :-**
  - o Select ***File > New >Report***, then the opening screen of Report is displayed. (Do not enter any data in it) or
  - o Select ***Report > Quick Report*** option.

<u>Generating a Report:</u>- Generating means to display the output of the created report on the screen. Before generating a report, the database file must be opened.

Use .dbf file

REPORT FORM <report file name> (if file name is not specified, then select dialog box will get opened)

<u>Previewing a Report</u>:- You can preview a report while designing it. The preview mode of the report form allows you to view the report page by page.

Select **Report > Page Preview** option

Or

Enter the following command in the command window-

REPORT FORM <filename> PREVIEW

<u>Printing a Report:-</u>

USE SALES

REPORT FORM SALES FOR PRODUCT = "TV" TO PRINT

Characteristics or Advantages of Quick Report :-

- The quick report allows you to generate the report in a faster way.
- Using this option, you can customize our report.
- Click on ***Expression*** button (It is in report expression dialog box)
- It invokes the expression builder.
- For formatting click on ***Format*** button (in Report expression dialog box)
- Save the created report.

MAILING ADDRESS LABELS:-

The process of designing of mailing labels is similar to that of designing report:-

- Open the database file that contains the name and address.
- Open the label design window.
- Select and position the fields and other text in the label.
- Select the margins and label layout etc
- Save the label in a label format file.

Creating Labels :-

CREATE LABEL <label file name> *(it will open the label design window)*

- If we do not specify the name with the CREATE LABEL command, then a file named UNTITLED.LBX is created
- Extension of label file can be .LBX or .LBT
- The label window displays the default size and their layout, if we want to change the layout then-
    - o Invoke the ***Label*** menu.
    - o Select the ***Label > Layout***, FoxPro displays the list of available label layouts.
    - o Select the desired label layout from the list.
- Then, enter the field expression and other text to be printed in labels. We can directly enter the fields of a database in any row of the label. If we want to use the fixed text, we can specify it within " "or use the expression builder by selecting ***Label > Expression...***

Displaying and Printing Labels :-

- Open the database file with the USE command.
- Use the LABEL FORM command with the name of label format file. Specify the necessary options if required.

  e.g. USE ADDRESS

  LABEL FORM ADDRESS (the labels get scrolled out on the screen)

To display labels in page mode :-

LABEL FORM ADDRESS PREVIEW

To Print labels :-

LABEL FORM ADDRESS TO PRINT

LABEL FORM ADDRESS TO PRINT NEXT 10

LABEL FORM ADDRESS TO PRINT FOR CITY = "New Delhi"

LABEL FORM ADDRESS FOR CITY = "New Delhi" TO FILE MYLABEL.TXT

To arrange labels in alphabetical order of names :-

USE ADDRESS ORDER NAME

LABEL FORM ADDRESS TO PRINTER

For Saving and Printing Labels **:-** Use Ctrl + w or use File menu's Save option.

7

Structured System Analysis & Design

Introduction:

Life on on earth can be thought of as a complex web of interconnected natural and human-made systems. Our own human bodies and brains are individual sub-systems within networks of larger biological, economic and socio-political systems without which we couldn't exist. We therefore can be said to spend our lives enmeshed in interdependent living and non living systems.

Systems are created to solve problems. One can think of the systems approach as an organized way of dealing with a problem. A system is an arrangement (pattern, design) of parts which interact with each other within the system's boundaries (form, structure, organization) to function as a whole.

Example: A farm is an integrated system of both living (the farmer, crops, animals, weeds, insects) and non-living (the tractor, barn, house, machinery, fertilizer) subsystems.

System:-

According to Leitner-

*"A set of **related components** that **work together** in a particular **environment** to perform whatever **functions** are required to achieve the system's **objectives.**"*

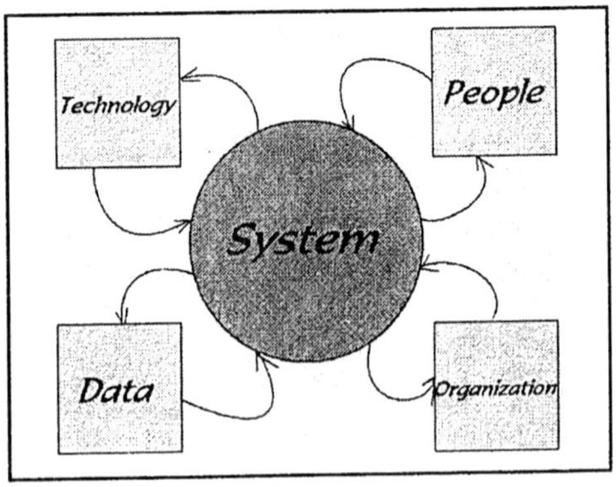

In other words, it can be defined as a group of interrelated components that have common ideas, principle or doctrines and the components work in a coordinating manner for achieving a common goal or objective. **e.g.** Transporting system, Banking System, Railway Reservation System, Computer System, Information System etc.

Basic Control Model of System :- *Systems use a basic control model consisting of –*

- A ***standard*** for acceptable performance.
- A method for ***measuring*** actual performance.
- A means for ***comparing*** actual performance against the standard.
- A method for ***feedback***.

System Design:-

It is a critical phase as a wrong design would result in considerable rework or waste of valuable resources. During this phase, the current physical model of the system is prepared. It is the process of planning a new system or to replace or to complement the existing system. In other words, it refers to the techniques on the basis of which a system will be implemented.

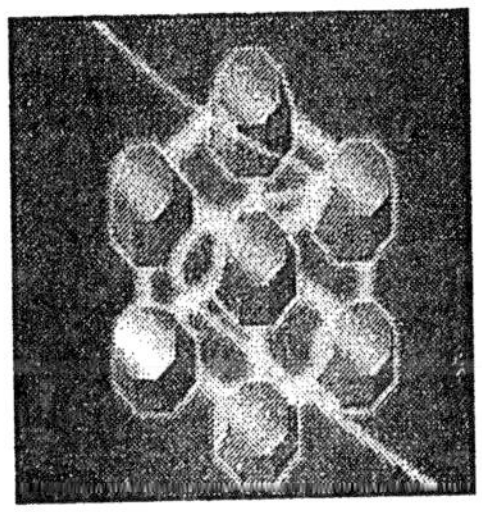

Once the analysis of what is required is done, the designing part begins. In this stage, the details of what the system will do are given. The system design also describes the logic for data to be input, calculated or stored. This model is discussed with the actual users to ensure that the model represents the reality. Based on the current physical model, the current logical model is worked out. According to the logical requirements, information technologist work out different alternative in terms of costs, efficiency, resource requirement and ease of maintenance etc. The design of a system is often expressed using software engineering tools such as DFDs (Data Flow Diagrams), ER diagrams, Data Dictionary etc.

System Analysis:-

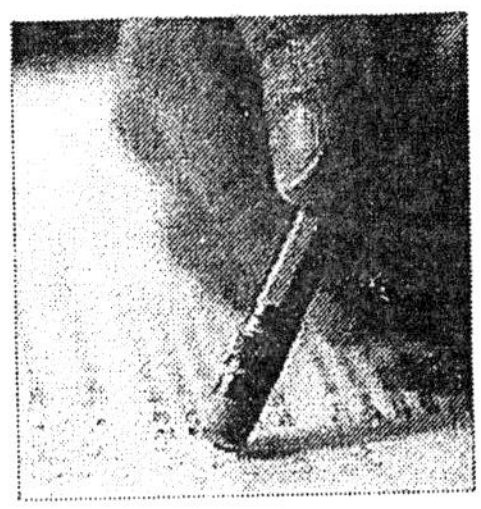

It is the process of gathering and interpreting facts, diagnosing problems and using the information to recommend improvements to the system. This job is performed by the system analyst.

In other words, it refers to the detailed study of various operations performed on a system with relation to it's external and internal environments. Thus, System analysis is done for the following reasons-

- problem solving
- Improving an organization
- Solving organizational problems

- Improve usefulness of information systems

  e.g. If we take an example of stockroom, then in that case to better control it's inventory and gain access to ore up-to-date information about stock levels and reordering, system analysis is done by the system analyst.

Thus, Analysis specifies 'what' the system should do. Design states 'how' to accomplish the objective.

In other words, Systems analysis is a process that combines the following activities-

- Identification and re-identification of objectives,
- Constraints,
- Alternative courses of action;
- Determination of probable consequences of the alternatives in terms of costs, benefits, and risks; presentation of the results in an effective way so that the decision maker can make an informed choice from among the alternatives.

Types of System Analysis

- ***Feasibility:*** That part or aspect of systems analysis that concentrates on finding out whether an intended course of action violates any constraints is referred to as ***"Feasibility"***
- ***Cost Effective Analysis:*** A systems analysis in which the alternatives are ranked in terms of effectiveness for fixed cost or in terms of cost for equal effectiveness is referred to as "***Cost Effectiveness"*** analysis.
- ***Cost Benefit Analysis:*** It is a study where the comparison and ranking of system present values are made in terms of net benefits (benefits minus cost) or the ratio of benefits to costs.

Examples of few other types are- *Decision Analysis, Risk Analysis & Policy Analysis etc.*

What System Analysis Is NOT-

✓ Studying a business to see which existing processes should be handled by computer and which should be done by non-computerized methods.

Reason : Analysis emphasize on understanding the details of a situation and deciding whether improvement is desired or feasible. The selection or non-selection of computer is secondary.

✓ Determining what changes should be made is not analysis.

Reason : The intent of system investigation is to study a business process & evaluate it. i.e. Change should be a result, not an intent.

✓ Determining how best to solve an information systems problem is not a part of analysis.

Reason : Regardless of the organization, the analyst works on business problems rather than system problems.

It's certainly possible, although uncommon, for a single individual to be skilled at both systems analysis and system design. It is then perfectly acceptable for him or her to do systems analysis some of the time and system design some of the time.

new topic System Analyst

System analyst is an individual who analyses the problem and then design the solution. System analyst is the central member of any system development project. The alternative name of System analyst is **Business Process Engineer**.

1. Role of System Analyst

The role of **Systems Analyst** evolved specifically to fill the gap between user clients and software designers. A systems analyst discovers the user organization's needs by interviewing key people, observing business processes (the old system), and examining relevant documents. They analyze business requirements in detail and prepare functional specification for new system. They also obtain rough estimates of the cost of operating and maintaining a proposed new system, considering use of appropriate technology, tools and methods. He or she then documents the requirements for a new system in a form that can be understood both by the responsible client organization participants and by the developers (or vendors). System analyst play a vital role in designing and developing user's manual and corresponding training programs for a system.

2. Qualification of System Analyst

- ✓ A System analyst should have a thorough knowledge of the functioning of the organization.
- ✓ He must have knowledge about recent developments in the computer system and software industry.
- ✓ He must be able to interpret what it that the organization expects from the system is.

3. Responsibilities of System Analyst

- ➢ **System Analysis Only :-**
  - ✓ The analyst's sole responsibility is conducting system studies to learn relevant facts about a business activity.
  - ✓ The emphasis is on gathering information and determining requirements.
  - ✓ Analysts are not responsible for system design.**(Information Analyst)**
- ➢ **System Analysis and Design :-**
  - ✓ Analyst carry out complete systems studies but have the added responsibility of designing the new system.
  - ✓ People who are responsible for both systems analysis and design, work on fewer projects than Information Analyst but spend more time on each one. **(System Designer)**

- **System Analysis, Design and Programming :-**
  - ✓ Analysts conduct the systems investigation, develop design specifications, and program software to implement the design. (Programmer Analyst)

newtopic Structured System Analysis & Design

At this point, you are familiar with the terms- System, Analysis and Design. Now, you might be thinking why it is called *Structured System Analysis and Design*? This is so because it deals with problems and determination of possible alternative solutions when implementing a structured approach to a system.

newtopic Need of System Analysis

System analysis is an explicit formal inquiry carried out to help decision maker to identify a better course of action and thus make a better decision. The typical use of systems analysis is to guide decisions on issues such as national or corporate plans, resource use and protection policies, research and development in technology, regional and urban development, educational systems, and other social services

According to ***Krippendorff***,

"Systems analysis provides a variety of analytical tools, design methods and evaluative techniques to aid in decision making regarding such systems."

Modern systems are too complex (it may be a computer system or a hotel system). Therefore, such systems make it harder than ever to find the correct requirements. System analysis has a proven track record for delivering the right requirements. System analysts filter out unimportant information and model only the significant aspects of system.

System analysis uses a comprehensive modeling approach to build a specification containing all the requirements. Models are not always an exact replica of the system. Some models are more useful if they show a "justified distortion" emphasizing significant aspects of the system. Thus, a model can filter out information which is irrelevant. Using working model, users and analyst work together, in order to reach, an identical understanding of the requirements. Thus, The task of system analyst is to study and specify it's requirement by building a working model of it. Once, the model is agreed the system is implemented by building a real-world version of the model.

newtopic System Analysis Of an Existing System

Assuming that a new system is to be developed, the next phase is system **analysis**. Analysis involved a detailed study of the current system, leading to specifications of a new system. Analysis is a detailed study of various operations performed by a system and their relationships within and outside the system.

A thorough analysis or study of the existing system is very important before embarking on a new system, in order to identify the current problems, possible root causes for the current problems, alternatives to overcome these problems. Findings are documented for analysis and discussion.

During analysis, data are collected on the available files, decision points and transactions handled by the present system. Interviews, on-site observation and questionnaire, Manuals are the tools used for system analysis in case of manual as well as automated systems. Using the following steps it becomes easy to draw the exact boundary of the new system under consideration:

- *Keeping in view the problems and new requirements*
- Workout the pros and cons including new areas of the system

All procedures, requirements must be analyzed and documented in the form of detailed data flow diagrams (DFDs), data dictionary, logical data structures and miniature specifications. System Analysis also includes sub-dividing of complex process involving the entire system, identification of data store and manual processes.

new topic System Analysis of a new Requirement

User requirements analysis should be planned from the beginning of a project.

User requirements analysis is not about asking users what system they want. User requirements analysis is about understanding users' current practices and the problems they encounter. They often don't know the possibilities and constraints of interactive systems. It's the job of an system analyst to vision a solution that answers real user needs.

People are not all that different. There are patterns in their practices and needs. User requirements analysis is about recognizing these patterns.

User requirements analysis can be scaled to the size of the project. It's better to do a 5-day analysis than no analysis at all.

Thus, the system analysis of a new requirement involves:-

- Specification of objectives of the new system according to the user requirements.
- Functional hierarchy showing the functions to be performed by the new system and their relationship with each other.
- List of attributes of the entities - these are the data items which need to be held about each entity (record) i.e. determining what data or information is required to be stored in the new system
- Defining the Hardware / Software Requirements
- Defining the Performance Specification
- Defining Safety Requirements
- Defining the User Interface
- Providing Installation Drawings/Instructions.

Differentiation of System Analysis Phase & System Design Phase

	Systems Analysis Phase	System Design Phase
Work performed by	Systems Analyst	Chief programmeror Lead software developer
Output	System Specification: everything about *what* the proposed system will do, nothing about *how* it is to be be built	System Architecture: platform choice, database design, program design, user interface design, etc.
users who read, under-stand, and accept the outputs	1. Sponsoring users 2. Chief programmer	Programmers and technical specialists

System Development Life Cycle

System development life cycle is an organizational process of developing and maintaining information systems.

It is a unified process, in which systems analyst, software engineers and programmers create new systems. It is also a management tool useful in planning, executing and controlling system development process.

SDLC involves various phases. At each phase certain activities are performed; the results of these activities are documented in a report identified with that phase. Management reviews the results of the phase and determines if the project is to proceed to the next phase.

Thus, it is a problem-solving process that will bring about a solution to the business situation.

1. Phases of SDLC

1. Preliminary Investigation or Analysis
2. Feasibility Study
3. Determination of System Requirements
4. System Design
5. System Development
6. System Testing
7. Implementation and Evaluation
8. Maintenance

1. PRELIMINARY INVESTIGATION or ANALYSIS: -

When the request for system analysis & development and is initiated from a manager, or employee or a system specialist; then the preliminary investigation begins.

The goal of preliminary investigation is simply to identify and select a project for development from among all the projects that are under consideration. Organizations may differ in how they identify and select projects for development. Some organizations have a formal planning process that is carried out by a steering committee (encompassing senior managers)

The objective of the systems-investigation phase is to answer the following questions:

- What is the business problem?
- Is it a problem or an opportunity?
- What are the major causes of the problem?
- Can the problem be solved by improving the current information system?
- Does a new information system needed?
- Is this a feasible information system solution to this problem?

The preliminary-investigation phase sets the stage for gathering information about the current problem and the existing information system. This information is then used in studying the feasibility of possible information systems solutions.

2. FEASIBILITY STUDY: -

- Feasibility study is carried out by experienced system analysts or managers to determine the resources required to provide an information systems solution, the cost and benefits of such a solution, and the feasibility of such a solution.

The goal of the feasibility study is to consider alternative information systems solutions, evaluate their feasibility, and propose the alternative most suitable to the organization. The feasibility of a proposed solution is evaluated in terms of its components. These components are:

- **Technical Feasibility :-**
  - § It determines- Can the work for the project be done with current equipment, existing software technology, and available personnel?
  - § If new technology is required, then how can it be developed?
- **Economic Feasibility :-**
  - § Economic feasibility determines the economic viability of the system.
  - § It determines - Are there sufficient benefits in creating the system to make the costs acceptable?
  - § A proposed system is said to be feasible, if it's Financial benefits equals or exceeds the costs.
  - § The purpose of financial & economic questions raised by analysis are for estimating the following:

- o Cost of H/W & S/W used.
- o Costs benefit analysis.
- o Cost to conduct the full system investigation.

- **Operational Feasibility or Functional Feasibility :-**
  - § This test is done to find whether the system will function as per the stated objectives or not.
  - § It determines whether the system be used by stakeholders, if it is developed and implemented? ***Stakeholders*** include management, employees, customers and suppliers.
  - § Is there sufficient support for the project from management and users?

3. DETERMINATION OF SYSTEM REQUIREMENTS

Analysts must study the business process (or system) to answer these key questions-

- o What is being done?
- o How great is the volume of transactions or decisions?
- o How well is the task being performed?
- o What are the desirable needs of stakeholders?

The system analyst gathers information using one or combination of the following methods-:

- o Observing or monitoring users of the current system to determine their needs as well as their satisfaction and dissatisfaction with the current system
- o Interviewing users, employees, managers, and customers.
- o Developing and administering questionnaires to potential users of the information system.
- o Collecting and analyzing documents, reports, layouts, procedures, manuals, and any other documentation relating to the operations of the current system.
- o Modeling and simulating the work activities of the current system.

After gathering the details, the analysts study the requirements data and produce a document containing the functional requirements of the new computer information system. The new system should have the following features-

- § Greater speed of processing
- § Effective procedure to eliminate errors.
- § Better accuracy.
- § Faster retrieval of information
- § Integration of data.
- § Larger capacity of storing data with reduced cost.

4. SYSTEM DESIGN

In this stage, the details of what the system will do are given. Design phase focuses on high level design like, what programs are needed and how are they going to interact, low-level design (how the individual programs are going to work), interface design (what are the interfaces going to look like) and data design (what data will be required). During these phases, the software's overall structure is defined.

- § It can be of two types-
  - o **Logical Design: -** The details that state how a system will meet the requirements identified during system analysis are referred to as logical design.
  - o **Physical Design: -** The process of developing actual information system (or software) is referred to as physical design.
- § The system design also describes the data to be input, calculated or stored.
- § Designers select file structures and storage devices such as magnetic disk, magnetic tape or even paper files.
- § Designers provide clearly outlined software specifications to the designers.

There are several tools and techniques used for designing. These tools and techniques are:

- Flowchart
- Data flow diagram (DFDs)
- Data dictionary
- Structured English
- Decision table
- Decision tree

5. SYSTEM DEVELOPMENT

- § Software developers may install purchased software or they may write new, custom-designed programs.
- § In this phase the designs are translated into code. Computer programs are written using a conventional programming language or an application generator. Programming tools like Compilers, Interpreters, Debuggers are used to generate the code. Different high level programming languages like C, C++, Pascal, Java are used for coding. With respect to the type of application, the right programming language is chosen.
- § The choice depends on the cost of each option, the time available to write software, and the availability of programmers.
- § Programmers are also responsible for documenting the program. Documentation is essential to test the program and carry on maintenance once the application has been installed.

6. SYSTEM TESTING :-

In this phase the system is tested. Normally programs are written as a series of individual modules, these subjects to separate and detailed test. The system is then tested as a whole. The separate modules are brought together and tested as a complete system. The system is tested to ensure that interfaces between modules work (integration testing), the system works on the intended platform and with the expected volume of data (volume testing) and that the system does what the user requires (acceptance/beta testing).

During system testing, system is used experimentally to ensure that the software does not fail, i.e. that it will run according to it's specifications and in the way users expect. Special test data are input for processing, and the results examined. In many organizations, testing is performed by persons other than those who wrote the original programs to ensure more complete and unbiased testing and more reliable software.

7. IMPLEMENTATION AND EVALUATION :-

§ Implementation is the process that involves-

- ✓ put new equipment into use.
- ✓ Train users
- ✓ Install the new application
- ✓ Construct data files.

§ Implementation is an ongoing process.

§ Evaluation of the system is performed to identify it's strengths and weaknesses. It involves the following :-

- o **Operational Evaluation :-** It includes the assessment of –
  - ✓ Ease of use
  - ✓ Response time
  - ✓ Suitability of information formats
  - ✓ Reliability
  - ✓ Level of utilization
- o **Organizational Impact :-**
  - ✓ Identification and measurement of benefits to the organization (i.e. cost, revenue and profit), competitive impact etc.
  - ✓ It includes impact on internal and external information flows.
- o **User Manager Assessment :-**
  - ✓ Evaluation of the attitudes of senior and user managers within the organization, as well as end-users.
- o **Development Performance :-**
  - ✓ Includes assessment of development methods and tools.
  - ✓ It only deals with the information (instead of merits) that can improve the effectiveness of subsequent application efforts.

8. MAINTENANCE

Inevitably the system will need maintenance. Software will definitely undergo change once it is delivered to the customer. There are many reasons for the change. Change could happen because of some unexpected input values into the system. In addition, the changes in the system could directly affect the software operations. The software should be developed to accommodate changes that could happen during the post implementation period.

Maintenance is necessary to eliminate errors in the system during its working life and to tune the system to any variations in its working environment. It has been seen that there are always some errors found in the system that must be noted and corrected. It also means the review of the system from time to time. The review of the system is done for:

- knowing the full capabilities of the system
- knowing the required changes or the additional requirements
- studying the performance

If a major change to a system is needed, a new project may have to be set up to carry out the change. The new project will then proceed through all the above life cycle phases.

Thus, The Systems Development Life Cycle (SDLC) is a conceptual model used in project management that describes the stages involved in an information system development project from an initial feasibility study through maintenance of the completed application.

2. Disadvantages of SDLC

- The use of bottom-up implementation (also known as waterfall model) i.e. building small modules to arrive at the final model)
- You cannot proceed to the next step until the previous step has been fully completed.

3. Practical Application of SDLC in Hospitality

- As the pace of globalization increases, hotels must not only provide a place for guests to relax, but an efficient place to conduct business as well. The hotel industry is also playing an increasing role in land use, urban development, and regional revitalization.
- Increased demand in the hotel industry has inevitably led to greater competition. Accordingly, hotels need to prepare forward-looking marketing strategies that reflect a full understanding of market conditions. At a time when society is rapidly evolving and values are diversifying, the requirements of hotel guests are clearly changing. The development of hotels that are in tune with the times and that have the required level of operational and service support is becoming an increasingly important factor in hotel management.
- The methodology of SDLC is used by Enterprise Consultants in developing Hotel Information Systems. Enterprise Consulting Services enable you to extend investment in your systems, software and people. Enterprise Consultants are available to assist hoteliers in planning, implementation and maintenance of information system for their hotels. They determine the technology needs of the hotel and then they design a solution to meet the entire technological requirements of the hotel.

Example: Generally speaking, for implementing a successful hotel plan, the SDLC methodology will prove to be the most suitable one.

new topic Models for System Development:-

1) Waterfall Model
2) Iterative Model
3) Prototyping Model
4) Spiral Model

1. WATERFALL MODEL :-

1. It is also known as the "*Classical life cycle*" or "*Linear Sequential model*".
2. It is called so, because of its diagrammatic representation.
3. All the steps have to be followed and an activity starts only when the previous activity has been completed e.g. maintenance phase is started only when the implementation phase has been completed.
4. Theoretically, it is the best model for development but it has some practical problems e.g it fails in some situations like, where the objectives are not clearly stated by the users.

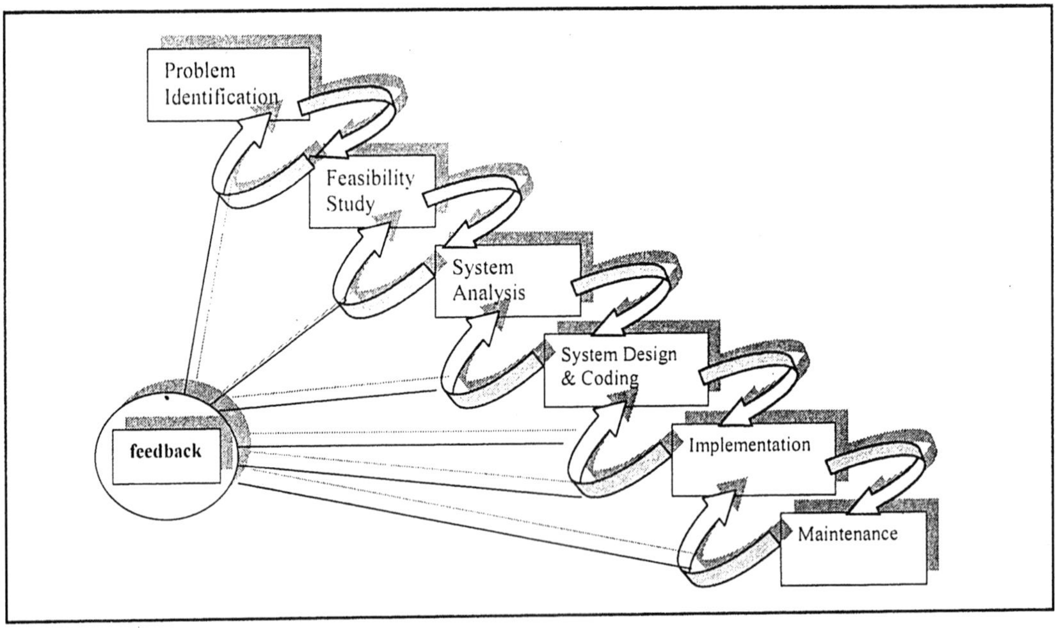

5. This model includes the following phases-

Disadvantages of Waterfall Model

Although the Waterfall Model has been used extensively over the years in the production of many quality systems, it is not without its problems. In recent years it has come under attack, due to its rigid design and inflexible procedure. Criticisms fall into the following categories-

- Real projects rarely follow the sequential flow that the model proposes.
- At the beginning of most projects there is often a great deal of uncertainty about requirements and goals, and it is therefore difficult for customers to identify these criteria on a detailed level. The model does not accommodate this natural uncertainty very well.
- Developing a system using the Waterfall Model can be a long, painstaking process that does not yield a working version of the system until late in the process.

2. ITERATIVE MODEL

The problems with the **Waterfall Model** created a demand for a new method of developing systems which could provide faster results, require less up-front information, and offer greater flexibility. With **Iterative Development**, the project is divided into small parts. This allows the development team to demonstrate results earlier on in the process and obtain valuable feedback from system users. Often, each iteration is actually a mini-**Waterfall** process with the feedback from one phase providing vital information for the design of the next phase. In a variation of this model, the software products which are produced at the end of each step (or series of steps) can go into production immediately as incremental releases.

Disadvantages of Iterative Model

While the **Iterative Model** addresses many of the problems associated with the **Waterfall Model**, it does present new challenges.

- The user community needs to be actively involved throughout the project. While this involvement is a positive for the project, it is demanding on the time of the staff and can add project delay.
- Communication and coordination skills take center stage in project development.
- Informal requests for improvement after each phase may lead to confusion — a controlled mechanism for handling substantive requests needs to be developed.
- The **Iterative Model** can lead to "scope creep," since user feedback following each phase may lead to increased customer demands. As users see the system develop, they may realize the potential of other system capabilities which would enhance their work.

3. PROTOTYPING MODEL:-

- Prototype model is an advantage over Water fall Model, because it is much beneficial in case, where the requirements of users are not clearly stated and the changed requirements are known by the developers at every iteration.
- It proves to be useful only if it is employed at the right time and in the appropriate manner.
- Basically, it is a working system that is developed to test ideas and assumptions about the new system.

- Thus, it's actually a test model.
- Once a prototype is made, it is evaluated by the users.
- The users then point out the features they like or dislike and also specify the shortcomings & additional features they require from the system.
- System prototyping is an interactive process that involves the users in it's analysis and design stages.
- This method constitutes the following steps-
- Identification of user's requirements and features needed in the system.
- Use the prototype and determine the enhancements & changes required in it.
- Modification of the prototype based on the information collected from the user.
- Keep revising these steps until the required system evolves.
- Thus, the process of developing the prototype continues until it reveals the essential design system.

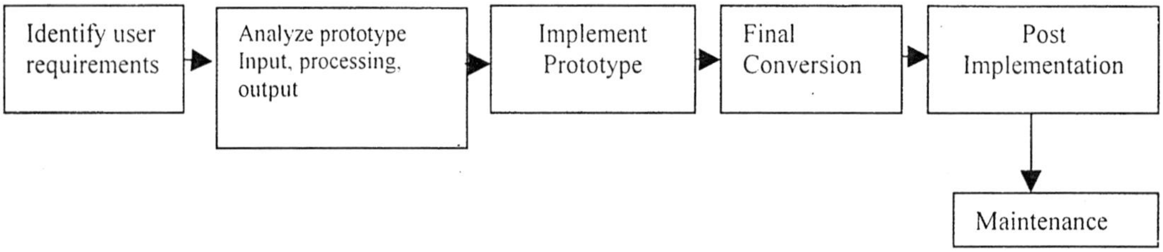

Disadvantages of Prototyping Model

- **Prototyping can lead to false expectations. Prototyping** often creates a situation where the customer mistakenly believes that the system is "finished" when in fact it is not. More specifically, when using the **Prototyping Model**, the pre-implementation versions of a system are really nothing more than one-dimensional structures. The necessary, behind-the-scenes work such as database normalization, documentation, testing, and reviews for efficiency have not been done. Thus the necessary underpinnings for the system are not in place.
- **Prototyping can lead to poorly designed systems.** Because the primary goal of **Prototyping** is rapid development, the design of the system can sometimes suffer because the system is built in a series of "layers" without a global consideration of the integration of all other components. While initial software development is often built to be a "throw-away, "attempting to retroactively produce a solid system design can sometimes be problematic.

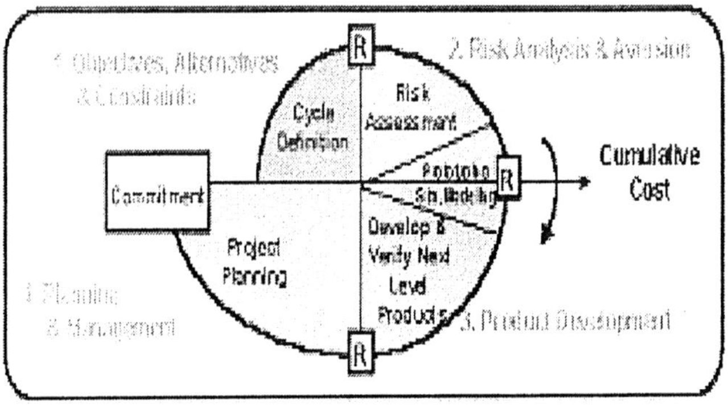

4. SPIRAL MODEL

- It couples the iterative nature or prototyping with the systematic aspect of linear sequential waterfall model.
- The spiral model is divided into a number of framework activities, called task regions.
- There are six task regions :-
  - **Customer/User Communication :-** Establish effective communication between developer and user
  - **Planning :-** It defines resources, timeliness, and other project related information.
  - **Risk Analysis :-** Uses both technical & management risk.
  - **Engineering :-** Build one or more representations of application.
    - **Construction & Release :-** Construct, test, install and provide user support.
    - **Customer Evaluation :-** User provides feedback based on evaluation of software.
      - In each iteration, three to six task regions may be involved.
      - A number of iterations lead to a system fully acceptable by the users.

Disadvantages of Spiral Model

Due to the relative newness of the **Spiral Model**, it is difficult to assess its strengths and weaknesses. However, the risk assessment component of the **Spiral Model** provides both developers and customers with a measuring tool that earlier **Process Model**s do not have. The measurement of risk is a feature that occurs everyday in real-life situations, but (unfortunately) not as often in the system development industry. The practical nature of this tool helps to make the **Spiral Model** a more realistic **Process Model** than some of its predecessors.

new topic Feasibility Study

- Feasibility means the probability or possibility whether they can meet the goals or not? If the goals which have been set are feasible, then how will they be met and what will be the cost.
- After the problem is stated, the feasibility of the system is to be determined.
- In the feasibility study, one has to study technical, economical and operational feasibility of the system.
- Once the goals for the given project are set, the analysts have to find out whether the goals are feasible i.e. whether they can meet the goals or not.
- If the goals which have been set are feasible, then how will they be met and what will be the cost.

- The feasibility study constitutes three levels of feasibility :-
  - § Technical Feasibility
  - § Economic Feasibility
  - § Functional Feasibility

1. TYPES OF FEASIBILITY STUDY:-

1. Technical Feasibility

1. The technical feasibility study should give answers to the following question-
2. Does the technology, equipment and personnel required for developing the given project exist?
3. Does the proposed equipment have the technical capacity to handle data required for the new system?
4. Will the proposed system provide adequate responses to inquiries, regardless of the number or location of users?
5. Is the system flexible to expansion after being developed?
6. Are there technical guarantees of accuracy, reliability, ease of access, and data security?
7. E.g if the proposal includes a printer, that is technically feasible but on the other hand, if a user is requesting voice input to write, read and change stored data, the proposal may not be technically feasible.

2. Financial or Economic Feasibility:-

1. A system that is technically feasible, should also be an asset to the company.
2. Financial benefits must equal or exceed the costs.
3. The analysts estimates the following-
   - ✓ Cost of Hardware & Software required for the application to be developed.
   - ✓ Cost to conduct a full system investigation.
   - ✓ Benefits in the form of reduced costs or fewer costly errors.

To be judged feasible, a project proposal must pass all these tests. Otherwise, it is not a feasible project. E.g. A medical system that can be developed at reasonable costs but the nurses will avoid using cannot be judged operationally feasible.

3. Operational or Functional Feasibility:-

1. A project will be beneficial to an organization only if they are able to meet the functional requirements of a system.
2. This feasibility test is done to find whether the system will function as per the stated objectives or not.
3. It also looks for the answer to the following :-
   - (a) Will the system be used if it is developed & implemented?
   - (b) Will it produce poor results in any area?

(c) Is there sufficient support for the project from management and users?

(d) Are current business methods acceptable to the users?

(e) Have the users been involved in the planning and development of the project?

4. Behaviourall Feasibility

1. People are inherently resistant to change like using computers for substituting the manual work.
2. Therefore, the staff requires special education and training for learning new ways of conducting business.

5. Social Feasibility

1. It is a determination of whether a proposed project will be acceptable to the people or not.

6. Management Feasibility :-

1. It is a determination of whether a proposed project will be acceptable to management.
2. If a management does not accept a project or gives a negligible support to it, the analyst will tend to view the project as a non-feasible one.

7. Time Feasibility :-

1. It is a determination of, whether a proposed project can be implemented fully within a desired time frame.
2. If a project takes too much time, it is likely to be rejected.

All these tests are equally important for determining, if the the project is feasible or not.

2. Objective of Feasibility Study

The major objective of feasibility study phase, are to find out the answers to these key questions-

- ✓ Is there a new and better way to do the job that will benefit the user?
- ✓ What are the costs and savings of the alternatives?
- ✓ What is recommended?

Providing answers to these question means, presentation of alternative systems, evaluation of the costs and savings and recommendation of the most suitable alternative.

3. Importance of Feasibility Study

1. If a system already exists, then studies of the shortcomings of the present system are made.
2. After studying the requirements of the user & the present system thoroughly, the goals & objectives for the new system are defined.
3. A feasibility study of the new system is also done to determine whether it is possible to develop a new system or not.

4. Thus, in feasibility study, an approximate estimate of the schedule, cost and time for the new system are determined.
5. After completing the task of feasibility study, the management may decide to accept or reject the proposal.
6. In other words, after the feasibility study is done, the organization decides whether to proceed further or not. If it decides to proceed, further analysis and designing starts.

4. Steps in Investigation for Generating Feasibility Report

1. *Form a Project Team and Appoint a Project Leader*

- § Firstly, separate teams for independent projects are formed by the project management group.
- § Each project team comprises of one or more System Analysts & Programmers with a project leader.
- § The project leader is responsible for planning and managing the development activities of the system.

2. *Start Preliminary Investigation :-*

- § The system analyst of each project team starts preliminary investigations through different fact finding techniques.

3. *Prepare the Current Systems Flow Chart :-*

- § The analyst prepare a flow chart of the current system, to analyse the working of the system effectively.

4. *Describe the Deficiencies in the Current System :-*

- § The analyst identifies and describes the deficiencies in the current system using the flow chart.

5. *Determine objectives of the Proposed System :-*

- § The major objectives of the proposed systems are listed by each analyst and are discussed with the project leader.

6. *Determine the Technical Feasibility :-*

- § The existing computer systems (H/W & S/W) of the concerned department are identified and their technical specifications are noted down.
- § The analysts decide, whether the existing systems are sufficient for the technical requirements of the proposed system or not.

7. *Determine the Economic Feasibility :-*

- § The analysts determine the costs and benefits of the proposed sytem in order to ensure that the project is economically feasible.

8. *Determine the Operational Feasibility :-*

- § The analyst identify the responsible users and mould the design of the project according to their requirements in order to ensure it's operational feasibility.

On the basis of the entire investigation, the analyst prepares a detailed report, which is called Feasibility Report.

new topic Cost Benefit Analysis

§ It is a method by which we find and estimate the monetary value of the development costs that produce the above mentioned benefits.

§ A cost benefit analysis is necessary to determine whether the project is feasible in terms of economic investment or not.

§ Cost –benefit analysis is performed by listing all the costs associated with the system.

§ The various kinds of costs incurred in development and implementation of the system include :-

1. **Hardware Costs :** cost incurred in purchase of hardware i.e. computer & it's peripherals.
2. **Personnel Costs :** include the salaries of the EDP staff, as well as the perks of personnel involved in the development of the system.
3. **Facility Costs :** include expenses incurred in the preparation of the physical site. This includes flooring, lighting etc.
4. **Operating Costs :-** include all costs associated with the day to day operation of the system.
5. **Supply Costs :-** include variable costs that increase with increased use of paper, ribbon, disks etc.

The first task it to identify each benefit obtained by the system and assign a monetary value to it for cost/benefit analysis.

1. Procedure for Cost/Benefit Analysis

1. Identify the various costs and benefits pertaining to the given project.
2. Categorize the various costs and benefits for analysis.
3. Select a method for evaluation.
4. Interpret the results of evaluation.
5. Take action.

2. Types of Benefits of a Project on the Basis of Advantage They Provide

1. Cost Saving benefit
2. Cost-avoidance benefit
3. Improved-service-level benefits
4. Improved-information benefits

1. Cost-saving Benefits

§ It means reduction in administrative & operational costs.

§ e.g. reduction in clerical staff, used in the support of an administrative activity.

2. Cost-avoidance Benefits

§ The benefits those eliminate future administrative and operational costs.

§ e.g. No need to hire additional staff in future to handle an administrative activity.

3. Improved Service-Level Benefits :-

§ The benefits due to which the performance of a system is improved by a new computer-based method.

§ e.g. Registering a student in fifteen minutes rather than an hour.

4. Improved-information Benefits :-

§ The benefits which lead to better information for decision making due to computer based methods are called improved-information benefits.

§ e.g. A system that reports of the updated sales of some particular goods, so that it can be decided, whether to produce more goods or not.

3. Classification of Cost and Benefits

1. Tangible or Intangible
2. Fixed or Variable
3. Direct or Indirect

Tangible Cost or Benefit	Intangible Cost or Benefit
The cost or benefit that can be easily measured.	The costs or benefit that exists but their financial value cannot be measured.
These can be accurately known.	These can only be approximated.
e.g. Tangible Cost • An outlay of cash for any specific item is tangible cost.	**e.g. of Intangible Cost** • Affect on moral of an employee cannot be measured in terms of financial values.
e.g. of Tangible Benefits • Saving made due to reducing expenditure. •Increase in production or cost.	**e.g. of Intangible Benefits** • Better service to consumers • Superior quality of products.

Fixed Cost or Benefit	Variable Cost or Benefit
The cost or benefit that remains constant, regardless of how a system is used.Therefore, it is also called Sunk cost.	The cost or benefit that is incurred/ realized on a regular basis.
It is not so.	Generally, they are proportional to work volume and continue as long as the system is in operation.
e.g. of Fixed Cost • computer purchased for a computer institute is fixed cost, regardless if it is being used or not.	**e.g. of Variable Cost** • cost of computer forms vary in proportion to the amount of processing done.

e.g. of Fixed Benefit • If 20 percent of staff members are reduced, we can call it as a fixed benefit.	e.g. of Variable Benefit • The benefit realized by personnel by saving monthly from his income.

Direct Cost or Benefit	Indirect Cost or Benefit
The costs or benefits which are directly associated with a system i.e. directly applied to the operator.	These are not directly associated with a specific activity in the system. Generally, referred to as Overhead expenses.
It is directly measurable in quantitative terms.	It is difficult to measure in quantitative terms.
e.g. of Direct Cost • The purchase of floppy for Rs. 600/- is a direct cost, because we can associate the floppy box with money spent.	**e.g. of Indirect Cost** • Time spent by system analyst in discussing problems with system analyst, gathering data about problem etc.
e.g. of Direct Benefit • The benefit realized by selling any item directly is direct benefit.	**e.g. of Indirect Benefit** • Benefit realized by Telephonic Marketing of a product to customers; because it is not directly measurable.

3. Methods for Evaluation of Cost and Benefits :-

1. Net benefit analysis
2. Present Value analysis
3. Net present Value
4. Payback analysis
5. Break even analysis
6. Cash-flow analysis

PRESENT VALUE ANALYSIS

1. It calculates the costs and benefits of the system in terms of today's value of the investment and then comparing across alternatives.
2. In this method, the amount we are willing to invest today is determined by the value of the benefit at the end of a given period. This is called the present value of the benefit.
3. e.g. if Rs. 300,000 is to be invested in a microcomputer and the average annual benefit for four years will be Rs. 150,000. In this case, the investment has to be made today, whereas the benefits are in the future.
4. We compare present value to future values by considering the time value of money to be invested.

PAYBACK ANALYSIS

1. Payback analysis is a simple and streamlined type of cost/benefit analysis.

2. It does not consider the time value of the money as it was in case of present value analysis.
3. It yields the number of years required for the improvement to pay for itself.
4. In this method, the total cost of the improvement is divided by the first-year energy cost savings produced by the improvement.
5. Shorter the pay back period, the sooner a profit is realized and more attractive is the investment.
6. While this analysis is an easy way to examine the overall costs and savings potentials for a variety of project options, it does not consider more unpredictable factors, such as operation and maintenance expenses, that can have a significant impact on cost savings.

BREAK EVEN ANALYSIS

1. Break-even analysis is a technique widely used by production management and management accountants.
2. It is based on categorizing pro-duction costs bet-ween those which are "***variable***" (costs that change when the production output changes) and those that are "***fixed***" (costs not directly related to the volume of production).
3. Total variable and fixed costs are compared with sales revenue in order to determine the level of sales volume, sales value or production at which the business makes neither a profit nor a loss (the "break-even point").

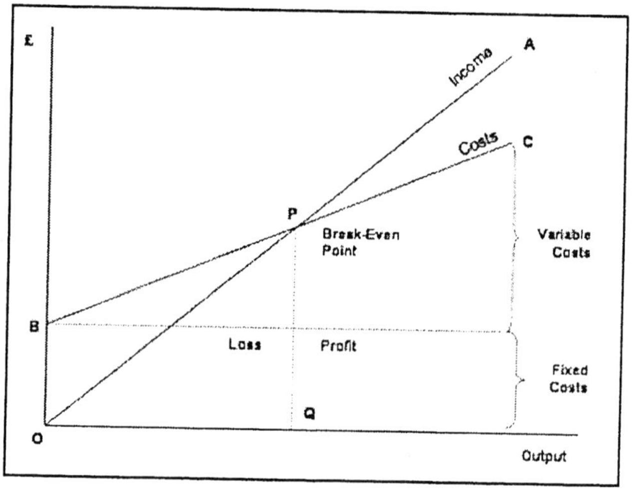

4. **The Break-Even Chart:** In its simplest form, the break-even chart is a graphical representation of costs at various levels of activity shown on the same chart as the variation of income (or sales, revenue) with the same variation in activity. The point at which neither profit nor loss is made is known as the ***"break-even point"*** and is represented on the chart below by the intersection of the two lines:
5. In the diagram above, the line OA represents the variation of income at varying levels of production activity ("output"). OB represents the total fixed costs in the business. As output increases, variable costs are incurred, meaning that total costs (fixed + variable) also increase. At low levels of output, Costs are greater than Income. At the point of intersection, P, costs are exactly equal to income, and hence neither profit nor loss is made.

FIXED COSTS Vs VARIABLE COSTS

Fixed Costs

Fixed costs are those business costs that are not directly related to the level of production or output. In other words, even if the business has a zero output or high output, the level of fixed costs will remain broadly the same. In the long term fixed costs can alter - perhaps as a result of investment in production capacity (e.g. adding a new factory unit) or through the growth in overheads required to support a larger, more complex business.

Examples of fixed costs:

- Depreciation
- Research and development
- Marketing costs (non- revenue related)
- Administration costs

Variable Costs

Variable costs are those costs which vary directly with the level of output. They represent payment output-related inputs such as raw materials, direct labour, fuel and revenue-related costs such as commission.

A distinction is often made between **"Direct"** variable costs and **"Indirect"** variable costs.

Direct variable costs are those which can be directly attributable to the production of a particular product or service and allocated to a particular cost centre. Raw materials and the wages those working on the production line are good examples.

Indirect variable costs cannot be directly attributable to production but they do vary with output. These include depreciation (where it is calculated related to output - e.g. machine hours), maintenance and certain labour costs.

Semi-Variable Costs

Whilst the distinction between fixed and variable costs is a convenient way of categorising business costs, in reality there are some costs which are fixed in nature but which increase when output reaches certain levels. These are largely related to the overall "scale" and/or complexity of the business. For example, when a business has relatively low levels of output or sales, it may not require costs associated with functions such as human resource management or a fully-resourced finance department. However, as the scale of the business grows (e.g. output, number people employed, number and complexity of transactions) then more resources are required. If production rises suddenly then some short-term increase in warehousing and/or transport may be required. In these circumstances, we say that part of the cost is variable and part fixed.

CASH FLOW ANALYSIS

1. **Cash flow** is essentially the movement of money into and out of your business; it's the cycle of cash inflows and cash outflows that determine your business' solvency.
2. **Cash flow analysis** is the study of the cycle of your business' cash inflows and outflows, with the purpose of maintaining an adequate cash flow for your business, and to provide the basis for cash flow management.
3. A quick and easy way to perform a cash flow analysis is to compare the total unpaid purchases to the total sales due at the end of each month.
4. Cash flow analysis involves examining the components of your business that affect cash flow, such as accounts receivable, inventory, accounts payable, and credit terms. By performing a cash flow analysis on these separate components, you'll be able to more easily identify cash flow problems and find ways to improve your cash flow.

8

Information Concepts

Introduction:

According to **Peter Drucker -** *"information is man's modern weapon."*

About thousands of years ago our ancestors fought with knives, swords, spears and other physical weapons. In today's competitive business environment, man has resorted to information as his weapon.

We have modified our environment so radically that we must modify ourselves in order to exist in this new environment. — ***Norbert Wiener***

Information is essential to human activity and, in fact, to the very nature of being alive. The following statements made in this context are-

"Information is the basic ingredient of social organization or it is the lifeblood of the organization"

"Information is integral to all living organisms'

newtopic Data

The term data is derived from a Greek word "Datum", which means a single piece of information.

"A representation of facts, concepts, or instructions in an organized manner; suitable for communication, interpretation or processing, by humans or by automated means. Data are intangible and include numbers, words, symbols, ideas, concepts, and oral verbalization."

Or

"Data refers to collection of raw facts or figures (which may or may not be true) gathered from the surroundings on the basis of which inferences can be drawn"

Example:

- Figures of revenue generated in a hotel on daily basis
- Figures of closing stock of each item... etc.

Data Processing

The process of converting data into information is called as data processing and the processed data is called information. A datum has to go through considerable amount of manipulations before it becomes meaningful information. The manipulations includes following steps-

- ***A***cquisition of data
- ***C***lassification of data
- ***S***torage of data
- ***R***etrieval of data
- ***E***diting of data
- ***H***ypothesis generation
- ***A***nalysis & testing of assumptions
- ***C***hoice of format for presentation of data
- ***R***eport Generation

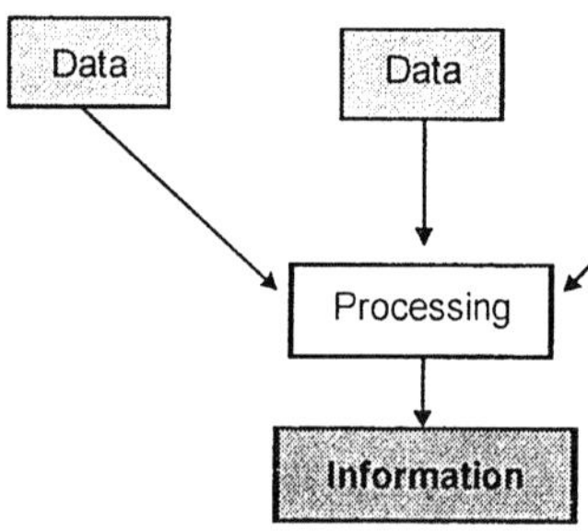

Information

In everyday language, the terms "*data*" and "*information*" are used interchangeably.

However, the two terms have different meanings. Data refers to what you collect, through observation, measurement and inference whereas the information refers to the systematically organized and analyzed form of data i.e. *processed data* or *meaningful data*. It means information is created from data. Thus, data (like bricks) are the building blocks of the information (like house).

Reporting is a common procedure of converting data into meaningful information.

Example:

- Monthly or Annually Generated Revenue Reports
- Month wise or Annual Inventory Report

1. Common Properties of Information

- Information is never consumed never deteriorated.
- One information item can be available to different persons at the same time.
- There is no unit for measuring information.
- The price of information is not linked to it's value in a particular situation i.e. you cannot quantify the benefit/value of information.

2. Common Sources of Information

- **Less Formal:**
  - People communication by telephone or e-mail
- **More Formal:**
  - Hard Copy or Electronic or Digital Document

3. Characteristics of Information

The value of information can be measured by evaluating the following characteristics of information-

1. **Timeliness:** Timeliness refers to the availability of information source in time. For evaluating the value of a given information, you must consider this question- *"Is it there soon enough to be meaningful?"*. The objective of MIS is *"right information at the right time"*. The information must be available for managerial activities at the right time. If the information is delayed, it reduces the usefulness of the information.
2. **Sufficiency:** It refers to the completeness of information. Insufficient information is worthless. For evaluating the sufficiency of information, you must consider the given question in your mind- *"is there adequate information for the purpose intended"*
3. **Accuracy:** The information is expected to be reasonably accurate. It is not necessary that the information must be absolutely accurate at perfection level; however increasing the accuracy level at times becomes uneconomical. That's why the expectation is of reasonable accuracy rather than absolute accuracy. Accuracy of information determines the actual reliability of the information.
4. **Preciseness:** Information should be precise as much as possible because at times, when unnecessary information elements are included, the information readability is adversely affected. Too much of information landing on a busy manager's desk can create a confusion and a situation called *"Information Overload"*.. Therefore, it should have certain decision relevance.
5. **Understandability:** The information should in a simple and understandable form i.e. the language and the presentation of information should be practical and free of perceptual errors. The information should contain such elements that have *freedom from bias.*
6. **Cost-efficiency:** The information collected must be cost effective. If the cost of acquiring information exceeds it's value, there are two alternatives-

a. Increase it's value by increasing accuracy

b. Or reduce it's cost by decreasing accuracy

More often, the first option is selected to maintain it's value in terms of both accuracy and utilities.

7. **Confidentiality:** Confidentiality refers to the possession of information by only authorized people thus restricting it's access from unauthorized people. This is so because the possessor of information strongly affects it's value by controlling it's dissemination to others. The information should have confidentiality to maintain it's authentication i.e. validity and genuineness.

8. **Update-to-Date:** In many business situations, the information needs to be updated. The frequency at which the information needs to be updated is very important. If the information is not updated frequently, there is a fear that decisions are based on old information that is not updated. Thus, the resulting decisions might be ineffective.

4. Types of Information

Facts: A unique bit of information that identifies an object, person, place, or date. More precisely, it refers to a particular situation or thing that is known to be true (and it can be proved) ***e.g***. "Earth is revolving around the Sun", "Moon is a natural satellite of the Earth" etc

Concepts: A concept generally refers to a category of items or ideas that share common features. ***e.g.*** Civilization, Social community etc.

Procedures: A formal series of steps for performing a particular task. ***e.g.*** Quality control procedures, Health and Safety Procedures etc

Process: A description of how something works or operates. ***e.g*** Reservation Process, Registration process etc

Principles: It may refer to a belief, rule, theory or law that influences your actions. ***e.g.*** Principles of Management, Principles of teamwork etc

newtopic Methods of Data & Information Collection

No one data collection method is ideal for every situation. For this reason, it is preferable to use multiple methods whenever possible. Using multiple methods to assess the same outcomes (e.g., using surveys and questionnaires to assess program management) provides a richer, more detailed picture.

1. Personal interviews:

Interviews are most often used to gather detailed and qualitative information. Interviews are conducted one-by-one. Questions are generally open-ended and responses are documented in thorough using either manual or electronic forms (or reports). Interviews may be of the following types-

a. Face-to-face Interviews

b. Telephonic Interviews

c. Computer Assisted Personal/Telephone Interviewing (CAPI / CATI)

Advantages

- Provide rich data that paint a broad picture
- May highlight issues not previously considered
- useful for interpreting quantitative data collected through other methods

Limitations:

- Can be difficult to elicit participation from individuals who have time constraints
- Documentation and analysis can be time consuming and may require the help of someone versed in qualitative analysis

2. DIRECT OBSERVATION:

Observations are a generally unobtrusive method for gathering information. They are usually conducted by system analysts or database architects to verify and supplement information gathered through other methods.

Observations can be highly structured, with protocols for recording specific behaviors at specific times, or unstructured, taking a "look-and-see" approach. They are most reliable when they are conducted over a period of time. This method may collect information about implementation, activities, interpersonal interactions, administration and management etc

Advantages

- Provide highly detailed information from an external perspective
- Provide less biased descriptions

Limitations

- Can be time consuming and expensive
- Observers must be trained and be consistent with one another
- Observations conducted on a sample of days may not be suitable for collecting sufficient Information

3. SURVEYS & QUESTIONNAIRES:

Surveys and questionnaires are usually administered on paper, in a structured or semi-structured format. Respondents often choose from among a set of forced-choice, or provided, responses. These can include yes/no or scaled responses. Surveys and questionnaires can be administered in person, by mail, over the phone, or via email/Internet. Therefore, Surveys may be of following types-

a. Door-to-Door Surveys

b. Mail Surveys (or Internet Surveys)

   A well-designed questionnaire efficiently collects the required data with a minimum number of errors. Data collected often include demographic information, satisfaction levels, and opinions about a particular issue (or matter). Questionnaires may be -

c. Printed Questionnaires

d. Electronic Questionnaires (like Electronic forms)

Advantages

- Less time consuming and expensive to administer than other methods
- Can be administered to large groups of individuals
- Effective for assessing program or system satisfaction

Limitations

- Data entry and analysis can be time consuming
- May be difficult to complete a particular survey efficiently

4. Document Reviews:

Document reviews analyze existing program records and other documents in order to extract valuable information. Examples include budget, staff records, and annual reports.

Advantages

- Reduce evaluation time and costs
- May elicit a high degree of information accuracy

Limitations

- May not be available or applicable for every situation

  The cost or budget, data quality & availability of time should be considered while selecting any of the given methods for collecting information. Often the most satisfactory information collection strategy uses a combination of the above methods. For example, mail surveys have proven to be quite efficient when designed as a follow-up for those who did not respond by telephone interview.

newtopic Barriers to Data or Information Collection

1. **Time:** Managers have to take lot of decisions, but they have less time to investigate each decision. Thus, managers do not spend much time for data or information collection. Moreover, they rely upon the information gathered (for decision making) in short span of time. Thus, time is a greatest barrier in the way of information collection.
2. **Decision making Techniques:** Some managers tend to use a short list of alternatives for taking a decision. That is instead of postponing decisions until all information is collected, they decide as they go; therefore breaking the search process before necessary information is collected.
3. **Structural barriers:** Organizations restrict access to some information for security reasons. Only authorized people within the organization have access to such information. When organization decentralize decision making and remove structural barriers to information, employees have more latitude (or freedom) in decision making and may follow various decision making procedures.
4. **Cultural factors:** Both the society and the organization affect the culture in which information is collected. Cultural factors draw the line between curiosity and intrusiveness. These factors restrict the collection of

information by making some topics taboo (i.e. topics against which people feel embarrass or offensive) or requiring the person to follow particular rituals for getting certain information.

5. **Technical unawareness:** Employees may not be aware of sources of information or procedures for access to these sources.
6. **Cost :** Cost is another factor that limits the scope of information collection. For seeking different types of information, a different value of cost is involved. The information collection is therefore bound by the budget of the organization or the team collecting the data.

newtopic Retrieval of Information

Accessing stored information from the database is called retrieval of information. The information is collected in a database and thus a certain language has to be used for interacting with database, in order to access desired information. The personnel involved in retrieval of information are known as "end-users". There exists some common problems related with information retrieval-

1. Perfect information system does not exist practically.
2. Users gets confused by the large influx of information (i.e. information overload)
3. In many cases, it is not completely clear to the user of an information retrieval system which information is infact required.
4. A lot of information cannot be obtained or atleast not free of charge.
5. Computer systems are machines. This may cause difficulties related to language and vocabulary.
6. The need of information cannot be completely expressed in the form of a query.

newtopic Information and Organization

The design of the organizational structure should take into account and take advantage of the information and information- processing techniques. The technology itself is neutral, but it can greatly increase humanity's welfare, depending on how efficiently it is used. Organizations collect and distribute information. In the process, they also distort it. Some distortions are intentional and some are intentionally done to change the value and meaning of information. Sometimes employees are asked to summarize data and report it to their supervisors. Summarizing data means leaving some parts of it out. ***Example:*** *In a hotel, reports are generated for providing an insight of sales trend, demand of guests and also future employee requirement.*

Managing large amounts of information is one of the leading challenges for organizations. As new means of communication increase, the amount of messages we send and receive, and the speed of those messages increase. Therefore, the communication of information is vital in determining the success of an organization.

Lets say for an example, getting the right information from corporate HQ to stores, restaurants or hotel locations is a frequent challenge in retail and hospitality organizations.

Information is a valuable asset of an organization that has to be managed through an information system. Information technology investments must be thought of in terms of a firm's overall information system. Information system model requires an analysis of the following factors- the IT hardware and software itself, the people with direct involvement in the information system, the process that those people follow in completing a business activity, and the business's structure, including its organizational design and formal and informal reporting relationships.

In particular, it's worth noting that IT initiatives cannot precede organization change (although implementing an IT system will undoubtedly affect the entire business), one does not always need to purchase the "best" or most recent technology, and information systems are constantly evolving as a business changes.

newtopic Information and MIS

"When information systems are designed to provide information needed for effective decision making by managers, they are called MIS"

Information processing and computing is pervasive. MIS is a formal system for providing management with accurate and timely information necessary for decision making. There is hardly any management activity that does not involve active or passive information seeking. Information seeking is the first step in bringing about individual or organizational change. It helps prepare and lead managers to action. Information generally reduces the alternatives available to the manager so that effective decisions can be made. The essential element of management is information processing and thus computers are expected to heavily influence management. Computers influence what decisions are made, when decisions are made, what information is available at the point of decision and who is asked to decide.

Many managers believe that decision making is an art not a science and that they can do it without training. Consequently, they commit some type of errors in processing information. Hence they do not check routinely to see if they are falling victim to any of the following traps.

Most decision makers commit some type of error in processing information. ***Russo and Shoemaker*** have provided the following summary of the ten most dangerous decision traps:

1. **Taking Early decisions** — Some mangers reach conclusions whether sufficient information is available for the decision or not. The decision maker has little or no understanding of how the decision was made or should be made.
2. **Ignorance of real problems** - Some managers focus on problems defined by available data and ignore the real problems, the organization faces. In such cases, the information systems collect data that is easily available instead of seeking information actually required by the organization.

3. **Lacking Broad Perspective** — Some managers see the problem in one perspective i.e. they do not consider all the aspects of the problem. Therefore, an appropriate solution could not be found for a particular problem. The manager should not have narrow perspective in order to avoid biased judgments.

4. **Avoiding Decision Aids due to Overconfidence –** Some managers think themselves to be very smart and efficient in decision making. Therefore they show less or no interest in availing decision aids from the efficient group of people or any committee. Some information systems contribute to the problem by providing information but not decision aids.

5. **False Assumptions** — Some managers are overconfident of themselves because they keep false assumptions about them and their success. They fail to believe that success is a journey but not the destination. Also they could not understand the simple fact that in this journey they could meet various uncertainties and therefore they should learn from their experiences. In the end, no matter how poorly they have decided, they only see their own success and fail to notice their failures.

9

System Concepts

Introduction:

Systems exist to fulfil a purpose. Purposes can be described in terms of one or more objectives. These objectives then become the output standards. Feedback mechanism will be required to ensure objectives are achieved. Feedback involves measuring the output of the system, comparing the output with a standard and using the difference to modify subsequent input to ensure that the output conforms to the required standard. Feedback requires a flow of information, which brings us back the idea of a System.

newtopic Definitions

"A system can be defined as a group of interrelated components that have common ideas, principle or doctrines and the components work in a coordinating manner for achieving a common goal or objective."

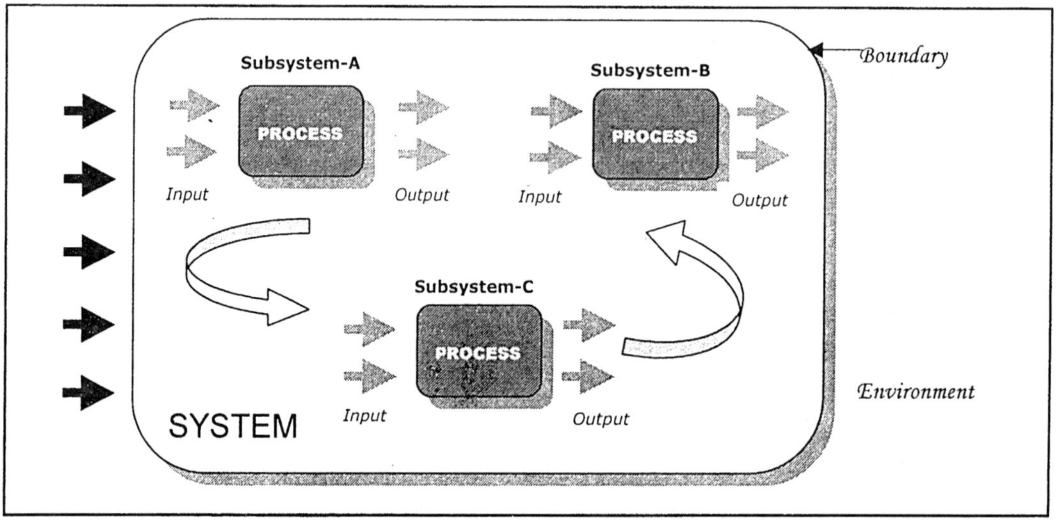

"An organized set of doctrines, ideas, or principles, usually intended to explain the arrangements or working of a systematic whole."

"A system is composed of interacting parts that operate together to achieve some objective or purpose. A system is intended to "absorb" inputs, process them in some way and produce outputs. Outputs are defined by goals, objectives or common purposes"

newtopic Important Components of a System

- People
- Organization
- Data
- Technology
- Decision

Example of Systems are:- Transport System, Airline System, Payroll system etc.

newtopic Elements of System Reconstruction

A System can be reconstructed by considering the following six elements :-

- Outputs & Inputs
- Processors
- Control
- Feedback
- Environment
- Boundaries and Interface

OUTPUTS & INPUTS

1. Output refers to goods, services or information.
2. A major objective of a system is to produce an output that has value to it's user.
3. Input refers to the materials, human resources, information.
4. Input is given to the system to produce some desired output.
5. ***e.g.*** A Business system, which incorporates human, financial and material resources to produce goods and services.

PROCESSOR(S)

1. The processor is an element of the system, which takes the input and transforms into output ***ie.*** It is the operational component of the system.
2. Processors may modify inputs totally or partially, depending on the specifications of the output.

CONTROL

1. It is the decision making subsystem that controls the pattern of activities governing input, processing and output.
2. Management support is required for securing control and supporting the objective of the proposed change.
3. ***e.g.*** In a computer system, Operating System will control all the activities of the entire system.

FEEDBACK

1. In a dynamic system, control is achieved by feedback.
2. Feedback refers to measuring output against a standard and then modifying the input or processing in order to alter the output in a desired manner.
3. It can be positive or negative, routine or informational.
4. Negative feedback results in enhancements to meet the user requirements.

ENVIRONMENT

1. It is the ***Supersystem*** within which an organization operates.
2. It is everything that interacts with the system elements but it is not a part of the system.
3. e.g. if we look at a factory as a system, then vendors, competitors etc which provide constraints and may influence the actual performance of the business ,are categorized as environment.

BOUNDARIES AND INTERFACE

1. Each system has boundaries that determine it's sphere of influence and control.
2. The interfaces are points of interaction between the system and environment i.e boundaries and external entities.

new topic Characteristics of a System

1. **Organization:** Organization is a system that is made up of number of subsystems. These subsystems must be properly organized in order of the proper functioning of the system. Each subsystem performs a specific set of activities. These activities are triggered by information. ***e.g.*** Sales activities are triggered by receipt of an order from a shop. These activities in turn will generate information flows within the organization. ***Example:*** Order Processing generates flow of information flow to the warehouse & Accounts (for financial or sales trend analysis). Organizations comprise human and technological resources to achieve certain goals. For some organizations the "***goal***" is to make money. In other organizations (***e.g.*** schools, hospitals, prisons) the goal could be quite different. The "***three pillars***" of any organization are: -
   a. People (***e.g.*** education, training, employee attitudes)
   b. Organization (***e.g.*** strategy, policy, culture, bureaucracy)

c. Technology (***e.g.*** hardware, software, telecommunications, information systems)

2. **Interdependence:** In a system the different components are connected with each other and they are interdependent. If any component is independent or unreliable to the system, then it is not a part of the system. The components of a system should work in coordination with each other in order that system work properly. ***For example***, Human body represents a complete natural system in which number of subsystems (like Respiratory system, Nervous system, Circular System etc) are involved to achieve a common goal i.e. harmony with life.

3. **Integration:** A system should be integrated in such a manner that each component should perform it's own task in order to obtain a common result. ***For example,*** a hotel is a system which is formed by the integration of various departments (like Front Office, HouseKeeping, Food and Beverage etc) and all the departments work in a unified manner to achieve best possible satisfaction of guest.

4. **Interaction:** System and environment are in general separated by a boundary i.e. all the systems have its defined boundary. Boundary of a system acts as an interface (communication medium) for other sub-systems. (*Example to understand: for living systems the skin plays the role of the boundary.)* The subsystems of a system must be interactive with each other. Besides this, a system may also interact with the external entities (like vendors, suppliers etc.) in the ***environment***.

   a. ***For example:*** Front Office department maintains interaction with several other departments of a hotel for the smooth functioning of the hotel. Housekeeping department should be informed of all the arrivals, so that the room cleaning schedule can be planned accordingly. The Sales Department will need to have information on the room availability. Thus, to make your system successful, you must understand the other systems with which it will interact

   b. ***For example***, a group of interacting people may form a family, a firm, or a city..

5. **Input and Outputs:** Anything that enters a system from it's external environment is called as input. Output is the result that a system provides to it's external environment. Input and output are quite different. The system is not just a passive tube, but an active processor. ***For example***,

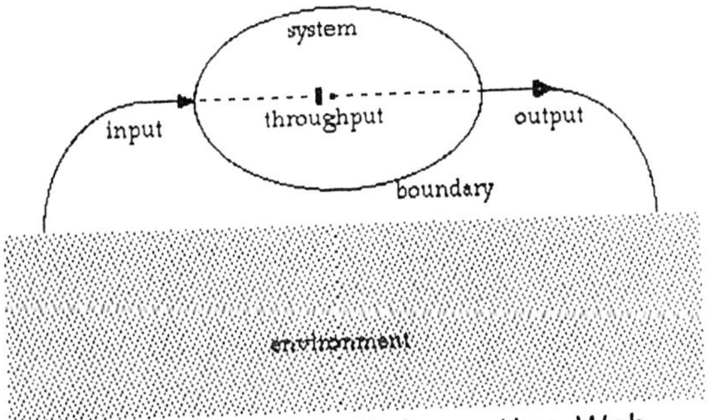

Source: Principia Cybernetica Web

the food, drink and oxygen we take in, leave our body as urine, excrements and carbon dioxide. The transformation of input into output by the system is usually called throughput. For establishing a system, the following objectives should be kept in mind-

a. What essential outputs must the system produce to satisfy user requirements?
b. What type of information does the system need to store?
c. What inputs are necessary for transformation to produce their outputs?
d. What transformations are necessary to produce these outputs?

6. **Central Objective:** It is the most important characteristic of any system. The central objective is the basis on which the whole system is built. All the subsystems of a system should have a common objective to achieve. The approach of having a central objective may lead to inseparable integration and effective functionality of a particular system.

newtopic Types of System

Virtually everything that we come into contact with during our day-to-day life is either a system or a component of a system (both). Broadly speaking, the common types of system are-

1. Natural System:

All the "***God***" made systems are referred to as Natural Systems. These systems exist in nature on its own i.e. these are not man made.

Examples:

i. Stellar System (like Galaxies, solar system etc)
ii. Geological System (like mountains, rivers, valleys etc)
iii. Molecular System (organization of complex atoms)
iv. Living System (Plants and animals)

2. Man-Made System

Man is creation by "***God***" and all the creations of man are termed as man-made systems.

Examples:

i. Social System (like organization, communities etc)
ii. Transportation System (like Railways, Airways, Road transportation system etc)
iii. Communication System (like Telephone, Fax, E-mail etc)
iv. Reservation System (like Hotel Reservation, Train Reservation system)
v. Manufacturing System (like Factory, Mill, Water Plants etc)
vi. Financial System (like Accounting, Inventory etc)
vii. Information System

3. AUTOMATED SYSTEM:

The systems those are man-made and controlled by one or more computers are called automated systems.

a. **Batch System**: A ***batch system*** is one in which jobs are bundled together with the instructions necessary to allow them to be processed without intervention. The main idea behind a batch processing system is to reduce the interference of the operator during the processing or execution of jobs by the computer. Most often, the similar nature jobs are bundled together. However, several batches could be formed on the basis of criteria of priorities. So, the batch having the highest priority could be made to run earlier than other batches. This would give a better turn around service to the selected jobs. **Example:** System Software like Operating System, Speech

b. **On-line System:** It refers to a system that is connected to a large network of computers. Such type of network could be either MAN or WAN.

Example:

i. Electronic Banking System

ii. Online Reservation System

iii. Online Examination System

c. **Real time System:** It is that system which responds back fast so that it is able to an impact on the environment in which it is working. The real time system is mostly applied in those systems where the response or the feedback is immediately required. ***Examples*** included guided missile systems and medical monitoring equipment. The operating system on real-time computers is severely constrained by the timing requirements. Another ***example*** of real time system application is airline seat reservation system in which, the availability of a seat is checked, reserved and booked while the operator is interacting with the customer.

new topic Comparison of Systems

• PHYSICAL SYSTEM VS ABSTRACT SYSTEM:

The systems that are visible and tangible are called physical systems. In other words, Physical System refers to those systems that comprise matter and energy. In other words, physical system consists of physical objects. ***e.g.*** Lake, Human being, Classroom. On the basis of it's entities, it can be of two types-

- **Static Physical System :-** It refers to those systems whose components do not change with time rather than that they remain constant ***e.g.*** chair, table, computer etc.
- **Dynamic Physical System :-** It refers to those systems whose inputs & outputs keep on varying ***e.g.*** Finance Department.

On the contrary, *The systems that are non physical or conceptual are called abstract system.* Abstract systems are also called Conceptual systems because these are based on human concepts and ideas. These are not visible and tangible. Thus, such systems are the outcome of thought process and assumptions of living beings. ***e.g.*** Education system and Social System etc.

- **OPEN VS CLOSED SYSTEM**

Open System refers to a system that freely interacts with its external environment i.e. a system that accepts inputs & deliver outputs to the outside system.

Example: **Organisms are open systems:** they cannot survive without continuously exchanging matter and energy with their environment. Such systems are flexible in nature i.e. they tends to adapt changes easily. Thus such systems have two components- input and output. Input refers to *"what enters the system"* and output refers to *"what leaves the system"*;

Another Example: **.** Purchase Department, interacting with its vendors is an example of open system.

On the contrary, closed system refers to a system that do not interacts with it's external environment. ***Example:*** a person taking the toll ticket when he enters the toll road and pays the tax when he exit out toll road. Another ***example*** can be an e-mail sent by you to a friend or sister...

- **STATIC SYSTEM VS DYNAMIC SYSTEM**

Static system refers to a physical system that is fixed and do not adapt to changes in environment. ***Example:*** Table, Computer.

On the contrary, Dynamic system refers to a physical system that continues on changing from time to time. ***Example:*** Finance department, Share Market.

- **DETERMINISTIC OR PROBABILISTIC SYSTEM:-**

A deterministic system is one in which the occurrence of all events is perfectly predictable. In a deterministic system, every action, produces a reaction, and every reaction, in turn, becomes the cause of subsequent reactions e.g. Electronic computers, Universe.

On the contrary, *Probabilistic system* is one in which the occurrence of events cannot be perfectly predicted.

e.g. Warehouse and it's contents, Miracles, Radioactive decay etc

newtopic System Approach to an Organization:-

The "Systems Approach" establishes performance optimization by assuring system components operate efficiently and effectively in concert with each other.

System approach integrates both ***holism*** and ***reductionism.*** **.** It was first proposed under the name of "***General System Theory***" by the biologist ***Ludwig von Bertalanffy***.

According to this approach, organization is a system that consist a number of subsystems. All the subsystems interact with each other as well as also interact with the external environment like suppliers, vendors etc. Each subsystem accepts some input and gives output accordingly. The output produced from one subsystem can act as input to another subsystem. But all the subsystems work in a united manner to achieve common objective of the organization.

The effectiveness of an organization can be measured with respect to its input, transformations (process), output (or feedback) and interrelationships.

System approach is suitable for an organization because Systems-oriented managers anticipate as many crises as possible and have plans in place to deal with them. They apply a framework when solving problems or implementing change that incorporates a broad range of perspectives and integrates a variety of employee tools.

Example: System Approach to Hospitality Industry: The main purpose of hospitality industry is to provide best possible services to the guest, in order to attain guest satisfaction. According to this approach, a hotel is a system that may consists of numerous departments like Front Office, Housekeeping, Food and Beverage Service etc. that works in a coordinating manner to achieve a common objective i.e. guest satisfaction or providing superior quality of services to guest. Practically speaking, this approach is not implemented by all the hotels successfully. One of the hotel company named as Ritz-Carlton Hotel Company is an example of a hospitality business that has been successful in implementing systems approaches without losing its sense of urgency in guest satisfaction. The main reason behind the failure of system approach to most hospitality organization can be illustrated by the following phrase-

"Assume that four people are sitting in a sinking rowboat. Two of the people are high and dry at the bow of the boat, while the other two are desperately bailing water at the stern. One of the people at the bow says to the other, "I'm glad the problem is not on our end."

This phrase illustrates disconnect (or lack of communication) that can occur between causes and symptoms in hospitality organizations that are seeking to improve service quality. This disconnect can occur between leaders or departments at the senior level and those on the front lines, or between department leaders and the people who come directly into contact with guests.

System Approach to MIS:-

The term ***"systems"*** is derived from the Greek word ***"synistanai***," which means ***"to bring together or combine."*** The systems approach emerged as scientists and philosophers identified common themes in the approach to managing and organizing complex systems. *Four major concepts underlie the systems approach:*

- ***Specialization:*** A system is divided into smaller components allowing more specialized concentration on each component.
- ***Grouping:*** To avoid generating greater complexity with increasing specialization, it becomes necessary to group related disciplines or sub-disciplines.
- ***Coordination:*** As the components and subcomponents of a system are grouped, it is necessary to coordinate the interactions among groups.
- ***Emergent properties:*** Dividing a system into subsystems (groups of component parts within the system), requires recognizing and understanding the "emergent properties" of a system; that is, recognizing why the system as a whole is greater than the sum of its parts. For example, two forest

stands may contain the same tree species, but the spatial arrangement and size structure of the individual trees will create different habitats for wildlife species. In this case, an emergent property of each stand is the wildlife habitat.

The systems approach considers two basic components: elements and processes. *ELEMENTS* are measurable things that can be linked together. They are also called objects, events, patterns, or structures. *PROCESSES* change elements from one form to another. They may also be called activities, relations, or functions. In a system the elements or processes are grouped in order to reduce the complexity of the system for conceptual or applied purposes.

MIS is a formal system for providing management with accurate and timely information necessary for decision making.

System Control

According to Jemmy Allen (1998),

"Controlling is directly related to planning. The controlling process ensures that plans are being implemented properly. In the functions of management cycle - planning, organizing, directing, and controlling - planning moves forward into all the other functions, and controlling reaches back. Controlling is the final link in the functional chain of management activities and brings the functions of management cycle full circle. "

Control is the process through which standards for performance of people and processes are set, communicated, and applied. The control process is a continuous flow between measuring, comparing and action. Effective control systems use mechanisms to monitor activities and take corrective action, if necessary. The supervisor observes what happens and compares that with what was supposed to happen. He or she must correct below-standard conditions and bring results up to expectations. Effective control systems allow supervisors to know how well implementation is going. Control facilitates delegating activities to employees. Since supervisors are ultimately held accountable for their employees' performance, timely feedback on employee activity is necessary.

A control chart displays the results of measurements over time and provides a visual means of determining whether a specific process is staying within predefined limits. As long as the process variables fall within the acceptable range, the system is in control. Measurements outside the limits are unacceptable or out of control. Improvements in quality eliminate common causes of variation by adjusting the system or redesigning the system.

Examples:

- **Time controls** relate to deadlines and time constraints.
- **Material controls** relate to inventory and material-yield controls.
- **Equipment controls** are built into the machinery, imposed on the operator to protect the equipment or the process.
- **Cost controls** help ensure cost standards are met. Employee performance controls focus on actions and behaviors of individuals and groups of employees. Examples include absences, tardiness, accidents, quality and quantity of work.

- **Financial controls** facilitate achieving the organization's profit motive. One method of financial controls is budgets. Budgets allocate resources to important activities and provide supervisors with quantitative standards against which to compare resource consumption. They become control tools by pointing out deviations between the standard and actual consumption.
- **Operations control** methods assess how efficiently and effectively an organization's transformation processes create goods and services. Methods of transformation controls include Total Quality Management (TQM) statistical process control and the inventory management control. Statistical process control is the use of statistical methods and procedures to determine whether production operations are being performed correctly, to detect any deviations, and to find and eliminate their causes.

1. Steps in the Control Process

There are four steps in the control process: establishing performance standards, measuring actual performance, comparing measured performance against established standards, and taking corrective action.

***Step 1.* Establish Performance Standards:** Standards are created when objectives are set during the planning process. It is a precise, explicit statement of expected results from a product, service, machine, individual, or organizational unit. It is usually expressed numerically and is set for quality, quantity, and time.

***Step 2.* Measure Actual Performance.** Supervisors collect data to measure actual performance to determine variation from standard. Personal observation, statistical reports, oral reports and written reports can be used to measure performance.

Computers are important tools for measuring performance. In fact, many operating processes depend on automatic or computer-driven control systems. Computers give supervisors direct access to real time, unaltered data, and information. On line systems enable supervisors to identify problems as they occur. Database programs allow supervisors to query, spend less time gathering facts, and be less dependent on other people. Supervisors have access to information at their fingertips. Employees can supply progress reports through the use of networks and electronic mail. Statistical reports are easy to visualize and effective at demonstrating relationships. Written reports provide comprehensive feedback that can be easily filed and referenced.

***Step 3.* Compare Measured Performance Against Established Standards.** Comparing results with standards determines variation. Some variation can be expected in all activities and the **range of variation** - the acceptable variance - has to be established. **Management by exception** lets operations continue as long as they fall within the prescribed control limits. Deviations or differences that exceed this range would alert the supervisor to a problem.

***Step 4.* Take Corrective Action.** The supervisor must find the cause of deviation from standard. Then, he or she takes action to remove or minimize the cause. If the source of variation in work performance is from a deficit in activity, then a supervisor can take immediate corrective action and get performance back on track. Also, the supervisors can opt to take basic corrective action, which would determine how and why performance has deviated and correct the source of the deviation. Immediate corrective action is more efficient, however basic corrective action is the more effective.

An *example* of the control process is a ***thermostat.***

Standard: The room thermostat is set at 68 degrees.

Measurement: The temperature is measured.

Corrective Action: If the room is too cold, the heat comes on. If the room is too hot, the heat goes off.

2. Types of Controls

- **Feedforward controls:** These controls focus on operations before they begin. Their goal is to prevent anticipated problems. An example of feedforward control is scheduled maintenance of kitchen equipments of a hotel. Regular maintenance feeds forward to prevent problems. Other examples include safety systems, training programs, and budgets.
- **Concurrent controls:** These controls are applied to processes as they are happening. Concurrent controls enacted while work is being performed include any type of steering or guiding mechanism such as direct supervision, automated systems (such as computers programmed to inform the user when they have issued the wrong command), and organizational quality programs.
- **Feedback controls** : These type of controls focus on the results of operations. They guide future planning, inputs, and process designs. Examples of feedback controls include timely (weekly, monthly, quarterly, annual) reports so that almost instantaneous adjustments can be made.

new topic Handling System Complexity:-

According to Charle Perrow,

"The systems have become so complex & closely coupled that accidents are normal and cannot be assured against. These components are tightly coupled, so that failure propagates through the system quickly (& perhaps not visibly)

A System is complex when it is composed of a group of related subsystems for which the degree and nature of the relationships is imperfectly known. In other words, system complexity increases when the interaction between the subsystems occurs in an unexpected sequence. Increasing complexity is the biggest cause of cost-overruns. The higher the system complexity, the harder it is to upgrade, maintain, and develop the system.

e.g. Transportation systems are complex and dynamic i.e. they vary in space & time; therefore modeling the entire system is just a difficult task.

• Examples of System Complexity

1. ***Project complexity:*** Project complexity can involve both technical and organizational complexity. Technical complexity arises because a system has to interact with a large number of other applications, inter-

dependencies, and the complexity of the interfaces to other systems. Technical complexity raises following problems-

a. difficulty of estimating the resources that must be allocated to a project

b. exposing the project to feasibility, budget, and scheduling risks.

Therefore, software project managers tend to accept complexity as a known driver of project risk.

2. ***Organizational complexity:*** *Organizational complexity is the amount of differentiation that exists within different elements constituting the organization.* It grows with the number of departments or organizations involved in and affected by the system. Organizational complexity raises coordination challenges and exposes the development process to unpredictable coordination failure.

   Organizational complexity is considered a response to complexity with the internal or external environment. The internal environment consists of the processes and technologies. The external environment includes customers, markets, suppliers and competitors etc. For example: a restaurant have low complexity whereas a five-star hotel have high complexity due to large number of departments and various kinds of job specifications and so on.

   When *organization complexity is low,* organizational members can succeed in their daily routine. When *organization complexity is high,* organizational members are forced to constantly solve existing problems and scan new ones. When *organization complexity is moderate,* organization members learn new skills & solve problems within the limitations of their ability to process information. ***e.g.*** "Learning" is reported to be low in steel industry, as it has low complexity whereas learning is more emphasized in computer firms having high complexity (due to complex technology)

   For Handling organizational complexity, an organization may follow the given steps-

   - Smoothing input and output transactions.
   - Organization will segment itself to make it's sub-environments relatively homogeneous ***e.g.*** division of products for effective marketing
   - An organization will adopt rules as a means to coordinate the less complex aspects of it's internal and external environment.

newtopic Post Implementation Problem to a System:-

Post-Implementation Review is used to evaluate the effectiveness of the system or project functionality after the system has been in production (or operation) for a period of time (generally 6 months).

Post Implementation includes Operation and Evaluation. It is generally used to assess the risk elements involved in a system. It is the final activity of a system design process. A detailed plan should be developed prior to post-implementation review.

System implementation can be faultier if the new system encounters problems once installed. Every new system will have bugs, but thorough acceptance testing must be completed in order to minimize post-installation problems. After implementation, system or project is shifted into "maintenance" phase.

The post-implementation review process establishes conclusions about whether the project solved

the business problem by achieving the stated business goals and objectives. In other words, Post implementation review is an opportunity to highlight what worked well and what did not do to make possible recommendations for improvement i.e. it is used to realize the changes projected by implementation.

A post-implementation project report can be a good tool to quickly help senior management ascertain whether a project achieved it's objectives. Post implementation project report describes actual events, problems, issues and results.

Some of the common objectives of post-implementation review are stated below-

- Provide feedback from department employees concerning satisfaction or difficulties with the implementation.
- Providing training to the employees
- Identifying and solving issues regarding successful implementation of the system
- To develop various metrics in order to measure the system performance. It may include metrics for- identifying the number of people working on a project, comparison of the projected budget to the actual project expense etc.

10

Management Information System

Introduction:

It refers to Management Information System or Management Information Services.

DEFINITION & CONCEPT

According to Davis-

"MIS an integrated man/machine system for providing information to support the operation, management, and decision-making functions in an organization'

"MIS refers broadly to a computer-based system that provides managers with the tools for organizing, evaluating and efficiently running their departments. In order to provide past, present and prediction information; an MIS can include software that helps in decision making, data resources such as databases, the hardware resources of a system, decision support systems, people management and project management applications, and any computerized processes that enable the department to run efficiently. "

"A management information system is an organized procedure that provides past, present, and prediction information. It plays nowadays an important and decisive role in the planning and decision-making by furnishing uniform and timely information. Modern management information systems are computer-based systems with built in automation for data retrieval, data capture, selection, sort, data processing, and data analysis and data exchange."

- (Walter J. Kennevan)

"MIS is an information system that integrates data from all the departments it serves and provides operations and management with the information they require. Within companies and large organizations, the department responsible for computer systems is sometimes called the MIS department."

Thus A Management Information system is -

✓ an integrated user-machine system

✓ for transforming data into useful information

✓ to support the operations, management, analysis and decision making functions

✓ in an organization.

- **ELABORATION OF DEF.**

➢ *The output of an MIS is information that sub serves managerial functions. However, if a system provides information to persons who are not managers, we will not consider it as a part of MIS.*

Example:

1. Processing a lot of data (in an organization) in order to provide processed data (i.e. information) to various govt. regulatory agencies. Such a system may have interfaces with an MIS, but would not be a part of MIS. **i.e.** preparing salary disclosures and excise duty statements.
2. Using computer aided design system for engineering purposes.

➢ *An MIS deals with information that is systematically & routinely collected in accordance with a well-defined set of rules. However, the information that may be very systematically collected but not collected on a regular basis will not be a part of MIS.*

Example:

1. Information collected for managerial planning significance.
2. Information collected to enhance the potential of a new product.

➢ *The information provided by an MIS assists managers to make planning and control decisions. However, the information that supports operations and has no managerial decision-making significance will not be a part of MIS.*

Every organization has to perform certain operations in order to function. Therefore, for performing these operations, an organization must make plans for them. Also, an organization must control the operations according to the plans and targets developed in the planning process **i.e.** the organization is required to know if the operations are in-line with targets and if not, the organization must make decisions to correct or revise the plans.

Example:

Information assisting managers:

A car manufacturer must decide on how many and what type of cars to make next month. The car manufacturers must know if manufacturing operations are in-line with targets and if not he must make decisions to revise the plans.

Information having no managerial decision-making significance:

If the car manufacturers has a system that provides information to the workers on the top floor about the job that needs to be done on a particular batch of material. *On the contrary, if the system provides information of productivity,* machine utilization or rejection rates etc, then it would be considered as a part of MIS.

➢ *An MIS includes all the ingredients that are employed in providing information support to managers in making planning & control decisions.*

e.g. Managers often Managers use historical data of all the organization's activities as well as current status data to make planning and control decisions. Such data comes from a database which is contained in files (paper or electronic) maintained by the organization. Thus, database is an essential component of MIS. Besides this, manual procedures and computer hardware, software and operation research models employed to collect and process data also forms part of the MIS.

Components Utilized by MIS

1. **Computer H/W**
   a. Hardware refers to physical computer equipment and associated devices. Hardware must provide five major functions-
   i. Input or entry of data
   ii. Output results
   iii. Secondary storage for data and programs
   iv. Central processor
   v. Communication

   b. ***Example:*** Keyboard, Mouse, Speech Recognizer, Touch Screens etc.

2. **Computer S/W**
   a. Software is a broad term given to the instructions that direct the operation of the hardware. The software can be classified into -
      i. System software (***e.g*** Operating systems, Compilers etc)
      ii. Application software (***e.g.*** Ms-Office, Fidelio, Micros etc)

3. **Manual Procedures**
   a. Formal operating procedures are physical components because they exist in a physical form such as a manual or instruction booklet. Three types are-
      i. User instructions (for users of the application to record data, employ a terminal to enter or retrieve data or use the result)
      ii. Instructions for preparation of input by data preparation personnel.
      iii. Operating instructions for computer operations personnel

4. **Models**
   a. Data usually needs to be processed and presented in a systematic manner.
   b. The well-prepared data models are then used for analysis, planning, control and decision making.
   c. ***Example***: Data Model of a Reservation System

5. **A database**

   a. The database contains all data utilized by application software. The database is a collection of data related to an organization. So, for the success of MIS, it should be well designed by a professional Database Architect.

6. **GUI Interface**

   a. A Graphical User Interface (GUI) is important in the success of a MIS.

   b. It refers to the visual data-entry screen or environment through which end users perform database related operations like inserting data, deleting or updating data and so on.

   c. In designing a GUI for a MIS, you need to consider the following-

      i. Make use of pictorial forms

      ii. Extensibility so that new functionality can be added to the system.

      iii. Make use of logically designed forms and reports

      iv. Communication (the screen should be user friendly so that user feel interacting with the interface. This can be achieved using dialogs and message boxes etc)

7. **Operations Personnel**

   a. Operations Personnel includes computer operators, system analysts, programmers, data preparation personnel, data administrators, data architects etc.

newtopic MIS Concept

A Management Information System (MIS) converts data from internal & external sources into information in an appropriate form to managers at different levels in an organisation to enable them to make effective decisions or to track or control the performance of their employees.

Example: a Bar Manager of a hotel needs to decide how many bottles of rum is required in a week To accomplish this he could see-

- The number of rum bottles currently in stock
- Orders to be served to guest
- sales of rum bottle last week
- sales of rum bottle last year (during a particular month)

MIS has been described as a pyramid structure. Each level of information processing may make use of data provided for lower levels; but new data may also be introduced.

• Description of Pyramid Layers

Layer 1 Or Top Layer: Information required by senior Managers (like General Manager of a hotel) for strategic and policy planning and decision making (or forecasting)

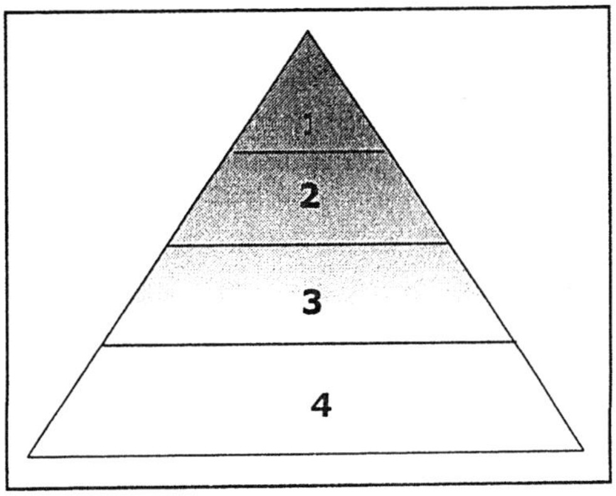

Layer 2: Management Information for tactical planning and decision making. Middle managers (like Head of the departments of a hotel) often require tactical information to take certain decisions. Data models can be used by them to obtain tactical information. **e.g.** monthly sales report of a hotel

Layer 3: Management information for operational planning, decision making and control. Operations managers (like Supervisors of a hotel) are usually responsible for tracking day-to operations and transactions in an organization, in order to take further decisions. **e.g.** Obtaining information about number of rooms sold in a day, controlling inventory etc.

Layer 4 Or Bottom Layer : It deals with the Management Information of Transaction processing & inquiry response **e.g.** Room occupancy report generated on daily basis. This layer constitutes people like Receptionist, Reservationist, Bell boy, Attendants etc.

> ***For Example:*** In a football club, the *Chairman* has a strategic role, the *Coach* has a tactical role, the team *Captain* has an operation role.

To conclude - the pyramid structure is a traditional one. The recent trend is to have a less hierarchical structure in organizations in order to reduce layers of management. In the "***Pyramid Structure***", roles are clearly defined. Each layer of the pyramid is responsible to the layer above.

But, Pyramid Structure have following problems -

- This type of organization can be slow to change
- Decisions can be slow to make and even slower to be implemented.
- Senior staff can be remote

A "***horizontal structure***" has become increasingly popular. ***Example:*** Most businesses are divided into "departments i.e. production, sales and marketing, personnel (responsible for training and hiring), finance and accounting." There are fewer layers and problems can, therefore, be moved up the line more quickly. More people are directly answerable to the top management and, therefore, more decisions are taken by middle management. Employees have more responsibility and this leads to greater motivation.

Limitations of Horizontal Structure:

- Individual departments can become isolated from each other.
- Fewer levels in the organization may mean fewer promotion opportunities.

newtopic MIS INVOLVES

1. **Data Gathering:** Data pertinent to the operations of the organization are gathered from the external and internal sources.

2. **Data Entry:** The above data is entered and stored in a database at the information processing core of the system.
3. **Data Transformation:** Data is transformed into useful information through the application support staff and other system users.
4. **Information Utilisation:** This useful information is retrieved as needed by management and technical personnel and applied to a wide variety or decisions related to the conduct of organizational operations.

Objectives of MIS

1. To provide requisite information support for managerial functions within the organization.
2. To make available, right information at the right place at the right time at the lowest cost.
3. To ensure that wrong and unwanted information is not generated, the condition of data overload is avoided.

Facts about MIS or Characteristics of MIS

1. Information provided to persons who are not managers will not be a part of MIS.
2. The information that may be very systematically collected but not collected on a regular basis will not be a part of MIS.

   e.g. Information collected to enhance the potential of a new product.

3. The information that supports operations and has no managerial decision making significance will not be a part of MIS
4. A MIS should be flexible enough to allow different users to access data in different ways.
5. It should be capable of supporting users with a range of skills and knowledge.
6. It should be quick and easy to use.
7. It should protect the user against "*information overload*".

Advantages of MIS

1. MIS is used to keep track of the flow of information within an organization.
2. MIS is involved in the planning stages of a project to avoid having to retrofit Hardware and software in order to make everything work.
3. Reduction of user frustration levels by having support within reach in the MIS department.
4. Reduction of labor costs for updating software maintaining licenses, warranties & maintenance of equipment.
5. Provides justification for additional staff or to maintain existing staff.

Limitations of MIS

1. **Unsuitability for certain tasks :**

   There are many managerial roles such as leading, negotiating and disturbance handling that cannot be accomplished with an information system.

2. **Unrealistic Expectations :**

   When a new information system is installed, it is natural the organization have few expectations with respect to the new system's contributions to it's success. However, it is natural for people to expect too much from technological devices, but they should understand that technology cannot replace the manager, it can only support and facilitate the tasks of manager.

3. **Information not Tailored to user needs :**

   A major problem arises when new and on-going systems does not exactly meet user needs. As managerial problems change, the kind of problem-solving information needed continues to change as well. Thus, it is quite obvious that systems specialists give continuous attention to matching the system's information to the needs of the operating managers.

4. Poor identification of information needs
5. Poor communication between management and people of the system

MIS SERVICES

The MIS offers the user organization a wide range of possible services for all levels and for all functional areas. The MIS provides line managers with quality, accurate, timely complete and relevant information through-

1. **Routine Performance Reports:** These are usually scheduled summaries, such as periodic sales reports, production reports, quality control reports, inventory control reports and wide range of accounting reports.

- **Examples of reports used in hotels :** Maintenance Report and Annual Appraisal Report

2. **Exception Reports :** These are produced only when actual performance deviates from predetermined standards. These are generally used for controlling activities such as production output, machine efficiencies, product quality etc.
   - **Examples of reports used in hotels :** Guest History Report and Department Expenditure Statement
3. **On-demand Reports:** These are occasional reports that are requested by management. e.g. A purchasing manager may ask for a report on stock status of a item or on a list of outstanding orders.
   - **Examples of reports used in hotels :** Guest History Report and Department Expenditure Statement
4. **Predictive Reports :** These are based on ***"what-if"*** analysis and are used in strategic analysis and planning activities. The MIS software is used to simulate past, present and future conditions.
   - **Examples of reports used in hotels :** Sales Forecasting Report and Reservation Forecast report

newtopic Steps of MIS establishment or Implementation

To be able to establish a MIS, you need to acquire the resources (computer-hardware and software) and to acquire or develop instructions (MIS) to direct the work. The MIS development involves following steps-

1. ***Conceptualization:*** The information needs of an organization are defined. Few alternative solutions are designed to meet the required needs. Finally, selection of an optimal solution is made. In other words, the objectives are defined.
2. ***Detailed assessment and design:*** The organization carefully assesses systems under consideration for purchase. If it has decided to modify an existing system or to develop a custom system, it will thoroughly address design issues.
3. ***System development and implementation:*** The organization develops (or refines or adapts) the system it has chosen. Implementation of the new system requires the following steps-
   a. Purchase and set-up of hardware
   b. Choice of appropriate software (purchasing *"off-the-shelf"* software or customizing commercial software or developing custom 'in house' software)
   c. Preparation and revision of documentation

d. Configuration of the system (integration of hardware, database, software along with appropriate controls)

e. Testing

f. Staff training

4. ***System maintenance and MIS audits:*** In this final step, the organization focuses on post-implementation issues like system maintenance, modifications, and periodic audits to ensure that the system is functioning efficiently,

newtopic Factors Facilitating Implementation of MIS :-

- Involvement of top management in the computerization effort, in defining the purpose and goal of computers within the organization.
- Selection of an EDP Manager who has the political skills to involve managers in choosing application areas, identifying information needs and designing reports.
- A computer staff having good skills in computers, management and operation research.
- A balanced expenditure on hardware and software.

newtopic Criteria for MIS

Crowe and Avison (1982) suggested five criteria for an MIS:

1. ***Relevance:*** Information should be relevant to the individual decision-makers at their level of management.
2. ***Accuracy:*** The database from which information is extracted should be up-to-date, contextually relevant and validated.
3. ***Timeliness***: The information should be provided at the time required.
4. ***Management by exception:*** Managers should get precise information pertaining to factors critical to their decision making.
5. ***Adaptability:*** The information system should have an in-built capability for re-design so that it can suitably adapt to environmental changes and changing information requirements.

newtopic Strategies for determining MIS design

MIS design should be specific to an organization with respect to its structure and operations.

Following Strategies are suggested by Bluemental (1969)for determining MIS design :

- ***Organization-chart approach:*** Using this approach, the MIS is designed based on the traditional functional areas, such as finance, administration, production, R&D etc. These functional areas define current organizational boundaries and structure.

- ***Integrate-later approach:*** Largely a ***laissez faire*** approach, it does not conform to any specified formats as part of an overall design. There is no notion of how the MIS will evolve in the organization. Such an MIS becomes difficult to integrate. In today's environment - where managers demand quick and repeated access to information from across sub-systems - the integrate-later approach is becoming less and less popular.
- ***Data-collection approach:*** This approach involves collection of all data which might be relevant to MIS design. The collected data are then classified. This classification influences the way the data can be exploited usefully at a later stage. The classification therefore needs to be done extremely carefully.
- ***Database approach:*** A large and detailed database is developed, stored and maintained. The database approach is more and more accepted for two main reasons: first, because of data independence it allows for easier system development, even without attempting a complete MIS; and, second, it provides management with immediate access to information required.
- ***Top-down approach:*** The top-down approach involves defining the information needs for successive layers of management. If information required at the top remains relatively stable in terms of level of detail, content and frequency, the system could fulfill MIS requirements (Zani, 1970). The usefulness of this approach depends on the nature of the organization. It can be suitable for those organizations where there is a difference in the type of information required at the various levels.
- ***Total-system approach:*** In this approach the interrelationships of the basic information are defined prior to implementation. Data collection, storage and processing are designed and done within the framework of the total system. This approach can be successfully implemented in organizations which are developing.

new topic Approaches For Installing MIS

1. **Crash or Direct Installation :** It requires that the new system replace the old system entirely all at once.
2. **Parallel Installation :** In this, the new system is installed and operated alongside the old one. The old system is deactivated until the new one works satisfactorily.
3. **Pilot Installation :** It is first installed in small part of the organization on a trial basis. The rest of the organization uses the old system until the pilot system proves satisfactory.
4. **Phased Installation :** It allows the organization to implement the new system segment by segment.

Role of MIS

1. Role of MIS in Planning
2. Role of MIS in Control
3. Role of MIS in
4. Role of MIS in Business Organization
5. Role of MIS in Hospitality Industry
6. Role of MIS at Management Levels

1. Role of MIS in Planning:- .

1. Planning is one of the vital functions of management.
2. Planning set the direction for future actions. Planning is defined as a process of establishing the goals and objectives as well as identification and selection of policies, strategies and actions need to achieve the objective.
3. Planning consists of the following phases-
   a. Objective setting
   b. Formulation and Evaluation of Alternatives
   c. Selection of Optimum Alternative by Decision Making
   d. Implementation
   e. Feedback
   f. Control

In all the phases of the planning process, information support is required. The information support is provided through MIS

Planning activities take place at different levels in the business organization

Types of Planning	Organization Structure
1. Strategic Planning....................	Top Management
2. Tactical Planning.....................	Middle Management
3. Operational Planning.................	Operational Management

Strategic Planning :-

❖ The planning activities that are undertaken at the top management level of the business organization are identified as **"Strategic Planning".**

- The planning horizon of the top management is measured in years. The typical planning horizon of the top management is ***3 years, 5 years*** and in some cases ***10 years*** as well.
- Such planning include the plans for making available required resources in terms of money, materials, manpower etc
- Support of MIS in strategic planning is often manifested through projections, trend analysis and simulation models.

Tactical Planning :-

- Planning activities undertaken by the middle management layer of the business organization is termed as Tactical Planning.
- The planning horizons in case of tactical plans are 12 months or 18 months.
- The tactical plans include activities such as new product introductions, achieving market growth, sales plans etc.

Operational Planning :-

- Planning activities that are carried out at the operational level of the business organization are termed as operational plans.
- The planning horizon for such operational plans is often expressed in terms of days or weeks.
- The operational plan, like tactical plans are oriented towards facilitating monitoring and control.
- Such plans include machine loading plan, distribution plans, inventory plans, monthly sales planning etc.

2. Role of MIS in Control

1. Control can be defined as a systematic effort by business management to compare the performance against predetermined standards, plans or objectives
2. The working of control activities in business organizations can be explained through the model called as **"Feedback Control Mechanism".**
3. Feedback Control mechanism has four stages-
   a. Performance Standard
   b. Measurement
   c. Comparison
   d. Corrective Action
4. The stage of performance standard is closely linked with planning activities. The plans provide the performance standard against which the actual performance is to be compared.
5. Based on the comparison between the performance standard and the measured performance, the need for corrective action is identified.
6. In the entire process of this measurement, comparison, initiation of corrective action and evaluating the effects of corrective actions was supported by management information systems.

3. Role of MIS in Business Organization:-

1. Management Information Systems (MIS) is important because all businesses have a need for information. The task before businesses is to use information and technology as a tool for solving problems, and providing opportunities by increasing productivity and quality.
2. Information has always been important but it has never been so available, so current, and so overwhelming. Great strides have been made in the collection, storage, and retrieval of information. The challenge remains in the selection, analysis and interpretation of the information to produce useful intelligence that will improve decision making and productivity.
3. As we approach the end of the century and the millennium, we witness the growing importance of computerized information systems. Increasingly, businesses are realizing the importance of computerized information systems simply to remain competitive.
4. MIS provides information support at different levels or layers. These layers are-
    a. Transaction Processing
    b. Operational Control
    c. Managerial Control
    d. Strategic Planning
    e. Decision Support

In typical manufacturing organizations, the functional areas where MIS provides support are-

Marketing: The role of MIS in marketing planning and control is often manifested through Product Mix decisions, market segmentation decisions, Product Pricing decisions, market research analysis etc.

Manufacturing: The role of MIS in manufacturing is seen through production planning and control activities, manufacturing planning and scheduling, work distribution etc.

Materials: Materials MIS is observed to generate various types of reports that provide the information support for the managerial functions in materials management.

Finance: Finance MIS deals with activities such as financial and profitability ratio analysis, cost benefit analysis etc

Human Resource: MIS for human resource includes subsystems such as performance appraisal, employee development plan, training & development activities etc.

4. Role of MIS in Hospitality

1. To explain it, let's take an example of a mini-computer based information system installed in a restaurant. In a restaurant, a waiter takes an order at a table and then enters it online via one of the six terminals located in the restaurant dining room.

2. The order is routed to a printer in the appropriate preparation area: the cold-item printer if it is a salad, the hot-item printer if it is a hot sandwich or the bar printer if it is a drink.
3. A customer's meal- check listing the items ordered and the respective prices is automatically generated.
4. This ordering system eliminates the old three-carbon copy guest check system as well as any problems caused by a waiter's handwriting.
5. When the kitchen runs out of a food item, the cooks send an "out of stock" message, which will be displayed on the dining room terminals when waiters try to order that item.
6. This gives the waiters faster feedback, enabling them to give better service to the customers.
7. This system also provides up-to-the minute information on the food items ordered and breaks out percentages showing sales of each item versus total sales. This helps management plan menus according to the customer's tastes.
8. It also compares the weekly sales totals versus food costs, allowing planning for tighter cost controls.

5. Role of MIS at various Management Levels

1. A manager usually performs the following functions: - ***P***lanning, ***O***rganizing, ***S***taffing, ***D***irecting, ***C***oordinating, ***R***eporting and ***B***udgeting.
2. Infact, management is a process of achieving goals & objectives of an organization by making best utilization of resources (men & materials). Machines, money, methods and information. Management can be structured into three hierarchical levels-
    a. Top Level
    b. Middle Level
    c. Bottom Level
3. Top Management establishes the policies, long-term plans and objectives of the company as well as a budget under which the various departments will operate. These factors are passed to the Middle Management. They are translated into specific revenue, cost & profit goals. The operational level has the responsibility of producing goods and services to meet the revenue, profit & other goals to achieve the overall plans and objectives.
4. The hierarchical view of management is important for two reasons-
    a. Information needs tends to be different at different levels of management & the amount of time devoted to different levels also varies respectively.
    b. In the context of MIS, Management can be defined as a process of-
        i. Selection of objectives.
        ii. Allocation of resources.
        iii. Determining operational plans and schedules.

iv. Keeping control of progress .

v. Evaluation through feedback.

5. Thus, we take strategic decisions at the top level, tactical decisions at the middle level and operational decisions at the bottom level.

Example of a Pizza shop: A shop manager (operational) might need a daily list of all Pizzas sold. The Regional Manager (tactical) might want a weekly or monthly report showing sales figures in each region. The Marketing Manager (strategic) of the company might want to forecast sales trends over the next few years.

new topic Types of MIS

According to Mason (1981), MIS can be categorized as follows:

1. ***Databank information systems***: It refers to creation of a database by classifying and storing data which might be potentially useful to the decision-maker. The decision-maker has to determine contextually the cause and effect relationships. MIS designs based on the databank information system are better suited for unstructured decisions.
2. ***Decision-making information systems:*** It provides expert advice to the decision-maker either in the form of a single recommended course of action or as criteria for choice, given the value system prevailing in the organization. The decision-maker has just to approve, disapprove or modify the recommendation. Decision-making information systems are suitable for structured decisions. ***Examples:*** Operations research and cost-effectiveness studies.
3. ***Predictive information systems:*** It provides source and data along with predictions and inferences. The decision-maker can also enquire as to *'what if a certain action is taken?'* and whether the underlying assumptions are true. This type of MIS is useful for semi-structured decisions.
4. ***Decision-taking information systems:*** Such systems integrate predictive information and decision-making systems.

new topic Managerial Duties of Various Personnels involved in Hotels

In hotels, managerial duties vary significantly by job title or you can say designation. Some of the examples of hoteliers involved in a hotel and their duties are listed below-

General Managers: He has the overall responsibility for the operation of the hotel. The General manager (with assistance from owner of hotel or executives of hotel chain) sets room rates, allocates funds to departments, approves expenditures, and ensures expected standards for guest service, decor, housekeeping, food quality, and banquet operations.

Resident or hotel managers: Hotel managers are responsible for the day-to-day operations of the hotel. At least one manager, either the general manager or a hotel manager, is on call 24 hours a day to resolve problems or emergencies.

Assistant managers: They help in running the day-to-day operations of the hotel. In large hotels, they may be responsible for activities like accounting, office administration, marketing and sales, purchasing, security, maintenance, and recreational facilities etc.

Executive Committee: This committee comprises of senior managers of the hotel. These managers may belong to different departments like Front Office, Housekeeping, Food and Beverage etc. They assist the general manager, in setting hotel policy and collaborate on efforts to ensure efficient guest services throughout the hotel.

Executive housekeepers: They ensure that guest rooms, meeting and banquet rooms, and public areas are clean, orderly, and well maintained. They also train, schedule, and supervise the work of housekeepers, inspect rooms, and order cleaning supplies.

Front office managers: They coordinate reservations and room allotments. They also train and direct the hotel's front desk staff. They ensure that guests are treated courteously, complaints and problems are resolved, and requests for special services are carried out.

Convention services managers: They coordinate the activities of various departments to accommodate meetings, conventions, and special events. During the meeting or event, they resolve unexpected problems and monitor activities to ensure that hotel operations are carried out smoothly.

Food and beverage managers: They supervise the ordering of food and supplies, direct service and maintenance contracts within the kitchens and dining areas, and manage food service budgets. They coordinate menus with the Executive Chef for the hotel's restaurants, lounges, and room service operations.

Catering managers: They arrange for food service in a hotel's meeting and convention rooms. They coordinate menus and costs for banquets, parties, and events with meeting and convention planners or individual clients. They coordinate with kitchen personnel to ensure appropriate food service.

Sales or marketing directors: They are responsible for the advertising and promotion of hotel operations and functions, including lodging and dining specials and special events, such as holiday or seasonal specials. They also coordinate media relations and answer questions from the press.

Human Resources Directors: They are responsible for hiring employees and providing special training programs for them. They manage the personnel functions of a hotel, ensuring that all accounting, payroll, and employee relation matters are handled in compliance with hotel policy and applicable laws.

Finance (or Revenue) Directors: They are responsible for accounting and tracking the cash-flow at the hotel. They monitor room sales and reservations, as well as decide which rooms to discount and when to offer special rates.

Computer & MIS

Using computerized MIS rather than manual is very efficient in terms of time and reliability. The system provides up-to-the minute information on the food items ordered and breaks out percentages showing sales of each item versus total sales. This helps management plan menus according to customer's tastes. The system also compares the weekly sales totals versus food costs, allowing planning for tighter cost controls. It will help in saving time and overhead of paperwork.

e.g. In a Restaurant, a waiter takes an order at a table, and then enters it online via one of the six terminals located in the restaurant dining room. The order is routed to a printer in appropriate preparation area: i.e. the cold-item printer if it is a salad, the hot-item printer if it is a hot sandwich or the bar-printer if it is a drink. A customer's meal check listing the items ordered and the respective prices is automatically generated. This ordering system eliminates the old three-carbon-copy guest check food item, the cooks send an "out of stock" message, which will be displayed on the dining room terminals when waiters try to order that item. This gives the waiters faster feedback enabling them to give better service to the customers.

11

Decision Support System

Introduction:

Practically, one of the most important human skills is decision-making (judgments and choice). Decision-making skill strongly affects the quality of life and success both at a personal level and in the context of organizations. Every decision that we make (or don't make) shapes our future.

Decision is a situation in which, you have more than one option. The option you choose can have some effect on the outcome. You can think about which option to choose. There are four things to consider when making a decision - Goals, Options, Outcomes and Probabilities.

Decision-making consists of a number of steps or stages such as: recognition, formulation, generation of alternatives, information search, selection, and action.

The study of attitudes, creativity, and problem-solving is closely associated with decision-making. If you can learn to make timely and well-considered decisions, then you can often lead your team to spectacular and well-deserved success. However, if you make poor decisions, your team risks failure and your time as a leader will, most likely, be brutally short.

new topic Decision Making Process:-

According to Harris (1980),

"Decision making is the study of identifying and choosing alternatives based on the values & preferences of the decision maker. Making a decision implies that there are alternative choices to be considered, and in such a case we want not only to identify as many of these alternatives as possible but to choose the one that best fits with our goals, objectives, desires, values and so on"

According to Baker (2001),

"Decision making should start with identification of the decision maker(s) and stakeholder(s) in the decision, reducing the possible disagreement about problem definition, repair, goals and criteria.

1. Elements of Decision Making Process:-

- **System** : System refers to an or surrounding environment or organization in which the decision has to be made.
- **Problem** : Problem refers to a situation which requires a decision. According to ***Sabherwal and*** Grover (1989)-

  "*The term problem refers to the existence of* a gap between the desired state and the existing state".

  Consequently, the decision making process aims to fill, or at least reduce, this gap and thus solve the problem.

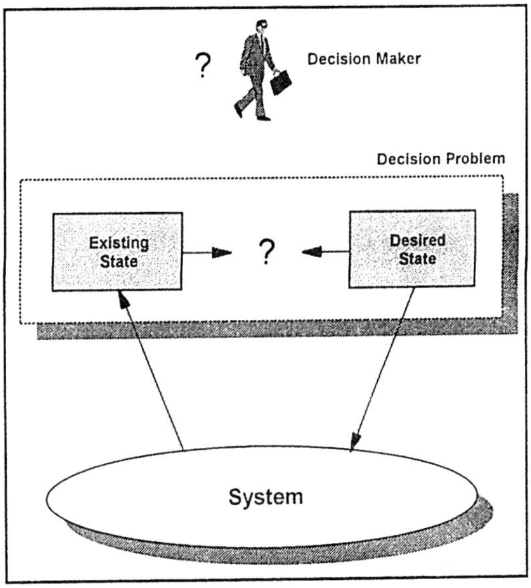

- **Decision Maker**: Decision maker may refer to an individual or group of individuals in an organization, who is required to decide upon the action or a set of actions which are to be undertaken in order to achieve certain objectives (fill or reduce the gap between the existing and desired state of the system). These objectives are provided by those to whom the decision maker is responsible.

2. Steps of Decision Making Process:-

- ***Identify the decision to be made:*** The first step is to identify the problem in a given situation for which the decision has to be made. For this a thorough analysis of the given system is required and various factors affecting the problem must be considered for taking a good decision to solve the problem.
- ***Gather relevant information:***. Most decisions require collecting pertinent information. For collecting precise and relevant information, you most know about the valuable sources of information and procedures of accessing information. You can access required information from various sources like newspaper, T.V, Journals, Books, Internet etc..
- ***Identify alternatives***: For solving a problem, you are required to consider at least two or more than two alternatives i.e. identify two or more possible paths of action. You may also use your imagination and information to construct new alternatives.
- ***Assign Priority to identified Alternatives:*** Analyze the different path of actions or alternatives logically and assign a priority order to each alternative. In other words, arrange all the identified alternatives according to a particular order of priority. You can assign priority to each alternative according to a predetermined criterion.
- ***Choose among alternatives:*** Then choose or select the best suitable alternative available. You may even choose a combination of alternatives.

- ***Take action:*** Implement the chosen alternative. Use a positive approach during the implementation process. Thus finally take a good decision that may tend to solve the actual problem.
- ***Review decision and consequences***: In this step you experience the results of your decision and evaluate whether or not it has "solved" or helped to solve the stated problem. If yes, you may stay with the decision. If no, you may repeat certain steps of the process in order to make a new decision.

3. Types of Decisions :-

1. **Structured or Programmed Decisions :** A structured decision-making process ensures that important decisions are made on time and are based on facts, research, and analysis. In other words, the decisions where the choice is made in accordance with predetermined logic or rules can be called as structured or programmed decisions.

   Successful decisions are based on reliable information and verifiable data. Adequate time should be spent to thoroughly research the options and their implications. Structured decision-making requires analysis of the four decision components - context, objective, options, & criteria. The analysis must be based on reliable data. MIS approaches have been used successfully in organizations for aiding programmable decisions.

   These are mostly repetitive and routine in nature. Computer based systems are found useful for making structured decisions as the logic and business rules can be

   incorporated in the computer programs. In business organizations, the decision made at lower levels of organization structure are generally structured decisions. The extent of predetermined rules or logical conditions goes on reducing as the decision making level rises to middle management level.

2. **Semi-structured Decisions:**

   There are certain decisions where the choice is partly as per predetermined logic or rules and partly without predetermined logic or rules. Such decisions can be considered as semi-structured decisions. Middle management is involved in semi structured or non-structured decisions. ***For example:*** when a director of a company is making a decision about the site for the proposed new plant, there would be no predetermined logical rules available for that purpose.

3. **Unstructured or non-Programmable Decisions**

   There are certain decisions where the choice is made without following any set of rules or regulations. Such decisions are termed as non-structured decisions. With unstructured decisions, for example, each decision maker may use different data and processes to reach a conclusion. In addition, because of the nature of the decision there may only a limited number of people within the organization that are even qualified to evaluate the decision. ***Example,*** Decision related to a crisis **i.e.** a civil war in a country or decisions related to such matters where conditions or situation changes recurrently.

So, when the conditions or actions do not fit the decision rules, the decision is considered as non-programmed or unstructured and is passed to higher level decision making.

Generally, unstructured decisions are made in instances in which all elements of the business environment—customer expectations, competitor response, cost of securing raw materials, etc.—are not completely understood (new product and marketing strategy decisions commonly fit into this category).

The key to support of unstructured decisions is to understand the role that individuals experience or expertise plays in the decision and to allow for individual approaches.

Semi structured and unstructured decisions can be particularly problematic for small businesses, which often have limited technological or work force resources. According to ***Gupta and Harris*** *"many decision situations faced by executives in small business are one-of-a-kind, one-shot occurrences requiring specifically tailored solution approaches without the benefit of any previously available rules or procedures". The unstructured or semi-structured nature of the decisions situations aggravates the problem of limited resources and staff expertise available to a small business executive to analyze important decisions appropriately.*

Subsequently, small businesses have increasingly turned to DSS to provide them with assistance in business guidance and management.

4. Structured Vs Unstructured Decisions:-

Structured	**Unstructured**
Established Situation	Emergent Situation
Programmable Decision	Creative Decision
Situation Fully Understood	Situation Unclear
Routine	One-shot
Specialized Mfg. Processes	General Processes

newtopic Decision Support System (DSS):-

The term DSS was born in the early 1970s. DSS have evolved from two main areas of research: the theoretical studies of organizational decision making conducted at the Carnegie Institute of Technology during the late 1950s and the technical investigations carried out at Massachusetts Institute of Technology in the 1960s

According to Scott Morton(1971)

"DSS are interactive computer-based systems which help decision makers utilize data and models to solve unstructured problems"

According to Keen & Scott Morton(1978)

"Decision support system couples the intellectual resources of individuals with the capabilities of the computer to improve the quality of decision. It is a computer based support system for management decision makers who deal with semi structured problems"

In other words, A Decision Support System is an interactive computer-based system or subsystem intended to help decision makers use communications technologies, data, documents, knowledge and/or models to identify and solve problems, complete decision process tasks, and make decisions.

DSS refers to a class of systems that gathers and presents data from a wide range of sources, typically for business purposes. DSS applications help people make decisions based on data that is culled from a wide range of sources. The emphasis is on "support" rather than on automation of decisions.

Decision making is a very important activity in business organizations. In fact, decisions making is considered as an essence of managerial tasks. Managers in business organization have to make decisions. In order to make decisions, managers need information support. If the information input is insufficient or incorrect, the decision making activity suffers and possibility of wrong decisions increase.

Many DSSs are oriented toward individual decision support. There is growing interest in DSSs that directly support distributed decision making at the group, organization, and inter-organization levels.

Decision support systems also differ with respect to the kinds of knowledge they help manage. The majority of conventional DSSs have been devised to help manage primarily descriptive and procedural knowledge. In contrast, there is a class of artificially intelligent DSSs concerned mainly with the representation and processing of reasoning knowledge.

DSS integrates decision model with information system. Decision support system enables the decision maker to retrieve data and test alternative solutions during the process of problem solving.

1. Characteristics of DSS :-

- Support for various managerial levels
- Support to individuals and groups
- Support all phases of the decision making process
- Support a variety of decision making process and styles
- Have user friendly interfaces
- The decision maker controls the decision making process
- Utilizes models for analysis
- Provides access to a variety of data sources, formats and types
- Provides support in semi-structured & unstructured situation

2. Why use DSS:-

- Improve decision quality
- Improved communication
- Cost reduction
- Increased productivity
- Time Savings

- Improved Customer & employee satisfaction
- User friendliness
- Generate more alternatives
- Promote lateral thinking
- Utilize all available data
- Examining all decision impacts

3. Types of DSS:-

- ***Data-Driven DSS***: It emphasizes using data and include Executive Information Systems (EIS)
- ***Model-Driven DSS:*** emphasize using models to support decision making. A Communications-Driven or Group decision support system (GDSS) is an interactive computer-based system intended to facilitate the solution of problems by decision makers working together as a group and includes groupware.
- ***Knowledge-Driven DSS:*** attempt to capture the knowledge of a human expert in a computer system. This computer system can then be used by less expert users.
- ***Document-Driven DSS:*** access and display text and multimedia information to support decision making.

4. Limitations of DSS :-

- Overemphasize on decision making
- Assumption of relevance
- Unintended transfer of power from decision maker to DSS

newtopic Decision Methods:-

According to Roozenburg & Eekels (1995),

Decision methods aim at helping people to make decisions. The determined values and the effectiveness of an alternative with regard to a criterion have to be aggregated into a score for the overall value of the alternative.

Methods of Decision Making-

- Ordinal Methods (or Qualitative Methods)
- Cardinal Methods (or Quantitative Methods)

newtopic Decision Tools:-

1. Pareto Analysis:

Vilfredo Pareto was an Italian economist who noted that approximately 80% of wealth was owned by only 20% of the population. Pareto analysis is a formal technique for finding the changes that will give the biggest benefits. Thus, it helps you to choose the most effective changes to make. In Pareto analysis,

Pareto principle is followed. ***For example,*** by doing 20% of work you can generate 80% of the advantage of doing the entire job.

It is useful where many possible courses of action are competing for your attention. To start the analysis, write out a list of the changes you could make. If you have a long list, group it into related changes. Then score the items or groups. The first change to tackle is the one that has the highest score. This one will give you the biggest benefit if you solve it. The options with the lowest scores will probably not even be worth bothering with because solving these problems may cost you more than the solutions are worth.

2. Paired Comparison:

Paired Comparison Analysis helps you to work out the importance of a number of options relative to each other. It is particularly useful where you do not have objective data to base this on.

This makes it easy to choose the most important problem to solve, or select the solution that will give you the greatest advantage. Paired Comparison Analysis helps you to set priorities where there are conflicting demands on your resources.

It is also an ideal tool for comparing *"apples with oranges"* - completely different options such as whether to invest in marketing, a new IT system or a new piece of machinery. These decisions are usually much harder than comparing three possible new IT systems, for example.

You can use this to compare each option with each other option, one-by-one. For each comparison, you will decide which of the two options is most important, and then assign a score to show how much more important it is.

Generally, paired comparisons can be used any time you have a set of items, issues, or concerns that you would like to rank or prioritize. The situations can be as trivial as where to dine out with the family, or as complex as allocating resources for research or even social improvements. The use of paired comparisons can be found in situations as common as getting your eyes examined for glasses. The doctor has you look at an eye chart through a number of different lenses. The goal is to find "Which of these lenses enables you to see the eye chart better? This first one or this second one?" They switch the lenses back and forth until you tell the doctor which one makes your vision better. Then the doctor goes on to another set of lenses and repeats the process until the best lenses are identified to correct your vision. The exam is a systematic process of presenting pairs of different lenses and eliminating lens options until the best lens is found.

Paired comparison is a practical technique for comparing up to; say 10-15 items (ideas, options or criteria etc.) – i.e. too many to rank easily just by inspection, but not so many that the table size becomes unmanageable. However, if a larger comparison is necessary then you can use the same principle with computer aided methods.

3. Grid Analysis:

Grid Analysis helps you to decide between several options, while taking many different factors into account. Grid Analysis is also known as Decision Matrix analysis or MAUT (Multi-Attribute Utility Theory). It is a useful technique for making a decision. Decision matrices are most effective where you have a number of good alternatives and many factors to take into account. To use this tool, perform the following options-

- The first step is to list your options (as rows) and then the factors (as columns) that are important for making the decision.
- Next work out the relative importance of the factors in your decision. This is done by allocating weight to each factor.
- Then score each option for each of the important factors in your decision. Score each option from 0 (poor) to 3 (very good). It should be noted that you can assign same score for each option for a particular factor in your decision.
- Finally add up these weighted scores for your options. The option that scores the highest will be the most appropriate one to solve a particular problem.

Example Grid Analysis Showing Weighted Assessment of How Each Type of Car Satisfies Each Factor

Factors:	Cost	Board	Storage	Comfort	Fun	Look	Total
Weights:	***4***	***5***	***1***	***2***	***3***	***4***	
Esteem	4	0	0	2	9	12	**27**
Ford	0	13	2	4	3	4	**26**
Zen	8	8	0	6	0	0	**22**
Scorpio	8	15	3	6	0	4	**36**

4. Decision Trees:

Decision Trees are used to choose between several courses of action. Decision trees are excellent tools for making financial or number based decisions where a lot of complex information needs to be taken into account. They provide an effective structure in which alternative decisions and the implications of taking those decisions can be laid down and evaluated. They help you to form a balanced picture of the risks and rewards associated with each possible course of action. Decision trees provide an effective method of Decision Making because they:

- Clearly lay out the problem so that all options can be challenged
- Allow us to analyze fully the possible consequences of a decision
- Provide a framework to quantify the values of outcomes and the probabilities of achieving them
- Help us to make the best decisions on the basis of existing information and best guesses.

Drawing a Decision Tree

Squares represent decisions, and circles represent uncertain outcomes. Write the decision or factor above the square or circle. If you have completed the solution at the end of the line, just leave it blank. You start a decision tree with a decision that needs to be made. This decision is represented by a small square towards the left of a large piece of paper. From this box draw out lines towards the right for each possible solution, and write that solution along the line. Keep the lines apart as far as possible so that you can expand your thoughts.

At the end of each solution line, consider the results. If the result of taking that decision is uncertain, draw a small circle. If the result is another decision that needs to be made, draw another square.

5. PMI (Plus, Minuses and Implications behind any decision)

Edward de Bono has given the concept of PMI. PMI stands for plus, minus, and interesting. It is a very powerful and much neglected technique. According to this technique, firstly list all the plus or good points of the idea are listed, then all the minus or bad points, and finally all the interesting points (like consequences, areas of curiosity or uncertainty, or attributes). Thus, it is a technique that is used to identify the pros and cons of an idea. PMI helps to improve the decision making quality.

This technique is used only in case if you have decided a particular course of action. To use the technique, draw up a table with three columns headed Plus, Minus and Interesting. Within the table write down all the positive points of following the course of action, all the negatives, and all the interesting implications and possible outcomes.

If the decision is still not obvious, you can then score the table to show the importance of individual items. The total score should show whether it is worth implementing the decision.

For example, suppose you are on a jury and must decide the guilt or innocence of the accused. What happens on most juries is that after the members meet in the room and choose a foreman, a preliminary vote is taken. "Let's find our where we all stand now," the foreman might say. Unfortunately, beginning a decision making session this way creates more problems than it solves. Before the jurors have had time to think over the issues or to discuss them to clarify the facts, they are asked to give their opinions. Giving an opinion is, in our society, accompanied by an ego investment, because we do not like to be wrong. As a result, each juror becomes emotionally committed to his first opinion and will very often proceed to look for arguments and facts that support this opinion (and hence defend his ego), rather than listen thoughtfully to the facts and decide the case on its merits.

If, on the other hand, the foreman said, "Instead of a preliminary vote on the case, let's work together to draw up a list, first of all the evidence that would argue for the defendant's guilt, then all the evidence that would argue for his innocence. And as we make the lists, we can also write down facts that are interesting but that don't necessarily argue either for guilt or innocence." Now all the jurors will work together, have the opportunity to ask questions and resolve doubts, consider evidence they might not otherwise have remembered, and can change their minds back and forth as many times as they want, all without a threat to their egos or their need to be correct. Notice that the PMI technique turns the jurors into collaborators, working together, instead of competitive debaters arguing for victory (rather than truth).

6. Six Thinking Hats

Dr. de Bono invented the Six Thinking Hats method in early 1980s. He organized a network of authorized trainers to introduce the Six Thinking Hats.

The six hats represent six modes of thinking and are directions to think rather than labels for thinking. That is, the hats are used proactively rather than reactively. Six Thinking Hats is a good technique for looking at the effects of a decision from a number of different points of view. The technique also helps, for example, persistently pessimistic people to be positive and creative.

Organizations such as Prudential Insurance, IBM, Federal Express, British Airways, Polaroid, and Nippon Telephone and Telegraph, possibly the world's largest company, use Six Thinking Hats.

The method promotes fuller input from more people. **According to De Bono's,** it "***separates ego from performance***". The six hats system encourages performance rather than ego defense. People can contribute under any hat even though they initially support the opposite view.

The key theoretical reasons to use the Six Thinking Hats are to:

- encourage Parallel Thinking
- encourage full-spectrum thinking
- separate ego from performance

The following is an excerpt from ***John Culvenor*** and **Dennis Else Engineering Creative Design**, 1995)

White Hat on the Hats

There are six metaphorical hats and the thinker can put on or take off one of these hats to indicate the type of thinking being used. This putting on and taking off is essential. The hats must never be used to categorize individuals, even though their behavior may seem to invite this. When done in group, everybody wear the same hat at the same time.

White Hat thinking

This covers facts, figures, information needs and gaps. "I think we need some white hat thinking at this point..." means let's drop the arguments and proposals, and look at the data base."

Red Hat thinking

This covers intuition, feelings and emotions. The red hat allows the thinker to put forward an intuition without any need to justify it. "Putting on my red hat, I think this is a terrible proposal." Usually feelings and intuition can only be introduced into a discussion if they are supported by logic. Usually the feeling is genuine but the logic is spurious. The red hat gives full permission to a thinker to put forward his or her feelings on the subject at the moment.

Black Hat thinking

This is the hat of judgment and caution. It is a most valuable hat. It is not in any sense an inferior or negative hat. It is also called negative hat. The black hat is used to point out why a suggestion does not fit the facts, the available experience, the system in use, or the policy that is being followed. The black hat must always be logical.

Yellow Hat thinking

This is the logical positive. Why something will work and why it will offer benefits. It can be used in looking forward to the results of some proposed action, but can also be used to find something of value in what has already happened.

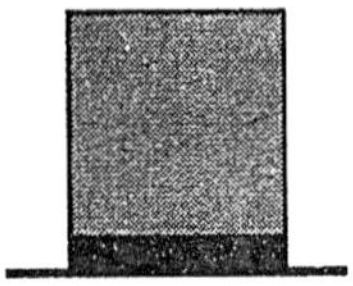

Green Hat thinking

This is the hat of creativity, alternatives, proposals, what is interesting, provocations and changes.

Blue Hat thinking

This is the overview or process control hat. It looks not at the subject itself but at the 'thinking' about the subject. "*Putting on my blue hat, I feel we should do some green hat thinking at this point*." In technical terms, the blue hat is concerned with meta-cognition.

Example:

The directors of a property company are looking at whether they should construct a new office building. The economy is doing well, and the amount of vacant office space is reducing sharply. As part of their decision they decide to use the 6 Thinking Hats technique during a planning meeting.

Looking at the problem with the White Hat, they analyze the data they have. They examine the trend in vacant office space, which shows a sharp reduction. They anticipate that by the time the office block would be completed, that there will be a severe shortage of office space. Current government projections show steady economic growth for at least the construction period.

With Red Hat thinking, some of the directors think the proposed building looks quite ugly. While it would be highly cost-effective, they worry that people would not like to work in it.

When they think with the Black Hat, they worry that government projections may be wrong. The economy may be about to enter a 'cyclical downturn', in which case the office building may be empty for a long time. If the building is not attractive, then companies will choose to work in another better-looking building at the same rent.

With the Yellow Hat, however, if the economy holds up and their projections are correct, the company stands to make a great deal of money. If they are lucky, maybe they could sell the building before the next downturn, or rent to tenants on long-term leases that will last through any recession.

With Green Hat thinking they consider whether they should change the design to make the building more pleasant. Perhaps they could build prestige offices that people would want to rent in any economic climate. Alternatively, maybe they should invest the money in the short term to buy up property at a low cost when a recession comes.

The Blue Hat has been used by the meeting's Chair to move between the different thinking styles. He or she may have needed to keep other members of the team from switching styles, or from criticizing other peoples' points.

7. COST-BENEFIT ANALYSIS:

Cost/Benefit Analysis is a powerful, widely used and relatively easy tool for deciding whether to make a change. To use the tool, firstly work out how much the change will cost to make. Then calculate the benefit you will from it.

Cost/Benefit Analysis can be carried out using only financial costs and financial benefits. You may, however, decide to include intangible items within the analysis.

Example:

A sales director is deciding whether to implement a new computer-based contact management and sales processing system. His department has only a few computers, and his salespeople are not computer literate. He is aware that computerized sales forces are able to contact more customers and give a higher quality of reliability and service to those customers. They are more able to meet commitments, and can work more efficiently with fulfillment and delivery staff.

The cost-benefit analysis involves the following general steps: Specify a list of all possible courses of actions. Assign a value (positive or negative) to the outcome for each action, and determine the probability of each outcome. Compute the expected outcome for each action. Take the action that has the best-expected outcome.

The best strategy can be found diagrammatically by plotting both benefits and costs on the horizontal axis and choosing the point where the distance between them is the greatest, as shown in the following figure:

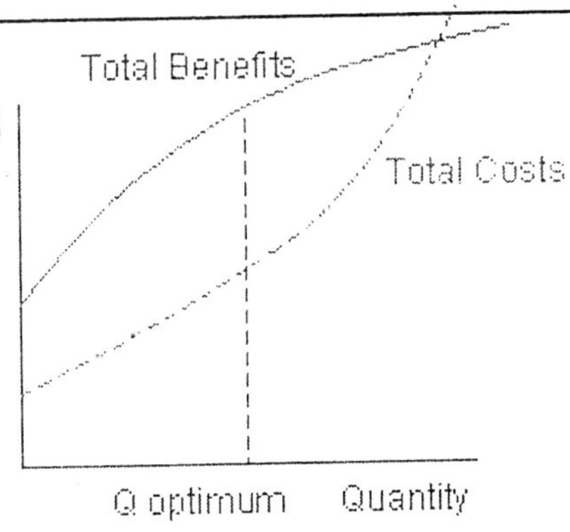

Total Benefits and Total Costs

Alternatively, one may plot net profit and find the optimal quantity where it is at its maximum as depicted by the following figure:

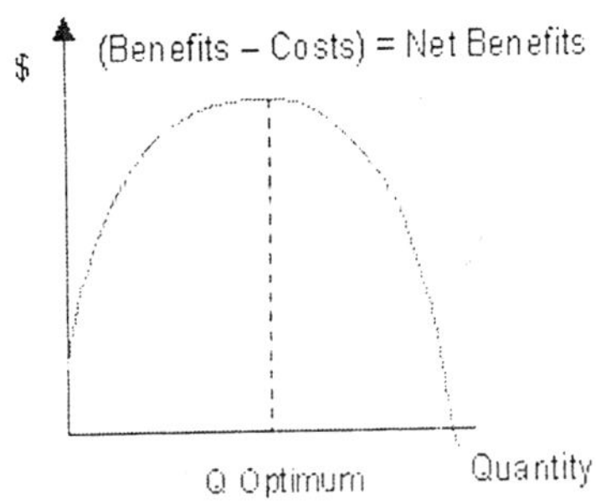

new topic Levels of Decision Making

DECISION LEVELS

We all recognize that some decisions are more important than others, whether in their immediate impact or long term significance. As a means of understanding the significance of a decision so that we can know how much time and resources to spend on it, three levels of decision have been identified:

1. ***Strategic:*** Strategic decisions are the highest level. Here a decision concerns general direction, long term goals, philosophies and values. These decisions are the least structured and most imaginative; they are the most risky and of the most uncertain outcome, partly because they reach so far into the future and partly because they are of such importance.

   For example: Decisions about what to do with your life, what to learn, or what methods to use to gain knowledge (travel, work, and school) would be strategic. Whether to produce a low priced product and gain market share or produce a high priced product for a niche market would be a strategic decision.

2. ***Tactical:*** Tactical decisions support strategic decisions. They tend to be medium range, medium significance, with moderate consequences.

   For example: If your company decided to produce a low priced product, a tactical decision might be to build a new factory to produce them at a low manufacturing cost.

3. ***Operational:*** These are every day decisions, used to support tactical decisions. They are often made with little thought and are structured. Their impact is immediate, short term, short range, and usually low cost. The consequences of a bad operational decision will be minimal, although a series of bad or sloppy operational decisions can cause harm. Operational decisions can be preprogrammed, pre-defined, or set out clearly in policy manuals.

   For example: If your tactical decision is to read some books on forestry, your operational decision would involve where to shop for the books.

   Issues should be examined and decisions should be made at all of these levels. If you discover that nearly all of your thinking and decision making is taking place at the operational level, then you are probably not doing enough strategic thinking and planning. As a result you will lead a reactive life, responding only to the forces around you and never getting control of your life, your direction or your goals.

new topic Organization Decision Making

Decisions are not made in isolation — a network of influence affects all important decisions. Who is highly influential when important decisions are made in your organization? Is it internal people? External experts? Do some managers include subordinates' inputs, while others only seek out superiors, or external experts?

According to Kieron J. Meager and Andrew Wait,

"Quality and timely decision making is essential for the success of any firm. In fact, how an organization chooses to design its decision-making rules are one of the most fundamental aspects of its internal design"

An organization is a system of resources structured by power centers to achieve some purpose within some environment. A manager is an entity having the power to structure some monetary, material, human & knowledge resources existing in an organization with the intent of pursuing some purpose of the organization with respect to it's environment. An organization's managers transform it's resources from one state to another in the interest of confirming to it's purpose within a changing environment.

Decision making in organizations is often pictured as a coherent and rational process in which alternative interests and perspectives are considered in an orderly manner until the optimal alternative is selected.

In an organization, the decision maker may want uncertainty avoidance. The behavioral theory defines the methods for uncertainty avoidance which may need to be supported by information. The information system design should recognize the practical, behavioral limitations of organization with optimization models because these models assume consistent organization. Organizational learning and adaptive behavior is important in the design of information procedures for planning and control systems because of the need to recognize changing goals and aspirations. Information system support can aid decision makers to avoid incremental decision making for policy decisions.

newtopic MIS & Decision Making

MIS stands for Management and Information System. It is a kind of system that is used to collect, organize and display information for workers and managers in an organization to support them in making decisions.

A MIS can include software that helps in decision making, data resources such as databases, the hardware resources of a system, decision support systems, people management and project management applications, and any computerized processes that enable the department to run efficiently.

A MIS manipulates data collected by a transaction processing to generate reports that workers and managers can use to make routine decisions in response to structured problems.

Various kinds of reports used in MIS are-

§ ***Detail Reports:*** lists all transactions or inventory items,

§ ***Summary Reports:*** condenses information in a detail report,

§ ***Control Line Reports:*** groups data and provides subtotals by category,

§ ***Exception reports***: calls attention to values that are outside of normal or acceptable ranges.

Generally these reports are produced on a scheduled basis (e.g., daily, weekly).

Decision support system (DSS) allows users to manipulate data directly and produce on-demand reports. These reports help managers and workers make non-routine decisions or solve semi-structured problems. A decision support system is used to make a decision model of a real-life situation which can then be manipulated to provide data used in making a decision.

1. Sources of Information for MIS

Internal information: Such information is generated by the organization. ***Examples*** are inventory levels, cash flow, customers, orders, personnel, sales. Such information is entered into system by Keyboard operators or through the use of scanners.

External information:- information about market trends, the economy, competitors, mailing lists of potential customers. This kind of information can be accessed from news sources, company publications, industry magazines, and increasingly through the World Wide Web. External information is not stored permanently in a company's MIS.

Managers and IS professionals must share responsibility for the effectiveness of information systems and share responsibility for dealing with the problems and opportunities presented by rapidly changing information technologies. Managers must consider both information systems and information technology issues when they design jobs, supervise subordinates, work with customers and suppliers, formulate strategy, develop goals and plans and implement management controls.

Within companies and large organizations, the department responsible for computer systems is sometimes called the MIS department. Other names for MIS include IS (Information Services) and IT (Information Technology).

Management Information Services Department provides hardware and software information systems and technologies that enable us to accomplish your mission. These systems and technologies provide our department personnel with information relative to their operations, support strategic planning, promote effective resource management, enhance customer service, and promote internal and external communications.

The role of MIS in decision making can be explained by taking Simon's Model of Decision Making in consideration. Simon was a central figure in several developments of twentieth-century science: behavioral economics, political science and public administration, artificial intelligence, cognitive psychology, and computer science.

DSS refers to an interactive computerized system that gathers and presents data from a wide range of sources, typically for business purposes. DSS applications are systems and subsystems that help people make decisions based on data that is culled from a wide range of sources.

For example: a national on-line book seller wants to begin selling its products internationally but first needs to determine if that will be a wise business decision. The vendor can use a DSS to gather information from its own resources to determine if the company has the ability or potential ability to expand its business and also from external resources, such as industry data, to determine if there is indeed a demand to meet. The DSS will collect and analyze the data and then present it in a way that can be interpreted by humans. Some decision support systems come very close to acting as artificial intelligence agents.

DSS applications are not single information resources, such as a database or a program that graphically represents sales figures, but the combination of integrated resources working together.

2. Simon's Model of Decision Making

According to the Simon's model, the decision making constitutes three phases-

- ***Intelligence:*** The intelligence phase is characterized by search of the environments for situations that demand decisions. Information is gathered during the Intelligence phase. In the intelligence phase, the role of MIS is seen through making the right information available at the right time and to help in processing and evaluating the information accurately and quickly.
- ***Design:*** In the design phase, different alternatives are identified, invented or developed. The viability and practicability of the alternatives is evaluated to eliminate or weed out impractible alternatives. In the design phase, the MIS provides information support for creation and evaluation of alternatives.
- ***Choice:*** It consists of only refined and practical alternatives of decision making. During the choice phase, the optimum alternative is chosen. The alternative so selected is the decision that is implemented. In general, the three phases are sequential and takes place in a logical order. However, there could be some amount of rollback that would take place on a need basis. If the decision maker in the choice phase realizes that the choices available are inappropriate or inadequate, the rollback to design phase occur. The process of decision making is some what iterative. The process of decision making involves creativity, judgment, backtracking and application of knowledge gained through education, experience and training and even intuition. Thus, MIS has a role to play in all types of decisions. The role would vary according to the type of decision. MIS bridge the environment and the decision makers through information availability. The role of MIS in decision making is manifested through activities such as optimization techniques, simulation, what-if-analysis, trend analysis and projections, cost-benefit analysis etc.

Sales Analysis is a typical example of information for decision making. The Marketing Manager uses the sales analysis reports for a variety of decisions such as target setting for subsequent period, to make decisions about the performance of salespersons, to make decisions about product strategies, introduction of new products, product withdrawal etc.

12

Enterprise Resource Planning

Introduction:

1. **ERP** refers to ***Enterprise Resource Planning.***
2. *It is the latest planning tool in an organization. (Examples of few other planning tools- MIS, EIS, CIS etc.*
3. It is an integrated software solution to all the functions of an organisation. In other words, the ERP solutions integrate operation processes and information flows in the company to synergise the resources of an organisation like men, material, money and machine etc.
4. **ERP** solutions use technology to handle business issues providing a user-friendly interface. Thus, **ERP** provides a strategic competitive advantage for the organization.
5. The ERP software actually attempts to integrate all departments and functions across a company/ organization onto a single computer system that enables various departments to easily share information and communicate with each other.
6. This integrated approach would prove to be useful, if the software is installed correctly.
7. Besides, ERP software provides several administrative tools, which are beneficial for the IS (Information System) Managers. Thus, ERP has an important role to play for ***Top management***.
8. According to the present scenario, Chartered Accountants play an important role in managing, controlling and supporting the business. It does not matter that if they have some knowledge about ERP or not. But in the future (sooner or later), when ERP solutions are implemented in organizations, then such organizations would require Chartered Accountants with the in-depth knowledge of ERP; otherwise they will be considered less important to a particular organization.

9. In the ERP implementation, ***Change Management*** occupies a very significant role. The reason being change is need in every sphere, i.e. People, Systems and Organization.

10.SI (System Integrator) is appointed by the organization to act as a single point source for all that is required to make it's ERP project successful.

Definition & Explanation

"ERP is group of integrated, comprehensive set of software products to help organization's different functional groups to work together as a single entity and service the external world, efficiently and cost effectively"

Or

"ERP Systems are a set of integrated business software modules providing operational, managerialand strategic information for improving productivity, quality and competitiveness of business"

Example to Understand the Functionality of ERP

1. Let us assume the organization to be a human body that consists of—
   a. **nervous system** (analogous to networks that link and carry data)
   b. **brain & spinal chord** (analogous to distributed servers hosting applications)
   c. **vascular system** (analogous to ERP)and
   d. **blood** (information carrier flowing on the network which assists in the information interchange)
2. The manner in which these parts function is predefined to carry out several planned activities essential to our body.
3. Likewise, ERP works similar to a nervous system and immune system, so that the organization stay fit and be competitive. ie. It helps to avoid the development of any crisis by tracking the right symptoms and intimating the immune systems in time.

Top vendors of ERP are-

1. SAP
2. PeopleSoft
3. Oracle
4. Microsoft
5. BAAN (now owned by SSA Technologies)
6. J D Edwards
7. Platinum

Role of BPR in ERP

1. BPR refers to ***Business Process Reengineering.***
2. Firms often use **ERP** as a reengineering process.
3. Reengineering process involves redesigning of business process to achieve improvements in cost, quality, service or speed of transactions.
4. Thus, BPR is a pre-requisite for implementing ERP in an organization. As it brings out deficiencies of the existing system and attempts to maximize the production and consequently the profit of the organization.
5. Business Process Engineering involves the following steps-
   a. Study the current system
   b. Design and develop new systems
   c. Define Process, organisation structure and procedures
   d. Customization of ERP software
   e. Training
   f. Implementing new system

Features of ERP

1. ERP facilitates company-wide Integrated Information system. (i.e. it integrates all the departments of a company to form a single system)
2. ERP also provides integration of companies, which are under the same management.
3. ERP allows automatic introduction of latest technologies like Electronic Fund Transfer (EFT), Electronic Data Interchange (EDI), Internet, Intranet, Video conferencing, E-Commerce etc.
4. ERP eliminates most of the business problems like Material shortages, Productivity enhancements, Customer service, Inventory problems, Quality problems etc.
5. ERP provides business intelligence tools like Decision Support Systems (DSS), Executive Information System (EIS), Reporting, Data Mining and Early Warning Systems (Robots) for enabling people to make better decisions and thus improve their business processes.

Functional Areas of ERP:-

- To enable the easy handling of the system the ERP has been divided into the following Core subsystems:
  1. Planning & Analysis
  2. Customer Order Management

3. Material Management
4. Manufacturing
5. Sales and Marketing
6. Supply
7. Purchasing
8. Finance & Accounting
9. Asset Management
10. Decision Support

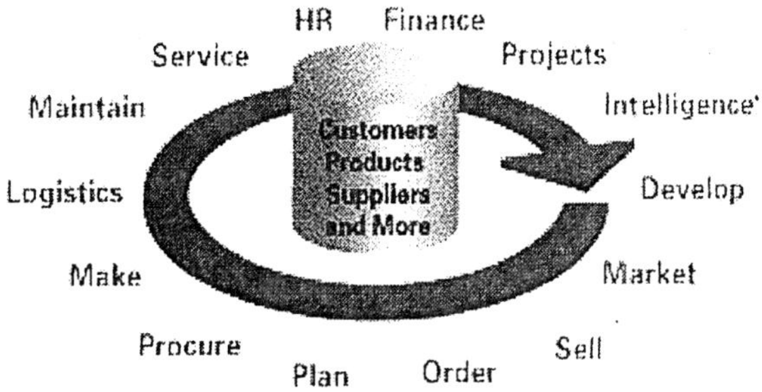

Depending on the type of busi. functional areas to manage and control them.

newtopic Need of ERP

1. **Integrated Approach:** An ERP **integrates** the information needs of various functions and processes and provides - consolidated information.

Courtesy: erpfans.com

2. **Lack of IT Talent:** The inability of organizations to retain the best IT talent as they would normally prefer to work for the IT industry.
3. **Rapid Implementation: -**
   a. Ready-made functionality
   b. Well tested
   c. High-level documentation
4. **Focus on Business Process Reengineering (BPR)**
   a. Based on 'Best Practices' resulting in cost reduction
   b. Focus is on Business Process and not on automation of activity
5. **Standardization and Built-in Integration**
   a. Integration and Feedback thus, improves decision making capability
   b. common repository of data
   c. seamless flow of information across modules
6. **User Ownership**
   a. User-friendly interfaces
   b. Configuration through user driven parameters
7. **Long Term Cost-Effectiveness**
   a. Continuous vendor upgrades
   b. Vendor training support
   c. Lower maintenance effort

new topic Evolution of ERP

1. Enterprise Application systems have evolved along with the growth in Information Technology. The key steps in the evolution are-

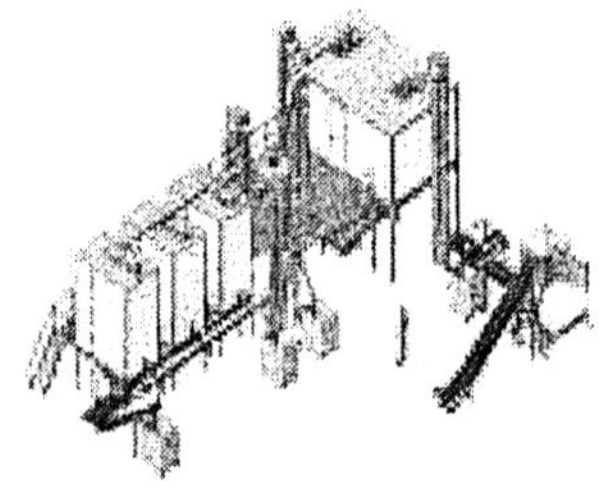

   a. MRP-I

   i. It refers to Material Requirement Planning.

   ii. It basically deals with basic inventory control, material management and production management.

   b. MRP-II

   i. It stands for Manufacturing Resource Planning.

   ii. It deals with machine loading and scheduling and some of the accounting functions in addition to material requirement planning

   iii. It is implemented by a central IT department.

   iv. The scope of this system was limited to the requirements of a single company.

MRP and MRP-II systems were fairly successful due to the advantages of organized databases, computational logic and processing power of computers.

   c. ERP :-

   i. The lacking flexibility in the above two is fulfilled by ERP.

   ii. ERP integrates corporate strategy with a latest technology to meet the changing market conditions.

   iii. ERP systems span the requirements of the entire enterprise.

   d. DEM :-

   i. It stands for Dynamic Enterprise Modeling.

   ii. It is an on-going configuration.

   iii. It will be used across WAN.

   iv. It will overcome the shortcomings of ERP

   v. It will also extend the scope beyond the enterprise to include the extended value chain.

Evolution of Enterprise Systems can be viewed as-

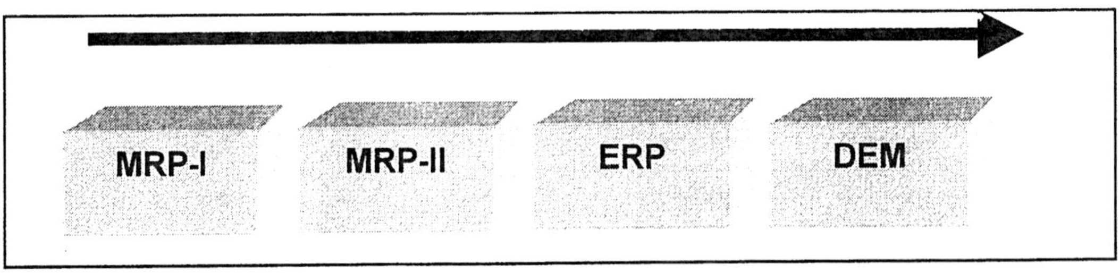

Benefits of ERP-

1. Improved decision making
2. Increased productivity
3. Improved customer services
4. Defining metrics & measuring
5. Cycle time reduction in all areas
6. Effective Cash Collection
7. Working capital reduction
8. Improves International operations by supporting a variety of tax structures, invoicing schemes, multiple currencies, multiple period accounting and languages.
9. Greater accuracy of information with detailed content and better presentation.
10. Reduces Paper work
11. Enables quick response to change in business operations and market conditions.

Selection of ERP

Evaluation of right ERP solution is the most crucial step. It is the next step followed after finishing BPR (Business process Reengineering). Evaluation and selection involves the checking of the following conditions-:

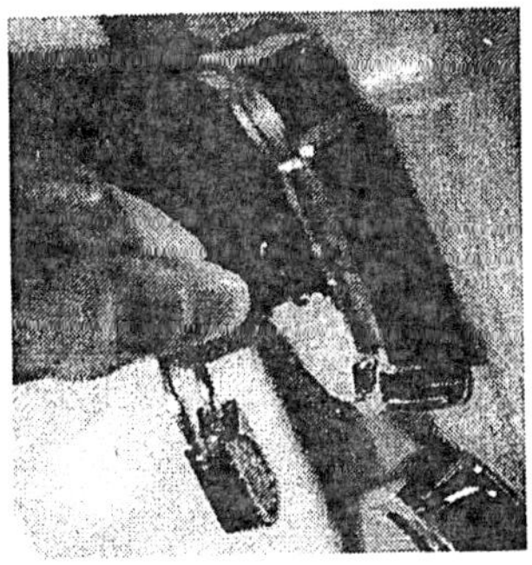

1. It should cover all functional aspects of the Business
2. It should fully integrate all the business functions and processes
3. It should introduce latest IT trends
4. The vendor of ERP solution should have customization capabilities
5. It should be financially feasible
6. It should be easily implemented
7. It should be user friendly
8. It should be flexible and scalable

Implementation of ERP

The growing Information needs of an enterprise make it imperative to improve or replace old systems. The time for implementing of an ERP package cannot be estimated correctly. Because successful implementation of ERP depends on multiple factors like size of the business organization, tendency of people to adapt change etc. Approximately, the total time required for successful implementation of an ERP package will be anything between 18 and 24 months. The implementation of ERP should be done step-by-step to achieve optimal results of it. The normal steps involved in implementation of an ERP are as below:

- Project Planning
- Analysis of Business Operations
- Business Process Reengineering
- Installation and configuration
- Project team training
- Determining Business Requirement
- Module configuration
- System interfaces
- Data conversion
- Documentation
- End user training
- Acceptance testing

newtopic Why Companies Undertake ERP

1. To Integrate financial information
2. To Integrate customer order information
3. To Standardize and speed up manufacturing processes
4. To Reduce inventory
5. To Standardize HR information
6. To Efficiently manage all the resources
7. To attain flexibility as per the trends or changes in the business

newtopic Factors Responsible for ERP Failure:-

1. Long Implementation times (users get demoralized & fatigued)
2. Communication gap (difference between the language of business users & IT professionals)
3. Inability of most applications to support continuous improvement and change management
4. Inability to take advantages of shared experiences
5. Inadequate training and documentation

Factors responsible for ERP effectiveness: -

1. Establish the Need and set the stage for ERP
2. Set Performance Measures and Review them
3. Assess Value to the Company
4. View ERP as an integrated process

Evaluating Cost of ERP Solution-

The cost of EPR solution cannot be determined correctly because it is determined by several varying factors like the amount of integration required in an organization, the number of modules to be implemented and so on. ERP cost can be segregated into-

Technical costs

- Hardware, software and communication
- Technical and functional personnel deputed for implementation
- Integration and Testing
- Customization of Modules according to changing business trends

Data creation costs

- Creation of master files
- Conversion of data from one format to another
- Data Analysis

Training costs

- Education and training of personnel in use of the ERP system
- Consultancy fees given to outside professionals/Consultants.

13

Role of IT in Hotels

Introduction:

Information technology, as the name suggests deals with the technology that is used to handle information. This information could be about hotel reservation, weather information, guest history etc. In simple words, it refers to computer technology (hardware & software) for processing and storing information. It also includes network technology that is used for transmitting and sharing information. This typically includes computers, networking equipment, telephony, video distribution equipment, multimedia and similar computer-based audiovisual equipment, electronic or digital printing equipment, and other related hardware.

Information Technology is concerned with the planning, introduction and use of IT resources for the benefit of the entire organization. Before implementing this strategy, it is important to identify the information needs of the organization. It must be led by the needs of the organization and not by the availability of the technology. The main factors that contribute to the success of an IT strategy are commitment from top management, adequate resources and sufficient training to the end users.

An organization tends to incorporate existing and future technologies in order to remain competitive. Investments in technologies and effective application of these technologies in hotel operations and services will become one of the most decisive factors differentiating successful hotel organizations globally.

Following is a quotation by ***John Diebold,*** 1984***:***

"Technological innovations have often led to changes in society. Seldom, however, have so many fundamental social issues been posed so rapidly as has been the case in the veritable explosion of information technology-computers and communications. The technology is changing far more rapidly than the rules that are supposed to contain it, often leaping over national as well as regulatory boundaries. Dealing as they do with the principal determinant of human organization- information and it's communication – this technology promises to change the very fabric of society, and in the process a wide range of the most basic ethical, and moral questions must be faced if we are to make our future work."

new topic Components of IT

1. **Hardware :** All the physical components of computer constitutes hardware. In other words, you can say all the visible & tangible (touchable) parts of computer, are collectively called hardware. Hardware incorporates the following-
    a. **Input Devices** (***e.g***. Keyboard, Mouse, Scanner etc)
    b. **Secondary Storage Devices** (***e.g***. Magnetic Tapes, Magnetic Disk & Optical disk etc)
    c. **Output Devices** (***e.g.*** Monitor, Printer, Plotter etc)
2. **Software :** Software refers to the collection of related programs used for performing a peculiar task. Software can be broadly divided into-
    a. **System Software:** Those software, which are used for controlling & managing various operations related to a computer system, are called system software **e.g.** Operating System (WINDOWS, UNIX, LINUX etc)
    b. **Application Software:** The software that serves a particular purpose of the user or in other words, it refers to that software which is used for some serving some definite purpose of the end-user. ***Examples of some commercial software*** are Text Editors, Spreadsheets, DBMS, and CAD, CASE etc.

Today, the decline in rates of Hardware & Software has made the computers available even in case of small business organization.

CAD/CAM:

- CAD is an acronym for "*Computer Aided Design*" and CAM stands for "*Computer Aided Manufacturing*".
- CAD is a kind of software which helps engineers to translate their concepts and requirements into digital form and then manipulate the same to test various design alternatives.
- Using this software, three dimensional designs can be made, the rotation of drawing is also possible to perform various design analysis.
- These tools enable the designer to locate a large number of shortcomings and remove them by means of interactions with the CAD software.
- Design is entered by means of keyboard, mouse or digitizer and hard copies of the drawings may be printed using inkjet printer or laser printer or plotters.
- ***CAM:*** It is a special software used to schedule and control automated factory equipment like machine tools, industrial robots etc and make available up-to-date performance information to the concerned managers.

CASE:

- CASE stands for Computer Assisted System Engineering.
- These tools are used to improve software development and maintenance in less time and at reduced cost.
- In CASE approach, the entire system development can be divided into following phases- Design, Coding, Testing, and Maintenance.
- By using a selected set of CASE tools, the Project Manager can generate useful estimates of efforts, cost and duration of software project in order to plan a workable project schedule, on a continuous basis.

3. **Networking:** It includes-

   a. **Client Server Technology:** Client server technology in the hospitality industry offers significant opportunities to improve guest services and hotel operations. Client server technology is probably the most viable strategic option for medium to large multi-property owners. It decouples (or separates) the database on the "***server***" from the applications running on the client PCs. Data access is faster because the "server" is not burdened with running applications. Data access is more evenly distributed, and users have the ability to query and create their own reports. The applications on different clients can utilize the same database on the server. Even more, the applications running on different clients may belong to different vendors. Thus, client server technology is inevitable for most hotel operations. ***Examples*** *of services utilizing Client server technology:-*

      i. **In-room Guest Services:** It means guest can navigate through audio and video aids provided to him and can automatically be connected the outside services. Such guest services provided by the staff typically involve a PC running a front-end application that allows access to outside services, as well as access to guest-specific information maintained in a central database.

      ii. **Database Marketing:** Database can be used a powerful marketing tool. Client server technology now permits a hotel chain to maintain one single customer database which can be accessed by all of the properties connected to the server over the network. The database may contain a hotel's customer information to develop profiles of frequent guests, target prospective customers and improve retention.

   b. **Internet:** Internet can be defined as a global network of numerous computers and computer networks all over the world, allowing one to access and exchange information over the network. The five basic advantages of Internet are-

      i. **Communication:** ***e.g.*** Electronic Mail

      ii. **Documentation or File Transfer:** ***e.g.*** FTP (File Transfer Protocol)

iii. **Interactive Browsing:** ***e.g.*** Browsers like Internet Explorer, Netscape Navigator can be used for surfing the World Wide Web.

iv. **Reading and Posting:** ***e.g.*** Messages can be read or posted to particular Bulletin Boards (online)

c. **World Wide Web:** The two terms "Internet" and "WWW" are not synonymous; therefore these should not be used interchangeably. Internet refers to a collection of computer networks. Whereas, World Wide Web refers to the way of accessing information via Internet. Therefore, World Wide Web is a portion of the Internet. WWW uses HTTP protocol. HTTP stands for Hypertext Transfer Protocol. The documents present on World Wide Web are called Web pages. These pages are linked via hyperlinks. (if you click on a hyperlink on current web page, then you would be automatically taken to another web page (or sometimes same web page) containing the linked information.

d. **Intranet:** It is a private network that is designed using Internet protocols like TCP/IP & HTTP. It generally belongs to a group or an enterprise i.e. only the people employed in that enterprise could access the information available on Intranet. Sometimes, a portion of the intranet is made available to the customers, dealers or suppliers (that are not the part of the organization). Thus, the small portion available to the people other than the members of organization is termed as ***Extranet.***

e. **Wireless Networks:** The computer networks in which computers are interconnected and would be able to communicate without wires, are known as wireless networks. Using wireless networking, any fixed devices like PC (Personal computer) or mobile devices like Laptops, Palmtops, and Notebooks can be connected. These devices having wireless connectivity are referred to as "*Wireless clients*" or simply "*Stations*". The stations (devices having wireless connection) should have ***WNIC*** i.e. Wireless network interface card, in order to be the active participant of the wireless network. Such networks are flexible, and cost efficient.

newtopic Disadvantages of Information Technology

1. Electronic and information technology may be inaccessible to people with physical disabilities (like color blindness, deafness or impaired vision); if it provides only one way for users to gain access to or manipulate information.

   For example, people who are blind cannot read instructions presented only in a visual format; people who are deaf cannot understand content that is presented only orally; people who are color-blind cannot discriminate between color-coded options and so on.
2. Technical failures of equipment.
3. Unsatisfactory for complex Interpersonal communication, such as negotiation or bargaining.
4. The accuracy of information cannot be judged.
5. Valuable information can be misused by unauthorized people.

Advantages of Information Technology

1. Information Technology is driving the world's business.
2. Information technology can be used for Accounting purpose-
   a. Payroll (overlap with HR)
   b. Accounts Payable / receivable
3. It can be used to facilitate Human Resources Support-
   a. Payroll (overlap with Account)
   b. Managing employee records
4. It can be used for Customer Resource Management (CRM)
5. It can be used for Enterprise Resource Planning.
6. It can be used for managing inventory efficiently.
7. It can be used for developing Point of Sale Systems.
8. It can be used in Manufacturing-
   a. Design Systems (CAD/CAM)
   b. Production System (Robotics)
9. Advances in technology are creating new opportunities for faculty to teach and students to learn.

Above mentioned are the fewer advantages of Information Technology. Nowadays, IT is involved in every field to support the operations particular to that field. Therefore, it is impossible to quote every usage of information technology in this unit.

Application of Information Technology

❖ BUSINESS:

1. Computers began their business careers in the banking and insurance industries, where massive amounts of data have to be processed daily. Computers are used in bans for magnetic coding of checks and for providing ATM facility.
2. Credit cards are used for automatic and instantaneous banking transactions through computers.
3. The concept of "bank anywhere, anytime" depends on the computer based expansion of EFT (Electronic Fund Transfer) technology.
4. Computers are used for almost all aspects of business administration bookkeeping, accounting, inventory control, forecasting and record keeping.
5. In the field of Office Automation, computers interconnected by telecommunication are applied to such tasks as the text and document

processing and keeping in touch with the outside world through electronic mail and information browsing.

❖ EDUCATION:

1. In education, computers are becoming increasingly useful tools of education.
2. For some applications, such as routine instructions, they can be superb adjuncts to the teacher.
3. These are ideally suited for self-placed instructions where the course objectives and contents are well defined.
4. Computers are not good at teaching "fuzzy" situations, where tasks cannot be defined in simple terms.

❖ HOME:

1. Computers have entered the homes in large numbers.
2. Many home computers are used mainly for entertainment but have great potential for education household management and household control.
3. There are some other examples of some automated systems like microwave ovens, fully automatic washing machines, programmable recorders and radios, home security systems and intelligent telephones etc. These all are consist of built-in computing devices.

❖ ELECTRONIC MAIL:

1. An electronic system which can store and deliver message that would otherwise be sent through postal services or over telephone lines.

❖ FASCIMILE MACHINES:

1. These are used to electronically send a printed copy of the document at the receiver's end. Thus, it is an electronic system which can store and deliver message that would otherwise be sent through postal services or over telephone lines.

❖ MIS:

1. Managers need Management Information Systems to help them monitor and control the performance of the organization and plan for the future.
2. Knowledge Workers or Operation professionals (**e.g**. accountants, lawyers, teachers, engineers etc) require facilities like word processing, spreadsheets, databases etc. to help them with their work. They also need communication tools, **e.g.** Email, video conferencing, fax machines.
3. Production Workers might use data processing systems. Transactions are the events that are recorded when goods are bought and sold. There are two types: batch systems (where transactions are processed in a "batch") and online systems (where data is processed as soon as it is generated (could be used for a hotel reservation system).

4. Using IT, many low level jobs have disappeared (**e.g.** robots have replaced production workers, automated data entry has replaced many secretaries) and, therefore, some levels of the MIS pyramid have disappeared altogether.
5. IT systems can now take decisions that are generally taken by middle managers.

❖ TELECONFERENCING FACILITY:

1. Teleconferencing refers to an interactive group communication (three or more people in two or more locations) through an electronic medium.
2. In general terms, teleconferencing can bring people together under one roof even though they're separated by hundreds of miles.
3. It can be of following types-
   a. ***Video conferencing:*** All the members of the meeting will be able to see and hear each other, with the help of cameras and microphones (even if they are remotely sitting at their places)
   b. ***Computer conferencing:*** Printed communication through keyboard terminals **e.g.** Chatting via Internet
   c. ***Audio-conferencing:*** It refers to verbal communication via internet **e.g.** Voice chat
   d. ***Data Conferencing:*** It means sharing of data via internet using Whiteboards. Whiteboards are electronic application (like a Notepad), similar to chalk boards. People sitting at remote locations can simultaneously write or draw on these boards thereby giving an impression that they are working together.

❖ HOTEL INDUSTRY:

1. Information Technology has a great impact on the Hotel industry. It has proven itself to be a valuable aid to hotel industry.
2. Every business organization requires up-to-date information. Thus, information technology helps the hospitality industry to store & manage important information required in various areas of industry.
3. According to J. Lyons, *"Catering company of U.K was the first commercial users of computers. They developed LEO (Lyons Electronic Office) LEO was used for management of hotel business"*
4. It is responsible for reducing cost and enhancing efficiency of hotel industry.
5. It is an important tool used for marketing and online reservations.
6. It facilitates internal operations of hotels like inventory management, reservations, billing, property management, accounting & Human Resource Management.
7. It provides various Information systems that deal with guest comforts and also maintain interaction with the external environment.
8. Consequently, the Hotel Industry is using computers in all the departments like front office, Housekeeping, Food and Beverage etc.

9. Computers are used to provide essentially efficient and better services. They are used for booking bills, taking care of room services and also other food and beverage services, website optimization, email marketing etc.

new topic Information Systems (IS)

1. Information system is one of the essential components of Information technology.
2. The systems which take information as input and provide information as output are called information systems.
3. The information can be processed either manually or using computers.
4. The information systems, which are developed by man to produce some meaningful information, are called man made systems. ***e.g.*** Railway Reservation system, Telecommunication system, Sales monitoring software etc.
5. Broadly speaking, it plays two important roles- Operational Support and Decision Support.
6. Computer and information systems managers play a vital role in the technological direction of their organizations. They do everything from constructing the business plan to managing network and Internet operations.
7. They determine technical goals in consultation with top management, and make detailed plans for the accomplishment of these goals.
8. Computer and information systems managers direct the work of systems analysts, computer programmers, support specialists, and other computer operators.
9. However the duties of information system managers vary according to their job titles. ***For Example:*** The Chief Technology officers keep themselves upgraded with the current advancements in IT and determine how these advancements can bring a change in the improvement of the organization. They reports to the Chief Information Officers who are responsible for determining the standards of technology to be adopted to enhance the current information system of the organization. MIS directors often work under Chief Information Officer. They generally make recommendations for hardware and software upgrade in order to manage the information system of the organization successfully.

1. Characteristics of an Information System

- Ease of data input into a storage medium
- Data validation during input of data
- Flexible data storage and retrieval procedures
- Availability of data for analysis and forecasting

2. Types of Information System

1. Formal Information Systems

2. Informal Information Systems
3. Computer Based Information Systems

FORMAL INFORMATION SYSTEM

1. It is an organization based system, represented by the organization chart.
2. The chart is a map of positions and the relationships among different positions are indicated by boxes and connected by straight lines.
3. It is concerned with the pattern of authority, communication and work flow.

INFORMAL INFORMATION SYSTEM

1. It is an employee-based system.
2. It is designed to meet personnel and vocational needs.
3. It also funnels information upward through indirect channels.
4. It is considered to be a useful system because it works within the framework of the business and it's stated policies. E.g. a peon directly explaining his problem to the Chairperson to maintain the privacy of his matter.

COMPUTER BASED INFORMATION SYSTEM (CBIS)

1. It uses computers for handling business applications.
2. It can be classified as-
   a. Transaction Processing System (TPS)
   b. Management Information System (MIS)
   c. Decision Support System (DSS)
   d. Office Automation System (OAS)

Transaction Processing System

1. It includes record-keeping applications.
2. It assists in carrying out the day-to-day activities of the organization.
3. These are operations-oriented.
4. Manual procedures are substituted by computer programs.
5. It is operated at First Line Management in the hierarchical view of CBIS.

Management Information System

1. These are decision oriented and utilize transaction data to formulate future decisions.
2. It is an information system that assists managers in decision making and problem solving.
3. The information must be precise, accurate, relevant, complete, timely and economically feasible.
4. It deals with supporting well structured decision situations.
5. It is operated at Middle Management in the hierarchical view of CBIS.

Decision Support System

1. It basically deals with taking decisions in unique situations, by determining what information to consider.
2. Decision support systems should be flexible enough to meet the changing needs of managers.
3. The decision system supports, but does not replace the judgement of manager.
4. It is applicable to the Top Management.

Office Automation System

1. It is a multi-function, integrated computer based system that allows many office activities to be performed in an electronic mode.
2. Such systems are used to increase the efficiency and productivity of office workers-typists, secretaries, administrative assistants and managers etc.

new topic Business System

1. A business system combines policies, personnel, and equipment and computer facilities to coordinate the activities of a business organization.
2. A business organization refers to any organization which produces goods or services for customers with an objective of gaining profit.
3. If we want to study the business system, the best approach is the System approach i.e. we look at the organization as a system.
4. Business is an open and adaptive system.
5. A business is typically subdivided into various organizational subsystems. These can represent functional areas such as Marketing, Manufacturing & Finance.
6. The firm may also be divided into subsystems, such as a project team, product groups or any other work group. This process is called decomposition.
7. It is very difficult to define the boundaries of a system and it's subsystems.
8. In private business organization, the main purpose is to satisfy the producer-consumer relationship and to provide a minimum invested capital with maximum profit.
9. In State-owned business (steel, coal, petrol, rail etc), the investment is done by the state itself and a virtual monopoly exists in the home market.
   - Their systems and subsystems need to be controlled in the same manner as the private enterprises.
   - The performance is controlled by accounting system and measured by the profit-and-loss concept.
10. There are also various non-commercial businesses, such as charitable organization, Educational establishments and government departments (health, water supply, police, fire, water etc).

11. Elements of a business system are-
    - ***Physical :*** *e.g.* Buildings, raw material, furnished products
    - ***Procedural :*** *e.g.* Order processing routines, Credit checking procedures
    - ***Conceptual :*** *e.g.* Statement of policy, Market for products
    - ***Social :*** *e.g.* Workers, Departments

Examples of some information systems used in hotels are-

1. Reservations Systems (RS)
2. Point-of-Sale Systems (POS)
3. Property Management System (PMS)
4. Stock Control System (SCS)
5. F & B Management System (FBMS)
6. Event Management System (EMS)
7. Customer Relationship Management (CRM)

1. Reservation Systems

1. Reservation system is basically a set of programs integrated together to perform reservation operations of a hotel.
2. The main function of the reservation process is to match ***room requests*** with ***room availability***.
3. The room reservation system of star hotels has been computerized almost all over India.
4. The computerized reservation introduced in 1980's. Computerized reservation system takes off from the manual system. The common manual system used is Whitney's system, in which reservation is basically maintained on paper mounted metal frames, arranged according to date and also alphabetically (in wardrobes)
5. The reservation process includes the following steps-
   a. Conduct the reservation inquiry
   b. Determine room and rate availability
   c. Create the reservation record
   d. Confirm the reservation record
   e. Maintain the reservation record
   f. Produce reservation reports
6. Well managed reservation systems can strengthen the relationship between a hotel and its guest.

Functions of Reservation Systems

1. Managing reservation inventory (guest profile, arrival & departure dates, details of passport, visa or credit card etc)
2. Track reservations i.e. selling of rooms
3. Track advance deposits
4. Automatically generate daily charges
5. Update sales information daily
6. Control front and back end office functions
7. To generate breakdown of the Room Revenue and Profitability analysis

Sources of Reservations:

- Central Reservation Systems
- Property Direct Reservation System
- Travel Agencies

❖ **CRS (Central Reservation System):-**

1. The majority of Lodging Properties (hotels, resorts etc) belongs to one or more Central Reservation Systems.
2. A central reservation system is composed of a central reservation office, member hotels connected together via communication devices, and potential guests.
3. Hotel members of the central reservation system shall provide and exchange accurate room availability data to central reservation offices. This is done through the communication equipment given to the member hotels by the CRO. Such equipment may be Telephone, facsimile machines, to personal computers, Internet connections...... etc.
4. Central reservation office (CRO) charges a fee for the utilization of its services from the member hotels.
5. ***Examples:*** *WorldSpan, Amadeus, ABACUS International, Galileo etc.*
6. Central Reservation Offices are divided into two: -
   - o ***Affiliate Reservation System: -*** It refers to a hotel chain's central reservation systems (CRS) in which all participating properties are contractually related. Most affiliate systems process reservation on the basis of a declining inventory of both room types and room rates. It reduces the overall system cost.
   - o ***Non-Affiliate Reservation System: -*** It refers to a subscription system linking independent properties. It process reservation solely on the basis the availability of room types. This method helps participating properties to maximize revenue potential and occupancy.
7. ***Some of the important features of central reservation system are listed below-***
   - o Instant Booking and Confirmation

- o Online Room Inventory
- o Booking Acceptance for an Event
- o Arrival List generation
- o Revenue Report Generation
- o Maintaining Guest Profile
- o Performance Auditing
- o Centralized Control
- o Scalability due to parameterized database design

The flow of information in Central Reservation System is as under-

1. A network is installed at the central reservation office, including the RDP (Reservation Data Processing) system and database.
2. A network is also installed at the property, including an independent copy of the RDP system and database.
3. All reservations are made at the central reservation location, including Internet Reservations.
4. When the central reservation department closes for the day, they create a transfer file that holds all new reservations, changes, and deletions. This file is sent via E-Mail to the property.
5. If there is more than one remote location, the process is repeated for each property.
6. The property runs a program that automatically loads all information from the transfer file into their database.
7. Guests are checked in and checked out on the system at the property.
8. The property performs a normal night audit. After this audit, the property has the option of creating a transfer to send all new information back to Central Reservations, so that Central has complete history.

❖ **Property Direct Reservation System**

Most of the properties install software solutions according to their own requirement for carrying out reservation operations. This is so because potential guests might still find it convenient, and personal to call directly the hotel to communicate a reservation inquiry. ***Example-*** Fidelio, Micros etc.

❖ **Travel Agencies**

Most reservation agents work for large hotel chains or airlines, helping people to plan trips and make reservations. Reservation agents quote fares and room rates, provide travel information, and make and confirm transportation and hotel reservations. Most agents use networks to obtain the information related to reservation confirmation or deletion. They usually work in large reservation centers, answering telephone or e-mail inquiries and offering suggestions and information about travel arrangements, such as routes, schedules, rates, and types of accommodation. Travel agents can access hotel availability, rental car, airline availability etc through a computer network, which is known as **GDS** (Global Distribution System). Some of the examples of ***GDS*** companies are ***Sabre*** and ***Apollo***. Nowadays, guests can make room reservations via ***GDS*** through travel agents or directly via direct interface with GDS on Internet. (i.e. GDS websites) ***Example of Travel Network is:*** *American Express*

2. Point-of-Sale Systems

According to Ruffin,

"A good POS allows you to allocate your human resources to the customer service area of the business that means they no longer have to be counting, calculating, ordering and checking cash-register accuracy."

According to Melvin

"POS lends itself to a better overall customer experience — the sorts of things a customer expects when he walks through the front door".

Most POS (Point Of Sale) software has an on-board database where all of your transactions are stored. POS software is expandable also, i.e. if you need more merchant accounts because of opening a new business, you can add new accounts to the software. The basic function of POS systems is managing inventory and performing accounting operations like billing, generating reports, ledgers etc. ***Example:*** Retail Management System, CREST System. In hotels, POS systems (or software) are generally installed in the following functional areas- Restaurants, Retail counters, and Liquor Store. A POS system involves pre-configured software on the basis of the inventory or vendor or guest of a particular hotel. A POS system involves following hardware-

- Monitor (9 or 10 inch; touch screen technology- most desirable)
- Keyboard (Keyboards have various configurations for the Point-of-Sale environment. Some are standard 101-key keyboards, with integrated magnetic stripe readers, bar code scanners, decoders and programmable keys)
- Barcode Scanner
- Printer
- Modems
- UPS
- Zip drives
- Cash drawer etc

Advantages of POS

1. **Improved Margins** - A POS system protects margin as it requires the entry of a specific item code to process a sale. Margins are also improved and protected by knowing what and when to order to reduce shipping costs and take advantage of supplier promotions.
2. **Preventing Stealing & Unauthorized discounts** - Your employee's may steal from your restaurant (if you are a restaurant owner). They may be giving away items or food, discounting at the register for friends or family and so on. You can match purchase orders against packing slips. Thus, by installing POS at your site (i.e. restaurant or retail counter), you have

control without having to watch over everything by standing at a cash register.

3. **Inventory Control** – POS system enables to view all the details of inventory i.e. the number and types of items present in the stock, the items to be ordered and the items not available currently etc. Thereby, a hotel can control it's inventory by frequently tracking the information provided by POS system.
4. **Time Savings –** Once the correct details of inventory and transactions are entered in POS system, then all the other operations are carried by the POS system automatically i.e. you don't have to bother about the analysis of records or generating reports and purchase orders etc. Thus, you can accomplish this by just giving instruction to the POS system.
5. **Sales:** A POS system enables you to respond to customer buying habits quickly and profitably. A POS system allows you to know exactly what your customers are buying, enabling you to respond with mailings, special promotions, etc.

Disadvantages of POS

1. Problems with cash flow
2. Lack of capital
3. Lack of Planning
4. Lack of Customer Knowledge
5. Lack of flexibility

3. Property Management Systems (PMS)

Property Management System emphasizes the highest level of individual guest services through comprehensive guest profile; seamlessly integrating rooms, dining, and retail, with information contained in reservations and guest history.

Regardless of your hotel size, your hotel property management system must be compatible with your clientele and growing changes in technology. Property Management software must be flexible enough so that it can be customized to meet your Property management needs.

PMS refers to Property Management System. It is used for automating-

- Inquiry & guest contacts management
- Mail Merge Capabilities
- Online Reservation
- Occupancy & Availability Management
- Revenue Reporting
- Room Occupancy Analysis
- Housekeeping & Maintenance Management
- Night Audit
- Guest Messaging Service

- Lost & Found Database
- Marketing Analysis
- Guest Billing.

BILLING :-

The billing of the rooms, room services and restaurant services are all done using computerized receipt printing. The rates of the different rooms per day are already there in the computer software package. While billing a guest, the check-in and check-out data and time is typed and auto processing allows computerized bills to be prepared and the guest does not have to wait for bill, while checking out. The room service and restaurant bills or any other bills such as laundry, gifts etc, if not paid earlier by the guest are also attached or added to the bill. The unpaid bill is automatically added to the guest bill through guest ID and room no. The guest whether or not a resident of the hotel, get the bill with each menu item ordered along with it's individual price, taxes applicable and total made out. The clean and neat print out makes it easier for the guest to understand the bill.

4. Stock Control Systems (SCS)

1. Manual Stocktaking involves making an **inventory**, or list, of stock, and noting its location and value. The simplest manual system is the stock book, which suits small businesses with few stock items. Stock cards are used for more complex systems. Each type of stock has an associated card, with information such as:
   - description
   - value
   - location
   - re-order levels, quantities and lead times (if this method is used)
   - supplier details
   - information about past stock history
2. More sophisticated manual systems incorporate coding to classify items. Codes might indicate the value of the stock, its location and which batch it is from, which is useful for quality control. Codes (example- barcodes), can make the whole process much easier but it can still be quite time-consuming.
3. Any stock control system must enable you to:
   - track stock levels
   - make orders
   - issue stock
4. On the contrary, A computerized stock control system (or software) program is fully integrated with Point-of-Sale software. It assists in keeping tight fiscal and physical control over the stock of the restaurant by:

a. Automatically adjusting stock levels based on the sales made throughout the restaurant.

b. It incorporates a recipe system. This system can be developed to accurately gauge the specific amounts and costs of raw product that are incorporated into each dish, as well as being able to provide the capability to calculate the gross revenue & profitability of each item.

c. It can also determine the cost to produce an item.

d. This system even has the capability to account for wastage in the restaurant

e. It provides an interface for the exporting of sales data and debtor data from the Point-of-Sale into accounting packages.

5. Food & Beverage Management Systems

1. Technology influences the jobs of food service managers in many ways, enhancing efficiency and productivity.
2. However, the technology used by the restaurant depends upon the need of the management and also on the type of restaurant.
3. F & B applications rely upon electronic cash register (ECR) and point-of-sale (POS) technology to monitor service area transactions using computers.
4. Such applications track orders, inventory, and the seating of guests. Point-of-service (POS) systems allow servers to key in a customer's order, either at the table, using a hand-held device, or from a computer terminal in the dining room, and send the order to the kitchen instantaneously so preparation can begin.
5. The same system also tracks sales i.e. Managers tally the cash and charge receipts received and balance them against the record of sales.
6. To minimize food costs and spoilage, many managers use inventory-tracking software to compare the record of sales from the POS with a record of the current inventory.
7. Food service managers use the Internet to track industry news, find recipes, conduct market research, purchase supplies or equipment, recruit employees, and train staff.
8. Many restaurants maintain Web sites that include menus and online promotions, provide information about the restaurant's location, and offer patrons the option to make a reservation.
9. F & B Systems are also used for menu preparation, which includes taking account of the ingredients used, calculate the applicable taxes and other overhead costs and decide upon a price, which will prove profitable to the organization.

6. Customer Relationship Management (CRM)

1. CRM is the acronym that stands for Customer Relationship Management.
2. Such systems are used to determine customers needs & behaviors in order to develop stronger or you can say good relationships with them.

3. In other words, CRM is an information system that will help to gather lots of valuable information about customers, sales, marketing effectiveness, responsiveness and market trends.
4. Thus, CRM helps organizations maximize customer acquisition, loyalty, retention and profitability.

new topic General Information Systems not used in Hotels

Examples of some General Information Systems not used in Hotels are-

- LMS (Library Management System)
- CMS (Content Management System)
- ECMS (Enterprise Content Management System)
- RMS (Record Management System)

new topic Information System does not mean Information Technology (IT)

Information systems don't have to mean information technology....This can be clearly understood by considering the following anecdote (Professor Vicki L. Sauter):

A CEO with hotel chain "A" found himself having to spend a night in a hotel from hotel chain B. Naturally, he was very curious as to what kind of information systems they had, and resolved to keep an open eye for competitive use of IT. As he approached the reception for first time, the woman behind it smiled at him and said "Welcome back, Sir!"

Flabbergasted, he said "But...it is 12 years since I was here last! How could you know that I have stayed here before, what kind of advanced information systems do you have that can store and find the fact that I was here 12 years ago?"

"Well, it is really very simple", she said. "When the doorman opened the door to your cab, he asked if this was your first stay with us. You answered no, and as you walked through the door, the doorman looked at me through the window and touched his nose. That told me that you should be welcomed back...."

14

Microsoft Word

Introduction:

Ms-Word is a powerful word processing program contained in Ms-Office. A word processor is a computer program that enables you to create, edit, print, format and save the documents for future retrieval and revision. One of the major advantages of a word processor over a non-conventional typewriter is that a word processor enables you to make changes to a document without retyping the entire document. Another thing, in case of a typewriter, you need to hit the return key whenever you want to end the line. On the other hand, in case of WORD, when a word does not fit on a line, it automatically flows to the beginning of the next line. This feature is called ***WORD-WRAP*** feature. However, you can press enter key to end a short line or to end a paragraph or to create a blank line.

Following are the technical points to remember-

- File of Ms-Word is called ***Document.***
- A document consists of ***pages***.
- By default name of Document is ***Document1***.
- By default extension of a Document is ***.doc***

newtopic Starting Ms-Word

If you wish to open Ms-WORD directly from the desktop, double click on Microsoft Word icon

Microsoft Word

OR

1. Click on ***Start*** button  on the Taskbar, then a popup menu appears

2. Then click on the ***Program*** option
3. Then choose ***Microsoft WORD*** sub-option

Above three steps will successfully launch or start Ms-WORD on your desktop.

Or

1. Press ***Windows key*** on the keyboard to open Start menu
2. Then click on the ***Program*** option
3. Then choose ***Microsoft WORD*** sub-option

Screen Elements

1. ***Title Bar:*** Name of application program & name of currently opened document is displayed on it. It also contains control buttons

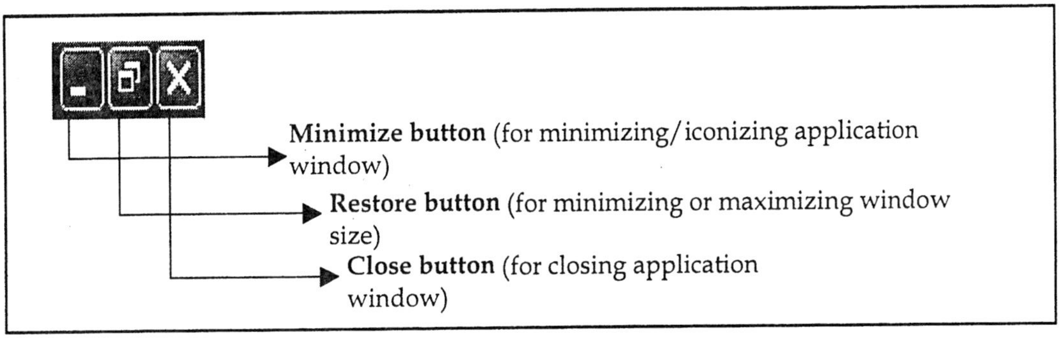

2. ***Toolbar:*** It refers to the graphical or pictorial representation of commands present under different menu items like File, Edit etc. Some common Toolbars are-
   - ***Standard Toolbar:*** contains tools for managing operations related to file & editing operations
   - ***Formatting Toolbar:*** contains tools for changing the appearance of text i.e. Text formatting or object
3. ***Menu Bar :*** It refers to the horizontal bar containing menu items or pads like File, Edit, View etc. Menu items can be accessed using mouse, just by clicking on related menu item. Although these can be accessed using keyboard shortcut key : Alt + Underlined character in menu items name e.g. Alt + F is used for accessing File Menu. For navigating through commands under a menu item, Arrow key can be used. For executing a particular command, Enter key can be used.
4. ***Ruler Bar :*** used for setting or clearing tabs. It is of two types -
   a. Horizontal Ruler bar
   b. Vertical Ruler bar
5. ***Scroll Bar :*** used for navigating in document window. Navigation refers to moving up & down through the pages in a document. We have horizontal & vertical scroll bars.

6. ***Document Window:*** It refers to the actual work area in Ms-Word window, where the actual typing, editing and formatting of text is done.
7. ***Office Assistant:*** It is basically an online help. It aids user to work conveniently by displaying related messages.
8. ***View Buttons:*** These are used for switching among different views of Ms-Word.
9. ***Drawing Toolbar:*** It contains several tools used for drawing pictures & various shapes.
10. ***Status Bar :*** It is used to display important information related to document like page no., line no., ...& so on. Besides this it also displays help messages. It also indicates the status of few keys e.g. the status of Insert key (i.e. on/off) is shown by the OVR pane.
11. ***Application Window:*** It refers to the main Word Window that contains all the above components. This is also called parent window due to it's prior existence than document window. Thus, document window is referred to child window.

new topic Moving in a Document using Keyboard

To move	***Press key***
To the beginning of a line	Home
To the end of a line	End
To the next line	Down arrow key
To the previous line	Up arrow key
Up one screen	PgUp
Down one screen	PgDown
To the top of the Document	Ctrl + Home
To the end of the Document	Ctrl + End

new topic Text Related Operations

1. Inserting Text

Click the mouse at desired place, and then an insertion point or cursor appears. You can type the text. However, there are two modes of typing-

a. ***Insert Mode:*** If Insert key is turned on, then it means we are working in Insert mode. Insert mode refers to a mode in which; one of more than one characters can be inserted in pre-typed text. In this case, OVR pane (displayed on the status bar) seems to be dimmed or grayed.
b. ***Overtype Mode:*** If Insert key is turned off, then it means we are working in overwrite mode. Overwrite mode refers to a typing mode in which new text overwrites or replaces pre-typed text, in a case if we wish to insert characters in between. In this case, OVR seems to be highlighted. It

should be noted that if overtype mode is on, then pressing spacebar would delete the words instead of putting space between the typed characters.

Insert key is a toggle key i.e. it can be either turned on or off.

2. Deleting Text:

- To delete the text / characters to the right hand side of cursor, press ***Delete*** key
- To delete the text/ characters to the left hand side of cursor, press ***Backspace*** key.

3. Selecting Text:

For performing the majority of operations in WORD like deleting, moving, formatting, you always need to select the text in advance. So, for selecting text, there are many methods, some of them are as follows-

For Selecting	***Method***
Single Word	Double click on that word
Single Sentence	Ctrl + click on the desired sentence
Single Paragraph	Tripple click on the desired paragraph
Entire Document	Ctrl + A
Selecting Entire Line using Selection bar	Move the mouse pointer to the selection bar. The mouse pointer will change its shape from I-bar to an arrow. Click the mouse once then the entire line to the right of where you have clicked will be selected
Selecting Entire Paragraph using Selection bar	Move the mouse pointer to the selection bar. The mouse pointer will change its shape from I-bar to an arrow. Double Click the mouse then the entire para to the right of where you have clicked will be selected
Selecting desired text	Either use click & drag method via mouse **Or** Use Shift + arrow keys
Selecting Graphics or other objects	Click anywhere on the graphic or other object

new topic Document Related Operations

1. Creating a Document: (Ctrl+N)

1. Select ***File > New*** option
2. Then select ***Blank document*** option in ***New*** dialog box
3. Click on OK

Or

Click ***New*** tool on the standard toolbar.

In both the cases, a new blank document is created.

2. Saving a Document: (Ctrl +S)

1. Select ***File > Save*** option, then Save As... dialog box is displayed
2. Then specify location, where you wish to save the file
3. After then, specify the desired file name
4. Click on ***Save*** button

Or

Click ***Save*** button on the standard toolbar.

In both the cases, existing document will be saved.

3. Closing a Document

Select ***File > Close*** option.

In this cases, active document will get closed

4. Opening a Document (Ctrl + O)

1. Select ***File > Open*** option, then Open dialog box is displayed
2. Then specify location of existing file
3. After then, select the desired file or specify the desired file name
4. Click on ***Open*** button

Or

Click **Open** tool on the standard toolbar.

In both the cases, existing document will get opened.

5. Creating a Copy of a Document (Save As)

1. Select ***File > Save As*** option, then ***Save As*** dialog box is displayed
2. Then specify location, where you wish to save the file
3. After then, specify the new file name
4. Click on ***Save*** button

Or

Press ***F12 s***hortcut key

6. Save As Web Page:

1. Select ***File > Save as Web Page*** option, then Save as dialog box is displayed
2. Specify the desired location for saving html document
3. Specify the file name for html file
4. Make sure the file type should be web page and not Word document
5. The html document so created can be viewed using browser like Internet explorer as a web page
6. You can change the title of the page that would appear in the title bar of the browser

   In this case, active document will get saved as a web page

7. Print Previewing a Document

- Print preview is used to view the document for printing.
- In print preview mode, you cannot type or edit. However, you can change the alignment settings or margins of the text.
- Print Preview is also called ***WYSIWYG,*** which refers to — **W**hat **Y**ou **S**ee **I**s **W**hat **Y**ou **G**et i.e. As you see your document in print preview mode, exactly the same print or hard copy you get from the printer.
  - Select ***File > Print Preview*** command

    Or

1. Click the ***Print Preview*** button  on the standard toolbar
2. Then, WORD switches to the print preview mode.
3. For exiting out of print preview mode, click ***Close*** button on the Print Preview toolbar.

8. Page Setup of a Document

Select ***File> Page Setup*** command then Page Setup dialog box is displayed. In this dialog box, you can change margins, paper source and page orientation for the entire document or for selected sections of a document. Page Setup dialog box consists of following tabs-

➢ *Margins Tab*

Click this to set Left, Right, Top & Bottom margins. You can also give binding margins through ***Gutter*** margins from this tab.

➢ *Paper Size Tab*

Click this to set paper size and page orientation. There are two types of page orientation-

- ***Landscape:*** To set up horizontal printing
- ***Portrait:*** To set up vertical printing

➢ *Paper Source Tab*

Click this to set option for printing pages including the type of printer, paper tray and manual feed.

➢ *Layout Tab*

Click this to set option for headers and footers, section breaks, vertical alignment and line numbers etc.

9. Printing a Document (Ctrl + P)

File> Print option is used to print your active document. The printer must be installed and selected before printing a document. The options available in the Print dialog box are-

- ***Status:*** It describes the state of the selected printer i.e. busy or idle
- ***Where:*** It displays to which port the output is sent i.e. LPT1 Or LPT2
- ***Copies:*** To set the number of the copies to print
- ***Collate:*** To organize pages when you print multiple copies of the document, select the Collate check box. A complete copy of the document is printed before the first page of the next copy is printed.
- ***Page Range:*** It lets you choose the page range to be printed. It may be-
    - o ***All*** (to print all pages)
    - o ***Current Page*** (to print current page)
    - o ***Pages*** (to specify range. For example 2-8)
    - o ***Selection*** (to print the selected portion of a document)

new topic Editing Operations

1. Cut, Copy and Paste

- ***(Ctrl + X) Edit > Cut*** command is used to cut the selected text. The selected text will disappear from the screen and will be placed on clipboard.
- ***Edit > Copy*** command is used to copy the selected text. It is generally used to duplicate items or text. The copied item will also be placed on clipboard.
- ***Edit > Paste*** command is used to paste the cut or copied item. If you already cut or copied a item, then you can place the insertion point at the desired location and then perform paste operation. Thus, Paste command is used to place clipboard items (Cut or Copy) to Word document.

Cut-Paste operation is equivalent to Move operation

2. Undo and Repeat

- ***Edit > Undo*** command allows to revert the last done action. If you press ***Ctrl + Z*** repeatedly, it will reverse your previous actions. Word allows reverting the modifications like cut and paste, formatting actions like fonts, changing styles etc.
- ***Edit > Repeat*** command is used to repeat the last reverted change using Undo. You can repeat as many actions that you have reverted using Undo.

3. Find and Replace

- ***Edit > Find*** command is used to search a particular word in a document. For this, specify the desired word in ***Find what*** box in **Find** dialog box and click ***Find Next*** button. By doing so, the word found with the specified criteria becomes highlighted in the document. Click on ***More*** button to specify a search criteria. For example, you can select ***Match Case*** checkbox if you want to make your search case sensitive (i.e. an exact match of the word in ***Find what*** box will be searched in the document with respect to its case like Uppercase or lowercase)
- ***Edit > Replace*** command is used to replace an existing word with a new word. For this the word that is already present in your document (that need to be replaced) is typed in ***Find what*** box and the replacement of that word (i.e. new word to be used as a replacement) will be typed in ***Replace*** box.

Shortcut of Editing Operations

Editing Operations	***Shortcut Keys***
Cut	Ctrl + X
Copy	Ctrl + C
Paste	Ctrl + V
Undo	Ctrl + Z
Repeat	Ctrl + Y
Find	Ctrl + F
Replace	Ctrl + H

newtopic Views of Ms-Word

1. Normal View:

a. It shows your text as you have typed it, and displays graphics where you have inserted them.

b. It does not show header and footer.

c. Only horizontal ruler is displayed

d. Automatic page breaks are shown as dotted lines.

e. Normal view keeps repagination and screen redraw delays to a minimum.

f. For switching to normal view, select ***View > Normal*** command.

2. Web Layout:

a. It is used for viewing your document as a web page.

b. Only horizontal ruler is displayed in this view.

c. There is no distinction of hard and soft page break.

3. Print Layout:

a. In this view, the screen resembles a white sheet of paper. A dark background is also displayed behind the "***paper***".

b. In this view, you can see all graphics, hidden text, headers and footers.

c. In this view, both the horizontal and vertical rulers are displayed.

d. You can also edit the document in print layout view.

e. It is the default view of Ms-Word.

4. Outline Layout:

a. It displays document in traditional outline format with text indented beneath headings in a hierarchical structure.

b. Outline view lets you quickly navigate reorganize even large, complex documents.

c. Outline view is useful to move text from one page or section to another page or section without cut and paste.

d. In outline view you can see page breaks in dotted line.

5. Document Map:

a. In this view, the document is divided into two panes-

   i. Document Map (left pane to display headings of document)

   ii. Document (right pane to display the actual document)

b. If you click on a particular heading in the document map, then the corresponding text is displayed in the document pane.

c. This view lets you quickly navigate the entire document.

d. Select ***View > Document*** map command for switching to Document map view of a document.

new topic Formatting a Document

Formatting means to enhance the appearance of your document. This can be done by the application of different font, font style, font size, font color or effects on the selected text. You can format a document either using Font dialog box (Format > Font) or by Formatting toolbar.

FONT TAB For Setting Font related options

1. Select the desired text.
2. Select ***Format > Font***, then Font dialog box is displayed.
3. In Font Dialog box, select Font tab. Then, set the following options -

   a. **Font :**
      i. It refers to style of writing a character.
      ii. **e.g.** Times New Roman, Tahoma, Courier New etc.
      iii. By default font is **Times New Roman**.

   b. **Font Size :**
      i. It refers to the size of the font.
      ii. It is measured in **Points.**
      iii. Min. font size is **8 points**. Max. font size is **72 points**. However, minimum and maximum number varies from one font to other font.
      iv. By default font size is **12.**

   c. **Font Style :**
      i. It refers to different styles of font like- Regular, Bold, Italic, Bold Italic.
      ii. By default Font style is **Regular.**

   d. **Font Color :**
      i. It refers to color of the Font.
      ii. You can use the available colors in the color palette or you can use the standard or customized colors by using More Colors option in Color Palette.
      iii. By default Font color is ***Automatic*** (Black)

   e. **Underline Style :**
      i. It refers to style of underline.
      ii. **e.g.** This is an underline style, This is a words only underline style
      iii. By default font underline style is none (i.e No underline)

   f. **Underline Color :**
      i. It refers to the color of underline.
      ii. Using color palette, desirable color can be selected for underline.

   g. Effects : (You can apply required effects by selecting the appropriate checkbox)

- ✓ Strikethrough
- ✓ Double Strikethrough
- ✓ Shadow
- ✓ Outline
- ✓ Superscript
- ✓ Subscript
- ✓ Emboss
- ✓ Engrave
- ✓ Small Caps
- ✓ All Caps
- ✓ Hidden

CHARACTER SPACING TAB For Setting Spacing between characters

1. Select the text.
2. Select ***Format > Font***, then Font dialog box is displayed.
3. In Font dialog box, select the ***Character Spacing*** tab.
4. You can specify the following options-

   a. ***Scale :*** Scaling refers to increase or decrease the size of selected text. In scaling box, enter the scaling percentage.

   b. ***Spacing :*** Spacing refers to the gap between the consecutive characters (excluding gap left using spacebar). You may set the spacing as-

   i. Expanded
   ii. Condensed
   iii. Normal.

   c. ***Position :*** Position refers to the placement of text with respect to baseline. You may set it as

   i. Lowered
   ii. Raised
   iii. Normal

   d. ***Kerning :*** Kerning means adjusting the space between two consecutive characters to improve the clarity. Kerning is required in case of few fonts. For Kerning, select the Kerning checkbox and specify a numeric value for kerning.

TEXT EFFECTS TAB For animating text

1. Select the desired text.
2. Select ***Format > Font***, then ***Font*** dialog box is displayed.

3. Select the ***Text effects*** tab.
4. You can select any animated effects from the list.
5. Then, click Ok.

Formatting a Paragraph

1. Select the desired paragraph.
2. Select ***Format > Paragraph***, then Paragraph dialog box is displayed.
3. Select the ***Indent and Spacing*** tab.
4. You can specify the following parameters for changing the appearance of a paragraph-
   a. ***Alignment:*** Alignment refers to the position of text with respect to page. You may select any one of the alignment-
      i. Left
      ii. Center
      iii. Right
      iv. Justified

   b. **Indents :** Indentation refers the distance of paragraph from the left or right edge of page. You may enter a numeric value for specifying the left distance and Right distance.
   c. **Spacing :** Spacing refers to the space between two consecutive paragraphs. In a document, you may have two or more paragraphs. Therefore, there are two options related to a paragraph spacing-
      i. ***Before:*** Specify the space before a selected paragraph, by entering a number.
      ii. ***After:*** Specify the space after the selected paragraph, by entering a number.
   d. ***Line Spacing:*** It refers to the spacing between two consecutive lines in a paragraph. It may be-
      i. Single
      ii. Double
      iii. Half (1.5)

Applying Bullets & Numbering to a List

APPLYING BULLETS TO LIST

1. Select the list of items
2. Select ***Format > Bullets and Numbering*** command
3. Click on the ***Bullet*** tab
4. Select the bullet style & click Ok

REMOVING BULLETS FROM A LIST

1. Select the bulleted list of items
2. Select ***Format > Bullets and Numbering*** command
3. Click on the ***Bullet*** tab
4. Select the ***None*** style & click Ok

APPLYING NUMBERING TO A LIST

1. Select the list of items
2. Select ***Format > Bullets and Numbering*** command, then Bullets and Numbering dialog box will be displayed.
3. Click on the ***Numbered*** tab
4. Select the Numbering style & click Ok

REMOVING NUMBERING FROM A LIST

1. Select the numbered list of items
2. Select ***Format > Bullets and Numbering*** command, then Bullets and Numbering dialog box will be displayed.
3. Click on the ***Numbered*** tab
4. Select the ***None*** style & click Ok

For applying and removing bullets, select the list and click on ***Bullet*** tool on the formatting toolbar (it is a toggle button). Likewise, for applying and removing numbering, select the list and click on ***Numbering*** tool on the formatting toolbar (it is also a toggle button)

newtopic Applying Borders and Shading

APPLYING BORDERS

You can apply various border and shading to single paragraphs or groups of paragraphs. You can also put border around graphics. The steps of applying borders to a paragraph or graphics is as follows-

1. Select the paragraph/group of paragraphs or graphics around which border is to be applied
2. Choose ***Format > Borders and Shading*** command. Then, Borders and Shading dialog box will be displayed.
3. Click on ***Borders*** tab, and then choose the following options-
   a. a border setting like Box, Shadow, 3D etc
   b. Line Style
   c. Color
   d. Width

4. A border will be displayed in the ***Preview*** box according to the above settings. However, you can alter the border using the buttons with the preview diagram.
5. Click Ok.

Removing Borders

1. Select the paragraph/group of paragraphs or graphics around which border is already applied.
2. Choose ***Format > Borders and Shading*** command. Then, ***Borders and Shading*** dialog box will be displayed.
3. Click on ***Borders*** tab, and then choose ***None*** option from the ***Border setting*** options.
4. Then, border will disappear in the ***Preview*** box.
5. Click Ok.

Applying Shading

1. Select the paragraph or elements to be shaded.
2. Choose ***Format > Borders and Shading*** command. Then, Borders and Shading dialog box will be displayed.
3. Click on ***Shading*** tab, and then choose ***Fill*** color from the color palette.
4. If you want to apply pattern to the selected elements, then choose one of the ***Pattern style*** and ***color.***
5. Click Ok.

Removing Shading

1. Select the paragraph or elements that are already shaded.
2. Choose ***Format > Borders and Shading*** command. Then, Borders and Shading dialog box will be displayed.
3. Click on ***Shading*** tab, and then choose ***No Fill*** under ***Fill*** option.
4. Likewise, to remove pattern, choose ***Clear*** in the Pattern ***Style*** list box.

new topic Changing Background Color

1. Select ***Format > Background*** command, and then choose a color from the color palette. For applying shading, texture, pattern or selected picture to the background of document, choose ***Fill Effects*** option.
2. For removing the color/shading/texture/picture from the background, choose ***No Fill*** option after clicking ***Format > Background*** option.

new topic Insert Related Operations

1. Inserting Picture

1. For inserting Picture from clipart, place the insertion point (or cursor) at the desired position in document.

2. Select ***Insert > Picture > ClipArt*** option, then Clipart gallery is displayed.
3. Select a Picture Category and click the desired picture. Then click on Insert Picture option.

2. Inserting Chart *(Chart is the pictorial or graphical representation of data)*

1. Place the cursor at the desired position in document.
2. Select ***Insert > Picture > Chart*** option, then datasheet is displayed along with the chart.
3. Then, you can edit the data on the datasheet in order to modify the chart.
4. It should be noted that by *right clicking* on the blank area of the chart, you can edit various options like - Chart Type, Chart options like legend, axes, title etc. However, for performing formatting of chart, *double click* on the desired area (like walls, floor, bar/columns etc) of the chart.

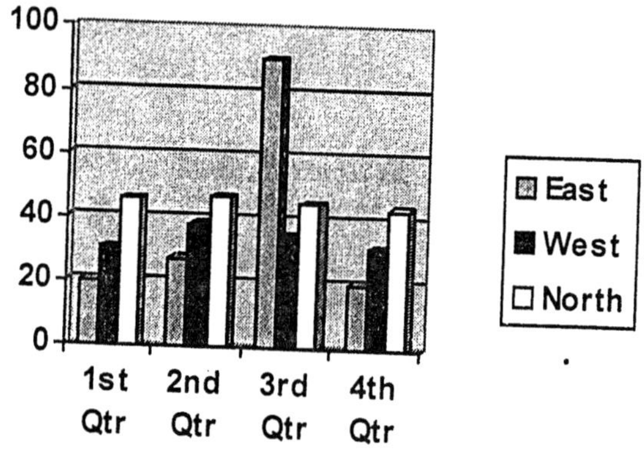

3. Inserting WordArt (*WordArt refers to decorative text*)

1. Place the cursor at the desired position in document.
2. Select ***Insert > Picture > WordArt*** option, then WordArt gallery is displayed.
3. Select the desired WordArt style & click Ok. Then, ***Edit WordArt Text*** dialog is displayed.
4. Finally, enter the desired text and set options like Font & Font size and click Ok.

4. Inserting AutoShapes

1. Select ***Insert > Picture > AutoShapes*** option, then AutoShapes toolbar will get displayed.
2. Click on the desired Shapes category and then click the desired shape. The mouse pointer will become crosshair shaped.
3. Click the crosshair shaped mouse pointer at the desired place in the document and then drag it to draw the selected shape.

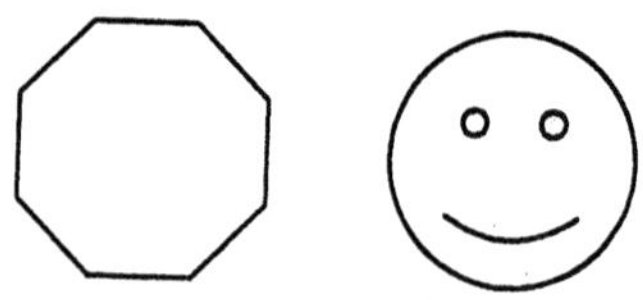

5. Inserting Page Numbers

1. Select ***Insert > Page Numbers*** command, then ***Page Numbers*** dialog box will be displayed.

2. Select the desired ***Position*** (like Top or Bottom) & ***Alignment*** (like Left, Right, Center, Inside, Outside) and then click Ok.
3. However, in order to change the Page Number format (like a,b,c ..... or i, ii, iii ... .etc), click on ***Format*** button in the ***Page Numbers*** dialog box.

> 3. Click the crosshair shaped mouse pointer at the desired place in the document and then drag it to draw the selected shape.
>
> ***Inserting Page Numbers***
>
> 1. Select *Insert>Page Numbers* command, then *Page Numbers* dialog box will be displayed.
> 2. Select the desired *Position* (like Top or Bottom) & *Alignment* (like Left, Right, Center, Inside, Outside) and then click Ok.
> 3. However, in order to change the Page Number format (like a,b,c...... or i, ii, iii.....etc), click on *Format* button in the *Page Numbers* dialog box.
>
> ***Inserting Symbols***
>
> ***Inserting Hyperlink***
>
> newtopic **Spell Checking a Document**
>
> newtopic **Mail Merge**

6. INSERTING SYMBOLS

1. Select ***Insert > Symbol*** command, then ***Symbol*** dialog box will be displayed. (***Examples of symbols:*** c& e" k& ")
2. Select the desired font and then choose the desired symbol from the given symbols.
3. Click ***Insert*** button to insert the symbol in the document; otherwise click ***Cancel*** button.

Note: After clicking on ***Insert*** button, ***Cancel*** button becomes ***Close*** button, if you wish to insert another symbol, continue using above steps otherwise click ***Close*** button

7. INSERTING HYPERLINK

(Hyperlink refers to highlighted text to which a particular link is attached. Shortcut key for inserting hyperlink is Ctrl + K. For activating the hyperlink press Ctrl + Click on the desired link)

1. Select ***Insert > Hyperlink*** command then Hyperlink dialog box will be displayed.
2. Set the following options in Hyperlink dialog box-
   - **a.** ***Text to display:*** Enter the text you want to appear as hypertext (i.e. underlined highlighted word)
   - **b.** ***Link to:*** Select an appropriate option like existing document or place in this document or e-mail address and then choose the corresponding link you want to attach with the hypertext. Finally, click Ok.

newtopic Spell Checking a Document

Spell check is one of the powerful features of Word. It is also possible to check the spellings of the entire document including the header, footer and the hidden text.

STEPS FOR CHECKING THE SPELLINGS-

Choose ***Tools > Spelling and Grammar*** command, and then ***Spelling and Grammar*** dialog box will be displayed. It contains the following boxes and buttons-

1. ***Not in Dictionary:*** The first spelling error if any is shown in ***Not in Dictionary*** box.
2. ***Suggestion:*** List of suggestions related with the spelling error are displayed in the ***Suggestion*** box.
3. ***Ignore:*** Click ***Ignore*** button to ignore the spelling error and to retain the original word.
4. ***Ignore All :*** Click ***Ignore All*** to ignore all the occurrences of the spelling error.
5. ***Change:*** Click ***Change*** button to change the erroneous word.
6. ***Change All :*** Click ***Change All*** to change all the occurrences of the erroneous word.
7. ***Add:*** To add the misspelled word (if you find it as correct) into the WORD dictionary, click ***Add*** button.

new topic Mail Merge

1. Mail merge feature is used to combine information from two documents to produce merged documents e.g. mailing labels, mailing letters, envelopes, catalog etc. Mail merge involves 3 documents. The two documents combined to produce ***merged document*** are –
   a. ***Data source :*** Data source is an organized collection of records and fields.
   b. ***Main Document :*** It is the file containing the static contents of the document and the fields from data source are merged into main document to produce a merged document.

Steps for creating a Merged Document-

1. Create a main document
2. Create a data source
3. Create a merged document

First Step: Creating a Main Document

1. Select ***File > New***, to create a new document or open an existing file. This becomes the active window. Type in the desired contents (that remain static in all the copies of merged document)
2. Choose ***Tools > Mail merge***, then ***Mail merge Helper*** dialog box is displayed.
3. In dialog box, click the ***Create*** button under Main Document header, then a pull down menu appears containing the options like Form Letters, Mailing Labels etc.
4. Select ***Form Letters***, then a message will be displayed.
5. In the message window, click ***Active window*** button.
6. Then, the path of the currently opened or created document (i.e. active window) is displayed as the path of the main document below the Create button (in Mail Merge Helper dialog box)

Second Step: Creating a Data Source

1. In Mail Merge Helper dialog box, click on ***Get Data*** button.
2. Select ***Create Data source*** for creating new data source or ***Open data source*** for opening existing data source.
3. On clicking ***Create Data Source***, the Create Data Source dialog box is displayed. It provides you with a list of suggested field names-
   a. To add a new field to the field list, enter the field name in Field name box and click ***Add field name***
   b. To remove a field from the field list, select the field and click ***Remove field name.***
   c. Then, click OK.
4. The above step is followed by a ***Save As*** dialog box, wherein you can specify the location and name of the data source.
5. Then a message box is displayed that would inform you that the data source has no records. If you wish to enter records then click ***Edit Data Source*** button.
6. A data form is displayed, in which you can enter the desired number of records. Also you would be able to delete, find or restore the records, then click OK button to exit data form.

Third Step : Creating the Merged Document

1. Click on the ***Insert Merge field*** on the Mail Merge toolbar. Then, a drop down menu is displayed, containing all the fields present in recently created or opened data source.
2. Place the cursor at desired location in the main document, then click on the desired field you wish to insert at current location.
3. Repeat the above steps to insert all the required fields in a particular manner.
4. Then, choose ***Tools > Mail Merge***, Mail Merge Helper dialog box is displayed.
5. Click on ***Merge*** button under the Merge the data with the document header, and then Merge dialog box is displayed.
6. In Merge dialog box, specify the output of mail merge, number of records to be inserted and other merge related options, then click Merge button.
7. In this case, a merged document is produced that would consist of number of pages equivalent to the records merged from the data source. Each page contains the static contents of main document combined with each record from the data source.

newtopic Creating Letters and Labels

1. Select ***Tools > Envelopes and Labels***, then Envelopes and Labels dialog box is displayed. It has following tabs-

ENVELOPES TAB – Envelopes and Labels

1. Select ***Envelopes*** tab, then enter or edit ***Delivery Address*** in Delivery Address box and ***Return Address*** in Return Address box.
2. You can select ***Omit*** checkbox, if you do not want the Return Address to appear on the Envelope.
3. To print your envelope, click ***Print*** button, provided with that the envelope has been already fed in the printer tray.
4. To add the designed envelope in the active document, for later printing, click on ***Add to Document*** button. If you once add the envelope in the document, Add to Document button will become ***Change to Document***.
5. For setting other options like envelope size and font & font size of the delivery address and return address, click on ***Options*** button.

LABELS TAB – Envelopes and Labels

1. Select ***Labels*** tab, then enter or edit Address in Address box or use address book available in Ms-Outlook.
2. You can select any of the following Printing options-
   a. Full page of same label
   b. Single Label
3. For adding the label in a document, click ***New Document*** button.
4. For setting other options like Printer information, Label Products, Product Number etc, click on ***Options*** button.
5. For getting detailed information about the height, width, margin, pitch etc, click Details button.
6. For making a customized label, click ***New Label*** button.
7. For deleting an existing label, click on ***Delete*** button.

newtopic Creating Resume

A Resume is a document that outlines your skills (or talents) and experiences in order to communicate your objective or your contribution to the employer's organization. For a resume to be effective, you should know about the duties and skills required for the job and how to organize your resume around the points known in advance.

METHODS OF CREATING RESUME

1. Using Tables Menu :

This is the simplest method, of learning how to work with tables & make the resume in your own way. Example-For a simple resume containing headings on left side, heading - specific text entries on right side, both separated by a colon; Do the following:

1. Create a document by choosing ***File > New*** & then selecting ***Blank document*** option.
2. Insert a Table using ***Table > Insert Table*** command. Table should contain three columns and say ten number of rows (if your resume contains 10 headings)
3. Type the headings in first column.
4. Put a colon (:) in second column & using copy-paste, paste it in the rest of the rows of second column.
5. Enter your text entries in right column corresponding to each left-side heading.
6. If you type more than one statements or points in a row, apply bullets or numbering to them.
7. Finally, remove the borders of the table, by choosing ***None*** from the available Table Border options in ***Table > Table Properties*** command.
8. Then, see the Preview using ***File > Preview***. You will not find the grid of the table displayed in the final document.
9. Finally, to get a hard copy of it, choose ***File > Print*** command.

2. *Using Resume Template:*

Resume template refers to the pre-designed format of resume, which can be reused to create your resume. In this case, you have to perform only editing and not have to worry about formatting etc. For creating resume, using resume template do the following-

1. Select ***File > New*** command and click ***Other Documents*** tab in ***New*** dialog box. Choose one of the available resume templates-
   - i. Elegant Resume
   - ii. Contemporary Resume
   - iii. Professional Resume

   b. Finally, Click Ok.

   c. In this case, you will get a readymade resume. You can finally edit it according to your own requirements.

   d. Then select ***File > Print*** command to get a hard copy of your resume.

This method is best suitable when you wish to create a resume having the same layout and formatting features as that of the existing templates. In this case, you only require performing editing.

3. *Using Resume Wizard :*

Resume wizard is a step-by-step procedure of creating resume. Using resume wizard, you can modify or tailor your resume according to your requirements, while creating it. Resume wizard prompts you to specify or select desirable options in each step.

For creating a resume using resume wizard, do the following:

*Select **File > New** and click **Other Documents** tab. Then choose Resume Wizard & click Ok. Then Resume wizard dialog box is displayed. It consists of the following steps-*

- ***Step 1:*** Select one of the available Style for your resume. It may be Professional, Elegant or Contemporary. Click ***Next.***
- ***Step 2:*** Then, select the desired Type of resume you want to create. It may be- Entry-level, Chronological, Functional or Professional. Click ***Next.***
- ***Step 3:*** Enter your name and mailing address. Click ***Next***.
- ***Step 4:*** Select the desired headings from the available list of headings by checking corresponding checkbox. Click ***Next.***
- ***Step 5:*** This is also to select the available headings. However, it is an optional step. Click ***Next.***
- ***Step 6:*** The final step lets you to add or remove headings and also to sort the headings in required order. Click ***Finish.***

After clicking ***Finish***, you will get a resume having the desired style and headings as you have selected or specified in the wizard. At this stage, you are only required to enter the heading-specific entries.

newtopic Table Related Operations

A table is actually a grid of row and columns. A table may have any number of rows and columns

1. Inserting a Table/Row/Column

1. Place the insertion point at the desired location.
2. Select ***Table > Insert***, then, following sub options are displayed-
   a. ***Table :*** to insert table at the desired location
   b. ***Column to the Left:*** to insert the column to the left of selected column
   c. ***Column to the Right :*** to insert the column to the right of selected column
   d. ***Rows Above :*** to insert the rows above the selected row
   e. ***Rows Below :*** to insert the rows below the selected row
   f. ***Cells :*** to insert the cells in a table
3. ***On Selecting Inserting Table :*** If you select ***Table > Insert > Table*** option, then in Table dialog box, you have to specify the – (For the same you can also use Insert Table tool present on Table toolbar or standard toolbar)
   a. Number of columns by entering a numeric value
   b. Number of rows by entering a numeric value

2. Deleting a Table/Row/Column

1. Select the desired table, column, row or cell or just place the cursor in desired table, row, column or cell.
2. Select ***Table > Delete***, then, following sub options are displayed-
   - ***a. Table :*** select this to delete selected table
   - ***b. Column to the Left:*** select this to delete the column to the left of selected column
   - ***c. Column to the Right:*** click this to delete the column to the right of selected column
   - ***d. Rows Above:*** click this to delete the rows above the selected row
   - ***e. Rows Below:*** click this to delete the rows below the selected row
   - ***f. Cells :*** click this option to delete the cells in a table
3. You can select any of the above option, according to your requirement.

3. Selecting a Table/Row/Column

1. Place the cursor in desired table, row, column or cell.
2. Select ***Table > Select***, then, following sub options are displayed-
   - ***a. Table:*** Click this to select the desired table
   - ***b. Column:*** Select this option to select the desired column
   - ***c. Row:*** Click this to select the desired row
   - ***d. Cell:*** Click this to select the desired cell
3. Then, the corresponding table, column, row or cell will get selected.

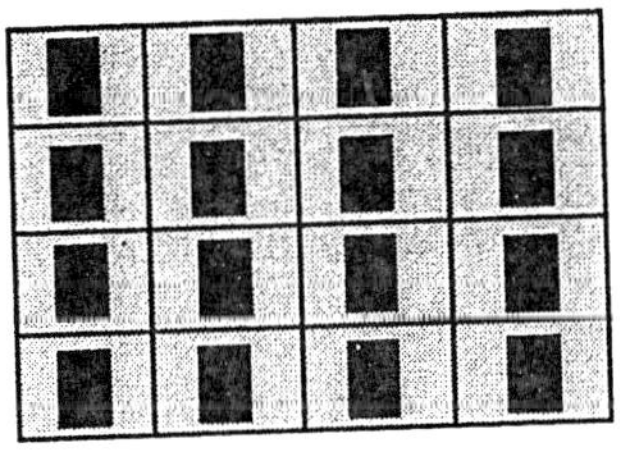

4. Merging Cells

1. Select the desired cells.
2. Select ***Table > Merge Cells*** option

   Or

   - Click ***Merge cells*** tool on the ***Table*** toolbar.
3. Then, the selected cells are combined to form a single cell.

ü **Example of Merged cells —**

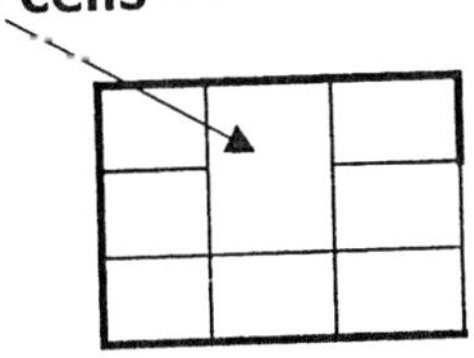

5. Sorting a Table

1. Select the desired items in a table or place the cursor in the column containing the list.
2. Select ***Table > Sort***, then, Sort dialog box is displayed.
3. Then, set the following option-
   - **a.** ***Sort by :*** Select the column name or column number from the given list under Sort by option.
   - **b.** ***Type :*** It refers to the type of the entries in a given list or column. It may be-
     - ***i. Text :*** If this type is selected, then list is sorted alphabetically
     - ***ii. Numeric :*** If this type is selected, then list is sorted numerically
     - ***iii. Date :*** If this type is selected, then list is sorted date wise.
   - **c.** ***Order :***
     - ***i. Ascending :*** It means from A to Z or from 1 to 9 or from earliest date to latest date.
     - ***ii. Descending :*** It means from Z to A or from 9 to 1 or from latest date to earliest date.
   - **d.** ***My list has :***
     - ***i. Header row :*** Select this if your list contains heading in the first row.
     - ***ii. No header row:*** Select this if your list do not contain headings in the first row
4. Then, click OK.

6. Setting Table Properties

1. Select the table or Place the cursor in the table.
2. Select ***Table > Properties***, then Properties dialog box is displayed.
3. ***Properties*** dialog box consists of following tabs-

TABLE TAB – **Table Properties**

Under this tab, set the following options-

1. ***Size:*** Select the preferred width check box and enter a numeric value for specifying the width
2. ***Measure in:*** Specify the unit for measuring the width of table.
3. ***Alignment:*** Select the desired alignment. Alignment may be- Left, Center or Right
4. ***Text Wrapping:*** Select the text wrapping property as None or Around (if you wish to wrap the text around table)
5. ***Borders and Shading:*** Select the desired border width, border color, border style and shading etc to perform grid formatting

ROW TAB – Table Properties

Under this tab, you can specify the height of each row explicitly by using ***Previous row*** and ***Next row*** buttons

COLUMN TAB – Table Properties

Under this tab, you can specify the width of each column explicitly by using ***Previous Column*** or ***Next Column*** buttons

CELL TAB – Table Properties

Under this tab, you can specify the width of the cell as well as the vertical alignment i.e. alignment of text with respect to a cell. Vertical alignment may be - Top, Center or Bottom.

7. Converting Text to Table and Vice-Versa

1. Select the Table or text.
2. Select ***Table > Convert***, then two sub options are displayed-
   a. *Text to table:* used to convert selected text into table
   b. *Table to text:* used to convert selected table into text.

Select the appropriate option.

Case of Text to Table:

1. On clicking this option, ***Convert Text to Table*** dialog box is displayed, in which you can specify the following options-
   1. ***Table size:*** specify the number of columns and number of rows
   2. ***AutoFit behavior:*** select the appropriate options for setting the AutoFit behavior of table.
   3. ***Separate text at:*** select the mark by which you wish to separate text

Case of Table to Text :

1. On clicking this option, ***Convert Table to Text*** dialog box is displayed, in which you can specify the separator characters to be used to separate the text.
2. Separator characters may be tab, comma, paragraph mark or any other specified character.
3. Generally, row endings are converted to paragraph marks and column endings are converted to comma, tab or other specified mark.

8. Splitting a Table

Split Table option is used to split table

1. Place the cursor at the desired place, in the table.
2. Select ***Table > Split Table***, then the table gets splitted into two.

Creating HTML Document

*A Html document or a web page can be created in **MS-WORD** by using one of the following methods-*

a. Creating a web page based on **Template.**

b. Creating a web page from the **existing WORD document.**

c. Creating a web page using **Web Page Wizard.**

1. Creating a Web Page Based on Template :-

1. On the **File** menu, click **New**.
2. Do one of the following:
   - On the **General** tab, click **Web Page** to open a blank Web page.
   - On the **Web Pages** tab, click the template that you want to base your Web page on.

2. Creating a Web Page from the Existing WORD Document

1. Open an existing WORD document using ***File > Open*** option.
2. On the **File** menu, click **Save as Web Page**.
3. In the **File name** box, type a name for the document.
4. In the ***Save as Type*** box, select Web Page (or HTML document)

3. Creating a Web Page Using Web Page Wizard

1. On the **File** menu, click **New**, and then click the **Web Pages** tab.
2. Click **Web Page Wizard** and follow the given steps (instructions) in the wizard-

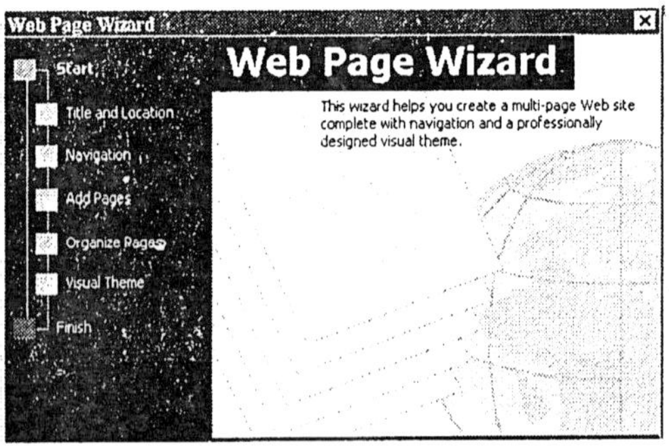

Steps 1: *Specify the title and location of saving the web site.*

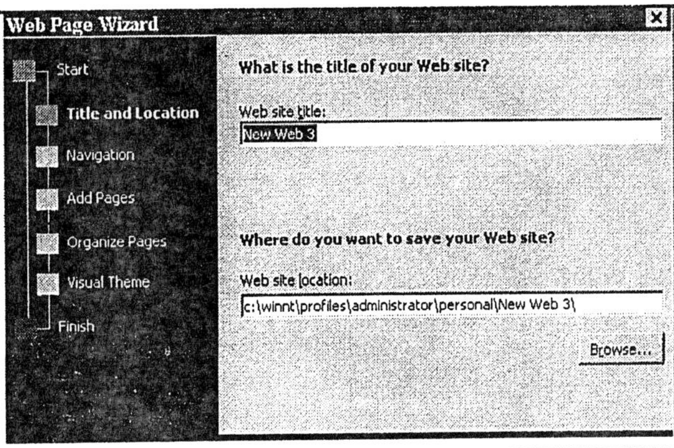

Step 2: *Specify the type of navigation that you want for your web site. It can be-*

- Vertical Frame
- Horizontal Frame
- Separate Page

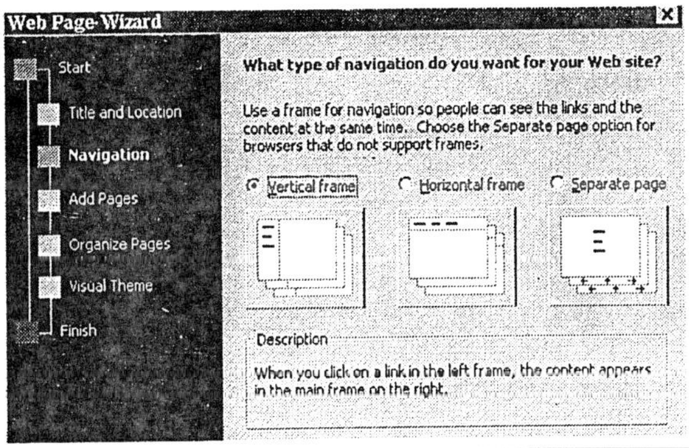

Step 3: *Specify the pages to be added to your web site from the current file or from the existing file(s).*

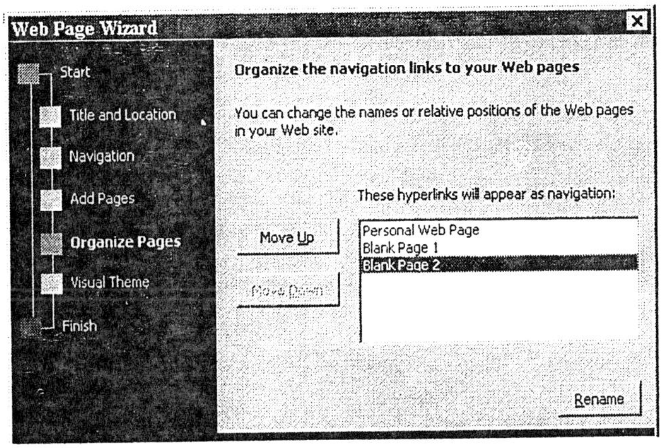

Step 4: *You can customize the order of the web pages of your web site.*

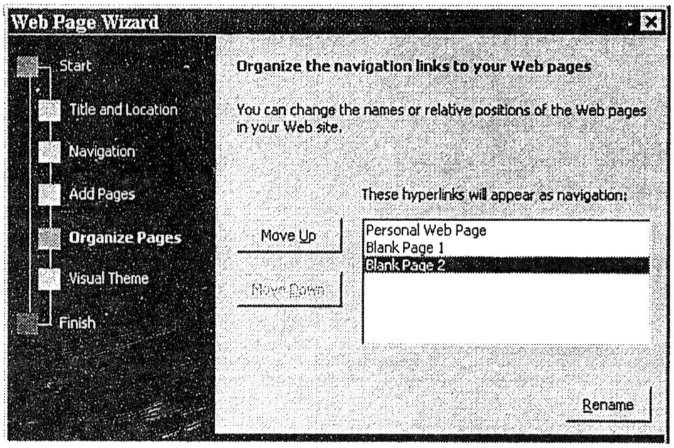

Step 5 : *Specify the theme you want to set for the web site. The application of a theme changes the appearance of your web site like it's background, font color, font etc.*

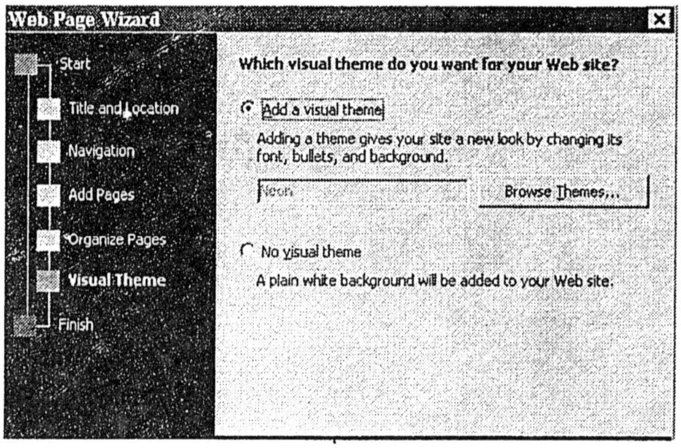

Step 6 : *Click* ***Finish*** *to view your web page.*

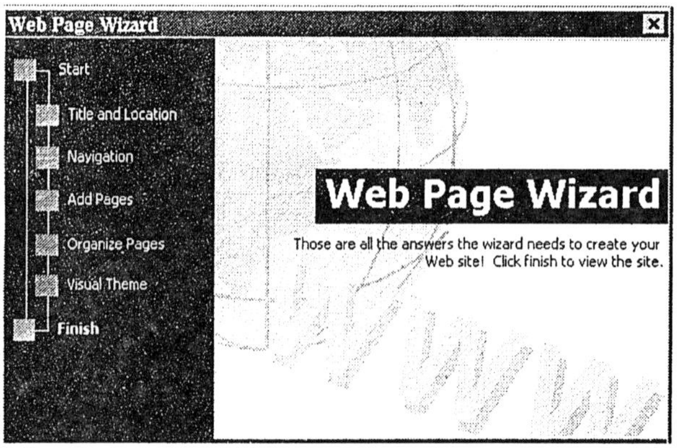

15

Microsoft Excel

Introduction:

1. Excel is a very powerful window based spreadsheet developed by Microsoft Corporation.
2. The concept of spreadsheets emerged, when the need of the business community grew with the growth in the size of organizations. Thus, the need to automate the manual business procedures using computer is responsible for the emergence or development of spreadsheets.
3. Electronic Spreadsheet packages are application programs used for analysis of data, planning and modeling in order to substitute the paper work in offices. It is basically an electronic grid of horizontal rows and vertical columns.
4. It is basically a number processor. It helps in calculations involving standard formula and representing data in various forms like graphs or charts.
5. It contains **65,536** rows and **256** columns. A cell is referenced using unique column name and row number. The columns are labeled from A....Z, AA...AZ....up to IV and the rows are numbered from 1 to 65, 536.
6. The first spreadsheet invented was **Visi Calc**.
7. **Other Examples of spreadsheets** are- Lotus 1-2-3, Excel, QuattroPro etc.
8. Spreadsheets also help managers in decision making by performing what-if analysis.
9. There are various functions available in the electronic spreadsheet for calculating mean, mode, median, average, standard deviation etc.
10. It also provides **OLE** support ie. Object Linking and Embedding. It means that using this feature, objects of different application programs can be inserted in Ms-Excel and vice-versa.

STARTING MS-EXCEL

Click ***Start > Programs > Microsoft Excel*** option

Or

Double click on the Microsoft Excel icon present on the desktop.

COMPONENTS OF EXCEL WINDOW

- **Title Bar:** Name of application program & name of currently opened workbook is displayed on it. It also contains control buttons.

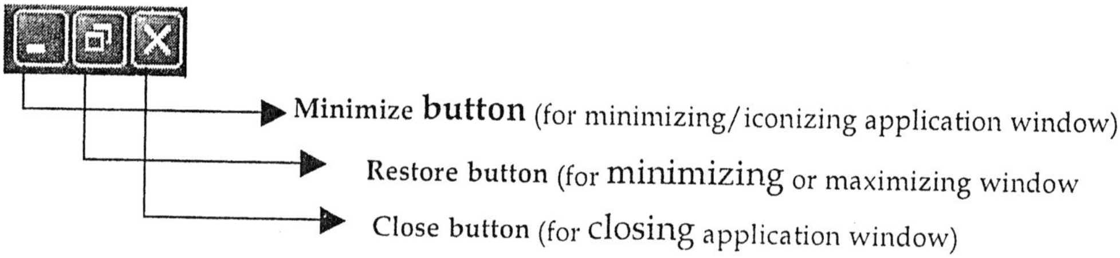

- **Menu Bar:** It refers to the horizontal bar containing menu items or pads like File, Edit, View etc. Menu items can be accessed using mouse, just by clicking on related menu item. Although these can be accessed using keyboard shortcut key: Alt + Underlined character in menu items name e.g. Alt + F is used for accessing File Menu. For navigating through commands under a menu item, Arrow key can be used. For executing a particular command, Enter key can be used.
- **Toolbar:** It refers to the graphical or pictorial representation of commands present under different menu items like File, Edit etc. Some common Toolbars are-
    - o Standard Toolbar: **contains tools for managing operations related to file & editing operations**
    - o Formatting Toolbar: **contains tools for changing the appearance of text i.e. Text formatting or object**
- **Address Box:** It displays the address of the active cell.
- **Formula Bar**: It is used for entering/editing/displaying formula used in the target cell.
- **Columns & Row Headings:** The rows headers are numbered as 1,2,3..... 65536. The column headers are labeled as A, B...Z, AA, AB....AZ,....IV
- **Scroll Bar:** used for navigating in worksheet window. Navigation refers to moving up & down through the cells in a worksheet. We have horizontal & vertical scroll bars.
- **Office Assistant:** It is basically an online help. It helps user to work conveniently by displaying related messages.
- **Grid of cells/Worksheet Window:** The worksheet window (spreadsheet) is actually a grid (group of horizontal rows & columns) of cells. A cell refers to the intersection of rows and columns.
- **Sheet Navigator Buttons:** These are used to switch over among first, last, next or previous sheet.
- **Sheet Tabs:** Sheet tabs represent the entire number of individual sheets present in the workbook.

- **Drawing Toolbar:** It contains several tools used for drawing pictures & various shapes.
- **Status Bar:** It is used to display important information related to worksheet. Besides this it also displays help messages like READY. It also indicates the status of few keys **e.g.** the status of CAPS LOCK key & NUM LOCK Key is displayed as CAPS & NUM respectively in different panes of the status bar.

newtopic WorkBook Related Operations

1. CREATING A NEW WORKBOOK

1. Select **File > New** option, then **New** dialog box is displayed.
2. Select **General** tab and click **Workbook** option in **New** dialog box
3. Click on **OK**

   Or

   Click **New** tool on the standard toolbar. *(or press Ctrl + N shortcut key)*

In both the cases, a new blank workbook is created. By default name of workbook is Book1 and extension is .xls

Excel can work with the following types of cell entries-

1. ***Labels:*** Text values such as names and addresses.
2. ***Numbers:*** Numeric values such as 34, -897, 987.876 and 0
3. ***Formulas:*** Expressions that compute numeric results.
4. ***Date and Time Values:*** These values are treated as numbers, thus right aligned.
5. ***Data Series:*** A collection of data values having a uniform relationship between each other.

2. SAVING A WORKBOOK

1. Select **File > Save** option, and then ***Save As...*** dialog box is displayed
2. Then specify location, where you wish to save the file
3. After then, specify the desired file name
4. Click on **Save** button

   Or

   Click ***Save*** button on the standard toolbar *(or press Ctrl + S shortcut key)*

In both the cases, existing workbook will be saved.

3. CLOSING A WORKBOOK

1. Select **File > Close** option

In this case, active workbook will get closed

4. OPENING A WORKBOOK

1. Select **File > Open** option, then **Open** dialog box is displayed
2. Then specify location of existing file
3. After then, select the desired file or specify the desired file name
4. Click **Open** button

Or

Click **Open** tool on the standard toolbar. *(or press Ctrl + O shortcut key)*

In both the cases, existing workbook will get opened.

5. MAKING SELECTION IN EXCEL

A single cell	Click the cell or use arrow keys to activate a desired cell
Range of cells within a column/row	Click the first cell and drag up to the last cell.
All cells on a worksheet	Press Ctrl+A or choose Edit > Select all option
Rectangular Range of cells involving multiple columns/rows	Click the first cell. Hold down the shift key pressed and click on the last cell of the range
Non-contiguous range of cells	Click the first cell. Hold down the Ctrl key pressed and then click on other non-contiguous cells to be selected
Entire Row	Click on the desired row header like 1, 2, 3 and so on.
Entire Column	Click on the desired column header like A, B, C and so on.
Contiguous columns/rows	Click on first column/row header. Drag up to the last column/row (or Shift key is pressed before clicking on last column/row)
Non-contiguous columns/rows	Click on the first column/row header. Press down Ctrl key, click on desired column/row headers.

6. CREATING A COPY OF A WORKBOOK

1. Select **File > Save As** option, then **Save As** dialog box is displayed
2. Then specify location, where you wish to save the file

3. After then, specify the new file name
4. Click on **Save** button

Or

Press **F12** shortcut key

In both the cases, a new copy of the existing workbook will be created.

7. PRINT PREVIEWING A WORKSHEET:

In this mode, worksheet cannot be edit. However it is only used to set the margins and contents of the worksheet.

- Select **File > Print Preview** command.

Or

1. Click the Print Preview button on the standard toolbar
2. Then, EXCEL switches to the print preview mode.
3. In Print Preview mode, print preview toolbar appears that consists of the following buttons-
   a. **Next :** Click it to switch to preview of next page
   b. **Previous :** Click it to switch to preview of previous page
   c. **Zoom :** Click it to switch between enlarged or reduced preview of active page
   d. **Normal /Page break view :** Click it to switch between Preview mode to Normal view or Page break view respectively
   e. **Setup :** Click it to open Page Setup dialog box for making certain page related options like margins, header/footer etc.
   f. **Print :** Click it to open Print dialog box, in order to give the actual print order to the active printer.
   g. **Margins :** Click it to display all the margin tabs, using which you can modify the height of row or width of column.
   h. **Close :** Click this to exit out print preview mode.

8. PRINTING A WORKSHEET:

Print command is used to obtain the hard copy of the worksheet.

1. Select **File > Print** option, then a dialog box is displayed.
2. Then specify the required information related to printing in dialog box.
3. Then, click OK

Or

Click the **Print** button on the standard toolbar

Set the following options in the Print dialog box & click OK-

1. ***Name:*** It indicates the name of active printer. For sending a fax, hereby, you can specify the name of fax machine currently attached to your system and then proceed the print command in usual manner.

2. ***Status:*** It indicates the status of the selected printer busy or idle
3. ***Where:*** It displays the port to which printing output is sent i.e. LPT1 or LPT2 or USB001 etc
4. ***Copies:*** Enter the required no. of copies to be printed
5. ***Collate:*** It is used to organize multi-page worksheet, in case if we wish to print multiple copies of it. If this option is selected, then worksheet pages will be printed set wise i.e.. First all the pages of a current worksheet will be printed, then a copy of the entire set of pages will be produced.
6. ***Print Range:*** It is used to specify the pages to be printed. The page range should be specified using hyphen in between i.e. 2- 8. For specifying non-consecutive pages to be printed, comma can be used to separate different page numbers like 4, 9, 20 and so on.
   a. ***All:*** Select this to print all the worksheets of the current workbook.
   b. ***Page(s) From:*** Select this to specify a desired range of pages to print like 2-6, 5-9 etc.
7. ***Print What:*** Select one of the following options to specify what has to be printed-
   - ***Selection:*** Click this in order to print only the selected range of cells.
   - ***Active Sheet:*** Click this in order to print only the active/current worksheet.
   - ***Entire Workbook:*** Click this in order to print all the worksheets of a current workbook.
8. ***Properties:*** Click this button to set the following properties. This is followed by a dialog box that contains following options-
   a. ***Size is :*** Click Size is list box to select the desired paper size.
   b. ***Type is:*** Click Type is list box to select the desired type of the paper.
   c. ***Print Quality:*** You can select the desired print quality like Normal, Draft, Best etc.
   d. ***Orientation:*** Select the desired orientation of page like Portrait or Landscape.
   e. ***Mirror Image:*** Click this checkbox, in order to print the mirror image of a given page.
   f. ***Page Order:*** Select one of the following to specify in which order the given page range will print. Let us take an example, you have 10 pages to print.
      - *Front to Back: If this option is selected then page order will be 1,2,3... ..10*
      - *Back to Front: If this option is selected then page order will be 10,9,8 .. ..1*
   g. ***Copies :*** Enter a numeric value to specify the count of copies (of the given pages) to be printed.

Editing Operations

1. UNDO & REPEAT

Undo is used to revert the currently done changes in the worksheet. The shortcut key for Undo is ***Ctrl + Z.*** Repeat command is used to repeat the changes reverted using Undo command. The shortcut key for Repeat command is ***Ctrl + Y.***

2. CUT, COPY & PASTE

Cut command is used to move the selected content (text or picture) into clipboard. The steps are as follows-

1. Select the desired content *(cell entry or range of cells)*
2. Select **Edit > Cut** option

   Or

   Click **Cut** tool on the standard toolbar *(or press Ctrl + X shortcut key)*

Copy command is used to copy the contents of worksheet into clipboard for further pasting it in the worksheet. The steps are as follows-

- Select **Edit > Copy** option

  Or

- Click **Copy** tool on the standard toolbar *(or press Ctrl + C shortcut key)*

Paste command is used to paste the contents from clipboard (cut or copied items) into the worksheet. The steps of performing Paste operation are as follows-

- Select **Edit > Paste** option

  Or

- Click **Paste** tool on the standard toolbar *(or press Ctrl + V shortcut key)*

3. FIND & REPLACE

FIND (Find is used to search a desired text in the entire worksheet)

1. Open a desired worksheet.
2. Select ***Edit > Find*** option, then a dialog box is displayed. Set the following options in the Find dialog box-

   a. ***Find What:*** In this box, enter the desired text you want Excel to find.

   b. ***Search:*** This is used to specify the search direction or the search method used in the worksheet. You may select either By Rows or By Columns.

   c. ***Look in:*** In Look in combo box, you may select Formulas, Comments or Values in order to specify the type of worksheet content or element in which you want to find the desired text.

d. Special options:

- ***Match Case:*** used to find the characters by matching the Case (uppercase or lowercase) of text.
- ***Find Entire Cells only:*** used to find the exact contents of the cell as specified in Find What box.

3. Specify the desired options related to text that has to be found.
4. Then, click Find Next button in order to find the text otherwise click Cancel button.

Or

Press **Ctrl + F**

REPLACE (Replace is used to replace selected cell entry with the desired string.

1) Select **Edit > Replace** option, then a dialog box is displayed.
2) Specify the desired options in the Replace dialog box. Set the following options in the dialog box-
   a) ***Find What box :*** In this, you must enter the text you want to find.
   b) ***Replace with box :*** In this, you must enter the replacement text.
   c) ***Search :*** This is used to specify the search direction or the search method used in the worksheet. You may select either By Rows or By Columns.
   d) ***Match Case :*** used to find the characters by matching the Case (uppercase or lowercase) of text.
   e) ***Find Entire Cells Only :*** used to find the exact contents of the cell as specified in Find What box.
3) Then, click Find Next button. If a match is found, then two options are there-
   a) ***Replace :*** To replace the first occurrence of the word found by the desired word
   b) ***Replace All :*** To replace all the occurrences of the word found by the desired word

Or

–Press **Ctrl + H**

new topic View Related Operations

1. VIEWS OF MS-EXCEL

a. A view consists of a variety of settings (like print setting etc) that affect the display of information on the worksheet.
b. You can set different views for different worksheets like- Normal view, Page Break Preview, Print Preview, Web Page Preview

c. You can also create custom views using **Views > Custom Views** command. Using this command you create new custom views as well as you can switch to the desired view that you have already created.

d. Different custom views of the same worksheet can be created so that you can view your data differently without saving the same data in different worksheets.

NORMAL VIEW:

Select **View > Normal** option, then your workbook will be displayed in Normal view.

Characteristics of Normal Layout:

1. Normal view is the by-default view.
2. Used for usual data entering and working on worksheets.
3. Print area & page breaks can be seen marked with dotted lines.

PAGE BREAK PREVIEW

Select **View > Page Break Preview** option

Characteristics of Page Break Preview: -

1. Page Break Preview displays the exact position of data on different pages. Thus, it lets you know about which data will get printed on each page.
2. Page breaks and print areas (print areas refers to range of cells marked for printing) are displayed clearly.
3. This view cannot be used for working with data entered on worksheets.

2. HEADER AND FOOTER

1. Header is the information, repetitively displayed at the top of each page.
2. Footer is the information, repetitively displayed at the bottom of each page.
3. Header and Footer are generally used for printed pages.
4. In header and footer, you can place text, image, graphics, date and page number etc.

How to insert header and footer

1. Select ***View > Header & Footer*** option to create, view or edit the header & footer of the worksheets. In this case, Header and Footer toolbar is displayed on the screen to edit or to switch between header and footer.
2. Then, **Page Setup** dialog box is displayed. Under the Header & Footer tab, select the desired built-in header or footer.
3. You can also customize built-in header or footer by clicking ***Custom Header*** or ***Custom Footer*** buttons respectively. (As explained earlier in Page Setup option)

3. COMMENTS

A comment is an extra information or note or additional supplement that you wish to attach to a particular cell entry. Comment is such information that is not directly included in a worksheet although it is linked or attached to a cell entry in the worksheet. Comments can be viewed as well as printed.

1. Select **View > Comments**, then all the comments are displayed in worksheet (comments are displayed at the same locations where they were created).
2. The cells to which a comment is associated, is indicated by a red mark on the top right corner of the cell.
3. Comments can also be viewed by resting the mouse pointer on the cell to which comment is associated.
4. You can review the comments in a sequential order (one by one) by using Reviewing toolbar. Besides this, you can insert, edit or switch between various comments in the worksheet, using this toolbar.
5. Click **Next Comment** button to move the focus to Next comment in the worksheet.
6. Likewise, click **Previous Comment** button to move the focus to Previous comment in the worksheet.
7. Comments can be inserted using **Insert > Comments** option.
8. Comments can also be deleted by selecting the desired cell containing comment and clicking **Delete Comment** button

newtopic AutoSum Feature

1. AutoSum is an important feature in Excel.
2. It provides a facility for adding a given range of cells just by clicking **AutoSum** button.
3. AutoSum button is displayed on the Standard toolbar & looks like a statistical symbol (sigma)

Steps of using AutoSum for calculating sum of given values-

1. Enter the desired values in a contiguous range of cells (horizontally or vertically)
2. Activate the target cell (in which the result has to be obtained) by clicking it.
3. Click AutoSum button Σ, then formula is displayed in the target cell.
4. Press Enter key to obtain the final result.
5. It should be noted that AutoSum button is making use of **SUM** function, which can be, used as-

   Syntax = SUM (range of cells)

newtopic AutoFill Feature

1. AutoFill is a special feature of Excel that provides a facility for filling cells with a series of values.

2. The fill handle (a small black square), which is displayed at the lower right corner of the selected cell is used to fill a range of values.

Steps for filling an in-built series like month series, days series are-

1. Activate a cell
2. Type the first value of the series (like Jan or Mon)
3. Then, drag the fill handle either horizontally or vertically to fill the navigated cells with the values of series.

Steps for filling a desired series like odd number series or even number series are-

1. Activate a cell
2. Type the first two values of the series in two contiguous/continuous cells (like 2, 4 in case of even series or 1,3 in odd series)
3. Select both the cells using the selector
4. Then, drag the fill handle either horizontally or vertically to fill the navigated cells with the values of series.

CREATING CUSTOMIZED SERIES

1. Besides the month and weekday names, Excel can fill in any list of values.
2. To add your own AutoFill list to Excel built-in lists, perform the following steps-
   a. Select **Tools > Options** command
   b. Click the ***Custom Lists*** tab to display the current AutoFill lists in effect.
   c. Click the ***Add*** button, in order to add a new AutoFill series.
   d. Type the desired values for creating a new AutoFill series. Hit Enter key after entering each value (to separate them) or insert comma after each entry.
   e. Click **Ok** to add your list to AutoFill current list.

Examples-

1. AutoFill series of Planets- Mercury, Venus, Earth, Mars, Jupiter, Saturn, Uranus, Neptune, Pluto
2. AutoFill series of types of cables used in networking- Twisted pair, Coaxial, Fiber Optics etc.
3. Suppose, in case if you are a frequent user of Excel for maintaining database of school, then in such case, you can create AutoFill series of students names of different classes. By doing so, whenever you require the list of names of students, there is no need to copy & paste from one file to another. Simply type in the name of first student and drag the fill handle across to fill in rest of the names.

Formatting

1. FORMATTING OF CELLS

1. Formatting refers to the change of appearance of selected cells.
2. The formatting characteristic of a cell or range in a worksheet includes the numeric display format, the alignment, the font selection, borders etc.
3. To change the format of cells, select **Format > Cells**, then Format Cells dialog box is displayed. It contains following tabs-
   a. Number
   b. Alignment
   c. Font
   d. Border
   e. Patterns
   f. Protection
4. Set the appropriate options under these tabs and click OK. (Tabs Discussed later in this book)

NUMBER TAB

1. The number format determines how numbers should appear on the sheet (both on the screen as well as when printed)
2. Most of the numbers in the workbook are initially formatted with the general format.
3. Some of the common Formats are-
   a. General: The numeric data has no special formatting and generally appears exactly the way you enter the data.
   b. Number: It is used for the general display of numbers.
   c. Currency: This format is used for displaying monetary value
   d. Date: It is used to display date values.
   e. Time: It is used to display time values.

ALIGNMENT TAB

1. **Text Alignment:** Alignment refers to the position of text with respect to cell. Text Alignment are of two types-
   a. Horizontal: The alignment of text with respect to horizontal axis (x-axis) is called horizontal alignment. It may be- Left, Right, Center. The default horizontal alignment is General (text values——left aligned, numeric values——right aligned, logical & error values——center aligned)
   b. Vertical: The alignment of text with respect to vertical axis (y-axis) is called vertical alignment. It may be — Top, Bottom, Center. The default vertical alignment is Bottom.

2. **Orientation:** It refers to the angular rotation of text within a cell. Either select a numeric value for specifying angle of rotation or select the desired type of orientation.
3. **Text Control:** You can check one of the given checkbox as per your requirement-

a. ***Wrap Text:*** Click this checkbox, if you want to type multiple lines within the same cell.

b. ***Shrink to Fit:*** Click this checkbox, if you want to shrink the selected text so that it would fit into containing cell (irrespective of its height & width)

c. ***Merge Cells:*** Click this checkbox, if you want to combine two or more cells to obtain a single cell. It should be noted that, desired cells should be merged before typing their contents. Otherwise, the contents of only first cell of the selected range of cells would be restored on merging.

FONT TAB

1. **Font:**
   a. It refers to style of writing a character. By default, font is Times New Roman.
   b. e.g. Times New Roman, Tahoma, Courier New etc.
2. **Font Size:**
   a. It refers to the size of the font. It is measured in Points.
   b. Max. font size is 72 points. However, this maximum number varies from one font to other font. By default font size is 12.
3. **Font Style:**
   a. It refers to different styles of font like- Regular, Bold, Italic, Bold Italic.
   b. By default Font style is Regular.
4. **Color:**
   a. It refers to color of the Font. By default Font color is Automatic (Black)
   b. You can use the available colors in the color palette or you can use the standard or customized colors by using More Colors option in Color Palette.
5. **Underline:**
   a. It refers to style of underline.
   b. e.g. This is an underline style, This is a words only underline style
   c. By default font underline style is none (i.e No underline)
6. **Effects:** (You can apply required effects by selecting the appropriate checkbox)
   a. **Strikethrough :** **e.g.** This is strikethrough effect
   b. **Superscript :** **e.g.** 7^2
   c. **Subscript :** **e.g.** H_2O

BORDER TAB

A border is a cell outline that you can apply to enclose selected cells. Set the following options under Border tab-

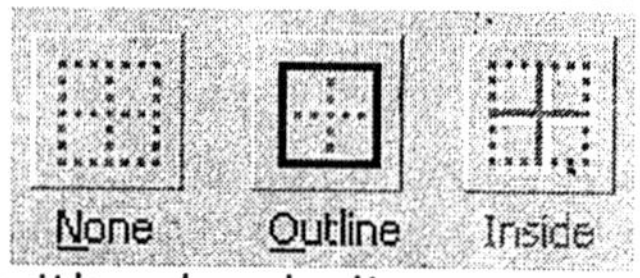

1. **Presets:** Select one of the following formats-
   a. ***None:*** Select this to remove borders.
   b. ***Outline:*** Select this to outline selected cells with a borderline.
   c. ***Inside:*** Select this to outline all the cells in the selected range individually i.e.. To apply Inside border to a selected range.
2. **Line Style:** Select the desired line style (dashed, dotted etc) from the Style box.
   a. ***Color:*** Select the desired color of the border from the color palette.
   b. ***Border:*** You can click the corresponding buttons to modify the border settings of even the different edges of selected cell. The modified settings can be visualized by the Preview diagram displayed in the dialog box.

PATTERNS TAB

Under this tab, you can set following options-

a. ***Shading:*** For shading a cell or a range of cells, select one of the desired color from the Color palette displayed under Cell Shading option. Select No Color button to remove cell shading. Then, click Ok.

b. ***Pattern:*** For shading a cell with desired pattern, click Pattern list box, select one of the given pattern (You can also select the color of the pattern from the color palette displayed in Pattern list box, otherwise pattern is applied using black color). Then, click Ok.

In each case, you can visualize the shading or pattern settings through the Sample box displayed.

2. FORMATTING OF ROWS

1. Select the desired row (by clicking on desired row number) or range of rows (by clicking and dragging along the range of row numbers)
2. Select **Format > Rows** and choose one of the formatting options from the sub menu desirably.
3. Formatting of Rows include following options-
   a. **Height:**
      i. On clicking this option, Row Height dialog box is displayed.
      ii. In Row Height dialog box, you can view current height or to edit it to set the desired height of the row. Click Ok.
   b. **AutoFit:**
      i. Click this option in order to fit the contents of cells by automatically modifying the height of the row. (You only need this option in case, if you have set wrap text option for that row using Format > Cells command)

c. Hide

i. Click this option if you want to hide selected rows temporarily.

ii. Hiding does not mean deleting rows from the worksheet.

iii. When you hide a given range of rows or simply one row, then, a smooth black line is displayed in place of the hidden row(s)

d. Unhide:

i. Click this option to unhide already hidden rows using Hide option.

3. FORMATTING OF COLUMNS

1. Select the desired column (by clicking on desired column label/header) or range of columns (by clicking and dragging along the range of column headers)
2. Select **Format > Columns** and choose one of the formatting options from the sub menu desirably.
3. Formatting of Columns include following options-

a. **Width:**

i. On clicking this option, ***Column Width*** dialog box is displayed.

ii. In Column Width dialog box, you can view current width or to edit it to set the desired width of the column. Click Ok.

b. **AutoFit Selection:**

i. Click this option in order to fit the contents of cells by automatically modifying the width of the column. (You only need this option in case, if length of text exceeds the size of column width)

c. ***Hide:***

i. Click this option if you want to hide selected column(s) temporarily.

ii. Hiding does not mean deleting columns from the worksheet.

iii. When you hide a given range of columns or simply one column, then, a smooth black line is displayed in place of the hidden column(s)

d. **Unhide:**

i. Click this option to unhide already hidden rows using ***Hide*** option.

e. ***Standard Width***

i. Click this option & enter desired width in ***Standard Width*** dialog box. This is used to set the same width for all the columns in a worksheet.

4. AUTOFORMATTING

AutoFormat is a built-in feature of Excel, using which you can select one of the pre-defined formats and apply to selected range of cells. AutoFormat including formatting features like Font, Borders, Pattern, Number, Alignment, and Width/ Height etc.

Performing AutoFormatting

1. Select the range of cells to which the format has to be applied.
2. Select **Format > AutoFormat** command, then AutoFormat dialog box is displayed.
3. Select a desired Format from the list of **Table Formats**.
4. Click Ok.

5. CONDITIONAL FORMATTING

Conditional formatting refers to formatting of a given range of cells on the basis of a particular criteria based on the cell value or the formula contained in a cell. Conditional formatting can be applied on the cells (e.g.. Applying borders) or on the contents of cells (e.g.. Applying Font color)

Performing Conditional Formatting

1. Select the desired range of cells to which you want to apply conditional formatting.
2. Select **Format > Conditional Formatting**, then Conditional Formatting dialog box is displayed.
3. Specify Condition 1 by selecting-
   a. ***The basis of condition:*** Select either Cell Value Is or Formula Is
   b. ***Operator :*** Select the desirable logical or relational operator like between, equal to, less than etc
   c. ***Value or Operands :*** Enter the values involved in condition.
4. Then, set the format of cells by clicking on **Format** button. It is followed by Format dialog box in which you can modify the options related to —— Font, Border or Pattern.
5. Click **Add** in order to add condition 1 and corresponding format features to the Condition list.
6. Likewise, you can enter up to three conditions. Click Ok.

Removing Conditional Formatting:

1. Select the desired range of cells on which conditions are already applied.
2. Select **Format > Conditional Formatting**, which is followed by Conditional Formatting dialog box.
3. Click **Delete** button, then **Delete Conditional Format** dialog box is displayed.
4. Select the checkbox corresponding to condition i.e.. Condition1, Condition2 or Condition3 & click Ok.

Sorting of Data

Sorting refers to the arrangement of records in ascending or descending order

Steps for Performing Sort

1. Select the desired range of the data that you wish to sort.
2. Select **Data > Sort** command, then Sort dialog box is displayed.
3. In the Sort dialog box, set the following options-
   a. **Sort by:** Click drop-down control in the Sort by box, then all the fields of the selected range is displayed. Select the desired field used for sorting.
   b. **Sort Order:** Select the desired sorting order- Ascending or descending.
   c. **Then by:** You can also specify the field name in the Then by box, in case if you wish to sort another column of the selected range on the basis of field specified in the Sort by box. (Sorting of a column on the basis of previously sorted column)
   d. **My list has:** You can also specify whether the selected range contains header row or not.
   e. **Options:** You can click on Options button for setting other options related with sorting like case sensitiveness or sorting orientation (sort top to bottom or sort left to right)
4. Click Ok.
5. After setting above options, Excel carries out sorting in the specified manner.

newtopic Insert Related Operations

1. CELLS/ ROW(S)/ COLUMN(S)

Inserting Cells

1. Select the desired location, where you want to insert cells.
2. Select ***Insert > Cells*** command. It is followed by ***Insert Cells*** dialog box.
3. Select one of the following options in the dialog box-
   a. ***Shift Cells right:*** Select this if you want to move the contents of active cell to the right cell, on inserting new blank cell.
   b. ***Shift Cells down:*** Select this if you want to shift cells down on inserting new blank cell.
   c. ***Entire Row:*** Select this if you want to insert an entire row.
   d. ***Entire Column:*** Select this if you want to insert an entire column.
4. Click Ok.

Inserting Rows

1. Select the desired row heading above which you want to insert a new row.
2. Choose ***Insert > Rows*** command.

3. Then, a single row is inserted above the selected row. *(In order to insert multiple rows, select the rows in advance then select Insert > Rows command)*

Inserting Columns

1. Select the desired column label before which you want to insert a new column.
2. Choose ***Insert > Columns*** command.
3. Then, a single column is inserted before the selected column. (*In order to insert multiple columns, select the columns in advance then select Insert > Columns command)*

2. PICTURE

This option is used to insert picture in the worksheet from clipart gallery.

1. Place the insertion point at the desired location in a worksheet.
2. Select **Insert > Picture**, then, select Clipart from the available sub options.

Or

1. Click **ClipArt tool** on the drawing toolbar.
2. Then, Microsoft Clipart Gallery dialog box is displayed, select one of the Category.
3. Then click the desired image and click **Insert picture tool.**

3. CHART

1. Chart is a graphical or pictorial representation of data placed on a worksheet.
2. Chart can either be placed on a separate **Chart Sheet** or can be placed on the same worksheet containing the actual data.
3. Charts are automatically updated as soon as you update data placed on the worksheet.
4. Chart Sheets can be printed like normal worksheets.
5. In Excel, charts can be either 2-Dimensional (2D) or 3-Dimensional (3D).
6. ***Examples:*** Line chart, Bar Chart, Pie chart, Radar chart, Area chart etc.

Steps of Inserting Chart

Select **Insert > Chart**, then Chart wizard is displayed. This wizard consists of four basic steps. Perform all the steps sequentially, by clicking **Next** each time. Finally, click **Finish**.

First Step : Select the type of chart and one of the chart types and click **Next.**

Second Step :

1. Select the data range by clicking on Collapse dialog button in **Data Range** box (Data Range is automatically displayed if you have already selected the data range)

2. Specify the type of series by selecting either **Rows** (for row wise series) or **Columns** (for column wise series) and Click Next.

Third Step :

It is the core step in the chart wizard. It lets you specify various properties of a chart by using following six tabs respectively-

a. **Titles:** Specify the title for chart, X-axis & Y-axis.

b. **Axes:** Specify whether you want to display the values of X-axis & Y-axis.

c. **Gridlines:** Specify the appropriate option, if you want to display the Minor or Major gridlines corresponding to X-axis and Y-axis respectively.

d. **Legend:** Check the **Show Legend** checkbox and specify the position for placing legends with respect to chart.

e. **Data Label:** Select a suitable option related to the display of Data Labels.

f. **Data Table:** Select Show data table checkbox, in case if you want Data Table to be displayed along with the chart.

Fourth Step :

This step is used to specify whether the chart has to be placed on a separate chart sheet or on the same worksheet on which data is placed.

Modifying a Chart

1. Charts can be modified after it's creation. It's attributes like labels, background colors etc can be changed by double-clicking on the desired element of the chart like Plot Area, Axis, and Legends etc. On double clicking corresponding dialog box is displayed, using which you can perform the required changes.
2. Once you create a chart, you can even modify all the basic steps you have performed to create a chart. For example- Chart Type, Chart Data, Chart Options, Chart Location etc. For doing so, right click on the chart area, then a pop up menu appears containing all the necessary options related to a chart.
3. Click the desired option to be modified in the pop up menu, and then corresponding dialog box is displayed. Perform necessary editing and click Ok.

Saving a Chart

1. Chart is automatically saved on saving the workbook.

Printing A Chart

1. Select the chart.
2. Select **File > Print** command. Then, Print dialog box is displayed.
3. Click on Selected Chart option under **Print What** option and Click Ok.

3. FORMULAS & FUNCTION

What are Formulas?

1. Formulas are the means of performing calculations. Calculation may be simple or advanced.

2. A Formula always begins with an equal to (=) sign
3. Using formula, you can add, subtract, multiply or divide values to carry out certain computations & comparisons.
4. A formula can be entered either in the formula bar (in this case, it is also displayed in the active cell) or directly in the target cell or active cell where you want the actual result to be displayed (in this case, the formula is also displayed in the formula bar)
5. The result of the formula is displayed on pressing Enter key.

Components of A Formula –

- Cell references
- Values
- Operators
- Worksheet functions
- Names

Steps for Entering Formula-

1. Activate (or Double click) the target cell
2. Type the equal to (=) sign
3. Type in the formula
4. Press Enter key

Operators Used in Formulas

Operators basically indicate the type of operation involved. Following types of operators are used in Excel-

Mathematical or Arithmetic Operators :

1. Addition (+)
2. Subtraction (-)
3. Multiply (*)
4. Divide (/)
5. Percentage (%)
6. Exponentiation (^)

Logical Operators:

1. Equality (=)
2. Less Than (<)
3. Less Than or Equal to (<=)
4. Greater Than (>)
5. Greater than or Equal to (>=)
6. Not Equal To (<>)

Textual Operators:

1. **<u>Concatenation operator</u> (&):** - It concatenates or joins two text values to produce single value. If operand used is a cell reference, then it concatenates the values stored in the cell.

   <u>Example of a Formula</u> (Below given is the formula for calculating simple interest)

   = (A1 * B1* C1)/100

   where, A1 cell contains the amount of Principal, B1 cell contains the amount of Rate and C1 cell contains the amount of Time

What are Functions?

1. Functions are the named set (or group) of commands used to perform a particular task.
2. In other words, Functions are the built-in programs that accept arguments and return some value.
3. Excel has many built-in categories of functions. Different category functions are used for performing distinguished tasks. **For Example** - Statistical function, Mathematical function, Financial, Date & Time etc.
4. Excel provides a function wizard that helps you to enter functions and their arguments correctly into a worksheet.

Using Functions

- **Inserting functions Manually:**
  1. Functions can be manually inserted in formula, placed in target cell.
  2. In this case, knowledge of proper syntax of a function is required in order to obtain the correct result.
- **Inserting functions using Function wizard: (or you can click function button)**For using function wizard, no previous knowledge is required for using functions.

<u>Steps of using function wizard are-</u>

1. Select **Insert > Function** command. Then, Function dialog box is displayed.
2. In the dialog box, select a category of function you want to use like Text, Mathematical etc.
3. Then, corresponding functions are displayed in adjacent list of functions.
4. Select a desired function & click OK.
5. Then, argument dialog box is displayed. Enter the required arguments or select the arguments directly from the worksheet by clicking on Collapse dialog button (Press escape to continue after selecting a range of arguments from the worksheet)
6. After entering all the arguments, the formula result is displayed in the same dialog box.
7. Click Ok to paste the result of the formula in the target cell.

List of Various functions and their purposes are given below-

TEXT FUNCTIONS	
UPPER (text)	Converts all lowercase letters in a string to uppercase
LOWER (text)	Converts all uppercase letters in a string to lowercase
VALUE (text)	Converts a text string(that represents a number) to a number
CHAR(ASCII code)	Returns the character corresponding to given ascii code e.g.. Char(97) will return "a"
LEFT	Returns the leftmost character of a string
RIGHT	Returns the rightmost character of a string
LEN	Returns the length of a text string

DATE & TIME FUNCTIONS	
DAYS360(start_date, end_date, method)	Returns the number of days between two given dates
DAY(serial_no)	Returns the day of the month (integer from 1 to 31)
DATE(serial_no)	Returns the number that represents a particular date
MONTH(serial_no)	Returns the month (integer from 0 to 12)
YEAR (serial_no)	Returns the year (integer from 1900 to 9999)
TIME (serial_no)	Returns the number that represents a particular time
SECOND (serial_no)	Returns the seconds (integer from 0 to 59)
HOUR (serial_no)	Returns the hours (integer from 0 {12:00 a.m.}to 23{11:00 p.m.})
WEEKDAY (serial_no, return type)	Returns a number from 1 to 7
NOW( )	Returns the current date and time
TODAY( )	Returns the current date

MATHS & TRIGNOMETRIC FUNCTIONS	
COS(number)	Returns the cosine of an angle
SIN(number)	Returns the sine of an angle
TAN(number)	Returns the tangent of an angle

STATISTICAL FUNCITONS	
MAX(num1, num2...)	Returns the largest value of the given numbers or values
MIN(num1, num2...)	Returns the smallest value of the given numbers or values
COUNT(value1, value2..)	Counts the total number of numeric values in the specified range
COUNTA(value1, value2..)	Counts the total number of all type of values in the specified range
COUNTBLANK(range)	Counts the total number of blank cells in the specified range
COUNTIF(Range, criteria)	Count the number of cells that follows the specified criteria
AVERAGE(num1,num2 ..)	Returns the average or arithmetic means of the given numbers
MODE (num1, num2...)	Returns the most repetitive or frequently occurring value in the given range
MEDIAN (num1, num2...)	Returns the mid value of the given range of numbers

LOOK UP & REFERENCE FUNCTIONS	
HLOOKUP	To search the topmost row of a range and return the corresponding value in another row of the range
VLOOKUP	To search the leftmost column of a range and return the corresponding value in another column of the range
INDEX	Returns the value or reference when column & row number is known
ROWS(reference)	Returns the number of rows
COLUMNS(reference)	Returns the number of columns

4. HYPERLINK

The term hyperlink is made up of two words- hypertext and link. Thus, you can say that it is a highlighted, colored and underlined text or graphics, by clicking on which, you can move to some other file or to some other location in the same file.

- Select **Insert > Hyperlink**, then Hyperlink dialog box is displayed.

  Or

1. Click hyperlink on the standard toolbar.

2. In Hyperlink dialog box, specify the text to be displayed as hyperlink (select text before opening Hyperlink dialog box)
3. Specify the file name or web page name, you wish to link with the highlighted text.
4. You can even specify the bookmark name, if you wish to link the text with some portion within the same workbook. (For this, bookmarks must be already created)
5. Thus, it means you can link highlighted text with any other workbook, web page (html file) or bookmark. (sheets or references of the same workbook)

newtopic Sheet Related Operations

1. INSERTING NEW WORKSHEET

1. Select the desired Sheet tab before which you want to insert a new worksheet.
2. Choose ***Insert > Worksheet*** command.
3. Then, a single worksheet is inserted before the selected worksheet.
4. In order to insert multiple worksheets, select the desired number of sheet tabs in advance and then select Insert > Worksheet option.

2. DELETING EXISTING WORKSHEET

1. Activate the desired worksheet.
2. Select **Edit > Delete Sheet** command.

Or

- Right click on the desired worksheet tab. Then select **Delete** command from the popup menu.

In both the above cases, Excel will warn you about the permanent deletion of the activated or selected worksheet(s). Click Ok to delete the selected worksheets or click Cancel button to cancel the deletion of worksheet(s).

3. RENAMING A WORKSHEET

1. Select the desired sheet (by clicking on desired sheet tab)
2. Select **Format > Sheet** and choose ***Rename*** option.
3. On clicking this option, the name of the selected sheet tab gets highlighted; you can either edit the name displayed or enter a new name for the sheet.
4. On renaming sheets, the contents or order of the sheets are not affected.

Or

- Right click on the desired worksheet tab. Then select ***Rename*** command from the popup menu. (or simply double click on the sheet tab and edit the name of the sheet)

4. COPY/MOVING A WORKSHEET

1. If you want to move or copy a worksheet to a different workbook, open both the source workbook and destination workbook. On the other hand, if you want to move a worksheet to a new location within a workbook, then only target workbook needs to be open.
2. Activate the source workbook and click on the desired worksheet tab that you want to move or copy.
3. Select **Edit > Move or Copy Sheet** Or **Right click** on the desired sheet tab and click **Move or Copy** option. Then **Move or Copy** dialog box appears.
4. Set the following options in the dialog box-
   a. ***To Book:*** Select the desired workbook into which you want to copy or move the selected worksheet.
   b. ***Before Sheet:*** Select the desired worksheet in selected workbook before which you want to place the moved or copied worksheet.
   c. ***Create a Copy:*** Select this checkbox, if you want to create a copy of the selected worksheet instead of actually moving the worksheet itself. In order to move the actual worksheet to a desired location in the same workbook or to different workbook, leave this checkbox unchecked.
5. Click Ok.

newtopic Cell Referencing

Cell referencing simply means addressing of cell or range of cells. In Excel, cell references are used in formulas instead of the actual values contained in cells. References would tell Excel about the location of the values (involved in formula) in the worksheet.

1. STYLES OF CELL REFERENCING

Excel supports following reference styles-

a. **A1 Style:**
   i. It is the by default style of addressing cell or range of cells.
   ii. According to this, a cell is referenced using column label and row number. Columns being labeled from A to IV & Rows being labeled from 1 to 65,536.
   - **Examples-**
     - Address of first cell : A1
     - Address of last cell : IV65536
     - Address of cell in third column & fourth row : C4
     - Range of cells is specified using colon (:) e.g. C3:C10

b. **R1C1 Style:**
   i. It is the alternative style used for addressing cells.

ii. According to this, a cell is referenced by using row subscript 'R' followed by row number & a column subscript 'C' followed by a column number.

- **Examples-**
  - Address of first cell: R1C1
  - Address of last cell: R65536C256
  - Address of cell in third column & fourth row : R4C3

2. TYPES OF CELL REFERENCES USED IN FORMULAS OR TYPE OF REFERENCING

a. Relative References

b. Absolute References

c. Mixed References

- **Relative Referencing:**

1. Relative referencing refers to addressing a cell with respect to the cell in which the formula is currently placed.
2. In this case, when formula is copied to another cell, the cell references would change accordingly.
3. **Example:** If the formula is = B4+B5+B6 and is currently placed in the B7 cell. If the formula is then copied to the E7 cell, then the references will change automatically & the formula would become =E4+E5+E6

To better understand, it can be compared to a situation, in which a person is told about the address of a particular person with respect to the address of one of the person known to him in the same area.

- **Absolute Referencing:**

1. Absolute referencing refers to exact (or fixed or static) addressing of a cell, in the formula.
2. In this case, when formula is copied to another cell, the absolute cell references do not change i.e.. It remains constant irrespective of the location of target cell (that contains formula)
3. For converting relative references to absolute, add a prefix **'$'** (dollar symbol) to both the elements involved in addressing **e.g**.. $A$1
4. **Example:** If the formula is =$B$4+$B$5 & is contained in B6 cell. Then, on copying it to another cell say E6 the formula would remain the same =$B$4+$B$5

- **Mixed Referencing:**

It is a combination of above two references i.e.. If both the relative as well as absolute references are used in a formula, then it is called Mixed referencing e.g.. = B2 +$B$3. In this case, cell reference B2 would change on copying it to another cell whereas $B$3 would remain constant irrespective of the place where it is placed.

16

Microsoft PowerPoint

Introduction:

PowerPoint is a sophisticated presentation graphics package. It is a stand-alone product, but most notably is an integral part of the Microsoft Office Suite. In simple words, PowerPoint is an application that lets you build, print and deliver presentations. It has tools to produce presentation in a professional manner. Different versions of the same presentation can also be created for different audiences.

A Presentation is a structured delivery of information and ideas to the audience. It has tools to produce presentation in a professional manner. Presentation involves text handling, inserting pictures, sounds and animations. Presentation can be produced on paper, on-screen, or on transparencies. Thus, it is a collection of handouts, slides, speaker's notes and outline- all packaged together in one file.

STARTING MS-POWERPOINT

Click ***Start* > *Programs* > *Microsoft PowerPoint*** option

Or

Double click on the Microsoft PowerPoint icon present on the desktop.

COMPONENTS OF POWERPOINT WINDOW

1. **Title Bar :** *Name of application program & name of currently opened document is displayed on it. It also contains control buttons*
2. **Toolbar :** *It refers to the graphical or pictorial representation of commands present under different menu items like File, Edit etc. Some common Toolbars are-*
   - *Standard Toolbar :* contains tools for managing operations related to file & editing operations
   - *Formatting Toolbar :* contains tools for changing the appearance of text i.e. Text formatting or object
3. **Menu Bar :** *It refers to the horizontal bar containing menu items or pads like File, Edit, View etc. Menu items can be accessed using mouse, just*

by clicking on related menu item. Although these can be accessed using keyboard shortcut key : Alt + Underlined character in menu item's name e.g. Alt + F is used for accessing File Menu. For navigating through commands under a menu item, Arrow key can be used. For executing a particular command, Enter key can be used.

4. **Ruler Bar :** *used for setting or clearing tabs. It is of two types -*
   a. Horizontal Ruler bar
   b. Vertical Ruler bar
5. **Slider or Scroll Bar :** *used for navigating in document window. Navigation refers to moving up & down through the pages in a document. We have horizontal & vertical scroll bars.*
6. **PowerPoint Development Area:** *PowerPoint Development area contains three panes— Outline Pane (on the left), Slide Pane (on the top right) & Notes pane (on the lower right).*
   i. Outline Pane : It consists of the slide number, title and the text of all the slides included in the presentation.
   ii. Slide Pane : It refers to the actual slide area in Ms-PowerPoint window, where the actual text or graphics can be placed for designing the presentation.
   iii. Notes Pane : It is used to place the notes related to each slide, so that the notes can be viewed by the speaker while giving presentation to the audience.
7. **Office Assistant :** *It is basically an online help. It aids user to work conveniently by displaying related messages.*
8. **Status Bar :** *It is used to display important information related to Presentation file like slide number, total number of slides and other help messages etc.*
9. Application Window : ***It refers to the main PowerPoint Window that contains all the above components.***
10. **Placeholders:** *A placeholder is displayed as a box with dotted outlines. Typing your text into a placeholder is the easiest way to add text to a slide. It should be noted that unused placeholders are not displayed on the screen. You can also move the placeholders by click & drag method.*

IMPORTANCE OF POWERPOINT IN HOSPITALITY INDUSTRY

1. A comfortable room, good food, and a helpful staff can make being away from home an enjoyable experience for both vacationing families and business travelers.
2. In the highly competitive hospitality industry, a satisfied customer is more likely to be a repeat customer. Today new technologies are adopted by hotels to help their staff to improve the overall guest experience.
3. Hotels increasingly emphasize specialized training. Postsecondary training in hotel, restaurant, or hospitality management is preferred for most hotel management positions.

4. PowerPoint, which can be found on two hundred and fifty million computers around the world, is software you impose on other people. It allows you to arrange text and graphics in a series of pages (or slides), which you can project, slide by slide, from a laptop computer onto a screen, or print as a booklet.

5. Thus, PowerPoint is an impressive way of communicating with a group of people. Most of the hotels are nowadays using PowerPoint for developing influencing presentations.

newtopic Presentation Related Operations

1. Creating a New Presentation

- **Using AutoContent Wizard**

  The Autocontent Wizard is used to build a dummy presentation that will guide you in developing the content of the presentation. The wizard is basically a step-by-step procedure that involves various dialog boxes for creating a presentation according to the requirement of user. At each step, it prompts user to give answers to several questions to modify the presentation accordingly. The steps for using Autocontent wizard are as follows-

  1. ***Select*** File > New ***option***
  2. Then select Autocontent wizard option under General tab.
  3. Click on OK
  4. *Then, the AutoContent wizard is displayed. It constitutes the following steps*
     i) Read the starting information and click ***Next***
     ii) Select the category & type of presentation you want to give and click ***Next***
     iii) Select the type of output you wish to use for giving presentation and click ***Next***
     iv) Specify the title, footer and other options related to presentation and click ***Next***
     v) Then, click ***Finish*** button to view the complete presentation

  In this case, a presentation is created automatically, with all the required slides and their respective points (that will guide user in developing contents)

- **Using Blank Presentation**

  Blank presentation refers to a presentation, in which no graphics & text is placed in advance. Using Blank presentation, one can place desired objects i.e. text & graphics at desired position & in required order on the slide. The formatting of slides & other objects placed on it can be done in desired manner. The steps for creating a blank presentation are as follows-

1. **Select** File > New **option**
2. ***Then, select*** Blank Presentation ***option under*** *General* ***tab in New dialog box***
3. Click on OK
4. ***Then, choose an*** Auto Layout ***from the*** New Slide ***dialog box and click OK.***

   Or

   Click New ***tool*** 🗋 ***on the standard toolbar.***

In both the cases, a new blank presentation is created.

- **Using Design Templates**

  The default color-schemes of PowerPoint are called Design Templates. Design Template allows you to establish the background and color scheme from the available templates prior to beginning work in the new presentation. You can apply Design templates to your presentation at any time during development. The steps of creating a presentation based on a design template are-

  1. **Select** File > New **option**
  2. ***Then select desired design template (presentation design) under Design Templates tab in*** New ***dialog box***
  3. Click on OK

  In this case, a new presentation is created that contains one slide on which the chosen design template has been applied. If you try to insert new slide using Insert > New Slide **option, then another slide will also be created with the same design template automatically applied to it.**

- **Using Pre-designed Presentations**

  These are pre-designed formats of complete presentation, using which you can create presentation quickly. Such presentation also contains formatting features and contents, just like presentations created using AutoContent wizard. The steps for creating blank presentation are -

1. *Select* **File > New** *option*
2. Then select the desired presentation from the available list of presentations under **Presentations** tab.
3. Click on OK

   In this case, a presentation is created automatically, with all the required slides and their respective contents. You can edit the contents according to your requirement.

2. Saving a Presentation

1. *Select* **File > Save** *option, then* **Save As...** *dialog box is displayed*
2. Then specify location, where you wish to save the file
3. After then, specify the desired file name

4. *Click on* **Save** *button*

   Or

   - Click Save button on the standard toolbar.

   In both the cases, current presentation will be saved.

3. Closing a Presentation

1. *Select* **File > Close** *option*

   In this case, active presentation will get closed

4. Opening an Existing Presentation

1. *Select* **File > Open** *option, then Open dialog box is displayed*
2. Then specify location of existing presentation file
3. After then, select the desired file or specify the desired file name
4. *Click on* **Open** *button*

   Or

   - *Click* **Open** *tool on the standard toolbar.*

In both the cases, existing presentation will get opened.

5. Creating a Copy of Presentation

1. *Select* **File > Save As** *option, then* **Save As...** *dialog box is displayed*
2. Then specify location, where you wish to save the file
3. After then, specify the new file name
4. *Click on* **Save** *button*

   Or

   - *Hit* **F12** *shortcut key*

In both the cases, a new copy of the existing presentation will be created.

6. Page Setup and Printing Slides

Page Setup

1. *Select* **File > Page Setup** *option, then page setup dialog box appears*
2. Set the desirable options like-
   a. ***Slide sized for:*** Select the desirable option to indicate for what purpose you wish to resize the slides.
   b. ***Width:*** Enter the desirable width of each slide in a presentation.
   c. ***Height:*** Enter the desirable height of each slide.
   d. ***Number of slides:*** Enter a numeric value for specifying the starting value for numbering of slides.
3. Orientation of slides, handouts, notes and outline: Orientation may be set as -
   a. ***Portrait:*** In this kind of orientation, height is more and width is less.

b. ***Landscape:*** In this type of orientation, width is more and height is less.

4. Then, click OK button.

Printing Slides

1. *Select* **File > Print** *option, then Print dialog box is displayed.*
2. Then specify the required information related to printing in dialog box.
3. Then, click OK

   Or

- *Click the* **Print** *button* *on the standard toolbar*

Set following options in Print dialog box-

Printer:

1. **Name :** *Specify the name of the currently installed printer.*
2. **Status :** *It indicates the status of the selected printer busy or idle*
3. **Where :** *It displays the port to which printing output is sent i.e. LPT1 Or LPT2 Or USB001*

Copies:

1. **Number of Copies:** *To set the required no. of copies of a presentation to be printed*
2. **Collate:** *It is used to organize multi-slide presentation, in case if we wish to print multiple copies of it. If this option is selected, then presentation will be printed set wise i.e.. First all the slides of a presentation will be printed, then a copy of the entire set of slides will be produced.*

Print Range

1. **Slides:** *It is used to specify the range of slides to be printed. The slide range should be specified using hyphen in between i.e. 2- 8. For specifying non-consecutive slides to be printed, comma can be used to separate different slide numbers like 4, 9, and 20 and so on.*
2. **All:** *Use to print the entire slides contained in a presentation*
3. **Current Slide:** *used to print only the current slide. Current slide refers to the selected slide or a slide in which the cursor lies currently.*
4. **Selection:** *used to print the selected portion of the slide. This option gets enabled only after selecting the desired text, in advance.*
5. **Custom Show:** *This option is used to specify the name of existing custom show, in order to print only those slides, which are contained in a custom show*

Print What:

1. **Print What:** *You can select desired option from the following- Slides, Handouts, Notes Pages or Outline view.*
2. **Color/Grayscale:** *You can select either color or grayscale or black and white printing option according to your requirement.*

3. **Slides per Pages:** *You can specify the number of slides you wish to print on one sheet of page. Generally, it prints the reduced size of slide.*
4. **Order:** *You can specify the order of slides, in case if you have specified 2 o:- more slides in Slides per Pages option. It may be horizontal or vertical.*
5. **Scale to Fit Paper:** *The size of slide is either increased or reduced in order to make it fit according to paper size. Thus, this check box must be selected in order to scale your slide to fit paper.*

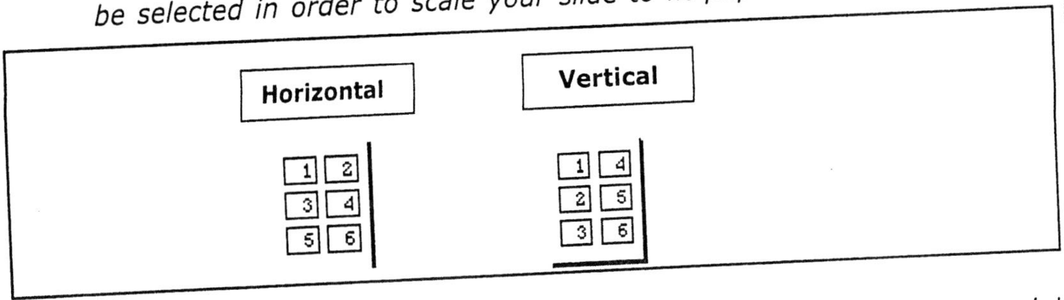

6. **Print Hidden Slides:** *This check box must be checked in order to print hidden slides in a presentation.*
7. **Frame Slides:** *This check box is checked in order to add a frame to each slide in a presentation.*

Properties : Click this button in order to specify the paper size, paper type used for printing as well as for specifying the print quality. Print quality is measured in dpi (dots per inches). It may be- Fast Draft, Normal, Best etc. This setting is essential in order to make the proper & efficient usage of your cartridge ink. In Properties dialog box, you can also select Print Preview checkbox in order to view the presentation before actual printing is done.

Editing Operations

1. Undo & Repeat

Undo is used to revert the currently done changes in the presentation. The shortcut key for Undo is ***Ctrl + Z.*** Repeat command is used to repeat the changes reverted using Undo command. The shortcut key for Repeat command is ***Ctrl + Y.***

2. Cut, Copy & Paste

Cut command is used to move the selected content (text or picture) into clipboard. The steps are as follows-

1. Select the desired content (text or graphics)
2. *Select* **Edit > Cut** *option*

   Or

   Click **Cut** *tool on the standard toolbar (or press Ctrl + X shortcut key)*

Copy command is used to copy the contents of worksheet into clipboard for further pasting it in the presentation. The steps are as follows-

- *Select* **Edit > Copy** *option*

  Or

- *Click* **Copy** *tool on the standard toolbar (or press Ctrl + C shortcut key)*

Paste command is used to paste the contents from clipboard (cut or copied items) into the presentation. The steps of performing Paste operation are as follows-

- *Select* **Edit > Paste** *option*

  Or

- *Click* **Paste** *tool on the standard toolbar (or press Ctrl + V shortcut key)*

3. Find and Replace

FIND: *Find is used to search a desired text in the entire presentation.*

1. Open a desired worksheet.
2. *Select* **Edit > Find** *option, then a dialog box is displayed. Set the following options in the Find dialog box-*
   a. ***Find What:*** In this box, enter the desired text you want PowerPoint to find.
   b. Special options:
      - **Match Case:** used to find the characters by matching the Case (uppercase or lowercase) of text.
      - **Find Whole Words only:** used to find the complete word as specified in Find What box. *(instead of its embedded form)*
3. ***Then, click*** Find Next ***button in order to find the text otherwise click Cancel button.***

   Or

   Press Ctrl + F

REPLACE: Replace is used to replace selected text with the desired string or text.

1) *Select* **Edit > Replace** *option, then a dialog box is displayed.*
2) Specify the desired options in the Replace dialog box. Set the following options in the dialog box-
   a) ***Find What box:*** In this, you must enter the text you want to find.
   b) ***Replace with box:*** In this, you must enter the replacement text.
   c) ***Match Case:*** used to find the characters by matching the Case (uppercase or lowercase) of text.
   d) ***Find Whole Words Only:*** used to find the text that is a word by itself and is not a part of another text

3) Then, click **Find Next** button. If a match is found, then two options are there-

   a) ***Replace :*** To replace the first occurrence of the word found by the desired word

   b) ***Replace All :*** To replace all the occurrences of the word found by the desired word

   Or

   – Press Ctrl + H

4. Delete Slide

- ***Select the desired slide***
- ***Choose Edit > Delete slide option.***

Views Related Operations

1. Views of Ms-PowerPoint

PowerPoint gives you four views in which you create and organize your presentation. As you create a presentation, you can switch among the four views as you work.

The five PowerPoint views and corresponding buttons are given below:

Normal View

1. Select ***View > Normal*** option, then your presentation will be displayed in

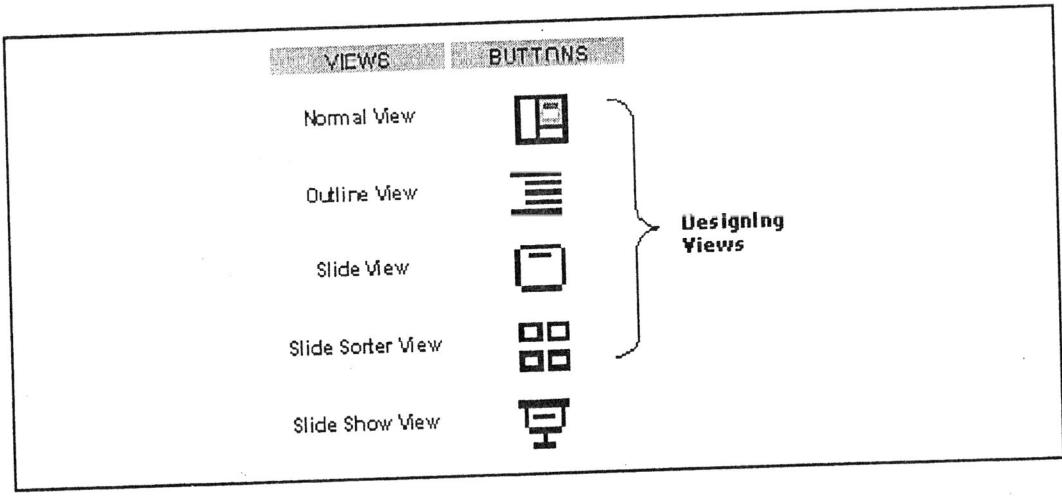

Normal view.

2. It is the by default view of a presentation in Ms-PowerPoint.

Characteristics of Normal Layout: - Presentation window is divided into three panes-

1. **Outline Pane:** It displays the number of slides along with their miniatures.
2. **Slide Pane:** It displays the current slide, so that you can edit it.
3. **Notes Pane:** In notes pane, you can keep the notes related to each slide. These notes are kept for the sake of speaker, but not the audience. These notes can be viewed by the speaker for recalling certain point or example, while showing the on-screen presentation to the audience.

Outline View

1. Click Outline view button, then your presentation will be displayed in Outline view.
2. The Outline pane occupies the major area of PowerPoint window.
3. It is most suitable for managing text in slides.

Characteristics of Outline View :- Presentation window is divided into three panes-

1. **Outline Pane:** It displays the number of slides along with respective text.
2. **Slide Pane:** It displays the miniature of current slide.
3. **Notes Pane:** In notes pane, you can keep the notes related to each slide. These notes are kept for the sake of speaker, but not the audience. These notes can be viewed by the speaker for recalling certain point or example, while showing the on-screen presentation to the audience.

Slide View

1. Click Slide view button, then your presentation will be displayed in Slide view.
2. The major area of PowerPoint window is occupied by the Slide pane.
3. Used for managing objects placed on slide and also for editing a slide.

Characteristics of Slide View: - Presentation window is divided into two panes-

- ***Outline Pane :*** It displays the number of slides along with their miniatures.
- ***Slide Pane:*** It displays the current slide, so that you can edit it.

Slide Sorter View

1. Select ***View > Slide Sorter*** option, then your presentation will be displayed in Slide Sorter view.
2. It is the best view for re-ordering and deleting the slides in a presentation.
3. Used for setting certain show related options like- Transition of slide, Animation, Rehearse timings, hiding a slide etc.

Characteristics of Slide Sorter View: - Presentation window is divided into one pane-

✓ ***Slides Pane :*** The miniatures or reduced versions of all the slides of a presentation are displayed. You can use click and drag (in forward direction) method to replace the position of two slides at a time. By reordering, the position of a slide and the slide number assigned to each slide by Ms-PowerPoint will change but the slide number placed on the slide (by the presenter) will not change. The slides marked as hidden will not be displayed in the actual show.

Slide Show View

1. Select ***View > Slide Show*** option, then your presentation will be displayed in Slide Show view (on full screen)
2. It is the best view for showing the presentation to the audience in Ms-PowerPoint.
3. Used for viewing or presenting an on-screen show of a presentation.
4. All the slides are shown one by one.
5. In case of manual slide show, for advancing the slides in, Enter key or mouse click can be used.
6. In case of automatic show (using timings), slide will advance/change automatically.
7. The shortcut key used for viewing the slide show is F5
8. For terminating the slide show in between, Escape (Esc) key is used.

Notes Page

1. The notes page is a place that you can add notes for each slide.
2. It is also used for adding extra information to a slide.
3. Adding Notes: select ***View > Notes Page*** command. PowerPoint displays a different view that has the slide at the top of the page and a text box at the bottom. Add your additional information to the text box.
4. You can resize the slide image and the text box on the notes page as per your requirement.
5. ***Printing Notes Pages :*** Select Notes Pages option under Print What option in the Print dialog box, while printing a slide or presentation (File > Print)

new topic INSERT RELATED OPERATIONS

1. INSERTING NEW SLIDE: SELECT INSERT > NEW SLIDE OPTION

2. INSERTING DUPLICATE SLIDE : SELECT THE SLIDE TO BE DUPLICATED THEN CHOOSE INSERT > DUPLICATE SLIDE OPTION.

3. INSERTING PICTURE

From ClipArt Gallery

1. Place the insertion point at the desired location in the current slide.
2. Select **Insert > Picture**, then, select Clipart from the available sub options.

Or

1. Click ***Clipart*** tool on the drawing toolbar.

2. Then ***Microsoft Clipart Gallery*** dialog box is displayed, select the ***Category.***
3. Then click the desired image and click ***Insert picture*** tool.

From File...(.jpg or .bmp or .gif)

1. Place the insertion point at the desired location in a current slide.
2. Select ***Insert > Picture***, then, select ***From File...*** from the available sub options.

   Or

   - Click ***Insert Picture*** tool on the Picture toolbar.

   3. Then, ***Insert Picture*** dialog box is displayed. In this, you have to specify the filename along with it's exact path or location (in your system).

Then click ***Insert*** button.

4. INSERTING CHART

1. Place the insertion point at the desired location in the current slide.
2. Select ***Insert > Picture***, then, select Chart from the available sub options.

   Or

1. Click ***Chart*** tool on the standard toolbar.
2. Then, a datasheet and a corresponding chart, having default setting is displayed.
3. You can alter the data in the datasheet and the chart will get automatically updated.
4. After making the required updations in Chart, you can close the datasheet.

5. INSERTING ORGANIZATION CHART

Organization charts are an extremely effective way to communicate organizational, employee and enterprise information. An org chart makes it easier for people to understand large amounts of information as a visual picture rather than as a table of names and numbers.

1. Select **File>New**, then **New** Dialog box is displayed.
2. Choose **Blank Presentation** option and click OK.
3. Then **AutoLayout** dialog box is displayed, click Organizational chart layout and click OK.
4. A presentation will be created having one slide displaying the title placeholder (type corresponding title of organization chart in this) and organizational chart icon.
5. Double click on the organizational chart icon to activate organizational chart tool that contains tools for creating organizational chart.
6. Create the desired organizational chart using appropriate tools.
7. Finally, when your chart is completed, click on the menu item **File > Update Presentation**, and then select **File > Close** and return to

PowerPoint. Your organizational chart will have been transferred to your presentation.

Editing an Organizational Chart

To further edit it at a later occasion, double-click on the organizational chart object to reintroduce the organizational chart tool.

Resizing an Organizational Chart

To resize your chart on your page, you can, as with the table object, click and drag on one of the sizing handles that appear on the perimeter of the selected organizational chart object.

6. Inserting Table

A table is a grid of row and columns. After inserting a table in the current slide, you can insert or deleted rows and columns in the table.

1. Select ***Insert > Table***, then, ***Insert Table*** dialog box is displayed.
2. Then, enter the desired number of rows and number of columns.
3. Then, click OK.

newtopic Formatting of Presentation

1. Font

1. Select the desired text.
2. Select ***Format > Font***, then Font dialog box is displayed.
3. In ***Font*** Dialog box, select Font tab. Then, set the following options -
   a. **Font :**
      i. It refers to style of writing a character.
      ii. e.g. Times New Roman, Tahoma, Courier New etc.
      iii. By default, font is Times New Roman.
   b. **Font Size :**
      i. It refers to the size of the font.
      ii. It is measured in Points.
      iii. Max. font size is 72 points. However, this maximum number varies from one font to other font.
      iv. By default font size is 12.
   c. **Font Style :**
      i. It refers to different styles of font like- Regular, Bold, Italic, Bold Italic.
      ii. By default Font style is Regular.
   d. **Font Color :**
      i. It refers to color of the Font.

ii. You can use the available colors in the color palette or you can use the standard or customized colors by using More Colors... option in Color Palette.

iii. By default Font color is Automatic (Black)

4. ***Effects :*** (You can apply required effects by selecting the appropriate checkbox)

- **Shadow :** ***e.g.*** This is shadow effect
- **Superscript :** ***e.g.*** 7^2
- **Subscript :** ***e.g.*** H_2O
- **Emboss** ***e.g.*** This is Emboss effect

2. Bullets and Numbering

1. Select the text to which you wish to apply bullets or numbers.
2. Select ***Format > Bullets and Numbering***, then Bullets and Numbering dialog box is displayed.
3. Select ***Bulleted*** tab, then you can select desired bullet style and click OK.

   Or

   - Click on ***Bullets*** tool on the Formatting toolbar.

Applying Picture Bullets : You can also apply Picture bullets by clicking on Picture button under Bulleted tab, then a list of picture bullets (in clipart) is displayed. You can select the desired bullet and insert it using insert clip tool

Removing Bullets: You can select **None** under Bulleted tab.

Applying Colorful Bullets: In ***Bullets and Numbering*** dialog box, select desired color from Color list box displayed under Bulleted tab.

3. Alignment

Alignment refers to the position of text with respect to page. You may select any one of the alignment-

- ***Left :*** All the lines are aligned towards left (uniform margin on left side)
- ***Center :*** The center of all the lines will lie at a common line (uniform center)
- ***Right :*** All the lines are aligned towards right (uniform margin on right side)
- ***Justified :*** All the lines are uniformly aligned towards left and right (uniform

1. Select the desired paragraph.
2. Select ***Format > Alignment***, then following sub-options are displayed-

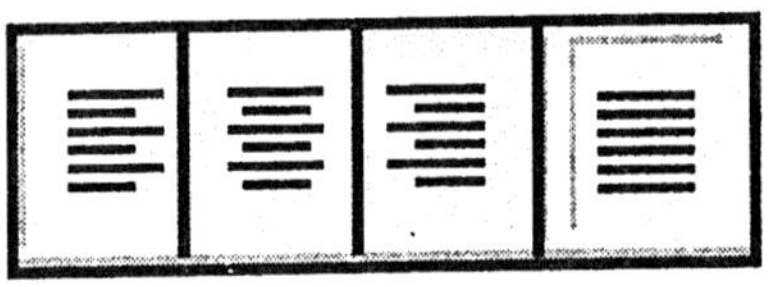

a. Align Left
b. Center
c. Align Right
d. Justified

3. Select the desired alignment, in order to apply desired alignment to selected paragraph.

4. Apply Design Template

Design template refers to a pre-formatted design of a slide that can be applied to a presentation. Design templates are applied to a presentation to achieve uniformity in the presentation.

1. Open the desired presentation.
2. Select ***Format > Apply Design Template***, then Apply Design Template dialog box will be displayed. In the dialog box, names of several design templates will be displayed along with their corresponding preview.
3. Choose the desired design template and click ***Apply*** button.

Or

1. Right click in the **blank area** (outside the placeholder) of the desired slide, then a context menu (or pop-up menu) appears.
2. Choose ***Apply Design Template*** option, which is followed by Apply Design Template dialog box.
3. Choose the desired design and click on ***Apply*** button.

5. Slide Layout

Slide Layout refers to the desired organization of the objects (or placeholders) placed on the slide.

1. Open the desired slide, of which you wish to change the layout.
2. Select ***Format > Slide Layout***, Slide Layout dialog box will be displayed.
3. Choose the desired layout from the given layouts and click on ***Reapply*** button.

Or

1. Right click in the **blank area** (outside the placeholder) of the desired slide, then a context menu (or pop-up menu) appears.
2. Choose ***Slide Layout*** option, which is followed by ***Slide Layout*** dialog box.
3. Choose the desired layout and click on ***Reapply*** button.

6. Slide Color Scheme

Color scheme is used in case If you have your own plans to design your slide/presentation. Once you set the color scheme of a slide/presentation, you don't have to worry about it's formatting later on.

1. Open the desired presentation/slide.

2. Select ***Format > Slide Color Scheme*** option, then ***Color Scheme*** dialog box is displayed. It has two tabs-
3. **Standard**
   a. Click **Standard** tab and select desired color scheme (by clicking on the given color schemes)
   b. Click **Apply** button (in order to apply desired color scheme to current slide) or click **Apply to All** button (in order to apply desired color scheme to all the slides of current presentation)
4. **Custom**
   a. Click **Custom** tab and modify colors of different objects like Background, Fills, Colors & Lines, Shadows etc. For doing so, choose the object (for color change) and click Change Color button.
   b. Click ***Apply*** button (in order to apply desired color scheme to current slide) or click ***Apply to All*** button (in order to apply desired color scheme to all the slides of current presentation)

7. BACKGROUND

Steps for Applying Background to a Slide

1. Select ***Format > Background***, then select desired color from the color or select More Colors sub option from the Colors list box.
2. Click ***More Colors*** sub option, then Colors dialog box is displayed. In Colors dialog box, select any of the following tabs-
   a. ***Standard tab :*** Select the color, by clicking on one of the given colors.
   b. ***Customize tab :*** You can customize the color setting according to your choice to generate a desired color. (It is achieved by placing the black cross bar shaped pointer on the desired color and then selecting desired color from the color bar)
3. Then, click Ok, to make your selected color as the new color used to fill the background.
4. Click ***Apply*** to fill the background of current slide or Click ***Apply to All*** to fill the background of all the slides of a presentation.

Applying Shading to Slide Background

1. Select ***Format > Background*** options, then few sub options are displayed.
2. Select ***Fill Effects*** option, then Fill Effects dialog box is displayed.
3. Select ***Gradient*** tab, and specify the shading options-
   a. ***One color*** [select the desired color and adjust it's intensity to make it dark or light]
   b. ***Two color*** [select two desired colors for shading]
   c. ***Preset*** [select one of preformatted shading formats from the Preset color list]
4. Then, select one of the shading style-

a. Horizontal
b. Vertical
c. Diagonal Up
d. Diagonal Down
e. From Corner
f. From Center

5. Then, click OK.
6. Click ***Apply*** button to apply shading to the current slide or click ***Apply to All*** to apply shading to all the slides in a presentation.

Applying Texture To Slide Background (formatted background resembling to natural things like wood, marble etc)

1. Select ***Format > Background*** options, then few sub options are displayed.
2. Select ***Fill Effects*** option, then Fill Effects dialog box is displayed.
3. Select ***Texture*** tab, then select one of the desired texture and click OK. Click ***Apply*** or ***Apply to All*** to apply texture to current slide or all the slides in a presentation respectively.

Applying Pattern or Picture in Background

Pattern

1. Select ***Format > Background***, then select Fill effects from the sub options.
2. In Fill effects dialog box, select the ***Pattern*** tab.
3. Select the desirable pattern from the available patterns.
4. Specify the foreground and background color and click OK.

Picture

1. Select ***Format > Background***, and then select Fill effects from the sub options.
2. In Fill effects dialog box, select the ***Picture*** tab.
3. Click the ***Select Picture*** button, and then specify the name and location of a picture file in the Select Picture dialog box and then, click ***Insert*** button.
4. Click OK to select the specified picture.
5. Click ***Apply*** to insert selected picture in the current slide or Click ***Apply to All*** to insert selected picture in all the slides of a presentation.

Removing Above Applied Effects from Background :

- Select ***Format > Background*** and then select ***Automatic*** sub option.

newtopic Slide Show Related Operations

1. Viewing Slide Show

- Select ***Slide Show > View Show***, then full screen view of the presentation is displayed.

Or

Hit **F5** shortcut key for viewing the on-screen presentation.

2. Set Up Show

1. Select ***Slide Show > Set Up Show***, then Set up Show dialog box is displayed.
2. In the dialog box, set the following options like-
   - ***a. Show type :*** It refers to the type of show that you wish to present or view. It may be-
     - **i. <u>Presented by a Speaker</u> (**full screen) [Facility of viewing speaker notes is available to the presenter]
     - **ii. <u>Browsed by an individual</u>** (window) [Suitable for displaying the presentation to different audience (or clients) in a network.
     - **iii. <u>Browsed at Kiosk</u>** (full screen) [No facility of viewing speaker notes]
   - ***b. Slide :*** Using this option, you can specify the slide range to be included in a show. It may be-
     - **i. <u>All</u>** (It includes all the slides of a current presentation)
     - **ii. <u>From ___ to ___</u>** (i.e.. Desired Range of slides)
     - **iii. <u>Custom Show</u>** (You can select the name of existing custom show)
   - ***c. Advance Slides :*** You can specify how to change or advance slides. It may be done either-
     - i. Manually
     - ii. Using timings, if present
   - d. Special Checkboxes-
     - **i. <u>Loop continuously until 'Esc'</u>** (Check this for viewing the show continuously i.e.. Without break until you Hit Esc key)
     - **ii. <u>Show without narration</u>** (Check this if you wish to present your show without any narration, that was previously attached to it)
     - **iii. <u>Show without animation</u>** (Check this if you wish to present static show i.e.. Show without animation)

3. Custom Show

Custom Show refers to a desirable group of slides chosen (for presenting later on) from a particular presentation. In simple words, custom shows are the different views of the same presentation. From one presentation, we can create any number of custom shows containing a different sequence of slides.

1. Select ***Slide Show > Custom Shows***, then Custom Shows dialog box is displayed.
2. In the ***Custom Shows*** dialog box, click ***New*** button to create a new custom show from the current presentation. A ***Define Custom Show*** dialog box follows it.

3. Specify the name of the Custom Show in ***Slide Show Name*** box.
4. Select the slides from the Slides in presentation list box and click ***Add*** button to move the selected slides to the Slides in custom show list box.
5. You can desirably click on ***Remove*** button, in order to remove selected slide form the Slides in custom show list box.
6. You can also change the order of slides in Slides in custom show list box by clicking on ***Move up*** or ***Move Down*** button.
7. Then, click Ok.
8. In ***Custom Shows*** dialog box, click ***Show*** button to view the created custom show otherwise click ***Close*** button to view the created custom show otherwise click ***Close*** button to view the show later on.

4. Custom Animation

Custom Animation refers to modifying the options related with the movement of objects on slide and so on.

1. Select ***Slide Show > Custom Animation***, then a Custom Animation dialog box is displayed.
2. In the Custom Animation dialog box, select the desired check boxes corresponding to an object that you wish to animate in Check to animate slide objects box.
3. Besides above mentioned option, Custom Animation dialog box has four tabs-
   - ***a. Order and Timing:-*** Under this tab, you can specify the order of animation of objects and select the method of starting animation (on mouse click or Automatically using timings)
   - b. **Effects :**
     - i. Under this tab, you can specify the animation type during the entry of an animated object on the slide.
     - ii. The sound produced during the entry is also specified under the same option.
     - iii. Here, you can also specify how you wish the text to appear on the slide ie. All at once, by word or by letter.
   - c. **Chart Effects:**
     - i. This tab contains some options related to the animation of a chart inserted in a slide.
   - d. **Multimedia Setting :**
     - i. These settings are done in case if you have inserted certain movie clips or sound object in the slide/presentation. Such settings are related about the playing of those movie clips or sounds.

5. Slide Transition

1. Select ***Slide Show > Slide Transition***, then Slide Transition dialog box is displayed.

2. In the Slide Transition dialog box, specify the following options like-
   - **a. *Slide Transition:*** Select the desired slide transition effect from the slide transition list box and also specify the mode of transition- slow, medium or fast.
   - **b. *Advancement:*** Select one of the following options in order to change or advance slides in a presentation -
     - i. On mouse click
     - ii. Or Automatically after (specify desired time for advancing or changing slide)
   - **c. *Sound :*** Select the desired sound you wish to play during slide transition

     Or

     - Specify the desired type of slide transition in the transition list box displayed on the Slide Sorter toolbar (in the Slide sorter view)

6. Hide Slide

1. Select the desired slide.
2. Select ***Slide Show > Hide Slide*** option, then selected slide will not appear in the on-screen show presented to the audience.

   Or

1. Click on the ***Hide Slide*** button on the ***Slide Sorter*** toolbar (in Slide Sorter View).
2. The selected slide number will be displayed as strike by a slant line (diagonally down) in the slide sorter view.

You can again unhide an hidden slide so that it would appear in the slide show. It can be achieved by repeating any of the above mentioned option.

Tips of Making an Effective Presentation

Microsoft PowerPoint is a very popular and effective means of delivering a presentation. Here are a few tips to help you create a great PowerPoint presentation-

1. Every slide should contain a meaningful title.
2. Remember to use a landscape orientation rather than portrait. The image will fit better on a computer display and a TV-type monitor.
3. Use bright letters against solid light backgrounds, or light letters against solid dark backgrounds. Avoid the use of red it tends to smudge into other colors.
4. Use uniform formatting and background throughout your presentation. Keep the background shading consistent across the screen so text is readable in all areas. Generally white, yellow and cyan colors are recommended for

foreground colors. Black, dark brown or dark blue are usually recommended for background colors.

5. Don't use more than seven or eight lines (maximum nine lines) per slide and keep your information concise. Remember a simple fact that- few words can convey a whole paragraph.
6. Slide titles should be no less than 44-point type.
7. Body text should be no less than 24-point type in order to remain clearly readable to all your audience.
8. Embed True Type fonts in file using "Tools > Save Options > Embed True Type Font" while saving your file using "File > Save" or "File > Save As".
9. Dim previous lines for more emphasize on current line.
10. Use illustrations, charts and clip art when appropriate.
11. Follow your presentation in a logical progression. Divide it into clear segments.
12. For your presentations to work, the visual images must convey exactly what you want to say and require the least possible effort on the part of your audience to "get it". Also remember to place minimum visuals on slides. A busy slide forces smaller font sizes to be used.
13. Avoid using sounds for introducing a new slide or bullet point.
14. Avoid using distracting & slow transition effects.
15. Use such diagrams and graphs that are simple, easy to understand and involve readable text.

Appendix A

Glossary

A

1 **Absolute Reference**	The cell reference that is made constant using $ symbol, as a prefix to a particular cell reference. Such references remains constant even when the formula is copied from one cell to another
2 **Access time**	In computing, the time taken by a computer, after an instruction has been given, to read from or write to memory.
3 **Action**	The basic unit of macro
4 **Active Window**	On graphical operating systems, the window containing the program actually in use at any given time.
5 **Address**	A specific location in a computer's memory that is used to store information.
6 **Algorithm**	It is a logical sequence of operations to be performed by a program.
7 **Alias**	A type of nickname (usually short and easy to remember) that refers to a type of network resource.
8 **Analog**	A method of storing information, used by most audiotapes, videotapes and laserdiscs. An analog device uses a physical quantity, such as length or voltage, to represent the value of a number.
9 **Anonymous FTP**	Method of retrieving a file from a remote computer without having an account on that computer.
10 **ANSI character set**	The American National Standards Institute 8-bit character set. It contains 256 characters.
11 **ANSII**	Stands for American Standard Code for Information Inter-change.This is a numerical code used to represent characters. For example A is 65 and B is 66.

12 **Application Program**	A computer program designed for serving a particular applicative purpose e.g. WORD, EXCEL etc
13 **Archive**	A backup of data or a program used in the event that the original data or program is destroyed.
14 **Argument**	A variable, expression or constant that is supplied to a function or action which modifies the result of the function or action
15 **ASCII File**	A file consisting of ASCII characters
16 **Assembler**	A translator program used to convert assembly language code/program to machine language
17 **Assembly Language**	A computer language consists of special codes, called Mnemonics, which are understandable by the assembler
18 **Asynchronous Transfer Mode**	A high-speed computer networking standard suitable for all types of data, including voice and video, that can be used on both private and public networks.
19 **Auto number**	Access field type that automatically inserts a sequentially numbered value in each record

B

1 **Backbone**	In networking, a high-bandwidth trunk to which smaller networks connect. The original backbone of the Internet was NSFnet.
2 **Backup**	A second, safe copy of a file, letter or data.
3 **Bad sector**	A fault in a floppy disk or hard disk. Disks are divided into tracks which contain many sectors. If you have a bad sector, it means the disk surface has been damaged at this point and that the disk drive cannot read the data there.
4 **Bandwidth**	This refers to the difference (measured in Hz), between the highest and lowest frequencies of a transmission. Most people loosely refer to bandwidth as the amount of data that can be transferred over a network connection.
5 **Baseband**	A network in which the entire bandwidth of the transmission medium is used by a single digital signal. Unlike broadband, no modulation techniques are used.

6 **BAT or batch file**	The three-letter file name extension given to batch program files that contain a series of commands to be processed sequentially.
7 **Baud rate**	A number representing the speed at which information travels over a communication line.
8 **BBS**	An acronym for bulletin board system.
9 **Beta software**	Pre-release version of a new software program still in development, which is handed out to users for testing.
10 **Binary**	The common name for base two maths. In binary, the smallest unit is a bit (short for a binary digit). This can have one of just two values: 0 or 1.
11 **Binary File**	A file consisting of binary digits i.e. bits. It is more space efficient than ASCII file
12 **Binary file**	A file containing information that is in machine readable form. It can be read only by an application or the operating system.
13 **BIOS**	Stands for Basic Input/Output System. This is a series of instructions that manages the basic functions in your PC.
14 **Bit**	Binary digit. It's may be 0 or 1
15 **Bit**	A binary digit, the smallest unit of data used in a computer; 7 or 8 bits are typically used to represent a single character of text.
16 **Bits Per Second (bps)**	The speed at which bits are transmitted.
17 **Boot disk**	Floppy disc containing the necessary files to boot a computer without needing to access its hard disc.
18 **Boot, Boot up**	To start up a computer. This is process carried out when your PC is switched on. First, a sequence of instructions stored with the BIOS in a chip are executed and they tell the computer to look on the boot disk for the main operating system.
19 **Breakpoint**	It refers to a point in a program, where the program is explicitly interrupted or terminated
20 **Buffer**	A part of the memory used to store data temporarily while it is waiting to be used. For example, a program might store data in a printer buffer until the printer is ready to print it.

21 **Bug**	An error in a program that means it does not work properly.
22 **Bus**	The internal communication path from the CPU to the rest of the motherboard and peripheral devices.
23 **Bus Topology**	A network topology in which nodes are connected to a single cable with terminators at each end.
24 **Byte**	It consists of 8 bits

C

1 **Cache**	A very high speed memory that is used to temporarily store data before it is used by the PC's processor.
2 **CAD**	Stands for Computer Aided-Design. It is a special software that allows designers and architects to draw precise blueprints on screen, then model them in 3D to see how the design will appear in real life before a product is manufactured or a building erected.
3 **Calculated control**	A control that displays the result of an expression rather than data stored in a an underlying table
4 **Capacity**	The storage size of the disk in megabytes.
5 **Cascading Windows**	A way of arranging lots of windows on screen so that they overlap, with only the title bar and caption showing. This is a neat and efficient way of displaying lots of windows at once.
6 **CD**	Stands for Compact Disc. A small plastic disc that is used to store up to 700 Mb of data. The data is stored in the form of tiny holes etched on to the surface of the disc. A CD drive spins the disc and uses a laser beam to read the holes in the surface.
7 **CD-ROM drive**	A computer accessory used to access CD-ROM discs.
8 **Cell**	A single rectangle of a datasheet or design grid that can contain data or instructions
9 **Cell Pointer**	The current cursor position within a Excel sheet. It can be moved from one cell to another using arrow keys.
10 **Chat**	Real-time exchange of messages between users of a particular system. Chat allows people who are geographically far apart to

type messages to each other which are sent and received instantly. Also, an acronym meaning Conversational Hypertext Access Technology.

11 **Check box** — A control that displays a check for a yes/ true conditioning or nothing (unchecked) for a no/false condition

12 **Chip** — An integrated circuit etched on the surface of a tiny wafer of silicon and enclosed in a plastic or ceramic package. Pins extend from this package for connection to other electronic circuits.

13 **Client-server computing** — A technique with which processing can be distributed between nodes requesting information (clients) and those maintaining data (servers).

14 **Clipboard** — The area of windows memory where any cut or copied information is stored and from which stored information is pasted. The clipboard is automatically overwritten each time a cut or copy operation is performed.

15 **Clock** — It is an electronic circuit that emits a regulated sequence of electrical pulses synchronizing the operation of the circuits in a computer.

16 **Clock speed** — This is the speed at which the computer's internal clock is running. The higher the clock speed, the faster the computer will operate. Clock speed is usually measured in megahertz (MHz.)

17 **Column Label** — The column name displayed at the head of column

18 **Combo box** — Controls that can display a drop-down list or accept user-typed data.

19 **Command** — An instruction to carry out a specific action.

20 **Command button** — Controls that can be set to run a macro or event procedure when it is clicked

21 **Compiler** — A computer program designed to convert high-level language (HLL) code/program to low level language (LLL) code/program.

22 **Compression** — Technique for reducing the amount of storage needed for a given amount of data.

23 **Concatenation** — Combining together two or more than two separate text values (strings) for display as one string

24 **Control**	It refers to graphical objects. A control can be bound, unbound or calculated and can take the form of a text box, label, command button, line, picture or rectangle
25 **Control key (Ctrl)**	This key is normally used in combination with some other key on the keyboard. For example, CTRL+F4 will close the current document in a Windows application.
26 **CPU**	The electronic nerve center of a computer which controls the processing done by the computer. The Central Processing Unit carries on all computer operations.
27 **Cracker**	Substantially different from hackers, crackers are users who try to gain illegal access to computers. They are usually malicious in their intentions.
28 **Criteria**	Instructions to limit records to be displayed in a query, form, or report
29 **Cursor**	A flashing bar that indicates the position where the characters are entered
30 **Cursor**	A highlighted or blinking block, line or underscore on a computer monitor that indicates where you are currently typing.
31 **Cyberspace**	The world of computers. It now loosely refers to the online world and even more loosely to the Internet.

D

1 **Data**	Facts, figures, and symbols, especially as stored in computers. The term is often used to mean raw, unprocessed facts, as distinct from information.
2 **Database**	A structured collection of data, which may be manipulated to select and sort desired items of information.
3 **Datagram**	A block of data that is "smart" enough (actually, which carries enough information) to travel from one Internet site to another without having to rely on earlier exchanges between the source and destination computers.
4 **DDE**	Abbreviation for dynamic data exchange, a form of communication between processes used in Microsoft Windows.
5 **Dedicated Line**	A communications line that is used solely for computer connections. If you buy an additional phone line for your modem, that's a dedicated line.

6 **Default**	An attribute, condition, value or option that is assumed when none is explicitly specified. A value or setting that takes effect when the equipment is turned on, reset or initialized, until redefined or changed.
7 **Defragmentation**	When a file is saved to disk the operating system does not necessarily save it over a continuous area. The defragmentation utility will reorganise your hard disk so that all the files are stored in continuous areas.
8 **Desktop**	A graphical representation of file systems, in which applications and files are represented by pictures (icons).
9 **Device Driver**	Software that controls how a computer communicates with a device. A low-level program (usually with a .DRV or .SYS file extension) that controls a hardware device such as a monitor, printer, hard disk, etc.
10 **Dialup**	A widely used method of accessing the Internet. A dialup connection uses regular phone lines to connect one computer to another via modem.
11 **Digital**	Used in computers to describe information that can be represented by a collection of bits.
12 **Digital Cameras**	Cameras that do not use photographic film. The light images are converted into computer data by special electronics and are stored in memory chips within the cameras.
13 **Directory**	It is used to group a number of files or sub-directories
14 **Disk**	A flat, circular piece of plastic that's coated with a substance that is capable of being magnetized and so store information. The disk spins at high speed and data is written to or read from the surface of the disk by a magnetic head much like the one in a cassette recorder that moves across the surface of the disk.
15 **Display Adapter**	The electronic device that controls what you see on your monitor. The display adapter takes instructions from the PC and converts them into electrical signals that define the color and character shapes you see on your screen.

E

1 **Editor**	A computer program used to create, edit and print text documents.
2 **E-mail**	An acronym for electronic mail. A way of sending and receiving messages between users on a network.
3 **Embed**	To insert a copy of an OLE object created in another application that can continue to be edited in that application
4 **Encryption**	The basis of network security. Encryption encodes network packets to prevent anyone except the intended recipient from accessing the data.
5 **Environment**	The environment is the imaginary space in which you work when you use your PC.
6 **Esc key**	A key on a PC keyboard, in the top left-hand corner, that is sometimes used to cancel an action.
7 **Ethernet**	The most popular protocol for local area networks. Ethernet was developed principally by the Xerox Corporation.
8 **Event**	An action that can be recognized by an object such as a mouse click or key press
9 **EXE**	File extension (.EXE) that denotes an executable file. Usually a program file.
10 **Execute**	To perform a computer operation or run an entire computer program.
11 **Export**	To convert a file from its native format to another format so that it can be read by a different program.
12 **Expression**	Combination of fields, constants, variables, operands and functions, that results in a single value
13 **Extended memory**	RAM memory that begins above 1 megabyte is extended memory.
14 **Extension**	The three-letter code at the end of a filename that generally indicates the type of format of the file. e.g. .doc is the extension of WORD document

F

1 **FAT**	Stands for File Allocation Table. A special data file that's stored on a disk and contains the name, size, date and location of all the files that are stored on the disk.

2 **Fax modem**	This is a modem that has the additional capability of interfacing with a standard FAX machine.
3 **Fiber optic cable**	Glass or plastic fibers over which modulated light pulses from laser or LED (Light Emitting Diode) can transmit data. It is not subject to interference.
4 **Field**	One item of information in a record of a table; i.e. it represents a column in datasheet view
5 **File**	A named group of characters or data bits in your computer or on the network. Files in a computer are similar to file folders in a filing cabinet. Such a file is made up of records.
6 **File Control Block (FCB)**	A file control block is used for maintaining the information related to file i.e. File's name, location & size. There is one FCB on the disk, for each file.
7 **File Format**	The type of file, such as picture or text; represented as a suffix at the end of the filename. Examples: text = .txt
8 **File sharing**	If you have two or more PCs linked together in a network, then you can share files between users. Sometimes only one user will use a file at any particular time, in other cases several users might be looking at a file at the same time.
9 **Filter**	Criteria applied to a group of records to limit the display or printing of records to a subset
10 **Find**	Criteria applied to a group of records to display only those records that meet the specified criteria
11 **Flame**	A negative response to an email or newsgroup posting.
12 **Floppy disk**	A portable storage device that stores information on a thin, flexible disk. The disk is coated with a magnetic material. The information is stored on the disk as a series of magnetic signals using a disk drive.
13 **Folder**	A container used to organize objects, programs, documents or other folders in OS.
14 **Font**	Particular style or design of the characters (alphabets, number & symbols) used to display data
15 **Font**	Complete set of printed or display characters of the same typeface, size, and style (bold, italic, underlined, etc.)

16 **Footer**	A section that appears at the bottom of a window or page or at the end of a report
17 **Form**	An object that contains a variety of controls organized for displaying data on the screen
18 **Format**	In context of disk, it refers to the division of disk into tracks and sectors. In context of an application program (**e.g.** Ms-WORD), it means to change the appearance of the text/ numbers.
19 **Format a disk**	To prepare a hard disk or diskette to hold information. Formatting a disk deletes all information that was previously on it.
20 **Frame**	A control that can contain an OLE object
21 **Freeware**	Software that is distributed for free, with no license fee.
22 **Front end**	The part of a software program that a user sees and interacts with.
23 **FTP (File Transfer Protocol)**	The most widely-used way of downloading and uploading (getting and putting) files across an Internet connection. The File Transfer Protocol is a standardized way to connect computers so that files can be shared between them easily.
24 **Full Duplex**	Communication providing simultaneous sending and receiving.
25 **Function**	A subprogram or sub procedure that accepts certain arguments and performs computation in order to return a value
26 **Function Key**	The special keys on a keyboard that are labeled F1 through F12. Software programs use these function keys to perform special actions within the program.

G

1 **GIF**	Stands for Graphics Interface Format. A commonly-used format for storing images and bitmapped colour graphics.
2 **Gigabyte**	A unit of measurement for computer memory equal to 1000 MB (megabytes) or one billion bytes.
3 **Graphical user interface (GUI)**	A type of user interface in which programs and files appear as icons (small pictures), user options are selected from pull-down menus, and data are displayed in windows (rectangular areas), which the operator can manipulate in various ways.

4 **Graphics card**	A peripheral device that processes and displays graphics.
5 **Grid**	A matrix of evenly spaced horizontal and vertical lines that help you align and measure drawings. The grid lines are not printed and serve only as a guide for drawing.
6 **Gutter**	1) The blank space between two adjacent columns of text. 2) Blank space or margin between two facing pages.

H

1 **Hacker**	Normally used to refer to someone who is trying to break into a secure computer system for criminal purposes, such as someone trying to discover a way into a bank.
2 **Half Duplex**	Communication that alternates between sending and receiving.
3 **Handshaking**	A procedure performed by modems, terminals, and computers to verify that communication has been correctly established.
4 **Hang**	A slang term that means your computer has stopped responding because of a temporary fault.
5 **Hard Copy**	A printed document or copy of an image that's stored on computer.
6 **Hard disk**	A rigid magnetic disk that is able to store many times more data than a floppy disk. Usually it cannot be removed from the disk drive that's located inside your PC.
7 **Hardware**	Any physical unit, hard disk, monitor or electronic circuit that is part of a computer system.
8 **Header**	Text that appears at the top of every page of a document when it is printed.
9 **Hertz (Hz)**	A unit of frequency measurement in cycles per second.
10 **Hexadecimal**	It is a base 16 number system. It contains digits 0 to 9 & alphabets A to F i.e. 0 1 2 3 4 5 6 7 8 9 A B C D E F
11 **High Density (HD)**	Refers to a diskette with higher than standard storage. High density diskettes include those capable of storing 1.2 and 1.44 MB of data. Also refers to the drive which uses high density diskettes.

12 **High Memory Area (HMA)**	RAM memory that exists between 1024KB and 1088KB.
13 **Host**	A computer that is attached to a network or the Internet. Hosts allow users on client machines to connect and share files or transfer information.
14 **Host Address**	The address of a host computer on the Internet.
15 **Hostname**	The name given a host computer connected to the Internet.
16 **HTML**	Stands for Hyper Text Markup Language. It is a standard for structuring and describing a document on the World Wide Web.
17 **Hue**	The position of a color along the color spectrum.
18 **Hypermedia**	The combination of hypertext and multimedia in an online document.
19 **HyperTerminal**	A communications program that is included with Windows 95 and allows you call a remote computer via a modem and transfer files.
20 **Hypertext**	A type of text that allows embedded links to other documents. Clicking on or selecting a hypertext link displays another document or section of a document.

I

1 **I/O Device**	Input device refers to the device by means of which we fed data into computer. Output device refers to the device by means of which we get thc required output/information produced by the computer
2 **I-beam cursor**	A flashing cursor shaped like a capital I used to indicate that you can edit text on screen.
3 **IBM Compatible Computers**	Computers that use the same software as the computers introduced by the IBM Corporation in the early 80's.
4 **Icon**	A small picture displayed on screen to identify a command or file.
5 **Image editor**	Software that lets you edit, change or paint new parts of an image.
6 **Import**	To bring a document or object created by another program into the current application and convert its format to the format of the current application.

7 **Inactive window**	A window in which you are not currently working. This window cannot receive input from the user.
8 **Input**	To transfer information into a computer. If you type text on your keyboard you are inputting data into the computer. Other examples are using a scanner or using a mouse to draw on screen.
9 **Install**	The steps involved in copying and setting up an application program on your hard disk.
10 **Integrated Circuit (IC)**	A miniature electronic circuit that is imprinted on the surface of a silicon chip.
11 **Internet**	An international network connecting governments, companies, universities, and many other networks and users.
12 **Internet Protocol (IP)**	An industry standard, connectionless, best-effort packet switching protocol used as the network layer in the TCP/IP Protocol Suite.
13 **Interrupt**	A signal received by the computer's central processing unit that causes a temporary halt in the execution of a program while some other task is performed.
14 **IP Address (Internet Protocol Address)**	Numbered address assigned to an Internet host. Traditionally, IP addresses are 32-bit, which means that numbered addresses have four sections separated by dots, each a decimal number between 0 and 255.
15 **ISDN (Integrated Services Digital Network)**	A relatively new technology which combines voice and digital network services in a single medium.
16 **ISO (International Standards Organization)**	An international organization that creates networking standards, including the OSI (Open Systems Interconnections) model.
17 **ISP (Internet Service Provider)**	An ISP is a company that maintains a network that is linked to the Internet via a dedicated communication line, usually a high-speed link. It sells dial-up access to the Internet.

J

1 **Jabber**	Network error caused by an interface card continually sending corrupted data onto the network.
2 **Jaggies**	Slang term for the jagged edges that you'll see along the sides of curves, graphics or round characters. Jaggies occur because the printer can only print individual dots rather than smooth lines.

3 **Jitter**	A fault on a monitor that causes annoying, tiny movements of characters.
4 **Joystick**	An input device that signals to a computer the direction and extent of displacement of a hand- held lever.
5 **JPEG**	A standard you may come across if you use graphic images. JPEG is a complex way of storing images in a compressed format so they take up a much less disk space.
6 **Jumper**	Rectangular plug used to make connections on a circuit board.

K

1 **Kermit**	A file-transfer protocol, originally developed at Columbia University and made available without charge.
2 **Keyboard**	An input device resembling a typewriter keyboard, used to enter instructions and data.
3 **KHz**	A measure of the frequency of a sound. One KHz (or Kilohertz) is equal to 1,000 cycles per second. The higher the number, the higher pitched the sound.
4 **Kilobyte (Kb)**	A measure of the capacity of a storage device that is usually written as Kb. A Kb is equal to 1,024 bytes.

L

1 **LAN**	Acronym for Local Area Network. It is a network restricted to a single room or building. It enable around 500 devices, usually microcomputers acting as workstations, as well as peripheral devices, such as printers, to be connected together.
2 **Laptop**	A small computer that you can carry around.
3 **Laser printer**	Printer that produces very high quality text and graphics using a laser beam.
4 **LCD**	An acronym for Liquid Crystal Display. A display screen with black characters on a white background. This display type is used on battery powered models like notebook and laptop computers.
5 **Leased Line**	A dedicated, full-time connection used to link a user or network to an Internet Service Provider or another network.

6 **Light pen**	A probe containing a light sensitive cell which, when pointed at the monitor screen, can make selections or input instructions to the computer.
7 **Log off**	The process by which a user identifies himself or herself to a multiuser computer and leaves the system
8 **Log on**	A command that tells the network that you want to use the network resources. Normally you need to enter your user name and password which is then verified by the network software before allowing you to access the resources.
9 **Loop**	A sequence of one or more instructions in a computer program that are executed repeatedly until certain conditions have been met.
10 **Low-level language**	A programming language designed for a particular computer and reflecting its internal machine code; low-level languages are therefore often described as machine-oriented languages.

M

1 **Machine language**	A computer's native language of binary code using 0's and 1's. All executable programs are converted into the binary code of machine language so the computer can process the information.
2 **Macro**	A series of instructions requiring multiple keystrokes or menu choices that are recorded and saved and can be played back at anytime with a single keystroke or action.
3 **Mailing List**	A list of email addresses used to forward messages to groups of people. When you subscribe to a mailing list, you receive all mail sent to that list.
4 **Mb or Mbyte**	Stands for Megabyte. A measure of the data capacity of the storage device that is equal to 1,048,576 bytes.
5 **Media**	Something that will store or carry information. It's a vague term, but it generally refers to floppy disks or CD-ROM discs.
7 **Megahertz (MHz)**	A unit of speed measurement in millions of cycles per second.

6 **Memory**	This means some device that can store information, but it's also used to refer to electronic components that can store data and are used to provide the RAM in your PC.
8 **Metropolitan Area Network (MAN)**	A network capable of high speed data communication over distances up to about 80 kilometers.
9 **Microphone**	A device that converts sound waves into electrical signals.
10 **Microprocessor**	Main computer chip that provides speed and capabilities of the computer.
11 **Modem**	A device that converts electronic signals from your PC into sound signals that can be transmitted over a phone line. To receive information the modem works in reverse and converts the sound signals back into digital electronic signals. Modems are used to connect to the Internet or to an online service, such as CompuServe.
12 **Monitor**	Device that displays the text and graphics from your PC. It looks and works rather like a TV set.
13 **Motherboard**	This is the main circuit board inside a computer that contains most of the components necessary for the proper operation of the computer including the CPU, clock, RAM memory, and others. Most of the peripheral devices are plugged into, or in some way connected to, the motherboard.
14 **Mouse**	Small hand-held device that's moved on a flat surface to control the position of a pointer on screen.
15 **Multitasking**	It is the ability of an Operating system to run several different programs at the same time. All the programs are held in memory together and each is allowed to run for a certain period, giving the impression of parallel activity. For example, one program may run while other programs are waiting for a peripheral device to work or for input from an operator.
16 **Multithreading**	It means executing two or more threads or sections of a program simultaneously. A thread is a separate path of execution. In other words, a thread is an independently running subtask. Multithreading is extremely useful in creating a responsive user interface. For example, a browser allows a user to view another page while it is downloading data.

17 **Musical Instrument Digital Interface (MIDI)**	A special interface that lets your computer control musical instruments, such as a synthesiser, keyboard or drum machine.

N

1 **Network**	A network is a group of entities connected together. An example of a network is the telephone system.
2 **Network Basic Input/ Output System (NetBIOS)**	A widely used protocol governing data exchange and network access.
3 **Network Interface Card**	Adapter board that provides the physical connection between a computer and the network medium. Also called Network Interface Controller.
4 **Network Operating System (NOS)**	Controlling software for a network, which may run on top of DOS, that oversees resource sharing and often provides security and administrative tools.
5 **Network Topology**	The arrangement of nodes usually forming a star, ring, tree or bus pattern.
6 **Newsgroups**	Electronic bulletin boards on the Internet that specialize on particular topics, such as nursing, aviation, football, gardening, piano tuning, and many aspects of computers.
7 **Node**	Any device, including servers and workstations, connected to a network. Also, the point where devices are connected.

O

1 **Object Linking and Embedding (OLE)**	System that lets you cut and paste data from one application to another, retaining the formatting and controls. You can select part of a spreadsheet, switch to a word processor and paste it in.
2 **Offline**	Not connected to a network.
3 **Online**	A modem that is connected to another modem via a telephone line and is currently transferring information.
4 **Operating System**	A program that controls the basic operation of a computer. A typical OS controls the peripheral devices such as printers, organizes the filing system, provides a means of communicating with the operator, and runs other programs.
5 **Operator**	A symbol that defines a mathematical action. X is the multiplication operator.

6 **Optical Character Recognition (OCR)**	This is a type of software that is used to convert text in a graphical image into a word processor format that can be used by a computer.

P

1 **Packet**	A bundle of data. On the Internet, data is broken up into small chunks called packets that each traverse the network independently.
2 **Packet Forwarding**	Copying the packet to another node without looking at the destination address.
3 **Packet Switching**	A method of transmitting data between computers connected in a network.
4 **Palmtop**	Tiny computers that contain keyboard, screen and storage.
5 **Parallel Port**	Socket at the back of your PC that lets you connect it to a printer. A parallel port sends data to the printer over eight parallel wires.
7 **Parity**	A setting of a terminal or modem related to the type of error correction system used when connected to a network.
6 **Partition**	A way of dividing a hard disk into chunks that can be addressed by separate disk drive letters.
8 **Peripheral**	Any item connected to a computer's central processing unit (CPU). Typical peripherals include keyboard, mouse, monitor and printer.
9 **Photorealistic**	A computer image that has almost the same quality and clarity as a photograph.
10 **Phototypesetter**	A device that can produce very high resolution text on photo-sensitive paper or film.
11 **PING (Packet Internet Gopher)**	The simplest way to test or time the response of an Internet connection. A PING sends a request to an Internet host and waits for a reply called a PONG. When you PING an address, you get a response telling you the number of seconds it took to make the connection. PING clients exist for a number of platforms, or you can use a UNIX or Windows 95 prompt to issue a PING command directly.
12 **Pirating**	When you buy a software program, you do not own the program; you only own a license to use the program. The program is owned

by the company that developed it. Thus, giving the program to others is stealing.

13 **Pixel** — The smallest single unit or point on a display or on a printer whose colour or brightness can be controlled.

14 **POP (Post Office Protocol)** — A protocol designed to allow single users to read mail from a server. There are three versions: POP, POP2, and POP3. When email is sent to you, it is stored on the server until accessed by you. Once you are authenticated, the POP is used to transmit the stored mail from the server to your local mailbox on your client machine.

15 **Port** — A connector on a computer to which cables for devices or communication lines are attached. Ports can be parallel or serial.

16 **Printer** — A device that produces text or an image on paper using ink or toner under the control of a PC.

17 **Processor** — Also called the central processing unit (CPU). It's an electronic device that contains millions of tiny components designed for basic arithmetic and control functions. A CPU can add or subtract numbers, move numbers from one location to another, or control an external device.

18 **Program** — Complete set of instructions which direct a PC to carry out a particular task.

19 **Protocol** — A protocol is a rule or a complete set of rules defining how computers communicate. In other words, a protocol is an agreement that must be obeyed by sender and receiver in order to communicate.

20 **Purge** — To empty the contents of the Recycle Bin in Windows.

Q

1 **Quantize** — To convert an analogue signal into a numerical representation.

2 **Query By Example (QBE)** — A database front end that requests the user to supply an example of the type of data to be retrieved.

3 **Qwerty keyboard** — English-language keyboard layout for a typewriter or computer, in which the top line of letters are QWERTY. The French use a different layout with the top line reading AZERTY.

R

1 **Ragged**	Text that is not straight or that has an uneven edge.
2 **RAM**	Stands for Random Access Memory. This memory allows access to any location in any order, without having to access the rest first.
3 **Read Only Memory (ROM)**	A computer memory that stores permanent information. This information is constant and cannot be erased, or changed, or lost, even if electrical power is turned off. All PC's contain programs in ROM that execute when the power is turned on (BIOS.)
4 **Real time**	Processing time which is of the same order of magnitude as the problem to be solved. Air-traffic control computers have to analyse the position of aircraft within a second so that they do not collide.
5 **Re-boot**	The equivalent of switching your PC off then on.
6 **Record**	A set of data (facts and figures) relating to a specific thing (e.g. person, car, etc.). The data are identified by field names.
7 **Refresh Rate**	This is the speed at which the screen is repainted. Typically, color displays must be refreshed at 60 times per second (60 Hertz).
8 **Registry**	A database that forms the basis of Windows and contains information about every program stored on the disk and the users, networks and preferences.
9 **Repeater**	A device that regenerates and often amplifies signals to extend transmission distance. It is independent of protocol and media.
10 **Resolution**	Number of pixels that a screen or printer can display per unit area.
11 **RGB**	High-definition monitor system that uses three separate input signals controlling red, green and blue color picture beam.
12 **Rich text format (RTF)**	A way of storing a document that includes all the commands that describe the page, type, font and formatting. The RTF format allows formatted pages to be exchanged between different word processors.
13 **Root directory**	The topmost directory from which all other directories branch.

S

1 **16-bit processor**	A processor which handles data in 16-bit words, providing much faster operation than older eight-bit systems.
2 **Safe mode**	A special operating mode of Windows that is selected if Windows detects a problem when starting. Safe mode does not let you do anything except try to work out and fix the problem.
3 **Sampling**	Measurement of an analogue signal (such as an audio or video signal) at regular intervals. The result of the measurement can be converted into a digital signal that can be electronically enhanced, edited or processed.
4 **Scalable font**	A font that can be displayed or printed at any size without changing shape. Each letter is described as a set of curves which can be altered to print at any size without looking jagged.
5 **ScanDisk**	A utility supplied with MS-DOS (which is also part of Windows) that check's your hard disk for problems.
6 **Scanner**	A device which uses photo-electric cells to convert a drawing, photograph or document into data which can be manipulated by a PC.
7 **Screen saver**	A moving picture or pattern that appears on your screen when you have not moved the mouse or pressed a key for a specified period of time. Screen savers prevent screen damage.
8 **Sector**	The smallest area on a magnetic disk which can be addressed by a PC. The disk is divided into concentric tracks, and each track is divided into sectors which can store 512 bytes of data.
9 **Server**	A dedicated computer which provides a function to a network, such as storing images, or printing data.
10 **Session**	The time period between when you "log in" to and "log off" from a network system.
11 **Shareware**	Software which is available free for you to sample. But if you keep it you are expected to pay a fee to the writer.

12 **SMTP (Simple Mail Transfer Protocol)**	A protocol used to transfer email. SMTP transfers mail from server to server, and the end user must use POP to transfer the messages to their machine.
13 **Software**	Computer programs that perform various tasks. Word processing programs (like WordPad or Microsoft Word), spreadsheet programs (like Lotus or Excel), or database programs (like dBase III+, Access, or Oracle) are all software.
14 **Software License**	An agreement between a user and a software house, giving details of the rights of the user to use or copy software.
15 **Soundcard**	Printed circuit board that, coupled with a set of speakers, enables a computer to reproduce music and sound effects.
16 **Startup disk**	A floppy disk which holds the system configuration files which can, in case of hard disk failure, be used to start the computer.
17 **System**	A general term that refers to a computer, and its associated peripherals or to the operating system software such as Windows.

T

1 **TCP/IP**	Set of network protocols, developed principally by the US Department of Defense. TCP/IP is widely used, particularly in UNIX and on the Internet.
2 **Telecommunication**	Communicating with other people through the computer using communication software and modems.
3 **Teleconferencing**	To link video, audio and computer signals from different locations so that distant people can talk and see each other.
4 **Telnet**	The Internet standard protocol to connect to remote terminals. Telnet clients are available for most platforms.
5 **Terminal**	A device connected to a computer network that acts as a point for entry or retrieval of information. Personal computers can be made to act as network terminals, by running terminal emulation (communication) programs.
6 **Thumbnail**	A miniature graphical representation of an image.
7 **TIFF**	An acronym for Tagged Image File Format, is usually created by scanners or image

processing programs. These bitmapped files come in a number of different versions.

8 **Time Slice** In a multitasking environment, this is the amount of processor time that the operating system allocates to an application, usually measured in milliseconds. Each application can run for this specified amount of time before the next application is given control.

9 **ToolTips** A feature of Windows that displays a line of descriptive text under an icon when you move the pointer over that particular icon.

10 **TrueType** An outline font technology introduced by Apple and Microsoft as a means of printing exactly what is displayed on screen. The technology is also capable of producing fonts that can be scaled to any point size while still remaining smooth.

U

1 **UNDELETE** A DOS command which restores files previously deleted with the DEL command. UNDELETE cannot restore a directory that has been removed or restore a file if you have removed the directory that contained the file.

2 **Undo** A function of some applications that will let you undo/revert the command that you've just carried out.

3 **UNFORMAT** A DOS command which restores a disk erased by the FORMAT command or restructured by the RECOVER command.

4 **Universal Serial Bus (USB)** A serial "information path" through which the CPU communicates with devices such as scanners. USB ports are being used on newer devices instead of the older COM ports.

5 **Unix** A multi-user, multi-tasking operating system developed by AT & T Bell Laboratories to run on almost any computer, from a PC, to minicomputers and large mainframes.

6 **Upload** The act of transferring computer files from an individual's computer to a web server.

7 **UPS** Stands for Uninterruptible Power Supply. It is a battery backup system to provide continuous power in the event of power failures or fluctuations.

8 **URL** Stands for uniform resource locator. Series of letters and/or numbers specifying the location of a document on the World-Wide Web.

9 **Usenet** — The world's largest bulletin board system, which brings together people with common interests to exchange views and information.

10 **User interface** — Software which operates between the user and the operating system, often to make the latter easier to use.

11 **User-friendly** — A description of software which is easy to use- particularly for novice or inexperienced computer users.

V

1 **Vector graphics, image** — A system of drawing objects using curves and lines. The images are described by line length and direction from an origin to plot lines and build up an image rather than a description of each pixel, as in a bitmap image.

2 **VGA** — An acronym for Video Graphics Array. Analog graphics standard introduced with the IBM PS/2 series computers. Compatible with EGA but has higher resolution. Supports a maximum resolution of 640 x 480 pixels in 16 colors.

3 **Video graphics card** — An expansion board that gives personal computers their display capability.

4 **Video-conferencing** — A system which allows people in different locations to interact via video and audio.

5 **Virtual** — Something which does not actually exist, except in an imaginary form in a computer.

6 **Virtual memory** — A technique whereby a portion of the computer backing storage, or external, memory is used as an extension of its immediate- access, or internal, memory.

7 **Virtual reality (VR)** — A simulation of a real-life scene or environment by a computer which you can interact with and explore.

8 **Virus** — A computer virus is an insidious piece of software that infects other software and moves from computer to computer when software is transferred.

9 **Volatile** — A term used in reference to a computer memory that requires electrical power to retain information. The random access memory in a personal computer is volatile memory.

W

1 **Wallpaper**	An image being displayed on the Windows desktop background.
2 **WAVE or WAV file**	A standard method of storing an analog signal in digital form under Microsoft Windows.
3 **White Pages**	Databases containing email addresses, telephone numbers, and postal addresses of Internet users. You can search the Internet White Pages to find information about particular users.
4 **WHOIS**	An Internet program (related to Finger and the White Pages) that lets you enter an Internet entity (such as domains, networks, and hosts) and display information such as a person's company name, address, phone number and email address.
5 **Wide Area Network (WAN)**	A network capable of transmissions over large geographic areas that uses transmission lines provided by a common carrier.
6 **Wildcards**	A symbol used when searching for files or data which represents all files; in DOS, UNIX and PC operating systems, the wild card character '?' will match any single character in this position.
7 **Windows**	A multi-tasking graphical user interface for the IBM PC developed by Microsoft that is designed to be easy to use. Windows uses icons to represent files and devices and can be controlled using a mouse.
8 **WWW**	Abbreviated to World Wide Web. It is a hypertext system for publishing information on the Internet.
9 **WORM**	Stands for Write Once, Read Many Times memory. An optical disc storage system that allows the user to write data to the disc once. The user can then read the data from the disc many times.
10 **WYSIWYG**	"What you see is what you get".

X

1 **Xmodem**	An FTP protocol designed to make transmitting files via telephone speedy and error-free.
2 **XT**	The original version of the first IBM PC, developed by IBM that used an 8088 processor and included a hard disk.

3 **XT keyboard** A type of keyboard used by the IBM PC which had ten function keys running in two columns along the left-hand side of the keyboard. The current standard is called the AT.

Y

1 **Yahoo** Search engine for the World Wide Web, based on a catalogue of indexed resources.

Z

1 **Zmodem** FTP protocol for transferring files across the Internet or other communications link.

2 **Zoom** To enlarge an area of text or graphics to make it easier to see or work on.

Appendix-B

MEMORY UNITS

Every piece of information stored within the computer's memory is encoded as some unique combination of zeros and ones. These zeros and ones are called bits. Each bit represents an electronic state i.e. zero represents **"pulse is off"**, one represents **"pulse is on".** Various units of memory and their corresponding relationships are given below in ascending order-

1Byte = 8 bits

1KB = 1024 Bytes = 10^3 = 2^{10}

1MB = 1024 KB (Kilo Bytes) = 10^6 = 2^{20}

1GB = 1024 MB (Mega Bytes) = 10^9 = 2^{30}

1TB = 1024 GB (Giga Bytes) = 10^{12} = 2^{40}

1PB = 1024 TB (Tera Bytes) = 10^{15} = 2^{50}

1EB = 1024 PB (Peta Byte) = 10^{18} = 2^{60}

1ZB = 1024 EB (Exa Byte) = 10^{21} = 2^{70}

1YB = 1024 ZB (Zetta Byte) = 10^{24} = 2^{80}

Note :-

- **Bit** refers to Binary digits
- **Decimal equivalent of 1024** is 1000 or 10^3
- **Binary equivalent of 1024** is 2 raise to power 10
- **YB** refers to Yotta Byte
- **In small computers**, memory is expressed in terms of **Bytes**
- **In large computers**, memory is expressed in terms of **Words**
- Each **word** may consist of 32 or 36 bits

Appendix-C

ASCII CHART

It should be noted that the first 32 characters and the last character are control characters. Usually they are not displayed. But, some computers support certain graphics characters for these ASCII values.

ASCII Table - I

Dec	Hex	Char	Dec	Hex	Char	Dec	Hex	Char	Dec	Hex	Char
0	00	Null	32	20	Space	64	40	@	96	60	`
1	01	Start of heading	33	21	!	65	41	A	97	61	a
2	02	Start of text	34	22	"	66	42	B	98	62	b
3	03	End of text	35	23	#	67	43	C	99	63	c
4	04	End of transmit	36	24	$	68	44	D	100	64	d
5	05	Enquiry	37	25	%	69	45	E	101	65	e
6	06	Acknowledge	38	26	&	70	46	F	102	66	f
7	07	Audible bell	39	27	'	71	47	G	103	67	g
8	08	Backspace	40	28	(	72	48	H	104	68	h
9	09	Horizontal tab	41	29	)	73	49	I	105	69	i
10	0A	Line feed	42	2A	*	74	4A	J	106	6A	j
11	0B	Vertical tab	43	2B	+	75	4B	K	107	6B	k
12	0C	Form feed	44	2C	,	76	4C	L	108	6C	l
13	0D	Carriage return	45	2D	-	77	4D	M	109	6D	m
14	0E	Shift out	46	2E	.	78	4E	N	110	6E	n
15	0F	Shift in	47	2F	/	79	4F	O	111	6F	o
16	10	Data link escape	48	30	0	80	50	P	112	70	p
17	11	Device control 1	49	31	1	81	51	Q	113	71	q
18	12	Device control 2	50	32	2	82	52	R	114	72	r
19	13	Device control 3	51	33	3	83	53	S	115	73	s
20	14	Device control 4	52	34	4	84	54	T	116	74	t
21	15	Neg. acknowledge	53	35	5	85	55	U	117	75	u
22	16	Synchronous idle	54	36	6	86	56	V	118	76	v
23	17	End trans. block	55	37	7	87	57	W	119	77	w
24	18	Cancel	56	38	8	88	58	X	120	78	x
25	19	End of medium	57	39	9	89	59	Y	121	79	y
26	1A	Substitution	58	3A	:	90	5A	Z	122	7A	z
27	1B	Escape	59	3B	;	91	5B	[	123	7B	{
28	1C	File separator	60	3C	<	92	5C	\	124	7C		
29	1D	Group separator	61	3D	=	93	5D	]	125	7D	}
30	1E	Record separator	62	3E	>	94	5E	^	126	7E	~
31	1F	Unit separator	63	3F	?	95	5F	_	127	7F	□

ASCII Table - II

Dec	Hex	Char	Dec	Hex	Char	Dec	Hex	Char	Dec	Hex	Char
128	80	Ç	160	A0	á	192	C0	└	224	E0	α
129	81	ü	161	A1	í	193	C1	┴	225	E1	ß
130	82	é	162	A2	ó	194	C2	┬	226	E2	Γ
131	83	â	163	A3	ú	195	C3	├	227	E3	π
132	84	ä	164	A4	ñ	196	C4	─	228	E4	Σ
133	85	à	165	A5	Ñ	197	C5	┼	229	E5	σ
134	86	å	166	A6	ª	198	C6	╞	230	E6	µ
135	87	ç	167	A7	°	199	C7	╟	231	E7	τ
136	88	ê	168	A8	¿	200	C8	╚	232	E8	Φ
137	89	ë	169	A9	⌐	201	C9	╔	233	E9	Θ
138	8A	è	170	AA	¬	202	CA	╩	234	EA	Ω
139	8B	ï	171	AB	½	203	CB	╦	235	EB	δ
140	8C	î	172	AC	¼	204	CC	╠	236	EC	∞
141	8D	ì	173	AD	¡	205	CD	═	237	ED	ø
142	8E	Ä	174	AE	«	206	CE	╬	238	EE	ε
143	8F	Å	175	AF	»	207	CF	╧	239	EF	∩
144	90	É	176	B0	░	208	D0	╨	240	F0	≡
145	91	æ	177	B1	▒	209	D1	╤	241	F1	±
146	92	Æ	178	B2	▓	210	D2	╥	242	F2	≥
147	93	ô	179	B3	│	211	D3	╙	243	F3	≤
148	94	ö	180	B4	┤	212	D4	╘	244	F4	⌠
149	95	ò	181	B5	╡	213	D5	╒	245	F5	⌡
150	96	û	182	B6	╢	214	D6	╓	246	F6	÷
151	97	ù	183	B7	╖	215	D7	╫	247	F7	≈
152	98	ÿ	184	B8	╕	216	D8	╪	248	F8	°
153	99	Ö	185	B9	╣	217	D9	┘	249	F9	∙
154	9A	Ü	186	BA	║	218	DA	┌	250	FA	
155	9B	¢	187	BB	╗	219	DB	█	251	FB	√
156	9C	£	188	BC	╝	220	DC	▄	252	FC	ⁿ
157	9D	¥	189	BD	╜	221	DD	▌	253	FD	²
158	9E	₧	190	BE	╛	222	DE	▐	254	FE	■
159	9F	ƒ	191	BF	┐	223	DF	▀	255	FF	□

Appendix-D

SHORTCUT KEYS

Working with WINDOWS

BASIC WINDOWS OPERATIONS	SHORTCUTS
Restarting Computer	Ctrl + Alt +Del
Closing or Exiting Window	Alt + F4
Select a file/folder/icon	Type the first letter of the file. If you have several files starting with the same letter, continue hitting the letter key until your cursor lands on the file or folder you want.
Search for a file/folder	F3
Rename a file/folder	Select the file/folder, click F2, and then re-type the name
Find out when the file or folder was created, by whom, and how big it is	Select the file, right-click, and then click **Properties**
Display the Start menu	Ctrl + Esc
Scroll between open items	Alt + Tab, then hold down Alt while clicking Tab to reach the desired file or program
Use these shortcut keys in order to minimize all windows on the desktop	1. Ctrl + Esc 2. Alt + M

Working with WORD

BASIC OPERATIONS	SHORTCUTS
Select text	Shift + Right Arrow, Left Arrow, Up Arrow, or Down Arrow to highlight text
Copy selected text	Ctrl + C
Cut selected text	Ctrl + X
Paste selected text	Ctrl + V
Undo your last action	Ctrl + Z
Select all the text within your document	Ctrl + A
Bold text	Ctrl + B
Italicize text	Ctrl + I
Underline	Ctrl + U
Decrease font size	Ctrl + Shift + <
Increase font size	Ctrl + Shift + >
Change font	Ctrl + Shift + F, then use the arrow keys to reach the new font
Change font size	Ctrl + Shift + P, then use the arrow keys to reach the new font size
Create page break	Ctrl + Enter
Create new document	Ctrl + N
Open My Documents window	Ctrl + O
Close a document	Ctrl + W
Save a document	Ctrl + S
Print a document	Ctrl + P

BASIC OPERATIONS	SHORTCUTS
Preview what you're about to print	Alt + Ctrl + I
Selecting all contents of the page	Ctrl + A
Copying selected text	Ctrl + C
Cut Selected Text	Ctrl + X
Paste Cut or Copied Text	Ctrl + V
Find a word	Ctrl + F
Inserting hyperlink	Ctrl + K
Reverting or Undo Recent done change	Ctrl + Z
Repeating the recent reverted change	Ctrl + Y
Change the font	Ctrl + Shift + F
Deletes word to right of cursor.	Ctrl + Del
Deletes word to left of cursor.	Ctrl + Backspace
Change the case of selected text	Shift + F3
Save As	F12

Working with Excel

Move right to left, cell by cell	Tab
Move up and down, cell by cell	Enter
Erase data in current cell	Backspace
Return to the beginning of the row	Home
Enter the date	Ctrl + ; (semicolon)
Enter the time	Ctrl + Shift + : (colon)

BASIC OPERATIONS	SHORTCUTS
Start a formula	= (equal sign)
Check the spelling of titles or words within the cells	F7
Find out about the style within the cell	ALT + ' (apostrophe)
Display the Format Cells dialog box	Ctrl + 1
Apply the general number format	Ctrl + Shift + ~
Turn numbers into dollars	Ctrl + Shift + $
Make numbers a percentage	Ctrl + Shift + %
Apply a border	Ctrl + Shift + &

Working with PowerPoint

Insert a new slide	CTRL+M
Switch to the next pane (clockwise)	F6
Switch to the previous pane (counterclockwise)	SHIFT+F6
Make a duplicate of the current slide	CTRL+D
Start a slide show	F5
Apply subscript formatting	CTRL+EQUAL SIGN (=)
Apply superscript formatting	CTRL+PLUS SIGN (+)
Open the **Font** dialog box	CTRL+T
Repeat your last action	F4 or CTRL+Y
Find	CTRL+F
View guides	CTRL+G
Delete a word	CTRL+BACKSPACE

BASIC OPERATIONS	SHORTCUTS
Capitalize	SHIFT+F3
Bold	CTRL+B
Italicize	CTRL+I
Insert a hyperlink	CTRL+K
Select all	CTRL+A
Copy	CTRL+C
Paste	CTRL+V
Undo	CTRL+Z
Save	CTRL+S
Print	CTRL+P
Open	CTRL+O

Working with Internet Explorer

Display the Internet Explorer Help, or when in a dialog box, display context help on an item	F1
Toggle between Full Screen and regular view of the browser window	F11
Move forward through the items on a Web page, the Address bar, and the Links bar	Tab
Move back through the items on a Web page, the Address bar, and the Links bar	Shift + Tab
Go to your Home page	Alt + Home
Go to Next Page	Alt + Right Arrow

BASIC OPERATIONS	SHORTCUTS
Go to Previous Page	Alt + Left Arrow or Backspace
Scroll toward the beginning of a document	UP ARROW
Scroll toward the end of a document	DOWN ARROW
Scroll toward the beginning of a document in larger increments	PAGE UP
Scroll toward the end of a document in larger increments	PAGE DOWN
Move to the beginning of a document	HOME
Move to the end of a document	END
Refresh the current web page	F5 or Ctrl + R
Stop downloading a page	ESC
Opens a new window	Ctrl + N
Closes the current window	Ctrl + W
Saves the current web page	Ctrl + S
Print the current web page	Ctrl + P
Open Search in Explorer bar	Ctrl + E
Open Favorites in Explorer bar	Ctrl + I
Open History in Explorer bar	Ctrl + H

Appendix-E

Abbreviations (365)

A

Sno.	Abbreviations	Full Forms
1	A	Accumulator
2	ACE	Automatic Computer Engine
3	ADC	Analog to Digital Converter
4	ADP	Automatic data processing
5	ADSL	Asymmetric digital subscriber line
6	AGP	Accelerated Graphics Port
7	AI	Artificial Intelligence
8	ALGOL	Algorithmic Language
9	ALU	Arithmetic & Logical Unit
10	ANSI	American National Standard Institute
11	API	Application Program Interface
12	AR	Address Register
13	ARIN	American Registry for Internet Numbers
14	ASCII	American Standard Code for Information Interchange
15	ASM*	Source code file for assembly language
16	ASP	Application Service Provider
17	ATM	Asynchronous Transfer Mode/ Automatic Teller Machine
18	ADBS	Advanced Data Broadcast System
19	ACL	Access Control List
20	AF	Audio Frequency
21	ANANDI	Area Networking Development Initiative
22	ARPANET	Advanced Research Project Agency Network

	23	AT & T	American Telegraphic and Telephone Co. Ltd.
	24	ATC	Air Traffic Control
	25	ANMC-21	Asian Network of Major Cities-21
B	1	BAK*	Backup Files
	2	BAS*	Source code file for Basic
	3	BASIC	Beginners All Purpose Symbolic Instruction Code
	4	BAT*	Batch Files
	5	BBS	Bulletin Board Service
	6	BCD	Binary Coded Decimal
	7	BIOS	Basic Input Output System
	8	Bits	Binary Digits
	9	BMP*	Bitmap
	10	BOC	Bell operating company
	11	bps	Bits per second
	12	BSD	Berkley standard distribution
	13	B2B	Business to Business
	14	B2C	Business to Consumer
	15	BLOB	Binary Large Objects
	16	BPO	Business Process Outsourcing
	17	Bps	Bytes per second
C	1	C*	Source code file of C
	2	CAD	Computer Aided Design
	3	CAM	Computer Aided Manufacturing
	4	CAS	Content Addressable Storage
	5	CASE	Computer Aided Software Engineering
	6	CAT	Computerized Axial Tomography
	7	CBT	Computer based training
	8	CCD	Charged Couple Devices
	9	CCIE	Cisco certified internetwork expert
	10	CCNA	Cisco certified network associate
	11	CD/W	Compact Disk-rewritable
	12	CD/R	Compact Disk-recordable
	13	CDMA	Code division Multiple Access

	14	CE/RW	
	15	CGA	Color Graphic Adapter
	16	CGI	
	17	CGM*	Graphic file
	18	CIM	Computer Integrated Manufacturing
	19	CISC	Complex Instruction Set Computer
	20	CLEC	Competitive Local Exchange Carrier
	21	CMOS	Complimentary Metal-oxide semiconductor
	22	CMS	Content Management System
	23	COBOL	Common Business Oriented Language
	24	COM	Computer Output Film
	25	COM*	Program file having COM Format
	26	CPU	Central Processing Unit
	27	CRM	Customer Relationship Management
	28	CRT	Cathode Ray Tube
	29	CSMA/CD	Carrier Sense Multiple Access/Collision detection
	30	CTO	Chief Technical Officer
	31	CUI	Character User Interface
	32	CVT	Constant Voltage Transformer
	33	CMC	Computer Maintenance Corporation
D	1	DA	
	2	DASD	Direct Access Storage Device
	3	DAT	Digital Audio Tape
	4	DAT*	Data files
	5	db	Decibel
	6	DBF*	Database File
	7	DBMS	Database Management System
	8	DCE	Data communication Equipment
	9	DDE	Dynamic Data Exchange
	10	DDR	Double data rate
	11	DEC	Digital Equipment Corporation
	12	DEF*	Module Definition Files
	13	DHCP	Dynamic host configuration protocol

	No.	Abbreviation	Full Form
	14	DLL*	Dynamic link library
	15	DLT	Digital linear tape
	16	DMA	Direct Memory Access
	17	DNS	Domain Name Service
	18	DOC*	Word Document
	19	DOS	Disk Operating System
	20	DOS	Denial of service (attack)
	21	dpi	Dots per inches
	22	DRAM	Dynamic Random Access Memory
	23	DRO	Destructive Read-out
	24	DRV*	Device Drivers
	25	DSL	Digital subscriber line
	26	DSLAM	Digital subscriber line access multiplexor
	27	DSS	Decision Support System
	28	DTE	Data Terminal Equipment
	29	DTP	Desktop Publishing
	30	DVD	Digital Video/Versatile Disk
	31	DWG*	AUTOCAD drawing file
	32	DXF*	Graphic files
	33	DHSD	Duplex-High Speed Data Service
	34	DSB	Digital Satellite Broadcasting
	35	DSIDC	Defence Scientific Information and Documentation Centre
	1	EBCDIC	Extended Binary Coded Decimal Interchange Code
E	2	ECC	Error correcting code
	3	EC	Execute Cycle
	4	ECIL	Electronics Corporation of India Ltd.
	5	EDP	Electronic data processing
	6	EDSAC	Electronic Delay Storage Automatic Computer
	7	EDVAC	Electronic Discrete Variable Automatic Computer
	8	EFT	Electronic Fund Transfer
	9	EGA	Enhanced Graphics Adapter
	10	EIA	Electronics Industries Association

	11	EISA	Extended Industry Standard Architecture
	12	EMMS	Electronic Mail/Message System
	13	ENIAC	Electronic Numerical Integrator & Calculator
	14	EPABX	Electronic Public Access Branch Exchange
	14	EPROM	Erasable-Programmable Read Only Memory
	15	EPS*	Encapsulated post script files
	16	ESD	Electrostatic Discharge
	17	EU	European union
	18	EULA	End User License Agreement
	19	EDI	Electronic Data Interchange
	20	EGP	Exterior Gateway Protocol
	21	EIS	Executive Information System
	22	EM	Electronic Mailing
	23	ERS	European Remote Sensing Satellite
	24	ESC	Electronics and Computer Software Export Promotion Council
	25	ERNET	Educational and Research Network
	26	EVM	Electronic Voting Machine
F	1	FAQ	Frequently Asked Questions
	2	FAT	File Allocation Table
	3	FAX	Fascimile
	4	FC	Fetch Cycle
	5	FDC	Floppy Disk Controller
	6	FDD	Floppy Disk Drive
	7	FM	Frequency Modulation
	8	FON*	Font file
	9	FOR*	FORTRAN source code file
	10	FORTRAN	Formula Transfer
	11	FTC	Federal Trade Commission
	12	FTP	File Transfer Protocol
G	1	GB	GigaByte
	2	Gb	Gigabit
	3	GC	Graphics card

	4	GIF*	Graphic Interchange Format
	5	GIGO	Garbage in Garbage out
	6	GPRS	General Packet Radio Service
	7	GSM	Global system for mobile communication
	8	GUI	Graphical User Interface
H	1	H*	C Header file
	2	HDD	Hard Disk Drive
	3	HDTV	High definition Television
	4	HGA	Hercules Graphics Adapter
	5	HLL	High Level Language
	6	HTML	Hypertext Markup Language
	7	HTTP	Hypertext Transfer Protocol
	8	HF	High Frequency
	9	HVNET	High Speed VSAT Network
I	1	IBG	Inter-block gap
	2	IBM	International Business Machine
	3	IC	Integrated circuit
	4	IC	Instruction Cycle
	5	ICO*	Icon files
	6	IDE	Integrated Development Environment
	7	IGP	Integrated graphics processor
	8	IGS*	Graphic file
	9	ILEC	Independent local exchange carrier
	10	ILEC	Incumbent local exchange carrier
	11	IMAP	Internet message access protocol
	12	INI*	Windows Configuration file
	13	IP	Internet Protocol
	14	IPO	Initial Public Offering
	15	IrDA	Infrared data
	16	IR	Instruction Register
	17	IRG	Inter-record gap
	18	IRQ	Interrupt request
	19	ISA	Industry standard architecture
	20	ISA	Internet security and acceleration (Microsoft server)

	21	ISDN	Integrated Services Digital Network
	22	ISO	International Organization for Standardization
	23	ISP	Internet Service Provider
	24	ISS	Interrupt Service Subroutine
	25	I & B	Information & Broadcasting
	26	IDD	International Direct Dialing
	27	IIIT	Indian Institute of Information Technology
	28	INFINET	Indian Financial Network
	29	INFLIBNET	Information & Library Network Centre
	30	INTELEX	International Teleprinter Exchange
	31	INTELSAT	International Telecommunication Satellite Consortium
	32	INSAT	Indian National Satellite
	33	INTELSAT	International Telecommunication Satellite Consortium
	34	ISD	International Subscriber Dialing
	35	ITI	Indian Telephone Industries
J	1	JIT	Just in time
	2	JMS	Java Message Service
	3	JPG/JPEG	Joint Picture Expert Group
K	1	K	It represents 2 raise to power 10 i.e. 1024
	2	KB	Kilobyte
	3	KIPS	Knowledge Information Processing System
	4	Kb	Kilobit
L	1	LAN	Local Area Network
	2	LCD	Liquid Crystal Display
	3	LEC	Local Exchange Carrier
	4	LED	Light Emitting Diode
	5	LEO	Lyons Electronic Office
	6	LIB*	Library files
	7	LIPS	Logical Inferences per second
	8	LLC	Logical Link Control
	9	LLL	Low Level Language

	10	LSI	Large Scale Integration
	11	LTO	Linear Tape Open
	12	LASER	Light Amplification by Stimulated Emission of Radiation
M	1	MAC	Media Access Control
	2	MAN	Metropolitan Area Network
	3	MAR	Memory Address Register
	4	MB	Megabyte
	5	MBR	Memory Buffer Register
	6	Mb	Megabit
	7	MCGA	Multicolor Graphics Array
	8	MCP	Microsoft Certified Professional
	9	MCSD	Microsoft Certified Software Developer
	10	MCSE	Microsoft Certified System Engineer
	11	MDA	Monochrome Display Adapter
	12	MFLOPS	Millions of floating point operations per second
	13	MICR	Magnetic Ink Character Reader
	14	MIDI	Musical Instrument Digital Interface
	15	MIME	Multipurpose Internet Mail Extension
	16	MIPS	Millions of Instructions per second
	17	MIS	Management Information System
	18	MITS	Micro Instrumentations and Telemetry
	19	MMU	Memory Management Unit
	20	MMS	Multimedia Messaging Service
	21	MODEM	Modulator Demodulator
	22	MPEG	Moving Picture Expert Group
	23	MRI	Magnetic Resonance Imaging
	24	MUART	Multifunction universal asynchronous receiver-transmitter
N	1	NAS	Network Attached Storage
	2	NDRO	Non-destructive Read-out
	3	NIC	Network Interface Card
	4	NIC	National Informatics Centre
	5	NOS	Network Operating System
	6	NSC	National Semi Conductor

	7	NTFS	New Technology File System
	8	NVRAM	Non-volatile random access memory
	9	NASSCOM	National Association of Software and Service Companies
	10	NFSIT	National Venture Fund for Software and IT Industries
	11	NICO	New Information and Communication Order
	12	NIIT	National Institute of Information Technology
O	1	OCR	Optical Character Reader
	2	OEM	Original Equipment Manufacturer
	3	OFDM	Orthogonal Frequency Division Multiplexing
	4	OLE	Object Linking & Embedding
	5	OLTP	Online Transaction Processing
	6	OMR	Optical Mark Reader
	7	ORDBMS	Object Oriented Relational Database Management System
	8	OS	Operating System
	9	OSI	Open Systems Interconnection
P	1	P3P	Platform for privacy preferences
	2	PAN	Personal Area Network
	3	PC	Personal Computer
	4	PC	Program Counter
	5	PC-AT	Personal Computer with Advance Technology
	6	PCL	Printer Control Language
	7	PC-XT	Personal Computer with Extended Technology
	8	PDA	Personal Digital Assistant
	9	PDAs	
	10	PERL	
	11	PET	Positron Emission Tomography
	12	PGP	Pretty good privacy
	13	PIC	Programmable Interrupt Controllers
	14	PKI	Public key infrastructure

	15	PMML	Predictive model markup language-xml based
	16	POP	Post Office Protocol
	17	POST	Power on Self Test
	18	POTS	Plain Old Telephone Service
	19	PPP	Point to Point Protocol
	20	PROLOG	Programming Logic
	21	PROM	Programmable Read Only Memory
	22	PSDN	Packet Switching Data Network
	23	PUC	Public utility commission
	24	PVAM	Protected Virtual Address Mode
	25	PBS	Public Broadcasting Service
	26	PBX	Private Branch Exchange
	27	PERT	Project Evaluation & Review Technique
	28	PCM	Public Code Modulation
	29	PIM	Personal Information Management
	30	PSLV	Polar Satellite Launch Vehicle
Q	1	QoS	Quality of service
R	1	RADIUS	Remote authentication dial in user service
	2	RAM	Random Access Memory
	3	RDBMS	Relational Database Management System
	4	RF	Radio Frequency
	5	RFC	Request for comments
	6	RFID	Radio frequency identification
	7	RGB	Red Green Blue
	8	RISC	Reduced Instruction Set Computer
	9	ROM	Read only memory
	10	RQBE	Relational Query By Example
	11	RSA	Rivest.Sharnir & Adelman (encryption inventors)
	12	RADAR	Radio Directing and Ranging
	13	RAD	Rapid Application Development/ Research and Development

	14	RAX	Random Access Exchange
	15	RPV	Remote controlled Pilotless Vehicle
S	1	SAN	Storage Area Network
	2	SC	Sound Card
	3	SCL	Semiconductor Complex Ltd.
	4	SIMD	Single-instruction stream, multiple-data stream
	5	SISD	Single-instruction stream, single-data stream
	6	SISD-M	SISD with multiple functional units
	7	SISD-S	SISD with single functional unit
	8	SMS	Short Messaging Service
	9	SMTP	Simplex Mail Transfer Protocol
	10	SNMP	Simple network management protocol
	11	SOAP	Simple Object Access Protocol
	12	SOHO	Small Office Home Office
	13	SONET	Synchronous Optical Network
	14	SP	Stack Pointer
	15	SQL	Structured Query Language
	16	SRAM	Static Random Access Memory
	17	SSAD	S
	18	SSD	Solid state disk
	19	SSL	Secure socket layer
	20	STP	Shielded twisted pair
	21	SLV	Satellite Launch Vehicle
	22	SITE	Satellite Instructional Television Experiment
	23	STARS	Satellite Tracking & Ranging Station
	24	STD	Subscriber Trunk Dialing
T	1	TAC	Terminal Access Controller
	2	TB	Terabyte
	3	TCO	Total cost of ownership
	4	TCP/IP	Transmission control protocol/Internet Protocol
	5	TDM	Time Division Multiplexing
	6	TDMA	Time Division Multiplex access

	7	TFT	Thin Film Transistor
	8	THD	Total Harmonic Distortion
	9	TLD	Top level domain
	10	TMS	Texas Instruments
	11	TPI	Tracks per inches
	12	TIFAC	Technology and Information Forecasting & Assessment Council
U	1	UART	Universal asynchronous receiver/ transmitter
	2	UDP	User Datagram Protocol
	3	ULSI	Ultra Large Scale Integration
	4	UNIVAC	Universal Automatic Computer
	5	UPI	Universal Peripheral Interface
	6	UPS	Uninterrupted Power Supply
	7	URL	Uniform Resource Locator
	8	USART	Universal synchronous-asynchronous receiver-transmitter
	9	USB	Universal serial bus
	10	UTP	Unshielded twisted pair
	11	UUID	Universal unique identifier
	12	UC	Upper Case (capital letters)
	13	UVPROM	Ultra violet Programmable Read only Memory
V	1	VB	Visual Basic
	2	VDSL	Very high data rate digital subscriber line
	3	VDT	Visual Display Terminal
	4	VDU	Visual Display Unit
	5	VFAT	Virtual File Allocation Table
	6	VGA	Visual Graphics Adapter
	7	Visi Calc	Visible Calculator
	8	VLSI	Very large scale integration
	9	VoIP	Voice over Internet Protocol
	10	VPN	Virtual Private Network
	11	VR	Virtual Reality
	12	VT	Vacuum Tubes
	13	VAM	Virtual Area Network

	14	VAN	Value Added Network
	15	VSAT	Very Small Aperture Terminal
W	1	W3C	World Wide Web Consortium
	2	WAN	Wide Area Network
	3	WAP	Wireless Application Protocol
	4	WDD	Winchester Disk Drive
	5	WECA	Wireless Ethernet Compatibility Alliance
	6	WLAN	Wireless Local Area Network
	7	WML	Wireless Markup Language
	8	WORM	Write-Once Read-Many (optical disk memory)
	9	WWW	World Wide Web
	10	WILL	Wireless in Local Loop
	11	WYSIWYG	What You See Is What You Get
X	1	XML	Extensible Markup Language

Update Your NET Knowledge

INTERNET

"The Internet is a network of networks, linking computers to computers sharing the TCP/IP protocols."

The Internet is a global computer network made up of thousands of networks worldwide. The Internet is a self-publishing medium. It is not a library of evaluated publications selected by professionals. Rather, the Internet is a bulletin board containing everything from the definitive to the spurious.

According to ***Tim Berners-Lee***, founder of the WWW Consortium-

"It's a bit like a postcard with a simple address on it. If you put the right address on a packet, and gave it to any computer which is connected as part of the Net, each computer would figure out which cable to send it down next so that it would get to its destination. That's what the Internet does. It delivers packets—anywhere in the world, normally well under a second."

No one knows exactly how many computers are connected to the Internet. It is certain, however, that these number in the millions and are growing.

Private companies own the Internet backbone, through which Internet traffic flows. There are organizations, which develop technical aspects of this network and set standards for creating applications on it, but no governing body is in control.

All computers on the Internet communicate with one another using the Transmission Control Protocol/Internet Protocol abbreviated as TCP/IP. Computers on the Internet use client/server architecture. This means that the remote server machine provides files and services to the user's local client machine. Software can be installed on a client computer to take advantage of the latest access technology.

An Internet user has access to a wide variety of services: electronic mail, file transfer, interest group membership, interactive collaboration, multimedia displays, real-time broadcasting, breaking news, shopping opportunities, and much more.

The Internet consists of a variety of access protocols. Many of these protocols feature programs that allow users to search for and retrieve material made available by the protocol. Today, more than 120 countries and 60 million people use the Internet.

HISTORY OF INTERNET

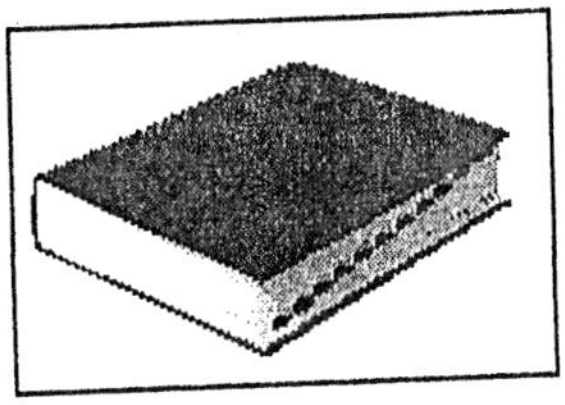

The ARPANET was the precursor to the Internet. ARPA is the acronym used for Advanced Research Projects Agency. The Department of Defense in conjunction with several universities developed it. The goal of ARPANET was to allow university-based researchers working for the Defense Department to share information with their colleagues in other U.S. cities. The main motive behind this project was to develop a secure network that survives and works even after nuclear attack. By 1971, there were about 30 universities participating in ARPANET.

ARPANET was also used for research, education and government organizations.

Computers in ARPANET used certain rules to communicate with each other. These set of rules are termed as Protocols. The protocol used by ARPANET was NCP (National Control Protocol). By the time, NCP was out of use and TCP/IP came in the world of networking. TCP converts the messages into stream of packets at the source, which could be transmitted easily and reassembles all these packets at the destination. IP handles the dispatch of these packets. This way, ARPANET started growing and became a massive network of networks - the Internet. The term "***Internet***" was used for the first time in 1982. By 1984, the network had grown to include 1,000 host computers.

TIMELINE OF INTERNET

1984

- Domain Name System (DNS) is established, with network addresses identified by extensions such as .com, .org, and .edu.
- ***William Gibson*** coins the term "***cyberspace***"

1985

- Quantum Computer Services, which later changes its name to America Online, debuts. It offers email, electronic bulletin boards, news, and other information.

1989

- The World (world.std.com) debuts as the first provider of dial-up Internet access for consumers. Tim Berners-Lee of CERN (European Laboratory for Particle Physics) develops a new technique for distributing information on the Internet. He calls it the World Wide Web.

1990

- The first effort to index the Internet is created by Peter Deutsch at McGill University in Montreal, who devises Archie, an archive of FTP sites.

1991

- Gopher, which provides point-and-click navigation, is created at the University of Minnesota and named after the school mascot. Gopher becomes the most popular interface for several years.
- Another indexing system, WAIS (Wide Area Information Server), is developed by Brewster Kahle of Thinking Machines Corp.

1993

- Marc Andreeson at the National Center developed "Mosaic" for Supercomputing Applications (NCSA). It becomes the dominant navigating system for the World Wide Web.

1994

- The White House launches its website, www.whitehouse.gov.
- Initial commerce sites are established and mass marketing campaigns are launched via email, introducing the term "spamming" to the Internet vocabulary.
- Marc Andreessen and Jim Clark start Netscape Communications. They introduce the Navigator browser.

1995

- CompuServe, America Online, and Prodigy start providing dial-up Internet access.
- Sun Microsystems releases the Internet programming language called Java.

1996

- Approximately 45 million people are using the Internet, with roughly 30 million of those in North America (United States and Canada), 9 million in Europe, and 6 million in Asia/Pacific (Australia, Japan, etc.). 43.2 million (44%) U.S. households own a personal computer, and 14 million of them are online.

1997

- On July 8, 1997, Internet traffic records are broken as the NASA website broadcasts images taken by Pathfinder on Mars. The broadcast generates 46 million hits in one day.

1999

- College student Shawn Fanning invents "Napster", a computer application that allows users to swap music over the Internet.
- "E-commerce" becomes the new buzzword as Internet shopping rapidly spreads.

2000

- This year is known for the development and frequent spreading of viruses. "Love Bug" and "Stages" are two examples of self-replicating viruses that send themselves to people listed in a computer user's email address book. The heavy volume of email messages being sent and received forces many infected companies to temporarily shut down their clogged networks.

2003

- In December, President Bush signs the Controlling the Assault of Non-Solicited Pornography and Marketing Act of 2003 (CAN-SPAM Act), which is intended to help individuals and businesses control the amount of unsolicited email they receive.
- Apple Computer introduces Apple ***iTunes*** Music Store, which allows people to download songs for 99 cents each.

2004

- Internet Worm, called MyDoom or Novarg, spreads through Internet servers. About 1 in 12-email messages was infected.

newtopic REQUIREMENTS TO ÒGET ON THE INTERNETÓ

1. Computer
2. Modem
3. Internet Service Provider
4. Telephone Connection
5. Browser Software

newtopic FUNCTIONS PERFORMED ON THE INTERNET:-

- Communication (E-mail)
- Document or File Transfer (FTP)
- Browsing or Surfing world wide web
- Remote Login (TELNET)
- Reading and posting to topic specific Bulletin Board

- Business Transaction
- Chatting / Instant Messaging
- Videoconferencing
- On-line Reservation (Flight Reservation, Railway Reservation or Hotel Reservation etc)
- On-line Banking
- On-line Employment
- On-line Matrimonial
- On-line Advertisement
- E-commerce (e-business)

- Downloading Software or programs (or files)
- Listening or Downloading Music
- Watching movies
- Playing games

new topic WORLD WIDE WEB (WWW)

*WWW is described as a **"wide-area hypermedia information initiative, which aims to give universal access to a large set of documents"***

The ***World Wide Web*** (abbreviated as the Web or WWW) is a system of Internet servers that supports hypertext to access several Internet protocols on a single interface.

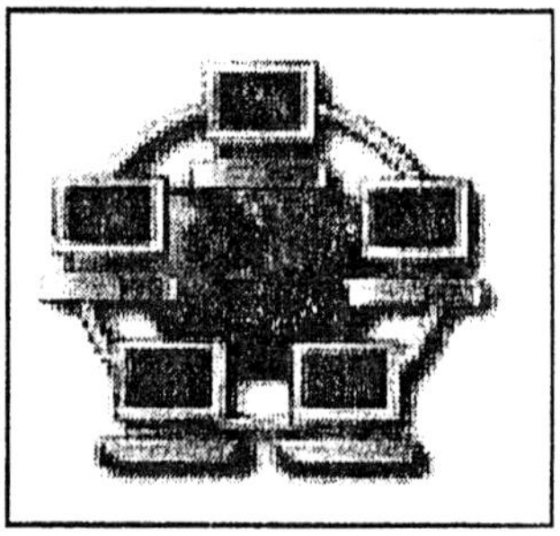

Tim Berners-Lee (a young scientist of CERN-European Laboratory for Particle Physics) in Switzerland developed the World Wide Web in 1989. The initial purpose of the Web was to use networked hypertext to facilitate communication among its members, who were located in several countries. The World Wide Web consists of files, called pages or home pages, containing links to documents and resources throughout the Internet.

The World Wide Web Consortium now manages it. World Wide Web Consortium (W3C) is funded by a large number of corporate members, including AT&T, Adobe Systems, Inc., Microsoft Corporation and Sun Microsystems, Inc. Its purpose is to promote the growth of the Web by developing technical specifications and reference software that will be freely available to everyone. The Consortium is run by MIT with INRIA (The French National Institute for Research in Computer Science) acting as European host, in collaboration with CERN.

The National Center for Supercomputing Applications (NCSA) has developed the earliest web browser "***Mosaic***" and distributed free to the public. It led directly to the phenomenal growth of the World Wide Web.

According to Tim Berners-Lee,

"The Web is an abstract (imaginary) space of information. On the Net, you find computers—on the Web, you find document, sounds, videos, information."

Almost every protocol type available on the Internet is accessible on the Web. **Internet protocols** are sets of rules that allow for intermachine communication on the Internet. The following is a sample of major protocols accessible on the Web:

- **E-mail** (Simple Mail Transport Protocol or SMTP): Distributes electronic messages and files to one or more electronic mailboxes
- **Telnet** (Telnet Protocol): Facilitates login to a computer host to execute commands
- **FTP** (File Transfer Protocol): Transfers text or binary files between an FTP server and client

- **Usenet** (Network News Transfer Protocol or NNTP): Distributes Usenet news articles derived from topical discussions on newsgroups
- **HTTP** (HyperText Transfer Protocol): Transmits hypertext over networks. This is the protocol of the Web.

Many other protocols are available on the Web. **For example**, the Voice over Internet Protocol (**VoIP**) allows users to place a telephone call over the Web.

When you log onto the Internet using a web browser (**e.g.,** Internet Explorer, Firefox, Netscape, Opera, Safari), you are viewing documents on the World Wide Web. The operation of the Web relies primarily on ***hypertext***. Hypertext is text, which contains links to other texts. Ted Nelson coined the term "***hypertext***" around 1965.

A single hypertext document can contain links to many documents. In the context of the Web, words or graphics may serve as links to other documents, images, video, and sound. It is HTML and other programming languages (like ASP, PERL etc) embedded within HTML that makes possible hypertext. Thus, web is a collection of virtual connections among a vast number of documents, graphics, videos, and sounds.

This "***clickability***" using Hypertext links is the feature, which is unique and revolutionary about the Web.

new topic DIFFERENCE BETWEEN INTERNET & WWW

The World Wide Web, or the Web, is often confused with the Internet. In fact, it is just one part of the Internet, along with email, videoconferencing, and streaming audio channels. In other words, ***World Wide Web is a big slice of Internet Pie.***

On the Net, you find computers—on the Web, you find documents, sounds, videos, information. On the Net, the connections are cables between computers; on the Web, connections are hypertext links. The Web exists because of programs, which communicate between computers on the Net. The Web could not be without the Net. The Web made the net useful because people are really interested in information (not to mention knowledge and wisdom!) and don't really want to have know about computers and cables."

new topic HYPERLINK

World Wide Web is a collection of millions of pages of information. The pages are linked together using ***Hyperlinks***. Remember these three rules about a hyperlink:

- A hyperlink is usually colored in **blue** and underlined (although they can be lots of different colors sometimes!)
- If you move your mouse over a <u>hyperlink</u>, it will change to the shape of a hand, like this...

- If you click on a hyperlink, you will go to a different page.

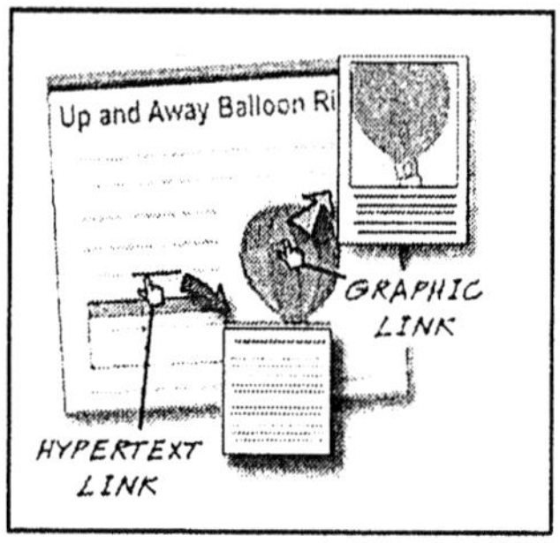

Hyperlink can be some text or graphic image. If one picture is serving as the hyperlink to different pages (i.e. on clicking different portion of image, you will move to different pages), then such a picture is called ***Image Map***.

MODEM

It is the acronym used for Modulator-Demodulator.

"MODEM is a device that allows remote computers to communicate, to transmit and receive data using telephone line."

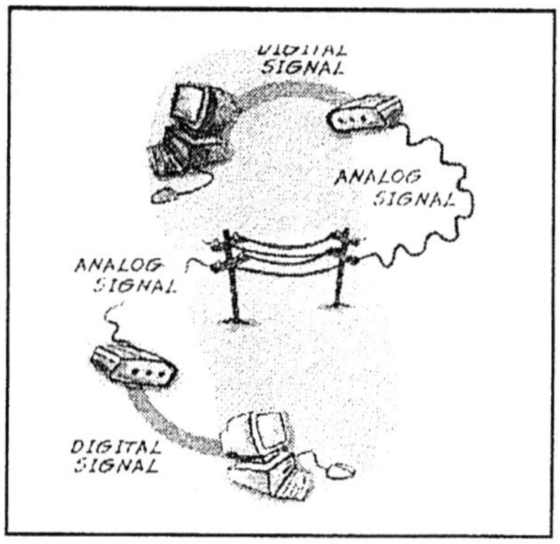

Telephone lines were designed to transmit the human voice, not electronic data from computers. Therefore, modems were invented to convert digital computer signals into a form (analog) that allows them to travel over phone lines and *analog signals into a form (digital)* accepted by remote computer.

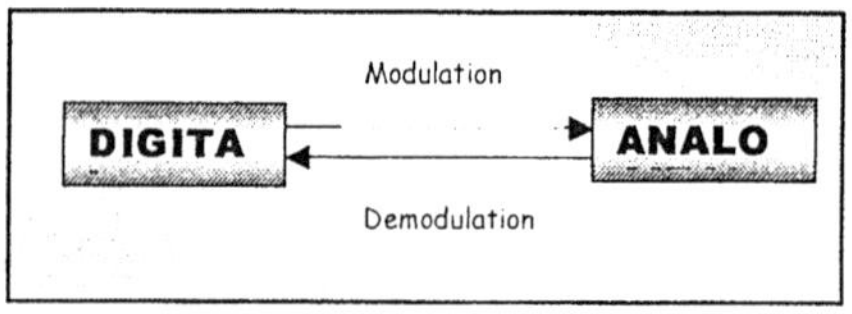

Both the communicating computers must have separate MODEMs in order to allow exchange of information between each other. MODEMs can be Internal or External.

Modems come in different speeds and are measured in bps or bits per second. A 28.8 Kbps modem transmits data at speeds up to 28,800 bits per second. A 56 Kbps modem is twice as fast, sending and receiving data at a rate of up to 56,000 bits per second. Almost all modems today are 56 Kbps.

HOW WEB WORKS

1. To access a website, you first enter its web address (or URL) in Address box of browser.
2. URL contains- ***http://*** indicates that the browser & web server will communicate using hypertext transfer protocol; ***www*** indicates a resource on world wide web; ***domain*** identifies which web server will host the site.
3. Your web browser sends request to appropriate web server on Internet.
4. Web server, then locates the files and download to your computer.
5. Finally, web browser assembles the page on your screen.

new topic INTERNET SERVICE PROVIDER (ISP):-

A company that provides access to the Internet is known as ISP. The service provider charges a certain amount/fee for giving you a software, username, password and access phone number. ISP are also called IAP (Internet Access Provider). ISPAI refers to ***Internet Service Providers Association of India.***

EXAMPLES OF ISP:

- MindSpring
- CompuServe
- AOL (America Online)
- AT&T WorldNet
- Hotmail (An e-mail only service)
- Juno (An e-mail service)
- MSN (The Microsoft Network)
- Prodigy Internet
- Yahoo Mail (An e-mail only service)

LIST OF WEB ADDRESSES OF INDIAN ISPs

1	**Asianet Satellite Commns. Ltd.**		www.asianet.co.in
2	**Bharti Infotel Ltd.**		www.airtelenterprise.com
3	**Broadband Pacenet (India) Pvt Ltd**		www.pacenet-india.com
4	**C. J. Online Pvt Ltd**		www.cjnet4u.com
5	**Cisco-Systems (India) Pvt. Ltd.**		www.cisco.com/in
6	**del DSL Internet Pvt. Ltd.**		www.deldsl.com

7	**Dishnet Wireless Ltd**		www.dwl.co.in
8	**Estel Communication Pvt. Ltd.**		www.estelcom.com
9	**Estel Communications PVT LTD**		www.estelcom.com
10	**Exatt Technologies Pvt. Ltd.**		www.exatt.com
11	**GTL Ltd.**		www.gtllimited.com
12	**Guj. Info Petro Ltd.**		www.gipl.com
13	**Hathway C & D Pvt. Ltd.**		www.hathway.net
14	**HCL Infinet Ltd**		www.hclinfinet.com
15	**HFCL Infonet Ltd**		www.hfclconnect.com
16	**Hughes Escorts Commn. Ltd**		www.hughes-escorts.com
17	**I2i Enterprises Ltd.**		www.i2ienterprise.net
18	**In2Cable (India) Ltd.**		www.in2cable.com
19	**Indianspider.com**		www.pbcnet.com

No.	Company	Website
20	NetMagic Solutions Pvt. Ltd.	www.netmagicsolutions.com
21	Ortel Communications Ltd	www.ortelcom.com
22	Pacific Internet (India) Pvt. Ltd.	www.pacific.net.in
23	Primus Telecommunication India Ltd	www.primus-direct.com
24	Railtel Corporation of India Ltd.	www.railtelindia.com
25	Rajesh Multi Channel Pvt Ltd	www.myrajeshnet.com
26	Reach Network India Pvt. Ltd.	www.reach.com
27	Reliance Commn. Infastructure Ltd	www.relianceinfo.com
28	Rolta India Ltd	www.rolta.com
29	Sify Ltd	www.sifycorp.com
30	Software Tech. Parks of India	www.stpi.in
31	Spectra Net Ltd.	www.spectranet.com
32	SpectraNet	
33	Tata Internet Services Ltd.	www.tatanova.com

34	**Telegolbe America Inc.**		www.teleglobe.com
35	**Trak Online Net India Pvt Ltd**		www.net4india.in
36	**Tulip IT Services Ltd**		www.tulipit.com
37	**Vasnet Commns. Pvt Ltd**		www.vasnet.co.in
38	**Vebtel Obconic Internet Protocol Pvt. Ltd.**		www.vebtel.com
39	**World Phone**		www.worldphone.in
40	**Worldcom Communications India Pvt Ltd**		www.mci.com

TECHNOLOGY OR CONNECTION TYPES USED BY ISP TO PROVIDE INTERNET FACILITY: -

Dialup Connection

- Dial-up connections are the most common type of internet connection available from ISPs,
- These are also the slowest, inexpensive and widely available Internet connections.
- A dial-up connection allows you to connect to the Internet via a local server using a standard 56k modem.
- Your dialer Software calls an access number. Then, your modem converts the signals from your computer to signals that travel over telephone lines to an ISP. Finally, your ISP provider serves a connection to the Internet.
- The telephone line used for dialup connection cannot be simultaneously used for dialing or receiving telephone calls. If connected to Internet, the telephone would give a busy signal.
- The cost is usually the same, as you would pay for a local phone call so as long as they are used sensibly they can be a very cost effective Internet connection.

ISDN

- ISDN refers to Integrated Services Digital Network.
- It is an older service, but still a viable technology offered by phone companies in some parts of the U.S.

- ISDN requires a so-called ISDN adapter instead of a modem, and a phone line with a special connection that allows it to send and receive digital signals.
- An ISDN line has a data transfer rate of between 57 Kbps and 128 Kbps.
- ISDN provides faster data transfer rates as compared to a dial-up connection.

DSL or Leased Line

- DSL refers to "***Digital Subscriber Line***"
- It is a high-speed or broadband technology. The connections work by splitting your phone line into two separate channels—one for "*voice*" and another for "*data*".
- A DSL line remains connected to the Internet, so you don't need to dial-up when you want to go online.
- DSL provides a dedicated connection — a connection that is not shared with other subscribers.
- Typically with DSL, data is downloaded to your computer at rates up to 1.544 Mbps and you can send data at 128 Kbps. ***Example:*** Average Web Page (50 Kilobytes; including images) is downloaded at a speed of 256kbps and can be viewed in roughly 1.56 seconds). On the other hand if the download speed is assumed to be 512kbps, then the 50kb page can be viewed in 0.78 seconds.
- You can use your existing phone line to establish DSL service because it can carry both voice and data.
- DSL service requires a digital modem and a network card in your computer.
- ADSL connections are not available to everyone; you should always ensure that you have ADSL (Asymmetric Digital Subscriber Line) coverage in your area.

Cable Modem

- This technology allows Cable TV providers to deliver high-speed services over the same cable lines used to carry TV signals. Cable connections are shared with other users, so actual speed is affected by what others around you are doing.
- When a cable company offers Internet access over the cable, Internet information can use the same cables because the cable modem system puts *downstream data* — data sent from the Internet to an individual computer — into a 6-MHz channel. On the cable, the data looks just like a TV channel.
- Upstream data — information sent from an individual back to the Internet — requires even less of the cable's bandwidth, just 2 MHz, since the assumption is that most people download far more information than they upload.
- Putting both upstream and downstream data on the cable television system requires two types of equipment: ***a cable modem*** on the customer end and a ***cable modem termination system (CMTS)*** at the cable provider's end.

WIRELESS (WI-FI) INTERNET

- It refers to ***Wireless Fidelity***.
- It is a technology of wireless local area networks, licensed by ***Wi-Fi Alliance*** (an organization of ***Austin*** that certifies 802.11 wireless Ethernet devices for interoperability)
- It is based on ***IEEE 802.11*** technology (IEEE refers to Institute of Electrical & Electronics Engineering Standards Association). IEEE standards are designed for Wireless LANs to extend 802.3 (wired Ethernet)
- Wireless LAN is the linking of two or more computers without using wires. It uses radio waves to enable communication. All the computers in WLAN are called ***stations.*** All stations are equipped with wireless network interface cards (**WNICs**)
- **Examples of Wi-Fi devices**
    - A ***wireless access point*** (WAP) is a stand-alone device that connects a group of wireless stations to an adjacent wired local area network (LAN). An access point can relay wireless data to all other compatible wireless devices as well as to hub or switch. (as WAP plug into an Ethernet hub or switch). One IEEE 802.11 WAP can typically communicate with 30 client systems located within a radius of 100m. Every WAP has a unique IP address. ***Hotspots*** are locations where you can connect your computers (**e.g.** Laptop or PDA) to the Internet via wireless access points.
    - A ***wireless router*** integrates a wireless access point with an Ethernet switch and an Ethernet router.
    - A ***wireless Ethernet bridge*** connects a wired network to a wireless network.
    - **Others:** Computer, Telephone, PDA (Personal Digital Assistants : handheld computers)
- ***Repeaters*** and ***Reflectors*** are used to extend the range of WAP (used for amplification of radio signals)

BROWSERS:-

Browser is a software program that enables users to surf the World Wide Web and view web pages. They "translate" HTML-encoded files into the text, images, sounds, and other features you see.

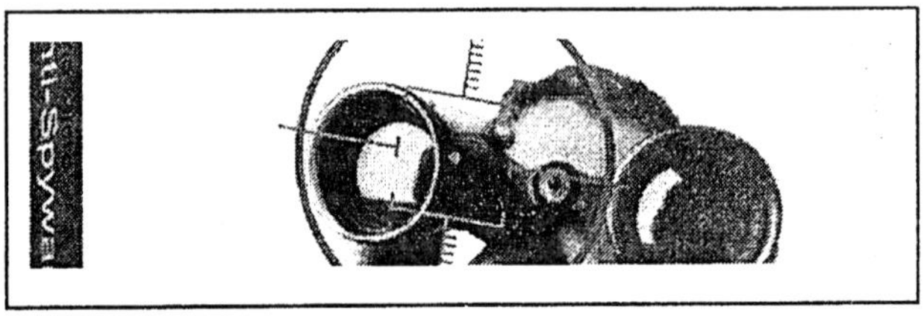

In other words, ***Browser*** is software developed specifically to retrieve information from Internet and present them as web pages to the viewer.

The first browser, called NCSA ***Mosaic***, was developed at the *National Center for Supercomputing Applications* in the early 1990s. ***Firefox*** and ***Internet Explorer*** are currently the leading "graphical browsers" in the world (meaning they facilitate the viewing of graphics such as images and video and more).

Browsers rely on "***plug-ins***" to handle the retrieval of files you find on the Web. Plug-ins are sub-programs stored within a browser or elsewhere in your computer especially to support special types of files you may click on. If you click on a link, and your computer does not currently have the plug-in needed for the file you clicked on, you are usually prompted with an opportunity to get or install the plug-in.

Example of Oldest Web Browser

Mosaic *(Developed at NCSA)*

Examples of Most Popular Browsers

Microsoft Internet Explorer

Netscape Navigator *(owned by AOL)*

Examples of Other Browsers

Firefox

Opera

Safari *(Apple)*

NeoPlanet

Lynx *(Text based Browser)*

SeaMonkey

A browser may be launched by double clicking the browser icon (available one) on the desktop or by simply clicking the browser icon on task bar (at the bottom of the desktop). On launching the browser, a predefined web page appears, which is called **Home Page** or **Start Page**. For viewing a desired web page, type the **URL** or web address of the website in the address bar of your browser and press enter or click ***Go***.

1. Types of Browsers

- **Text Browser:** Text browser provides access to the Web in text-only mode. Navigation is accomplished by highlighting emphasized words in the screen with the arrow up and down keys, and then pressing the forward arrow (or Enter) key to follow the link. ***Example :*** Lynx
- **Graphical Browser:** Graphical browser provides access to text, images, audio and video and all types of files. Pointing and clicking with a mouse on highlighted words and graphics accomplish navigation. These browsers are available for Windows, Apple and Linux. ***Example:*** Internet Explorer, Firefox, Netscape, Mozilla and Opera.

2. Example of Browser Window (Internet Explorer):

3. Important tools of a Browser window toolbar-

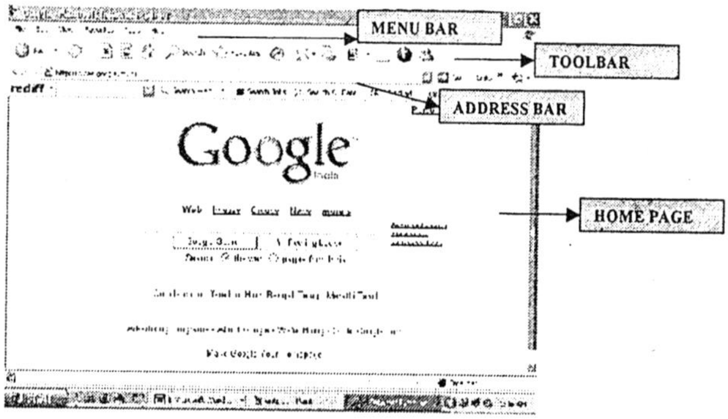

- **Back:** Back button returns you the previous page you have visited.

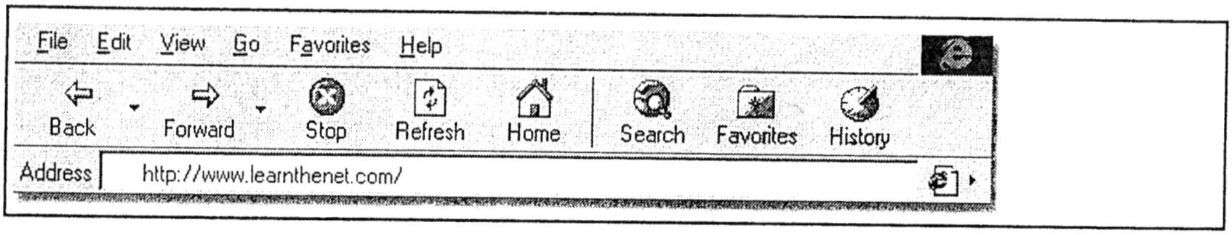

- **Forward:** Forward button is used to return to the page you just came from.
- **Stop:** Stop button stops the browser from loading the current page.
- **Refresh:** Reload or Refresh is used to load the web page again. By reloading the page, the data on the current web page is updated from the web server.
- **Home:** It is used to return to a previously defined start page or home page.
- **Search:** It lets you connect to directories and search tools on the websites.

- **Favorites:** It lets you add the webaddress of desired web pages that you want to revisit.
- **History:** It lets you view the web addresses you have already visited during a specific period of time.

WEBSITES AND WEBPAGES

The World Wide Web consists of files, called websites.

In other words, a website is a collection of various types of files like Text files, graphic files, audio files and video files etc.

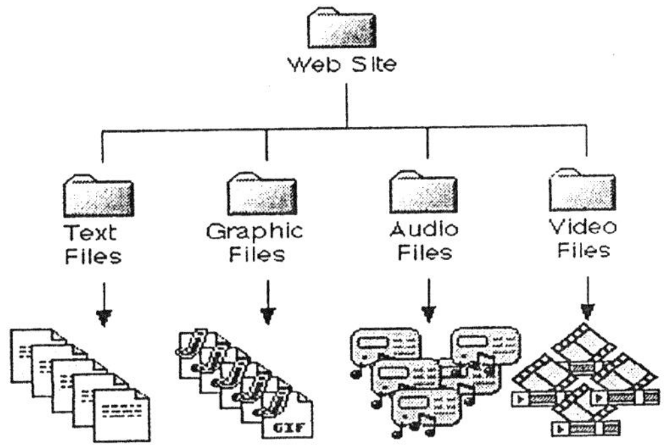

A website has one or more related web pages, depending on how it's designed. Web pages on a site are linked together through a system of hyperlinks, enabling you to jump between them by clicking on a link. On the Web, you navigate through pages of information according to your interests.

A web page is an electronic document written in a computer language called HTML, short for Hypertext Markup Language. Each web page has a unique address, called a URL or Uniform Resource Locator that identifies where it's located on the network.

URL

URL stands for Uniform Resource Locator. Each web site has an address, or Uniform Resource Locator (URL). The URL contains a set of instructions that are read by the browser.

Every file on the Internet, no matter what its access protocol, has a unique URL. Web browsers use the URL to retrieve the file from the host computer and the specific directory in which it resides. This file is downloaded to the user's client computer and displayed on the monitor connected to the machine.

URLs are translated into numeric addresses using the **Domain Name System (DNS)**. The DNS is a worldwide system of servers that stores location pointers to Web sites. The numeric address, called the IP (Internet Protocol) address, is actually the "real" URL. Since numeric strings are difficult for humans to use, end users employ alphanumeric addresses. Once the translation is made by the DNS, the browser can contact the Web server and ask for a specific file located on its site.

As the technology of the Web evolves, URLs have become more complex. This is especially the case when content is retrieved from databases and served onto Web pages

ANATOMY OR FORMAT OF A URL

The beginning of the URL contains the protocol. This is usually "http" (Hypertext Transfer Protocol) or "ftp" (File Transfer Protocol). The second section of the URL reveals the domain. Directories follow the domain. Lastly is the name of the document. *(If no document is named the browser will automatically open any document in the directory named "default" or "index.")*

- ***Some Important URLs (Internet Resources)***

Animals

- *American Zoo and Aquarium Association:* www.aza.org
- *Animals A-Z:* www.oaklandzoo.org/atoz/atoz.html
- *Kid's Planet:* www.kidsplanet.org/
- *National Wildlife Federation:* www.nwf.org/kids/

Art

- The @rt Room: www.arts.ufl.edu/art/rt_room/index.html
- Metropolitan Museum of Art, New York: www.metmuseum.org/htmlfile/education/kid.html
- Worldwide Art Gallery: www.theartgallery.com.au/kidsart.html
- National Gallery of Art for Kids: www.nga.gov/kids
- Smithsonian Institution, Washington, D.C.: www.mnh.si.edu/

Geography

- *Atlapedia Online:* www.atlapedia.com/
- *National Geographic for Kids:* www.nationalgeographic.com/ngforkids/
- *CIA World Factbook:* www.cia.gov/cia/publications/factbook/index.html
- *50 States.com:* www.50states.com

Government and Politics

- *White House:* http://www.whitehouse.gov/kids/
- *Congress for Kids:* www.congressforkids.net
- *State and Local Governments:* www.cia.gov/cia/publications/factbook/index.html
- *50 States.com:* lcweb.loc.gov/global/state/stategov.html

News

- *Yahooligans! News:* www.yahooligans.com/content/news/
- *The Internet Public Library:* www.ipl.org/div/news/
- *New York Times:* www.nytimes.com
- *TIME for Kids:* www.timeforkids.com/TFK

Reference

- Fact Monster: www.factmonster.com
- Internet Public Library: www.ipl.org
- Kids Zone: www.lycoszone.lycos.com/
- *Refdesk:* www.refdesk.com

Science and Math

- *Ask Dr. Math:* mathforum.org/dr.math
- *Astronomy for Kids:* www.ipl.org
- *BAM! Body and Mind:* www.bam.gov/
- *Bill Nye the Science Guy:* www.billnye.com
- *Cool Science for Curious Kids:* www.hhmi.org/coolscience/
- *FunBrain:* www.funbrain.com
- *How Things Work:* rabi.phys.virginia.edu/HTW//
- *KidsHealth:* www.kidshealth.org/index2.html
- *NASA Kids:* kids.msfc.nasa.gov/
- *National Science Foundation (NSF):* www.nsf.gov
- *Space Kids:* www.spacekids.com

Sports

- *Major League Baseball:* www.mlb.com
- *Major League Soccer:* www.mlsnet.com
- *National Basketball Association:* www.nba.com
- *National Football League:* www.nfl.com
- *National Hockey League:* www.nhl.com
- *Sports Illustrated Kids:* www.sikids.com
- *Women's National Basketball Association:* www.wnba.com

Internet Protocol Address or IP Address

Every machine that is on the Internet has a unique IP address. If a machine does not have an IP number, it is not really on the Internet.

A unique number consisting of 4 parts separated by dots, **e.g.** 165.113.245.2

DOMAIN

The domain is the name of a network or computer that is linked to the Internet.

You can find the domain in an email address after an @ sign. ***For example:*** **aasthasoni@rediffmail.com**. Here, rediffmail.com is the domain name. The ending of a domain tells you what type it is:

These top-level domains are currently in use:

.aero	For the air-transport industry
.biz	Reserved for businesses
.com	For businesses, commercial enterprises, or online services like America Online. Most companies use this extension.
.coop	Reserved for cooperatives
.edu	For educational institutions and universities
.gov	Reserved for United States government agencies
.info	For all uses
.int	For organizations established by international treaties
.mil	For the United States military
.museum	For use by museums
.name	For use by individuals
.net	For networks; usually reserved for organizations such as Internet service providers
.org	For non-commercial organizations
.pro	For use by professionals, such as attorneys and physicians

Many countries have an official extension or country code that appears at the end of a URL (website address) or email address. The extension identifies where the host website or network is located. For example, the web address for the Nobel Museum is http://www.nobel.in. The extension ".in" indicates that the information on the Nobel site originates in India.

Examples of countries extensions-

.fr = France

.in = India

.it = Italy

.jp = Japan

.pe = Peru

.zr = Zaire

newtopic WEB PORTALS

Web portals are simply referred to as ***Portals.*** A Portal is basically a Web site on the World Wide Web that offers a broad array (or range) of resources and services, such as e-mail, forums, search engines, and on-line shopping malls etc.

The web portals can be categorized as - Voice portals, Regional portal, Govt web portal, Corporate web portal, Community portal and so on.

Examples of Web Portals

- Webplace.it (ITALY)
- Rediff (INDIA)
- Sina.com (CHINA)
- FirstGov.gov (U.S)
- Businesslink.gov.uk (UK)

newtopic BOOKMARKS AND FAVOURITES

The terms "Bookmarks" and "favorites" are analogous (same). These are web addresses of the desired web pages; which the users have asked the web browser to remember for convenient access in the future. Microsoft Internet Explorer uses the term "***favorite.***" Most other products, including the very first web browsers and the modern ***Firefox*** browser, use the term "***bookmark***." In Microsoft Internet Explorer, you can add a favorite by visiting the page you want the browser to remember, pulling down the "Favorites" menu and selecting "Add to Favorites." In Firefox, you can do the same thing by pulling down the "Bookmarks" menu and selecting "Bookmark This Page."

newtopic WEB SERVER

Web server refers to an actual, physical computer that is running web server software.

In other words, the term "web server" refers to the software that runs on those computers, which accepts HTTP connections from web browsers and delivers web pages and other files to them, as well as process form submissions.

EXAMPLES

- APACHE
- Microsoft Internet Information Server (IIS)

PROXY SERVER

Proxy servers are specialized web servers that allow web browsers to receive web pages from web servers without communicating with them directly. When there are many users sharing a single proxy server, the proxy server can also speed up web browsing by caching popular web pages. Most of the major Internet Service Providers (ISPs) now run "***transparent***" proxy servers without your browser being directly aware of it. This is done by intercepting Internet packets that are recognized to be part of the HTTP protocol and silently redirecting them to the proxy server rather than sending them directly to the intended web server.

CACHING

Caching refers to the strategy of keeping a copy of a page or image you have already seen; web browsers typically cache files that they display for you, and simply ask the server if the page has actually changed rather than always downloading the entire thing. This speeds up your next visit to the page.

In browsers, "cache" is used to identify a space where web pages you have visited are stored in your computer. A copy of documents you retrieve is stored in cache. When you use GO, BACK, or any other means to revisit a document, the browser first checks to see if it is in cache and will retrieve it from there because it is much faster than retrieving it from the server.

COOKIES

A "cookie" is a small message from a WEB SERVER computer, sent to and stored by your browser on your computer.

When you visit a web site, then browser stores a small amount of information on your computer. When your computer consults the originating server computer, the cookie is sent back to the server, allowing it to respond to you according to the cookie's contents. The main use for cookies is to provide customized Web pages according to a profile of your interests.

Cookies play a vital role in session management and long-term user identification. Some web sites require users to log in to access certain features. The web site behaves differently depending on who is logged in. Everything that happens between logging in to the web site and logging out is called a "session."

E-MAIL (Electronic Mail)

It is the acronym used for electronic mail. It is the paperless method of sending messages, notes or letters from one person to another or even many people at the same time.

E-mail is a service provided by internet that allows computer users locally and worldwide to exchange messages. Each user of e-mail has a mailbox address to which messages are sent. An e-mail address directs a message to the recipient. Messages sent through e-mail can arrive within a matter of seconds.

E-Mail is very fast and too economic method of communication as compared to the normal mail.

You can also attach files to e-mail messages to send picture, sound, documents, video clippings and other types of file with your email. These files are referred to as ***MIME*** attachments. ***MIME*** stands for Multimedia Internet Mail Extension, and was developed to help e-mail software handle a variety of file types.

1. Important Historical Events Related to E-Mail

- Electronic mail was introduced by ***Ray Tomlinson***, (a computer scientist) in **1972.** He uses the symbol "@" to distinguish between the sender's name and network name in the email address.
- In **1976**, Presidential candidate ***Jimmy Carter*** and ***Walter Mondale*** use email to plan campaign events. Queen Elizabeth sends her first email.

2. Setting up an email account

There are many ways to set up an email account but the basics of emailing remain the same. Three important means of creating an email account are given as follows-

- Setting up an account through your Internet Provider. In other words, who ever set up your connection to the Internet provides email accounts as part of your Internet access charges.
- Some email programs such as Outlook Express or Eudora can be used for creating your mail account provided with you have internet connection.
- Several Web "portal" sites like-

  www.yahoo.com, **www.rediffmail.com**, **www.hotmail.com** provides free email service.

3. E-mail Message

An e-mail message consists of following two parts-

- ***Header information:*** It constitutes recipient's address (To), the subject, sender's e-mail address and so on.
- ***Body:*** It refers to the actual content of the message.

  Usually, email is accessed through a web browser (online). However, messages can be composed off-line (when not connected to Internet) also.

4. E-mail Address

The Internet Service Provider assigns an e-mail address to you. Usually you can choose your user name. The first part -of the address (before the @) is a user name. The second part, or domain name, defines the Internet provider where the mail is sent. The two parts are separated by an @ sign. The domain name is followed by an extension that indicates the type of organization to which the network belongs.

Here is an example of an address: ***company@yahoo.com***

5. How e-mail works

1. Compose (or type) the email, then send it.
2. The message is sent to your ISP's mail server.
3. The mail server examines the address, deciding how to route the message.
4. The message then travels over the Internet, arriving at the mail server of the recipient's Internet Service provider, where it is held in an electronic mail box.
5. To read the message, log on to the mail server and retrieve new messages waiting on the server.

6. E-mail Discussion Group

The Internet is home to a large community of individuals who carry out active discussions organized around topic-oriented forums distributed by e-mail. These are administered by various types of software programs.

Discussion groups cover a great variety of topics. When you subscribe to a group, messages from other subscribers are automatically sent to your electronic mailbox. You subscribe by sending an e-mail message to the address of the group. You must have an e-mail account to participate in a discussion group.

You can ask questions from the experts and read the answers to questions that others ask. Belonging to these groups is somewhat like receiving a daily newspaper on topics that interest you.

Software programs manage e-mail discussion groups. There are three programs, which are in common use- Listserv, Majordomo, and Listproc.

A good Web-based directory to assist in locating e-mail discussion groups is Tile.net, located at http://tile.net/.

7. Unrequested or Spam e-mail

The unwanted or unrequited mail present in Inbox is called spam e-mail. It has become a major problem on the Internet. Some ISP Providers provide software that will filter out the unrequited mails.

8. Popular e-mail Softwares

Microsoft Outlook Express

Eudora

Mozilla Thunderbird

Becky! Internet Mail

9. Popular e-mail Websites

- Excite Mail
- HotMail
- GMail
- Lycos Mail
- Mall Clty
- Yahoo! Mail
- Netaddress

10. Websites for Locating e-mail addresses

- 411 Locate
- FreshAddress.com
- Yahoo! PeopleSearch
- Internet Add Finder
- Friends Reunited
- Email_Lookup.com
- Comrades and Colleagues.com

11. Smileys

Smileys are also called **emoticons.** These emoticons are used to convey more than just words. Here are some common (keyboard smileys) smileys used in Internet e-mails and chat rooms.

Symbol	Meaning
:-)	*smiling*
;-)	*winking*
:-(	*frowning*
:'-(	*crying*
:-p	*sticking your tongue out*
:-*	*oops!*
:-[	*pouting*
:-Y	*a quiet aside*
:-,	*smirking*
:-#	*my lips are sealed*
:-D	*laughing*
:-O	*yelling*
:-I	*hmmm; perplexed*
:-/	*undecided*
C=:-)	*I am a chef*
***<:-)**	*I am Santa Claus*
[:-)	*I am wearing a Walkman*
:-))	*I have a double chin*

12. E-mailese

In email and online chat rooms, people often try to type as fast as they can. Using acronyms or abbreviations helps them keep up their speed. Such abbreviations are sometimes known as "***emailese***" or "***chatroomsy.***"

- **ACE:** am confused, explain

- **BIF:** before I forget
- **BRB:** be right back
- **DTS:** don't think so
- **FWIW:** for what it's worth
- **FYEO:** for your eyes only
- **GMTA:** great minds think alike
- **GTG:** got to go
- **HAW:** homework a-waiting
- **ICBIGBA:** I can't believe I got booted again
- **ICCL:** I couldn't care less
- **IMHO:** in my humble opinion
- **KWIM:** know what I mean?
- **LOL:** laughing out loud
- **MMBS:** mail me back soon
- **MMD:** made my day
- **PIR:** parent in room
- **PXT:** please explain that
- **TTFN:** ta ta for now
- **URATPM:** you are a total Pokémaniac

newtopic Newsgroups

"A newsgroup or forum is like a community bulletin board. You can post a message, reply to a message or just read messages"

Newsgroups provide a mechanism whereby mail messages are systematically made available to large groups of people. In other words, ***Newsgroups*** are just email, but distributed to a broad audience.

In this case the mail message is said to be "***posted***" to the newsgroup. You can write a message and post it to a newsgroup. Then news server posts it for everyone to read.

You can also reply to other's messages (& other members of the newsgroup can also respond to your messages). The replied messages are also posted to the newsgroup. Group of related messages are known as ***"threads".***

Therefore, subscribers can participate in discussions that may go on for very long periods and range over many topics related to the subject matter of the newsgroup.

Many newsgroups have a publicly accessible ***FAQ***. A FAQ is a collection of frequently asked questions that have been posted many times to a newsgroup.

Newsgroups and their Frequently Asked Questions (FAQs) can be one of the richest sources of information on the Web.

Examples of Newsgroups

- Austin
- Bionet
- Cern
- Comp
- Demon
- Info
- talk

CHATTING

Chat is a way to "talk" in real time (event happening with the same speed as it happens in real life) with people all around the world. During a chat, you're not really talking to anyone, just typing and reading messages. Thus, using online chat, you can meet new people in an anonymous environment. Once you enter a chat room, you can choose to only read the messages, known as lurking, or you can join in and post your own. Typically chat rooms are based around certain themes, such as Teen Chat, Educational Chat, or Religious Chat.

1. Chat Room

A chat room, meantime, is a virtual room where a chat session takes place. Technically, a chat room is really a channel, but the term "room" is used to promote the chat metaphor. In other words, a chat room is a web page that runs special software that lets you type messages to one or more people.

2. Lurker

A lurker is a person that hangs out in chat rooms, reading messages, but rarely writing any.

3. Post

Post means to send a note you wrote to a chat room or other group of people on the Internet.

4. Safety Tips of Chat Rooms

1. Don't use your real name.
2. Do not give out personal information such as your last name, home address, parent's work address, or telephone number.

3. Never share a password for an Internet game or chat room.
4. Never agree to meet with someone you met in a chat room.
5. Notify the teacher and/or parent if you receive an obscene message.
6. Because you can't see or hear the person you are chatting with, they may be fooling you as to whom they really are.
7. If someone is being rude to you, ignore them or just log-off and find something else to do.
8. Learn how to use emoticons to express your feelings. (*Discussed above*)

5. Popular Chat Web Sites

Yahoo! Chat

MSN Chat

Spinchat.com

UK Chatterbox

INSTANT MESSAGING (IM)

Instant messaging (IM) is a form of real-time communication (via internet) between two or more people based on typed text. Instant messaging allows you to chat, send messages and files and various other features but only with people you choose.

Thus, IM is a type of communications service that enables one to create a private chat room with another individual. Typically, the IM system alerts you whenever somebody on your buddy or contact list is online. You can then initiate a chat session with that particular individual.

While IM is used by millions of Internet users to contact family and friends, it's also growing in popularity in the business world. Employees of a company can have instant access to managers and co-workers in different offices and can eliminate the need to place phone calls when information is required immediately. Overall, IM can save time for employees and help decrease the amount of money a business spends on communications.

Instant messaging also exists, to a certain extent, in the wireless world. Short-messaging services (SMS) are a system that sends short text messages to mobile phones. The process isn't quite as "instant" because SMS messages are stored on servers and then sent to recipients

There's a big difference between chat rooms and IM, though: A chat room environment, typically handles two or more people involved in one or many discussions. Instant messaging almost always involves one conversation between two people.

1. Popular Instant Messaging Services

Yahoo! Messenger

AOL Internet Messenger (AIM)

GoogleTalk

ICQ

RediffBol

Windows Live Messenger

2. Companies Involved in Providing IM Services

- Microsoft
- IKimbo
- Ecrio (Rich Instant Messaging in wireless environment)
- Presence Works (lets business keep track of its customers)

DIFFERENCE BETWEEN EMAIL, CHATTING AND INSTANT MESSAGING (IM)

E-mail is a way of sending individual messages to people using an e-mail server to relay the message. Because the server holds the messages for a person until he or she retrieves them, e-mail can be sent whether or not a person is online.

Online Chat is a way of talking online in real-time with many people at once. Online chat rooms allow multiple users to join in a conversation and see what all the other people are typing.

Instant Messaging, or "***IMing***" is a way of communicating online with a selected group of people, usually individually. To instant message someone, you need to know his or her screen name. You can save your friends' screen names in a list called a "***Buddy List***." In the instant messaging world, your screen name is likely to be more permanent than with online chat. While online, you can open IM windows with many of your friends at once and type messages back and forth.

PROTOCOL

"***Protocol***" refers to a set of rules used for communicating. Two programs or computers that follow the same rules are able to exchange information, even if they don't run the same operating system and are not made by the same company. To understand, it can also be said that protocol is a type of language used by the browsers in order to communicate with web server.

EXAMPLES OF INTERNET PROTOCOLS

- FTP
- TELNET
- TCP/IP
- HTTP

1. FTP (File Transfer Protocol)

It is the acronym used for File Transfer Protocol. It is an Internet tool that allows us to move/transfer a file (i.e. any digital entity like documents, images, sounds, software) from one place to another.

The file that you are sending does not travel to your friends computer directly, or even in a single continuous stream. The file you are sending gets broken up into separate **data packets**.

The Internet Protocol side of TCP/IP labels each packet with the unique Internet address, or IP address of your friend's computer. Since these packets will travel separate routes, some arriving sooner than others, the Transmission Control Protocol side of TCP/IP assigns a sequence number to each of packets. These sequence numbers will tell the TCP/IP in your friend's computer how to reassemble the packets once he receives them. Amazingly, the complicated process of TCP/IP takes place in a matter of milliseconds.

The packets are then sent from one "router" to the next. Each router reads the IP address of the packet and decides which path will be the fastest. Since the traffic on these paths is constantly changing each packet may be sent a different way.

Mode of Sending Files

FTP can move files in two major ways: "***binary mode***" and "***ASCII mode***." Binary mode just moves the file down the wire without modifying anything. "ASCII mode" is sometimes used for plain-text (usually, .txt) files. ASCII mode, named for the American Standard Code for Information Interchange which determines what byte stands for each letter, number or other character in text. ASCII mode doesn't do us much good. These days ASCII mode is mostly an annoyance.

The norm today is for FTP to simply ship files unchanged in binary mode.

2. TCP/IP

TCP/IP refers to Transmission Control Protocol/Internet Protocol. It is the protocol that is responsible for entire communication on the Internet. The HTTP protocol is layered on top of TCP/IP.

TCP/IP is a communications protocol used to transfer digital data around the internet. TCP and IP were developed by a Department of Defense (DOD) research project to connect different networks designed by different vendors into a network of networks (the "Internet"). TCP/IP is often referred to as the ***'internet protocol'***.

As with all communications protocols, TCP/IP is composed of layers:

IP -

The Internet Protocol (IP) is a network-layer (Layer 3) protocol in the OSI model that contains addressing information and some control information to enable packets being routed in network. Along with the Transmission Control Protocol (TCP), IP represents the heart of the Internet protocols. IP is equally well suited for both LAN and WAN communications.

Each computer (known as host) on a TCP/IP network is assigned an unique logical address (32-bit in IPv4) that is divided into two main parts: the ***network number*** and the ***host number***. The network number identifies a network and must be assigned by the Internet Network Information Center.

When you send or receive data (for example, an e-mail note or a Web page), the message gets divided into little chunks called packets. Each of these packets contains both the sender's Internet address and the receiver's address. Because a message is divided into a number of packets, each packet can, if necessary, be sent by a different route across the Internet. Packets can arrive in a different order than the order they were sent in. The Internet Protocol just delivers them. It's up to another protocol, the Transmission Control Protocol (TCP) to put them back in the right order.

TCP -

Transmission Control Protocol (TCP) is the transport layer protocol in the TCP/IP protocol suite. Along with the Internet Protocol (IP), TCP represents the heart of the Internet protocols.

Since many network applications may be running on the same machine, computers need something to make sure the correct software application on the destination computer gets the data packets from the source machine and some way to make sure replies get routed to the correct application on the source computer. This is accomplished through the use of the TCP "***port numbers***". The combination of IP address of a network station and its port number is known as a ***socket*** or an "***endpoint***

TCP offers reliability by providing connection-oriented, end-to-end reliable packet delivery. It does this by *sequencing bytes* with a forwarding acknowledgment number that indicates to the destination the next byte the source expects to receive. Bytes not acknowledged within a specified time period are retransmitted. The reliability mechanism of TCP allows devices to deal with lost, delayed, duplicate, or misread packets. A time-out mechanism allows devices to detect lost packets and request retransmission.

In case of Full-duplex operation, TCP processes can both send and receive packets at the same time.

Numerous simultaneous upper-layer conversations can be multiplexed over a single connection.

3. HTTP

HTTP refers to Hypertext Transfer Protocol. Simply speaking, it is a language used by web browser to communicate with a web server. ***Example:*** For fetching a web page, this language is used by the browser to retrieve requested web page from the web server.

4. TELNET

It refers to ***Terminal Emulation*** program. Telnet is a user command and a connection oriented protocol for accessing remote computers. In other words, Telnet is the ability to access and control another computer somewhere on the internet.

Telnet is the main Internet protocol for creating a connection with a remote machine. It gives the user the opportunity to be on one computer system and do work on another, which may be across the street or thousands of miles away. Where modems are limited, in the majority, by the quality of telephone lines and a single connection, telnet provides a connection that's error-free and nearly always faster than the latest conventional modems.

On the Web, HTTP and FTP protocols allow you to request specific files from remote computers, but not to actually be logged on as a user of that computer. With Telnet, you log on as a regular user with whatever privileges you may have been granted to the specific application and data on that computer.

Telnet is most likely to be used by program developers and anyone who has a need to use specific applications or data located at a particular host computer.

new topic USENET

It is a global bulletin board service that uses the internet as an access point. It is a set of "***newsgroups***" with names that are classified hierarchically by subject. "***Articles***" or "***messages***" are posted to these newsgroups by people on computers with the appropriate software — these articles are then broadcast to other interconnected computer systems via a wide variety of networks. It is an excellent tool for science professionals.

In other words, Usenet News is a distributed computer conferencing system. Conferences in Usenet News are called newsgroups, and messages are called articles.

The basic principle of Usenet News is that a local server handles most of the functionality. The Usenet News protocol is called network news transfer protocol (NNTP) Usenet News standardizes two variants of the NNTP protocols: One for communication between adjacent servers and another one for communication between a client and a server. Each server can download as much as it wants of what is available on any of the adjacent servers. Loop control is handled both by a trace list and a list of the Message-IDs of received messages stored by each server, so that the server can reject the same message coming back again. The procedure for distribution of news can be compared to pouring water onto a flat surface; the water flows out in all directions.

Flame: A "***Flame***" on usenet is an insult. To be flamed means that you've sent an e-mail to a person(s) that has caused that person(s) to respond in many, not-so-nice words. It's basically a verbal attack in electronic form.

FREQUENTLY ASKED QUESTIONS (FAQs)

FAQ stands for "Frequently Asked Questions." In general, it refers to a collection of some questions, with answers. These are the documents created by internet users all over the world, who are often experts in the particular topic area.

Nat Torkington started the original WWW FAQ in 1993. FAQ contains questions that are infact frequently asked in a newsgroup. Almost every website contains a FAQ, which in turn is specific to that website.

DOWNLOAD

Downloading refers to the method by which you access digital information from a remote computer. In simple words, downloading refers to the actual transferring of the document from the Internet to your own computer. When you access a web page, for instance, you are actually downloading the text document and its entire associated graphics from a web server. Once the digital data arrives, your web browser looks at the file extension (the letters following the "."). If it recognizes the type of file, it will display it. If it doesn't recognize it, it will ask you if you want to configure a viewer (tell the browser which software program to use to view the file). You also have an option to save the file to your hard drive.

Another way to download files is to click on the link to the file with your right mouse button (or hold the mouse button down if you are using a Mac), and select **Save to Disk** or **Save Target As...** from the pop-up menu. In some cases, you will be prompted to save the file somewhere on your hard drive, or the file may download automatically to your desktop, depending on how your browser is configured.

UPLOAD

The term "***upload***" refers to transmission of data from a computer to a bulletin board service, mainframe or network. You can upload documents, pictures, music and movies. There are several websites that provides uploading facility. A file may be uploaded to multiple recipients simultaneously. Examples of free uploading sites are: ***Uploading.com***, ***UploadIt.org*** etc.

ECOMMERCE

Electronic commerce or e-commerce is a term for any type of business, or commercial transaction that involves the transfer of information across the Internet.

Ecommerce allows consumers to electronically exchange goods and services with no barriers of time or distance. It covers a range of different types of businesses, from consumer based retail sites, through auction or music sites, to business exchanges trading goods and services between corporations. It is currently one of the most important aspects of the Internet to emerge.

Electronic commerce has expanded rapidly over the past five years and is predicted to continue at this rate, or even accelerate. In the near future the boundaries between "conventional" and "electronic" commerce will become increasingly blurred as more and more businesses move

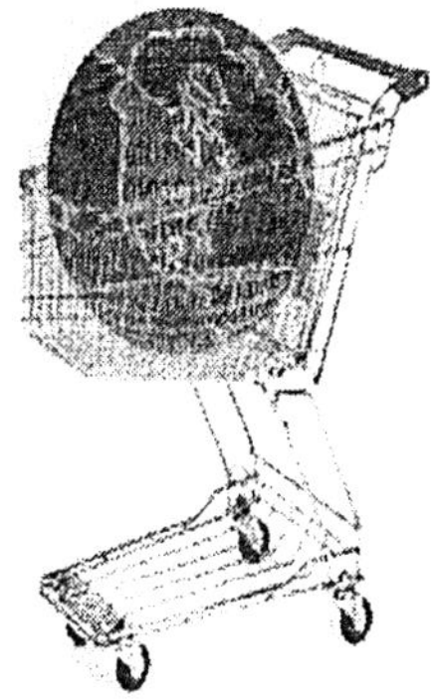

sections of their operations onto the Internet. Electronic commerce has also led to the development of electronic marketplaces where suppliers and potential customers are brought together to conduct mutually beneficial trade.

Business to Business or B2B refers to electronic commerce between businesses rather than between a business and a consumer..

E-Commerce is about setting your business on the Internet, allowing visitors to access your website, and go through a virtual catalog of your products / services online. When a visitor wants to buy something he/she likes, they merely, "add" it to their virtual shopping basket. Items in the virtual shopping basket can be added or deleted, and when you're all set to checkout...you head to the virtual checkout counter, which has your complete total, and will ask you for your name, address etc. and method of payment (usually via credit card).

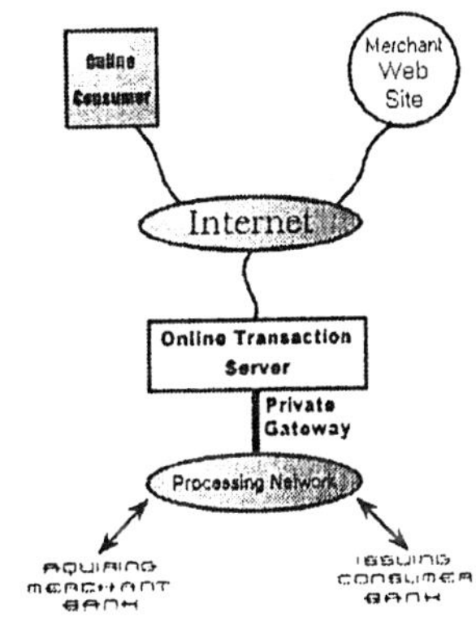

In short, by implementing E-Commerce, you save money, are online 24 hours-a-day, 7 days-a-week, no traffic jams, shopping crowds, carrying overloaded heavy shopping bags etc.

There are several basic steps involved in becoming eCommerce Enabled-

- Getting an Internet Merchant Bank Account
- Web Hosting
- Obtaining a Digital Certificate
- Finding a Provider of Online Transactions
- Creating or Purchasing a Shopping Cart Software

1. Essential elements to conduct e-commerce:

- ☑ A product
- ☑ A place to sell the product i.e. a Web site displays the products in some way and acts as the place
- ☑ A way to get people to come to your Web site
- ☑ A way to accept orders - normally an on-line form of some sort
- ☑ A way to accept money - normally a merchant account handling credit card payments. This piece requires a secure ordering page and a connection

to a bank. Or you may use more traditional billing techniques either online or through the mail.

- ☑ A fulfillment facility to ship products to customers (often outsource-able). In the case of software and information, however, fulfillment can occur over the Web through a file download mechanism.
- ☑ A way to accept returns
- ☑ A way to handle warranty claims if necessary
- ☑ A way to provide customer service (often through email, on-line forms, on-line knowledge bases and FAQs, etc)

2. Top E-commerce Companies:

- **M**erchant **O**nline
- **C**yber**S**ource
- **I**nternet **B**illing
- **P**ayment **N**et
- **M**aster **M**erchant

new topic SEARCH ENGINES

"A search engine is a searchable database of Internet files collected by a computer program (called a wanderer, crawler, robot, worm, spider)."

A search engine might well be called a **search engine service** or a **search service.** As such, it consists of three components:

- Spider
- Index
- Search engine mechanism

Search engines use software called **Spiders,** which comb the Internet looking for documents and their web addresses. The document and web addresses collected and sent to search engines indexing software. Indexing software extracts information from the documents, storing it in a database. The kind of information indexed depends on the particular search engines. Search engine mechanism is such software that enables users to query the index.

1. Examples of Search Engines

- AltaVista
- BabelFish
- Ask.com
- Google
- Yahoo
- Lycos

- Clusty
- DonBusca
- AOL Search

2. How to Formulate Queries (for searching using search engines)

- Identify your concepts *e.g.* Sales and Marketing
- List keywords for each concept *e.g.* Sales, Marketing, Sales Trend, Marketing Strategy, Sales Analysis etc.
- Specify the logical relationships among your keywords *e.g.* use logical operators like AND, OR, NOT to specify the relationship between keywords.

DIFFERENT CATEGORIES OF INTERNET SOFTWARES

Freeware: Freeware is software that you can download and use without ever paying a dime. This software is sometimes developed by kind hearted souls who create software for the simple joy of creating it. Other times it's created by large companies who want you to test the software and find any bugs before they sell it to the general public (beta versions).

Shareware: Shareware is basically "***try it before you buy it***." You can download it and try it out. If you decide that you want to keep it you should pay the developer the "shareware fee." This fee is usually minimal. Sometimes all the developer asks in return for the software is an email from you proclaiming how much you've enjoyed using it.

INTERNET SECURITY

As technology advances and more people come to rely on the Internet for information, leisure, and business. Security tools are designed to be used to protect computer systems and networks. Internet is an open system. There are many reasons and many ways to set up a secure or closed system with in this 'open' framework. Any information you send or receive is scrambled or 'encrypted' using a mathematical formula and then reassembled or 'decrypted' at the other end. The computer user will not even notice this happening as they perform the transaction.

Programs having negative influence on internet security are as follows-

- ✓ **Malware:** Malware refers to malicious software, which is designed specifically to damage or disrupt a system, such as a virus or a Trojan horse. Examples of Malware are as follows-
  - **Virus:** Viruses are "programs" that modify other programs on a computer, inserting copies of themselves. They cannot run on their own, and

need to become part of some host program. When such an infected program is executed, the virus attaches itself to another and so on.

- **Worm:** A worm is a malicious program that copies itself from one computer to another on a network. A worm is an independent program, in the sense described above, unlike a virus which is a part-program that must insert itself into a whole-program. A worm typically does not modify other programs.
- **Trojan Horses:** Trojan horses are programs that appear to have one function but actually perform another function. Trojan horses are named after the Trojan horse of the Greek Trojan War.
- **Bacteria:** Bacteria, or rabbit programs, make copies of themselves to overwhelm a computer system's resources. Bacteria do not explicitly damage any files. Their sole purpose is to replicate themselves. A typical bacteria program may do nothing more than execute two copies of itself simultaneously on multiprogramming systems, or perhaps create two new files, each of which is a copy of the original source file of the bacteria program. Both of those programs then may copy themselves twice, and so on. Bacteria reproduce exponentially, eventually taking up all the processor capacity, memory, or disk space, denying the user access to those resources.
- **Drooper:** A dropper is a program that is not a virus, nor is it infected with a virus, but when run it installs a virus into memory, on to the disk, or into a file. Droppers have been written sometimes as a convenient carrier for a virus, and sometimes as an act of sabotage. Some anti-virus programs try to detect droppers.
- **Adware: A**dware is any software application in which advertising banners are displayed while the program is running. The authors of these applications include additional code that delivers the ads, which can be viewed through pop-up windows or through a bar that appears on a computer screen. The justification for adware is that it helps recover programming development cost and helps to hold down the cost for the user. Adware has been criticized because it usually includes code that tracks a user's personal information and passes it on to third parties, without the user's authorization or knowledge.
- **Spyware:** In general, spyware is any technology that aids in gathering information about a person or organization without their knowledge. In context of Internet, Spyware is software that transmits information back to a third party without notifying the user. Here are some common signs that you have been infected:
    - Your PC is running unusually slow.
    - Ads are popping up even when your browser isn't running.
    - Your home page has been hijacked.
    - Antispyware or antivirus applications aren't working correctly. Some spyware programs will sabotage the programs designed to detect and eliminate them.
    - There's been a dramatic increase in your network's traffic, eating up bandwidth and crippling performance.

1. General Characteristics of viruses, worms, Trojan Horses and malicious code include:

- Causes harm
- Propagates by multiple methods
- Attacks from multiple points
- Spreads without human intervention
- Exploits vulnerabilities

2. Threats to Internet Security

Spyware / Adware / Malware Security Threats

- Installs invisibly on a user's computer
- Collects and transmits private information such as keystrokes, Web surfing habits, passwords, e-mail addresses and other sensitive data through employee Internet access activities
- Corrupts workstations and depletes bandwidth

Ilegal Music Security Threats

- Illegal music or movie downloads can result in legal liability
- Leaves computers open to viruses and worms
- Consumes bandwidth
- Allows transmission of confidential information

Phishing Security Threats

- Steals private information such as passwords, bank account numbers, social security numbers, PINs, and credit card numbers
- Businesses are especially vulnerable because phishers mass mail every e-mail account available, multiplying an organization's risk for informational loss

Viruses, Trojan Horses, Worms and Macros Security Threats

- Cause odd system behavior such as applications crashing, freezing or incorrect operation
- Not only harm host computers but replicate and invade a whole network
- Corrupt and delete files, causing networks to shut down

new topic NETIQUETTE

The term "Netiquette" is derived from two words- "*Internet*" & "*etiquette*". Netiquette describes the rule for online behavior especially in newsgroups, forums & chat rooms.

EXAMPLES -

- Do not type in capitals (DO NOT TYPE CAPITALS) as it is seen as shouting.
- Do not defame people

- Responding appropriately to request
- Not sending bulk email or spam
- Using Internet acronym or emoticons

1. Rules for being a good Netizen-

- What is inappropriate in the real world is inappropriate in the cyber world.
- Do not take undue advantage of your Anonymity (your identity remain unknown on net)
- Do not steal
- Do not hack
- Do not flame *(discussed previously)*

BROADBAND

Broadband is the latest and fastest mode of connecting to the Internet. With Broadband, your connection will generally be ten times faster than with a standard dial up modem connection. Standard broadband technologies are DSL & Cable modem.

Broadband is a transmission medium that is capable of supporting a wide range of frequencies, typically from audio up to video frequencies. It can carry multiple signals by dividing the total capacity of the medium into multiple, independent bandwidth channels, where each channel operates only on a specific range of frequencies.

Broadband does not depend on the telephone line and is capable of carrying "heavy" packets on the Internet at incredible speeds. Examples of organization providing Broadband connection are **BSNL & Sify.**

1. Advantages of Broadband-

- High speed "***always on***" connection
- Use of Phone and Internet at the same time
- You can share the connection
- No call charges when you use Internet
- Compatible with latest Game consoles

2. Technologies used to deliver Broadband-

- Leased lines
- Cable
- Satellite

- DSL (Digital Subscriber Line)
- PowerLine

new topic CONFERENCING

"Conferencing refers to the ability to communicate in real time, via Internet. With the Internet, you can see, hear, talk to and collaborate with people in different locations around the world, without the expense of travel."

Conferencing can be done one-to-one, one-to-many (called multicast), and many-to-many (called multipoint). Most conferencing software is built on open industry standards so that a dial-up connection is enough to get you in the game. However, broadband connections give far better results.

Microsoft Internet Explorer (version 4.0 and higher) has a built-in conferencing program, called NetMeeting. This versatile software can be used for audio and videoconferencing, as well as for sharing applications and collaborating on documents.

You can use video and audio simultaneously, just audio, or use the screen-sharing capability to collaborate on documents without either audio or video.

1. Types of Conferencing:

1. ***Video-conferencing:*** Videoconferencing technology allows two or more people at different locations to see and hear each other at the same time. In addition, it is often possible to share computer applications such as Internet pages, library catalogs, documents, or software. Placing a video call is a lot like placing a telephone call. After you connect, you see the other person in color video and may be able to transfer files or collaborate. A videoconference system must have audio-visual equipment (monitor, camera, microphone, and speaker) as well as a means of transmitting information between sites. For Example: ***CU-SeeMe*** is a free videoconferencing program from ***Cornell University*** which is available to anyone with a Macintosh or Windows and a connection to the Internet. With Cu-SeeMe, it is possible to have a videoconference with another site anywhere in the world.

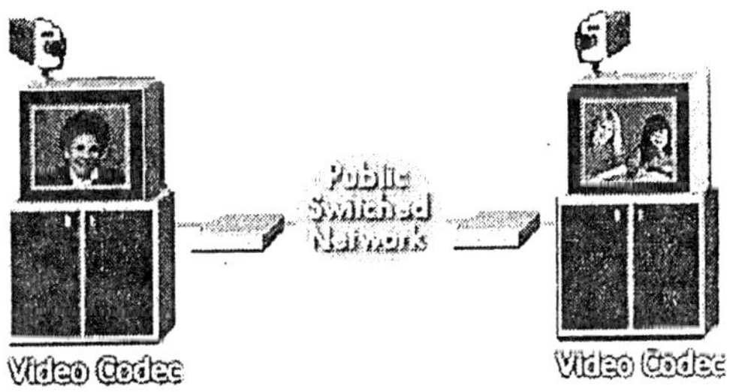

2. ***Audio-conferencing:*** Audio conferencing allows you to communicate verbally, rather than typing messages. The Internet can also be used to make telephone calls around the world, for only the cost of a local connection. To make Internet calls, you need a headset with earphones and a microphone, as well as the telephony software. It works by digitizing your voice, then sending the digital data to its final destination over the Internet.

PRACTICAL KNOWLEDGE OF ? INTERNET

HOW TO START WORKING ON INTERNET

Using Dial-Up Connections

1. Click **Dial up Connection** icon available on your desktop.
2. In the **User Name** box, type your user name.
3. In the **Password** box, type your password.
4. Choose one of the following options:
   a. To save the user name and password so that you will not have to type them in the future, select the **Save this user name and password for the following users** check box.

   b. If you want only the current user to have access to the saved user name and password, select the **Me only** option.
   c. If you want all users to have access to the user name and password, select the **Anyone who uses this computer** option.
5. Click **Dial** or **Connect.**

Dialer software is responsible for making the physical connection with the ISPs computer and the Internet. Once configured you simply run the software to connect your computer's modem to the ISP's modem, giving you access to the Internet.

Using Broadband Connections or Leased Line

1. Double click on the **Internet Explorer** icon (or other browser icon, whatever available) on the desktop or simply click browser Icon on the task bar. This will led you to the browser window. *(In this case, connection establishes itself automatically or within few seconds as soon as you boot your system)*

USING INTERNET EXPLORER 6

Internet Explorer is a Web browser released by the Microsoft Corporation in 2001. Internet Explorer 6.0 is the standard browser in the latest version of Windows (Windows XP). Internet Explorer 6.0 is the most commonly used browser today.

1. How to open Browser (For Example: Internet Explorer)

Click this icon on the task bar

Click this icon on the desktop

OR

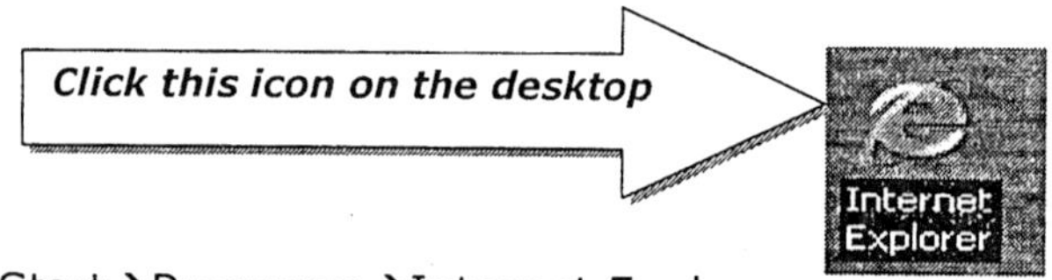

OR

Click on Start→Programs→Internet Explorer

2. TOOLBARS IN INTERNET EXPLORER 6

IE 6 has two toolbars at the top of the browser window:

Menu Bar: Contains menu items that open up dropdown lists for related options.

Navigation Toolbar: Contains icons for a variety of features including navigating among Web pages, searching the Web using a selection of search tools, accessing and managing Favorites, viewing a History of visited pages, printing, and accessing email and newsgroups.

3. Navigating the Web Site with IE6

Internet Explorer 6 allows you to move back and forth among the Web pages that you visit during a session.

To go back to previous sites:

Click on the small **Back** left arrow on the navigation bar near the top left corner of your screen. Each time you click on this arrow, you will return to the next previous site that you visited. If you hold your mouse over the **Back** arrow, the title of the upcoming page will briefly appear.

To skip farther back, click on the small black triangle to the right of the word ***Back****. This will bring up a list of pages you have visited. Click on any one* *of these choices to return to the desired page. This is the equivalent of clicking on the **Back** arrow several times.*

To move Forward:

When you have returned to previous sites with the **Back** arrow, you can go forward again by clicking on the small right-pointing arrow next to the **Back** arrow. If you hold your mouse over this arrow, the title of the upcoming page will briefly appear.

*To move farther ahead, click on the small black triangle to the right of the Forward arrow in the menu bar at the top of the screen. This presents a list of several sites you have visited. Click on any of the choices to return to the desired site. This is the equivalent of clicking on the **Forward** arrow several times.*

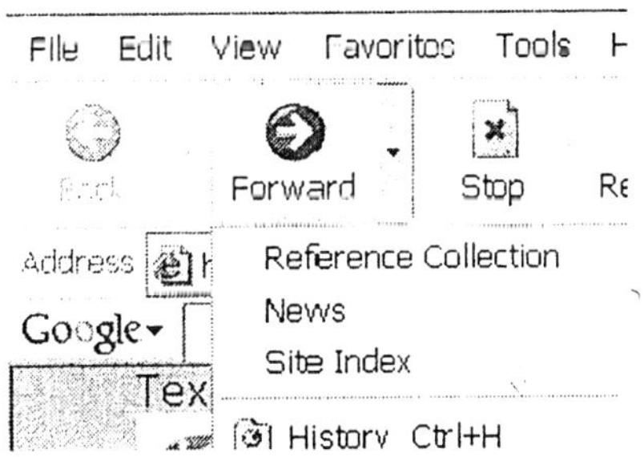

4. Important Tools of Navigation Toolbar

Stop: This button will stop a page while it is in the process of loading This is useful if a page is not successfully or speedily retrieving.

Refresh: This button is used to re-retrieve the page you are currently viewing. This is useful if the page does not load successfully or completely.

Home: The home icon takes you back to the page that was on the screen when you first started IE 6.

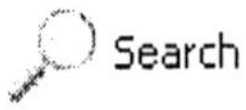

Search: The search button opens up a function that uses one or more Web search tools. You can choose the search tool(s) you want as your default.

You can also customize your search experience. After clicking on ***Search,*** *choose the* ***Customize*** *option and make your selection. A pop-up window called "****Customize Search Settings****" will appear. If you choose to "****Use Search Assistant****" broad search topics will be displayed and the appropriate search tool will be queried. You can also opt to have IE 6 remember your last 10 searches so that you can easily repeat them.*

*Also notice that you can click a button called "****Autosearch settings****." This allows you to choose the search tool you want when you use the Address bar as a search window. You can also customize this option on the "When searching" line. You can even choose to turn off the use of the Address bar as a search window. If you do this, all words you type into the Address bar will be interpreted as URLs.*

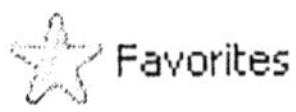

Favorites: Favorites are Web sites you have visited that you would like to store for easy access. You can add, delete and organize your Favorites.

To add the current Web page as a favorite, click on **Favorites** and then **Add**. To choose the folder where you want to store this listing, click on **Create in** and choose the folder you want. At this point, you also have the option to create a new folder.

To delete a Favorite, simply right click on the item and choose **Delete**. Or, you can choose **Organize Favorites** select the desired item, and click on the **Delete** button.

To move a favorite to another folder, click on **Organize Favorites**, select the desired item, and click on **Move to folder**. In the pop-up window, select the folder where you would like to store this listing.

History: The history function allows you to view and select Web pages you have recently visited. You can sort your items by clicking on the black triangle to the right of the word **View**. You can sort by size, date, the number of times visited, and the order you have visited today.

Mail: You can read email from this window. Choose the email software you wish to use by going back to the Menu Bar and choosing **Tools/Internet Options/Programs**.

Print: Allows you to print the current page. This option will be explained in more detail below under Printing.

Edit: You may edit the current page in the HTML editor of your choice. Choose the editor by going back to the Menu Bar and choosing **Tools/Internet Options/Programs**.

Discuss: You may set a default Usenet newsgroup server.

Useful Options on the Menu Bar

5. Useful Options on the Menu Bar

The menu bar at the top of the screen includes some useful options. Here are a few highlights.

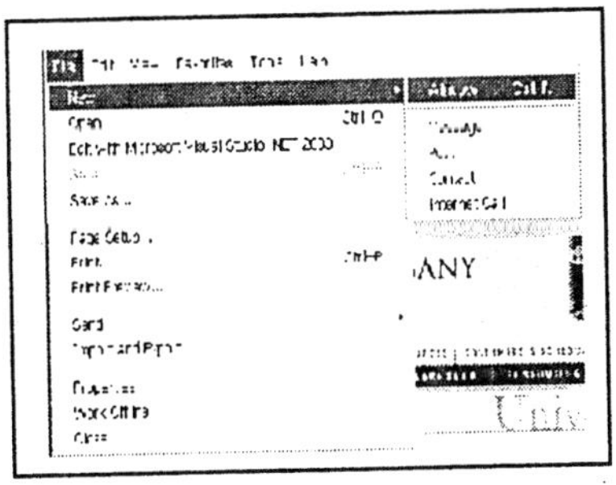

File/New/Window: You can open up a second copy of IE 6 by using this feature. This allows you to visit more than one Web page at a time.

File/Edit with...: You can edit the current Web page using the editor of your choice. Select the editor by going back to the Menu Bar and choosing **Tools/Internet Options/Programs**. You choices will be determined by software installed on your computer.

Edit/Find (on This Page): IE 6 allows you to do a text search of the document on your screen. Choose this option and type in the word or phrase you wish to search.

Tools/Show Related Links: IE 6 will display pages that are related in content to the current page. This is a service of ***Alexa***, a Web content and traffic analysis company.

*The **Tools** menu offers you many ways to customize IE 6. This will be covered below under Customizing Internet Explorer.*

newtopic SAVING A WEB PAGE (or Download)

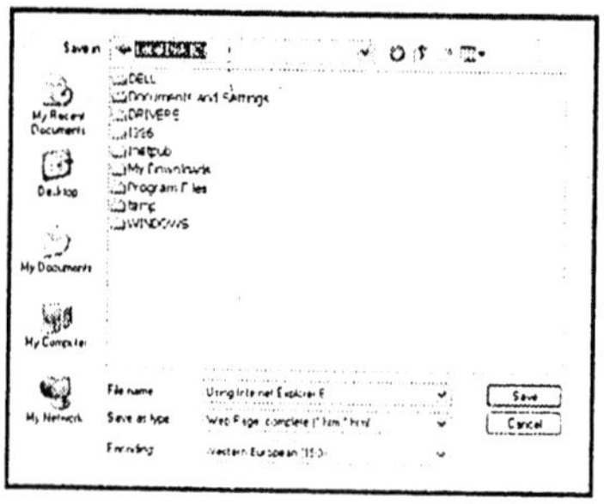

1. Click on **File/Save As** (top left of screen). A pop-up window will appear.
2. ***Save in:*** Choose the desired drive.
3. ***Save as type:*** Make sure you save the page to the file type that will be useful to you. If you save the page as a Web page, you will need a Web browser or HTML editor to view it. A text file (txt) can be viewed in a word processing program such a Word or WordPerfect.
4. Click on ***Save***

newtopic PRINTING THE ENTIRE WEB PAGE

1. Click on the **Print** icon on the Tool Bar
2. Click on **OK**

newtopic PRINTING THE SELECTED WEB PAGES

1. Click on **File/Print Preview** (top left of screen)
2. Click through the pages using the navigation arrows and make a note of which pages you want to print
3. Click on **Print** (top left of screen)
4. Click on the "***Pages***" option.
5. Type in the pages separate by commas, ***e.g.*** 1,5, 6, Or, to print the page displayed in the Print Preview window, choose **Current Page**
6. Click on OK.

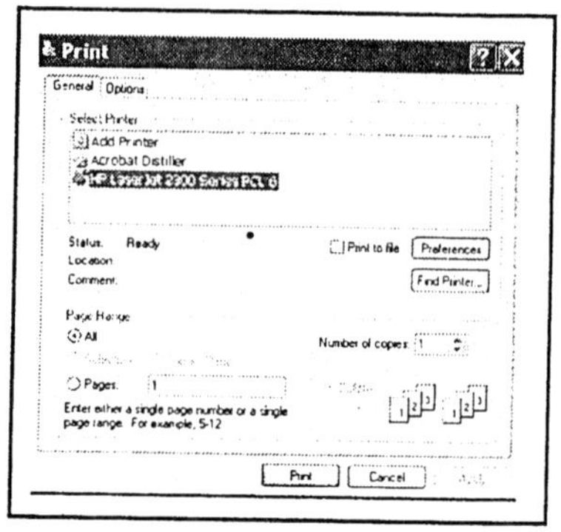

newtopic PRINTING SELECTED PORTIONS OF A WEB PAGE

1. Select the desired portion of a web page
2. Click on **Print** (top left of screen)
3. In the **Print** dialog box, click on the "***Selection***" option.
4. Click on OK.

newtopic USE OF RIGHT MOUSE BUTTON

The right mouse button offers a number of useful features if you are using a PC. To view the possibilities, press down on the right mouse button and hold it. Options will display in a pop-up window.

1. WHEN THE MOUSE POINTER IS ON THE SCREEN (but not on a link or an image)

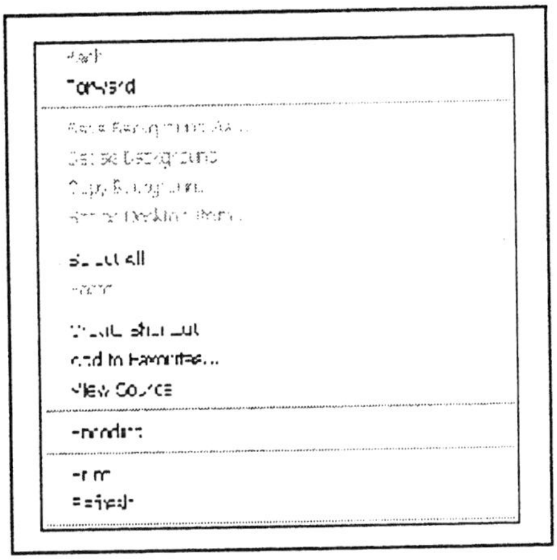

1. **Back:** Moves back to the previously visited page in your history list (same as **Back** icon)
2. **Forward:** Moves forward to the next page in your history list (same as **Forward** icon)
3. **Select All:** Selects all the text on the page for copying and pasting
4. **Create Shortcut:** Creates a shortcut to the current Web page on your desktop
5. **Add to Favorites:** Adds the current Web page to your Favorites
6. **View Source:** Brings up the HTML source code of the current page
7. **Encoding:** Allows you to choose a language.
8. **Print:** Prints the current document
9. **Refresh:** Reloads the current page from the server

2. WHEN THE MOUSE POINTER IS OVER A LINK

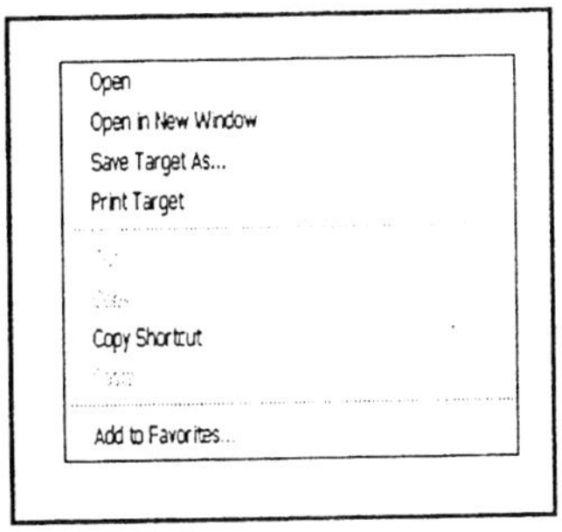

1. **Open:** Opens the page
2. **Open in New Window:** Opens the link in a new copy of IE 6
3. **Save Target As:** Saves the link as a file
4. **Print Target:** Prints the link
5. **Copy Shortcut:** Copies the URL to the Clipboard for pasting into a text editor or word processing program
6. **Add to Favorites:** Adds the selected page to your Favorites

3. WHEN THE MOUSE POINTER IS OVER AN IMAGE

1. **Save Picture As:** Saves the image to a disk drive of your choice
2. **E-mail Picture:** Opens your default email program and attaches the image to the message

3. **Print Picture:** Prints the image on your default printer
4. **Set as Background:** Uses the image as your desktop wallpaper
5. **Set as Desktop Item:** Sets the image as an Active Desktop item
6. **Copy:** Copies the image to the Clipboard for pasting into a graphics editing program
7. **Add to Favorites:** Adds the selected images to your Favorites

new topic CUSTOMIZING INTERNET EXPLORER

IE 6 offers a number of customization options. This section will highlight some of the more useful features available under **Tools/Internet Options** on the Menu Bar.

Tools/Internet Options is divided into six tabs. Each one is explained below.

1. General

- **Home Page:** Specify the URL of the page you want to appear whenever you open IE 6, or whenever you click on the Home icon
- **Temporary Internet Files:** This option allows you to view the files in your browser's cache. The cache holds viewed Web pages for subsequent quick viewing. Retrieving a file from the cache is much faster than repeated trips to the remote Web server where the file originated. Click ***Delete cookies*** button in order to delete all the cookies saved on your computer. (because cookies may somewhat slowdown the computer) Likewise, click ***Delete Temporary Files*** button to delete temporary files stored in IE6 cache.
- **History:** This option customizes your access to pages you have visited with the **History** function. Here you can set the number of days to keep pages in your history. Click on ***Clear History*** button in order to delete the list of viewed web pages from IE6 history.
- **Colors:** Choose colors for links, visited links, and link hovers (the color appearing when your mouse is over a link). You can also set a default text and background color.
- **Fonts:** Select the language script, the font displayed in Web pages, and the font displayed as plain text.
- **Languages:** Select the language that will display Web pages accessed with IE 6.
- **Accessibility:** Choose to ignore colors, font sizes and font styles on Web pages. You can also set a style sheet as the display template for all Web pages viewed with IE 6.

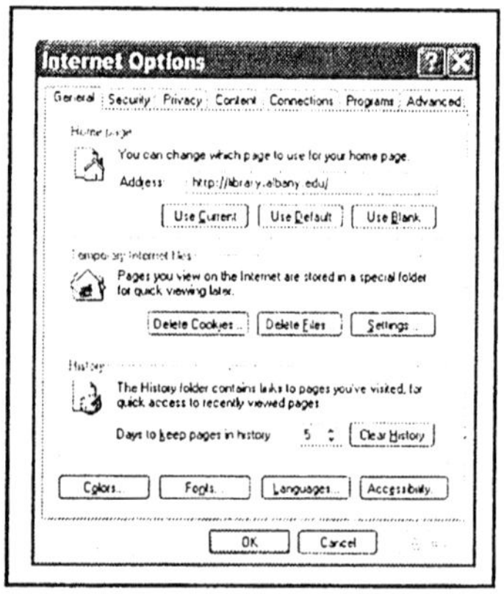

2. Security

Using Security tab, you can set levels of security for individual Web pages. Also, you can customize Security settings of the Internet Explorer by clicking on ***Custom Level*** button.

3. Content

Content Advisor: You can enable ratings of objectionable content to control the pages that may be viewed with this browser.

Personal Information: This consists of two options.

i. **AutoComplete** will store entered Web address, information entered into forms, and usernames and passwords needed to access sites you have visited. When you are using your browser, previous entries will come up as choices so that you don't have to retype the information. This can make your work go much faster. You can customize these options, and delete your settings. Click ***AutoComplete*** button, then *AutoComplete Settings* dialog box is displayed. In dialog box, you can choose the options like Web addresses, forms etc for which you want to use AutoComplete. Besides this, you can also click ***Clear Forms*** button & ***Clear Passwords*** button in order to delete the previously typed entries (typed in text box while using the browser) and passwords respectively.

ii. ***My Profile*** offers a template for entering personal information. If a Web site requests this information, you can give permission for it to be used.

4. Connections

Here you can store the information about your Internet Service Provider, configure your LAN settings, or send your browser requests through a proxy server.

5. Programs

Here you can set the programs you want the browser to use for HTML editing, email, Usenet news, collaboration ("Internet Call"), your calendar and contact list.

6. Advanced

This screen offers a number of options in the categories of accessibility, browsing, HTTP settings, Microsoft VM (Virtual Machine), multimedia access, printing, searching and security. Set these options if you are comfortable with them.

How to Open Websites

1. If the web address is known, then type the address in the Address bar (using appropriate protocol)

2. Press ***Enter*** or Click ***Go***

Or

1. Simply type the name of the website in the address bar

2. Then press ***Ctrl + Enter***. After doing so the appropriate URL of Yahoo would appear in the address bar. (http://www.yahoo.com)

newtopic How to search text using Google

(*Assume that you have opened Google site in IE6*)

1. Identify your concepts ***e.g.*** Hospitality & Tourism
2. List keywords for each concept ***e.g.*** Hospitality, Tourism, Hospitality industry, Tourist places, Role of Hospitality in Tourism etc.
3. Type a keyword (*one at a time*) in Google Search text box & click on ***Google Search*** button.

4. It should be noted that in order to search text, "***Web***" link must be already selected.

Result: Links to various websites (containing the specified keywords) would get displayed. Click on them one by one and explore.....related knowledge.

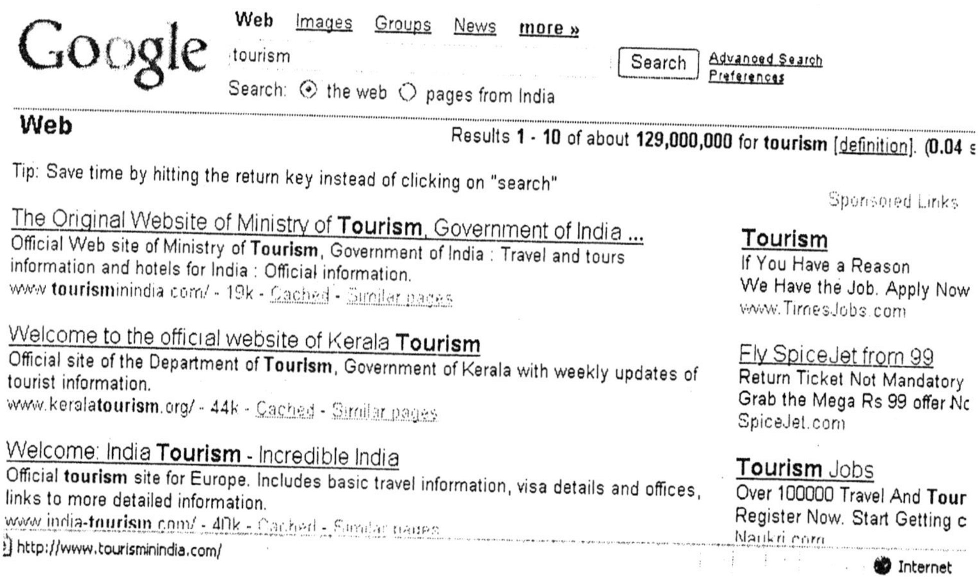

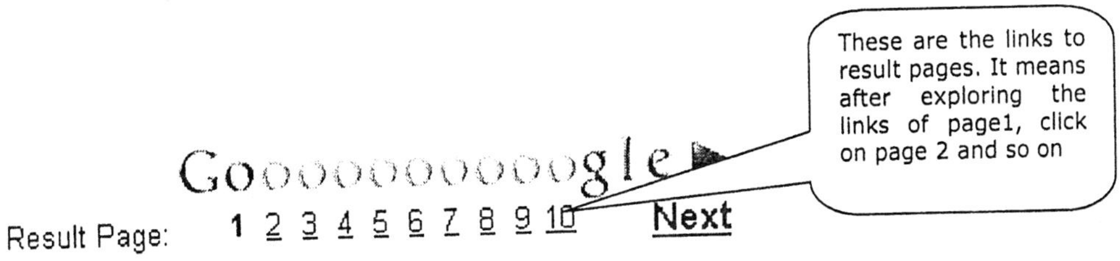

How to search & save images using Google

1. List keywords related to the image.
2. Type a keyword in Google Search text box & Click on ***Google Search*** button.
3. It should be noted that in order to search images, ***"Images"*** link must be already selected.

Result: Links to various images (related to the keyword) would get displayed.

For saving images: Right click on the desired image, and click on ***Save Picture As*** or ***Save target As*** option. Then, specify the name and the location for saving the picture in the respective dialog box and click ***Save*** button.

How to create E-mail id

For creating e-mail id, open the desired website (*using Internet Explorer*) on which you wish to open your email account. ***For example:*** Rediff, Yahoo, Hotmail, Sify etc. Here, we take the example of ***Yahoo*** (www.yahoo.com)

Step 1: Click on ***Sign Up*** hyperlink.

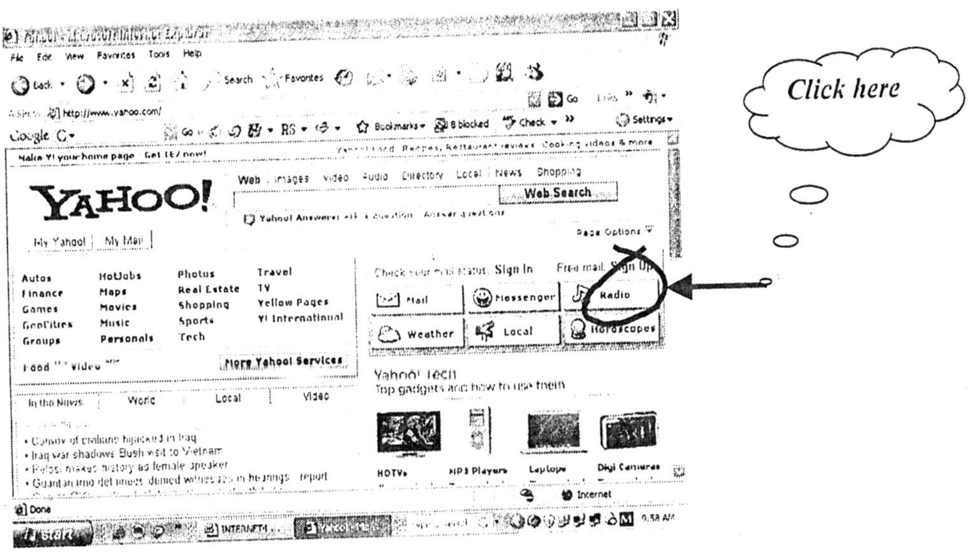

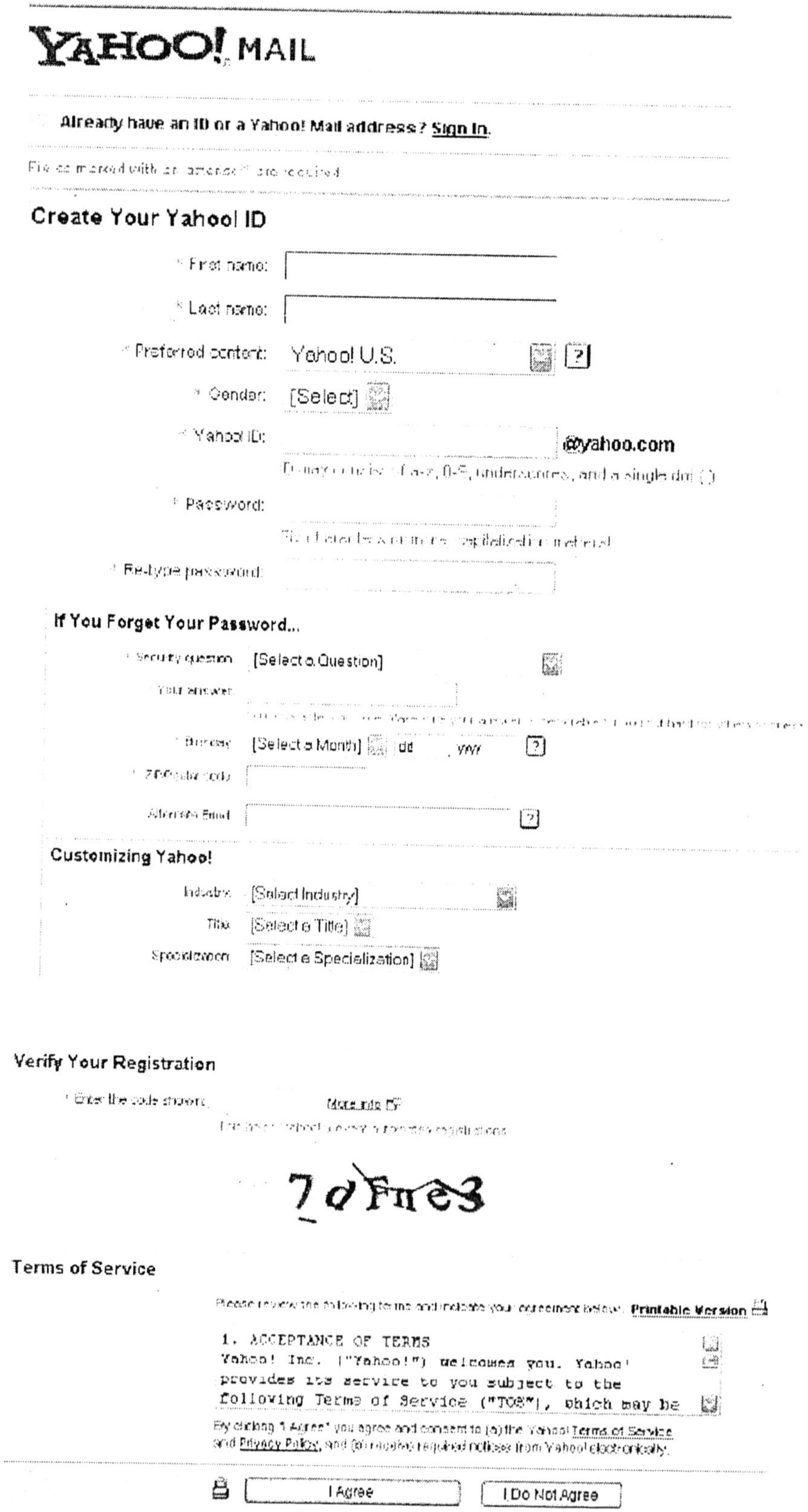

YAHOO! MAIL

Already have an ID or a Yahoo! Mail address? Sign In.

Create Your Yahoo! ID

* First name:

* Last name:

* Preferred content: Yahoo! U.S.

* Gender: [Select]

* Yahoo! ID: @yahoo.com

* Password:

* Re-type password:

If You Forget Your Password...

* Security question [Select a Question]

Your answer

* Birthday [Select a Month] dd , yyyy

Alternate Email

Customizing Yahoo!

Industry [Select Industry]

Title [Select a Title]

Specialization [Select a Specialization]

Verify Your Registration

* Enter the code shown: More info

7dFne3

Terms of Service

Printable Version

1. ACCEPTANCE OF TERMS
Yahoo! Inc. ("Yahoo!") welcomes you. Yahoo! provides its service to you subject to the following Terms of Service ("TOS"), which may be

I Agree | I Do Not Agree

Step 2: Enter all the required entries to register yourself with Yahoo. Finally, click ***I Agree*** button. If the e-mail id specified by you already exists, then it will highlight that particular entry with yellow bar. It also notifies you that the mail_id is already used by another user on the Internet. So, you have to fill this entry again and click on ***Submit*** button.

After completing the registration process; the confirmation of registration is displayed.

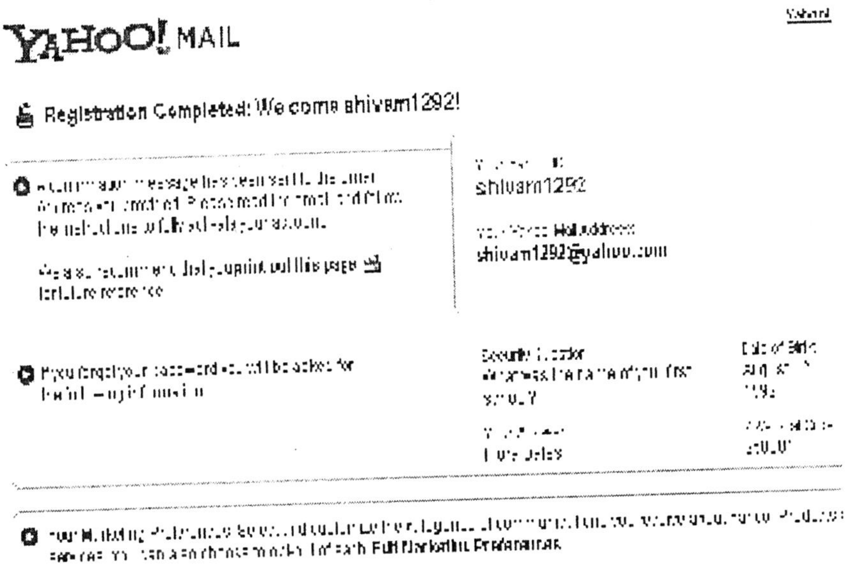

How to Sign-in & Logout of a particular mail-Id

For signing-in your mail account, the steps are as follows- (*You must be online*)

Step 1: Open Yahoo website (*as you have created your mail account on Yahoo*)

Step 2: Click on ***Sign-in*** hyperlink.

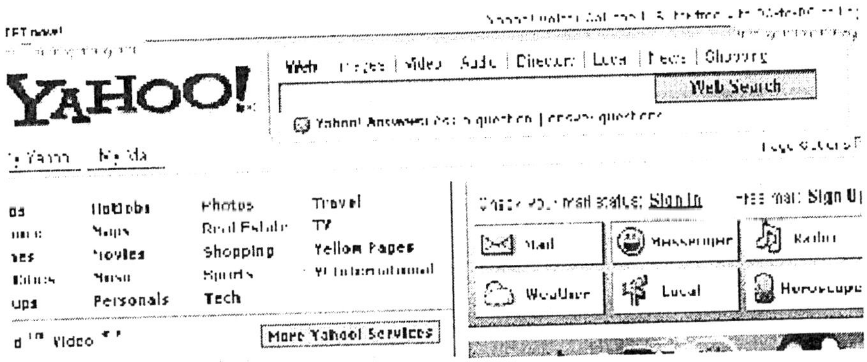

Step 3: Then, following screen will be displayed. Enter your email ID and password and click on ***Sign In*** button.

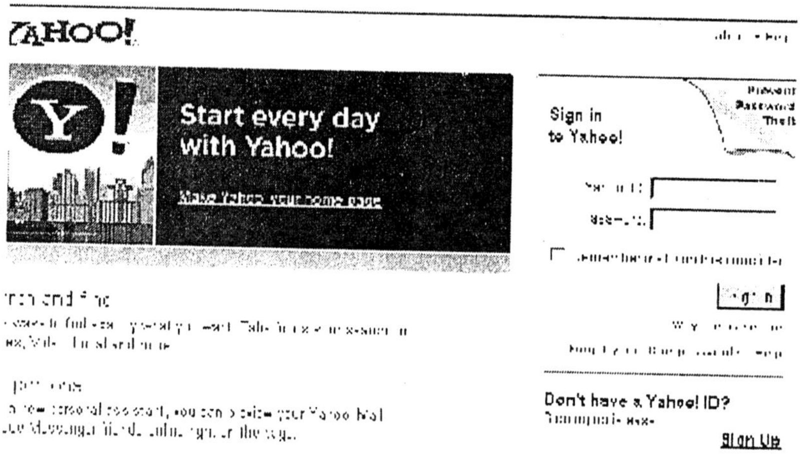

Then, following screen is displayed. This screen shows that you have successfully signed in your mail account.

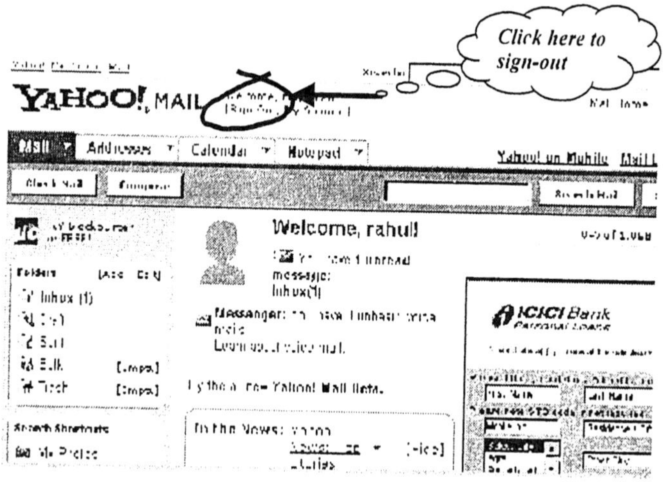

TO LOGOUT OR SIGN-OUT YOUR MAIL ACCOUNT

Step 1: Click Sign-Out hyperlink displayed in the above screen.

new topic How to Compose & Send Mail

1. Open your e-mail account

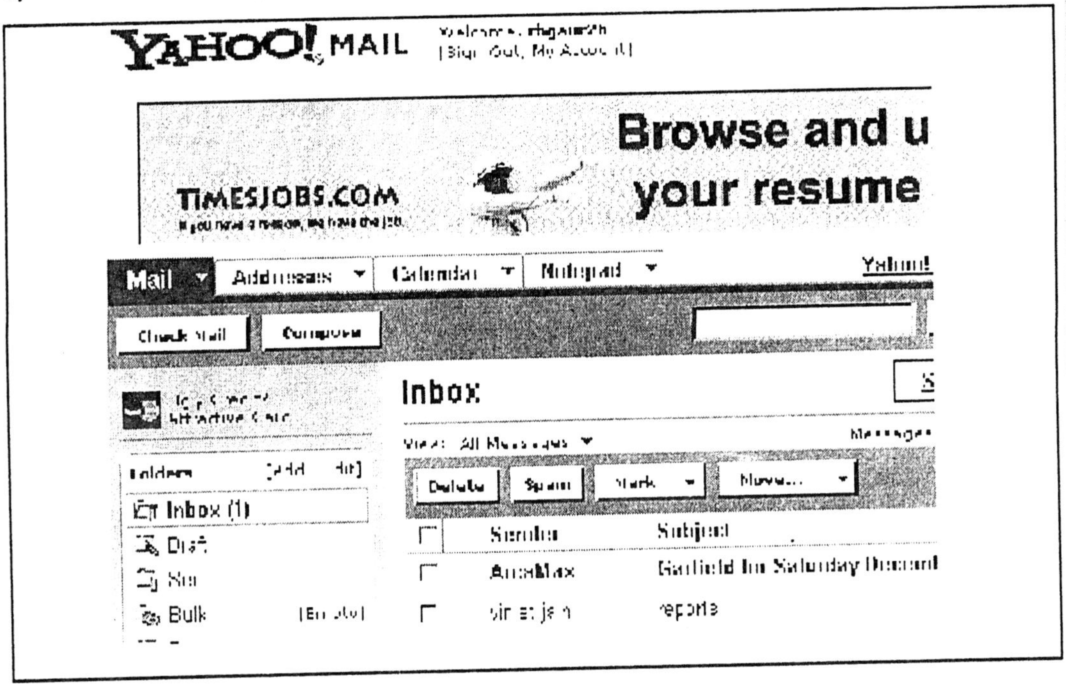

Step 2: Click ***Compose*** button.

Step 3: Then type recipient e-mail address in ***To*** box.

Step 4: Type the purpose of your mail in ***Subject*** box, so that it could be identified by the recipient.

Step 5: Type the actual content of the message in Message box.

Step 6: Click on ***Send*** button.

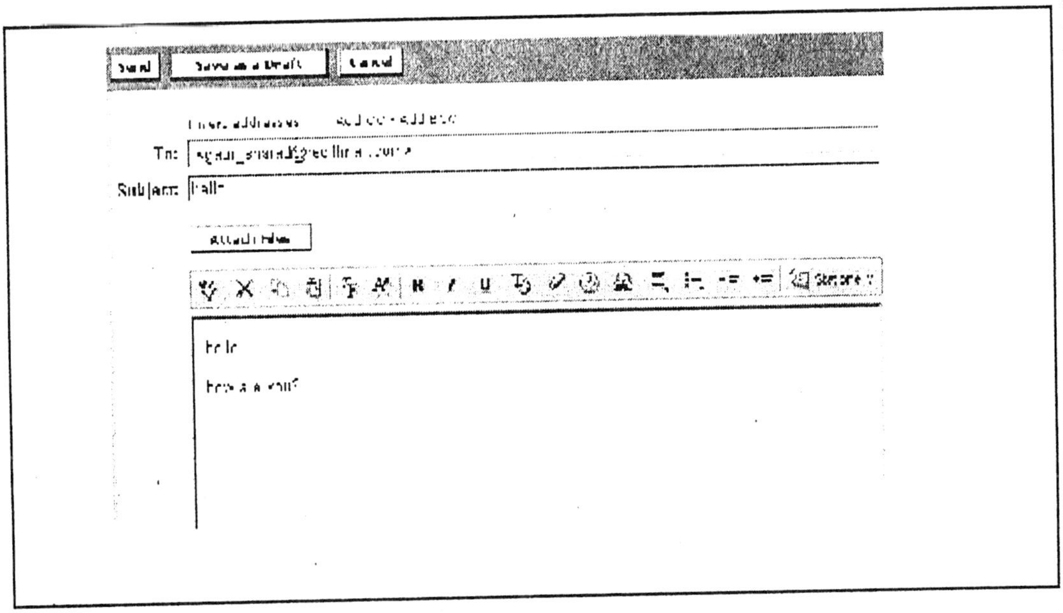

How to send Attachment with a Mail

Step 1: Click on ***Attach Files*** button.

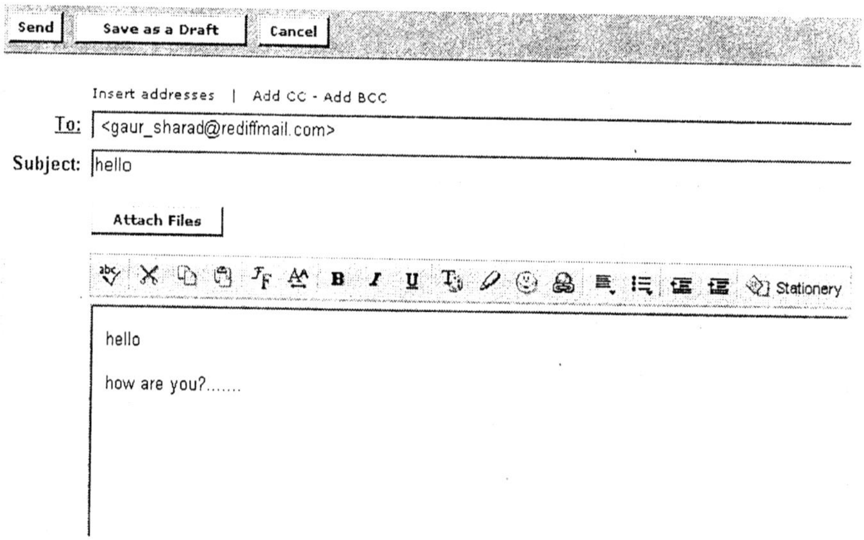

Step 2: Click on ***Browse*** button to attach one or more files respectively.

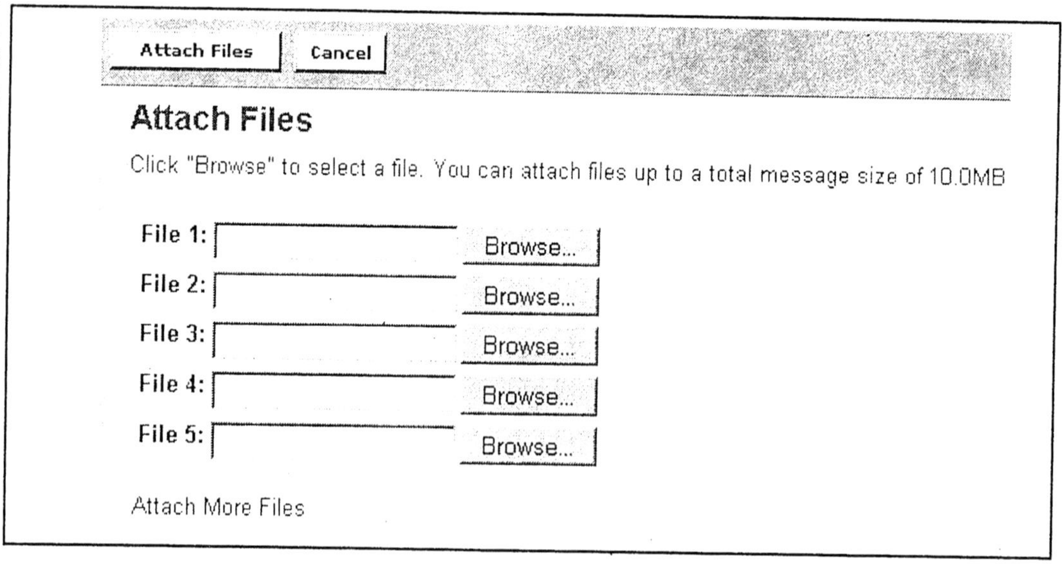

Step 3: Then, in the ***Choose File*** specify the location (File path) and the file name to be attached with the mail. Then, click ***Open*** button. Finally, click on ***Attach Files*** button. (after this wait for some time)

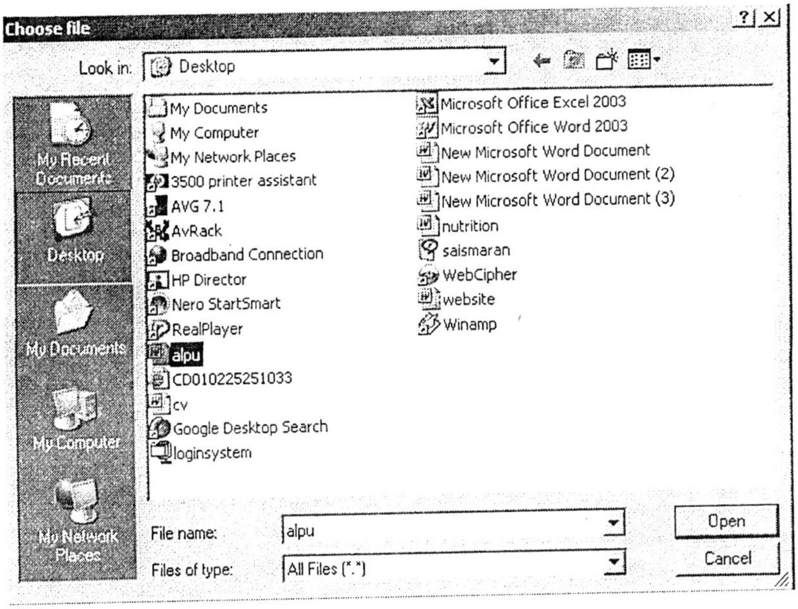

Step 4: Then, the following message is displayed indicating you that the required files have been attached with the e-mail message. Finally, click ***Continue to Message*** button.

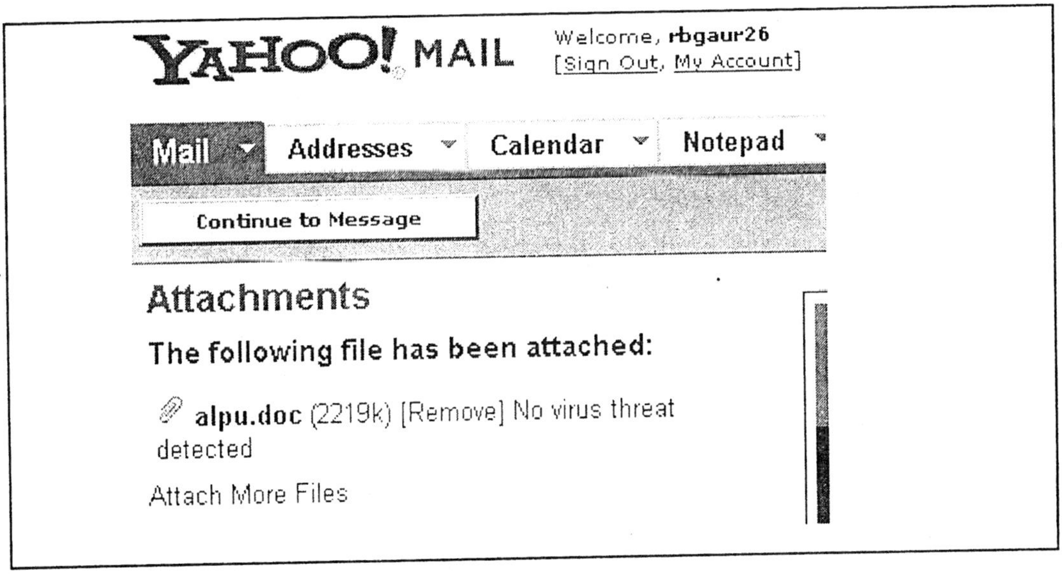

Step 5: The name of the attachment file is displayed.[If you want to delete the attachment from the message itself. Then, click on ***Remove*** hyperlink displayed along side with the name of attached file.] Finally, to send the message with attachment, simply click on ***Send*** button.

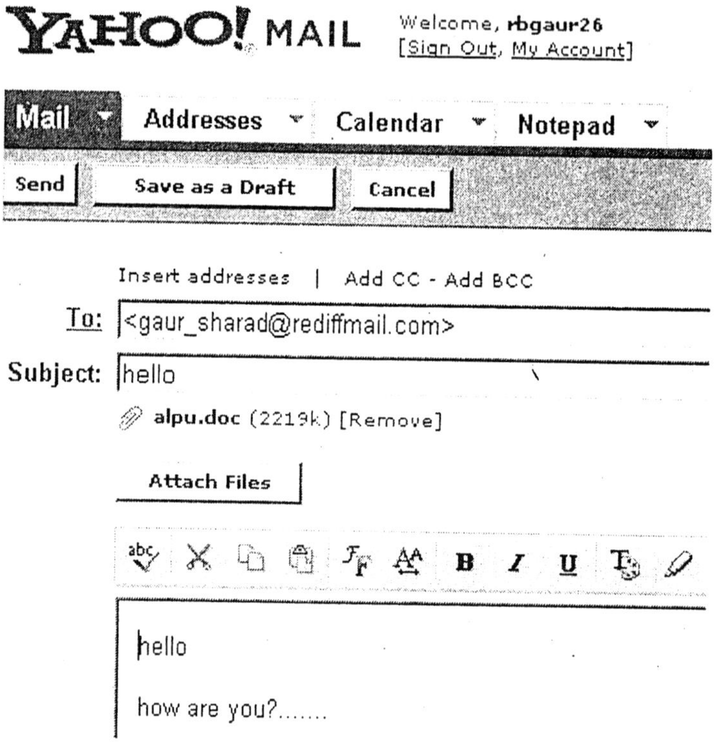

How to delete Mails from Inbox

Step 1: Select the checkboxes of the desired mail that you want to delete.

Step 2: Then, click ***Delete*** button.

(It means by selecting multiple checkboxes at the same time, you can delete them at once by clicking ***Delete button.)***

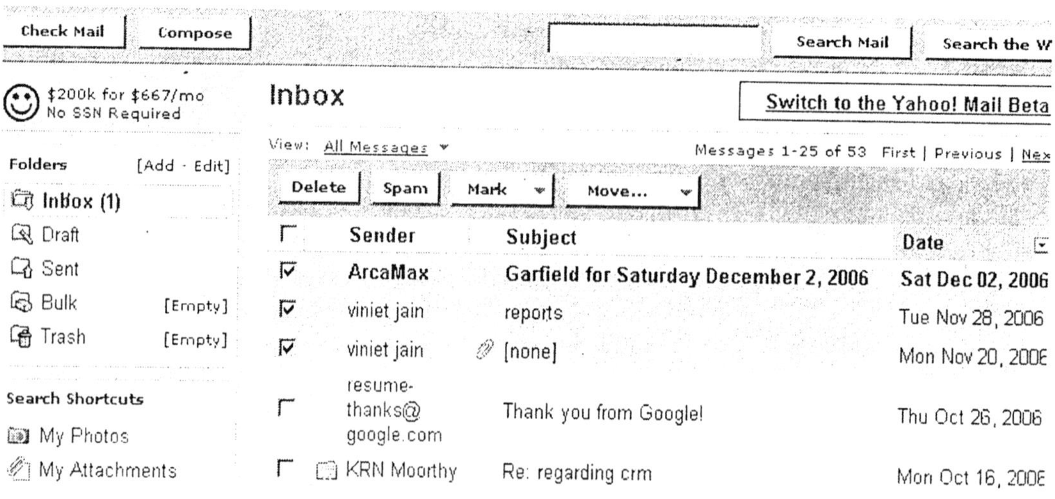

newtopic How to check Mails (or receive mails)

Step 1: Sign-in your mail account by entering username and password.

Step 2: Click ***Inbox*** hyperlink or click ***Check Mail*** button. Then, all the mails send to you are displayed.

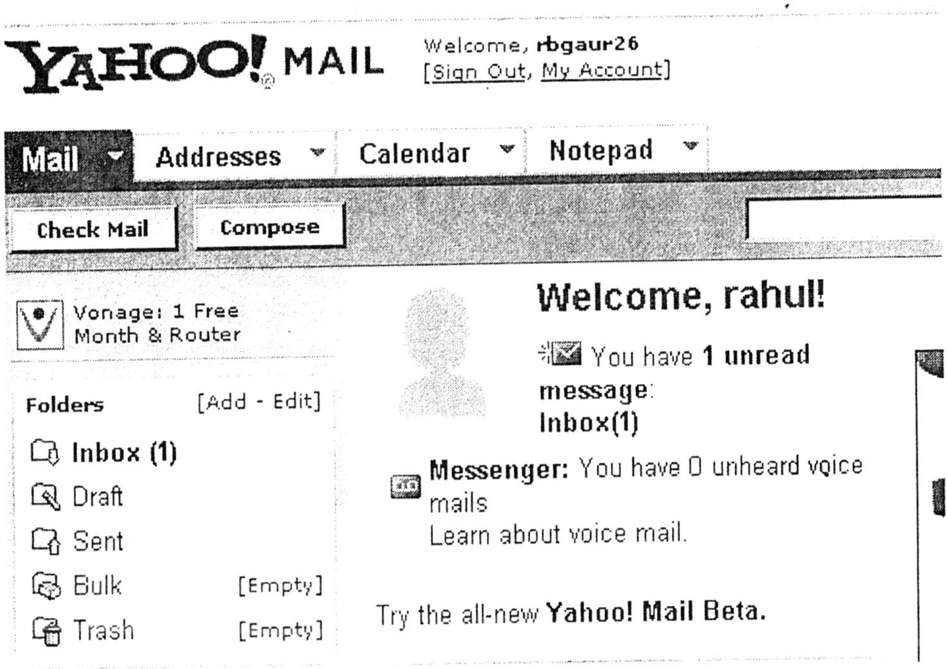

Step 3: Click on the ***Subject*** of the mail that you want to view. (or check)

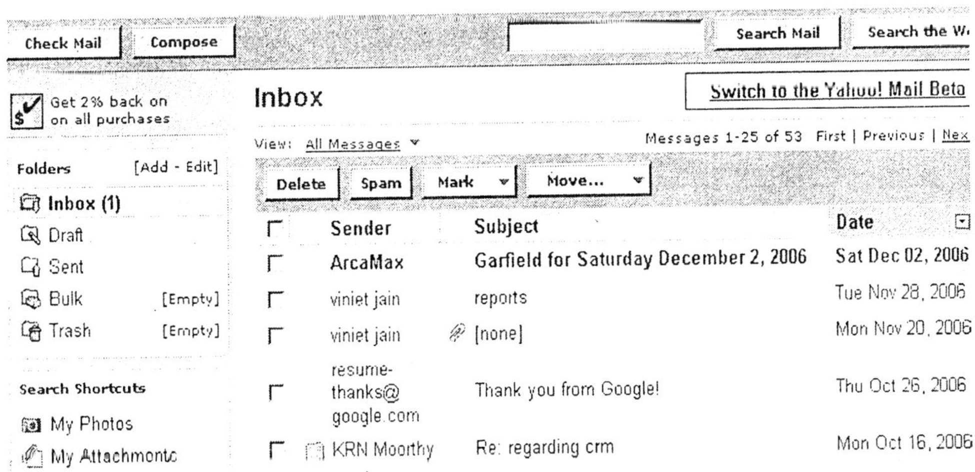

LIST OF WEBSITE ADDRESSES (URLs) & E-MAIL IDs OF HOTELS IN METROPOLITAN CITIES OF INDIA

DELHI

☆☆☆☆☆ FIVE STAR DELUXE HOTELS

Sno	Hotel Name	Website Addresses	E-mail Addresses
1	ASHOK HOTEL	www.theashokgroup.com	ashoknd@ndb.vsnl.net.in
2	CENTAUR HOTEL	www.centaurhotels.com	centaur@ndf.vsnl.net.in
3	CROWNE PLAZA SURYA	www.sixcontinentalhotel.com	suryahot@ndf.vsnl.net.in
4	HYATT REGENCY	http://www.delhi.hyatt.com	hrdelhi@hyattintl.com
5	INTERCONTINENTAL EROS	www.intercontinental.com	del-nehruplace@interconti.com
6	INTERCONTINENTAL THE GRAND	www.thegrandhotels.net	newdelhi@interconti.com
7	ITC HOTEL MAURYA SHERATON & TOWERS	www.welcomgroup.com	mauryaguest@hotmail.com
8	JAYPEE VASANT CONTINENTAL	www.jaypeehotels.com	hvc@del3.vsnl.net.in
9	LE-MERIDIEN	www.lemeridien-newdelhi.com	info@lemeridien-newdelhi.com
10	RADISSON HOTEL	www.radisson.com	raddel@del2.vsnl.net.in
11	SHANGRI-LA HOTEL	www.shangri-la.com	sind@shangri-la.com

12	TAJ PALACE HOTEL	tajhotels.com	palace.delhi@tajhotels .com
13	THE GRAND	www.thegrandnewdelhi .com	reservation@unison hotels.com
14	THE IMPERIAL	www.theimperialindia.com	luxury@theimperial india.com
15	THE METROPOLITAN HOTEL NIKKO	www.nikkohotels.com	nikko@hotelnikkodelhi.com
17	THE OBEROI	www.oberoihotels.com	reservations@ oberoidel.com
18	THE PARK	www.theparkhotels.com	gm.del@thepark hotels.com
19	THE TAJ MAHAL HOTEL	www.tajhotels.com	tmhbe@tajhotels.com
20	UPPAL'S ORCHID- AN ECOTEL HOTEL	www.uppalsorchidhotel .com	info@uppalsorchid hotel.com

☆☆☆☆☆ FIVE STAR HOTELS

Sno	Hotel Name	Website Addresses	E-mail Addresses
1	HOTEL SAMRAT	www.theashokgroup.com	hotelsamrat1@yahoo.co.in
2	JAYPEE SIDDHARTH	www.jaypeehotels.com	jhl@del2.vsnl.net.in
3	THE AMBASSADOR HOTEL	www.tajhotels.com	
4	THE CLARIDGES	www.claridges.com	info@claridges.com
5	THE QUTAB HOTEL	www.qutabhotel.com	qutabhotel@qutabhotel .com

☆☆☆☆ FOUR STAR HOTELS

Sno	Hotel Name	Website Addresses	E-mail Addresses
1	HOTEL ALKA	www.hotelalka.com	hotelalka@vsnl.com
2	HOTEL CITY PARK	www.hotelcitypark.com	hotelcitypark@vsnl.net
3	HOTEL DIPLOMAT		diplomat@nda.vsnl.net.in
4	HOTEL JANPATH	http://travel.vsnl.com/ hoteljanpath	janpath@ndf.vsnl.net.in

5	HOTEL MARINA	www.hotelmarina.com	hotelmarina@airtel broadband.in
6	MAIDENS HOTEL	www.oberoihotels.com	bsparmar@tomdel.com
7	THE CONNAUGHT	www.hotelconnaught delhi.com	PROMINENT.HOTELS@ gems.vsnl.net.in
8	THE HANS PLAZA	hansgroup.com	hansotel@nde.vsnl.net.in

☆ ☆ ☆ THREE STAR HOTELS

Sno	Hotel Name	Website Addresses	E-mail Addresses
1	GRAND SARTAJ	www.maharanigroupof hotels.com	grandsartaj3216@ yahoo.co.in
2	HOTEL BROADWAY	www.booadwaydelhi.com	broadway@vsnl.net
3	HOTEL THE MANOR	www.themanordelhi.com	info@themanordelhi.com
4	HOTEL TOURIST DELUXE	www.schandgroup.com	touristdeluxe@vsnl.net
5	HOTEL VIKRAM	www.hotelvikram.com	hotelvikram@vsnl.com
6	NIRULA'S HOTEL	www.nirulas.com	delhihotel@nirulas.com
7	THE RETREAT MOTEL /RESORT	www.theretreatre sort.com	contact@theretreatre sort.com
8	YORK HOTEL	www.indiamart.com /hotelyork	hotelyork@yahoo.com

MUMBAI

☆ ☆ ☆ ☆ ☆ FIVE STAR DELUXE

Sno	Hotel Name	Website Addresses	E-mail Addresses
1	EASTERN INTERNATIONAL HOTEL	www.holidayinbombay .com	reserve@holidayinn bombay.com
2	GRAND HYATT	www.mumbai.grand. hyatt.com	granahyattmumbai@ hyattintl.com

3	HILTON TOWERS	www.mumbai.hilton.com	mumbai@trident-hilton.com
4	HYATT REGENCY	www.mumbai-regency.hyatt.com	hyattregencymumbai@hyattintl.com
5	INTERCONTINENTAL THE GRAND	www.intercontinental.com	mumbai@thegrandhotels.net
6	ITC HOTEL GRAND CENTRAL SHERATON & TOWERS	www.itcwelcomgroup.in	www.itcwelcomgroup.in
7	ITC HOTEL GRAND MARATHA SHERATON & TOWERS	www.welcomgroup.com	itcgrandmaratha@welcomgroup.com
8	JW MARRIOTT HOTEL	www.marriott.com	mail@jwmarriottmumbai.com
9	LE ROYAL MERIDIEN	www.leroyalmeridien-mumbai.com	lmmumbai@vsnl.com
10	MARRIOTT EXECUTIVE APARTMENTS & RENAISSANCE MUMBAI HOTEL & CONVENTION CENTRE	www.marriott.com	rhi.bomb.reservations@renaissancehotels.com
11	SUN-N-SAND	www.sunnsandhotel.com	reservations@sunnsandhotel.com
12	TAJ LANDS END	www.tajhotels.com	landsend.mumbai@tajhotels.com
13	TAJ PRESIDENT	www.tajhotels.com	
14	TAJ WELLINGTON MEWS	www.tajhotels.com	twmgm.bom@tajhotels.com
15	THE LEELA KEMPINSKI	www.theleela.com	reservations@theleela.com
17	THE OBEROI	www.oberoihotels.com	mohit.nirula@oberoi-mumbai.com
18	THE RESORT	www.theresortmumbai.com	the_resort@vsnl.com
19	THE RETREAT	www.krahejahospitality.com	retreat123@vsnl.net
20	THE TAJ MAHAL HOTEL	www.tajhotels.com	tmhresv.bom@tajhotels.com

☆☆☆☆☆ FIVE STAR HOTELS

Sno	Hotel Name	Website Addresses	E-mail Addresses
1	HOTEL MARINE PLAZA	www.hotelmarineplaza.com	hotelmarineplaza@vsnl.com
2	RAMADA PLAZA PALM GROVE	www.krahejahospitality.com	palmgrove@krahejahospitality.com
3	SEA PRINCESS	www.seaprincess.com	seaprincess@vsnl.com
4	THE ORCHID HOTEL	www.orchidhotel.com	ohmu@orchidhotel.com

☆☆☆☆ FOUR STAR DELUXE

Sno	Hotel Name	Website Addresses	E-mail Addresses
1	BEST WESTERN THE EMERALD	www.theemerald.com	info@theemerald.com
2	FARIYAS HOTEL	www.fariyas.com	info@fariyas.com
3	HOTEL BAWA INTERNATIONAL	www.bawahotels.com	sales@bewahotels.com
4	HOTEL MIDTOWN PRITAM	www.pritamhotels.com	pritam@bom3.vsnl.net.in
5	KOHINOOR CONTINENTAL	www.kohinoorgroup.co.in	info@kohinoor-group.com
6	RAMEE GUESTLINE HOTEL	www.ramee-group.com	rameeguestlinedadar@rediffmail.com
7	RITZ HOTEL		ritz_hotel@vsnl.net
8	THE AMBASSADOR	www.ambassadorindia.com	sales@ambassadorindia.com
9	THE MIRADOR HOTEL	www.themirador.com	themirador@themirador.com
10	THE SHALIMAR HOTEL	www.theshalimarhotel.com	theshalimarhotel@vsnl.com
11	WEST END HOTEL	www.westendhotelmumbai.com	westhotel@hathway.com

☆ ☆ ☆ THREE STAR HOTELS

Sno	Hotel Name	Website Addresses	E-mail Addresses
1	ASCOT HOTEL	www.ascothotel.com	ascothotel@vsnl.com
2	ASTORIA HOTEL		astoria@hathway.com
6	CITIZEN HOTEL	www.citizenhotelmumbai.com	citizen@vsnl.com
7	DAYS IN NAVI MUMBAI	www.daysindia.com	manjeet@bom3.vsnl.net.in
8	EXECUTIVE ENCLAVE	www.executiveenclave .com	enclave@vsnl.com
9	GOLDEN MANOR	www.goldenmanor.com	contact@goldenmanor.com
10	HOTEL AIRLINK	www.hotelairlink.com	unversal@vsnl.com
11	HOTEL AJANTA	www.benluxhotels.in	hotelajanta@vsnl.com
12	HOTEL ATITHI		atithi@bom8.vsnl.net.in
13	HOTEL BENZY PALACE		benzypal@vsnl.net
14	HOTEL COMFORTINN HERITAGE	www.comfortinnheritage .com	reservation@comfort innheritage.com
15	HOTEL FOUR SEASONS		season4@bom3.vsnl.net.in
16	HOTEL GODWIN	www.cybersols.com \godwin	godwinht@vsnl.in
17	HOTEL HIGHWAY VIEW	www.shikarahospitality .com	info@shikarahosp itality.com
18	HOTEL KING'S INTERNATIONAL	www.kinginternational .com	kings@bom5.vsnl.net.in
19	HOTEL PARLE INTERNATIONAL	info@hotelparle international.com	
20	HOTEL RAMEE INTERNATIONAL	www.ramee-group.com	
21	HOTEL RANG SHARDA	www.rangsharda.org	hotelrangsharda@ vsnl.com
22	HOTEL SUN-N-SHEEL		hotelsunsheel@vsnl.net
23	HOTEL TRANSIT	www.hoteltransit.in	transit1@vsnl.com
25	K STARS HOTEL	www.kstarshotel.com	kstarshotel@rediffmail.com
26	REGENCY HOTEL		regencyhotel@vsnl.com

27	REGENT HOTEL	www.regentmumbai.com	hregent@vsnl.com
28	RESIDENCY HOTEL	www.residencymumbai.com	residencyhotel@vsnl.net
29	RODAS	www.rodashotel.com	info@rodashotel.com
30	SEA PALACE HOTEL	www.seapalacehotel.com	seapalacehotel@vsnl.net
31	SUPREME HERITAGE	hotelsupremeheritage.com	supremeheritage@vsnl.net
32	THE GORDON HOUSE HOTEL	www.ghhotel.com	dutymanager@gh hotel.com
33	THE RESIDENCE HOTEL & CONVENTION CENTRE	www.theresidence hotel.com	reservation@there sidencehotel.com

CHENNAI

☆ ☆ ☆ ☆ ☆ FIVE STAR DELUXE

Sno	Hotel Name	Website Addresses	E-mail Addresses
1	ITC HOTEL PARK SHERATON AND TOWERS	www.itcwelcomgroup.com	gm.park@itchotels.co.in
2	LE ROYAL MERIDIEN	www.leroyalmeridien-chennai.com	reservation@leroyal meridien-chennai.com
3	TAJ COROMANDEL		coromandel.chennai@taj hotels.com
4	THE PARK	www.theparkhotels.com	

☆ ☆ ☆ ☆ ☆ FIVE STAR HOTELS

Sno	Hotel Name	Website Addresses	E-mail Addresses
1	CHOLA SHERATON	www.welcomgroup.com	chola@md2.vsnl.net.in
2	FISHERMAN'S COVE	www.tajhotels.com	
3	RADISSON GREAT HOTEL	www.radisson.com	radissongrt@vsnl.net
4	TAJ CONNEMARA HOTEL	www.tajhotels.com	tajcon@giasmd01. vsnl.net.in

5	THE ACCORD METROPOLITAN HOTEL	www.theaccord metropolitan.com	hotel@theaccord metropolitan.com
6	THE RAINTREE	www.raintreehotels.com	mail@raintreehotels.com
7	TRIDENT HILTON, CHENNAI	www.trident-hilton.com	sanju.soni@trident-hilton.com

☆ ☆ ☆ ☆ FOUR STAR HOTELS

Sno	Hotel Name	Website Addresses	E-mail Addresses
1	AMBASSADOR PALLAVA	www.ambassadorindia .com	pallava@ambassador india.com
2	BENZ PARK TULIP	www.benzzpark.com	reservation@benz zpark.com
3	GREEN PARK	www.hotelgreenpark.com	chennai@hotel greenpark.com
4	GRT GRAND	www.grtgrand.com	admin@grtgrand.com
5	HOTEL PRESIDENT	www.presidenn.com	reserve@presidenn.com
6	QUALITY INN SABARI	www.qualityinnsabari.com	sabariinn@vsnl.net
7	RAMADA RAJPARK	www.ramadachennai.com	reservation@ramada chennai.com
8	SAVERA HOTEL	www.saverahotels.com	hotsave@md2.vsnl.net.in
9	THE RESIDENCY TOWERS	www.theresidency.com	restowers@vsnl.net

☆ ☆ ☆ THREE STAR HOTELS

Sno	Hotel Name	Website Addresses	E-mail Addresses
1	AADITHYA HOTEL	www.aadithya.com	aadithyamdsind@eth.net
2	AMBICA EMPIRE	www.ambicaempire.com	ambicaem@md4. vsnl.net.in
3	AMPA CRYSTAL INN		ampa@touchtelindia.net
4	BEVERLY HOTEL	www.beverlyhotels.com	beverly@vsnl.net
5	BREEZE HOTEL	www.breezehotel.com	breeze@vsnl.com
6	COURTYARD BY MARRIOTT	www.marriott.com	cy.maacy.asst.reserva tions.mgr@marritt.com

7	DAYS IN DECCAN PLAZA	www.deccanhotels.com	info@deccanhotels.com
8	GRAND ORIENT	www.empeehotels.com	empeegrandorient@ vsnl.com
9	HOTEL DEE CEE MANOR	www.dcmanor.in	dcmanor@vsnl.com
10	HOTEL KANCHI	www.hotelkanchi.com	reservations@ hotelkanchi.com
11	HOTEL MARS	www.hotelmars.net	hotelmars@yahoo.com
13	HOTEL PALMGROVE	www.ballalgrouphotels. com	kmballal@vsnl.com
14	HOTEL ROYAL PLAZA	www.hotelroyalplaza online.com	reservations@hotel royalplazaonline.com
15	HOTEL SHAN ROYAL	www.hotelshanroyal.com	contact@hotelshan royal.com
16	HOTEL SHELTER	www.hotelshelter.com	shelter@vsnl.com
17	MADRAS HOTEL ASHOKA	www.ballalgrouphotels .com	**madras** ashoka **@vsnl.net**
18	NEW VICTORIA HOTEL	www.hotelnewvictoria .com	hotelnewvictoria@vsnl.com
19	NEW WOODLANDS HOTEL	www.newwoodlands.com	newwoodland@vsnl.com
20	RADHA PARK INN	www.sarovarparkplaza.com	rpi@sarovarhotels.com
21	SRM HOTEL		royalsouthern@vsnl.com
22	THE ARUNA	www.arunahotels.com	hotelaruna@ touchtelindia.net
23	THE MARINA TOWERS	www.cimtchennai.com	cimt@cimarinatowers.com
24	THE RESIDENCY	www.theresidency.com	resmds@vsnl.com
25	THE SINDOORI HOTEL	www.sindoori.com	info@sindoori.com
26	THE VIJAY PARK	www.thevijaypark.com	vj-park@hotmail.com

KOLKATTA

☆☆☆☆☆ FIVE STAR DELUXE HOTELS

Sno	Hotel Name	Website Addresses	E-mail Addresses
1	HYATT REGENCY	www.kolkata.regency.hyatt.com	Kolka-Hrk@hyattintl.com
2	ITC HOTEL SONAR BANGLA SHERATON & TOWERS	www.welcomgroup.com	itcsonarbangla@welcomgroup.com
3	OBEROI GRAND	www.oberoihotels.com	reservations@oberoi-cal.com
4	TAJ BENGAL	www.tajhotels.com	bengal.cal@tajhotels.com
5	THE PARK	www.theparkhotels.com	tpcl@theparkhotels.com

☆☆☆☆☆ FIVE STAR HOTELS

Sno	Hotel Name	Website Addresses	E-mail Addresses
1	HOTEL HINDUSTHAN INTERNATIONAL	www.hindusthan.com	reservation@hindusthan.com
2	MBD AIRPORT HOTEL		mbdhotelk@vsnl.net

☆☆☆☆ FOUR STAR HOTELS

Sno	Hotel Name	Website Addresses	E-mail Addresses
1	THE KENILWORTH	www.kenilworthhotels.com	kenilworthkol@kenilworthhotels.com
2	THE PEERLESS INN	www.peerlesshotels.com	pik@sarovarparkplaza.com

☆☆☆ THREE STAR HOTELS

Sno	Hotel Name	Website Addresses	E-mail Addresses
1	HOTEL RUTT DEEN		ruttdeen@vsnl.com
2	LYTTON HOTEL	www.lyttonhotelindia.com	lytton@giascl01.vsnl.net.in
3	THE FFORT- A RADISSON	www.ffort.com	ffortcal@cal.vsnl.net.in

LIST OF BEST TOP TEN WEBSITES (URLs) OF INDIA

TRAVEL SITES

S.No	Site Name
1.	IndianHoliday.com
2.	MakeMytrip.com
3.	Indiaprofile.com
4.	Travelport.com
5.	Cleartrip.com
6.	IndiaTravelog.com
7.	Indiaatitsbest.com
8.	India-tourism.com
9.	Palacesonwheels.com
10.	Expresstravelandtourism.com

HOTEL SITES

S.No	Site Name
1.	Tajhotels.com
2.	Hotelskerala.com
3.	Itcwelcomgroup.in
4.	Travelmasti.com
5.	Cruisingindia.com

6.	Hotelspointindia.com
7.	Indiaatitsbest.com
8.	India-tourism.com
9.	Palacesonwheels.com
10.	Expresstravelandtourism.com

MAP SITES

S.No	Site Name
1.	Mapsofindia.com
2.	Worldmapstore.com
3.	Indiamapstore.com
4.	Maps.eicherworld.com
5.	Indiamap.com
6.	Lonelyplanetindia.com
7.	Mapblast.com
8.	Maptell.com
9.	Maps-india.com
10.	India.gov.in/maps

NEWS SITES

S.No	Site Name
1.	Aajtak.com
2.	Zeenews.com
3.	Ndtv.com
4.	starnews.indya.com
5.	Ibnlive.com
6.	Samachar.com

7.	Saharasamay.com
8.	Ddinews.gov.in
9.	Timesnow.tv
10.	Headlinesindia.com

EDUCATION SITES

S.No	Site Name
1.	Indiaedu.com
2.	Planetvidya.com
3.	Indiaeducation.info/
4.	Zeelearn.com
5.	Vidyaonline.net
6.	Indiaresults.com
7.	Esiksha.com
8.	Youngbuzz.com
9.	Indiaeducation.info
10.	Login4career.com

JOB SITES

S.No	Site Name
1.	Naukri.com
2.	Monsterindia.com
3.	Timesjobs.com
4.	Cybermediadice.com
5.	Clickjobs.com
6.	Placementindia.com
7.	Jobsahead.com
8.	Naukrihub.com
9.	Careerkhazana.com
10.	Itplacementsindia.com

CRICKET SITES

S.No	Site Name
1.	Cricinfo.com
2.	Cricketvideo.com
3.	Cricket.123india.com
4.	Cricketscorelive.com
5.	Cricketindex.com
6.	Cricket.indiatimes.com
7.	Cricketfundas.com
8.	Cric8.com
9.	Cricmania.com
10.	Icc-cricket.com

MUSIC SITES

S.No	Site Name
1.	Raaga.com
2.	Musicindiaonlinc.com
3.	Bollywoodmusic.com
4.	Themusicmagazine.com
5.	Indianmelody.com
6.	Musiconnet.com
7.	Music-today.com
8.	Dishant.com
9.	Indiamp3.com
10.	Bollywoodworld.com

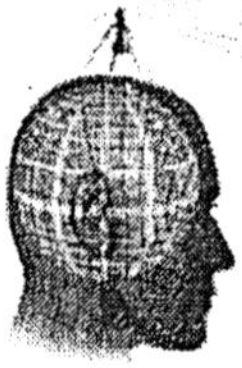

ADVANCED QUESTION BANK

- ? Sample Theory Questions
- ? Viva-Voice Questions & Answers
- ? G. Proficiency Computer Questions
- ? IT QUIZ

Sample Theory Questions

1. What is memory? Write down the main difference between the primary and the secondary memory.
2. What do you understand by the DOS internal and external commands? Give three examples for each along their syntax.
3. What is the function of CPU in a computer system? Name the parts of CPU.
4. How can you perform the following operations in Ms-WORD-
   a) Find and replace text
   b) Correct spellings in your document
   c) Change font size and style of a word
   d) Underline a Word
   e) Centre alignment of a line
   f) Drop Cap in a Paragraph
5. Write down what the following commands will perform-
   a) DIR /P
   b) CD..
   c) DEL *
   d) MD MYDIR
   e) FORMAT A:
   f) EDIT XYZ.TXT
6. Answer the following questions in one line-
   a) What is a web browser?
   b) Name any two web browsers.
   c) What is URL?
   d) What is the purpose of Recycle bin in Windows 2000
   e) What is a modem?
   f) What is search engine?

7. Define Computer. What are the various characteristics of Computer?
8. What do you understand by Hardware and Software? Give two examples of each.
9. Define Input and Output Devices. List three examples of each.
10. Draw a neat and labeled block diagram of computer.
11. Differentiate-
    1. RAM & ROM
    2. Application Software & System Software
    3. Interpreter and Compiler
    4. CUI and GUI
    5. Internal Commands & External Commands
    6. Impact Printer and Non-Impact Printer
12. Give the classification of computers-
    1. On the basis of Size and Speed
    2. On the basis of Computations Performed
13. Briefly describe the history of computers. Give advantages & disadvantages of various generations of computer.
14. List out various applications and limitations of computer.
15. What is Ms-Office? Name various constituent programs of Ms-Office.
16. Explain in brief-
    1. Formatting
    2. Drop Cap
    3. Mail Merge
    4. Word Processor
17. What is Ms-WORD? Draw a neat & labeled diagram of WORD window.
18. What do you understand by Editing? Also, give the shortcut keys used for Cut, Copy & Paste. Is Cut-Paste & Copy-Paste are the same kind of operations? Justify your answer.
19. Contrast between Undo & Redo. Also explain in brief, how you can apply Change Case option to change different types of cases of the same text.
20. Explain in brief-
    a) Excel
    b) Workbook
    c) Worksheet
    d) Cell
21. What is Ms-Excel/ Spreadsheet? List any five features. Also, draw a neat-labeled diagram of Ms-Excel Window.

22. What do you understand by Auto sum? How can you apply this feature- Explain?

23. Describe Auto fill feature? Explain how to create a -

    a) Even number series

    b) Jan, Feb, Mar..... series

    c) a list where you have the same item copied throughout the list e.g. 1,1,1,1,

24. Explain in brief-

    a) PowerPoint

    b) Slides

    c) Speaker Notes & Use

    d) DBMS

25. What is FoxPro? Also explain Sorting & Indexing in detail.

26. What do you understand by Views in PowerPoint? List them and describe briefly about each view.

27. Give purpose and syntax of the following commands -

    1. USE
    2. MODI STRU
    3. SKIP
    4. CREATE

28. Explain in brief-

    a) Word Processing

    b) Ms-Office

    c) Find & Replace

    d) Cut, Copy & Paste

29. What is Ms-WORD? List any five features. Also, draw a neat-labeled diagram of WORD Window.

30. List different cases available in Ms-WORD and give appropriate examples of each case.

31. List different types of alignment and draw a diagram of a page to show each type of alignment.

32. What do you understand by Referencing? Name them & also explain about it's various types.

33. What do you understand by-

    (i) Secondary Storage Devices

    (ii) Output Devices

34. Draw hierarchical representation of term computer.

35. Define the term Computer. Explain it's functioning using a block diagram.

36. Differentiate between the following-
    a) Software and Hardware
    b) RAM and ROM
37. List the following -
    a) Any three input devices
    b) Any three output devices
    c) Any three storage devices
38. Give full forms of the following-
    a) UPS
    b) CPU
    c) ALU
    d) CU
    e) CD
39. Explain in brief-
    a) Protection in Excel
    b) Function
40. What are Charts? Give the suitable example and option used for the same. Explain in detail.
41. Give-
    a) Address of first cell
    b) Mouse Pointer shapes and use
    c) By default extension of spreadsheet
    d) Max. no. of sheets in a workbook
    e) By default no. of rows
    f) Address of last cell
42. Explain in brief-
    a) Customized Auto fill series
    b) Formatting Cells in Excel
43. What is the meaning of Freeze in Excel? Give the suitable example and option used for freezing.
44. What are the special features of Excel? How many sheets (maximum), columns, and rows you have in Excel.
45. Differentiate MS-WORD & MS-EXCEL

46. Give-
    a) By default name of workbook
    b) By default name of worksheet
    c) By default extension of workbook
    d) Max. no. of sheets in a workbook
    e) By default no. of rows
    f) By default no. of columns
47. Give suitable guidelines to a person who wishes to create a presentation using PowerPoint.
48. Give one word answer for - "What is FoxPro?" What is the extension of a database file?
49. Give the commands for the following -
    a) Creating a table in FoxPro
    b) Opening a existing database file
    c) Modifying the structure of a database file
    d) For editing a database file in a tabular form
    e) For temporary deletion of database file
    f) For permanent deletion of database file
    g) For exiting out of FoxPro
50. Explain in brief-
    a) Mail Merge
    b) Drop Cap
51. Give the shortcut keys for the following-
    a) Cut
    b) Copy
    c) Paste
    d) Spell Check
    e) Creating a new document
    f) Accessing File menu
52. Give the DOS commands for the following -
    a) Creating a Directory
    b) Changing a Directory
    c) Deleting a Directory
    d) Creating a file
    e) Viewing contents of file
    f) Listing subdirectories and files
    g) For Moving a file

53. Give one word answer-
    a) Extension of Document
    b) Extension of Spreadsheet
    c) Extension of Database
    d) Shortcut-key for Spell Check
    e) Function for performing ranking of students in a list
    f) Function for evaluating multiplication of given numbers
54. What is an Operating system. Explain it's various characteristics.
55. What is Booting? Differentiate between warm booting & cold booting.
56. Differentiate between DOS & WINDOWS. Is there any difference between the terms 'WINDOW' & 'WINDOWS'? If yes, then briefly explain it.
57. Explain the steps required for performing-
    a) Creating a short-cut of a file/folder on the desktop
    b) Restoring any deleted item from recycle bin
    c) Deleting file/folder
    d) Copying from hard disk drive to floppy disk
    e) Copying from floppy disk to hard disk
58. Write short notes on-
    a) Recycle bin
    b) My Computer
    c) Windows Explorer
    d) Desktop
59. Give one line answer-
    a) In an article, the first letter is capitalized, stylized & made decorative. Name this feature.
    b) When you type continuously, the cursor automatically gets shifted to next line. Name this feature.
    c) The information displayed at the bottom of the page is called______.
    d) The buttons Bold, Italic & Underline has been given some specific name. What is it?
    e) Give some other name for Print Preview.
60. What do you understand by Bullets & Numbering in MS-WORD. How can you apply bullets on desired text. Can you apply picture bullets also?
61. Explain the following with examples-
    (i) Toolbar
    (ii) Checkbox
    (iii) Format Painter
    (iv) Superscript
    (v) Subscript

62. Give the shortcut keys for the following-
    a) Accessing menu
    b) Selecting a word.
    c) Selecting a sentence
    d) Making desired text bold
    e) Restarting computer
63. What do you understand by 'Header' & 'Footer'? Which option is used to set the header and footer of a document? Can we have different header for odd and even pages? If yes, then name only the option to do the same
64. How computers play an important role in Hospitality industry. Explain with suitable examples.
65. Today computer has become part of life and man has become fully dependant on computers. Is it good for man? Discuss.
66. Computer helps human being in taking certain decisions, even then its intelligence is called "Artificial Intelligence" why?
67. Computer and man though fully dependent on each other even then both tries to superior over one another. Comment.
68. Explain the following terms-
    a) Server
    b) Client
    c) Communication cable
    d) TCP/IP
    e) Modem
69. Define Networking of computers. What are its advantages and disadvantages? What are the different types of topologies used in LAN? What type of topology would you suggest installing in your organization and why?
70. Give features of the following-
    a) LAN
    b) MAN
    c) WAN
71. What is the importance of Management Information System in a hotel? Explain with examples.
72. Describe the type of computer setup a modern hotel requires to boost its performance. Discuss both software packages and hardware.

73. Explain the following-
    a) Virus
    b) Anti-Virus
    c) High Level Language
    d) Assembler
74. What is the difference between an application program and a system program? Can an application program run in a computer if the computer does not have a system program? Specify the reason to support your answer.
75. Expand the following-
    a) OCR
    b) OMR
    c) UPS
    d) CPU
    e) CU
    f) LAN
    g) WAN
    h) MAN
    i) MHZ
    j) GB
    k) VDU
    l) DTP
    m) DBMS
    n) WYSIWYG
    o) ASCII
    p) DOS
76. What is information? What is the difference between information and the raw data? Highlight the important aspects of information needed by managers.
77. Write down any HTML script. Explain the purpose of all the lines written in your HTML document. Your HTML document must use at least five different tags.
78. Write down the advantages of computer networking. What are some of the factors that determine whether a communication system is a LAN, MAN or WAN.

79. What is the purpose of following files in DOS-
    a) Autoexec.bat
    b) Config.sys
    c) IO.SYS and MSDOS.SYS
    d) DISKCOPY.COM
    e) XCOPY.COM
80. What is search engine? Name any two search engines. Also explain that what you mean by advanced searching.
81. What is the Mail Merge facility in Ms-WORD 2000? Explain the process of creating documents with the help of mail merge facility.
82. Name the components of a traditional communication system.
83. What do you understand by user interface? Write down the differences between the graphical using interface and command line interface.
84. Define what you mean by Management Information System. What role does MIS lay in an organization?
85. What is the scope and purpose of an Information System?
86. State the difference between MIS and a computer system.
87. Discuss why management needs information. Is it possible for the management of an organization to make effective decisions without the aid of an information system? Discuss.
88. Describe the three main categories into which information can be classified.
89. Explain in brief the basic principles that should be considered while designing an organization structure.
90. What are the various methods of data and information collection?
91. Explain the concept of database? List the advantages of DBMS over file processing system.
92. What is the purpose of Decision Support Systems in MIS? List few characteristics of DSS.
93. What are Artificial Intelligence System?
94. What is the concept of Enterprise Resource Planning? Discuss some of the basic features of ERP.
95. What do you understand by-
    a) Feasibility Study
    b) Cost-Benefit analysis
96. What is SSAD? What are the various phases of SDLC (System Development Life cycle)? Explain in brief.
97. Define System. List and explain various characteristics of a system.
98. What are Data Models? Give the significance of different data models.
99. How is system analysis approach different in new system requirement as against an existing one?
100. List and describe various information systems used in Hotel industry.

VIVA-VOICE QUESTIONS AND ANSWERS

Q1. What is a Computer?

A1. Computer is an electronic device that accepts input, process it to produce desired output.

Q2. What is the full form of Computer?

A2. **C**ommon **O**perating **M**achine **P**urposely **U**sed for **T**raining **E**ducation & **R**esearch

Q3. What is Input device? Give examples.

A3. Input device is a device which is used to enter (or feed) data into computer. ***Examples:*** Keyboard, Mouse, Scanner, Light Pen etc.

Q4. What is Output device? Give examples.

A4. Output device is a device which is used to display output (or processed result) to the user. ***Examples:*** Printer, Plotter, Monitor (Visual Display Unit or V.D.U)

Q5. What is Hardware? Give examples.

A5. Hardware refers to all the physical components of the computer (or we can say that all the tangible and visible components constitute Hardware) ***Example:*** CPU, Monitor, Keyboard, Printer etc.

Q6. What is Software? Give examples. What are the different types of software.

A6. Software is a set or collection of programs. ***Examples:*** Ms-Word, Excel, PowerPoint, Operating System (like Windows- XP, Vista, DOS, UNIX, LINUX etc)

Types: System software (that is used to control and manage the system related operations) and Application software (the software that serves a definite purpose for the end-user)

Q7. What is Memory? How many types of memory are there?

A7. Memory refers to the storage area which is used to store data and programs. It is of two types- Primary Memory and Secondary Memory.

Q8. What is Primary Memory?

A8. Primary memory refers to RAM, which is used to temporarily store the data.

Q9. *What is Secondary Memory?*

A9. Secondary memory is used to store the data permanently. ***Examples:*** CD, Floppy, Hard disk, Magnetic tapes.

Q10. *What is the smallest unit of measuring the capacity of memory?*

A10. Bytes (1 byte = 8 bits)

Q11. *Which is the largest unit of measuring the capacity of memory?*

A11. Terabyte (1 TB= 1024 GB)

Q12. *What are Bits and Bytes?*

A12. A bit refers to the binary digits. According to binary number system there are two binary digits 0 & 1, which are used to represent the characters. Binary code of each character is made up of 8 bits. A Byte is a group of 8 bits.

UNITS FOR MEASURING THE CAPACITY OF MEMORY	
1Byte	= 8 bits
1 KB (Kilobyte)	= 1024 bytes
1 MB (Megabyte)	= 1024 KB
1 GB (Gigabyte)	= 1024 MB
1 TB (Terabyte)	= 1024 GB

Q13. *Which has got the maximum storage capacity- CD, Floppy or Hard disk?*

A13. Hard disk

Q14. *Which has got the minimum storage capacity- CD, Floppy or Hard disk?*

A14. Floppy (only (1.44 MB)

Q15. *Describe the structure of floppy.*

A15. Floppy is divided into ***tracks*** and ***sectors.*** Floppy has ***concentric*** tracks.

Q16. *Describe the structure of CD.*

A16. CD (Compact disk) is also divided into ***tracks*** and ***sectors.*** CD has ***spiral*** tracks.

Q17. *Give Full forms-*

- **CD :** Compact disk
- **CPU :** Central Processing Unit
- **ALU :** Arithmetic and Logical Unit
- **UPS :** Uninterruptible Power Supply
- **CU :** Control Unit
- **DVD :** Digital Video Disk

- **RAM :** Random Access Memory
- **ROM:** Read Only Memory
- **PC:** Personal Computer
- **MICR:** Magnetic Ink Character Recognition
- **OCR:** Optical Character Reader
- **OBCR:** Optical Bar Code Reader
- **OMR:** Optical Mark Reader
- **WWW:** World Wide Web
- **RDBMS:** Relational Database Management System
- **CUI:** Character User Interface
- **GUI:** Graphical User Interface
- **LAN:** Local Area Network
- **MAN:** Metropolitan Area Network
- **WAN:** Wide Area Network

Q17. Give the classification of computer on the basis of size and speed.

A17. Supercomputer ***e.g.*** **PARAM 10000**(largest size and highest speed), Mainframe, Minicomputer, Microcomputer or PC (smallest size and comparatively lowest speed)

Q18. Give the classification of computer on the basis of computations performed.

A18. Digital, Analog and Hybrid

Q19. Give one word for each-

- Computer used nowadays belongs to which category according to the above classification: **Microcomputer, Digital**
- Computer used nowadays belongs to which generation: **Fourth Generation**
- Technology used in fourth generation computers : **IC (Integrated Circuits) with VLSI (Very large scale integration)**
- Most Recently launched Operating System : **Windows Vista**
- Most Recently launched version of Ms-Office: **Ms-Office 2007**
- Computer generation on which research is continuously carrying on: **Fifth generation**
- Technology used in Fifth generation: **AI (Artificial Intelligence)**
- Fastest memory used in computers for enhancing processing capacity: ***Cache Memory***

Q20. Define each of the following in one line-

1. **Operating System:** It is a software that is used to control and manage the entire resources of the computer. It acts as an interface between

the computer and the user or you can say an interface between the hardware and software.

2. **Virus:** It is a program that infects and damages computer programs and files. It has the ability to replicate itself.
3. **Antivirus:** It is a program that is used to protect the data and programs from the infection caused by computer virus.
4. **Ms-Office:** It is a software package that consists of numerous application programs like Word, Excel, PowerPoint, Access etc.
5. **Ms-Word:** It is a word processor that is used for typing, editing and formatting of textual information.
6. **Ms-PowerPoint:** It is a program used to design presentation.
7. **Ms- Excel:** It is a spreadsheet that is used to process numbers.
8. **Ms- Access:** It is a RDBMS that is used to create and manage database.
9. **DTP:** It refers to Desktop Publishing.
10. **Corel Draw:** It is an application program that is used for the purpose of designing
11. **PageMaker:** It is an application program that is used to develop publications like brochures, books, thesis etc.
12. **Photoshop:** It is an application program that is used to create and edit images.
13. **ClipArt Gallery:** It is collection of bitmap images or pictures.
14. **WordArt:** It refers to decorative text.
15. **Drop Cap:** It refers to capitalized & decorative initial letter of paragraph.
16. **Mail Merge :** It is an important feature of Ms-Word using which large number of mails can be prepared quickly by merging the main document and data source.
17. **Function: is** the named set of instructions. A Function accepts some arguments and returns a value.
18. **Referencing:** Referencing means addressing of cell. Types- Absolute, Mixed & Relative
19. **Presentation:** It is a collection of slides.
20. **Slide:** A slide is an individual page of presentation.
21. **Document:** Word file is called document.
22. **Workbook:** Excel file is called workbook
23. **Design Template:** These are the pre-designed formats of a presentation.
24. **Auto content Wizard:** It is a wizard that is used to develop presentation with predefined contents.
25. **Hyperlink:** It refers to hypertext to which a certain link is attached.

26. **Superscript:** It refers to a text that is reduced in size and raised above the normal text.
27. **Subscript:** It refers to a text that is reduced in size and lowered below the normal text.
28. **Clipboard:** It is a temporary storage area that is used to hold cut or copied items.
29. **RDBMS:** It is a software that is used to create and manage database.
30. **Database:** It is an organized collection of records.
31. **Tables:** Table is a collection of records.
32. **Forms:** Forms are used for entering records in tables.
33. **Queries:** Queries are used to retrieve particular data from one or more table.
34. **Reports:** Reports are used to display retrieved data to the user.
35. **Network:** A network is a collection of computers that are connected in a way so that they can communicate with each other.
36. **Topology:** Topology refers to the way in which computers are arranged in a network.
37. **Internet:** Internet is the collection of numerous computer networks worldwide.
38. **Intranet:** Intranet is an in-house computer network within a company. Enterprise or a closed user group that uses the standard internet technologies, software and protocols.
39. **Window:** It is a rectangular area on the screen that is used to display application programs.
40. **WINDOWS:** It refers to an Operating System.
41. **RAM:** It is the primary memory of computer that is used to store the data and programs temporarily. It is volatile in nature (if power turned off, contents get automatically deleted)
42. **ROM:** It is a permanent memory that contains the instructions of starting the computer (booting)
43. **Editing:** It means changes or modifications like cut, copy, paste, undo etc
44. **Formatting :** It refers to the change in appearance of the text.

Q21. FILES & EXTENSIONS

Word Document	.doc
Excel Workbook	.xls
PowerPoint Presentation	.ppt
Access Database	.mdb
PageMaker	.pmd
Corel Draw	.cdr
Photoshop	.psd

Q22. SHORTCUT KEYS

Closing an application window	Alt + F4
Restarting Computer	Ctrl + Alt + Del
Checking Spelling and Grammar	F7
Cut	Ctrl + X
Copy	Ctrl + C
Paste	Ctrl + V
Find	Ctrl + F
Replace	Ctrl + H
Bold	Ctrl + B
Italic	Ctrl + I
Underline	Ctrl + U
Undo	Ctrl + Z
Repeat	Ctrl + Y
Saving a file	Ctrl + S

GENERAL PROFICIENCY COMPUTER QUESTIONS

✪ True/False

1. By default name of document is Document1.
2. For deleting selected text, Enter key is used.
3. Table's grid can be made hidden using Properties option in Table menu.
4. Print Preview is used for viewing the document before printing.
5. Spelling & Grammar check can be invoked using F7 shortcut key.
6. Save & Save As options have no difference at all.
7. Format painter is used to apply the format of selected text onto another text.
8. Bold is not a toggle button.
9. One document consists of only 20 pages.
10. Hard copies refers to the printed pages.
11. The extension of a file is always made up of three letters.
12. There are 258 columns in a worksheet.
13. Ms-EXCEL is not a constituent of Ms-Office.
14. For selecting an entire column, we click on the first cell of a column.
15. The columns are labeled as A1, A2, A3.......& so on.
16. Ctrl + X is used to paste any item i.e. text or picture that had been cut or copied.
17. Workbook1 is the by default name of the workbook.
18. The number of maximum sheets contained in a workbook is 240.
19. Workbook in Excel is analogous to Document in Word.
20. Excel is also termed as Word processor.
21. The extension of a file is always made up of five letters.
22. The maximum number of slides in a presentation is 444.
23. Ms-PowerPoint is not a constituent of Ms-Office.

24. For deleting slide, Del key is used.
25. The desired slides can be made hidden so that to avoid them in the actual presentation.
26. Present3 is the by default name of the presentation.
27. Speaker notes are the notes kept in the notes pane.
28. FoxPro is a RDBMS.
29. Bold, Italic and Underline are toggle buttons.
30. Alignment refers to the position of text with respect to the page.
31. Comic Sans is the name of a font.
32. By default name of a document is Document10.
33. The commands to open, close and print a document are available under Edit menu.
34. To select a word, double click on that word.
35. Resume wizard is used for making letters.
36. The Slide Sorter View is the most appropriate view for ordering the slides.
37. We can have different design templates applied on different slides of the same presentation.
38. Slide View option is used for showing the on-screen presentation.
39. Rehearse Timings option is present under Edit menu.
40. Slides in a presentation can be advanced using mouse click.
41. Handouts can be developed in Powerpoint.
42. Office Assistant is an online help.
43. No two files (of the same type) in the same folder can have same names.
44. Word Wrap is a feature using which the first letter is made decorative & capitalized.
45. Ctrl+ Z is used to paste any item i.e. text or picture that had been cut or copied.
46. Redo is used to revert back the recent done change.
47. Minimizing Windows is same as closing Windows.
48. The commands to open, close and print a worksheet are available under the file menu.
49. Alt+ Click is used to select a sentence.
50. Header is the information that is displayed at the bottom of the page.
51. DIR command is used to display the list of only files.
52. Ctrl + V is used to paste any item i.e. text or picture that had been cut or copied.
53. Times New Roman is the name of a font.
54. To zoom the document, use the zoom option.

55. Bus is used for data storage.
56. In one presentation, only one slide can be created.
57. Powerpoint is a textual editor.
58. Different slides can have different backgrounds.
59. FoxPro is a language.
60. Slide transition means the way in which the picture on the slide appears.
61. Autocontent wizard cannot be used for creating presentations.
62. MODI STRU command is used for creating table in FoxPro.
63. Notes pane is used for typing the notes related to a slide.
64. Skip command is used for selecting the next record.
65. Spell check can be performed in case of typewriter.
66. Scroll bar are of two types- Left & Right.
67. Menu items like File, Edit, View etc can be accessed using Ctrl key along with the underlined character.
68. Toolbars are the pictorial representation of commands.
69. Resume wizard is used for making envelopes of the resume.
70. There are two modes of typing - Insert & Overwrite.
71. Caps lock key is used for switching between the lowercase and uppercase while typing.
72. Home key is used for switching between the Insert & Overwrite modes.
73. Memory is of two types- Primary & Secondary.
74. Microsoft Office 2007 is the recently launched version of Ms-Office.
75. "Feelix" is the name of a robot having childhood emotions.
76. Microsoft Vista is the name of recently launched operating system.
77. Several Operating systems can be run simultaneously on IBM Mainframes.
78. AI technology is used in fifth generation of computers.
79. Bill Gates is the father of Computers.
80. Toplogy refers to the manner in which the computers are arranged in a network
81. Word Processing is a type of system software.
82. CREATE command in FoxPro is used to create database files.
83. Database is a collection of interrelated data.
84. Feasibility study is the last phase of System Development Life Cycle.
85. WWW and Internet are one and the same concept.
86. Programmes written in high level languages are faster in execution as compared to machine language.
87. Scanner is an output device.

88. DOS is a type of application software.
89. In computer terminology processing of data takes place in the form of decimal number system.
90. FORTRAN is one of the high level language.
91. Interpreter acts a good debugging tool.
92. One of the features of computer is Versatility.
93. Compiler translates machine code to high level language code.
94. Modem stands for Modulation Demodulation.
95. IC stands for International Circuits.
96. PROM stands for Polar ROM.
97. CD contains spiral tracks.
98. One byte is a collection of ten bits.
99. Assembler is a translator program for converting high level language code to machine code.
100. CRS refers to Central Reservation System.

ANSWERS OF TRUE / FALSE

1	True	19	True	37	False
2	False	20	False	38	False
3	True	21	False	39	False
4	True	22	False	40	True
5	True	23	False	41	True
6	False	24	True	42	True
7	True	25	True	43	True
8	False	26	False	44	False
9	False	27	True	45	False
10	True	28	False	46	False
11	True	29	True	47	False
12	False	30	True	48	True
13	False	31	True	49	False
14	False	32	False	50	False
15	False	33	False	51	False
16	False	34	True	52	True
17	True	35	False	53	True
18	False	36	True	54	True

55	False	75	True	95	False
56	False	76	True	96	False
57	False	77	True	97	True
58	True	78	True	98	False
59	False	79	False	99	False
60	False	80	True	100	True
61	False	81	False		
62	False	82	True		
63	True	83	True		
64	True	84	False		
65	False	85	False		
66	False	86	False		
67	False	87	False		
68	True	88	False		
69	False	89	False		
70	True	90	True		
71	True	91	True		
72	False	92	True		
73	True	93	False		
74	True	94	True		

✪ Fill-in the Blanks

1. ___________ is a device which converts analog to digital signals and *vice versa*.
2. ___________ is the smallest measuring unit of computer.
3. One GB is equal to ________ MB.
4. WWW stands for ______________.
5. BASIC is a type of _____________ language.
6. HTTP stands for ___________________.
7. FoxPro is a type of __________ software.
8. Three types of languages are machine language, high level language and ________ language.
9. Full form of BASIC is __________.
10. ROM stands for __________.

11. Monitor is a type of ________ device.
12. First Indian super computer manufactured in India ____________.
13. Word Document consists of ________.
14. _______________feature is used to make the first letter of a paragraph capitalized, stylish and decorative.
15. _________ menu is used for saving a document.
16. By default name of a document is ____________.
17. By default extension of document is ____________.
18. Toolbar is a ______________ representation of commands.
19. _____________shortcut key is used to make the text bold.
20. _____________ key is used to restart computer.
21. _______________ is the unit for measuring font size.
22. Excel is also called as ______________.
23. In Ms- Excel, we have a ____________ of rows and columns.
24. _______________ buttons are used for navigating through the sheets.
25. _________ menu is used for open, close and save a workbook.
26. By default name of workbook is ______________.
27. _____________ is used to display the address of the active cell.
28. A formula always begins with an ____________ sign.
29. There are ___________number of rows in a sheet.
30. _______________symbol, on the standard toolbar is used for performing Autosum.
31. Powerpoint is an _____________program
32. In Ms- Powerpoint, we have ____________, which are analogous to 'Pages' in Word Document.
33. _______________ pane is used to display the number, order and contents of the slides.
34. By default name of presentation is _____________.
35. By default extension of presentation is _____________.
36. _____________shortcut key is used to show the presentation.
37. ____________ key is used to terminate an on-going presentation in between.
38. There are __________ number of views in Powerpoint.
39. PC stands for ______________.
40. _____________ shortcut key is used to cut selected text.
41. __________menu is used for performing editing operations.
42. By default font name is _______________.
43. Toolbar is a ______________ representation of commands.

44. Uppercase, Lowercase, Sentence cases are the examples of ____________ in Ms-WORD.
45. ____________ shortcut key is used for UNDO.
46. ________________ shortcut key is used for paste any item that has been cut or copied.
47. There are __________ number of columns in Excel.
48. A clipboard is a ______________ storage area.
49. Drop Cap option is present under _______ menu.
50. __________ refers to the physical components of computer.
51. There are _______ case options present in Change Case dialog box.
52. 2^3 : This effect can be created using __________ option under Format menu.
53. pAPER iS fINE : It is an example of ___________ case.
54. ____________ key plus the underlined character is used for accessing the menu items.
55. _________ shortcut key is used for performing the spelling and grammar check in document.
56. ___________ was the first electromechanical computer.
57. __________ is used for exiting out of a window.
58. ____________ is the called the Father of computer.
59. ____________ technology is used in fifth generation computers.
60. PARAM 10000 is the name of a __________________.
61. Delete option is present under _______ menu.
62. The field name can be upto _____ characters long.
63. Database is a collection of ____________.
64. Slides are individual ___________ of a presentation.
65. ___________ wizard can be used for creating presentation.
66. _________ shortcut key is used for viewing the slide show on full screen.
67. ___________ & ___________ are the characteristics of computer.
68. The processed data will be known as ______________.
69. Computer is comprised of _______________ & __________________.
70. CPU & ___________ are the two categories in which H/W can be divided.
71. CPU stands for _______________.
72. ___________ is used for the purpose of data storage in computers.
73. Mike is an ___________ device.
74. _________________ is used in banks for the verification of signatures on cheques.

75. MIS stands for ________________.
76. FAT stands for ________________.
77. RD command is used for __________ directory.
78. Warm booting means to ____________the computer.
79. __________ is the example of single user Operating system.
80. ______________ was the first invented Operating system.
81. CLS command is used for __________ the screen.
82. Floppy is divided into __________ and __________.
83. Screen is divided into tiny dots, which are called __________.
84. Black & White computer is called ______________.
85. For working with multiple files, FoxPro uses the concept of ______________.
86. The extension of program file in FoxPro is ________________.
87. __________number of documents are created in the process of mail merge.
88. ______________ is a feature in WORD due to which incorrect spellings are corrected automatically (as you type them)
89. To quickly format a table, ________________ option is used.
90. ______________is used for controlling data traffic in LAN.
91. ______________refers to the type of value a field can store.
92. ____________ command is used to display all the records contained in a database file.
93. ____________ command is used to move a file from one directory to another in DOS.
94. ____________ refers to a set of instructions defined to perform a particular task.
95. ____________ refers to an equation for performing arithmetic calculation.
96. ___________ feature of Excel is used for creating series.
97. ___________function returns the current time.
98. ___________function returns the current date and time.
99. ______________option is used for customizing the animation of a presentation.
100. The computer designed by Charles Babbage is called ______________.

ANSWERS OF FILL-IN THE BLANKS

1	Modem
2	Byte
3	1024
4	World wide web
5	High Level
6	HyperText Transfer Protocol
7	DBMS
8	Assembly
9	Beginners All Purpose Symbolic Instruction Code
10	Read Only Memory
11	Output
12	PARAM 10000
13	Pages
14	Drop Cap
15	File
16	Document1
17	.doc
18	Pictorial
19	Ctrl + B
20	Ctrl + Alt + Del
21	Points
22	Spreadsheet
23	Grid
24	Scroll
25	File
26	Book1
27	Address box
28	equal to
29	65536
30	(Sigma) "

31	application
32	Slides
33	Outline
34	Presentation
35	.ppt
36	F5
37	Esc
38	Five
39	Personal Computer
40	Ctrl + X
41	Edit
42	Times New Roman
43	graphical
44	Case
45	Ctrl + Z
46	Ctrl + V
47	256
48	Temporary
49	Format
50	Hardware
51	five
52	Superscript
53	Toggle
54	Alt
55	F7
56	MARK-I
57	Alt + F4
58	Charles Babbage
59	Artificial Intelligence
60	Supercomputer
61	Edit

62	10
63	data
64	pages
65	AutoContent
66	F5
67	Diligence, Automation
68	Information
69	Hardware, Software
70	Peripherals
71	Central Processing Unit
72	Memory
73	input
74	MICR
75	Management Information System
76	File Allocation table
77	deleting
78	restart
79	DOS
80	UNIX
81	clearing
82	tracks, sectors
83	Pixels
84	Monochrome
85	Workareas
86	.prg
87	Three
88	AutoCorrect
89	Table AutoFormat
90	Hub/Switch

91	Datatype	94	Function	98	today( )
92	LIST	95	Formula	99	Custom Animation
93	MOVE	96	AutoFill	100	Analytic Engine
		97	now( )		

1. A digitizer tablet and the graphic plotter mean the same thing
   a) the above statement is true
   b) the above statement is false
   c) it is unpredictable
   d) None
2. The operation carried out on an input data for examining it's acceptability is termed
   a) Verification
   b) Moderation
   c) Validation
   d) None of the above
3. A suite of programs that handle an organisation's database responsibilities is called a
   a) DBMS
   b) Database Processing System
   c) DMS
   d) All of the above
4. The most efficient and well designed computerized payroll system would be —
   a) On-line real time system
   b) Batch Processing System
   c) Both (a) & (b)
   d) All of the above
5. ______ is a set of programs, documents, procedures, routines and functions associated with the operation of a computer system
   a) Compiler
   b) Software
   c) Utilities
   d) Languages
6. Computer languages can be classified into __________ and ________ language-
   a) Compiler and Interpreter
   b) High Level Language and Low Level Language
   c) Application Software and System Software
   d) None
7. Which of the following in not an Operating System-
   a) WINDOW
   b) WINDOWS
   c) UNIX
   d) WINDOWS-ME
8. NCSA stands for —
   a) National Council of System Analysts
   b) National Center for Supercomputing Applications
   c) New codd Software Analysis
   d) None

9. GIAS stands for-
   a) Garbage In Analysis System
   b) Gateway Intranet Access System
   c) Gateway Internet Access Services
   d) None of the above
10. WIAS stands for-
    a) Windows In Accessible State
    b) WHITE Association of Andrew Schultz
    c) Wide-Area Information Service
    d) None of the above
11. An in-house computer network within a company/enterprise or a closed group that uses the standard Internet technologies, software and protocols-
    a) Internet
    b) Intranet
    c) WWW
    d) Browser
12. NLP stands for —
    a) Natural Language Processing
    b) New local prgoramming
    c) Nible level programming
    d) All of the above
13. Which of the following is not a type of a browser-
    a) Line Browser
    b) Page Browser
    c) Graphical Browser
    d) Service Specific Browser
14. Which of the following technology is used by Fifth generation computers-
    a) LSI
    b) VLSI
    c) AI
    d) None of the above
15. Name the register in ALU, that is used for performing actual computations-
    a) Adder
    b) Accumulator
    c) Super computational unit
    d) Active register
16. Which of the following is a semi conductor device that emits light when connected to an electric current-
    a) LCD
    b) LED
    c) LVD
    d) All of the above
17. Groupware is-
    a) collection of hardware equipments
    b) collection of various softwares
    c) combination of H/W & S/W
    d) None of the above
18. Which of the following device is used to process huge number of cheques in banks-
    a) MICR
    b) OBCR
    c) OMR
    d) All of the above

19. The smallest computer in size is-
    a) Mainframe c) Minicomputer
    b) Microcomputer d) Macrocomputer
20. The five functions of computer hardware are ____________
    a) Input, Output, Memory, Printing, Processing
    b) Printing, Displaying, Input, Processing
    c) Input, Output, Primary Memory, Secondary Memory, Processing
    d) Data Input, Data Display, Processing, Memory, Printing
21. Another name for the motherboard is the
    a. main circuit board.
    b. keyboard.
    c. control panel.
    d. operating system.
22. CPU is another name for
    a) a microprocessor.
    b) RAM cache.
    c) clock speed.
    d) megahertz.
23. Resolution is
    a) the maximum number of pixels a monitor can display.
    b) the distance between pixels in a graphics display.
    c) the number of rectangles in a character-based display grid.
    d) dot pitch in a graphics display.
24. The _______ chart is a standardized reference to the representation of characters by microcomputers.
    a) PCMCIA
    b) LAN
    c) ASCII
    d) COBOL
25. A series of eight bits is called a(n) ____________________.
    a) binary number
    b) serial data
    c) byte
    d) ASCII code

26. The storage capacity of a computer is conventially measured in
    a) bits.
    b) bytes.
    c) binary digits.
    d) ASCII characters.
27. Which of the following is the largest unit of measurement?
    a) a bit
    b) a gigabyte
    c) a megabyte
    d) a kilobyte
28. Megahertz and gigahertz are measurements of
    a) the amount of memory.
    b) the amount of RAM.
    c) the speed of the microprocessor.
    d) cache memory.
29. Where is program and data information that is being used temporarily stored by your computer?
    a) cache
    b) RAM
    c) ROM
    d) CMOS
30. A ________ is a computer that controls access to hardware and software on a network.
    a) server
    b) controller
    c) filter
    d) micro computer
31. A computer connected to a server is called a ________.
    a) server
    b) workstation
    c) personal computer
    d) application computer
32. A set of computer Instructions that carries out a task on your computer is called a(n) ________.
    a) shortcut
    c) user interface
    b) GUI
    d) program

33. _______ software helps the computer carry out its basic operating tasks.
    a) Virus protection
    b) Hardware
    c) System
    d) Application
34. Which type of software is used to analyze financial and other numerical data?
    a) word processing
    b) electronic publishing
    c) spreadsheet
    d) Web authoring
35. Bundled software refers to _______.
    a) software included with a new computer
    b) games and applications copied from friends
    c) special utility programs used by advanced users
    d) programs which can be downloaded from the Internet
36. Which one of these softwares is the most specialized for creating brochures, posters, and newsletters?
    a) spreadsheet
    b) presentation software
    c) multimedia authoring software
    d) desktop publishing software
37. The three major functions of operating systems are to manage _________:
    a) System software, applicaton software, user interface
    b) Resources, data, processes
    c) Input/Output, storage, processing
    d) Hardware, software, system updates
38. Which of the following software programs is NOT considered an application?
    a) Word-processing
    b) Database management
    c) MS-Windows
    d) Graphics editor
39. The three major advantages of MS-Windows are:
    a) Comes with most computers, user-friendly, multitasking.
    b) WYSIWYG, icons, uses a mouse.
    c) Multitasking, WYSIWYG, Clipboard.
    d) Clipboard, easy-to-use, never crashes.

40. If a menu command is followed by a(n) ____, a dialog box opens that allows you to enter specifications for how you want a task carried out.
    a) check mark
    b) ellipsis
    c) triangular arrow
    d) grayed-out command
41. When you first start Windows XP, what kind of settings does it use?
    a) custom
    b) basic
    c) default
    d) advanced
42. ________ is the most efficient technique for scrolling long distances.
    a) Clicking the scroll bar
    b) Dragging the scroll bar
    c) Pressing the ENTER key
    d) Clicking the scroll arrows
43. A user interface that displays graphics in addition to text when it communicates with the user is called a(n) ________.
    a) application interface
    b) graphical user interface
    c) user friendly interface
    d) desktop interface
44. The ________ button maximizes a window so that it fills the entire screen.
    a) Expand
    b) Fill Screen
    c) Maximize screen
    d) Restore
45. When you right-click an object, a(n) ________ displays.
    a) ToolTip
    b) full menu
    c) shortcut menu
    d) active menu
46. The window currently being used is called the ________.
    a) active window
    b) object window
    c) open desktop
    d) desktop window

47. When you delete an item from the desktop, it is placed in the ________.
    a) Recycle Bin
    b) Garbage Can
    c) Deleted Items folder
    d) Desktop Junk folder
48. What do you do to an object when you point to it and then click it?
    a) drag the object
    b) select the object
    c) copy the object
    d) move the object
49. To open an item, you can _____ it.
    a) click
    b) select
    c) double-click
    d) drag
50. What must you do to an item to open its shortcut menu?
    a) click it
    b) double-click it
    c) right-click it
    d) None of the above
51. The ability of Windows XP to run more than one program at a time is called _____.
    a) layering
    b) multitasking
    c) tiling
    d) simultaneous programming
52. Which of the following window controls contains basic window control buttons?
    a) menu bar
    b) title bar
    c) status bar
    d) toolbar
53. You can use the mouse to change the size of a window by dragging the window's _____.
    a) title bar
    c) outline
    b) sizing handle
    d) workspace

54. Which of the following menu conventions indicates a submenu?
    a) triangular arrow
    b) check mark
    c) ellipsis
    d) grayed-out option
55. Which of the following toolbar buttons reverses the effects of your last action?
    a) Delete
    b) Erase
    c) Undo
    d) Back
56. Which of the following dialog box controls allows you to scroll through a set of numbers to choose the setting you want?
    a) spin boxes
    b) tabs
    c) option buttons
    d) check boxes
57. Use the ________ to launch a program, find or open a document, or shut down the computer.
    a) taskbar
    b) Standard toolbar
    c) dialog box
    d) Start button
58. _____ is a convenient place to store documents, graphics, and other work.
    a) My Computer folder
    b) All Programs menu
    c) My Documents folder
    d) Both A and B
59. Which of the following contains specialized tools used to change the way Windows XP looks and behaves?
    a) My Computer
    b) Control Panel
    c) My Documents
    d) Help and Support Center
60. The ________ contains buttons to indicate which programs are open.
    a) Taskbar
    b) title bar
    c) tray status area
    d) Launch toolbar

61. You can click the button located in the upper-right corner of a program window to _____ that program.
    a) Maximize
    b) Minimize
    c) Close
    d) Restore
62. A file is often referred to as a(n) _____.
    a) wizard
    b) document
    c) pane
    d) device
63. To rename a file, _________ the file name and click Rename on the shortcut menu.
    a) drag
    b) select
    c) right-click
    d) click
64. You organize files by storing them in _____.
    a) archives
    b) folders
    c) indexes
    d) lists
65. Which of the following is NOT a removable medium?
    a) CD
    b) Zip disk
    c) floppy disk
    d) hard disk
66. The floppy disk drive is drive _____.
    a) A:
    b) B:
    c) C:
    d) F:
67. Windows organizes files and folders in a _____ system.
    a) task management
    b) folder
    c) document
    d) file

68. The location at the top of the Windows hierarchy is the _____ directory.
    a) root
    b) base
    c) origin
    d) home
69. _____ uses two panes to show drives, folders, and files on your computer and allows one to navigate from one location to another within a hierarchal disk structure.
    a) Microsoft Internet Explorer
    b) Windows Explorer
    c) My Computer
    d) Folders Manager
70. The left pane in the Windows Explorer window is called the _____ pane.
    a) View
    b) Explorer
    c) Folders
    d) Computer
71. The _____ pane in the Windows Explorer window lists the contents of the folders and other locations selected in the opposite section.
    a) right
    b) left
    c) top
    d) bottom
72. If a folder contains subfolders, a(n) _____ icon appears to the left of the folder icon.
    a) collapse
    b) expand
    c) view
    d) display
73. _________ a folder displays a list of indented subfolders.
    a) Expanding
    b) Collapsing
    c) Right-clicking
    d) Copying
74. To expand a folder in the Folders pane, _______ the plus sign.
    a) drag
    b) right-click
    c) click
    d) double-click

75. The drive from which a file was copied is called the ________.
    a) destination drive
    b) source drive
    c) destination folder
    d) source folder
76. The ____ folder is designed to store the files and folders you work with regularly.
    a) Frequently Used Files
    b) My Documents
    c) Recent Files
    d) My Files
77. The file ____ leads you through the Windows file system to your file.
    a) navigation
    b) path
    c) trail
    d) link
78. In the file path A:\Computer\Tutorial\Joystick.bmp, Tutorial is a ____.
    a) root folder
    b) extension
    c) filename
    d) subfolder
79. Which of the following can be used in a folder name?
    a) :
    b) |
    c) ?
    d) %
80. Which of the following cannot be used in a folder name?
    a) *
    b) &
    c) ^
    d) $
81. To select files that are listed together in a window, click the first file in the list, hold down the ____ key, and then click the last file in the list.
    a) Ctrl
    b) Esc
    c) Alt
    d) Shift

82. To select files that are not listed together, click one file, hold down the ____ key, and then click the other files.

a) Ctrl

b) Shift

c) Esc

d) Alt

83. Compressed folders are sometimes called ____ folders.

a) Batched

b) Extracted

c) Expanded

d) Zipped

84. The ____ is a collection of files that resides on computers located all over the world and that are connected to each other.

a) HTML

b) IP

c) Web

d) LAN

85. ____ is the amount of data that can travel through a communications circuit in one second.

a) Frequency

b) Data volume

c) Bandwidth

d) Resolution

86. A Uniform Resource Locator is an addressing scheme that tells the Web browser

a) the name of the file.

b) the domain name of the computer on which the file resides.

c) what protocol to use when transporting the file.

d) All of the above

87. The most common transfer protocol on the Internet is ____.

a) FTP

b) Gopher

c) HTTP

d) Telnet

88. _____ provides a variety of text-formatting tags used by browsers to display the text on Web documents.

a) HTML

b) FTP

c) URL

d) HTTP

89. The _____ protocol is a set of rules for establishing a remote terminal connection to another computer.

a) FTP

b) Gopher

c) HTTP

d) Telnet

90. On most computers, the filename extension of an HTML document is _____.

a) .html

b) .htm

c) .http

d) Either A or B

91. When you move the pointer over a(n) _____, the pointer changes shape to indicate that if you click that text, the Web browser will open a Web page.

a) hyperlink

b) status bar

c) bolded text

d) italicized text

92. The term "home page" means

a) the main page for a particular Web site.

b) the first page that opens when you start your browser.

c) the Web page that a particular browser loads the first time you run it.

d) All of the above

93. In most Web browsers, if you click and hold the mouse button down on either the Back or Forward button, a portion of the _____ list appears.

a) bookmarks

b) favorites

c) history

d) Both A and B

94. A browser stores a copy of every Web page it displays on your computer's hard disk in a(n) _____ folder in the Windows folder.

    a) URL Cache
    b) Temporary Internet Files
    c) URL Repository
    d) Internet Explorer

95. Web sites use _____ transmission to send and receive information, such as credit card numbers, to ensure privacy.

    a) encrypted
    b) certificate
    c) decoded
    d) double-key

96. To save a graphic in Internet Explorer, right-click it in the browser window, and click

    a) Store Picture.
    b) Save Picture As.
    c) Save Graphic.
    d) Save Image.

97. The _____ protocol transfers mail from your ISP's email server to your computer at home.

    a) SMTP
    b) router
    c) FTP
    d) POP

98. The _____ protocol enables users to transfer files between computers.

    a) Telnet
    b) Janet
    c) FTP
    d) MILNET

99. A Web page's _____ is its address.

    a) HTML
    b) HTTP
    c) URL
    d) FTP

100. All search engines provide a series of _____ pages.

a) results	c) expression
b) resource	d) keyword

101. When you use a search engine, you are searching ________
   a) the Internet
   b) a database
   c) only the World Wide Web
   d) all online library indexes

102. Which of the following top level domains typically indicates a not-for-profit organization?
   a) .net
   b) .org
   c) .npo
   d) .ngo

103. Which of the following suggest a low-quality resource?
   a) Graphics that serve no purpose
   b) Loud colors
   c) Flashing text
   d) All of the above

104. ________ are a convenient way of distributing information which is requested often. They are public, authoritative, and they are copyrighted.
   a) Search engines
   b) Newsgroups
   c) FAQs
   d) mailing lists

105. The ____ format is widely used on the Internet for images that have only a few distinct colors.
   a) JPEG
   b) GIF
   c) TIFF
   d) BMP

106. The ____ format is used extensively for photographs on the Web.
   a) GIF
   b) TIFF
   c) BMP
   d) JPEG

ANSWERS OF QUIZ

1	B	31	b	61	c
2	C	32	d	62	b
3	A	33	c	63	c
4	d	34	c	64	b
5	b	35	a	65	d
6	b	36	d	66	a
7	a	37	b	67	b
8	b	38	c	68	a
9	c	39	a	69	b
10	a	40	b	70	c
11	b	41	c	71	a
12	a	42	b	72	b
13	d	43	b	73	a
14	c	44	d	74	c
15	a	45	c	75	b
16	b	46	a	76	b
17	b	47	a	77	b
18	a	48	b	78	d
19	c	49	c	79	d
20	d	50	c	80	a
21	a	51	b	81	d
22	a	52	b	82	a
23	a	53	b	83	d
24	c	54	a	84	c
25	c	55	c	85	c
26	b	56	a	86	d
27	b	57	d	87	c
28	c	58	c	88	a
29	b	59	b	89	d
30	a	60	a	90	d

91	a	97	a	103	d
92	d	98	c	104	c
93	c	99	c	105	a
94	b	100	a	106	d
95	a	101	a		
96	b	102	c		